BY THE THAMES DIVIDED

BY THE THAMES DIVIDED:
CARDINAL BOURNE IN
SOUTHWARK AND WESTMINSTER

MARK VICKERS

GRACEWING

First published in England in 2013
by
Gracewing
2 Southern Avenue
Leominster
Herefordshire HR6 0QF
United Kingdom
www.gracewing.co.uk

No part of this publication may be reproduced, stored in a retrieval system, or transmitted in any form or by any means, electronic, mechanical, photocopying, recording or otherwise, without the written permission of the publisher.

The right of Mark Vickers to be identified
as the author of this work has been asserted in accordance
with the Copyright, Designs and Patents Act 1988.

© 2013 Mark Vickers

ISBN 978 085244 823 6

Typeset by Gracewing

Cover design by Bernardita Peña Hurtado

CONTENTS

CONTENTS..v

LIST OF ILLUSTRATIONS.....................................xiii

ABBREVIATIONS...xv

FOREWORD..xvii

INTRODUCTION..xix

1 THE BOURNES AND THE BYRNES..........................1
   'I know very little of his family'..1
   'The secrets and consolations of the worship of the Church'........3
   'True happiness and peace are only to be found in the service of God'..5
   'The more affluent Londoners moved further out'..............6

2 A VERY VICTORIAN CHILDHOOD............................11
   Modernity..11
   'A very holy, happy home, Catholic in the fullest sense'........12
   'It is time we left Clapham'..14
   'This peaceful locality'..15

3 *IN HAC LACRIMARUM VALLE*................................21
   'A hard school for young boys far from home'..................21
   'A martyr to his zeal'..22
   'Constant anxiety and self-sacrifice'....................................25
   'Making plenty of row'...26
   'Poor Harry'..28

'Unduly influenced by sad thoughts'..................................29
St Edmund's, Ware..30

4 PUTTING ON THE CASSOCK..................................35
'Unless the question is put to them'..............................35
Seminary Life..37
'I have no call for religion'.....................................38
Hammersmith..40
St Sulpice...42
'A humble stranger'..46
Louvain..46

5 *SACERDOS IN AETERNUM*......................................51
Ordination...51
Blackheath...52
Mortlake...54
'Dispensed from the missionary oath'..............................56
West Grinstead...58

6 'A SEMINARY IN THE MAKING'...................................63
A Seminary for Southwark...63
Henfield...65
The Move to Wonersh..67
'Training more by example than by words'..........................69
A Time of Trial..72
Audi Alterum Partem..73
Expansion and Development..75

7 BISHOP OF SOUTHWARK: 'PRACTICALLY A STRANGER'................81
Coadjutor: 'I have a great preference for the third'..............81

Bishop of Southwark..83
'Crushing debts'...84
The Society of Secular Priests...87
Promoting Priestly Vocations...91
Military Chaplains..91
Public Business and Personal Loss...96

8 CROSSING THE THAMES..103
A Dying Cardinal...103
Three Candidates...104
The Fourth Man...107
Roma locuta est..109

9 A LITTLE LOCAL DIFFICULTY...115
The New Archbishop..115
'This unpleasant business'...117
'A veritable campaign of slander'..123

10 EDUCATION, EDUCATION, EDUCATION...................133
The Background...133
Cares and Anxieties..137
'A damned bad Bill!'...140
A Ducal Spat..157
The McKenna Bills...162
The Runciman Bill...170
Fisher's Proposals..172
Trevelyan's Bills..181
Schools in General—and a Proposal in Particular...................185
Universities..188

11 THE FORBIDDEN PROCESSION 197
- The Nineteenth International Eucharistic Congress 197
- 'This d—d procession' 200
- 'Not abandoned but modified' 202

12 'NO NARROW MIND' 211
- Modernism 211
- Wonersh: 'A hotbed of Modernist thinking' 212
- 'An ailing little soul': Loisy 214
- 'A great name': Newman 216
- 'A highly nervous, eccentric and erratic person': Tyrell 218
- 'Our leader': Von Hügel 220
- 'Ward who is so unsafe' 222
- Pastorals and Encyclicals 225
- 'My fullest sympathy' 230
- 'Leanings towards Modernism' 231
- 'The brighter ecclesiastical atmosphere' 233

13 THE RED HAT 239
- Liberalising in Theology? 239
- 'We don't know' 242
- 'Unspeakably painful' 243
- 'Not bound by precedent' 245
- 'A great surprise' 246

14 'TROUBLE AND SADNESS' 251
- 'Mgr Amigo, whom I believed I knew intimately' 251
- 'Your own child' 252
- 'The first cause of friction' 256
- 'Cast away as useless' 260
- 'A direct and public insult' 264

'Send it up to Rome'...266
'A better state of things'?...272
'Too human a love'...274

15 'HOW GOOD AND HOW PLEASANT IT IS, WHEN BROTHERS LIVE IN UNITY'...281

'My confidence in the Archbishop has not abated'.................281
'To augment the number of Dioceses'....................................281
'The unfortunate division of this important city'.....................282
'Such an upheaval'...290
'An opportunity now in England'...295
'Some very strong speaking'...300
'A veritable obsession'...308
The Primate of England & Wales..311
Standing Committee...313
'An autocracy'..316

16 A CARDINAL AT WAR..325

'These times of sadness'..325
'At the end of our resources'...331
Episcopus Castriensis..336
Conscription..341
'The Shepherd and Teacher of the whole flock': Pope Benedict XV 342
Peace: 'Not the greatest gift'...349

17 ON THE INTERNATIONAL STAGE........................357

'All that concerns international dealings'................................357
'An ill-advised intrusion'...358
'What is Cardinal Bourne doing in the East?'.........................362
'Without the smallest anti-Jewish prejudice'..........................367
The League of Nations..371

    The Dictators..373
    'The Vatican: where incidentally he is *not* popular'..................376

18 IRELAND..386

    'Irish blood'..386
    'I am a Home Ruler'..388
    'This tragic farce in Dublin'..391
    'The Black and Tan Cardinal'?..394
    'The son of an English father and an Irish mother'..410

19 AND AT HOME..417

    'The Imperial Crown of England'..417
    'A mild contempt for party politics'..418
    Federation and Union..422
    'Words of outrage'..426
    'A Party to which a Catholic should not belong'..430

20 TO 'GUIDE SOCIETY ARIGHT'..441

    'Definite principles'..441
    The Demon Drink..442
    The Nation's Crisis..444
    COPEC..450
    'Real scandal to the Christian mind'..456
    Women and Children..460

21 SEPARATED BRETHREN..469

    The Strange Death of Protestant England..469
    'Part and parcel of the State'..470
    'May they be led to seek unity'..472
    'To cooperate when cooperation is possible'..475

22 TO MALINES AND BACK..479
- 'The first streaks of that dawning day'........................479
- 'Close and intimate contact'..................................484
- 'Our war against the English Catholics'.......................487
- 'Altogether sympathetic'......................................488
- 'You wished our Conversations ill'............................494
- 'His constant prayers for reunion'............................500
- 'A few fireside, informal talks over tea'.....................504

23 THE GENERAL STRIKE...515
- 'A sin against the obedience owed to God'.....................515
- 'The charge of disingenuousness'..............................520

24 METROPOLITAN OF METROLAND..................................527
- 'A good organiser'..527
- 'He was a father to me'.......................................529
- 'The Lay People's Cardinal'...................................533
- 'The extension of God's Kingdom'..............................538
- 'To retain a place within the national system of education'...540
- Westminster Cathedral: 'a true centre of the spiritual life'..542
- 'Our venerable College of St Edmund'..........................549
- 'The Central Seminary is doomed'..............................549
- 'Separated to some extent'....................................553
- 'The use of arms'...557
- 'His concentration on St Edmund's'............................559

25 *NOCTEM QUIETAM ET FINEM PERFECTEM*.........................567
- 'I have not been very well of late'...........................567
- 'Sorrow and grave anxiety'....................................568
- 'Not completely cured'..569
- Go forth, faithful Christian..................................571

'An unending stream of silent mourners'....................572

26 'FROM FIRST TO LAST A MAN OF GOD'...............575

'Little indeed on which to form any idea of the man'...............575
'A great English Cardinal'...575
'A great churchman'..578
'The Cardinal is a sphinx'...580
'The freedom of the soul'..583
Ne cede malis..585

SOURCES AND BIBLIOGRAPHY.........................589

INDEX..599

LIST OF ILLUSTRATIONS

Cover Picture: Cardinal Bourne by Sir Leslie Ward

1. Francis Bourne in (?) 1869
2. Seminary superior, aged 28
3. The first love: St John's Seminary, Wonersh
4. Southwark: friend and foe
   - Canon Edward St John
   - Bishop Peter Amigo
5. The Roman Curia
   - Cardinal Merry del Val
   - Cardinal Gasquet
6. Archbishop Bourne, 1908
7. The new Cardinal, November 1911
8. A Cardinal at War
   - Visiting the Fleet, 1916
   - With the Dublin Fusiliers at the Western Front, 1917
9. Cardinal Bourne in 1924
10. Cardinal Mercier
11. Centenary of Catholic Emancipation, September 1929
12. At Folkestone, April 1934
13. Golden Jubilee of priesthood
    - On the balcony of Archbishop's House
    - Outside the Cathedral
14. The burial place: the Galilee Chapel, St Edmund's College, Ware

ABBREVIATIONS

AAW	Archives of the Archbishop of Westminster
ACA	Arundel Castle Archives
ABSI	Archives of the British Province of the Society of Jesus
AGOSM	Servite General Archives, Rome
BAA	Birmingham Archdiocesan Archives
BDA	Brentwood Diocesan Archives
BIY	Borthwick Institute, York
CCIR	Catholic Council for International Relations
CDA	Clifton Diocesan Archives
COPEC	Conference on Christian Politics, Economics and Citizenship
CSG	Catholic Social Guild
CTS	Catholic Truth Society
CWL	Catholic Women's League
DAA	Downside Abbey Archives
FAB	Francis Alphonsus, Cardinal Bourne
GASSH	General Archives of the Society of the Sacred Heart
LCC	London County Council
LPL	Lambeth Palace Library
MAA	Malines Archdiocesan Archives
NLI	National Library of Ireland

NorDA	Northampton Diocesan Archives
NotDA	Nottingham Diocesan Archives
OUL	Oxford University Library
PDA	Portsmouth Diocesan Archives
PRO	Public Record Office
SAA	Southwark Archdiocesan Archives
SAUL	St Andrew's University Library
SCPF	Archives of the Sacred Congregation for the Propagation of the Faith
SDA	Salford Diocesan Archives
SEC	St Edmund's College Archives
UCA	Ushaw College Archives
WCC	*Westminster Cathedral Chronicle*
WCF	Westminster Catholic Federation
WO	War Office

FOREWORD

My son, if you aspire to serve the Lord,
Prepare yourself for an ordeal.
Be sincere of heart, be steadfast,
And do not be alarmed when disaster comes.
Cling to Him and do not leave Him,
So that you may be honoured at the end of your days.

Sirach 2:1-11

Those words from the opening chapters of the Book of Ecclesiasticus describe well the life of Francis, Cardinal Bourne. Born in 1861, he decided in his early youth that the priesthood was for him. His early years were marred by the death of his closest family members. Many of the later characteristics and actions of his life can be traced to these pivotal events.

Fr Mark Vickers has scrutinised the life and times of the longest serving Archbishop of Westminster in this scholarly work. His attention to detail and his scholarly research are second to none. In *By the Thames Divided* we have been given a rounded picture of a man who reached high office in the Church at a very early age: appointed Coadjutor Bishop of Southwark at thirty four, Archbishop of Westminster at forty two. Perhaps it was inevitable that this rapid rise should cause misunderstanding amongst some, resentment amongst others. Bourne's autocratic style of leadership made relationships with his fellow Bishops often tense and difficult. The complex social, political and educational issues with which he dealt throughout his tenure of office demanded clear analytical thought and action. Often his motives and methods were deliberately misunderstood by his colleagues. His austere and somewhat cold public persona belied a highly sensitive individual. His Sulpician spirituality sustained his conviction that all he did was not for popularity but for the greater glory of God and the well-being of the Church.

All this is chronicled in meticulous detail: Bourne's passion for seminary formation; his brave stance on Catholic education; diocesan reorganisation; ecumenical explorations; his personal wartime effort; the turmoil of the General Strike. All demanding and receiving his dedicated attention, despite sometimes bitter criticism of his position on matters of faith and morals.

> Cling to Him and do not leave Him,
> So that you may be honoured at the end of your days.

At the Silver Jubilee of Bourne's episcopate the *Daily Telegraph* wrote: 'Never has the Roman Church during the last three hundred years been in a stronger position in this country than it is today, and never has it made more rapid strides in the course of any period of eighteen years, than it has in the eighteen years since Cardinal Bourne came to Westminster.'

Perhaps even more telling were the words of Archbishop Downey of Liverpool on the death of his fellow Archbishop: 'He was, indeed, the just and determined man whom nothing could shake from his settled purpose. His episcopal motto is a true index to his character: *ne cede malis*, "yield not to the powers of evil." And the Virgilian line continues: *sed contra audentior ito*, "but meet them with still greater firmness."'[1]

+George Stack
Archbishop of Cardiff

24 May 2013
Feast of Our Lady Help of Christians

Notes

[1] Archbishop R. Downey, 'Francis Cardinal Bourne,' *WCC*, April 1935, p. 49.

INTRODUCTION

Bishops are not always noted for their prophetic voice. In one respect, however, Francis, Cardinal Bourne proved remarkably prescient. Created cardinal in November 1911, he travelled to Rome to receive the Red Hat from Pope Pius X. Staying at the national seminary, the Venerable English College, he threw a reception for Roman ecclesiastical society. Waiting to make his entrance, he paced the corridor outside known as 'the Cardinals' corridor,' so called from the portraits lining the walls of his compatriots who down the ages had also been members of the Sacred College. As he did so, the new Cardinal mused 'that in a hundred years from now he would be no more than one of those portraits of British Cardinals which hung on the walls.'[1]

In fact, Bourne fared less well than most other occupants of the Cardinals' Corridor. At more than thirty-one years, his is by far the longest reign of any Archbishop of Westminster. Yet mention 'Bourne' to a priest of the Diocese today, and they invariably mistake his name for that of his immediate predecessor, 'Vaughan.'

The obscurity is unmerited. Bourne's reign in Westminster covered some of the most momentous events of the modern English Catholic Church: the Education Question at the turn of the twentieth century, the Modernist Crisis, the First World War, the Irish Troubles and Treaty, the Catholic response to the emergence of the Labour Party, the Malines Conversations, the General Strike, the stirrings of Catholic social policy and the growing menace of the European dictators. By temperament and preference, Bourne played a quiet role in all these issues, but it was neither passive nor negligible. In the internal affairs of the Church, he devoted himself consistently to the cause of seminary education and the proposal for diocesan division. Bourne had his faults, but, in the main, he led the Catholic Church intelligently and conscientiously in difficult times.

Bourne's reputation has suffered in two respects. He was neither a self-publicist nor a prolific correspondent beyond the limits of the call of office. He leaves precious little documentation by way of apology for his objectives and achievements. Consequently, he has been viewed through the eyes of his contemporaries, and those the most critical.

Then Bourne is the subject of one of the worst ecclesiastical biographies of the last century. Ernest Oldmeadow was not Bourne's choice as biographer; he made no such nomination. Instead, Cardinal Hinsley, who had little interest in protecting Bourne's legacy, awarded Oldmeadow the task of writing the official biography as a consolation prize for firing him as editor of the *Tablet*. His two volume work is saccharine and sycophantic, at times petty and partisan. Often it is less a biography than an apologetical work aimed at an imaginary non-Catholic audience. Contemporaries were only too aware of Oldmeadow's limitations. 'The very sad lack of a comprehensive and understanding biography of this great priest is an indication, not that the subject is deficient, but that biographical capacity in the world has sadly deteriorated,' wrote one Catholic.[2] An Anglican Archbishop was more damning: 'A dull and narrow account of a humourless and rigid man. Absurd adulation mingled with spitefulness against all non-Roman Catholics. Parochial Romanism at its worst.'[3]

To be fair to Oldmeadow, much relevant and revealing documentation simply was not available at the time he wrote; access may have been deliberately withheld in some cases.[4] The quantity of archival material accessible today is far greater and, therefore, a balanced picture easier to achieve. There is now a consensus amongst Church historians that Bourne is overdue for re-assessment, but globally this has yet to occur.

My involvement with Cardinal Bourne is twofold in origin. After the death of Cardinal Hume and prior to the appointment of his successor contemporaries at the English College mooted the possibility of a brief study of all the Cardinal Archbishops of Westminster. The project did not materialise at that point, but I was assigned the figure of Bourne. My curiosity was awakened. It was increased a few months later when a diocesan priest suggested that there was a tale to be told of the turbulent relationship between Bourne and his successor across the Thames, Peter Amigo. Indeed there was.

In undertaking research on the English Martyrs of the sixteenth century, I was left grasping for any documentary evidence whatsoever. Even if not much given to social and conversational correspondence, there is no such paucity of evidence in relation to Bourne. An obituary recognised, 'Cardinal Bourne's biographer, whoever he may be, will have a formidable task in the choice of his material. During an episcopal life of nearly thirty-nine years, the Cardinal engaged so closely in a multitude of undertakings that there cannot be many aspects of Catholic activity in the country as to which we can say, "His Eminence had nothing to do with that."⁵

I am enormously grateful, therefore, to those who have guided and assisted me as I have worked my way through some of this material including the following : Dr John Martin Robinson at Arundel Castle; Fr John Sharp and Margaret Harcourt-Williams at Birmingham; Colin Harris at the Bodleian; Fr Stewart Foster at Brentwood; the Redemptorist Fathers in Clapham; Fr Tony Harding at Clifton; Abbot Aidan Bellenger at Downside Abbey; Margaret Osborne at Northampton; Canon Anthony Dolan and Graham Foster at Nottingham; Dr Val Fontana at Portsmouth; Sr Eileen Foster at Roehampton and Sr Margaret Phelan at the General Archives of the Society of the Sacred Heart in Rome; Jacky Hodgson at Sheffield University; Fr Michael Clifton and Fr Charles Briggs at Southwark; Dr Norman Reid at St Andrew's University; Dr Alastair MacGregor at Ushaw College; and the late Fr Ian Dickie and Fr Nicholas Schofield at Westminster. I also wish to thank the staff at Lambeth Palace Library, the National Library of Ireland and Propaganda Fide in Rome, and the staff and seminarians at Allen Hall, Oscott, Ushaw and Wonersh. I was kindly allowed the use of the libraries of the Oratory Fathers, London and Heythrop College.

I am extremely grateful to those who so generously provided hospitality on my travels as I undertook research: Michael and Susan Clark in Sussex, the Carmelite Fathers in Dublin, Fr David Barrett in Northampton, David Crookes in Durham, Allen and Elizabeth Mills in Oxford.

I owe a particular debt to Fr Seán Finnegan for sharing his thoughts on Bourne and his, then unpublished, history of St John's Seminary, Wonersh. Fr Stewart Foster provided a thorough list of suggestions and corrections of the draft of this work. Like Bourne, Archbishop Stack has his roots in the London Irish, to which the Catholic Church in the capital city owed its growth and vibrancy from the mid-nineteenth century. He has been a constant source of encouragement during my formation and priesthood. I have further reason to thank him for writing the Foreword to this biography.

This book has been too long in its gestation. Life as a curate provided the opportunity for reading and research. The duties of parish priest and university chaplain meant the task of writing proceeded at a slow and uneven rate. I wish to thank friends who lent their homes to permit more prolonged periods of writing: Fr Christopher Colven and Michael and

Veronica Hodges. Finally, I must thank Tom Longford at Gracewing for allowing this work finally to see the light of day.

Bourne belongs to the age of my grandparents and great-grandparents. As I began my research, therefore, he was already slipping from living memory. As a deacon in Pimlico, I met a dwindling number of an older generation who had been confirmed by him or served his Mass at Westminster Cathedral; but their encounters were those of youth with a distant prelate of the Church. A more intimate picture came from a remarkable survivor, Canon Reggie Fuller. He knew Bourne for two decades as a family friend, and then as his seminarian and priest. Ordained by Bourne in 1931, he was sent to Rome for doctoral studies and would meet up with the Cardinal on his visits to the Eternal City. When I interviewed the late Canon Fuller he was already in his mid-nineties, but able to recall with extraordinary clarity the events of three-quarters of a century earlier. His impressions and interpretation of Bourne invariably confirmed those of more immediate contemporaries. I count myself fortunate to have been able to establish this living link with the subject of this biography.

As the last living person to have known Bourne personally, it is perhaps right to hear Canon Fuller's assessment of the man who ordained him. Not denying Bourne's failings, Fuller recalled, 'He could be the kindest of men; he was a father to me.' His long episcopacy covered a number of difficult times and issues, but Bourne 'always kept his head.'[6] This work aims in some small way to re-examine those times and issues and Bourne's contribution to them.

This book is dedicated to Michael and Vron—a small repayment on a huge debt of gratitude.

Fr Mark Vickers
Feast of St Alban
20 June 2013

Introduction

Notes

1. FAB at the English College, Rome, 1 December 1911, *Tablet*, 9 December 1911, p. 934.
2. G. Wheeler, 'The Archdiocese of Westminster,' G. Beck (ed.), *The English Catholics 1850–1950* (London: Burns & Oates, 1950).
3. C. Smyth, *Cyril Foster Garbett*, (London: Hodder & Stoughton, 1959), p. 380.
4. C. Cowderoy to Editor of *Tablet*, 11 August 1944, SAA, Bourne Papers, Biographical Materials.
5. E. Anstruther, 'Francis Cardinal Bourne,' *Dublin Review*, April 1935, p. 177.
6. Interview with Canon R. Fuller, 7 November 2001.

Chapter 1

The Bournes and the Byrnes

'I know very little of his family'[1]

The resurgence of the Catholic Church in England from the mid-nineteenth century, its 'Second Spring,' was founded largely upon two constituent elements: Anglican converts and, numerically far more significant, Irish immigrants. Francis Bourne's immediate ancestry encompassed both groups.

As a Prince of the Church, others exerted themselves on the Cardinal's behalf to discover for him a knightly pedigree; he himself never exhibited more than a passing interest in his remote antecedents.[2] In fact, he claimed to know little of his genealogy beyond his own paternal grandfather, Henry Bourne. The Cardinal believed that his family originated in Herefordshire, in the vicinity of Leominster.[3] However, official documentation has his grandfather's birthplace as Thames Ditton in Surrey in 1796.[4]

At the end of the Napoleonic Wars Lady de Roos presented the young Henry Bourne for a position in the General Post Office at St Martin's-le-Grand in London.[5] Competent and industrious, from the 1840s he was entrusted with negotiations to bring economy and efficiency to the international postal service on which Britain's expanding commercial and imperial interests increasingly relied. In 1844 he was sent to negotiate a postal treaty with Pasha Mohammed Ali of Egypt. The attempt was frustrated by corruption and evasion at the Egyptian court. During the many interludes in the discussions he occupied himself in seeing the sites of ancient Egypt.[6] More productive was his attempt in 1847 to conform the postage rates between the British colonies in North America and the West Indies.[7] This was followed by a trip to the United States to pursue postal negotiations there.[8]

This worthy public servant married Sarah Sophia Hodson, a lady from a Staffordshire medical family, but, like her husband, born in the environs of the rapidly-expanding capital. They were to have three sons, the first, also Henry, the Cardinal's father, was born in 1826. At the time the family were living at Strahan Terrace in Islington, then still deemed fashionable and salubrious; the elder Bourne's status was sufficiently secure for him to be described as a 'gentleman.'[9] The two younger sons were Edward and Charles. The former was to play an active role in his nephew's early life, the latter virtually none.

The Cardinal's father's schooldays were far from happy. He and his brother, Edward, were sent to a private establishment in Islington where they were schooled in classics and mathematics. Even by contemporary standards, the treatment meted out to them was severe. Three generations later the Cardinal recalled, 'I often heard from my Mother of the horror of Protestant schools which his own schooldays left in my Father's memory. It was the treatment he there received that caused the hesitation in his speech of which those who knew him have often told me.'[10] During this time the family moved to Sussex Place, just off Canonbury Square, and then in the late 1840s to Cornwall Terrace on the southern boundary of Regent's Park.[11] We find them there at the time of the 1851 Census with two maidservants completing the household.[12]

The elder Henry Bourne used his influence to find positions in the Post Office for all three of his sons.[13] As he turned twenty a place was found for the younger Henry as a clerk in the Accountant-General's Office of the Post Office.[14] He joined Edward, who had been pursuing the family career for eighteen months already—although he was not to persevere, leaving the Post Office within a couple of years to work in the office of a City merchant. Also choosing to change employment, the youngest son, Charles, took up his mother's family profession, qualifying from the Charing Cross Hospital[15], and practising for a while as a physician in Australia before returning to England.

Nothing distinguishes the Bournes in the mid-1840s from hundreds of other middle class families serving conscientiously the growing bureaucracy of the British Government. Their religious beliefs and practice are also unlikely to have marked them out from their peers in the mid-Victorian metropolis. Sarah Hodson's family had been followers of the Swedenborgian sect, but by the time of her marriage and the birth of their children the family were worshipping in the classical surroundings of St Mary's, Islington, with its Low Church Anglican tradition.

'The secrets and consolations of the worship of the Church'[16]

In 1839 the Anglican clergyman Frederick Oakeley took charge of the Margaret Chapel, an unprepossessing place of worship just off Regent Street which he proceeded to transform. A Fellow of Balliol, Oakeley was a relative late comer to the Oxford Movement, which sought to free the Church of England from State control and to emphasise for it a catholic and apostolic basis, with the doctrinal and liturgical consequences that implied. Convinced of the Movement's aims, Oakeley collaborated with its leading lights, Newman, Pusey and Ward. Oakeley later explained his objectives on arriving in London: 'I can honestly say that the motive which actuated me in trying to improve the ceremonial practice… was to give worship as much reverential beauty as was consistent with the strict observance of such rubrics as were plain and incontrovertible… I must maintain that the ritual of the Margaret Chapel, whatever may be said for or against it, was simplicity itself… no Catholic, however uneducated, could possibly have mistaken the communion service at Margaret Street for High Mass.'[17]

Although sincere in his protestations, Oakeley's innovations aroused suspicion in an uncompromisingly Protestant Church of England. The Margaret Chapel was the first outpost of Tractarianism in London. The use of candles, cross and liturgical colours, daily services, setting Anglican psalms to Gregorian chant tones and the eastward position adopted at communion services aroused controversy. Such practices brought Oakeley into conflict with the Bishop of London, but also attracted a large, influential and devoted congregation, including the young William Gladstone.[18] From Oxford even Newman was concerned at the pace of change being forced by Oakeley, urging the barrister Samuel Wood to remain at the Margaret Chapel as a force for moderation, 'You are older than most of the persons likely to be there.'[19]

Newman's fear that the excesses of the London church were the work of its younger adherents was well founded. When Henry and Edward Bourne's father left for Egypt at the end of the summer of 1844 the two teenage brothers seized the opportunity to investigate the Margaret Chapel's exotic practices. Edward describes the experience: 'To be in the Margaret Street Chapel was to be in the van of the Oxford Movement; and therefore it was to be conscious of every forward step and thrilled with every fresh emotion of that enthusiastic time.'[20] A heady concoction for the religiously-inclined youth of the day. Still more controversially,

Oakeley established a quasi-monastic community with two young men in the clergy house, where together they recited the daily monastic office.[21] While Oakeley was on holiday in Ireland in the summer of 1844, the two fellow members of his 'community,' without his knowledge, were received into the Catholic Church. This is the situation into which the two Bourne brothers arrived, and of which they readily imbibed.

The situation was much in flux, but the catalyst for their own conversion was provided by events in Oxford. Determined to make a stand against the allegedly Romeward tendency of the Tractarians, in February 1845 the University Convocation deprived one of the leading protagonists, W. G. Ward, of his University degrees. When Oakeley's defence of his friend failed, he invited the University to strip him of his own degrees.[22] Edward Bourne recalls: 'Mr Ward lost his case, and was deprived of his degree, and we saw Mr Oakeley return to Margaret Street, knowing that there was thunder in the air.'[23] While Oakeley hesitated concerning his own position, the younger members of his congregation saw the Ward case as a watershed and acted immediately. Apostolicity and catholicity had to be sought elsewhere.

Henry and Edward Bourne took themselves off to the church of St Aloysius in Somers Town, receiving instruction in the Catholic Faith from Fr Holderstock. Needless to say, feathers were ruffled in the Protestant parental home. Given their father's absence in Egypt, Mrs Bourne sought guidance from an Anglican clergyman named Dodsworth.[24] His advice was not particularly helpful. He simply counselled that the boys 'must be very much in earnest to contemplate such a step.'[25] After six months' instruction, the two brothers were received into the Catholic Church—prior to the conversions of both Newman and Oakeley.

This defection to Rome led to no long term breakdown in family relationships. Henry Bourne continued to live with his parents for the next seven years, and both parents were themselves eventually to be received into the Catholic Church. Sarah Bourne lived into her mid-eighties, but her husband died in Hastings in 1858, leaving her the sole executrix and beneficiary of a respectably-sized estate valued at £3,000.[26] This was more than two years before the birth of his younger grandson. While his paternal grandfather played no part in Francis Bourne's life, he seems to have passed on certain physical characteristics. Forty years later Francis Bourne's mother sent a photograph of her son, the youngest English bishop, to an elderly relative. He commented in reply, 'There is much that reminds me of his grandfather, one of the very best men I ever knew; the same features and expressions only more spiritualised.'[27]

The Cardinal's father continued his work at the Post Office, but his free time was given largely to pursuing his enthusiasm for the Catholic faith. This brought him into contact with a pious Irishwoman called Miss Matilda Byrne, who seems to have lived in Dorset Square. There in the early 1850s Henry Bourne met a niece with a soft Irish accent visiting from Dublin.[28]

'True happiness and peace are only found in the service of God'[29]

An air of mystery pervades the person of Ellen Byrne. She was never to sit for the photographer. She was reluctant to disclose or commit to paper her own personal history. There is even doubt—shared by her own son—as to her age. Marriage and death certificates disagree with annuity papers.[30] (The destruction of records in Dublin during the Easter Rising prevents a conclusive determination.) Either there was an error in the annuity papers, or Ellen Byrne was born in 1824 while admitting to being three years younger. If the latter, she was two years older than Henry Bourne.

Yet a certain amount is known of Ellen Byrne's early life. She was one of three children, the daughter of a Dublin merchant, John Byrne. Her brother disappeared after setting out for Australia, but her elder sister, Mary, was to be her lifelong companion. Ellen's father died when she was very young and her mother while she was still in her teens. Although orphans, the Byrne girls were not left penniless. They were raised by their maternal grandmother, Mary MacDermot, and Ellen received a £3,000 legacy from her grandfather. Both sisters were educated overseas; Ellen at convent schools in Roulers and Amiens. In the latter she was in the charge of the Faithful Companions of Jesus. Ellen was bright, attracting the attention and affection of the Order's foundress, Marie Madeleine d'Houet, whom Ellen accompanied on journeys to Carthage and Turin as she attended to the affairs of the Order.[31]

Having completed their education, Mary and Ellen Byrne were taken in by an uncle. They were well treated and the European travels continued in his company, but his motives were not altogether altruistic. The Cardinal records: 'While treating them kindly their uncle managed to spend the money that rightly belonged to them and seems to have been very averse to the idea of their marriage, probably fearing that, in that case, he might be called to give an account of his stewardship.'³² Her grandfather's inheritance was thus frittered away. When she appeared in her aunt's London drawing room, Ellen Byrne was approaching thirty—accomplished and well-travelled, but more than a little anxious to establish her own home away from an over-protective uncle.

The Cardinal was proud of his ancestry spanning the Irish Sea and later claimed a right to speak with particular authority on Anglo-Irish matters, making public reference to his Irish mother. Yet his personal contact with Ireland was limited and his sympathy for Irish political aspirations questioned. His mother's nationality hardly gave him the close ties he sought with his flock. It is questionable the extent to which they would have related to Ellen Byrne, who lived only the earliest of childhood years in Ireland, who came from an affluent mercantile family and whose adult life was divided between France and England.

Henry Bourne and Ellen Byrne were quite different characters. Henry Bourne was affable and given to sentimentality. Ellen Byrne can appear cold and hard in pursuing what she perceived to be the best interests of those for whom she had responsibility. (It could be said that their younger son inherited much of his father's personality, but well concealed beneath an exterior moulded under his mother's influence.) Yet we need not doubt the affection and love of the young couple, fired by a natural attraction and a shared zeal for the Catholic faith. They were married on 3 June 1852 in the Royal Bavarian Chapel—now the Assumption, Warwick Street, just off Regent Street. The witnesses to the ceremony were the immediate family, Edward Bourne and Mary Byrne.³³

'The more affluent Londoners moved further out'³⁴

The newly-weds initially took up residence in Islington.³⁵ In moving, uppermost in Henry Bourne's mind was always the quality of the liturgy offered by the local Catholic church and his opinion of the clergy. The return to Islington, therefore, was largely determined by the presence of Frederick Oakeley, formerly of the Margaret Chapel, now parish priest of St John the Evangelist, Duncan Terrace. But Islington was no longer the genteel neighbourhood of Henry Bourne's childhood. Systematically developed from the 1830s—and not for the most discerning or prosperous clientele—it had become an area of 'trumpery allotments dealt out to the builders [from which] closely packed streets and terraces have arisen.'³⁶

With so many of their middle class contemporaries, the Bournes deserted Islington in its long period of social decline.

They went south of the River. Like Islington, Clapham has experienced considerable fluctuations in its social status. 'Discovered' in the eighteenth century, the new bridges across the Thames made this Surrey village accessible to Londoners. Its proximity to the City—just four miles away—made it a fashionable location for the country villas of mercantile magnates. More substantial development took place from the 1820s under the auspices of Thomas Cubitt, the developer of Belgravia and Pimlico. Clapham's proximity to his office was no doubt an incentive to Henry Bourne. The sixpenny horse-drawn omnibuses leaving for the City every five minutes were superseded by the arrival of the railway and the opening of new stations at Wandsworth Road and Clapham High Street in 1863.

Also important in determining the location of their new residence was the presence of St Mary's, Clapham, the Catholic church just fifteen minutes' walk from the Bournes' new home. Clapham's Anglican heritage was distinctly Low and Evangelical, the home of the Clapham Sect and William Wilberforce. Holy Trinity on Clapham Common was the epitome of a Protestant preaching box: 'an ugly, square, comfortable building ... built in an age when church architecture had reached its lowest depth.'[37] It would have gladdened the heart of the historically romantic Henry Bourne that just a few hundred yards away was the noble stone edifice of St Mary's, with its soaring spire and peal of six bells, solidly within the Roman communion and paid for by the convert, Fr Douglas. The church belonged to the Redemptorists and the parish priest from 1855—the year of the Bournes' arrival—was another Anglican convert, Fr Robert Coffin, an Old Harrovian and Oxonian, and intimate of Newman and Manning. He enjoyed a considerable reputation as a preacher, spiritual director and retreat giver. He and his church acted as a magnet to Catholics, convert or otherwise, who came in considerable numbers. Fr Coffin's interests lay in the development of St Mary's liturgical and musical tradition. With at least half a dozen priests, the parish had a full devotional life.[38] Henry Bourne could have wanted for nothing more when he found a fine organ and choir under the direction of yet another Oxford Movement convert.[39] Here indeed was somewhere he could call home.

Henry and Ellen were married four years before the birth, after a difficult pregnancy, of their first child, Henry Joseph, known as 'Harry.'

Born on 5 November 1856, he was baptised by Fr Coffin two days later. The couple had to wait a further four and a half years for the arrival of their next child.

Notes

1. FAB, 'Notes on my Life,' 8 June 1917, AAW, Bo. IV/1/1.
2. E. Oldmeadow, *Francis Cardinal Bourne*, i (London: Burns Oates & Washbourne Ltd, 1940), pp. 4–5.
3. FAB, 'Notes,' AAW, Bo. IV/1/1.
4. 1851 Census Return, UCA, Bourne Family Papers, OS/K (unsorted).
5. Post Office Record Room, 9 June 1904, AAW, Bo. IV/1/18.
6. Oldmeadow, *Francis Cardinal Bourne*, i, pp. 8–10.
7. UCA, Bourne Family Papers, OS/K1/10.
8. UCA, Bourne Family Papers, OS/K1/14.
9. Birth certificate, UCA, Bourne Family Papers, OS/K1/1.
10. FAB, 'Notes,' AAW, Bo. IV/1/1.
11. UCA, Bourne Family Papers, OS/K1/16, 21.
12. UCA, Bourne Family Papers, OS/K (unsorted).
13. Post Office Record Room, 9 June 1904, AAW, Bo. IV/1/18.
14. UCA, Bourne Family Papers, OS/K1/8.
15. Henry Bourne to Harry Bourne, Good Friday 1868, UCA, Bourne Family Papers, OS/K2/50.
16. R. W. Church, *The Oxford Movement, 1833–1845*, (London: 1891), p. 371 referring to the Margaret Street Chapel.
17. F. Oakeley, *Memoirs*, pp. 15–16, cited P. Galloway, *A Passionate Humility: Frederick Oakeley and the Oxford Movement* (Leominster: Gracewing, 1999).
18. Galloway, *A Passionate Humility*, pp. 51–62.
19. J. H. Newman to Samuel Wood, 6 January 1842, cited Galloway, *A Passionate Humility*, p. 129.
20. Edward Bourne to Wilfrid Meynell, 1885, cited Oldmeadow, *Francis Cardinal Bourne*, i, p. 13.
21. Galloway, *A Passionate Humility*, p. 66.
22. *Ibid.*, pp. 165–168.
23. E. Bourne to W. Meynell, 1885, cited Oldmeadow, *Francis Cardinal Bourne*, i, p. 13.
24. FAB, 'Notes,' AAW, Bo. IV/1/1.
25. *Ibid.*
26. UCA, Bourne Family Papers, OS/K1/21.
27. UCA, Bourne Family Papers, OS/K4/130.

28 J. Stuart, 'Notes of what the Bishop told me about his Mother and about himself, December 1900,' AAW, Bo. IV/1/27.
29 Ellen Byrne to FAB, 21 December 1882, AAW, Bo. IV/1.
30 Marriage certificate; General Annuity Fund to FAB, 7 January 1901, UCA, Bourne Family Papers, OS/K4/132.
31 FAB, 'Notes,' AAW, Bo. IV/1/1.
32 *Ibid*.
33 Copy marriage certificate.
34 P. Ackroyd, *London: The Biography* (London: Chatto & Windus, 2000), p. 529.
35 FAB, 'Notes,' AAW, Bo. IV/1/1.
36 *Building News*, (1863), cited Ackroyd, *London*, p. 528.
37 J. W. Glover (1877), cited G. Clegg, *Clapham Past* (London: Historical Publications Ltd, 1998).
38 *Catholic Directory*, (1861).
39 G. Stebbing, *History of St. Mary's, Clapham* (London: Sands & Co, 1935), pp. 32–55.

Chapter 2

A Very Victorian Childhood

Modernity

Francis Bourne belongs to the modern era. Born on 23 March 1861, he entered an England which was already an urban, industrial and imperial power. Victoria had been on the throne for almost a quarter of a century; by the end of the year the Prince Consort was dead and the Queen had entered her long widowhood. Abraham Lincoln was being inaugurated as the President of the uncertainly 'United' States, with America on the brink of Civil War. There were disturbances elsewhere—in Bosnia and Poland. The temporal power of Pope Pius IX in Rome was to be upheld for a little longer by the French troops of Napoleon III, but the rest of Italy had been largely united by Garibaldi for Victor Emmanuel II of Piedmont-Savoy. Closer to home, the discontented forces of Irish nationalism rumbled not too far below the surface.

The mid-Victorians were conscious that a watershed had been passed: the agrarian society of Merry England had disappeared with the Hanoverian Georges. In the decade preceding the Cardinal's birth alone, the population of England and Wales had increased by an astonishing 10% to stand at over 20 million. At the forefront of the growth was the imperial metropolis.[1] Much of the capital resembled one, huge building site—with all the inconvenience and dislocation that entailed—even if, in March 1861, activity was temporarily paralysed by a strike in the London building trade.[2] All this was underpinned by the extraordinary feats of Victorian engineering. Joseph Bazalgette had begun the development of London's sewerage system, hailed as 'the most extensive and wonderful work of modern times.' 165 miles of main sewers and 1,100 miles of local sewers were laid.[3] (The Bournes were to be directly affected.) On 10 January 1863 the world's first underground railway opened between Paddington and Farringdon Road.

Christianity too was being confronted with the full impact of modernity. The publication of Darwin's *Origin of the Species* in 1859 brought for many a crisis of faith—felt more keenly by the Established Church. The Catholic Church in England was engaged, on the one hand, in a certain triumphalism; on the other, in the provision of the most basic needs for its adherents. It was no longer the marginalised institution of penal times ministering to a scared and scattered population of recusant descent. Anglican converts brought confidence and Irish immigrants added numbers. No one knew for certain the Catholic population in England in the early 1860s. It was estimated at over one million— concentrated upon Lancashire and London.[4] By 1870 'there were more Irish living in London than in Dublin, and more Catholics than in Rome.'[5] With the Restoration of the Hierarchy in 1850, English Catholics were brought within the normal system of Church governance of bishops and dioceses. Given the poverty of the immigrant community, the statistics for the third quarter of the nineteenth century are staggering. The number of Catholic churches rose from 586 to 1,025; the number of Catholic priests doubled to 1,634. In the field of Catholic education the figures are even more extraordinary. There were just 99 elementary schools with 7,769 pupils in 1850. In 1874 the numbers were 1,484 and 100,372 respectively.[6]

'A very holy, happy home, Catholic in the fullest sense'[7]

There was no delay in bringing the future Cardinal into the fold of the holy Roman Church. He was taken to St Mary's for baptism the day after his birth. Like his brother, he was baptised by Fr Coffin. His bachelor uncle and maiden aunt were the godparents.[8] Known to the family as 'Frank,' at the font he received the names Francis Alphonsus. Francis was chosen after a relative of his father's whom he never knew. Alphonsus was an unwonted exoticism for the Bournes explicable by the fact that, following Ellen Bourne's near death in the delivery of her first son, the Redemptorists lent the Bournes a relic of their founder, St Alphonsus Liguori, to ensure his protection during the second pregnancy.[9] It worked, although there were to be no further children in the Bourne household.

The family home was 5 Larkhall Rise[10] in the north-eastern corner of the parish. The road is one of Clapham's ancient country lanes. Even today it enjoys a certain leafy seclusion on its ridge affording views across the River to Chelsea, but the tone of the neighbourhood changes markedly as it approaches South Lambeth. The house was part of a terrace set amidst substantial detached villas. Researching his biography, Ernest

Oldmeadow visited the road in the late 1930s and described the house: it 'cannot have been new because some of its windows are of the blind type belonging to the period of the window tax. In its prime, although not in the same class with the stately mansions of City magnates which still stand in Clapham, [it] must have had a modest dignity. A flight of many stone steps ascended to the front door and the façade had a width of about forty feet.'[11] The house disappeared shortly afterwards, a victim of the development of the Springfield Estate by the London County Council.

The externals of moderate middle class gentility were mirrored by the domestic arrangements within. Although the immediate Bourne family numbered just four, this was not the age of the nuclear family and the house was seldom quiet or empty. Henry and Ellen Bourne accepted into their home their young niece, Agnes, after the return to England of her widowed father, Charles, Henry's youngest brother. For a few short years she was raised as a sister to Harry and Frank. The spinster aunt, Mary Byrne, made her home there, and Henry's mother and brother, Edward, were also taken in while searching for a property of their own in the late 1860s. To these can be added maidservants, a dog and a couple of cats, poultry and pigeons, and a constant stream of visitors, mainly clerical, invited by the ever sociable Henry Bourne. There was much to interest and amuse a bright, young child.

Remembering the unhappiness of his own schooldays, their father determined that Harry and Frank Bourne should fare better. He relished the effort. There was more than a little of the child in Henry Bourne. He entered into their world and activities with a schoolboy's enthusiasm. Outings and presents were showered upon his sons. When Frank was cutting his second set of teeth, his father wrote to Harry, 'I do all I can to amuse him—I have got him a real sword, an old mail guard's cutlass ... you can imagine how proud he is of it.'[12] There were trips to the father's office and the theatre. The house emptied a little as Harry went off to school in 1865 and Frank's cousin, Agnes, to convent school in Belgium in 1867. His aunt went to the same country later that year. Frank's health was not of the most robust—there are frequent references to trips to the dentist and a susceptibility to colds—but nothing serious. There were children's parties and playfriends visiting Larkhall Rise, where 'they kicked up a great row.'[13] His early education was in the hands of his mother and aunt who taught him Latin and French, which was constantly spoken in the home.[14]

Thus far, Frank Bourne's childhood was indistinguishable from that of so many other middle class boys in mid-Victorian England. However, even by nineteenth-century standards, religion featured prominently. Henry Bourne was eager to communicate his love of the Mass and all things liturgical. His Ultramontane views punctuated his correspondence: 'Frank talks of being a Zouave when he is old enough—God bless him for the thought.'[15] Together father and son visited London churches, and were often at St Mary's. They were present when Bishop Grant of Southwark unveiled an image of Our Lady of Perpetual Succour—a copy of the original in the Redemptorists' mother house in Rome. They were back in the Redemptorist house a couple of weeks later: 'On Sunday Frank and I paid a long visit to Fr Coffin—I had not seen him for some months before—he was very unwell and saw us in his bedroom … Fr Coffin gave Frank a medal of Our Lady of Perpetual Succour … Br Joachim took Frank into the Fathers' Oratory upstairs which delighted him very much.'[16]

Frank Bourne would not have been conscious of a single moment in his life when he was not thoroughly immersed in the ceremonies, doctrine and conversations of the Catholic Church. He was soon playing his own part in the life of the Church. Having made his first Confession in January 1868,[17] Frank proceeded to serve at the altar at St Mary's. His aunt returned from Belgium with a most unusual present for her seven year old nephew: 'a purple velvet stole, in which he officiated with great dignity.'[18]

'It is time we left Clapham'

By the mid-1860s, however, Henry Bourne's enchantment with Clapham was waning. He suffered the same predicament as so many middle-class nineteenth century Londoners. He sought to remain within easy proximity of his work as a civil servant, while escaping the capital for the country. Of course, he and his contemporaries, restless to keep ahead of the onward march of the capital's boundaries, blighted all they touched with suburban development. Clapham had been doomed from the eighteenth century when one resident wrote, 'If they go on building at such a rate, London will soon be next door to us.'[19]

The pace of development accelerated in the mid-nineteenth century as Clapham's rural pretensions were finally abandoned. The population increased by almost 30% in the 1850s alone. Even when the Bournes arrived in 1855, other than the Common itself, the only significant open space in Clapham were the grounds of the Retreat, a substantial lunatic asylum on the southern side of Larkhall Rise. This was demolished in the 1860s as more new streets were laid out.[20] The ordinary disruption of building development was exacerbated by work on Bazalgette's sewerage system. Henry Bourne had had enough, 'I am looking forward to the change with great pleasure as I think it would be far nicer in the country. Just now Larkhall Lane is very disagreeable as they are making the new sewer, and the place is almost impassable.'[21] He deplored declining local standards. The family's poultry and pigeons were stolen on Christmas Day 1867.[22] The determining factor for Henry Bourne, however, was the ecclesiastical situation. Here too he was disaffected. Fr Coffin's promotion as Redemptorist Provincial in 1865 took him away from St Mary's. The new regime did not match up to our civil servant's exacting requirements. 'The *church* at Clapham seems quite strange—Br Philip has gone and there is a sacristan we do not know—and there are new Fathers, and altogether it seems quite dull and queer. It is time we left Clapham—it is no longer the same place to us.'[23]

'This peaceful locality'

The search for a new home began in earnest in the autumn of 1867. Barnet was rejected on account of its distance from the station.[24] When the family did move, it was in the opposite direction, to Greenhithe in Kent. Again, ecclesiastical concerns were significant. This time, however, it was not the prospect of convert clergy and grand liturgy. Henry Bourne wrote to his elder son, 'We are thinking of taking a house at Greenhithe—I have been in correspondence with one of the clergy there and he says there are several houses to let … There are two Capuchin Fathers there who serve that and two adjoining missions—they are very poor and we might be of some help to them.'[25]

On the southern edge of the Thames estuary, Greenhithe is just three miles beyond Dartford. Although twenty miles from London, the rail links were good. Today Greenhithe is still a separate settlement, but rather less isolated. It lies in the shadow of the Dartford Crossing, faced by oil storage depots and refineries at Thurrock on the other bank of the Thames. There has been much infill and the arrival of housing estates; the Bluewater Shopping Centre is little more than a stone's throw away. Yet when the Bournes arrived in March 1868 this really was the rural idyll they sought. 'Greenhithe is not a town at all—it consists of a railway station, a gentleman's house and park—one little street with a few shops, and a pier into the river, and one terrace of nice houses, quite in the country with nothing but fields and woods around them, and one of these houses we are going to take.'[26]

Both house and terrace are still there, at a slight distance from Greenhithe, on an old country lane which linked the village to the former A2. There is now a noisy, new road below, but the area retains a wooded aspect. Cobham Terrace comprises twenty semi-detached properties built into the hillside. They come as a surprise: three floor houses (now divided into flats), Italianate villas seemingly dropped into the Kent countryside from Bayswater or St John's Wood. The Bournes took a lease of 14 Cobham Terrace. They were delighted by their new home and 'the profound obscurity in which this peaceful locality is immersed.'[27] The house had its own grounds, but the family took a further lease of a kitchen garden 'on the other side of the lane at the back of the flower garden and goes up a steep hill, twice as high as the house, and from the top there is a magnificent view of the Thames. We are having an arbour planted and it will be delightful to sit there and see the vessels passing up and down the river which is very broad and sometimes quite rough.'[28]

For the young Frank life just seemed to get better and better. Greenhithe offered attractions undreamt of in suburban Clapham. Living on the banks of the Thames when Britain really did rule the waves was one constant adventure for a boy who from the earliest age displayed a fascination with matters military and naval. Imagine the excitement: 'There are now two Spanish men-of-war moored off Greenhithe—Frank and I took a boat and asked permission to go over one of them the other day. The officer in command was very polite and ordered a marine to show us everything ... Frank was delighted and one of the sailors gave him a great sea biscuit which he brought home in triumph.'[29] There were holidays to Belgium, Jersey, Lyme Regis and Deal,[30] and Frank was taken swimming in Boulogne by his father.[31] Again, there were trips to the theatre and galleries, and to the world's largest ship, The Great Eastern, when she came to Sheerness.[32] Henry Bourne was just as enthusiastic about providing entertainment indoors too. 'I have today bought Franky a little toy theatre,'[33] proceeding to write productions for it himself for the benefit of the household and its neighbours.

Henry Bourne's interest in the local parish began altruistically. Four years before the Bournes' arrival the Capuchins had founded the Mission in the most grinding of circumstances. One of the priests told the sorry tale: 'I have been in several missions, but I have never got so discouraged as I did on the first day I arrived here. For I found many and very heavy bills to pay, and no coal and no altar wine, no candles, no oil for the lamp, in a word I might say nothing of the necessary things. And we even had to borrow several things to sleep on.'[34] There were plans to build a permanent church for the 400 or so poor Catholics spread across the vicinity; lack of funds meant this was not quickly realised. Instead, the Capuchins operated out of four old cottages on the waterfront, one serving as a school, one as their residence and two as a chapel. 'During the summer the poor people have been able to stand in the garden during the Mass which was offered up in a room of one of the cottages; but we cannot expect them to do this in the cold weather that is now coming on. We have therefore begun to convert the cottages, which are to be replaced by a church, into a temporary chapel.'[35]

The image of his family as welcome benefactors to this poor outpost of Catholicism gradually lost its attraction for Henry Bourne. He made arrangements for the superior, Fr Maurice, to teach Latin to Frank, who was kitted out with cassock and cotta to serve at the altar, but he soon tired of attending a chapel that 'is nothing but an old wooden cottage.' This was not the standard to which he had become accustomed at St John's, Duncan Terrace or St Mary's, Clapham. Deciding the Greenhithe liturgy insufficiently dignified and polished, Henry Bourne sought a more worthy setting for the Mass in Gravesend, Dartford or Woolwich, taking Frank with him and teaching him about the ritual he loved so much.[36] He even proposed converting a room in Cobham Terrace into a chapel so visiting priests might offer Mass there. For Henry Bourne, everything was steeped in the vocabulary of the Church. He replied to a letter from his elder son, 'Frank was very pleased with yours of yesterday, but it was hardly Pontifical enough to satisfy him—he has published his Pastoral today which I send you for your edification.' It is little wonder that Frank had a great sensitivity towards the religious. 'We went to the National Gallery, and Frank was delighted with the paintings, especially the ones on sacred subjects, but they had such an effect on him that he dreamed about them, and began talking about them in his sleep and crying about them in the most excited manner during the night.'[37]

This was an isolated incident in an otherwise remarkably happy early childhood. No wonder the Cardinal reminisced fondly fifty years later: 'I could not have had a better home. There was no room for extravagance but there was real comfort, and everything reasonable in the way of good wholesome amusement for a child. My father's salary gradually increased, and he had every hope of making suitable provision for the education and future of his two boys.'[38] That future seemed set fair.

Notes

[1] Bourne was the first Archbishop of Westminster to be born in the capital city—and was proud of the fact. 'I am a Londoner by birth and the son of a Londoner; and I know London as intimately as most,' *Tablet*, 10 October 1925, p. 477.

[2] *Tablet*, 30 March 1861.

[3] Ackroyd, *London*, p. 344.

[4] *Tablet*, 1 February 1862, p. 73.

[5] Ackroyd, *London*, p. 576.

[6] P. Hughes, 'The Coming Century,' Beck (ed.), *The English Catholics*, p. 20.

[7] FAB, 'Notes,' AAW, Bo. IV/1/1.

[8] Baptism register, St Mary's, Clapham.

[9] FAB, 'Notes,' AAW, Bo. IV/1/1.

[10] This is clear from Francis Bourne's birth certificate and from contemporary local directories. The numbering has, however, given rise to some confusion. A local architectural guide gives the current No. 5 Larkhall Rise, on the south side of the road, as the birthplace of the future Cardinal, while simultaneously dating the house more than a decade after his birth. The Cardinal's own autobiographical fragment written in 1917 identifies the family home as No. *10* Larkhall Rise. The answer lies in the development of new streets from the mid-1860s which led to the re-numbering of houses in Larkhall Rise. What had been No.5, on the north side of the road, now became No. 10.

[11] Oldmeadow, *Francis Cardinal Bourne*, i, p. 24.

[12] Henry Bourne to Harry Bourne, 23 October 1867, UCA, Bourne Family Papers, OS/K2/30.

[13] Henry Bourne to Harry Bourne, 5 December 1867, UCA, Bourne Family Papers, OS/K2/31.

[14] FAB, 'Notes,' AAW, Bo. IV/1/1.

[15] Henry Bourne to Harry Bourne, 5 December 1867, UCA, Bourne Family Papers, OS/K2/31. (A zouave was a papal soldier who fought to save the Temporal Power of the Popes.)

[16] Henry Bourne to Harry Bourne, 1 January 1868 (misdated 1867), UCA, Bourne Family Papers, OS/K2/24.

[17] Ibid.

[18] Henry Bourne to Harry Bourne, 4 March 1868, UCA, Bourne Family Papers, OS/K2/44.

19. Cited Ackroyd, *London*, p. 517.
20. Clegg, *Clapham Past*, pp. 22, 70.
21. Henry Bourne to Harry Bourne, 21 February 1868, UCA, Bourne Family Papers, OS/K2/43.
22. Henry Bourne to Harry Bourne, 1 January 1868 (misdated 1867), UCA, Bourne Family Papers, OS/K2/24.
23. Henry Bourne to Harry Bourne, 23 September 1867, UCA, Bourne Family Papers, OS/K2/26.
24. Henry Bourne to Harry Bourne, 29 September 1867, UCA, Bourne Family Papers, OS/K2/27.
25. Henry Bourne to Harry Bourne, 22 January 1868, UCA, Bourne Family Papers, OS/K2/38.
26. Henry Bourne to Harry Bourne, 1 February 1868, UCA, Bourne Family Papers, OS/K2/40.
27. Henry Bourne to Harry Bourne, 5 January 1869 (misdated 1868), UCA, Bourne Family Papers, OS/K2/35.
28. Henry Bourne to Harry Bourne, Good Friday 1869, UCA, Bourne Family Papers, OS/K2/50.
29. Henry Bourne to Harry Bourne, 3 May 1868, UCA, Bourne Family Papers, OS/K2/52.
30. FAB, 'Notes,' AAW, Bo. IV/1/1.
31. Henry Bourne to Harry Bourne, 7 July 1868, UCA, Bourne Family Papers, OS/K2/58.
32. Henry Bourne to Harry Bourne, 3 June 1869, UCA, Bourne Family Papers, OS/K3/82.
33. Henry Bourne to Harry Bourne, 12 February 1869, UCA, Bourne Family Papers, OS/K3/72.
34. Fr Louis to anon. recipient, 19 November 1869, SAA, Greenhithe file.
35. Fr O'Sullivan and Fr Maurice to the Editor, *Tablet*, 15 October 1864.
36. Henry Bourne to Harry Bourne, 1 April 1868, UCA, Bourne Family Papers, OS/K2/48.
37. Henry Bourne to Harry Bourne, 8 November 1868, UCA, Bourne Family Papers, OS/K2/66.
38. FAB, 'Notes,' AAW, Bo. IV/1/1.

Chapter 3

In hac lacrimarum valle

'A hard school for young boys far from home'[1]

Given his own miserable experience of school, it is a surprise to find Henry Bourne choosing to educate his two sons at Ushaw, over 250 miles from London on the northern moors outside Durham. What possessed him to do such a thing?

A respectable Catholic education was essential for Henry Bourne's sons. But the nineteenth-century Church viewed her immediate priority as the provision of elementary education to the working classes who constituted the bulk of her adherents. Catholic establishments for middle class boys—especially for day boys—were thin on the ground. Henry Bourne sought Fr Coffin's advice. As a result, in 1865 Harry, aged just eight, was sent off to St Cuthbert's College, Ushaw.[2] Ushaw was the northern successor to the English College in Douai; St Edmund's, Ware was its counterpart in the South. The closure of Douai during the French Revolution forced staff and students to seek sanctuary in England, where they went their separate ways, north and south. Both successor institutions maintained Douai's tradition of educating both seminarians and lay boys. Under energetic leadership in the mid-nineteenth century, Ushaw expanded rapidly. For a brief while, before the Jesuits and the Benedictines cornered the market, Ushaw could claim to be one of the major Catholic public schools. Henry Bourne wished his sons to benefit from this.

Henry Bourne was concerned that Frank's health might prevent him from following Harry to Ushaw in the immediate future. 'I fear he will not be able to go to the north so early as you, he is so very susceptible of cold.'[3] This anxiety for the future Cardinal's health was to dominate his childhood and adolescence, but the move to Greenhithe seemed to augur a change for the better. But then his father was fretting about the company his younger son was keeping. 'Frank is very much in want of companions here—we do not care for him to be too intimate with Protestant boys like Freddy Mounsey, and there is no one else with whom he can associate.

It will be a very good thing when he is old enough to go to College with you.'[4] Later that same year, Frank was sent to join his brother. In September 1869 Ellen Bourne accompanied her son on the long train journey north, stopping off at York, before arriving at Durham.[5] Then the final four miles were travelled west through Bear Park, to the College itself.

As Frank Bourne had plenty of opportunity to discover, Ushaw could be an exposed and desolate place in the depths of winter. Yet in the early autumn sun its aspect is extremely appealing—imposing buildings set back from the road and shaded by substantial trees. Built as seminary and school, it is a massive complex of Victorian neo-Gothic stone. For someone raised by his father to appreciate ecclesiastical architecture, Pugin's seminary chapel would have been a cause for great delight. The two Bourne brothers were, however, next door in the Junior House designed by Pugin's son, E. W. Pugin, and built just a decade earlier. It formed a self-contained unit with schoolrooms, dormitory, refectory and its own chapel, St Aloysius'.[6] In a very different Church, Ushaw today is a sad shadow of its former self. The Junior House was closed in 1973, the glazing has gone and plants grow from the walls and roofs where five generations ago Frank Bourne, a small and delicate boy, entered the Fifth Class of Rudiments, the lowest in the school. The major seminary followed suit in 2011.[7]

'A martyr to his zeal'[8]

Frank's reaction to his arrival in this new environment was natural enough. Reports of his homesickness at the end of October are rapidly replaced by news of his settling down to school life.[9] When he bade farewell to his father in September 1869, Frank could not have suspected that they were never to meet again in this life. Although Henry Bourne was just 43, there had been indications for some time that all was not well.

In later life the Cardinal was subjected to a good deal of very unattractive snobbery. Evelyn Waugh wrote for his own peculiar motives: 'His upbringing was singularly narrow. His predecessor had been an aristocrat, his successor was the son of the village carpenter, each with the generous candour of his origin. Bourne came from a home of genteel poverty.'[10] Others imply, given his employer, that the Cardinal's father had been a postman.[11] The Bournes were not of the same standing, socially or financially, as the Mannings or the Vaughans. Henry Bourne

In hac lacrimarum valle

was a civil servant in the employ of the General Post Office. He was proud of the fact. After twenty years of service to the State, he had risen to a senior position of considerable responsibility.

In the 1860s the British Government was attempting to buy out the private interests controlling the electric telegraph networks. Henry Bourne was involved in the negotiations. 'I am just starting out for the House of Commons—I have been there a good deal during the week—our arbitration [concerning the value of submarine cables] with Reuters Telegram Company is very interesting as the great electrical people and a great many of the best lawyers are engaged on it.'[12] Characteristically, the family are kept abreast of his work: 'Frank takes great interest in telegraphs, and we have long conversations together on the subject.'[13] Simultaneously, Henry Bourne was involved in auditing the accounts of the P&O Company on the Government's behalf.[14] He also threw himself into various voluntary activities connected to his employment; he was one of the main figures behind the founding of the Civil Service Stores, a cooperative enterprise, and a frequent contributor to his professional paper, *The Civilian*.[15]

All this took its toll on his health. He was worried about his standard of living and financial position. 'I have been working like a galley-slave since last August, and have not yet been paid a single sixpence for my labours.'[16] He was not returning to Greenhithe until eight in the evening—and then often resuming work back home late into the night.[17] Henry Bourne wrote a surprisingly candid letter to his elder son, aged just 12 at the time. 'And now, Harry, I want you to undertake a few prayers for me every day for a short time, especially to our Blessed Lady. I have a great deal of anxiety and trouble—I have been very much overworked and annoyed of late, and am also very unwell—so I want you to pray for me. When you write, don't allude to what I have said here, as neither mamma nor Aunty know that I have written to you in this way, but I am sure that you will not forget to do what I ask. God bless you, dear boy.'[18] Matters came to a head in the summer of 1869 when he collapsed at work, and was taken home to recuperate.

Relief was offered from an unlikely source. Appreciative of his auditing work, P&O gave free passage to Henry Bourne, his wife and sister-in-law to the solemn opening of the new Suez Canal. The family leapt at the opportunity. Not only did it promise advantages for his ailing health, but it also allowed Henry Bourne to follow in his father's footsteps– indeed, in Egypt he met some of his father's acquaintances from a generation earlier. Amid much excitement and planning, the eastern journey was eagerly anticipated as Frank travelled to Ushaw in September. The little party were outside Alexandria by early November. Their concerns marked them as typical British tourists: over-priced and over-filled hotels, fleas and mosquitoes, natives who are 'filthy' but 'picturesque.'[19] Dutifully, they saw the sights in Alexandria and Cairo. Climbing the Grand Pyramid, Ellen Bourne was forced to remove her crinolines—her only recorded act of informality.[20] There was time for a little souvenir shopping as well. Frank got the 'tarboosh,' or Turkish cap, on which he had set his heart.[21]

The highlight of the journey, of course, was the opening of the Canal itself. At Port Said, the Bournes' P&O vessel docked alongside the Emperor Franz Josef's yacht and they were spectators to the stream of visiting royalty and dignitaries. The Empress Eugenie made a particular impression upon the English bystander, 'looking charming, and her elegance of manner is most authentic. Singularly enough she and Ellen were dressed in exactly the same colour.' The Bournes were present at the blessing of the Canal: 'The Royal Pavilion—the two chapels [Christian and Muslim]—the costumes and the shipping, and the blue Mediterranean as a background, all formed a scene never to be forgotten.' Then there was the grand ball to be looked forward to.[22] It was a world away from the daily life of a London civil servant.

By the end of November the party were almost home. Writing onboard the SS Delhi in the English Channel, Henry Bourne looked optimistically to the future. 'There have been a few physical discomforts on the journey; but when they are once over, the benefit to health, and the pleasant reminiscences will remain.'[23]

Ten weeks later he was dead. The end came at the family home in Greenhithe on 18 February 1870. Obviously, he was not a well man before he left these shores, but the official cause of death was recorded as two months' dysentery.[24]

The news reached Ushaw two days later. The Rector of the minor seminary, Fr Francis Wilkinson, sent for the two brothers after the Sunday High Mass. 'I have communicated the sad news as tenderly as I could to Harry and Frank, and have done all in my power to console them in their sad affliction. They have just gone from my room at this moment and have gone to the Chapel to pray for their Papa.' As a concession the brothers were allowed to spend the remainder of the day in each other's company.[25]

To that point, it was the father, rather than his mother, who played the more significant role in young Frank Bourne's life. Frank spent his days in Clapham and Greenhithe with his mother and aunt while his father toiled at his civil servant's desk. The two sisters gave him his first lessons at home. Yet it was the father who captured the child's imagination, shared his hopes and joys, captivated him with his own career and interests. In particular he passed on the gift of faith. 'My father taught me a great deal about the Mass and the Liturgy, in which he was keenly interested … I was much with my father in his free time and he used to take me to visit various churches with him … He taught me how to use an English Missal when I was still very young. In all kinds of ways he made me interested in the work of the Church and to realise the grace of being a Catholic.'[26] It was Henry Bourne who corresponded with his sons when they went away to school. There was a generosity of character in the father, a warm sociability. Elements of these traits would be apparent in his son later in life, but often suppressed, hidden from the gaze of all save a favoured few. More to the fore was the steely determination supplied by his mother in her widowhood. Would the Cardinal have enjoyed easier relations with his peers, would he have been more expansive, less prone to misinterpretation had his father lived? Possibly; but then perhaps it was his mother's unbending drive which propelled him to ecclesiastical prominence.

'Constant anxiety and self-sacrifice'[27]

With Henry Bourne's death, the family income largely disappeared. The home in Greenhithe had to be given up and the furniture sold. For two decades Ellen Bourne and her sister led a peripatetic life. Mother and aunt stayed first with friends in Chislehurst, then in Belgium. Although their circumstances were inevitably straitened, the two sisters could have managed to make ends meet—just—by eking out the small annuity payable on Henry Bourne's death and their own family inheritance reduced, as it was, by their uncle's profligacy. There were, however, certain compromises Ellen Bourne never contemplated. Simple economics suggested the £100 or more spent annually on her sons' school fees and expenses was an unaffordable luxury. Ellen Bourne would not hear of it.

The two sisters tried to survive in a rented apartment in Dalston, on the fringes of Hackney, but the expense proved too great. Ellen was unable to afford a family holiday in 1872, with the result that her two sons spent their summer at Ushaw. She resolved that something had to be done. She and her sister took work across the Channel, Ellen first as a 'reader' to a blind Russian prince, and then, both of them, as governesses. By sheer hard work and considerable self-sacrifice, she continued to finance the two brothers' education.[28] Not for several years did her sons know the full truth of the situation.[29]

Frank was just eight at the time of his father's death. There is a real poignancy in the Cardinal's admission later in life that he 'remembers very little of his father's appearance, but can recall little things that happened in his lifetime, and felt the want of him very much as he grew up.'[30] Perhaps his age explains Frank's resilience in the face of the family bereavement. At thirteen Harry was affected to a far greater extent, although uncomfortable displaying his grief in his younger brother's presence.[31] While never showing anything approaching brilliance, Harry developed an application to his studies and a gravity not previously evident, one influence, no doubt, leading him to consider a vocation to the priesthood. Harry Bourne received the tonsure in Ushaw College Chapel three and half years later.

'Making plenty of row'

Frank, by comparison, rapidly bounced back and showed himself a normal and ebullient schoolboy. He was physically small and inclined to be delicate, so that, at least in the early days, as his contemporaries played sports, one of the seminarians was delegated to take him on country walks. Later, Frank was able to join in the games of handball and battledore (an early form of shuttlecock).[32] His stature and constitution proved no constraint. 'He was very persistent and persevering in expressing his opinions in the Playroom, and although the smallest and youngest among us, he would always have his say in the matter and got a clout or kick for daring to lay down the law to his elders.'[33] Much belied by his later dignity, the Cardinal seems to have been something of a tearaway in his early schooldays. His brother wrote to his mother, 'Frank seems to go in for making plenty of row... I hear he is quite a bother to the philosophers.'[34] (The philosophers were older students already studying for the priesthood who were frequently called upon to act as assistant tutors to their juniors in the classroom.)

Frank's inseparable companion during these years was Henry Patmore, son of the convert Victorian poet Coventry Patmore, himself showing considerable ability as a writer and poet until his early death from consumption. The two were irrepressible. One afternoon was spent 'catching bumble bees and putting them in a tin box. In the middle of the School they lifted the lid and the bees made for the window. You may imagine the pandemonium that ensued ... Poor Earnshaw sat at the rostrum helpless.' On another occasion a future bishop of Shrewsbury—then the seminarian responsible for the College Library—was their victim. As the librarian turned out the lights, the two miscreants, hidden under his desk, proceeded to stick pins into his legs. The future Cardinal was known among his Ushaw contemporaries as 'Punk'[35]—a fact he might not care to have been reminded of fifty years later.

His academic record was good rather than outstanding. 'The name of Francis Bourne usually appeared near the top of a school of thirty, in places varying from second to tenth, but more often nearer the former position.'[36] He was sufficiently hard working to be in line for a scholarship to supplement the family finances.[37] Inadvertently, the thirteen year old gave an insight into the state of those finances when writing to his mother in Paris, 'Though I have got a good many clothes, they are shabby and some are getting quite threadbare in parts.'[38] There are hints also of his father's influence and his own natural inclinations. 'Another classmate of his was the late Alexander de Verteuil. Both Bourne and de Verteuil were famous in the School for their knowledge of the Lives of the Saints, and if any of us wished to know anything in the life of a particular Saint, we always trusted Bourne or de Verteuil.'[39]

The normalities of family life virtually disappeared for Harry and Frank Bourne. The boys were able to cross over to Belgium for the first summer after their father's death to spend their holidays with their mother and aunt. In Ostend they were witnesses to the changing world order. The seaside resort was filled with French refugees fleeing the Franco-Prussian War.[40] The family re-assembled for the summer of 1873, courtesy of friends in Dundalk, Co. Louth. But in 1871 Frank's summer holiday was spent tramping the London pavements around Dalston and Camberwell. The following year the family circumstances permitted no travelling at all; the two brothers remained at the school for the entire summer. However melancholy this might seem to modern sensibilities, it was not rare then for middle class children whose family rhythms were dictated by bereavement and British military and imperial commitments.

Schooldays at Ushaw passed against the backdrop of mid-Victorian life. The brothers' letters are peppered with references to colonial wars and miners' strikes in the Durham coal fields. And always there was the cycle of the liturgical year in the midst of a Catholic seminary. Both brothers were present in October 1873 at the celebrations marking the fifty years of priesthood of Ushaw's President, Mgr Tate. Bishops and priests thronged the College for Pontifical High Mass and celebratory concerts and dinners.[41] The Victorians were accustomed to the presence of death, even among the young, in a way which we would find disturbing. But the Bourne brothers still found macabre and chilling the death of the sixteen year old student James Byrne in April 1870. He hung himself in an Ushaw dormitory, apparently, to experience 'the sensation of being hung by the neck.' The coroner's verdict of 'accidental death' must, however, be viewed with a certain suspicion.[42] There were deaths at home as well as at school. Charles Bourne died in 1871, his sister-in-law conditionally baptising him on his deathbed. His daughter, Agnes, Frank's cousin and childhood playmate, returned from her Belgian convent school to die the following year.

'Poor Harry'[43]

Frank's relations with his brother sound entirely normal and healthy. As his junior, Frank 'went in awe' of Harry, being no doubt alternately embarrassed and proud of the presence of an elder sibling in the same school.[44] Harry didn't see matters in quite the same light. Frank 'does not favour me with much of his company, no doubt his schoolfellows are more congenial companions.'[45] Frank's preferences are not surprising. Harry employs all the pomposity of an eighteen year old in his dealings with his younger brother, 'So Frank has deigned this time to pen you an epistle. The child is condescending. I have lately had one or two long talks with him; I think he does not much care for them.'[46]

Allowance must be made for Harry Bourne in the spring of 1874. He was listless and seriously ill. The doctor 'thinks my stomach very bad indeed, and has given me a mixture, which he says will set it right in three or four weeks. I certainly feel at present very far from right, headaches, sleepy by day, wakeful by night, no appetite, pains everywhere, especially

In hac lacrimarum valle

all about the shoulders, and as weak as a kitten.[47] The end of the three week period saw no such improvement. Harry was forbidden to continue his studies; the summer exams were out of the question. Suffering from bile, he was prescribed port wine and cod liver oil.[48] When he left Ushaw at the end of May, the future was ominously clear to his contemporaries.

Harry Bourne went to his grandmother and uncle's home in Camberwell. His mother hurried from Paris to be with him. For all her self-control and stern exterior, she must have been emotionally distraught. Only four years had elapsed since the burial of her young husband. Since then she had witnessed the premature deaths of her brother-in-law and niece. Now she was called upon to nurse her elder son on his deathbed. At the end of the summer term Frank joined the dismal family gathering. He too was present, therefore, at the end. Harry Bourne died of consumption, aged eighteen, on 3 September 1874.

'Unduly influenced by sad thoughts'

His brother's death affected Frank in a way his father's had not. At thirteen he was more sensitive to the loss. Frank had not seen his father for five months before he died; he was continually in the presence of his dying brother during those final six weeks. Frank returned to Ushaw much altered. Harry's death 'undoubtedly had a very marked effect on me, making me more serious and pensive than I would otherwise have been, and, perhaps, unduly influenced by sad thoughts … I was not happy. I did not get on with my work.'[49] Robert Laing, a young deacon and Harry's former tutor, promised Ellen Bourne to do all he could for her younger son. Despite Frank's assurances to the young cleric that he was recovering from his grief, it was clear that all was far from well.[50] With the onset of another severe northern winter, Frank developed a heavy cold. His health became precarious once more.[51] The authorities feared the worst and advised his removal to a milder climate. Faced with the prospect of losing the last remaining member of her own family, Ellen Bourne acted immediately. Frank was withdrawn from Ushaw in January 1875.[52]

For six months, all thought of study was abandoned. Frank returned to Camberwell under the supervision of the family doctor and the watchful eye of his grandmother and uncle. Only once they were convinced that he was fully restored to health was he permitted to travel. In July he went down to the Isle of Wight to stay with his aunt, working as a governess for the Montgolfier family. The following month he made his own way across the Channel to his mother in Paris. Ellen Bourne had to decide where Frank was to continue his education. She chose Ushaw's sister foundation in the south.

St Edmund's, Ware

Referred to as 'St Edmund's, *Ware*,' the College is, in fact, some miles distant from that town. Rather, it is located in the scattered settlement of Old Hall Green in north-eastern Hertfordshire, not far from the borders of Essex and Cambridgeshire. The buildings stand in pleasant parkland, just back from the old Cambridge road, the A10. Thirty-five miles north of London, it was still a secluded rural location. At the end of the eighteenth century a small Catholic school existed at Old Hall Green, and it was here that the clerical refugees arrived from revolutionary France. Douai was reconstituted on English soil on 16 November (St Edmund's Day) 1793. The original buildings of Old Hall Green were supplemented by a functional central block of white brick—what Pugin called 'The Priest Factory.' To this Pugin was commissioned to add a new chapel. He succeeded magnificently under irksome constraints. A shrine chapel dedicated to the College's patron was added in 1873. As in the north, Frank Bourne was able to practise his Catholic faith in Gothic splendour.

St Edmund's continued the old Douai tradition of educating Catholic lay boys alongside those destined for priestly ministry. However, just six years prior to Frank's arrival, Archbishop Manning had seriously changed the nature of the institution. In the sixteenth century the Council of Trent had called for a holy priesthood, properly formed in seminaries, where future priests would study and pray apart from the world. This was the model adopted across Catholic Europe. In its pure form, it was unknown in England. For more than two centuries all serious efforts at Catholic education in any guise had to be carried on overseas. When Douai did eventually settle in England, lack of money and significant numbers meant that the Tridentine decrees were still not implemented. However, in the new mood of triumphalism sweeping the English Church following the restoration of the hierarchy, Manning decided that the moment had arrived to bring this country into line with the European system of separate seminaries. In 1869 he withdrew the theological students from Old Hall Green, leaving behind those boys intended for a secular career and 'the church boys' still completing initial school studies or beginning their philosophy.

Ellen Bourne accompanied her son back to London and together they visited Mgr James Patterson, the President of St Edmund's, at St James's, Spanish Place.[53] The young schoolboy favourably impressed the priest and Frank entered St Edmund's as a lay boy on 28 August 1875.[54] He was to be intimately concerned with the College for the next six decades. Manning countered criticism of his changes and emphasized the traditional identity and objectives of St Edmund's in his Exhibition Day speech that year: 'It was a great joy to me to see so many coming down to me in cassocks, but I was glad when I saw others coming down in jackets. I was glad because we want good Catholic laymen—we want laymen in the world who will live the lives and speak the language of priests ... I rejoice to see our young laymen growing up in the midst of our young priests, and I rejoice to see our young priests growing up in the midst of our laymen. Their early formation is identical ... Upon that formation together they contract friendships which go through life binding the two together.'[55]

Twenty years later, on the day of his own episcopal consecration, Frank Bourne acknowledged his debt to the kindness shown by Mgr Patterson: 'For had it not been for the care taken of him when he was ill for a year at St Edmund's College, Ware, he would not have been there that day.'[56] Health remained a major concern. The family doctor maintained that, 'If he could only get to twenty-two without a cold he would be all right but, if he got a cold before that, he would be done for.'[57] A disturbing prognosis. During this time of adolescent anxiety, the young schoolboy turned for help to his confessor, Fr Le Grave.[58]

Frank's family also sought reassurance from Fr Le Grave. The priest replied to his aunt's enquiry in early 1876: 'I am very thankful to you for showing that you believe I take an interest in your nephew's welfare. I certainly do so for he is both a clever boy and a good boy, and I have asked him several times to come to me and have a quiet talk over anything that might be difficult to him, or a subject of anxiety. I did so because the same thing struck me that struck yourself, namely that he seemed very quiet for one of his age, and knowing the sad death of his brother, I feared he too might be delicate. However he has assured me that he was perfectly well, and that he had no source of anxiety, though I cannot help thinking he is sometimes a little low spirited ... I think his present state of seriousness may be due only to a certain feeling of vague responsibility that not infrequently comes over boys when they first begin to think seriously of their future life ...'⁵⁹ Frank Bourne was indeed thinking seriously of his future life.

Notes

1. FAB, Notes, 1917, cited Oldmeadow, *Francis Cardinal Bourne*, i, p. 45.
2. Oldmeadow, *Francis Cardinal Bourne*, i, p. 45.
3. Henry Bourne to Harry Bourne, 15 October 1867, UCA, Bourne Family Papers, OS/K2/29.
4. Henry Bourne to Harry Bourne, 4 February 1869, UCA, Bourne Family Papers, OS/K3/71.
5. Oldmeadow, *Francis Cardinal Bourne*, i, p. 47.
6. *St Cuthbert's Seminary, Ushaw College : A Brief History*, u/d, p. 18.
7. 'Cardinal Bourne and Ushaw,' *The Ushaw Magazine*, p. 2.
8. Obituary of Henry Bourne, *The Civilian*, February 1870.
9. Henry Bourne to Mr Melling, 21 October & 29 November 1869, UCA, Bourne Family Papers, OS/K3/92 & 96.
10. E. Waugh, *The Life of Ronald Knox* (London: Chapman & Hall, 1959), pp. 166–167.
11. S. Leslie, *The Passing Chapter* (London: Cassells, 1934), p. 205.
12. Henry Bourne to Harry Bourne, 20 March 1868, UCA, Bourne Family Papers, OS/K2/30.
13. Henry Bourne to Harry Bourne, 20 October 1868, UCA, Bourne Family Papers, OS/K2/64.
14. Henry Bourne to Harry Bourne, 20 June 1869, UCA, Bourne Family Papers, OS/K3/83.
15. W. Meynell (ed.), *Cardinal Bourne: A Record* (London: Burns & Oates, c. 1912), pp. 11–12.
16. Henry Bourne to Harry Bourne, 10 April 1868, UCA, Bourne Family Papers, OS/K2/49.
17. Henry Bourne to Harry Bourne, 20 June 1869, UCA, Bourne Family Papers, OS/K3/83 .
18. Henry Bourne to Harry Bourne, 3 December 1868, UCA, Bourne Family Papers, OS/K2/69.
19. Henry Bourne to Sarah Bourne, 6 November 1869, UCA, Bourne Family Papers, OS/K3/94.
20. Henry Bourne to S. Bourne, 17 November 1869, UCA, Bourne Family Papers, OS/K3/95.
21. Henry Bourne to Mr Melling, 23 December 1869, UCA, Bourne Family Papers, OS/K3/98.
22. Henry Bourne to S. Bourne, 17 November 1869, UCA, Bourne Family Papers,

In hac lacrimarum valle

OS/K3/95.
23   Henry Bourne to Melling, 29 November 1869, UCA, Bourne Family Papers, OS/K3/96.
24   Death certificate, UCA, OS/K4/101.
25   Fr Wilkinson to Ellen Bourne, 20 February 1870, UCA, Bourne Family Papers, OS/K4/101; Harry Bourne to Ellen Bourne & Mary Byrne, cited Oldmeadow, *Francis Cardinal Bourne*, i, p. 49.
26   FAB, 'Notes,' AAW, Bo. IV/1/1.
27   *Ibid.*
28   *Ibid.*
29   Harry Bourne to Ellen Bourne & Mary Byrne, 30 April 1874, Bourne Family Papers, UCA, OS/K4/114.
30   Stuart, 'Notes,' AAW, Bo. IV/1/27.
31   Harry Bourne to Ellen Bourne & Mary Byrne, cited Oldmeadow, *Francis Cardinal Bourne*, i, p. 49.
32   'Cardinal Bourne and Ushaw,' *The Ushaw Magazine*, March 1935, pp. 2–4.
33   Fr Kerr to Fr Corboy, 8 February 1935, UCA, Bourne Family Papers, OS/K4/136.
34   Harry Bourne to Ellen Bourne, 16 November 1873, UCA, Bourne Family Papers, OS/K4/106.
35   Kerr to Corboy, 8 February 1935, UCA, Bourne Family Papers, OS/K4/136.
36   'Cardinal Bourne and Ushaw,' *The Ushaw Magazine*, March 1935, p.3.
37   Henry Bourne to Ellen Bourne & Mary Byrne, 30 April 1874, UCA, Bourne Family Papers, OS/K4/114.
38   FAB to Ellen Bourne & Mary Byrne, 6 April 1874, UCA, Bourne Family Papers, OS/K4/113.
39   Kerr to Corboy, 8 February 1935, UCA, Bourne Family Papers, OS/K4/136.
40   FAB, 'Notes,' AAW, Bo. IV/1/1.
41   *Tablet*, 1 November 1873, p. 563.
42   *Ibid.*, 7 May 1870, p. 591.
43   Rev R. C. Laing to Ellen Bourne, 24 September 1874, UCA, Bourne Family Papers, OS/K4/117.
44   FAB, 'Notes,' AAW, Bo. IV/1/1.
45   Harry Bourne to Ellen Bourne, 16 November 1873, UCA, Bourne Family Papers, OS/K4/106.
46   Harry Bourne to Ellen Bourne & Mary Byrne, 2 April 1874, UCA, Bourne Family Papers, OS/K4/112.
47   Harry Bourne to Ellen Bourne & Mary Byrne, 30 April 1874, UCA, Bourne Family Papers, OS/K4/114.
48   Harry Bourne to Ellen Bourne & Mary Byrne, 19 May 1874, UCA, Bourne Family Papers, OS/K4/115.
49   *Ibid.*

50. Laing to Ellen Bourne, UCA, Bourne Family Papers, OS/K4/117.
51. Stuart, 'Notes,' AAW, Bo. IV/1/27.
52. FAB, 'Notes,' AAW, Bo. IV/1/1.
53. *Ibid.*
54. R. Butcher to Oldmeadow, 1936, AAW IV/1/32a.
55. Cardinal Manning, Exhibition Day, St Edmund's, 6 July 1875, *Tablet*, 17 July 1875, p. 83.
56. *Catholic Herald*, 8 May 1896.
57. Stuart, 'Notes,' AAW, Bo. IV/1/27.
58. FAB, 'Notes,' AAW, Bo. IV/1/1.
59. Fr Le Grave to Mary Byrne, 2 February 1876, UCA, Bourne Family Papers, OS/K4/118.

Chapter 4

Putting on the Cassock

'Unless the question is put to them'

When Francis Bourne entered St Edmund's the most immediate concern was his health. Assuming that held out, the wider question of his future life remained open. Was he destined for public service like his father, or commerce and the professions as his uncles? That priesthood was also considered should come as no surprise. The Bournes' was a devout Catholic home. Prayer and the presence of priests were a constant before the family were scattered by death, study and financial necessity. Francis had been his father's companion at the liturgy and in visiting churches. He had served at the altar from the earliest age. His playthings were purple stoles and the composition of pastoral letters. Both his schools were run by priests and doubled up as seminaries. His own brother studied for the priesthood at Ushaw. As a young boy he had automatically assumed that he would, in the fullness of time, follow the same path.

Yet when he arrived at St Edmund's he hesitated. The uncertainties raised by bereavement reinforced the natural doubt and self-questioning of adolescence. Thirty years later he recalled that on arrival at St Edmund's he had 'a boy's vague fancy that some day, perhaps at the end of Rhetoric, I might think of studying for the Church; but during my first years, even these uncertain thoughts passed completely away.'[1]

What caused him then to decide that the priestly vocation was the one God intended him to pursue? With the benefit of hindsight and his own experience as a seminary rector, Francis Bourne wrote about the discernment of a priestly vocation. He felt the essential criteria were a strong character, 'seriousness of disposition, piety, obedience, consideration, and "the *wish* for the priesthood."'[2] Francis more than adequately fulfilled most of these. But what about that last criterion, 'the wish for priesthood'? He specifically addressed this, 'There are undoubtedly cases in which no wish will be expressed unless the priest or confessor gives some opportunity for it. There are excellent boys with very clear vocations, who will not speak of them, unless the question is put to them.'[3]

The question was put to Francis Bourne in the spring of 1877 when the Lenten Retreat for the lay boys was led by Fr Francis Stanfield. As parish priest of Hertford, he was well known to the boys. An energetic character and great organiser, he composed numerous hymns, including 'O Sacred Heart' and 'Sweet Sacrament Divine.' Having heard Francis's confession, Fr Stanfield 'asked him point-blank if he had thought of the priesthood. He said that he had some thoughts of it but that no decision need be taken at present. However, the Director of the Retreat, whether by some special light on the question or some suggestion from the authorities, pressed very urgently that the decision should be made at once and said he would speak to the President.'[4] The Cardinal recalled, 'Acting on Fr Stanfield's advice, I put on the cassock, to Mgr Patterson's great satisfaction, after the Easter holidays.'[5]

Thereafter, although he might question how this vocation was to be exercised in practice, the priesthood itself was never in issue. 'My mind was led to see what God meant me to do with my life, and from that time it remained fixed and unmoved.'[6] The only occasion on which Francis raised other possibilities had nothing to do with internal doubt. After taking his decision, he realised the continuing sacrifice this would cause his mother. His studies would be extended by many years. There would be no future salary to support his mother and aunt in their old age. He offered to leave the College and seek employment. Ellen Bourne, with characteristic firmness, would not entertain the idea. She replied that her son 'was perfectly free to follow God's call, if he had one, to the priesthood, or to choose a career in the world, but as to the proper length of time for his studies, that was for her to judge and that he was going to remain at school until he was eighteen.'[7] End of discussion.

Which diocese Francis was to study, and eventually be ordained, for? The issue lay—as it would throughout his life—between Westminster and Southwark. The two dioceses comprised London north and south of the Thames respectively. Westminster covered the counties of Middlesex, Hertfordshire and—at that time—Essex. Southwark extended across the counties of Surrey, Sussex and Kent; before 1882 it also included Hampshire, the Channel Islands and Berkshire. Although St Edmund's was in the Westminster Diocese, most Southwark seminarians at the time also began their studies there. Then as now, those wishing to pursue a calling to the priesthood could apply to whichever they diocese they wished. Normally, residence, the location of the family home, was the determining factor. As Francis had been born and raised in Surrey and Kent, as the only place he could call home—his grandmother and uncle's house in Camberwell—was in south London, Southwark was the obvious choice. Francis applied there—to the Chapter, the canons of St George's Cathedral, Southwark, who, if so inclined, would recommend him to the bishop. But the canons delayed, concerned by his health. They sought someone strong enough for the rigours of parish ministry. They did not want the financial responsibility of lifelong care of an invalid. Yet Francis had impressed the President of St Edmund's. Mgr Patterson saw Southwark's hesitation as Westminster's opportunity and urged Francis to make an immediate decision in favour of his own diocese. It was Francis' confessor, Fr Le Grave, who counselled caution. Southwark's answer came eventually; it was acceptance.[8]

Seminary Life

Fifty years later the then Cardinal wrote about seminary education. Certain passages appear to border on the autobiographical, relating to this time at St Edmund's. 'A boy or youth is a very reserved and shy being, where his most intimate concerns are in question; an English boy especially so. Yet he craves for understanding and sympathy, and will give his confidence gladly, when it has been fully won.'[9] The work displays a surprising realism. 'No one will be surprised to find that those who are called to the priesthood do often experience in youth very strong temptations arising from their newly awakened instincts of manhood. It is the obvious attack on one who is called to perpetual continence, so obvious that the evil one rarely fails to make use of it ... Boys of apparently unemotional character have sometimes very deep-seated sources of feeling, sensation and temptation ... such temptations are no sign of absence of real vocation.'[10] The Cardinal acknowledged the boredom which may descend on the second year seminarian. 'The monotony of daily routine begins to tell ... though it may last several months, it is essentially transitory and *no decision should be taken while it lasts.*' [11] Yet above and beyond the daily seminary regime, never to be under-estimated, remained the noble calling of priesthood. 'There can be no state of life higher and in itself more holy than that of those who are called to be ministers of the real and of the mystical bodies of Jesus Christ. There is no room here for comparisons and contrasts ... The priesthood stands alone.'[12]

Academically, Francis experienced no difficulties. He was 'a diligent and careful student,'[13] consistently first, very occasionally second, in his studies in the humanities and sciences, and then philosophy.[14] The highlights of the year at St Edmund's were the patronal feast day in November and Exhibition Day at the end of the summer term. The latter was an opportunity for recitals, speeches and prize-giving. In July 1879 Francis recited in Latin 'The Death of Pan' for Cardinal Manning and other assembled guests.[15] By now he was already a cleric, having received the tonsure the preceding St Edmund's Day. Manning was supposed to have conferred this, but, suffering from a cold, Cardinal Howard, stepped in and did the honours.[16] A year later Francis received from Bishop Weathers the first two minor orders, doorkeeper and lector. His liturgical sensibility was acknowledged as we find him acting as master of ceremonies at the grander College ceremonies.[17]

Elsewhere he was deemed worthy of responsibility too. Aged eighteen, the College President asked him to accompany a younger boy home to his family in Turin at the end of the summer term. Summer holidays were invariably spent in France—amusing himself in Paris while his mother and aunt worked. In 1878 he was able to visit the magnificent Paris Exhibition. Then for a few brief weeks the small family party travelled in the French provinces.[18]

While a seminarian at St Edmund's Francis developed the thirst and capacity for spiritual reading which remained with him for life. His choice was significant. Here he discovered the writings of St Francis de Sales, that wise and gentle pastor of the Counter-Reformation. They exercised a profound influence upon him. One of Francis's future professors described the works of the seventeenth-century bishop as 'all redolent of the sweetness, the hopefulness, the reasonableness of that most lovable of saints.'[19] Years later Francis himself described the saint as 'my beloved patron and unfailing guide.'[20] But a contemporary writer had a more immediate impact.

'I have no call for religion'

In March 1880, his study of philosophy largely completed, Francis Bourne left St Edmund's. But he did not pursue the usual path to study theology at Manning's new seminary. English translations had recently appeared of the works of Jean-Baptiste-Henri Lacordaire (1802–1861), the lawyer turned Dominican orator, who captivated Parisian society from the pulpit of Nôtre-Dame. Over the years he had developed a brilliant series of apologetics rebutting attacks on the Catholic Church. They exercised a great influence upon the young seminarian. This was combined with the feeling—often experienced during priestly formation—that he might be called to some 'higher' form of the spiritual life than mundane parish ministry. Despite his mother's doubts, Francis wrote to Bishop Danell of Southwark asking for permission to try his vocation to the religious life.[21] That permission was granted.

In March 1880 Francis entered the Dominican novitiate at Woodchester in Gloucestershire. The Dominican presence in that secluded valley outside Stroud was due to the generosity of the wealthy convert, William Leigh. Those in formation lived a life of austerity, rising early to sing the Divine Office in choir. Although meals and accommodation were of the simplest, the spiritual apprenticeship of the novices was marked by a genuine joy and Anglo-Saxon practicality.[22] However, it rapidly became apparent that Francis had made a mistake. Three months later he wrote again to Bishop Danell to tell him so. While he felt no doubt as to his priestly vocation, 'my stay here has made it clear to me that I have no call for religion. Under these circumstances I write to beg your Lordship to admit me again to study for your diocese.' Francis returned to his uncle's home in Camberwell, to await the Bishop's response.[23]

It was not that simple. It was not so much that Southwark held this foray into religious life against Francis Bourne. It was more concerned with the perennial question of health. While at St Edmund's he had been prescribed a bottle of stout a day on medicinal grounds;[24] reports consistently recorded Francis's health as 'delicate.'[25] His uncle had to reassure Bishop Danell on the point: 'When he left St Edmund's he was carefully re-examined by Dr Munk who pronounced him capable of enduring the Dominican novitiate involving as it does perpetual abstinence and rising at midnight. While at Woodchester his health was excellent and I have a letter from the Prior expressing an opinion that he would have physically benefited by a continuance of the monastic discipline.'[26]

Not everyone accepted that optimistic assessment. The Southwark Chapter now sought to add a condition to its original acceptance: that 'if the youth's health broke down he should not be a burden on the diocese.'[27] Edward Bourne pleaded on his nephew's behalf. 'I cannot help thinking that if a formal announcement such as is proposed is now made to him that it will prove a heavy blow and great discouragement,' and he undertook that the family would protect Southwark against any financial liability.[28] Other factors, however, seem to have clinched the matter. Westminster tried its luck once more. This time Cardinal Manning himself offered to take on Francis as a seminarian—without any condition as to health. The news got back to Southwark, inter-diocesan rivalry prevailed and Southwark finally and definitively decided in his favour. Even while these discussions were taking place, Francis had already begun his study of theology.

Hammersmith

Manning had announced his plans for change while at St Edmund's on Exhibition Day 1868. His intention, giving effect to the wishes of the Council of Trent, was 'the removal of the theological students to the metropolis, where I may have them under my own eye.'[29] He wasted little time. The following September he founded St Thomas's Seminary in Hammersmith. Although still distinct from London at this period, Hammersmith was a good deal closer to the Archbishop's eye, especially to the pro-cathedral in Kensington, than Old Hall Green. The move was a little too hasty. The four professors and twenty-five seminarians had as their accommodation nothing but an 'old and ruinous building,' a former Benedictine convent.[30] Manning commissioned J. F. Bentley—architect of the future Westminster Cathedral—and the foundation stone of the new seminary buildings was laid in July 1876. Work proceeded piecemeal as money became available, and had only just been completed when Francis Bourne arrived at the end of the summer of 1880. Even then the south wing, completing the cloister, remained unbuilt.[31]

The entire establishment—teaching staff, seminarians and servants—amounted to just thirty in number.[32] Francis would have known most of his fellow students already; they had begun their priestly training together at St Edmund's. The Seminary President himself was an Old Edmundian, and Manning's auxiliary, Bishop William Weathers. Noted for his austerity of life, he was held in 'great esteem and respect ... especially by the great body of the secular clergy, who have been educated under his paternal care and gentle direction.'[33] There were a couple of Belgians on the staff, including Edmund Surmont, the professor of dogmatic theology. Some found his heavily-accented Latin impenetrable.[34] Francis Bourne gained rather more. He took Fr Surmont as his confessor and bore 'grateful testimony to the high ideals which he placed before us, and to the patient encouragement that he ever gave us.'[35] He was to remain in constant contact with his former seminary professor and, years later, appointed him his Vicar-General.

On the surface the path towards priesthood progressed smoothly. At the end of the year Bishop Weathers wrote, 'Mr Bourne is a very good student and has good abilities.'[36] Along with thirty-seven candidates from various dioceses and religious orders, he received in March 1881 the next two minor orders, as exorcist and acolyte, from his own seminary rector at the pro-cathedral, Our Lady of Victories in Kensington High Street.[37] His notes made in the preceding retreat led by the Oratorian Fr Keogh read like those of many other candidates for the priesthood of the period. There is the usual preoccupation with humility, self-denial and purity.[38]

He later confided that his time at Hammersmith was 'not a happy year.'[39] Perhaps it was because he was not stretched academically. A contemporary recalled, 'As there were no external examinations as at Rome and other places on the Continent, there was no particular incentive to study hard, the more so as no prizes of any kind were given for success at internal examinations. Virtue was its own reward.'[40] St Thomas's was not an institution that inspired affection among its alumni. It did not survive a generation beyond its foundation. Francis had other reasons for his unhappiness. He was still plagued by ill-health. Bishop Weathers wrote, 'He has, since he came to St Thomas's Seminary, suffered off and on from neuralgia.'[41] This is the first time his medical condition is specifically named. Neuralgia itself, however, is a symptom. It is a result of the irritation of a sensory nerve, manifest in intense pain, even paralysis, in that part of the body (often the head or face) supplied by the irritated nerve. Given the primitive state of neurology in the nineteenth century, the young seminarian must have suffered considerably.

Against this background, it is not surprising that Francis sought a move. He asked his diocese to transfer him to the English College in Rome. His request was addressed to the head of the Southwark Chapter, Provost Crookall, who administered the diocese during the illness of Bishop Danell and after his death on 14 June 1881. Considering the request is being made by a twenty-year old seminarian, whose relationship with the diocese had been somewhat rocky, it is couched in terms of surprising confidence and perhaps a lack of finesse. 'I write to remind you of my wish for several reasons to continue my studies in Rome ... Trusting that you will be able to arrange this for me.'[42] Francis did not get what he wanted. Officially, he was told that there were no vacancies in Rome at this point.[43] Confidentially, however, the Southwark authorities took soundings from the staff at St Thomas's who poured cold water on the proposal. 'Whether his health would stand the heat of Rome I cannot say. I think it doubtful.'[44] Francis Bourne was not to study in Rome—something that coloured his subsequent ecclesiology and antipathy for the Curia of the Universal Church.

St Sulpice

Nor, however, did he remain at Hammersmith. The place he was sent that autumn was to have a far more profound impact on his intellectual development and theological outlook. His destination was the left bank of the Seine in Paris, to the seminary founded in the seventeenth century by Fr Jean Jacques Olier. In contrast to the English seminaries, this was an institution organised on uncompromisingly Tridentine lines. Heirs to the 'mixed' tradition of Douai, the English were concerned at turning out 'Christian gentlemen.' The Sulpician regime was more intellectually rigorous, the objective more exclusive: the formation of disciplined Catholic priests.[45] Cardinal Bourne frequently acknowledged his debt to the Sulpician Fathers, paying testimony to his veneration and affection for them. Their students saw 'in them true examples and models of priestly life. They make no pretence of being more than priests; they find in their priesthood the source and reason of holiness of life. Their lives are simple; they are unassuming, and without exaggeration, in the simplicity of the furniture of their rooms and of their other surroundings. They are content with a small stipend. They lead the lives of their students, and are ever at their disposition in any matter of which they can be of service to them. By being true priests they lead their students to an efficacious desire to become like them.'[46] These were the models Bourne sought to emulate in the seminaries for which he was to have future responsibility.

The choice of Paris is not as surprising as it may seem today. During Penal Times Englishmen studied for the priesthood in a wide variety of institutions across Europe. The practice was maintained to a certain extent even after the repatriation of Douai. St Sulpice enjoyed a high academic reputation, and there were always a number of English-speaking seminarians in residence. Bishop Danell of Southwark himself was an alumnus.

Putting on the Cassock

For Francis Bourne it had the attraction of his mother's and aunt's presence in Paris, a language in which he was conversant and a city with which he was familiar.

But Paris in autumn 1881 was ill at ease with itself. The crushing military defeat by the Prussians, the collapse of the Second Empire, the German siege, civil war and the Paris Commune had occurred just a decade earlier. All the divisions and unresolved issues of the Revolution and the Restoration were once more to the fore. The Archbishop of Paris had been killed or, depending on one's perspective, martyred. One half of France, the Catholic half, insisted on the need for national reparation for the sins of 1789 and subsequently gave physical expression to this in Sacré-Coeur, the Church of the National Vow, overlooking Paris from Montmartre. The other half, represented by successive ministries, coalesced around a policy of anti-clericalism and persecution of the Church. Rumours of a Bourbonist coup disturbed the peace. The Church did little to bolster the regime. The Archbishop of Paris declared, 'The Republic has received neither from God nor from history any promise of immortality.'[47] Meanwhile the economy boomed as a consequence of post-war reconstruction. Arriving in Paris the new seminarian would have been struck 'by the amount of building that is going up in every direction. A new city is, in fact, growing around the old one. Long lines of avenues and streets bordered with handsome and spaciously planned houses.'[48]

It took Francis Bourne three or four months to warm to his new surroundings. Perhaps it was engrained Anglo-Saxon expectations, perhaps it was a reaction against the severity of the regime, but Francis initially experienced a 'cloud of prejudice' against St Sulpice.[49] But by January 1882 Fr Hogan was able to reassure Southwark, 'Mr Bourne promises well.'[50] Fr John Baptist Hogan was the single most important influence upon Francis Bourne during his years of priestly formation. A native of Co. Clare, he had lived in France from the age of fifteen. Following ordination, he taught at St Sulpice for 32 years and then at the Sulpician seminary in Boston. His methods and outlook are set out with great clarity in his book, *Clerical Studies*, a comprehensive programme for priestly formation. To understand the theology and ecclesiology of the future Cardinal, this work repays closer inspection.

Once he had adjusted to his new surroundings, it is easy to see why the Sulpician regime appealed to Francis Bourne. Although great emphasis was placed on the dignity of the priesthood, the Sulpician fathers themselves were humble men, living alongside their charges. There was a spiritual zeal sometimes lacking among the more pragmatic English. And they took academic study seriously. Catholicism must be made intelligible and attractive to the modern world. And this meant applying a radical critique to the intellectual formation of priests. Hogan was not interested in seminarians regurgitating the contents of Scholastic manuals. Rather, they were to think for themselves. 'To the student himself, nothing of what he learns is of any value unless he is thus taught to realise it and make it his own.'[51] After the complacent and mediocre environment of Hammersmith, theology suddenly became alive.

Hogan sought to instil in his students a love of Catholic truth, which they in turn would use to reawaken the fervour of the faithful and to win converts for the Church. In doing so, Hogan had no inhibitions in attacking anything he saw as tending towards obscurity or anti-intellectualism. All that prevented the faith being understood and communicated in a contemporary setting was to be swept away. Thus, he takes a swipe at a narrow application of Thomist philosophy, the use of Latin as the medium of instruction, Creationism, Biblical fundamentalism and much else besides. He is not afraid to acknowledge the debate surrounding the definition of papal infallibility, the potential problems raised by evolutionism and modern biblical scholarship. 'It is not, nor has it ever been, the policy of the Catholic Church to close her eyes to the evidence, and cling indiscriminately to all that is old.'[52]

Yet Hogan was no proto-Modernist. His willingness to engage with contemporary issues came from an absolute conviction of the strength of the Church's position. 'As regards the ascertained doctrines of the Catholic faith, modern criticism, fairly conducted, cannot weaken them. They rest ultimately on the authority of the Church ... Far from shunning inquiry in their regard, the true believer invites it.'[53] For Hogan, the debate raging among biblical scholars held none of the threat it did for his Protestant contemporaries. 'Catholics can afford to contemplate it with complete equanimity. Their faith is based, not on the Bible, but in the Church, and for all time.'[54] Having condemned a pure conservatism that led only to stagnation, Hogan is equally fierce in his criticism of that progressive tendency which, 'if unchecked, would soon emancipate itself from authority, and do away with all definite, settled beliefs.'[55] There is complete loyalty to Rome and the magisterium, a rejection of Gallicanism, a condemnation of liturgical innovation. 'Neither in public prayer nor in the administration of the sacraments is any room left for individual tastes or preferences ... In action so solemn and sacred no room is left for what ... might easily become undignified or irreverent. The religious sense of a priest invariably shows itself in his close adherence to the prescribed rules.'[56] Academic enquiry is to be based within the wider life of the Church. Hogan is emphatic in urging the need for spiritual, scriptural and patristic reading, prayer and devotions.

Francis Bourne might have lacked the sheer brilliance of his professor, but he learnt well and retained much of the methodology and content imparted to him—as seen throughout his ministry as priest, seminary rector and bishop. His critical faculty was aroused and, much to his credit, he would not allow it to be crushed in others, even in the most testing of times. Maisie Ward praised the Sulpician seminary of his day as 'proof indeed of true traditionalism, for the learning ever available in the bosom of the Church came to life in their hands and was by them communicated.'[57]

Yet he was pursuing his studies in Paris for a purpose, and its realisation edged ever closer. On 23 December 1882 Francis was ordained subdeacon by Mgr Richard, auxiliary bishop, and later Cardinal Archbishop, of Paris. The event occasioned an exchange of letters between mother and son giving a rare insight into the evident affection between them. Ellen Bourne welcomed the approaching realisation of their shared dream. 'Now my dearest boy, almost on the eve of the solemn step you are about to take, I must tell you, although I never tried to influence you in the step you have decided on with much care and thought, I feel happier than if you were about to attain the highest worldly position. The more I see of life in general, the more convinced I am that true happiness and peace are only found in the service of God in Whom there is no deception. My thoughts are always with you.'[58] There is real relief that his mother's approval has finally been articulated. 'I have just got your letter. Many, many thanks for it. I felt sure of all that it contains; but to hear it in so many words indeed fills up my joy in the step I shall take tomorrow. My vocation has been to you a source of expense and care probably greater than had I entered any other career, and yet you have always given me everything I asked for ... I can never thank you enough for everything you have done for me, and which you have done so lovingly ... Give my love to Noony [his aunt], she has always been my second mother, and she feels as you do; her joy is the same. Good-bye until tomorrow. I shall then be a subdeacon. Be at the church at 7 a.m. and take a good breakfast, for the ceremony is very long.'[59]

A humble stranger

Francis was ordained deacon by the same prelate on 19 May 1883. A few days previously the city had experienced an unusual phenomenon which directly affected the young cleric. 'For the last ten days Paris has had its attention diverted ... to the personality of a humble stranger who has come here to beg for his hundred and sixty thousand children ... When he did come the crowd besieged his door all day long and flocked to hear his Mass ... It is a good thing to find in the Paris of today ... there are still people as eager to see a poor priest, reputed a great servant of God and of the poor, as to secure places at the opera.'[60] That humble stranger was an ageing Italian priest, Don Bosco, later canonised as St John Bosco. Like the young Englishman, he too had been inspired by St Francis de Sales. From his own work in Turin arose the Salesian Order dedicated to the care and education of poor boys on Christian and humane principles. It enjoyed extraordinary success. Don Bosco arrived in the city to appeal for funds for the papal project with which he had been entrusted, the construction in Rome of a church dedicated to the Sacred Heart. His humility and evident sanctity took anti-clerical Paris by storm.

Francis Bourne's attention had already been drawn to the work of the saintly educator by a French priest the preceding Lent. He was inspired to obtain a biography. On 28 April 1883 he met Don Bosco as he visited the seminary of St Sulpice. His final words to the seminarians on parting were, 'Soyez saints prêtres,'[61] 'Be holy priests.' Those words and the work of the Salesian Congregation were not to be forgotten.

Louvain

Having completed all the studies in philosophy and theology required by canon law, the new deacon spent summer 1883 in London, to where his mother had recently returned. Yet Southwark decided against his early entry into parish ministry. Recognising his academic ability, Francis was sent to Belgium, to begin a doctorate at the Catholic University at Louvain.

The political situation in Belgium resembled that of the France he had just left. There too an anti-clerical regime held power. Catholics were under political disadvantages, schools had been secularised and Belgium had broken off diplomatic relations with the Holy See. (Unlike France, however, the situation improved dramatically for the Catholic Church with the election of a sympathetic ministry in 1884.) Belgium too was undergoing a construction boom. The month Francis Bourne arrived the new Palace of Justice was opened in Brussels described as 'the greatest monument of modern architecture to be found upon the continent of Europe.'[62]

Louvain was altogether a more traditional destination. The university was an ancient papal foundation dating from the fifteenth century, suppressed during the French Revolution, but re-established two generations before Bourne's arrival in October 1883. Set in the picturesque medieval Flemish town, it had at the time some 1,700 students and 70 professors. The full range of academic studies was represented, including not only the arts, but engineering and manufacturing.[63] While he himself, of course, went to the faculty of theology in the Holy Ghost College, the university was a much wider concern than the seminaries for boys and young men where Francis had previously studied. Indeed, even in the theology faculty there were no seminarians—only hand-picked priests and deacons from Belgium thought capable of pursuing higher studies together with a smattering of clergy from other countries.

Francis probably appreciated most the contacts he made at Louvain. There were a number of other English there, including Louis Casartelli, above him at Ushaw and to be a fellow member of the English hierarchy twenty years later. Someone else to feature large in later life was the young Mgr Desiré Mercier, the newly-appointed professor of Thomist philosophy. He made a favourable impression. When Francis returned home, he asked for a copy of Mercier's photograph as a keepsake.[64]

He was unable, however, to benefit from the academic opportunities offered by Louvain, spending less than six months there. Health, seemingly not a problem during two years in Paris, suddenly once more placed priestly ordination in doubt. There was a severe recurrence of neuralgia. On medical advice, he returned to England in a hurry in March 1884. A compatriot at the Holy Ghost College was left to tidy up his affairs in Louvain, forwarding some of his meagre possessions to England, arranging for the rest to be sold.[65] His doctorate abandoned and priesthood in the balance, the future seemed uncertain indeed.

Notes

1   FAB to St Edmund's Academia, 22 September 1904, *Tablet*, 1 October 1904, p. 529.

2. FAB, 'Vocations to the Ecclesiastical State,' *Pastoralia*, 15 June 1893, cited T. Hooley, *A Seminary in the Making* (London: Longmans, Green and Co Ltd, 1927), pp. 80–82.
3. FAB, *Ecclesiastical Education*, cited p. 82.
4. Stuart, 'Notes,' AAW, Bo. IV/1/27.
5. FAB, 'Notes,' AAW, Bo. IV/1/1.
6. FAB to St Edmund's Academia, 22 September 1904, *Tablet*, 1 October 1904, p. 529.
7. Stuart, 'Notes,' AAW, Bo. IV/1/27 .
8. *Ibid.*
9. FAB, *Ecclesiastical Education*, p. 24.
10. *Ibid.*, p. 36.
11. *Ibid.*, pp. 34, 35.
12. *Ibid.*, p. 36.
13. Prefect's Report, 18 December 1878, AAW, SEC XIV/12/67.
14. Oldmeadow, *Francis Cardinal Bourne*, i, p. 67.
15. Tablet, 5 July 1879 .
16. *Ibid.*, 23 November 1878, p. 659.
17. *Ibid.*, 22 November 1879, p. 659.
18. FAB, 'Notes,' AAW, Bo. IV/1/1.
19. J. B. Hogan, *Clerical Studies* (Boston: Marlier, Callnan & Co, 1898), p. 287.
20. FAB, *Ecclesiastical Education*, p. vi.
21. Stuart, "Notes," AAW, Bo. IV/1/27.
22. F. Valentine, OP, *Father Vincent McNabb* (London: Burns & Oates, 1955), pp. 43–44, 84.
23. FAB to Bishop Danell, 27 June 1880, SAA, Bourne Papers, Biographical Material.
24. Butcher to Oldmeadow, 1936, AAW, Bo. IV/1/32a.
25. Prefect's Reports, 1877–1879, AAW, SEC XIV/12/65–68.
26. Edward Bourne to Danell, 2 September 1880, SAA, Bourne Papers, Biographical Material.
27. Cited Oldmeadow, *Francis Cardinal Bourne*, i, p. 66.
28. Edward Bourne to Danell, 2 September 1880, SAA, Bourne Papers, Biographical Material.
29. *Tablet*, 4 July 1868, p. 420.
30. *Ibid.*, 20 May 1876, p. 659.
31. *Ibid.*, 24 April 1880, p. 531.
32. 1881 Census Return.
33. *Tablet*, 12 October 1872, p. 466.
34. W. Brown, *Through Windows of Memory* (London: Sands & Co, 1946), p. 19.
35. FAB, *WCC*, February 1932, p. 21.
36. Bishop Weathers to Provost Crookall, 13 July 1881, SAA, Bourne Papers, Biographical Material.

37 *Tablet*, 19 March 1881, p. 469.
38 Oldmeadow, *Francis Cardinal Bourne*, i, pp. 77–80.
39 Stuart, 'Notes,' AAW, Bo. IV/1/27.
40 Brown, *Through Windows of Memory*, pp. 18–19.
41 Bishop Weathers to Provost Crookall, 13 July 1881, SAA, Bourne Papers, Biographical Material.
42 FAB to Crookall, 4 July 1881, SAA, Bourne Papers, Biographical Material.
43 Stuart, 'Notes,' FAB annotation, AAW, Bo. IV/1/27.
44 Weathers to Crookall, 13 July 1881, SAA, Bourne Papers, Biographical Material.
45 Fuller, Interview, 7 November 2001.
46 FAB, *Ecclesiastical Education*, p. 65.
47 Cardinal Guibert, 1886, cited R. Jonas, *France and the Cult of the Sacred Heart* (Berkeley: University of California Press, 2000), pp. 235–236.
48 *Tablet*, 15 October 1881, p. 615.
49 FAB Note-book, Resolutions, Retreat, October 1882, AAW, Bo. IV/1/24.
50 Hogan to Crookall, 21 January 1882, SAA, Bourne Papers, Biographical Materials.
51 Hogan, *Clerical Studies*, p. 71.
52 *Ibid.*, p. 71.
53 *Ibid.*, p. 168.
54 *Ibid.*, p. 481.
55 *Ibid.*, p. 152.
56 *Ibid.*, p. 332.
57 M. Ward, *Insurrection versus Resurrection* (London: Sheed & Ward, 1937), p. 43.
58 Ellen Bourne to FAB, 21 December 1882, AAW, Bo. IV/1.
59 FAB to Ellen Bourne, 22 December 1882, AAW, Bo. IV/1.
60 *Tablet*, 5 May 1883, p. 695.
61 FAB Notebook, AAW, Bo. IV/1/24.
62 *Tablet*, 20 October 1883, p. 600.
63 *Ibid.*, 17 May 1884, pp. 774–777.
64 FAB to Iles, 12 May 1884, UCA, Bourne Family Papers, OS/K4/124.
65 FAB to Iles, 27 March & 7 April 1884, UCA, Bourne Family Papers, OS/K4/122–123.

Chapter 5

Sacerdos in aeternum

Ordination

Francis Bourne was fortunate that when he returned to England as an invalid in the spring of 1884: the Bishop of Southwark was an old family friend, the former parish priest of Clapham, Robert Coffin. He had been appointed Bishop two years earlier following the death of Bishop Danell. From the presbytery at Tunbridge Wells where he had been sent to convalesce, Francis came up to town at the beginning of April. He stayed with his family in Camberwell. He encountered the consequences of ill health there too. 'I left my uncle in a very bad state. I fear there is no hope of his recovery.' His visit to Bishop Coffin was more heartening. The Bishop was decisive and prepared to be generous. (Having supported Francis through so many years of study, he may have felt that the Diocese had little to lose in ordaining him.) That ordination was scheduled for early June when another Southwark candidate would return from his studies at St Sulpice.[1]

In the meantime, Francis returned to Tunbridge Wells to build up his health. In fact, his health recovered surprisingly rapidly, perhaps assisted by the knowledge his future was secure. Assisting in the parish and preparing for his canonical exams for priestly faculties was not a taxing existence. Francis was able to go into London to visit the Health Exhibition and the new church of the Brompton Oratory opened just two weeks earlier—'most magnificent, there is nothing like it anywhere else in London.'[2] More rigorous was the pre-Ordination retreat undertaken in Clapham. There, under the spiritual guidance of the Redemptorists, Francis spent the final days before priesthood contemplating in silence the sacred vocation that lay ahead of him.

Eight years after putting on the cassock, following study and discernment in three seminaries, a religious novitiate and a Catholic university, he was finally ordained priest at the age of twenty three on 11 June 1884. There was a certain symmetry to the occasion. The ordination took place in St Mary's, Clapham, by the very same man who had baptised him there, Bishop Coffin.³ Fr Bourne's first Mass the day after Ordination, the Feast of Corpus Christi, was said in the church of the Sacred Heart, Camberwell. His happiness was increased by the presence of his mother, aunt, uncle and grandmother.⁴ The day had arrived which, no doubt, at times they wondered whether they would live to see.

Blackheath

After so much anticipation, so many years of preparation, little time was lost in putting the new priest to work. He took up his first appointment on 20 June 1884. When Fr Bourne saw the Bishop and received an Ordination date in April, he had been informed his destination would be Heron's Ghyll, the seat of the Dowager Duchess of Norfolk, near Uckfield in Sussex.⁵ The Bishop presumably thought a rural posting as chaplain to the aristocracy not too demanding for someone not enjoying the best of health. Then just at the time of his Ordination, plans were changed. Perhaps the recovery in his health led the Bishop to believe that Fr Bourne was up to something more strenuous. At any event, Bishop Coffin celebrated the patronal festival at Our Lady Help of Christians, Blackheath, where the new parish priest was his former secretary, Fr Thomas Ford. ⁶ Discussions ensued, the upshot of which was that the curate of Blackheath was dispatched to minister to the spiritual needs of the Duchess of Norfolk, while Fr Bourne was appointed to Blackheath in his place.⁷

What sort of man was the new curate? Intelligent and industrious, certainly; a rather serious individual. Although perceived as shy or reserved, he was, even aged just twenty-three, capable of advancing and maintaining his own views. There was a fixedness of purpose noticeable to those who encountered him. The natural enthusiasm of a newly-ordained priest and the inevitable difference of approach to those of another generation, meant that a certain amount of tension could be anticipated. Added to this, as a product of the Continental Tridentine seminary, there was a zeal for priestly and academic excellence which could appear unsettling, even threatening, to those formed in the more relaxed environment of the English seminaries. In so far as he records it in retreat notes and elsewhere, Fr Bourne's spirituality was conventional enough: a love for Jesus present in the Blessed Sacrament, a veneration for Our Lady, his patron saints and guardian angel, a detestation of mortal sin. Indicative of his Sulpician training is his familiarity with, and love of, Scripture. The young priest commits himself to reading daily three chapters of the Old Testament and one from the New.

Blackheath was to the south east of London, between Greenwich and Lewisham—a stone's throw from the family home at Camberwell. It possessed commanding views over the Thames to the City of London. The eponymous heath was traversed by Watling Street, the Dover Road. Yet despite its proximity to London, systematic development had only begun in the late eighteenth century, and Blackheath remained the preserve of the middle and mercantile classes. On arrival Fr Bourne records his approval of his spacious and salubrious surroundings.[8]

The Catholic presence there was due to Dr William Todd, a convert clergyman from the Church of Ireland. Having pursued orphanage work in Anglican days, the socially well-connected Dr Todd promoted the same object in the Catholic Church. To that end he purchased an eighteenth-century mansion, Park House, to which he added a small chapel for the use of the boys and staff. Local Catholics soon began to attend and a separate parish was founded in Blackheath in 1873. Dedicated to Our Lady Help of Christians, the church was known popularly as St Mary's. Canon Todd, who died in 1877, was clear about the orphanage's purpose: 'the maintenance and education of Catholic fatherless children. These children are not to be chosen from the lowest class, because there are already several institutions suitable for them. St Mary's is expressly designed for boys of the better class who have become poor by the hand of death.'[9] Boys with whom Fr Bourne could readily identify.

Indeed, he owed his presence in Blackheath to the orphanage. Although there were 500 parishioners, the new curate thought the parish work would not be especially onerous. His time and responsibility were to be concentrated rather on the 'orphanage for middle-class boys and a boarding school united, containing at present about 90 boys.' In addition to its general management and supervision, the young priest was to teach French.[10] His responsibilities extended to supervising cricket matches on the heath.[11] The school expanded under the energetic leadership of the new parish priest. Supported by the extensive aristocratic patronage cultivated by Canon Todd, extensive additions including new dormitories were opened at the time of the curate's arrival.[12]

The current church is not the building known by Fr Bourne during his time in Blackheath. Development of the neighbourhood meant that a new church was needed by 1891. The original orphanage chapel had become inadequate for the needs of local Catholics long before this. It had been expanded back in 1879 to accommodate a congregation of up to 300, a chancel, side altar, sacristy, porch and new organ being added to the original structure. Regular reports in the *Tablet* attest to a fine liturgical tradition, with the orphanage boys commended for their accurate chant accompaniment of the Mass. The new curate delighted in what he found and proceeded to develop it further. Apart from one regrettable lapse into 'the florid Italian style,' Fr Bourne was praised for the purity and correctness of the Gregorian chant achieved by the boys under his 'zealous' direction.[13]

The fund-raising activities involving St Mary's prominent patrons gave Fr. Bourne publicity few newly-ordained priests would have anticipated. The interest he took in developing the liturgy at St Mary's also ensured that he came to the attention of the Bishop's House. One curial official returned from 'Blackheath, where he had been to preach, and brought back a most glowing account of the wonderful accuracy with which the boys of the school there had been taught to sing Mass and Vespers by the then curate, Fr Bourne.'[14] This was not, however, simply an aesthetic exercise. In seeking to develop his pupils' musical ability and in giving glory to God in the divine liturgy, Fr Bourne was consciously fostering priestly vocations among those in his charge.[15]

In the days of lengthy curacies, Fr Bourne's stay at Blackheath was remarkably brief—a mere fifteen months. He did not hit it off with the parish priest. We do not have the precise details of the difficulties. Perhaps it was just the clash of two strong personalities, Fr Ford expecting rather more compliancy and a little less opinion from his curate. The parish priest went so far as to take the matter to the Bishop.[16] Fr Bourne was moved, but, at the end of the day, he suffered little from the upset.

Mortlake

He left Blackheath on 28 September 1885 for Sheerness at the mouth of the Thames Estuary for reflection and the laying of new plans.[17] Ten weeks later Fr Bourne was back in London, assisting the Bishop at the consecration of the high altar at Camberwell.[18] He took up his second parish appointment on 22 December 1885.

Although the Diocese of Southwark stretched across south-east England, the bulk of Catholics were Irish immigrants, often in grinding poverty, in the parishes of south London. Bourne never experienced this normative aspect of the Diocese in his priestly ministry. His next appointment again was among the more affluent middle classes. 'A lovely village on the banks of the Thames,' was how George Eliot had described Mortlake in 1855. It might have outgrown its 'village' status a generation later, but Mortlake was still a desirable location. By the railway and set back from the River and the High Street and with its own burial ground adjoining, St Mary Magdalen's was a fine stone church opened in 1852 thanks to the generosity of Lady Mostyn. Unlike so many of his contemporaries, Fr Bourne was not in a place where the parish debt was a constant source of anxiety for the clergy.

The parish priest was an Oxford Movement convert, Canon John Wenham, who had been in Mortlake since the church opened. He was appointed Provost of the Southwark Chapter within six months of Bourne's arrival. His interest was education. He had opened the parish school, was in charge of the Southwark Catholic School Inspectorate and wrote the manual used in Catholic teacher training colleges. Whether or not attributable to Wenham's presence, there were some notable Catholic characters in Mortlake. After Lady Mostyn, the most prominent Catholic was the Hon William Towry Law, another convert clergyman. The explorer, Sir Richard Burton, was a rather more tangential connection. An agnostic himself, his devout wife, Isabel Arundell, had him baptised when he suffered a heart attack in 1887.[19]

These converts and Catholics of means had their spiritual needs too, but Fr Bourne was also exposed to more prosaic work. There was a smattering of Irish immigrants in Mortlake, brought there by the railways and the local market gardens. He went regularly to the neighbouring Sacred Heart Convent in Roehampton—somewhere he would come to know well over the years.[20] We also know he was involved in the parish school. Established by Wenham 'for the sons of persons of limited means, especially if they were designed for the service of the church,' it prospered, expanded and raised its sights to the education of the sons of gentlemen.[21] As in Blackheath, Bourne found fulfilment in teaching and promoting priestly vocations.

It ought to have been an ideal appointment. It was not. Once again, Bourne was unsettled. Canon Wenham was not an easy man to live with. He was no stranger to controversy—as the letters columns of the *Tablet* attest. As in Blackheath, it might have been a matter of the tension existing between two strong personalities. 'It is said that the good Canon was hypercritical of his juniors and that when Father Bourne passed on an unfavourable opinion on a book which he had been bidden to read the Canon said that there was nothing wrong with the book but only with the curate's mind!'[22]

This time, however, the curate took the initiative. There was more than a clash of personalities unsettling the young priest. He raised the matter just seven months after arrival in Mortlake, in the summer of 1886, probably when the Bishop came to St Mary Magdalen's for the patronal feast. Bourne had never forgotten his momentous meeting with Don Bosco three years earlier. Indeed, the desire to know more about his Salesian Congregation and to test his vocation with them pre-dated even that meeting. It went back to that Lenten retreat in 1882 when, as a seminarian at St Sulpice, his attention had first been drawn to the work of the Salesians and the sanctity of their founder. The Bishop asked him to wait.

'Dispensed from the mission oath'

Fr Bourne continued to discuss his wish to join the Salesian novitiate in Turin with his spiritual director and, in correspondence, with Don Bosco himself. By the end of the year his resolution to try this vocation was stronger than ever. He wrote to his Bishop,

> I have wished for a long time to give myself to the care and education of boys of the lower and middle classes, and I know of no congregation of priests devoted to this work save that of Don Bosco: moreover I admire the spirit and rule of his Institute very much ... I believe that this lasting attraction comes from God, for I have no trace of any attraction for other work. For these reasons, my Lord, I now send you a petition to be dispensed from the mission oath: I trust you will allow it to be granted. If possible and convenient to you, I should like to be free to leave the diocese at the end of February, or the beginning of March next year.[23]

Events did not progress at the pace the impetuous curate hoped for. The Bishop saw him in January 1887. He reminded the young priest of the need for character references and the fact that only Rome could dispense him from 'the mission oath,' the pre-Ordination vow to spend his life in service of the Church in England. It was a protracted process, but Bourne got what he wanted. The Bishop remarked, with justification, 'I had to let him go because he really thought it was his vocation, but if you ever want to look after boys, I can find you plenty in London, without going to Italy for them.'²⁴ It was not only the Bishop who agreed with reluctance. His mother had her doubts too. 'Walking with her one day in Richmond Park, he told her of his thought [of joining the Salesians]. As before, her true instinct said *No* and her faithful will said *Yes*, if God wanted it.'²⁵ Bourne pressed ahead. Rome finally granted the requisite dispensation, a passport was issued and he left Mortlake on 9 September 1887 after less than two years in the parish.

The Salesians were the religious phenomenon of the moment, a rare bright spot for the Church in an anti-clerical Europe. Don Bosco's simplicity and sheer goodness placed his work and that of his Congregation on another plane; often they could operate in areas where all other spheres of activity were closed to the Catholic Church—and this notwithstanding their utter loyalty to Rome and the Pope.

From a poor Piedmontese family, Don Bosco had to contend with poverty and discouragement to pursue his vocation. While pursuing post-Ordination studies he began his work among poor boys in Turin. Appointed chaplain to an orphanage, he founded the Oratory of St Francis de Sales in 1844. He taught the boys to read, to pray the rosary, instructing them in the rudiments of their Catholic faith—but he was equally happy engaging in their games and pastimes. The older boys were taught maths, French and Latin. As further oratories opened, a number of the boys went on to study for the priesthood. It is clear to see why Bourne was attracted by the work. The Salesian Congregation was approved by Rome in 1875, but there was no educational system as such. Don Bosco's secret lay in giving the boys what they so lacked: 'kindness and loving friendship.' The Salesians were to treat the boys as sons, living alongside them. 'Be not superiors, but fathers,' was the founder's advice and example. The results were astounding. Throughout Italy, across Europe and beyond, the Salesian movement spread, touching the lives of hundreds of thousands of boys.²⁶

To test his vocation Bourne travelled to Turin in September 1887, living as a guest in the Salesian mother house.²⁷ He cannot have been there more than six weeks. Something made him realise very quickly that this specific life was not for him. He came to his decision on the retreat prior to entering the Order. Don Bosco approved it.²⁸ But, in terms of the experience gained for his own future work and for the contacts made with the Salesians, this Italian interlude was not wasted time.

Don Bosco's parting words to Bourne were: 'In your own country you will do much for the Salesians.'[29] He knew what he was talking about. (The saint was a sick man. He offered his last Mass two weeks later and died only two months after Bourne last saw him.) Perhaps part of the reason for Southwark's willingness to release Bourne was the fact that the Bishop was already negotiating with the Salesians to take over a parish in the Diocese.[30] Bourne's early departure from Turin was made to serve a purpose. On 1 November 1887 he took possession of 26 Trott Street, Battersea on behalf of the Order and prepared it for their arrival. He was on the platform to receive the first Salesians (two priests, one Irish, one English, and an Italian lay brother) in London later that month and he was given permission to remain with them during their first few weeks in England. This was not, however, to be his own future.[31]

West Grinstead

What was to be done with this twenty-six year old who seemed incapable of holding down an appointment, of working alongside a parish priest? Twice he had demanded to be released by the Diocese, convinced of a calling to religious life. Twice he had returned within a matter of weeks. Many bishops would have despaired of making anything of the young curate at this point.

Not John Butt. He had been appointed auxiliary bishop in Southwark back in January 1885 to act in the place of the absent and ailing Bishop Coffin, whom he succeeded just five months later. He was the son of convert parents; his father had held a position in the Post Office before becoming a teacher. Ordained from St Edmund's, he was Cardinal Wiseman's secretary and tried his vocation at the London Oratory. Subsequently he served as a military chaplain in the Crimea and then as parish priest at Arundel. As Bishop, he saw Bourne in action in Blackheath and Mortlake. Although he did not agree with the young man's wish to join the Salesians, he acknowledged his ability and determination. Not that the Bishop was likely to have expressed his appreciation to Bourne. The men were too similar. Butt's Financial Secretary assessed him thus, 'He was a man of action rather than of words, and once having made up his mind that it was his duty to act, he cared absolutely nothing as to what others thought of him.'[32]

Bishop Butt gave Fr Bourne another chance. Once again he avoided the south London slums. He was sent to the parish of Our Lady of

Consolation, West Grinstead in Sussex. Even today there is no sign of human settlement near the church, just to the east of the A24 between Horsham and Worthing. The parish owed its existence to the accidents of recusant demography. The seventeenth-century Priest's House, into which Bourne now moved, had been given by the local Caryll family to serve the scattered Catholic community of west Sussex and Hampshire during penal times.

Bishop Butt had his reasons. It was not a question—as it might have appeared—of sending Bourne off to the country to repent at leisure away from the company of other diocesan clergy. The parish priest for the previous generation was Mgr Jean-Marie Denis. A Breton, he had been more likely to have sympathised with Bourne's Sulpician formation. Wise and gentle, he did not feel threatened by his younger colleague's zeal. Quite the contrary. The two men remained friends for life. Mgr Denis later wrote to Ellen Bourne that her son was 'one in a thousand' and he had nothing but 'esteem and respect' for him.[33]

For the first time secure in the knowledge that he enjoyed the approval and friendship of his immediate superior, Bourne flourished. Engaged in ministering to the rural congregation, these duties were not onerous; its numbers were not large. There was the liturgy in this new shrine church. During Penal Times and beyond, Mass was offered in a converted hay loft, under the house roof and concealed from the exterior. When Mgr Denis arrived in West Grinstead in 1863, he determined to address the problem and set about raising funds in England and France. The result was the fine church in the early decorated style which Bishop Danell had opened in 1875, although still lacking a sanctuary at that point. The church dedicated to Our Lady of Consolation was affiliated to the original shrine of that name in Turin. It is somewhat incongruous to find a Catholic church seating 400 in the midst of Sussex fields and woodland. Part of the reason was that this was now a pilgrimage site, especially for those from the Diocese of Southwark who came each summer to venerate Our Lady of Consolation.[34]

There was another reason too why so large a church—and the presence of Fr Bourne—were required. Bishop Butt had listened to the young priest and chosen his appointment with care. Mgr Denis had extraordinary energy and great vision in developing his rural parish. Simultaneously with the new church, he established a boys' school. This quickly expanded beyond a simple elementary school for the few children of the local

Catholics and by the 1870s had become an 'industrial' school for 100 boys. Mgr Denis called in Dominican sisters to help run it, building a convent and chapel for them in the process. There they ran 'a large home for poor but respectable boys, where they receive not only a sound English education, but also learn a trade if that is the wish of their parents or benefactors. The school is highly qualified; more than 88 passed at the last Government inspection. The trades are taught by very efficient masters.' Farming and market gardening were among the skills offered.[35]

By the late 1880s the school and convent had further expanded to accommodate 220 children and 50 sisters.[36] Mgr Denis had need of assistance in the management of the school and providing for its spiritual and educational requirements. It is exactly the apostolate Bourne had sought in travelling to Turin to join the Salesians. He had thrown himself into the work with great vigour when he received a visit from Bishop Butt one day in the summer of 1888.

Notes

[1] FAB to Iles, 7 April 1884, UCA, Bourne Family Papers, OS/K4/122.
[2] FAB to Iles, 12 May 1884, UCA, Bourne Family Papers, OS/K4/125.
[3] It proved to be almost his final episcopal act. Ill health forced him to leave the Diocese the next month; he died in Devon the following year.
[4] FAB, 'Notes,' AAW, Bo. IV/1/1.
[5] FAB to Iles, 21 June 1884, UCA, Bourne Family Papers, OS/K4/126.
[6] *Tablet*, 7 June 1884, p. 911.
[7] *Ibid.*, 14 June 1884, p. 931.
[8] FAB to Iles, 21 June 1884, UCA, Bourne Family Papers, OS/K4/126.
[9] Cited *Our Lady Help of Christians: Centenary History* (1973).
[10] FAB to Iles, 21 June 1884, UCA, Bourne Family Papers, OS/K4/126.
[11] *Tablet*, 16 July 1921.
[12] *Tablet*, 25 October 1884, p. 672.
[13] *Ibid.*, 22 November 1884, p. 830; 25 April 1885, p. 671; 20 June 1885, p. 990.
[14] E. St John, 'The Right Reverend John Butt,' Hooley, *A Seminary in the Making*, p. 179.
[15] FAB, *Ecclesiastical Training*, p. v.
[16] Oldmeadow, *Francis Cardinal Bourne*, i, p. 108.
[17] *Ibid.*, p. 109.
[18] *Tablet*, 12 December 1885, p. 951.
[19] St Mary Magdalen Church, Mortlake guidebook (2002).

20 A. Jackman, 'Reminiscences of Cardinal Bourne,' *Wonersh Magazine*, May 1935, p. 23.
21 *Tablet*, 16 August 1862, p. 526.
22 Oldmeadow, *Francis Cardinal Bourne*, i, p. 111.
23 FAB to Bishop Butt, 13 December 1886, SAA, Bourne Correspondence.
24 St John, 'The Right Reverend John Butt,' Hooley, *A Seminary in the Making*, p. 179.
25 Stuart, 'Notes,' 1900, AAW, Bo. IV/1/27.
26 A. Auffray, SDB, *Saint Don Bosco* (Macclesfield: St Dominic Savio House, 1964); St John Bosco, Letters 4, 201–205.
27 FAB address to Salesians in Alexandria, January 1919, *Tablet*, 8 February 1919, p. 166.
28 Stuart, 'Notes,' 1900, AAW, Bo. IV/1/27.
29 Cited Oldmeadow, *Francis Cardinal Bourne*, i, p. 113.
30 *Tablet*, 10 September 1887, p. 431.
31 *Tablet*, 26 November 1887, p. 471.
32 M. Clifton, *A History of the Archdiocese of Southwark* (London: The Saint Austin Press, 2000), pp. 17–18; St John, 'The Right Reverend John Butt,' Hooley, *A Seminary in the Making*, pp. 168–177.
33 Mgr Denis to Ellen Bourne, 2 January 1892 & 7 January 1900, UCA, Bourne Family Papers, OS/K4/129 & 131.
34 M. Clifton & D. Goddard, *The Shrine of Our Lady of Consolation & St. Francis, West Grinstead: A Short History; Tablet*, 1 July 1876, p. 20.
35 *Tablet*, 15 October 1881, p. 631; 15 May 1880, p. 627.
36 *Tablet*, 10 August 1889, p. 232.

Chapter 6

'A Seminary in the Making'

A Seminary for Southwark

Most Southwark seminarians, like Bourne himself, studied at St Edmund's, Ware and, later, at St Thomas's, Hammersmith. Yet, like the other English dioceses of the newly-restored hierarchy, Southwark was committed to establishing its own seminary for the training of priests. Bishop Danell set matters in motion. By 1874 he had identified a suitable site, seven acres of wooded land not far from St George's Cathedral, launching an appeal to raise the £17,000 needed for the 'New Seminary of St Mary's, Southwark.'[1] Two years later he had sufficient funds to commence the building work; but the project never materialised.[2] There were problems with the site and other calls upon diocesan finances. Bishop Danell died in 1881; in the ensuing interregnum the Diocese was divided. The new diocese of Portsmouth negotiated a favourable deal, taking 40% of the assets of the old Diocese. The Southwark seminary was put on hold.

Bishop Butt took up the project again, concerned by the high proportion of Southwark students failing to stay the course, leaving seminary before priestly Ordination. He concluded that he needed a seminary of his own, which he could supervise and control more closely.[3]

Butt had known the Carthusians at Parkminster from his time as parish priest at Arundel. He made his annual retreat there in the summer of 1888, seeking enlightenment with regard to his seminary plans. His prayers were answered. The Prior of Parkminster, Dom Doreau, made a suggestion. He had a high regard for his neighbour and spiritual directee, the young curate at West Grinstead. The Prior was aware of his passion for education. He knew of his initiative in teaching Latin to the brighter orphanage boys who showed signs of a priestly vocation.[4] The Bishop took note. He remembered the determined young priest who had sought to work among the youth of Turin. He recalled the pastoral visits when he had seen for himself the curate's involvement with the youth of Blackheath, Mortlake and West Grinstead.

Butt was accustomed to act cautiously and, at times, obliquely. Bourne recalls how he was first apprised of the project which was to be so close to his heart. 'On the day of his departure [from Parkminster], on his way to the station, he called at West Grinstead ... Just as he was leaving, he turned to me and said: "I have now made up my mind to begin a diocesan Seminary; pray a great deal about it." This was the first of many subsequent intimations that he contemplated calling me to some share in the important work that he had gradually been maturing in his mind.'[5] In fact, Butt's plans were less vague than this intimation suggests. On his return from the retreat his curial officials found those plans very well advanced.

The Bishop shared his vision with his secretary and treasurer. 'He told us that he intended to purchase a site and erect a Seminary as soon as possible, that he had decided not to move any of the existing students into the Seminary when he finished, but to begin at once to form junior classes ... He intended ... to install them, with Father Bourne, in temporary premises while the Seminary was being built. In a year's time he proposed to add another class of junior boys, and so on each year, thus gradually to fill the new Seminary with students who had been trained from the beginning within the diocese, as future Missionary Priests ... they were not to be brought up in luxury; they were to do some manual work. We were told that Father Bourne was to take charge of the temporary establishment, but that he was not to be called "Rector" of the Seminary, and the Bishop added: "I do not say he will never be Rector, but we shall see how he goes on."'[6]

Bourne spent another year at West Grinstead. In July 1889 he made his retreat in the familiar surroundings of St Mary's, Clapham. At the end of that retreat he received a summons to visit Butt, who appointed him superior of the new enterprise, while withholding the title of Rector. And so the Diocese of Southwark learned it was to have its own seminary under the patronage of St John the Evangelist and under the leadership of an unknown and untested young curate.[7] Bourne's own reaction no doubt was one of delight mixed with anxiety to please a difficult Bishop. Elsewhere the response was more likely astonishment tinged with disapproval, even jealousy. Who was this inexperienced young priest tainted by association with the alien methods of the Sulpicians? Were there not appropriate senior clergy in Southwark trained in English seminaries? Bourne's emergence into the ecclesiastical limelight was controversial—and clerical memories are notoriously long.

Henfield

The decision announced, matters moved swiftly. While the seminary's permanent home was being built, Bourne was entrusted with the responsibility of finding temporary premises. He suggested Henfield Place, a rambling old house just three miles from West Grinstead and 11 miles north of Brighton. The Diocesan Treasurer, Fr Edward St John, was sent to inspect. Satisfied with what he found, he arranged a two-year lease and furnishings. Thus in typically practical manner began a friendship of almost forty years that was to be another source of bitter controversy for Bourne.

All that was very much in the future, however, as he took possession of Henfield Place on 25 July. The 28 year old Bourne moved in with three boys to whom he had been teaching Latin at West Grinstead. Mass was first offered at Henfield on 4 August 1889, the date regarded as the foundation of St John's Seminary.[8] With other students arriving over the next few weeks, the Seminary began its first year with 15 boys aged 12 to 15. Even had he wanted to do otherwise, Bourne was obliged to give effect to the Bishop's wish that the Seminary be built from the bottom up.

In those early days both staff and regime were rudimentary. In addition to Bourne himself, there were just two other teachers. Joshua Pooley was a former seminarian who had given up his studies for health reasons, later to resume them again. George Barrett was a seminarian waiting to begin Philosophy, soon replaced by Edward Escarguel, a young friend of Bourne's and another budding seminarian. The emphasis was on informality, not academic rigour. At least, Pooley, Barrett and Escarguel's kindness ensured their popularity among the boys. In the second year numbers increased to 24. Three separate classes were formed, taught respectively by Bourne, Pooley and a newly-ordained priest from Ushaw. The boys' capacity and the staff's teaching methods were not the most advanced. 'Latin at Henfield was but painfully and slowly absorbed by some, and Mr Pooley would cheer up the weary plodders by pointing them out with an accusing finger and bellowing: *"You're* a duffer," to each one of them.'[9] The studies differed little from those of other late-Victorian schoolboys, save for the emphasis on religion, Latin and Gregorian chant.

However, the boys were never allowed to forget this was no ordinary school—they were studying to be priests. [10]

Spiritual formation was at the heart of the enterprise. A makeshift chapel with altar, statues and organ was established in the house. Each day began with short prayers and 20 minutes meditation before Mass. Each evening the boys made an examination of conscience. From the beginning, Bourne introduced distinctive elements into the regime, valued from his own seminary days in Paris. The most important of these was 'Spiritual Reading,' the Sulpician practice of *lecture spirituelle*. Every evening, except Sunday, Bourne gathered the house for an intimate talk in the classroom. At the beginning of the year, and again half-way through, he would speak on the Seminary's Rule of Life. At other times it could be any spiritual topic, a matter connected with daily life, or the general principles of priestly formation. 'These quiet, homely talks were a great influence working steadily towards forming the spirit of the house, inculcating sound common sense in spiritual things … It is hard to exaggerate the effect on the whole life of the place of this continual daily guidance. The students looked forward to it.' The first six (later extended to fifteen) months were a time of probation, after which, after discussion with his confessor and the approval of the staff, a boy would make a public consecration of his vocation to St John and put on the cassock. Weekly meetings of the Sodality of St John for those who had made the act of consecration increased a sense of *esprit de corps* among the young seminarians.[11]

St John's differed significantly from the established English seminaries in that it functioned primarily as a family. This was not simply a necessity forced on Bourne by the small numbers in those early days. It was a deliberate decision to emulate St Sulpice (and the Salesians)—a policy continued when the Seminary moved to its permanent home. Motivated by his own experience, Bourne believed passionately that future priests were best formed by continual and familiar contact with devout and committed priests responsible for that formation.

Our own age might look askance at a Church prepared to accept boys as young as 12 and place them in an institution to form them for priesthood. The fact that most of boys who passed through the system, both at Henfield and subsequently, regarded this time with unmixed affection was due largely to the character and approach of the superior. He never forgot Don Bosco's advice to be a father to those in his charge.

Study and spirituality were crucial, but so were play and human relationships. One of the first boys to arrive at Henfield recalled Bourne's easy-going informality. On a hot summer's afternoon, he was more than capable of walking into a classroom, putting an end to their scheduled activities and announcing, 'Now, boys, it's too hot for study; we'll go for a dip in the river, and continue our studies this evening. Come along!'[12] And off they would go to the River Adur, a mile down the road. Again, there was cricket and football, long walks in the Sussex countryside, and ghost stories read by the superior to the boys around him.

These were happy days, not least for Bourne himself. He had been entrusted with the task for which he cared above all others, the education of youth, specifically the formation of priests. He won the affection and respect of those placed in his charge. He was without the heavier cares and responsibilities later to come his way. As *pater familias*, he clearly enjoyed to the full the family life of which death had cheated him in his own youth.

What did the Bishop make of all this? Butt visited Henfield frequently to ensure compliance with his wishes, but he remained enigmatic. One of the Southwark Chapter recorded the anxiety Bourne felt prior to Butt's first visit to the fledgling Seminary:

> The Bishop came, made many inquiries, asked all kinds of questions, went into everything most carefully, but neither that day nor the next did he give any indication of approval or blame—hardly, indeed, did he make a suggestion. At last when the visit came to an end, the priest could take the suspense no longer, and when asking for the Bishop's blessing, he blurted out: 'If, my Lord, there is anything to be changed or—' 'Thank you', said the Bishop, 'if I have *any fault to find* I will tell you at once.'[13]

Hardly overwhelming affirmation, yet, with Butt, actions always spoke louder than words. With the move to the Seminary's permanent home, Bourne was finally accorded the title of Rector.

The Move to Wonersh

That move occurred in August 1891 as the two year lease on Henfield Place expired. The destination was Wonersh, in quintessentially English countryside a few miles south of Guildford. Butt had wanted bare land. Kent and Sussex were dismissed as likely to form their own separate dioceses in the future. So when Canon Connelly spotted a City hoarding advertising the sale of Surrey farmland as 'an admirable site for a mansion,' Curial officials and then the Bishop went off to inspect. Impressed by what they saw, sixty acres were purchased. F. A. Walters, the prolific architect of Catholic churches and institutions in southern England, was commissioned to draw up plans for the approval of Connelly, St John and Bourne.[14] The style of the red brick buildings designed to house one hundred seminarians was described fancifully, and variously, as French/Flemish/English Renaissance.

Bourne arrived at Wonersh with one of the seminarians, five servants and several cartloads of furniture on 18 August 1891. The remaining seminarians, some forty in total, arrived a week later. Bourne recorded, 'The students arrive between 5 and 6 p.m. The house is in a most unfinished state, but all the exercises began and continued as usual.'[15] That was something of an understatement. The Refectory was the only room finished and fit for purpose. The foundation stone had been laid in the presence of a great number of Southwark clergy in June of the preceding year, but progress had been slow.

Things were not made any easier by the Bishop's severity and insistence on strict economy. External decoration of the buildings was largely vetoed, and he ordered the removal of radiators from the *ambulacrum*—if anyone felt the cold, they could walk more quickly.[16] Alumni reminisced on Butt's eccentricities: 'Fr Bourne had some difficulty in persuading the dear old Bishop to install bathrooms, His Lordship's opinion being that a regular change of underclothing adequately met the case.'[17] A further difficulty was the sloping nature of the ground, requiring huge quantities of earth to be cleared. The only recorded instance of physical exertion by Bourne concerns his rolling up his sleeves and taking spade and wheelbarrow to level the Seminary's playing area.[18] The house had to wait another four years until wealthy benefactors allowed the construction of the permanent chapel.

Studies began, and Bishop Butt formally opened St John's Seminary, Wonersh on 8 September 1891. It was, of course, distinguished from the traditional English seminaries by the separation of clerical from lay students. 'A place in [Butt's] Seminary was only to be given to those who had the priestly career definitely in view.'[19] It was still at this stage, however, very much a *minor* seminary: boys and adolescents who felt called to the priesthood, but who were still pursuing the normal schoolboy studies. Not until September 1893 did 14 students commence Philosophy, and not until the following September did anyone study Theology at

Wonersh. (Butt had the Englishman's disdain for Philosophy, maintaining one year's study sufficient for his seminarians.)

'Training more by example than by words'

Bourne later wrote, '*A seminary is not primarily a place of study.*'[20] The spiritual formation of the Catholic priest took priority over all else. It was to remain Bourne's view that only a minority of clergy who showed an aptitude for such things should be selected for subsequent further studies. In the early days much of the teaching at Wonersh was in the hands of the older seminarians and newly-ordained clergy—following the custom of John Bosco in his oratories. This was partly so a new generation of priests imbibed the spirit of the house, partly for reasons of economy. When the Seminary was split in 1893, the Junior Side was entrusted to a newly-ordained priest, later to a deacon. (Wonersh was far from unique among secular and ecclesiastical institutions of the period in employing student-teachers.) And Bourne took great care in sharing his vision of the Seminary with those students selected as future members of staff.

Bourne frequently spoke of Christ's own example in training the apostles as his model for seminary formation. This was to be their guide for the staff. 'They were not merely instructors in learning, but primarily directors of those who were to be priests. They were to lead a community life with the students, sharing in the spiritual exercises made in common, having their meals with them in the refectory, joining freely in their games and recreation and training them more by their own self-denying example than by their words. The work in the Seminary was to be their whole occupation, so no priest could be absent from the Seminary on a Sunday, or take up any external work without the Rector's special permission.'[21]

Bourne led by example, living among his charges. They were taken into his confidence as future co-operators in the priesthood. They were to mix freely with the staff so that, if a crisis were to occur, they should have no hesitation in taking it to their superiors. The Seminary Rule specifically allowed the Seniors to 'go freely to the Directors' rooms, if they have need to do so.'[22] Bourne chaired the Seminary debating society and spoke in debates; seminarians were free to criticise the positions he adopted.[23] The loneliness of his own boyhood summers in mind, a seminarian with no home to return to in the holidays, was sent by Bourne at his own expense to his mother's house at Seaford. He 'was always extravagant where his students were concerned.'[24]

As at Henfield, there was a lightness of touch and informality which readily appealed to the boys. When classes were over the Rector read from *Alice in Wonderland* and *Three Men in a Boat*.[25] A rather more intimate encounter was recalled fifty years on, 'To be sent for to the Father Rector's room was rather alarming. One examined one's conscience with a strong lens, as it were, and a tooth-comb. I remembered quite a lot. But when I arrived I was received with a cheerful smile and bidden look into a hand-mirror. Brook's Monkey brand. Heavens! And I had not yet got anything sharper than a pocket knife. So Father Rector led me into his own bedroom and himself shaved me with his own razor. It is one of my proudest boasts that I got my first shave from a future Cardinal Archbishop.'[26]

Arthur Jackman went on to become Bourne's Private Secretary in both Southwark and Westminster. He recalled the atmosphere of the Seminary he entered in 1894. 'I don't suppose that anywhere in England was there such hero-worship and filial respect as we had for the Rector. The fact, that instead of avoiding, as is usually the case with boys, his company in recreation, we sought and desired it, was in itself a wonderful indication of our whole attitude. For purposes of practical organisation confessors were assigned to the students on arrival; and happy was the boy who was directed to the Rector.'[27]

Boys are astute. They do not give respect easily, not to the weak nor to those intent on currying their favour. Bourne could act firmly when necessary. Boys were dismissed, temporarily or permanently, for conceit and impertinence, or for persistently advancing doctrinally unorthodox views. Rather, it was his ability to inspire, combined with his paternal affection, which won such loyalty. Jackman again: 'Personally I was thrilled by all I quickly found, and I discovered that I had come to a place where one's highest ideals could be satisfied. It only remained to yield oneself to the training and to drink in all that the teaching of the place was intended to instil in willing if uncouth and simple souls. A wonderful spirit permeated the whole Seminary and the Rector's suppressed enthusiasm was catching.'[28]

Bourne was not cynical, a rare enthusiast in the English Catholic Church. The Sulpicians and the Salesians had awoken in him the vision of the spiritual beauty of the priesthood. He possessed the integrity and the ability to communicate this to his seminarians. 'Those who really desire to become priests are capable of very high aspirations and of great achievements if they are prudently and gradually led to conceive lofty ideals. If they be treated merely as schoolboys ... only a few will rise to higher thoughts.'[29] Bourne's object was 'to train to a truly spiritual and supernatural life those to whom God has made known, and who desire to accept, the Eternal Priesthood of His Divine Son.'[30]

Prayer was the foundation of everything. Bourne insisted on a sufficient number of spiritual directors to form the seminarians in prayer in addition to hearing their Confessions and offering spiritual direction. 'The success of the Seminary depends mainly on the personal holiness of the Directors.'[31] Spiritual direction took place monthly to allow priest and seminarian to build a relationship of trust and friendship. Yet prayer had always to be personal. Throughout his life Bourne set himself against the prospect of one spiritual counsellor imposing his ideas on prayer upon others. It was precisely in this dependence upon and converse with God that every priest, and every Christian, should be most free. There was meditation before daily Mass. The Eucharist was central. 'If an aspirant for the priesthood has not a real love for his Divine Lord in the Blessed Sacrament, he is not likely to be an earnest or zealous priest.'[32] There were monthly days of recollection and regular retreats. Bourne advised devotion to Mary. More unusually, he required every seminarian be trained in a special devotion to the Holy Spirit. All this, and so much more, was communicated in the practice of Spiritual Reading—continued from Henfield—when the Senior Side gathered around the Rector each evening. (The Regent undertook the same function for the Juniors.)

Bourne offered his seminarians an attractive ideal, but, simultaneously, he was a realist. He understood adolescent nature. 'Patience and forbearance should be exercised in dealing with students at this time, for their characters are often temporarily strangely altered by the physical changes and spiritual perplexities which are working within them.'[33] Great insight and kindness was shown towards those struggling with their own difficulties—at least up until the point of Holy Orders. Such wisdom and patience bore fruit. It is easy to understand why so many Wonersh alumni remained devoted to Bourne for life. One Southwark priest explains:

> A junior student, naturally nervous, and doubly so by reason of his errand, knocked at [Bourne's] door. He remembers that even this cost a deal of screwing up of courage. [Bourne] received him with more kindness of manner and word than can readily be expressed, and made it almost easy for the lad to stammer out that he had

already written to his mother his decision—communicated to no one else—to leave the Seminary. Then with consummate gentleness and understanding [Bourne] drew out the little story of the boyish trouble '*du coeur*'. The lad remained at Wonersh. It may not look much on paper, but it meant a lifetime, and a deal more besides, maybe, here and hereafter. The lad has now been a priest between fourteen and fifteen years, and, God willing, will be giving to his successors as junior students, their annual retreat at the end of October.[34]

Not all seminarians, then or now, have been so fortunate.

A Time of Trial

The young Rector needed to be both eminently practical and deeply rooted in his faith to surmount the early difficulties faced by St John's Seminary. From its foundation Wonersh was not without its critics, even within the Diocese of Southwark. Anonymous accusations lodged with Rome accused Butt of megalomania in building a seminary twice the size required by the Diocese and dedicated to his own patron saint.[35] He was charged with favouritism, employing only younger priests in the Seminary, men who would flatter his vanity, rather than drawing from the senior clergy who ought to have been his natural advisers.

An institution founded to engender a real *esprit de corps* was bound to be accused of elitism. Some Southwark priests later recorded their opinion that Wonersh introduced an element of division in the Diocese.

> There seems to have existed in the minds of some in authority that the Wonersh priest was going to be a quite superior and better type that any other that had so far 'appeared on the market' hitherto. Hence, I think, the reason of much want of respect for the older clergy who have borne the burden and heat of the many years of faithful service in Our Blessed Lord's vineyard. I myself always had the idea that a priest who parted his hair, who wore cuffs, etc., etc. (to quote a few trifling things) was worldly and worthy of little respect.[36]

Another thought likewise, 'All the boys from the Seminary had the name for want of deference and more or less despising the older clergy on the Mission.'[37] If true, the attitude was not attractive. It was, however, susceptible to the passage of time. Experience of parish life would knock some of the corners off the younger priests and, hopefully, result in an appreciation of their qualities by their elders. And time, of course, would ensure that an increasing proportion of Southwark priests shared the same seminary formation.

During the winter of 1891 the Seminary was struck by that same strain of influenza which carried off Cardinal Manning and the Duke of Clarence. Bourne himself and most of the senior boys went down sick. It heralded the beginning of the ordeal which told most heavily on Bourne. The attack seriously weakened Joseph Tonks, one of three boys whom Bourne had taught at West Grinstead and who had formed the nucleus of the new seminary at Henfield. He died of consumption at Wonersh in summer 1893. Then in the academic year 1896/97 a series of deaths not only deprived Bourne of future seminary professors, but also a number of those closest to him in affection and association. Fr Frederick Kent was another of the original three West Grinstead boys. Having been ordained early, he died in November 1896. The Rev Denis Larkin, a brilliant student earmarked as a future member of staff, died the following month. Fr Albert Brotherton had been at Henfield from the beginning. As Regent of the Juniors, Bourne entrusted him with a pivotal role at Wonersh. Falling sick at the same time, he was an invalid until his death in April 1898. Added to the tragedy of the deaths of all these young men Bourne had seen grow to maturity, in April 1897 Fr Albert Füchter, the newly-ordained priest he had brought from St Sulpice as Professor of Philosophy, also died. The pressure on the teaching staff to continue anything like a normal seminary programme was tremendous. And all this at a time when diocesan duties increasingly took Bourne away from Wonersh. It is testimony to his own trust in Divine Providence and the confidence he inspired in others that the Seminary survived these trials.

'Audi Alterum Partem'

The greatest threat to the very existence of Wonersh, however, was an external one. When Cardinal Manning died in January 1892 he was succeeded as Archbishop of Westminster by Herbert Vaughan, Bishop of Salford. No one claimed for Vaughan a great intellect, but he was a man of action and decided ideas. In Salford he had attempted the Tridentine ideal of a separate diocesan seminary. It had not been a success. It led Vaughan to pursue a vision opposed to that embodied by Wonersh. As far as he was concerned, 'Proficiency will not come about by multiplying theological seminaries, but rather by increasing their number of students, raising their standard of studies and prolonging their years of culture and training.'[38] Centralisation would provide the resources to ensure a more educated priesthood.

Vaughan lost little time in implementing this policy on arriving in Westminster. Few regretted the sale of Manning's seminary in Hammersmith, but there was, however, considerable unease at the proposal to remove all theological formation from the Archdiocese. Vaughan proposed a Central Seminary—if not for the whole of England, at least for the South. He considered St Edmund's as a potential venue—but rejected it as too complete a reversal of Manning's policy. In an attempt to bring other dioceses on board, Wonersh too was considered. However, Butt had not gone to the trouble of establishing his own seminary to ensure effective episcopal control to see that diluted at its very genesis.

The Central Seminary was founded in the Midlands, at St Mary's, Oscott. Control rested with a board of the seven bishops of Southern England and Wales (less Southwark, of course). Birmingham brought to the agreement the seminary premises and contents, and the right to nominate the rector. Other dioceses provided cash by way of a capital endowment, Westminster contributing by far the largest share. Rome approved the new arrangements in February 1893. The Westminster seminarians arrived the following month. Butt and Bourne held aloof from this joint enterprise, but there was no guarantee that a future Bishop of Southwark might not reverse their policy.

Vaughan ensured favourable coverage of the new venture in the *Tablet* leading article of 4 March 1893, written by Fr Victor Schobel, a Bavarian priest and former Oscott professor. Acknowledging the ideal of separate diocesan seminaries, he claimed

> Catholic England simply lacks the infrastructure and finances Trent assumes ... Consequently there is a danger that the handful of students in the diocesan seminary may miss the advantages of emulation and the eager contact of mind with mind, and the life and vigour which are born of numbers, and cannot flourish among isolated students ... Financially the result of the separate diocesan seminary is, of course, almost intolerable ... [A Central Seminary would ensure a] new sense of fellowship and community feeling, among priests separated by distance and poverty.[39]

The article aimed to explain and justify Vaughan's actions. Implicitly, however, it was too much an indictment of Southwark's new foundation to go unanswered. Writing anonymously, Bourne replied with a two part article for the *Tablet*, 'On Diocesan Seminaries—*Audi Alterum Partem.*' He added a further two articles to these for a booklet on the subject published by Burns & Oates in May 1893. There, as even his critics recognised, Bourne set out his vision of seminary formation with ability and zeal.

Dioceses such as Westminster and Southwark, he maintained, were surely large enough to justify their own separate seminaries. Students from smaller dioceses might readily be admitted to these. It was unhealthy that bishops lacked a choice in deciding where to train their future priests. A diocesan seminary created a sense of unity among the clergy. As expected, Bourne vigorously defended his preference for the separation of lay and clerical students. Their needs are different. The seminarian is being trained for that time when, aged 24 or 25, he 'is placed in the world, practically alone, with no one upon whom to lean, and all men depending upon him.' Bourne also takes issue with the suggestion that a seminary exists to give a university education to all seminarians. This is neither necessary nor desirable. Yes, of course, those ordained priests displaying the aptitude for further studies could be sent to Louvain, Paris or Fribourg or a future Catholic faculty to be established in England. However, the seminary's priority is the spiritual and practical formation of men for parish ministry.[40]

Bourne anxiously awaited the reaction, aware that he was explicitly rejecting the Cardinal Archbishop's policy. Vaughan, however, was magnanimous, untroubled that the young Rector held contrary views. He wrote reassuringly, 'Whatever it may be worth, your project is another way of dividing forces; and if such division be desirable your plan has distinct merits, which I gladly recognise.'[41] Bishop Ilsley of Birmingham similarly felt Wonersh offered little threat to the Central Seminary and confirmed he bore Bourne no grudge.[42] More severely, Victor Schobel argued a fundamental difference of principle. Vaughan and others felt the most pressing want was the intellectual one; Southwark chose to concentrate rather on the moral needs of the seminarian. By creating a separate clerical caste, Schobel felt Bourne's approach, if it prevailed more widely, would result in 'a national calamity.'[43]

Expansion and Development

Butt's decision to build on the grand scale was justified. Wonersh continued to grow throughout the 1890s. In 1897 nine priests were ordained for Southwark. There were 89 seminarians in total, 77 of them studying at Wonersh.[44] The proportion not persevering to ordination was high, around 60% of entrants in the first decade.[45] Bourne was not unduly troubled by the statistics. He argued that in a seminary composed entirely of clerical students, a large number would leave in the early stages when forced to confront the high ideals of the priesthood. Those remaining would be far stronger candidates.[46]

The growth in numbers necessitated organisational changes, which Bourne had envisaged from the outset. He deliberately emulated those French institutions which were simultaneously both minor and major seminaries. Thus, in 1893 the house was divided into a Senior and a Junior Side. The former comprised those seminarians studying Philosophy and Theology; the latter those, aged between 13 and 20, who were still pursuing studies of the humanities preparatory to this. Although under the same roof, the two Sides were quite distinct. They met only in the Chapel and the Refectory. The Rector had absolute executive power in respect of the Seniors, the Regent in respect of the Juniors, subject to the control of the Rector to whom he reported weekly.[47] The system ran smoothly enough in Bourne's time, given his force of personality and status as founding father. This dual structure, however, possessed the potential for tension under other leadership.

Academic standards were raised. Bourne was able to attract lecturers from Fribourg and St Sulpice, and he himself taught Scripture and Moral Theology. In 1898 Rome affiliated Wonersh to the *Institut Catholique*, enabling seminarians to attain undergraduate degrees from Paris in respect of their studies at St John's. The more promising students were sent for further studies overseas so that they might return to teach at Wonersh. In one of his final acts in Southwark Bourne came to an arrangement with the University of London whereby students might be awarded a BA for their pre-Philosophy studies. It was difficult to argue that Wonersh was failing in its duty to provide an appropriate intellectual formation.

Recognition was forthcoming for Bourne's achievement. Bishop Butt relaxed sufficiently at the Seminary's Patronal Feast Day in 1892 to toast the health of the Rector as one 'whom he had always found willing to act in perfect harmony with all his wishes.'[48] Early in 1895 the Rector accompanied his Bishop to Rome; at their audience he was able to tell Leo XIII something of the new diocesan seminary. Weeks later he was created a Domestic Prelate of Honour to the Pope at the age of 34. Cardinal Vaughan too was gracious in his praise. At the opening of the permanent chapel he remarked before the assembled company that 'no one could fail to be struck by the evidences of the affection and confidence that exist between [Mgr Bourne] and those under his charge.'[49]

Butt's had been the inspiration and initial impetus, but Bourne provided the spiritual and practical underpinning for the new Seminary. In doing so, he acquired a reputation for exemplary administration. A fellow member of the hierarchy subsequently extolled him, 'His Seminary was a triumph of order, method and careful thought; and that the whole of merit of this was due to Mgr Bourne for he had commenced the work as Rector, remaining Rector until he was made Bishop, and the whole scheme was his.'[50] One of Bourne's successors at St John's made the same observation, 'When he went there as rector he was astonished at the perfect organisation and wealth of detail which had been expended upon the college by [Bourne] during his rectorate.[51]

Less complimentary were Aidan Gasquet, Abbot President of the English Benedictines, and his Roman correspondent, the Irish Franciscan, Fr David Fleming. Gasquet complained Bourne's 'notion of education is too *foreign* to please most people.'[52] Fleming agreed: 'I look upon the attempt to engraft the Sulpician system on the Catholic Church in England as a calamity. The experience of France is not encouraging.'[53] Why such divergent opinions? Gasquet, Fleming and plenty of others in the Anglo-Saxon world feared that the creation of a tightly-knit priestly body, educated apart, would create suspicion and prejudice, the type of anti-clericalism then prevalent in France. Bourne, on the contrary, maintained that without a confident identity and an appropriate spiritual formation, the priest failed in his essential mission—the sanctification of souls, his own and those of the flock entrusted to him.[54] It is the unresolved debate—is the Church called to be that shining city on the hilltop, or the yeast which leavens from within?

What can be acknowledged, however, is the success of Wonersh. St John's survives into its second century. Of the various diocesan seminaries founded in the aftermath of the restoration of the English hierarchy, it alone remains, still training priests for Southwark and other dioceses. Despite changes, some of which he bitterly resented, much of that achievement is due to its first Rector. Bourne wrote, 'On [the rector] rests the chief government of the house; his character and personality are the determining factors in its ruling.'[55] In this respect, St John's had a firm foundation. Bourne had a passionate commitment to seminary education in general and to Wonersh in particular. He addressed the house on his name day in 1896: 'the one great wish of his heart was to continue to his death as our Rector, that he had devoted his life to us, and that no wish was nearer or dearer to him than that of our welfare'[56] He spoke sparingly about it subsequently, but the fact that wish was not to be granted caused him great pain.

Notes

1. *Tablet*, 5 December 1874, p. 727.
2. *Tablet*, 9 December 1876, p. 755.
3. St John, 'The Right Reverend John Butt,' Hooley, *A Seminary in the Making*, p. 178.
4. Hooley, *A Seminary in the Making*, p. 9.
5. FAB, Sermon at Wonersh, 29 September 1920, cited *Ecclesiastical Training*, p. 85.
6. St John, 'The Right Reverend John Butt,' Hooley, *A Seminary in the Making*, pp. 178–179.
7. Hooley, *A Seminary in the Making*, p. 85.
8. *Ibid.*, pp. 15–16.
9. E. Burt, 'Some Early Reminiscences of St John's Seminary,' *Wonersh Magazine*, November 1935, p. 61.
10. Hooley, *A Seminary in the Making*, pp. 17, 26.
11. *Ibid.*, pp. 26–27.
12. Burt, 'Some Early Reminiscences of St John's Seminary,' *Wonersh Magazine*, November 1935, p. 61.
13. Cited Hooley, *A Seminary in the Making*, p. 18.
14. St John, 'The Right Reverend John Butt,' Hooley, *A Seminary in the Making*, pp. 180–181.
15. Diary of the Southwark Diocesan Seminary, 27 August 1891.
16. Hooley, *A Seminary in the Making*, pp. 39–40.
17. Burt, 'Some Early Reminiscences of St John's Seminary,'*Wonersh Magazine*, November 1935, p. 63.
18. Hooley, *A Seminary in the Making*, p. 41.
19. FAB, Sermon, Wonersh, 20 September 1920, cited FAB, *Ecclesiastical Education*, p. 87.
20. FAB, *Ecclesiastical Training*, p. 10.
21. Hooley, *A Seminary in the Making*, p. 147.
22. FAB, 'The Government of the Seminary,' c.1901? SAA, Wonersh, Addl. Material, 1904–1970/4.
23. Hooley, *A Seminary in the Making*, p. 43.
24. E. Pritchard, 'Confessions of Melchizedek,' *Southwark Record*, September 1948.

25 Burt, 'Some Early Reminiscences of St John's Seminary,' *Wonersh Magazine*, November 1935, p. 63.
26 Pritchard, 'The Confessions of Melchizedek,' *Southwark Record*, July 1948.
27 Jackman, 'Reminiscences of Cardinal Bourne,' *Wonersh Magazine*, May 1936, p. 107.
28 *Ibid.*
29 FAB, *Ecclesiastical Training*, pp. 19–20
30 *Ibid.*, p. 3.
31 FAB, 'The Government of the Seminary,' c.1901? SAA, Wonersh, Addl. Material, 1904–1970/4.
32 FAB, *Ecclesiastical Training*, p. 52.
33 *Ibid.*, p. 38.
34 W. Taunton to FAB, 26 September 1920, AAW, Bo. I/142.
35 Anon. letter to Propaganda, 1 March 1895, SCPF, 102/1895, f. 68, rr. 615–616.
36 E. Corbishley to A. Doubleday, 6 January 1912, SAA, Wonersh 1904–1936.
37 G. Newton [to Doubleday?], 10 January 1912, SAA, Wonersh 1904–1936.
38 Vaughan, Preface to 1882 translation of life of St John Baptist de Rossi, cited M. McInally, *Edward Ilsley: Archbishop of Birmingham* (London: Burns & Oates, 2002), p. 153.
39 *Tablet*, 4 March 1893, pp. 323–324.
40 'On Diocesan Seminaries,' *Tablet*, 11 March 1893, pp.363–364 & 18 March 1893; FAB, 'Diocesan Seminaries and the Education of Ecclesiastical Students,' cited Hooley, *A Seminary in the Making*, pp. 56–75.
41 Vaughan to FAB, 18 November 1893, p. 99.
42 FAB to Ilsley, 13 June 1893, BAA, B 10981.
43 *Tablet*, 24 June 1893, pp. 967–969.
44 FAB, Advent Pastoral 1897.
45 Hooley, A Seminary in the Making, p.131.
46 FAB, 'Diocesan Seminaries … ,' cited Hooley, *A Seminary in the Making*, p. 75.
47 Memorandum, FAB to Joseph Butt, 30 December 1900, SAA, Wonersh, Addl. Material, 1904–1970/1.
48 *Tablet*, 14 May 1892, p. 791.
49 *Ransomer*, 14 May 1896.
50 Bishop J.–B. Cahill to Cardinal Gotti, u/d, SCPF, 102/1904, f. 289, rr. 54–55.
51 Doubleday, Consecration as Bishop, 23 June 1920, *Tablet*, 26 June 1920, p. 852.
52 Gasquet to Fleming, 2 June 1902, cited S. Leslie, *Cardinal Gasquet: A Memoir* (London: Burns Oates, 1953), p. 80.
53 Fleming to Gasquet, 16 February 1904, cited Leslie, Cardinal Gasquet, p. 87.
54 FAB notebook, 5 April 1920, cited Oldmeadow, *Francis Cardinal Bourne* (London: Burns Oates & Washbourne Ltd, 1944), ii, p. 169.
55 FAB, *Ecclesiastical Training*, p. 65.
56 Senior Diary of Wonersh, 28 January 1896.

By the Thames Divided

Chapter 7

Bishop of Southwark: 'Practically a stranger'

Coadjutor: 'I have a great preference for the third'

Although only in his mid-sixties Bishop Butt's health was deteriorating rapidly. Winter 1892 was spent in the south of France. There were other absences from Southwark on account of his health. Critics were not slow to point out his failings. 'The canons do not hesitate to say openly, "The poor Bishop is losing his faculties; his memory has gone already!" In all meetings of diocesan priests the only talk is of the ineptitude of the Bishop, his ignorance, his despotism and his favouritism."'[1] Even the loyal Bourne subsequently acknowledged that the administration of the Diocese, especially financially, suffered in this period.[2]

In November 1895 Butt accepted the inevitable, petitioning Rome for a Coadjutor—a bishop to assist him in Southwark with the automatic right of succession to the Diocese in the event of his death or resignation. Rome agreed, asking Vaughan to put the process in motion. That process involved two sets of people, the English Bishops and the Chapter of Southwark canons, each drawing up their *terna*, a list of three candidates for Rome's consideration.

The Chapter met first, on 27 January 1896, the Bishops two days later. Their deliberations followed a predictable sequence. This was a period when the right to nominate bishops was strongly contested in England— less a question of a centralising Vatican seeking to abrogate local rights, than canons feeling aggrieved that their traditional role in the appointment of the diocesan bishop was being ignored by the national hierarchy. The fact that Bourne was to be the Bishops' choice and not the canons' was another grievance to be held against him in certain quarters of the Diocese—not least among the Chapter itself.

The Southwark canons opted for three of their own number. The Bishops promptly set this list aside, naming three others. Of the Bishops' candidates, Dr John Prior was the Vice-Rector of the English College in Rome, Fr Frederick Antrobus the Provost of the London Oratory. The third was Francis Bourne. Little known outside his own Diocese, Bourne's name was only included in deference to Butt's wishes. The papers submitted by the English Bishops to Rome mistook his age—they have him as 37, rather than his actual 34 years. Whoever took the notes of the Bishops' meeting didn't even know Bourne's Christian name; a blank space remains.[3]

The result of these deliberations was sent off to Propaganda, to which, as mission territory, England was still subject. What decision Rome would have come to is anyone's guess. The English Bishops gave no clue as to their preference. Bourne's name was third on the list. He was commended for his zeal, prudence and administrative skills, but there was no indication of a particular desire to see him appointed. Someone told Butt that he had better make his views known in Rome. He was persuaded to write to the Prefect of Propaganda: 'I believe that all three [on the Bishops' *terna*] are good men, however I have a great preference for the third above the first two. The reason for this preference is that I know him best; and I am persuaded that he would work in the same spirit as I have, especially regarding the Seminary, which is vital … The other two are strangers to the Diocese.'[4] He was just in the nick of time. Normally inclining to the wishes of the diocesan bishop, the Cardinals duly obliged, recommending Bourne to Leo XIII. The appointment was confirmed on 13 March 1896.

Not yet 35 years old, Bourne became Bishop of the titular see of Epiphania in Asia Minor. He had never been a parish priest. Save for five years as a curate, virtually his entire life had been spent in seminaries. Not surprising, therefore, that the 15th Duke of Norfolk would later recall: 'When appointed our Bishop, you were practically a stranger to the large majority of the laity.'[5]

Bourne was conscious that there was much to be done to gain acceptance, lay and clerical, in the Diocese. But from the very start he indicated that he would not compromise to achieve this. His choice of episcopal motto (taken, uncharacteristically, from the classics) put down a marker. *Ne cede malis*: 'Yield not to the powers of evil.' And if doubt remained, one had only to proceed to Virgil's next line: *sed contra audentior ito*, 'but meet them with still greater firmness.'

Bourne was consecrated Bishop at St George's Cathedral, Southwark on 1 May 1896. The principal consecrator was to have been Bishop Butt. At the last moment Butt's health failed and Vaughan stepped in, assisted by Butt and Bishop Whiteside of Liverpool (an Ushaw contemporary and fellow former seminary rector). The Cathedral was packed well before the ceremonies began. Fr Serafino Banfi from the Seminary read the papal brief authorising the consecration. As Cardinal Vaughan offered Mass at the High Altar, Bourne began his own Mass at a temporary side altar until brought over to the High Altar. After the Litany was sung, the Book of the Gospels was held over his head and the hands of the consecrating bishops were laid upon him. As the *Veni, Creator* was intoned, his head and hands were anointed with the oil of chrism. Having been presented with the episcopal insignia of crozier, ring and Book of the Gospels, Bourne returned to his Mass at the side altar. Before the Last Gospel, he was given his mitre and gloves, and then, as the *Te Deum* was sung, the new Bishop processed around the Cathedral giving his blessing to all present.[6] There was lunch for 150 at Cathedral House, but it was typical of the man that, at the close of the day, he slipped quietly back to his beloved Wonersh.

Although he continued to live at Wonersh until moving to Bishop's House, Southwark in spring 1898, episcopal duties increasingly took him away from the Seminary. Butt immediately took six weeks leave from Southwark for health reasons. Administering the Diocese in his absence, Bourne travelled up to the Cathedral three days every week to transact business. He was thus obliged to give up his lectures at Wonersh. Fr George Barrett was appointed initially administrative director and then, in January 1898, Seminary Rector. When Barrett retired on health grounds in September 1900, Bourne resumed the office of Rector again briefly, until in January 1901, Fr Joseph Butt[7], the former Bishop's nephew, took his place.

Bishop of Southwark

Bourne was not given long to learn the ropes. In March 1897 Bishop Butt wrote to Rome again, this time asking to be relieved completely of the responsibilities of office. 'I lack the strength to undertake the pastoral work necessary in the Diocese and my loss of memory prevents me dealing with the administrative details. For several months this has been discharged by Mgr Francis Bourne ... The doctor gives little hope of the recovery of my health—as I am 71, strength is not easily recovered.'[8] The ailing Bishop's request was granted, and he retired back to Arundel, dying there on 1 November 1899.

The Southwark canons acted with unnecessary petulance, still smarting from the hierarchy's rejection of their *terna* the preceding year. At a Chapter meeting on 30 April they challenged the validity of various diocesan appointments made by Bourne and demanded sight of the documentation from Rome relating to his own appointment as Bishop. Failing which, they threatened to withdraw from Bourne's enthronement at St George's four days later. Incensed, and adamant he had canon law on his side, Bourne complied with their demands, simply to avoid public scandal.[9] Relations between Bishop and Chapter were soured from the outset.

Those first days as diocesan Bishop involved a significant amount of travelling. There was a month in Rome in the early summer, including an audience with Leo XIII. In October he was in France, with Cardinals Vaughan and Richard at St Sulpice for the inauguration of the Archconfraternity for the Conversion of England, at Arles for the celebration of the 1,300[th] anniversary of St Augustine's arrival in England. That event had already been marked in his own Diocese the previous month by the entire English hierarchy assembled at Ebbsfleet, where Augustine had first brought the Gospel ashore to pagan Kent.

More typical, however, was the everyday work of the Bishop begun while still a Coadjutor. In addition to the appointments and administration undertaken from St George's, Bourne was constantly on the move, around South London, across the counties of Surrey, Sussex and Kent. No mean feat in the days before the motor car. His diary was a constant round of confirmations, priestly ordinations and religious professions, visitations of parishes and convents, the laying of foundation stones and consecration of new churches. No wonder he is writing from Dieppe to one of his female confidantes, the Ursuline, Mother Clare Arthur, 'I had great need of rest, the last three months were full of work, and more than full of worries and anxieties.'[10]

'Crushing debts'

Foremost among those 'worries and anxieties' were money matters. Bourne was unusual among his clerical contemporaries in not having known the overwhelming burden of parish debt. As a curate, he had not ministered in the slums of South London. At Wonersh, Butt had ensured the flow of resources for his pet project. On his appointment as Coadjutor, Butt revealed to Bourne Southwark's true financial position.[11] It was not good. Bourne acknowledged this in his first Pastoral Letter: 'In many cases [the priests'] work, arduous in its own nature, is further weighted by crushing debts, which they strive generously to discharge, but at the cost of many a weary moment of anxiety, which takes them away from those spiritual duties for which they were ordained. The diocesan funds, too small for the general diocesan wants, can give but little help in these individual cases, and we appeal to the faithful of the various missions to relieve their pastors of these great burdens.'[12] Bourne made clear in subsequent Pastorals that a lack of funds restricted the creation of new parishes and the development of existing ones.

The position had arisen due to the massive population growth in South London in the late nineteenth century, with the consequent requirement to attend to the spiritual and material needs of poor Irish Catholics. The Diocese of Southwark had risen to the challenge. The pastoral zeal was admirable, but the methods employed to fund this expansion were questionable. Not alone among English Bishops, Butt had raised funds on the strength of mortgages secured on the new church buildings and the land on which they stood. The intention was, that as congregations grew, their offerings would meet the mortgage interest payments and, eventually, repay the capital too. Sadly, Bourne had to admit, parishes had taken advantage of his predecessor's illness. Mortgage payments had fallen into arrears, producing a spiralling deficit on the central episcopal fund. Promised donations had failed to materialise, the situation further compounded by Butt's expenditure elsewhere—on the Cathedral, the Seminary, new schools and an enlarged clerical staff at Bishop's House.[13] Fr St John's work for destitute children at the Southwark Rescue Society was threatened with closure as debts there also increased.[14]

On assuming responsibility for Southwark, Bourne placed the precarious financial situation of the Diocese before his priests and people. He had a gift for inspiring the generosity of wealthy benefactors. Yet, as all fundraisers know, it is easier to attract money for prestigious new projects than for general administration or debt repayment. On parish visitations, he urged a sense of realism and increased giving. He had some success. Several thousand pounds of parish liabilities were repaid; the annual deficit on central funds was reduced from £1,000 to £700, this liability still increasing, only at a reduced rate.[15]

Bourne identified a handful of parishes which couldn't or wouldn't pay their way. As the worst offender, he singled out Plumstead in south-east London, founded just a few years earlier when Butt had separated it from Woolwich. Visiting Plumstead Bourne infuriated the *forceful*—'hostile' and 'violent' were Bourne's preferred adjectives—Irish priest, Fr Thomas Whelahan, by telling the parish that they were responsible for the £5,050 debt incurred in building the church and school. Whelahan appealed to Rome, execrating his Bishop for spending Charles Dawes's bequest of £86,000 on Wonersh while making impossible demands on poor Irish labourers. The church and school at Plumstead, he alleged, were Butt's gift to the parish; there was never any intention to make the parishioners liable.[16] Bourne disputed Whelahan's version of events: he had waited until Butt's death to advance this claim; it was only Butt's age and ill health which prevented him proceeding against Whelahan. The Bishop was unable to touch the capital of the Dawes Trust; the income could not be used to discharge parish debts. Bourne consulted his Chapter and decided the only practical resolution was to return the pastoral care of Plumstead (together with its financial liabilities) to Woolwich. Whelahan's boastful defiance was undermining episcopal authority.[17] The matter dragged on, Rome generally agreeing with Bourne, sanctioning his removal of Whelahan and Plumstead's merger with Woolwich, insisting only on a resident curate at Plumstead.[18]

Bourne was forced to look wherever he could for funds to support ordinary diocesan expenditure. An attractive option was the parish of Petworth in Sussex. A wealthy benefactor had endowed the parish with an annual income of £300. With only six Catholics (the priest's domestic staff) at Sunday Mass, surely, the money could be better spent elsewhere. Such a small parish required only half the income.[19] Rome and Cardinal Vaughan[20] agreed with Bourne's proposal to add the surplus income to general diocesan funds. Subsequently, investigative journalists were to be fiercely critical of his action.

By autumn 1900 Bourne was becoming increasingly desperate. He was frustrated by Whelahan's appeal to Rome. The Diocesan solicitor, Edward Fooks, predicted disaster if the operations of the Rescue Society were not reined in, and queried the prudence of St John and the Director of Buildings, William Romaine, in funding diocesan activities through ever greater mortgages. The Diocesan debt was approaching £200,000—almost quadruple the combined liability of Southwark and Portsmouth twenty years earlier.[21] While rejecting Fooks's analysis of the underlying causes, Bourne did not dispute the critical nature of the situation. The solvency of the Diocese was at stake. The problem, he wrote went back 'much further back, it was not of my creation, and I have no personal responsibility for it. It has arisen out of undertaking liabilities, mortgages, etc, without the means of meeting them. For at least ten years expenditure has been far in excess of income ... I am never sure of having a sufficient balance available at the exact moment that it may be needed.'²² St John was served with a warrant for the non-payment of rates on the Catholic Boys' Homes.²³ In addition to all of this, Bourne discovered that Butt had financed a number of his initiatives with loans raised against funds given for a specific purpose. Bourne felt morally obliged to repay the £15,000 concerned but was unable to do so from commercial sources.²⁴

It is sometimes said that Bourne did not consult. Yet in his financial worries he sought counsel from the canons of the Diocese. He turned also to the place where he expected any bishop could seek advice, Rome. Perhaps he presumed too much, but he laid the full extent of his predicament before the Prefect of Propaganda. One feels for the 39-year-old Bishop having difficulty seeing the way ahead. 'Your Eminence, I would be grateful for a line of action to follow. Must I close these missions and sell the mortgaged properties, thus discharging the mortgages? Or are there other measures I can take?' Was it imprudent to finance expansion on the basis of mortgaging Church property?²⁵ What hurt—Bourne alluded to the incident years later—was the fact that the Vatican did not even trouble to reply. The experience explains his subsequent ambivalence towards the Roman Curia.

Believing himself let down by Rome, Bourne approached that great benefactor of English Catholicism, Henry, 15th Duke of Norfolk. The Bishop wrote explaining the situation 'of extreme financial anxiety' in which he found himself. The response was one of 'prompt and unstinted assistance.'²⁶ £4,000 was immediately made available to the Diocese. It did not solve all Southwark's financial difficulties, but they were no longer 'the crushing weight of the first years of [Bourne's] episcopate.'²⁷ He was now free to attend to some of the less prosaic aspects of diocesan life.

The Society of Secular Priests

Bourne's priority as Bishop of Southwark presents no surprise. He readily acknowledged the need for more churches, the urgent requirement for work among the young—but his emphasis was elsewhere. 'Having taken every need into consideration, we are convinced that the work most urgently calling for our attention is the provision of permanent and sufficient funds for the maintenance of our ecclesiastical students, for all other works must fail, if we have not a sufficient number of zealous priests, educated for and permanently attached to the diocese.'²⁸ However pressing the diocesan finances, the Seminary was to be protected at all costs. The bulk of the income from the Dawes Trust (amounting to some £3,000 p.a.) was set aside for this purpose.[29]

Good and holy priests, capable of meeting the demands of parish work while never losing sight of the need for their own sanctification, that was what Bourne sought. The seeds were to be sown, of course, in the Seminary, but a good formation, by itself, was insufficient. Again, Bourne looked to his experience of the French Church. He decided on the solution in 1896 during the retreat prior to his episcopal consecration: an association of diocesan priests, sharing the same vision and living a common rule of life.

At this point Peter Amigo enters the story, not that he and Bourne were strangers. They overlapped for a couple of years at St Edmund's, Ware, although, given Bourne was three years older and a seminarian while Amigo was a lay boy, contact was probably limited. Amigo was ordained priest for Westminster in 1888—as Bourne founded the Southwark Seminary. At some point, however, their acquaintance deepened. They shared the same high ideals of the priesthood; in other respects their friendship was most unlikely—this reserved and isolated Englishman, the expansive and extrovert Gibraltarian.

Bourne invited Amigo to lead the retreat for the senior seminarians at Wonersh in both the spring and autumn of 1897, but he had a more permanent and significant collaboration in mind. In October of that year he requested Amigo's transfer to Southwark. Vaughan replied that Amigo could not be spared from his work in the House of Pastoral Theology recently founded in London's East End. Undeterred, Bourne continued quietly to develop his plans. He studied the constitutions of French associations of secular priests. Foremost among these, of course, were the Sulpicians, who explained to Bourne their rule of life. 'We take no vows and remain under the jurisdiction of our respective bishops who might, strictly speaking, call us back to serve in our own dioceses. Each one of us can fully dispose of the income he may have provided he observes the rules regarding simplicity of life, etc.'[30]

Although made parish priest of Commercial Road in 1899, Amigo still sought something more. He considered the Redemptorists and even, at one point, founding a new religious order with the sole purpose of administering the Last Rites to the dying. In February 1901 Bourne and Amigo were together at the Benedictine convent at Stanbrook. The

Abbess threw her weight behind Bourne's proposals.[31] Amigo revealed his restlessness to the Bishop of Southwark. 'I have felt for many years now that God was calling me to a special work, but never having anything definite I am satisfied with the work of a secular priest, because I believe it possible to sanctify myself in it and to do a great deal of good. The difficulty is how to do this. Community life will be a help, expelling the desire of making money a necessity. Helping future priests as you suggest in connection with active mission life will be an ideal. The question is how to do it, and we must pray as you say for God's light.'[32]

Bourne seized the opportunity, writing again to Vaughan, this time successfully: Amigo was released from Westminster for five years.[33] Having the priest whom he felt best able to realise his designs, Bourne acted rapidly. He sent Amigo a copy of his draft constitution. The primacy of the spiritual life is evident.

'This Society of Secular Priests is composed of those who desire to unite themselves together under the protection of our Blessed Lady, Queen of the Clergy; of St Joseph, Patron of the Interior Life; and of St John the Beloved Disciple; and of St Francis de Sales; with the object of living a perfect life according to the vocation which their Divine Master has in His exceeding goodness bestowed upon them, and of devoting themselves with unhesitating generosity to any work which the Bishop of the diocese may call upon them to undertake.

Fundamental articles of Union

I. To this end they propose:

1. [Fidelity to their priestly vows]

2. To live, in imitation of their Master, a simple life, detached from this world ... all offerings from Masses, stole fees, and all other ecclesiastical sources shall be placed in a common fund ...

3. To keep a close interior union with their Divine Master ... [They are to commit themselves to daily Mass, recitation of the Office, one hour's daily prayer after Mass including the reading of Scripture, the Rosary and an examination of conscience.]

II. The normal condition of the associates will be to live in community either in the Seminary or in the Presbyteries assigned to them by the Bishop, but they will be ready to take up isolated work for a time ...

III. Each one shall choose a spiritual director from among the associates.

IV. The Bishop of the Diocese shall be always the Superior General of the associates ...

V. To maintain and renew their fervour, the associates will go to Confession at least once a week ... ; keep a day of recollection every month; and make a retreat every year ...

VI. ... the associates will take as their guides in the priestly life those holy men raised by God, in the seventeenth century especially for the reformation of clergy ... they will take as their guide the writings of St Francis de Sales ...

VII. [Associates will meet annually to renew their vows.]

VIII. [Associates are free to withdraw at any time, but the intention is to remain an associate for life.]'[34]

Remembering his own days as a curate, Bourne also entrusted the Society to the patronage of Our Lady of Consolation, intending one day the Society would care for her shrine at West Grinstead.[35]

Such associations were not unknown in England; Manning attempted something similar with his Oblates of St Charles. There were the Oratorians of St Philip Neri. But Bourne's Rule went much further. Some English priests, defensive of their independence, saw it as too foreign. They argued that Bourne was undermining the essence of the diocesan priesthood; they were not ordained to a religious community. Was it practical to include a provision that the superior would always be the diocesan bishop? What if a future bishop had no taste for such things? How would a bishop, a spiritual father to all his clergy, protect himself against accusations of favouritism towards members of the Society? Yet, membership of the Society was to be freely undertaken by those who felt called to such a way of life; there was no compulsion to join. There have always been those who maintained that the delay in the conversion of England has not been so much due to a lack of priests, but rather an inadequate supply of truly committed and zealous priests. Bourne's initiative was bold and exciting. We can only speculate as to the results had he been given to the time to see the Society established and flourishing.

Bourne threw his entire energy behind the project. The intention was that he and Amigo would visit France to see at first hand how the Sulpicians—and others—lived out their common life. In the event, circumstances prevented Bourne from travelling; Amigo went alone. He was impressed by what he found. One of the Sulpicians gave 'a very beautiful lecture impressing on the seminarists that the life of a priest is a life of sacrifice ... I have found that there are many works in France from which we may get ideas for ours.'[36] On his return to England, Amigo was made parish priest of St Augustine's, Walworth, as a centre to further the work of the Society.

Promoting Priestly Vocations

It was not the only work Amigo was to undertake. Bourne had had in mind for some years the creation of a house of formation for older aspirants to the priesthood, young men already pursuing careers in the world who were to live in community so that their free time could be devoted to prayer, study and missionary work. Those who showed an aptitude for this way of life where then to proceed to seminary. Having taught at St Edmund's and been involved in training newly-ordained priests at Commercial Road, Amigo was deemed the ideal candidate to implement Bourne's experiment.[37]

Bourne was nothing if not systematic in his promotion of priestly vocations. Having opened a house for late vocations at Walworth, he next established a house of formation for boys thinking of the priesthood but too young to be sent to Wonersh. One of his last acts as Bishop of Southwark was to open St Bede's, Clapham Park. The centre he inaugurated there was to have a triple purpose: a new parish to relieve the pressure of numbers on St Mary's, Clapham, a place of rest and retreat for Bourne himself away from the clamour of St George's, but also the St John Berchman's School for boys showing signs of a priestly vocation.

Military Chaplains

Another matter exercised Bourne considerably. In his diocesan history, Fr Michael Clifton accuses Bourne of 'wasting much time on matters relating to the relationship of [military] chaplains to their Bishops when these matters were already clearly delineated.'³⁸ That is not entirely fair. The Bishop of Southwark's historic involvement with military chaplains was practical and historic. Many military establishments were located within the old Southwark boundaries (in the days before the creation of Portsmouth). The first Bishop of Southwark, Thomas Grant, was the son of a soldier and a former army chaplain himself. It was natural, therefore, that the British Government turned to him as the point of reference in the English hierarchy when the Catholic chaplains were first commissioned in the British Army after the Crimean War.

The Bishop of Southwark's oversight of military chaplains was rather loose. He presented candidates to the War Office and granted them faculties to exercise their priestly ministry, but, otherwise, there was little contact or control. Most Catholic chaplains did excellent work in difficult circumstances, but the potential existed for chaplains to play off the Bishop of Southwark against the War Office, military commanders against the local ecclesiastical hierarchy, giving the occasional impression that chaplains were subject to no effective authority whatever.

That position could be tolerated while Britain maintained a minimal standing army and avoided major conflicts, but the experience of the Boer War persuaded many that reform was inevitable. Even prior to the War, Bourne acknowledged the difficulties. 'Though he was the ecclesiastical chief of the chaplains, his position was unfortunately ill-defined, which was an obstacle to his doing all that he would wish for the [chaplains'] department.'³⁹ There were criticisms—some justified—of the Church's ability to supply sufficient and appropriate chaplains to minister to mainly Irish Catholic soldiers during the War.⁴⁰ Although this rather undermines the contention that the old system worked fine, problems were perhaps inevitable given wartime troop movements and communication difficulties. In Southwark Bourne appointed Canon Connelly to attend to chaplaincy matters with a meagre annual stipend of £50 allowed by the War Office. Some alleged inefficiency, but not the War Office. An internal memorandum noted, 'I am sure the Bishop of Southwark and his deputy, Canon Connelly, do their best for us.'⁴¹

During the War the most significant call for change came from Bishop Cahill of Portsmouth, who asked Bourne to pursue with the War Office his preference for his own priests to minister to soldiers stationed in his Diocese.⁴² Although this would allow the local Bishop to satisfy himself as to the provision of pastoral care in his own Diocese, it did not address the situation of chaplains operating overseas in time of war nor the need for central coordination of chaplains by the Church. Bourne subsequently turned his attention to these omissions. The War Office saw the merits of Cahill's proposal for British garrison towns, but recognised its inadequacy in the wider international context. 'The War Office must have at command the services of chaplains who can be ordered about at a moment's notice, eg for war, manoeuvres and troopship services. This means that a certain number of commissioned chaplains must be retained at present.'

The War Office could be sensitive if it thought the Catholic Church was dictating terms to the British Government, but generally it was remarkably accommodating, if only to prevent awkward questions by Irish MPs. 'In view of parliamentary criticism it is of the first importance that if possible [the Secretary of State] should be able to show he is acting in accordance with the wishes of the Catholic Bishops.'[43] The Bishops and the War Office agreed that military chaplains should be subject to the ecclesiastical discipline of the bishop of the diocese in which they were stationed, the Bishop of Southwark to act as an intermediary between the local bishop and the War Office, if necessary.

The real catalyst for reform came with peace. South Africa had its own bishops. Prepared to accept British military chaplains during hostilities, after the War they expected their own priests to look after any remaining British troops. It was a view Bourne shared. 'It is important that we at Southwark should not go beyond the instructions of Propaganda or enlarge the sphere of our military responsibility. It is understood that we recommend chaplains for the Home Service and for active service in time of war, but not for an army of occupation. The local Ordinaries would in the ordinary course provide for this.'[44] Informed that the War Office intended retaining military chaplains, Bourne proposed consulting both Rome and the South African bishops.

Matters deteriorated due to the actions of military chaplains on the ground. Fr Morgan, the Senior Chaplain in South Africa, claimed the right to appoint his fellow chaplain, Fr Edward Ryan, to minister to British soldiers in Cape Town in the place of an unpopular local priest. But Bishop Leonard of Cape Town refused to grant faculties to Ryan. Morgan maintained faculties from the local bishop were unnecessary; military chaplains in South Africa operated under papal dispensation.[45] It was not an attitude shared by Bourne or the local bishops. Bourne was horrified that not only was Ryan acting in defiance of himself and Bishop

Leonard, but was supported in his actions by the War Office.[46] Certain chaplains vociferously supported the War Office, preferring the British Army as their immediate superior, to a local bishop. More impartial chaplains appreciated the difficulties. It was not possible to usurp a bishop's authority in his own diocese. There were claims that some chaplains were not up to the mark. They 'were roaming about in South Africa and neglecting their work partially or entirely.'[47]

Bourne pointed out the weakness of the chaplains' case. The War Office itself had previously asked the South African bishops to assume pastoral care of British troops in peace time. The South Africans had incurred significant expenses, including the building of chapels, in doing so. Bourne also pointed out that he had written almost two years earlier informing the War Office that the South Africans intended resuming these pastoral responsibilities with the return of peace—and had received no objection.[48] He argued (as he invariably did in disputes with officialdom) lucidly and forcefully, but always with courtesy. With implicit reference to military discipline, he repeatedly asked the War Office if they really wanted to encourage the insubordination of men such as Ryan.

The War Office blustered for a while: the British Government should not be dictated to by a Catholic bishop. Bourne stood firm. 'While the Catholic Church is ever ready to make all necessary provision for the spiritual needs of the soldiers who belong to her Communion, and trusts to the well-known equity and fairness of His Majesty's Government for the adequate remuneration of the Clergy attached to the service of the Army, the Ecclesiastical Authority is not the servant of the Government called upon merely to do its behests.'[49] He won his point. 'The chaplains are subject to a twofold jurisdiction, the Ecclesiastical and the Military. These two jurisdictions are co-ordinate, and neither is subordinate to the other. If a chaplain is punished for a Military offence, the Ecclesiastical Authority makes no claim to have cognisance of the matter and readily accepts the decision of the Military Authority; so, in like manner the Ecclesiastical Authority alone can judge when an Ecclesiastical offence has been committed and what punishment is due to it, and the Military Authority is bound to accept this decision.'[50] The War Office accepted this as the basis of a settlement. Rome too ruled in favour of Bourne and the local bishops against appeals by the chaplains—who were removed from South Africa after a face-saving temporary grant of faculties to Fr Ryan.

Bishop of Southwark: 'Practically a stranger'

How could such disputes be avoided in future? To whom were military chaplains ultimately responsible? Bourne pressed the issue on his *ad limina* visit to Rome in January 1903 'so that a new settlement of the whole question of Roman Catholic chaplains may be arrived at.'[51] The War Office itself had previously mused on the possibility of a Catholic Military Bishop—along the lines existing in Germany—but had felt the number of Catholic chaplains did not justify this.[52] The Vatican was now minded to place all military chaplains under the ecclesiastical control of the Bishop of Southwark, who would represent not only the English bishops, but also the Holy See, thus having the authority to resolve situations like that which had arisen in South Africa.[53] Bourne sought the views of the War Office. He did so not only directly but also—a trait which was to irritate others throughout his career—through personal contacts. In this case the intermediary was Lord Edmund Talbot, the Conservative MP and brother of the Duke of Norfolk. The War Official did not appreciate 'these non-official communications on strictly official subjects.'[54] Which was a little rich given Whitehall was not adverse to engaging in a little 'amateur diplomacy'[55] of its own, asking the Benedictine chaplain, Fr Rawlinson, to press its views at the Vatican.[56]

A settlement was achieved after months in which Bourne acted as intermediary between the English hierarchy, the Vatican and the War Office. His contribution was acknowledged by the British Government. 'Mr Brodrick and his predecessors have always attached great weight to the advice from time to time rendered by your Lordship and have not infrequently sought it.'[57] On 4 May 1903 Rome appointed the Bishop of Southwark the Ecclesiastical Superior of all commissioned chaplains in the British Army (outside Ireland and India). As Delegate of the Holy See he had the exclusive power to grant faculties to chaplains. Chaplains were to report to the local bishop but only required his permission to minister to the local population—not to the British soldiers they were sent to serve. A chaplain was required to return to his own diocese when his duties were completed to avoid the allegations that some had gone freelance in South Africa.[58] Here was a clarity the previous arrangements had lacked. The Secretary of State for War indicated his approval: 'Very satisfactory.'[59] (Bourne's ability is reflected by the War Office request that he remain as superior to Catholic chaplains after his move to Westminster to ensure the continuance of 'the satisfactory results invariably accruing from your personal interest in the spiritual welfare of the British Soldier.'[60])

Public Business and Personal Loss

Diocesan affairs and the chaplaincy negotiations kept Bourne in Rome for four months. He was confident, however, that he had left Southwark in Amigo's capable hands. Bourne wrote to Amigo from Rome saying, 'It is a great comfort to me in this prolonged absence to have appointed you Vicar-General, as I feel sure that you will neither allow business to get in arrears nor commit me to any decision of which I might not approve.'[61] Bourne's correspondence from Rome gives insights into his conduct of diocesan business—and it does not support his critics' charges of autocracy. Yes, he could issue directions to Amigo, but that was the relationship of Bishop to Vicar-General. What is telling is that Bourne is perfectly willing to be persuaded that he has made a mistake, for example when Amigo is able to demonstrate that he has been over-generous in the assessment of a particular priest.[62] Amigo and St John were both entrusted with the responsibility of conducting daily diocesan business.

There was criticism of Bourne's regime in Southwark. In addition to suspicion of his innovations in priestly formation at Wonersh, it focused on two areas: allegations of a failure to consult and a tendency towards favouritism. 'As to the Chapter—intended by the Church to be the Senate or Privy Council of the Bishop. He practically and studiously ignored it. He is required to take counsel—but if he took counsel with anybody, it was with his dependents, and not with his constitutional advisers.'[63] One has to examine, however, the identity of the critics. They tended to be disaffected members of the Chapter, those who had opposed Bourne's appointment and remained disaffected throughout his tenure at Southwark. In the days before the Church saw the need for cumbersome bureaucracies, it was essential the Bishop had complete personal confidence in the handful of men with whom he ran the Diocese. Bourne worked with those who were prepared to work with him. When certain members of the diocesan establishment went into opposition—an attitude they had also adopted with the previous Bishop—then it is scarcely surprising that Bourne turned to more cooperative individuals, including the young priests now being ordained from his Seminary. Yet his letters to Amigo do not bear out the accusations of arrogance. Before making clerical appointments, Bourne urged confidential consultation with members of the Chapter. He expresses sympathy and understanding for his priests' failings.[64] The overall picture is of an efficient, yet humane, Bishop.

Bishop of Southwark: 'Practically a stranger'

As he was consecrated Bishop, Bourne's mother and aunt sat in the front row of the nave of St George's Cathedral. The ceremony over, they slipped away without speaking to him. His mother told him that henceforth he belonged entirely to his Diocese. She did not want him to waste time writing letters to her; he was only to send postcards to let her know where he was. She visited him only once at Bishop's House.[65] Even by Victorian standards, Ellen Bourne's reserve was excessive. Bourne demonstrated that he desired something different. In November 1900 he was summoned one Sunday by letter to his mother, who was clearly failing. He administered the Last Rites. He returned to her bedside the following day, but was hurt by her reaction. 'She would not allow me to remain, so that I feel my last act was in obedience to her wish.'[66] On 26 November 1900 Ellen Bourne died, as she lived, very much alone.

Bourne confided his feelings to his elderly aunt—although her deafness meant communication had to be through jottings in a notebook. They reveal an affectionate son and a lonely man. He barely managed to conduct his mother's funeral and burial without breaking down. 'It was an awful day and Monday night was terrible. But I am much quieter and have felt much consolation ... I will come tomorrow for a cup of tea, for it does me good. The life at Bishop's House is all business and very solitary in many ways, and it is a great comfort to me to be with you during these sad days. No one ever comes to me except for business. Others stay away because they fear to disturb me, and thus a Bishop's life is a very lonely and solitary one.'[67]

The person who provided comfort to the young Bishop in that dark period was Mother Janet Stuart, the formidable Superior of the Society of the Sacred Heart. 'She felt the nature of my sorrow, and the special loneliness in which I stood owing to my having hardly any relative except my mother's elder sister who was already very infirm; and with extraordinary tact she sought to make those first days of loss less terrible to bear. She begged me to go to Roehampton the day after the funeral, arranged the next day a Requiem at which I could assist unseen, and, during my stay, in a wonderful way made it easy for me to speak to her of my mother's holy and self-sacrificing life to my own great comfort and relief ... It was those days which established between Mother Stuart and myself a closeness of mutual confidence which grew ever stronger; to me a source of much help.'[68]

Bourne was unable to attend his aunt's funeral; she died on 14 February 1903, while he was in Rome. The passing of Mary Anne Byrne left him with no immediate family.

Despite this personal loss, Bourne was utterly faithful to his episcopal duties. The Diocese appeared healthy, continuing financial pressures notwithstanding, with significant expansion. When Bourne became Bishop of Southwark there were 305 priests working in the Diocese. Seven years later there were 405.[69] Much of this was thanks to Bourne's work at Wonersh. That Seminary alone ordained 38 priests for the Diocese in the first four years of his episcopate with a further 83 preparing for priesthood.[70] The work of the Major Seminary was to be supplemented by Bourne's projects at Walworth and Clapham Park.

The *Tablet* recorded that 'no fewer than seventeen new churches have been built or finished while his Grace was Bishop of Southwark, and eleven churches have been consecrated.'[71] When Bourne became Bishop plans were drawn to provide for churches in the rapidly developing areas of South and South-West London. Lack of funds seemed to render such plans impossible. Bourne gratefully acknowledged what eventually made the work possible.[72] 'For all these things we are indebted to one generous benefactress who has helped us abundantly in other ways as well.'[73] That 'one generous benefactress' was Miss Frances Ellis. In his diocesan history Fr Michael Clifton acknowledges the significance of this wealthy convert, who paid for the sites and construction of eleven churches and presbyteries, many serving the Diocese to this day.[74] The motivation for her extraordinary generosity ought also to be recorded. Frances Ellis herself was quite clear. She gave £144,000 to Southwark because she was inspired by the vision of Bishop Bourne, having complete confidence in him and St John as his agent. Lacking that, these churches would never have been built.[75]

In 1898 the Catholic population of Southwark was 94,800; four years later it had risen to 104,000. Not only churches were built to meet their needs. In the same period the number of Catholic schools rose from 200 to 230, educating 24,150 Catholic children.[76] The Southwark Rescue Society and the Catholic Boys' Brigade undertook crucial social work, the former having responsibility for 2,600 boys in eleven institutions.[77]

Little wonder Bourne wrote to Mother Clare Arthur in the summer of 1902: 'Bishop Butt retired in April 1897. How much has happened in these years, and how much there is to do.'[78] There was no intimation that he was not the one to continue this work.

Bishop of Southwark: 'Practically a stranger'

Notes

1 Anon. letter to Propaganda, 1 March 1895, SCPF, 102/1895, f. 68, rr. 615–616.
2 FAB to Norfolk, summer 1909 (draft), AAW, Bo. III/124/1.
3 Vaughan to Ledochowski, 2 February 1896, SCPF, 102/1896, f. 93, rr. 510–514; AAW, Bo. III/23/2.
4 Butt to Ledochowski, 19 February 1896, SCPF, 102/1896, f. 93, r. 515.
5 Norfolk's address, 22 March 1904, *Tablet*, 26 March 1904, p. 501.
6 *Catholic Times*, 1 & 8 May 1896.
7 Mgr Joseph Butt (1869–1944) was educated at Wonersh and ordained for Southwark in 1897. Rector of Wonersh (1901–1907), having been dismissed by Amigo, he came to Westminster and was appointed Vice-Rector of the Beda College, Rome (1909–1911). He was appointed Auxiliary to Bourne in 1911.
8 Butt to Ledochowski, 22 March 1897, SCPF, 102/1897, f. 114, 453.
9 FAB to Provost Moore, 12 September 1903 (copy), AAW, Bo. III/124/5.
10 FAB to C. Arthur, 18 August 1899 (copy), BDA.
11 FAB to Norfolk, summer 1909 (draft), AAW, Bo. III/124/1.
12 FAB Pastoral, 1 May 1897, *Tablet*, 15 May 1897, p. 792.
13 FAB to Ledochowski, 22 September 1900, SCPF, 102/1900, f. 189, r. 519.
14 *Tablet*, 16 April 1898, p. 628.
15 FAB to Norfolk, 25 November 1900, (copy), AAW, Bo. III/8.
16 T. Whelahan to Ledochowski, 31 August 1900, SCPF, 102/1902, f. 234, rr. 218 et seq.
17 FAB to Ledochowski, 22 September 1900, SCPF, 102/1902, f. 234, rr. 232 et seq.
18 Ledochowski to FAB, 17 December 1900, SCPF, 102/1902, f. 234, r. 239.
19 FAB to Ledochowski, 28 March 1901, SCPF, 102/1901, f. 211, r. 450.
20 Vaughan to Ledochowski, 29 April 1901, SCPF, 102/1901, f. 211, r. 453; Note of Audience, 2 May 1901, SCPF, 102/1901, f. 211, r. 449.
21 Fooks to FAB, 24 November 1900, AAW, Bo. III/8.
22 FAB to Fooks, 25 November 1900 (copy), AAW, Bo. III/8.
23 *Tablet*, 15 September 1900, p. 402. (St John was to win his case eighteen months later, Bourne arguing that the high-handedness of the local authority was motivated by anti-Catholicism.)
24 FAB to Norfolk, 25 November 1900, (copy), AAW, Bo. III/8.
25 FAB to Ledochowski, 22 September 1900, SCPF, 102/1900, f. 189, r. 519.
26 FAB, *Ad Clerum*, 12 February 1917.
27 FAB reply to Norfolk, 22 March 1904, *Tablet*, 26 March 1904, p. 501.
28 FAB, Advent Pastoral 1899.
29 FAB to Ledochowski, 22 September 1900, SCPF, 102/1900, f. 189, r. 519.
30 Fr de Foville, St Sulpice, Paris to FAB, 14 March 1899, AAW, Bo. I/65.
31 Abbess Heywood of Stanbrook to FAB, 22 February 1901, AAW, Bo. I/65.

32. P. E. Amigo to FAB, 22 February 1901, AAW, Bo. I/65.
33. Amigo to FAB, 9 March 1901, AAW, Bo. I/65.
34. 'Diocesan Society of Secular Priests,' u/d Rule in FAB's handwriting, referred to in Amigo's letter to FAB of 22 March 1901, AAW, Bo. I/65.
35. FAB to Amigo, 1903, SAA, Amigo Papers, Letters Pre-1904.
36. Amigo, Issy, to FAB, 7 June 1901, AAW, Bo. I/65.
37. *Tablet*, 1 March 1902, p. 354 .
38. Clifton, *A History of the Archdiocese of Southwark*, p. 21.
39. FAB speech at a dinner for new chaplain-bishops, Bellord and Brindle, 1 May 1899, *Tablet*, 6 May 1899, p. 702.
40. T. Johnstone & J. Hagerty, *The Cross on the Sword* (London: Geoffrey Chapman, 1996), pp. 24–37.
41. Internal memo by E. V. Fleming, WO, 11 March 1901, PRO, WO 32/6442.
42. Cahill to FAB, 4 March 1901, PRO, WO 32/6442.
43. WO memo, u/d, [1901], PRO, WO 32/6442.
44. FAB to E. Ryan, SAA, Chaplains Papers, cited Johnstone & Hagerty, *The Cross on the Sword*, p. 34.
45. Fr Morgan, Pretoria, to St John Brodrick, Secretary of State for War, 17 September 1902, PRO, WO 32/6447.
46. FAB to Sir Guy Fleetwood Wilson, Under-Secretary of State for War, 19 October 1902, PRO, WO 32/6447.
47. Fr S. Rawlinson, OSB, Rome, to Fleetwood Wilson, 21 November 1902, PRO, WO 32/6447.
48. FAB to Fleetwood Wilson, 18 January 1903, PRO, WO 32/6447.
49. FAB to Fleetwood Wilson, 19 May 1903 (copy), PRO, WO 32/6447.
50. FAB to Fleetwood Wilson, 13 June 1903 (copy), PRO, WO 32/6447.
51. Fleetwood Wilson to Brodrick, 18 Febuary 1903, PRO, WO 32/6447.
52. WO memo, u/d [1901], PRO, WO 32/6442.
53. FAB to Lord Edmund Talbot, 27 February 1903 (copy), PRO, WO 32/6447.
54. Minute, Fleetwood Wilson to Brodrick, 10 March 1903, PRO, WO 32/6447.
55. Fleetwood Wilson to Brodrick's private secretary, u/d, PRO, WO 32/6447.
56. Fleetwood Wilson to Rawlinson, 14 October 02 (copy), PRO, WO 32/6447.
57. Fleetwood Wilson to FAB, 12 March 1903, PRO, WO 32/6447.
58. Gotti to FAB, 15 June 1903, AAW, Roman Letters, Misc./3.
59. Fleetwood Wilson to Brodrick's private secretary [annotated by Brodrick], u/d, PRO, WO 32/6447.
60. Fleetwood Wilson to FAB, 5 February 1904.
61. FAB to Amigo, 18 April 1903, SAA, Amigo Papers, Letters Pre-1904.
62. FAB to Amigo, u/d [1903], SAA, Amigo Papers, Letters Pre-1904.
63. Canon O'Halloran to Merry del Val, 28 January 1904, SCPF, 102/1904, f. 289, rr. 220–221.

64 FAB to Amigo, 18 April 1903, SAA, Amigo Papers, Letters Pre-1904.
65 Stuart, 'Notes,' AAW, Bo. IV/1/27.
66 FAB exercise book, AAW, Bo. IV/1/23.
67 *Ibid.*
68 Jackman, 'Reminiscences of Cardinal Bourne,' *Wonersh Magazine*, May 1935, pp. 23–26, citing FAB's own recollections of Janet Stuart written 13 August 1915, p. 24.
69 *Tablet*, 6 February 1904, pp. 234–235.
70 FAB to Clergy on Ecclesiastical Education Fund, *Tablet*, 8 June 1901, p. 911.
71 *Tablet*, 6 February 1904, pp. 234–235.
72 FAB, St Bede's, Clapham Park, 16 May 1932, *Tablet*, 21 May 1932, p. 672.
73 Pastoral, 5 October 1902, *Tablet*, 11 October 1902, p. 591.
74 Clifton, *A History of the Archdiocese of Southwark*, pp. 68–69.
75 Draft memo, 5 March 1911, AAW, Bo. III/1/23.
76 Relation of the State of the Diocese of Southwark, 2 February 1899, SCPF, 102/1899, f. 165, r. 5; Report on Southwark, 1903, SCPF, 102/1903, f. 259, r. 58.
77 *Tablet*, 6 February 1904, pp. 234–235.
78 FAB to Arthur, 20 July 1902 (copy), BDA.

Chapter 8

Crossing the Thames

A Dying Cardinal

At the end of August 1903 Bourne was ordaining Jesuits at their house at Hales Place near Canterbury. 'As he was walking in the garden, the Rector of the house came to him and handed him a telegram; it brought him news that he was being transferred to Westminster. The young Bishop knew very well what this was likely to entail, as well as many who, at the time, looked on the appointment with misgiving. He was the youngest of the hierarchy, he had little of that impressive personality which had so graced his predecessor, he knew, still more, that somewhere at the back of his mind were ideas and ideals which might be less than pleasing to many. He stood for a moment with the telegram in his hand, then he turned to the Father Rector and said, as if he foresaw failure: "This at least I will promise; God shall have the very best I can give Him."'[1] Bourne's was a shock appointment. Many at the time, and subsequently, asked how this 42-year-old Bishop, little known outside Church circles, came to be the fourth Archbishop of Westminster, head of the Catholic Church in England & Wales, ahead of better known and more experienced candidates.

Conspiracy theories abounded: the Roman Curia was foisting an obscurantist Archbishop on England, blocking the claims of better qualified liberal intellectuals. A curmudgeonly Irishman's prejudice against English Benedictines. Xenophobia. The intervention of the Duke of Norfolk. And that comprehensive explanation for all evil: it was the fault of the French. For Bourne himself, the reason for his appointment was much simpler: 'God's Will has been clearly manifest, and I can only follow Divine Providence.'[2]

Reading the archival material allows us to piece together what actually happened. The vacancy at Westminster was no surprise to anyone. Cardinal Vaughan had been failing for some years; in June 1902 he suffered a serious relapse. On the doctors' orders he was sent to the country and overseas to conserve his strength. Although he survived for another twelve months, Vaughan's active ministry was effectively over.

The clerical chatter began as to whom the Pope might appoint as his successor. Of course, even the Pope is constrained by the existing pool of qualified candidates—a rather limited pool in this case. On only three occasions to date Rome has looked to an outsider; generally it is felt that the position requires someone with local episcopal experience to preside over his brother bishops. In addition to Westminster itself, there were only sixteen other English and Welsh dioceses. One was vacant. Three bishops were very recent appointments themselves. Of the remaining twelve, most were elderly or northerners with little experience of the Church in London. Few were known by the wider English public or distinguished by scholarship or other accomplishments. As a former Westminster auxiliary, Bishop Robert Brindle might have appeared a possible contender. (His inability to work with Vaughan had ensured his transfer to Nottingham.) Yet he was not young himself, disliked the exposure to national life Westminster inevitably involved and was an eccentric who later suffered a breakdown. Fr Ethelred Taunton was a perpetual malcontent living in Rome, never happier than when furthering discord in the Church. His views—proffered liberally to anyone prepared to listen—are normally to be treated with complete disregard. In this case, however, one wonders whether there was perhaps a grain of truth. 'Among all our bishops there is none fit to be Archbishop.'[3]

Three Candidates

Vaughan died on 19 June 1903. The Westminster Chapter met on 30 June to vote on their *terna* for his successor; the Bishops of England and Wales met for the same purpose the following day. Unusually, the two lists contained the same three names, only their order of preference differed. The Canons placed Archbishop Rafael Merry del Val at the head of their *terna*, followed by Abbot Aidan Gasquet and Bishop Hedley of Newport. The Bishops simply reversed the order of Merry del Val and Hedley.[4]

During his lifetime Cardinal Vaughan had worked to secure the Westminster succession through the appointment of an auxiliary or coadjutor bishop. 'The person whom I wanted to have above all is Mgr Merry del Val. He is a man imbued with the apostolic spirit—a man who would be good with both the clergy and the people.'[5] Such an appointment would have been hugely controversial. Rafael Maria José Pedro Francisco

Borja Domingo Gerardo de la Santisma Trinidad Merry del Val y Zulueta was just 37 years old at the time of Vaughan's death. Born in London, where his aristocratic father was Secretary at the Spanish Embassy, he had British, Irish and Dutch blood in his veins. After studying briefly at Ushaw, he had been ordained a priest for Westminster, going on to become a papal diplomat destined for high office in the Church.

Merry del Val himself was a realist. 'Not to speak of my deficiencies, my name alone is an insuperable obstacle. I should always be branded as an alien however much as I may be English to all intents and purposes.'[6] He was right. Religious tolerance at the end of Victoria's reign was still an uncertain matter. The effort of three centuries to dissociate English Catholicism from the Armada would have been undone overnight. Many in Westminster admired Merry del Val—because of his undoubted personal qualities, his role in ensuring the pronouncement against Anglican orders and his stance against liberalism. However, he got wind of the attempt to promote his candidacy, and took steps to derail it. He wrote to Cardinal Gotti at Propaganda urging the impossibility of the suggestion. He persuaded his friend the Duke of Norfolk to write in similar vein. 'He is not sufficiently English to make it wise to appoint him ... I feel that everything he did would be open to being misunderstood, and that on many public questions ... our difficulties would be greatly increased and our position jeopardised. I quite admit that a great deal of this would arise from the stupid side of our insular character but we have to take facts as we find them and this sort of stupidity is one of our great obstacles.'[7] Rome was quite prepared to take facts as they found them—not least because it had its own very different plans for the young prelate. The English Bishops admitted to placing his name third on their *terna* after they too received 'a very strong letter' on the subject from Norfolk.[8] Merry del Val's candidacy was a non-starter.

Bishop Cuthbert Hedley was the most accomplished member of the English hierarchy, as the non-Catholic establishment acknowledged. 'Bishop Hedley is a man of considerable learning and a thoughtful writer on religious subjects, and he is much respected.'[9] A former editor of the *Dublin Review*, he was a prestigious preacher and had been considered for Westminster on Manning's death 11 years earlier. But by 1903 he was 66 years old and lame. He was Bishop of a small Welsh diocese with just 36 diocesan priests and no seminary. Norfolk advised Rome that Hedley 'would be the most fitting successor' to Vaughan, and then proceeded to damn him with faint praise. Noting Hedley's age and scholarly nature, he remarked obtusely, 'It is very difficult to go to sleep in London. If he does there will be plenty of people to wake him up.'[10] Hedley suffered another disadvantage which by itself may have proved insurmountable. He was a Benedictine. It would be another three generations before the English were prepared to countenance a monk as head of the Church in England & Wales.

To have proposed one Benedictine to lead the Church in England over a century ago was remarkable. But, quite extraordinarily, the third candidate on the *terna* was also a monk, another spiritual son of St Benedict. Aidan Gasquet was exotic only in having professed religious vows and bearing a French surname. Otherwise, he was undoubtedly the establishment candidate: 'an uncompromising Englishman, fearless and bluntly outspoken ... His common sense did not admit shades or innuendo in conversation. His yea was yea and his nay meant nay ... He was John Bull in a Benedictine robe.'[11] As Prior of Downside he had engaged in the very Victorian activities of promoting a public school and significant construction work.

The *Times* pressed his case: 'Abbot Gasquet possesses in particular two qualifications which will carry weight in Rome. In the first place, as a pupil of Manning, he is better able than any other could be to gather up the scattered threads of Manning's later policy and regain the position that Manning won for Roman Catholicism in England. In the second place, he is the only English Roman ecclesiastic who has a great reputation outside his own body, his historical works on the Reformation having made his name familiar to many.' Just days before the appointment was announced, the Thunderer opined that it was 'highly probable' that Rome would select Gasquet for Westminster.[12] When that appointment was not what he wished, one member of the Catholic establishment complained, 'Most good folk are more than vexed that Dom Gasquet is not to be our new archbishop, and I fear the immediate future.'[13]

In fact, Abbot Gasquet was not quite as uncomplicated as might appear. Yes, he was a noted historian, but his history was of a polemical variety. Evidence was not allowed to come in the way of the argument he was advancing. When Gasquet took up a matter, his loyalty was unquestioning. It was his strength and weakness. With Merry del Val and Vaughan, he had fought strenuously against the recognition of Anglican orders in the preceding decade. Bourne later accused Gasquet of being his inveterate enemy in Rome, embittered by his failure to gain the

Westminster appointment. He was not alone in questioning Gasquet's motivation. Baron Friedrich von Hügel suspected the Abbot 'of being desirous of ecclesiastical promotion.'[14] Gasquet's own correspondence confirms the suspicion: 'the Roman authorities should do something in the way of showing that they understand I have served them well. I certainly think I have in the Anglican Orders Commission and in settling our Benedictine business. The only return for work and money expended for them was the *snub* over the Westminster business. Such is life!'[15] Monks too are human.

It was also alleged that Gasquet lacked the unequivocal support of his own order, that Abbot Hemptine of Sant'Anselmo, the Benedictine headquarters in Rome, had intervened to point out Gasquet's administrative inadequacies. The rumour emanated from the *Daily Chronicle* and was vigorously denied by Hemptine himself.[16] More difficult to refute was the submission made directly to Rome by one of the English Bishops: Gasquet was 'without experience in secular ecclesiastical affairs.'[17] His life had been spent in monasteries and libraries. Was that adequate preparation to administer the diocese at the heart of the British Empire? Another Bishop who knew him well also queried 'whether his gifts lay in the direction of a very important administrative post.'[18]

The Fourth Man

The English hierarchy were conscious of presenting Rome with an impossible choice. All three candidates suffered serious handicaps: two monks and a Spaniard with no desire for the job. Two had no experience of running a diocese, the third was ageing with a physical disability. It was unconventional, but, in the circumstances, the Bishops thought it prudent to add a fourth name: that of Francis Bourne.

According to one account, the suggestion came from Arthur Riddell, the Bishop of Northampton.[19] His own schooldays at Downside had given him a lifelong aversion to the Benedictines. He was a supporter of diocesan seminaries, having established his own at Shefford. He viewed Bourne as the most likely instrument for unravelling the Central Seminary at Oscott, viewed by Riddell as an unnecessary expense. Although not on their *terna*, the Westminster canons had in their deliberations mentioned the names of both Bourne and Bishop Cahill of Portsmouth. At the meeting of the hierarchy the two were asked to step out of the room for a moment, but Cahill did so only after having urged Bourne's merits to his brother Bishops. They returned to discover that Bourne had been unanimously added as the fourth man.[20]

Despite his relative youth, Bourne's inclusion ought not to have caused undue surprise. For some time he had assumed an increasingly prominent role in Church affairs beyond the boundaries of Southwark. There was his military chaplaincy work, so recently brought to a successful conclusion. And then illness had caused Vaughan to turn to Bourne on occasion as the only other Catholic Bishop in London. Even prior to this the two had collaborated, Bourne himself noting that back in the 1890s he was 'a frequent visitor to Archbishop's House, where Cardinal Vaughan spoke fairly freely to him on whatever topic was uppermost in his mind.'[21] He met with Vaughan to discuss vacancies in the hierarchy and communicated their joint views to Rome. 'During Cardinal Vaughan's protracted ill-health, [Bourne] was frequently called upon to help or replace him in connection with questions arising out of the recent Education Act.'[22] His exposure to national life was steadily growing. He had also stood in for Vaughan at a priestly ordination in December 1902.

Bourne's name was linked to Westminster—not always with approval. As Vaughan sought an auxiliary or coadjutor to help administer his Diocese, the *Times* thought Bourne the most probable candidate—although there is no evidence to suggest that this was ever considered by either Vaughan or Rome.[23] It did not, however, prevent Taunton from giving his customary, unsought advice: Bourne was least 'fitted by nature, prudence and intelligence.'[24] Five months later Taunton was writing again, delating Bourne to the Vatican for taking part of the Petworth endowment for general diocesan purposes—unaware that Bourne's action had been sanctioned by both Rome and Vaughan. Taunton had been educated at Downside and only ill health had prevented his entering the Benedictine Order. He was one of Gasquet's principal cheerleaders, one whom Gasquet would have fared better without. Nor was Gasquet himself particularly flattering about the young Bishop of Southwark. 'One cannot help feeling that we might get a worse man than Cardinal Vaughan in his place. Bourne's name I am told is freely mentioned, but this would be very unpopular in the diocese and his notion of Education is far too *foreign* to please most people.'[25] The *Times'* correspondent was also in the Gasquet camp. Bourne was 'a well-meaning and energetic prelate,' but he had 'given no sort of indication that he possesses any conspicuous ability, or that he has those special gifts which ought to distinguish a successor of Wiseman and Manning.' The paper proceeded to repeat Taunton's allegations of financial misconduct.[26]

Roma locuta est

This was the state of play when Hedley, as the senior Bishop, submitted the *terna* to Rome on 3 July. Two and a half weeks later Pope Leo XIII was dead. Rome's energies were engaged in the consequent conclave, which saw Pius X elected on 4 August. In fact, the change of pontiff delayed the Westminster appointment barely at all. The Cardinals on Propaganda met for the first time in the new papacy on Monday, 24 August. After 3 ¼ hours of deliberations, which also involved recommendations for other vacant dioceses, Gasquet heard that they had voted two for Hedley, four for himself and five for Bourne. On the Friday Gotti took the recommendation to Pius X and secured his approval. In his initial disappointment Gasquet was magnanimous, if somewhat patronising. 'I am very sorry for Bourne. He wrote me a letter that was all and more than could be expected from anyone and I believe that tho' he will never be brilliant, he certainly won't be narrow-minded.'[27]

How had Bourne come out on top? Well, of all the candidates he was best served by his supporters, especially by the Bishop of Portsmouth. Various representations were made and views proffered to Propaganda concerning the Westminster vacancy. None, however, was as cogent as the closely-reasoned four page submission of Bishop Cahill. Cahill obligingly gave the Cardinals a convincing analysis of the current state of the Diocese of Westminster, together with compelling reasons as to why Bourne was the best man to affect the necessary reform.

Cahill began with the perfectly valid point that the first three Archbishops of Westminster (Wiseman, Manning and Vaughan) had all been men very much in the public eye, bringing considerable ability to bear on national life. This might have been a very good thing for the renascent Catholic Church in England, but the implications for ordinary diocesan life were more questionable. Cahill feared there was some truth in the allegations that these Archbishops 'had no personal knowledge of the priests of the diocese, or of the conditions and circumstances of the several parishes.' What was needed now was that the new 'Archbishop of Westminster should be rather a good organiser than a brilliant public man.' Cahill backed up his contention by pointing to the disparate and demoralised state of the Westminster clergy. Priests were drawn from three sources: converts, surplus Irish and a diminishing number of diocesan priests born and bred in the Diocese—only three men had been ordained for Westminster in 1902. Much of this, he contended, was due to the lack of 'a proper ecclesiastical seminary.'

Urging the need for a 'proper' seminary along Tridentine lines was music to the ears of a Roman congregation. And Cahill told them, as he had told the English hierarchy, where they could find the man to implement this. The Bishop of Southwark enjoyed 'great power of organisation, with a thorough grasp of details, that the diocese of Southwark was completely and perfectly organised, but most especially his Seminary was a triumph of order, method and careful thought; and that the whole of merit of this was due to Mgr Bourne.' Cahill contrived to maintain a certain objectivity. He acknowledged the objections to Bourne's candidacy, and then proceeded effectively to dispatch them. 'It has been said that the Canons of Westminster purposely omitted the name of Bishop Bourne from the *terna*, because he was unpopular in his own diocese. I think that in the earlier part of his episcopate he was unpopular, because he was very vigorous. But I believe that his justice and his zeal are now quite understood, and that he has now conciliated all the priests and the Canons of his diocese who completely appreciate his ability and his work. I have heard in many directions that the leading members of the laity would be glad to see him appointed Archbishop.'[28]

By comparison, other submissions were virtually worthless. They failed to address the specific situation of Westminster, and why their preferred candidate was qualified to lead the Diocese. The Duke of Norfolk's letter was no help to anyone. Although he scotched the candidacy of Merry del Val—unnecessarily given Rome's alternative plans for him—it is difficult to see whom Norfolk was actually promoting. And, in any event, the Cardinals may have taken a rather dim view of a layman, even a duke, offering his thoughts on high ecclesiastical appointments.

It is difficult to over-estimate the importance of Cahill's intervention. He admitted to being an 'intimate friend' of Bourne; his enthusiastic promotion of his candidacy was 'based entirely on my appreciation of his able and earnest work.'[29] Yet the appointment did not lie in Cahill's gift. When Propaganda met on 24 August most of the 11 Cardinals were Italians, with a German, a Spaniard and one from Australia. The curial Cardinals would have had the recent opportunity of seeing Bourne at first hand during his four month stay in Rome resolving the military chaplaincy issue. His contact with Cardinal Gotti during that time had certainly done him no harm. It was said that the Prefect of Propaganda strongly supported Bourne.[30] And then the Cardinals were also capable of exercising some common sense. 'It was also in his favour that he was the Bishop of the diocese nearest to Westminster.'[31] Put all these factors together and Bourne's appointment is no longer so improbable.

And what of the conspiracy theories? It suited Gasquet and his circle to publicise these to explain Gasquet's failure. Gasquet blamed the Media. 'The Newspapers frightened people with the idea that I was the candidate of the "queer party".'[32] Like Bourne, Gasquet was to show himself critical of the excesses of the anti-Modernists. However, it is ironic that one so influential in preventing the recognition of Anglican orders should be regarded as a liberal, just as Bourne, given his Sulpician education, should be labelled an 'obscurantist.' These were the claims of the Roman correspondent of the *Daily Chronicle*, alleging that Gotti had doubted the orthodoxy of both Benedictines : 'Peril beset her (the Church) from foes within, the Liberal Catholic party, of whose insidious growth only too much evidence had been brought to the notice of the Holy See by English Bishops and others. He regretted that two candidates on the *terna* had not shown themselves free from tendencies in that direction.'[33] England has never been particularly blessed by the religious correspondents of the national Press. The *Daily Chronicle*'s man was an ex-seminarian of the Beda College, wide of the mark in a number of his assessments. Gasquet took the matter sufficiently seriously, however, to write to Gotti, who denied everything. 'No such expression of opinion, not even such an idea was uttered by me; not a single phrase or statement there reported was used by me. The whole may be denied in the most explicit and absolute manner.'[34] Gasquet ensured publication of the denial in both the *Tablet* and the *Daily Chronicle*. It is possible that Gotti entertained doubts as to the vigour with which the English Bishops promoted orthodoxy. It is implausible, however, that the deliberations of Propaganda were influenced, as Gasquet alleged, by the musings of the English secular Press.

Although Merry del Val's candidacy may have foundered on his nationality, the appointment was not decided by xenophobia. Merry del Val was never going to go to Westminster; Rome had other plans for him. The French always provide easy scapegoats. His own antecedents didn't prevent Gasquet from casting them in this role. 'There was I am told much canvassing on the part of the French for Bishop Bourne—"absolutely indecent" was the expression used in a letter to the *Tablet* as to this French action. The Abbé P--- told me that the French regarded its result as a triumph for the Seminary system and worked for that end. I had already heard that the French were working a great deal.'[35] It was also alleged that this was payback time for Gasquet's role in the Anglican orders commission, the French having taken a more ecumenical line in the 1890s. There is little or no evidence for these claims. Were the French hierarchy really that interested in Anglican orders or imposing their seminary system on England at a time they were contending with persecution from their own anti-clerical government? In any event, French influence in Rome declined under the new pontificate and there were no French cardinals sitting on Propaganda when the Westminster appointment was made.

That leaves only one conspiracy theory to be considered: the involvement of Cardinal Moran. Moran was Archbishop of Sydney, but first and foremost an Irishman. The nephew of an archbishop of Dublin, he went on to become a seminary professor and bishop in Ireland himself. In 1882 he was transferred to the Antipodes. Relevant to this controversy is the fact that Moran was the successor to two English Benedictine archbishops. He did not approve of them. He had been involved in a bitter dispute concerning the burial of one of them. When the news reached Australia of Leo XIII's death, Moran embarked immediately for Rome, hoping to participate in the conclave. He arrived three weeks too late. But he was in time for the meeting of Propaganda, where he vented his hatred for the Benedictines by dispatching the candidacies of Hedley and Gasquet.

Gasquet was convinced that he had been thwarted by the Irishman. 'Cardinal Moran's arrival brought a strongly determined man determined to prevent a Regular. Moran is an aged Cuckoo, who having got possession of a Benedictine nest has always tried to ignore the work of his Benedictine predecessors.'[36] Bourne's biographer, Oldmeadow, was having none of this. It was a point of honour to refute any suggestion that his Archbishop owed his appointment to such an imperfect cause. He set out to disprove the claim. His research showed that Moran's arrival was too late to influence matters. 'That the Australian Cardinal was responsible for the choice is a theory incompatible with the timetable.'[37] Unfortunately, Oldmeadow got his facts wrong. A glance at back issues of the *Tablet* would have told him that Moran arrived in Rome on the evening of 22 August.[38] The papers of Propaganda prove he was present at the relevant meeting two days later.[39]

Oldmeadow had the good grace to acknowledge his mistake when he published the second volume of his biography. He had discovered new material in the Westminster Archives in which Bourne himself verified the account of Moran's intervention. 'Again, my being made Archbishop of Westminster turned on a small point. Cardinal Moran happened to be in Rome at the time the choice of a man for the post was being considered. He had never met me but heard that I had certain administrative qualities and feeling that these were needed in Westminster at the time, he attended the meeting at which the decision was to be made. He did not know that Cardinal—was a Cardinal Bishop and entitled to speak first, and spoke first himself—the other Cardinal graciously giving way to a foreigner. He proposed me and carried the meeting.'[40]

So did Westminster owe the thirty-one year reign of Cardinal Bourne to Aussie disregard for protocol? If the voting at Propaganda was as close as Gasquet suggested, then Moran's intervention may have been decisive. However, one cannot casually discount the weaknesses associated with Gasquet's candidacy (principally that of his being a monk), nor the strengths of Bourne's. That Bourne's appointment was due exclusively to this one factor is disproved by the letter he had already written to Propaganda. By the time the Cardinals met word had got back to him that he was a serious contender; he wrote urging that he might be passed over, feeling himself incapable of the immense task and the public role involved.[41]

Whatever the relative weighting of the reasons, Church historians know God writes straight with the crooked lines of humanity. Francis Alphonsus Bourne was, by the grace of God and the favour of the Apostolic See, the fourth Archbishop of Westminster.

Notes

1. Archbishop Alban Goodier, SJ, 'Cardinal Bourne,' *The Month*, (1935), p. 111.
2. FAB to Gotti, 16 September 1903, SCPF, 102/1904, f. 289, r. 66.
3. E. Taunton to Gotti, 19 January 1903, SCPF, 102/1903, f. 259, r. 34.
4. Bishop C. Hedley to Gotti, 3 July 1903, SCPF, 102/1904, f. 289, rr. 27–31.
5. Vaughan to Gotti, January 1903, SCPF, 102/1903, f. 259, r. 28.
6. Merry del Val to J. Broadhead, 2 April 1903, UCA, Broadhead Papers, OS/J/4.
7. Norfolk to Gotti, 12 July 1903, SCPF, 102/1904, f.289, rr. 32–38.
8. Cahill to Gotti, u/d, SCPF, 102/1904, f. 289, rr. 54–55.
9. *Times*, 17 August 1903.
10. Norfolk to Gotti, 12 July 1903, SCPF, 102/1904, f. 289, rr. 32–38.

11. Leslie, *Cardinal Gasquet*, p. 12.
12. *Times*, 17 August 1903.
13. E. Green to W. Ward, 3 September 1903, SAUL, Ward Family Papers, ms 38347/VII/118/3.
14. M. de la Bedoyère, *The Life of Baron von Hügel* (London: J. M. Dent & Sons Ltd, 1951), p. 170.
15. Gasquet to Fleming, 31 December 1904, cited Leslie, *Cardinal Gasquet*, p. 199.
16. Roman correspondent, *Tablet*, 12 September 1903, p. 407.
17. Cahill to Gotti, u/d, SCPF, 102/1904, f. 289, rr. 54–55.
18. Bishop W. Brown, *Through Windows of Memory* (London: Sands & Co Ltd, 1946), p. 117.
19. P. Hughes, 'The Bishops of the Century,' Beck (ed.), *The English Catholics, 1850–1950*, p. 213.
20. Cahill to Gotti, u/d, SCPF, 102/1904, f. 289, rr. 54–55.
21. FAB address, St Mary's, Twickenham, 23 June 1927, *Tablet*, 2 July 1927, p. 14.
22. *Tablet*, 29 August 1903, pp. 321–322.
23. *Times*, 21 October 1902.
24. Taunton to Gotti, 19 January 1903, SCPF, 102/1903, f. 259, r. 34.
25. Gasquet to Fleming, 2 June 1903, cited Leslie, *Cardinal Gasquet*, p. 80.
26. *Times*, 17 August 1903.
27. Gasquet to E. Bishop, 7 September 1903, cited Leslie, *Cardinal Gasquet*, p. 83.
28. Cahill to Gotti, u/d, SCPF, 102/1904, f. 289, rr. 54–55.
29. *Ibid*.
30. Fleming to Gasquet, 22 October 1903, cited Leslie, *Cardinal Gasquet*, p. 86.
31. *Times*, 25 August 1903.
32. Gasquet to Bishop, 7 September 1903, cited Leslie, *Cardinal Gasquet*, p. 83.
33. *Daily Chronicle*, cited Roman correspondent, 30 August 1903, *Tablet*, 5 September 1903, pp. 373–374.
34. Gotti to Gasquet, 7 September 1903, cited *Tablet*, 19 September 1903, p. 446.
35. 'Memorandum of Abbot Gasquet on the Election of the Archbishop of Westminster, 1903,' cited Leslie, *Cardinal Gasquet*, p. 85.
36. Gasquet to Bishop, 7 September 1903, cited Leslie, *Cardinal Gasquet*, p. 83.
37. Oldmeadow, *Francis Cardinal Bourne*, i, p. 209n.
38. Roman correspondent, 23 August 1903, *Tablet*, 29 August 1903, p. 333.
39. Propaganda *Relazione con Sommario*, SCPF, 102/1904, f. 289, r. 53.
40. Memo [by Fr Coote?], San Remo, 10 December 1912, AAW, Bo. III/124/5.
41. Bourne to Gotti, 22 August 1903, SCPF, 102/1904, f. 289, rr. 88–89.

Chapter 9

A Little Local Difficulty

The New Archbishop

It is telling that Baron Friedrich von Hügel, the lay theologian, with the best of social and ecclesiastical connections, knew nothing of Bourne. 'I have never exchanged one word with the new Archbishop, and have seen him only once. But I thought it right to write him a carefully thought out letter of congratulation, and his answer was somehow touching in its simplicity and humility.'[1] Like von Hügel, most Catholics knew little of their new Archbishop.

The new regime began slowly. Although Pius X made the appointment on 28 August, it took effect only when the Brief arrived in Bourne's hands—not until 14 September. He formally took possession of his new Diocese by presenting the documentation to the Westminster Chapter on 20 September. In the interim he continued to live in Southwark, not saying his first Mass in Westminster until 4 October—appropriately enough back at St Edmund's. His appointment of two Old Edmundians, Mgr Patrick Fenton and Manning's former secretary, Mgr William Johnson, as Vicar-General and Provost of the Chapter respectively reassured his new Diocese.[2] There was a certain amount of business transacted, the consecration of a new bishop of Salford, seminary affairs. But on 26 October Bourne travelled to Rome to receive the pallium, that strip of woollen cloth worn around an archbishop's neck as a symbol of his authority and his loyalty to the Apostolic See. He was away for almost two months. Rather tellingly, he took with him two Southwark priests, Edward St John and Charles Coote, rather than Westminster priests.

Bourne was only enthroned as Archbishop of Westminster four months after his appointment. There was a reason for the delay. The funeral rites of his predecessor had been conducted in an unfinished cathedral. He postponed his enthronement until the archiepiscopal throne on the sanctuary was ready. But the planning was meticulous. Everything emphasized continuity with the medieval English Church. The Feast of

St Thomas Becket was chosen deliberately—Westminster was the new Canterbury. English Catholics were proud that 'that the Archbishop has decided that his enthronement shall be carried out according to the ancient ceremonial which was prescribed for his predecessors the Catholic Archbishops of Canterbury before the Reformation. The reasons which have motivated his Grace's decision are of far-reaching importance. Catholics never forget their proud heritage of a thousand years of English history ... How much we have in common with those who witnessed the enthronement of the Archbishops in Catholic days! The same Catholic faith—the same devotion to the Apostolic See—the same veneration of the same sacred pallium—the same prayers and liturgy—the same Holy Sacrifice of the Mass—even the same melodies which were sung centuries ago by the monks of Canterbury.'[3]

The new Archbishop laid out his programme in his first Pastoral Letter read from the sanctuary steps at his enthronement. He identified his priority: 'Almost all the questions which demand our special care ... are connected with education.' Paramount was the task of restoring the diocesan seminary. (He did not reveal the extent to which he had already advanced this objective.) Again drawing on personal experience, Bourne next pressed the case for the better provision of education for middle-class Catholic boys in London. He dealt at greater length with the question of Catholic elementary schools, acknowledging both the imperfections of the 1902 Education Act and the benefits it accorded to denominational education. He committed Catholics to attempting to make the new system work, but, with Nonconformist Liberalism resurgent, he was under no illusions as to the dangers ahead. 'Our conflict is not ended, it may become acute at any moment, and we must be on the alert; for there is a section of our fellow-countrymen, loud-voiced and strident—nay, we may even say aggressive and intolerant—who would gladly rob us of that measure of justice which we have gained.'[4] Finally, he urged the need for vigilance against the demon drink.

His aims might appear parochial, but they were the immediate concerns of his co-religionists. Bourne's brief had been to play less of a role on the national stage, rather to build up the spiritual and temporal welfare of his Diocese. His proposals received praise and support. One Bishop wrote, 'I read your Pastoral, and the joy it has afforded me no words of mine can express ... Your words on my dearest friend the late Cardinal charm me, and the way you show up our deadliest enemies the

Nonconformists baffles description ... You have a most difficult work before you ... You *need* courage, and great guidance from the Holy Ghost. May you receive both.'[5]

Not that Bourne forgot the greater purpose of his appointment. 'We must have that same apostolic spirit, that faith and heart of St Augustine when he came to England: which made him go about among our forefathers, seeking to bring them to God. As Catholics, we have to go about in this country, longing to give them the immense gift which has been given to our own selves because we are Catholics. We must trust to that apostolic spirit—the spirit of inventiveness, the spirit of discovering and striving, year by year, and generation by generation, how we can get to the very heart of the English people.'[6] Bourne's long episcopacy had its controversies, but even his critics conceded he never lost sight of his ultimate objective: to 'get to the very heart of the English people ... to bring them to God.'

'This unpleasant business'[7]

This much about Bourne's early days in Westminster is a matter of public record and can be easily gleaned from Oldmeadow. However, his biographer made only passing reference to the 'unworthy intrigue' and 'unpleasantnesses of his reign'[8] which began at this point and continued in one form or another for the better part of three decades. Oldmeadow hoped posterity would judge such 'misunderstandings' to have been of minor significance. Wisely, he acknowledged he was privy to only one half of the story. He might have added it simply wasn't possible to give a full account so soon after Bourne's death with so many of the protagonists still living. Too much scandal would have been given to English Catholics.

When so much of Bourne's discomfort was to be occasioned by his relations with Peter Amigo, it is hugely ironic that his earliest difficulties as Archbishop were attributable to his championing Amigo's cause in the face of great opposition. It began with the appointment of his successor in Southwark. Addressing his new Diocese, Bourne made no secret of his regret in leaving Southwark. 'The last four months have been a time of extraordinary sorrow to our soul. It has been sad, indeed, to bid farewell to the diocese of our birth, every mission and institution in which had become familiar to us; to leave surroundings and priests and people that had every claim upon our affection.'[9]

Bourne wanted continuity in Southwark, continuity with his own policies and those of Bishop Butt. Above all, he feared the appointment of a bishop unsympathetic to the ideals of Wonersh, a bishop who might undo everything he had sought to achieve at the Seminary. 'It seems very necessary to me that my successor continues the same path on which Mgr Butt placed me. A change of direction would be deplorable.'[10] Bourne petitioned Rome to have himself made administrator of Southwark during the interregnum. Such an action had precedent in Italy, but was rare in England. Bourne used every argument he could with Cardinal Gotti at Propaganda to advance his case—the need for continuity in negotiations with the Minister of War, forthcoming municipal elections, the need to present a united front to protect Catholic schools in London. Bourne begged to be allowed to retain jurisdiction over Southwark, 'which I love with all my heart.'[11]

Certain Southwark canons got wind of the proposal and acted hastily—over-hastily—to prevent it. There followed the most spectacular and unseemly row. The Southwark Chapter possessed the right to appoint a Vicar-Capitular to administer the Diocese pending the new bishop's appointment. They could do so only after Bourne had ceased to be Bishop of Southwark when the papal document appointing him to Westminster was received and promulgated in England. Bourne's move was a matter of public knowledge from the end of August, but Rome never acts quickly. The papal document formalising this was only drawn up on 11 September and received by Bourne on 14 September. Provost Moore acted wrongly, therefore, when on 5 September he summoned the Chapter to meet four days later to elect a Vicar-Capitular.

Bourne pointed out that any appointment of a Vicar-Capitular while he was still officially Bishop of Southwark would be invalid.[12] However, his reaction was disproportionate, drawing up a writ of excommunication against any canon participating in an invalid election.[13] Fortunately, the two Vicars-General, Amigo and Mgr Johnson, displayed better judgment. They prevailed upon Bourne to hand over the writ before it was promulgated and upon the canons to abandon their meeting. Massive embarrassment was narrowly averted, but Bourne continued to fulminate against the offending members of the Chapter, 'demanding' Cardinal Gotti intervene.[14] The Roman Curia does not take kindly to such demands, even from archbishops. Gotti duly deprecated the canons' intended action, requiring

A Little Local Difficulty

them to apologise to Bourne, but when the Brief finally arrived in London he was content for custom to take its course. [15]

With Provost Moore's election as Vicar-Capitular on 21 September, Bourne's jurisdiction in the Diocese of Southwark ceased. He had lost the first round, but applied himself with renewed determination to ensure the appointment of a bishop of Southwark committed to a policy of continuity.

The battle lines were re-drawn. The Chapter defended their right to nominate the bishop against interference from the hierarchy. The Southwark canons wasted no time, drawing up their list of three names on 1 October: Mgr Patrick Fenton and Canons Keatinge and Scannell. The latter two were from their own number. Mgr Fenton was the Chapter's preferred candidate: the Westminster Vicar-General, a hard-working priest popular with the poor and his fellow clergy but not with all sections of society. When his appointment as a possible auxiliary to Vaughan had been mooted the previous year, the Fitzalan Howards were perturbed. Fenton was felt to be not 'quite a gentleman.'[16]

The Bishops voted on their own *terna* on 6 October. They too entertained doubts about Fenton, but rather in terms of his age. He was 66. The Bishops were irritated by the perceived interference of certain Southwark canons who had written urging acceptance of their own candidates. However, the Bishops were divided among themselves as to whether they had the right to add further names beyond those already chosen by the Southwark Chapter—forgetting that that was precisely what they had done just seven years earlier on Bourne's own appointment as coadjutor. The Archbishop was requested to seek clarification from Rome.[17]

Bourne leapt at the opportunity. Writing to Gotti, he systematically demolished the claims of the canons' three candidates. He admitted 'great regard' for Mgr Fenton, but, ironically in the light of his own subsequent suggestions, maintained that Fenton was physically unfit to administer a large diocese—something Fenton contested hotly. Keatinge and Scannell were acknowledged to be 'good priests,' but trouble-makers, financially reckless, the cause of Bourne's difficulties with his Chapter. Both were damned as 'reckless spirits.'[18]

Bourne then displayed his own hand—not that this caused any surprise. Amigo had written to Provost Moore deprecating rumours that the Southwark succession had been sewn up the preceding April. He was forced to do so due to the indiscretion of Bourne's secretary, Mgr Charles Coote, who had let slip that Bourne wished to see Amigo succeed him in Southwark.[19] Bourne now pressed Amigo's candidacy with Propaganda. 'During my long absence in Rome this year, he kept everything in order, and I had no worries ... He showed very great prudence, ability and efficiency in administration, and is fully in agreement with the other members of the diocesan curia.' Having shared intimately with him his Sulpician ideals of priestly fraternity and seminary education, Bourne's reasons for promoting Amigo were obvious. As an afterthought, Bourne also mentioned St John—with little conviction, however. He conceded that St John lacked theological training, the capacity for preaching, knowledge of foreign languages and parish experience. Otherwise, 'he would be a very good and capable Bishop'![20]

Now battle was joined in earnest. Canon O'Halloran asked the Duke of Norfolk to intervene to frustrate Bourne's 'desire to put in Fr Amigo, through whom he hopes to rule Southwark as well as Westminster ... We are trying to make a stand for constitutional law and right against those who habitually strive to subvert both, in the cause of personal absolutism and unabashed favouritism.'[21] Norfolk's replied with masterly ambiguity. He refused to countenance such an improper interference by a layman in ecclesiastical affairs, commented that the canons' behaviour led him to sympathise with Bourne and then proceeded to give the impression that he might favour O'Halloran's views after all.[22]

O'Halloran extended the field of his campaign. He arranged for the Southwark Chapter to petition the Pope and Propaganda urging respect for their *terna*, and had virtually every chapter in the country petition in respect of their own rights.[23] Clearly, this was about much more than the Southwark appointment; a principle was at stake. On his own initiative, O'Halloran sent Fr James Warwick to Rome to act as agent for the Chapter.[24] This proved too much for some. Three Southwark canons loyal to Bourne wrote to Propaganda stating Warwick had no right to hold himself out as representing the Chapter as a whole.[25]

If Bourne seemed prone to paranoia at times, his fears were not always unfounded. O'Halloran sought advice and encouragement from the Irish Franciscan, Fr David Fleming, who urged the Southwark Chapter to maintain its own agent in Rome. He was foolish to become involved. As a member of the Roman Curia, he ought to have shown greater prudence and impartiality. More damagingly, his friendship with Abbot Gasquet gave the impression that this was revenge for Gasquet's loss of Westminster. Gasquet himself did nothing to dispel such an impression. 'I am very pleased indeed to hear that the Archbishop has been defeated *re* Amigo. It would have been the cause of great trouble and soreness. As to myself, of course, if it comes, I should not refuse [Southwark] as I have always made it a point in life to be guided by what turns up. I believe that one could do good among the Bishops if one were there.'[26] Gasquet was to protest on numerous occasions that he bore Bourne no ill will. This was not always apparent in his correspondence and conversation.

Fleming and Gasquet felt that they constituted an interested party in English ecclesiastical affairs to whom the Vatican should give due consideration—and expressed irritation when others did not see matters in the same light. 'Merry del Val *could* help but he does not seemed inclined. I am afraid that the choice will lie between Fenton and Amigo. The English Bishops gave us no help. The anti-Regular bias has always to be reckoned with.'[27]

As Fleming intimated, Merry del Val was not willing to maintain the canons' grievances over episcopal claims. He reassured Bourne, 'I hear that the Southwark Chapter is not acting properly in your regard. I think that we can safely leave the matter in the hands of Cardinal Gotti and Propaganda.'[28] The Southwark Chapter did nothing to help their case when O'Halloran wrote to Merry del Val saying that, if they could not have their own *terna*, then they would be satisfied with him. Did they really think someone just appointed Secretary of State of the Holy Roman Church would abandon that position for a small diocese on the English south coast? Nor would Merry del Val have appreciated O'Halloran's intemperate dismissal of Amigo and St John. The former was 'a newcomer, without any special qualifications;' the latter 'a half-educated priest—essentially unfitted by his past and his present.' The reason why they were being pushed? 'The Archbishop disregards alike *qualifications* and *disqualifications*. What he looks for is a man who will be ready to surrender himself and the Diocese to his guidance and control.'[29]

Not that Bourne exercised particular moderation in championing Amigo's candidacy. He was active throughout the autumn of 1903 and into the winter. He sought to remove Fenton as a potential candidate for Southwark by requesting his appointment as a Westminster auxiliary. He had to explain why Fenton was fit for one episcopal appointment, but not the other. 'Mgr Fenton has the necessary qualities [to be a Westminster auxiliary]: he is trusted by the clergy; he knows all the administrative details; his nomination would give great satisfaction within the diocese.' Yet, he argued, Fenton lacked the intellectual ability and a knowledge of educational and social questions to be diocesan Bishop of Southwark, claiming he would find it difficult to write Pastorals and direct a seminary.[30]

The Archbishop arranged for Bishops and laity to write in support of Amigo—and in opposition to Fenton. Men like John Gilbert[31] and Thomas King had worked hard for the Diocese of Southwark over many years and were prominent in civic life. Their views deserved consideration. They were particularly dismayed at certain priests' prejudice against Amigo's Gibraltarian background. 'I feel bound to say the leading laity of Southwark do not agree with their action and a very large number with whom I am personally acquainted are far from edified at their action … I have intimate knowledge of that good and holy priest of Walworth, he is the most zealous, holy and perfect mission priest I have ever met.'[32]

Bourne himself wrote to Propaganda, and visited while in Rome, with a frequency and insistence Gotti may have found irritating. Gasquet later alleged that Bourne had threatened to resign as Archbishop of Westminster if he failed to get his way with the Southwark appointment.[33] There is no actual evidence of this, but it is implicit in Bourne's dealings with Gotti. 'If Mgr Fenton is nominated, my situation will not only be difficult, but *impossible*.' He let it be known that he felt unable to use his influence with British Government on behalf of the Holy See concerning a situation in New Guinea until his authority had been vindicated.[34] Bourne's lack of a Roman formation is only too apparent. This is not the way the Vatican transacts business. Far more is achieved by courtesy, indirect suggestions and face-saving formulae. As a young Archbishop with powerful critics, Bourne was over-sensitive. It is understandable that he would have felt undermined if, immediately after his transfer, all his work in Southwark had been unravelled, yet he displayed little finesse in attaining his objective.

Bourne had not only to convince Rome, but also his brother Bishops in England. Propaganda ruled that the Bishops did indeed have the right, if dissatisfied with the *terna* of the Southwark Chapter, to add further names of their own choosing.[35] They met again on 22 December. They knew they were to be asked to add the names of Amigo and St John. They were not prepared for the Archbishop's tactics. He made the most emotional of appeals. 'Twice he spoke with great feeling on the matter, saying it would be "agony" for him to see his own work in Southwark going to pieces, and if the bishops did not support him in his first appeal for their aid, he felt he would not be able to count on their support in any further matter.'³⁶ Bourne also advanced cogent arguments on Amigo's behalf. He was a very able priest, valued in both Westminster and Southwark. It was rumoured that he had been considered for the Diocese of Gibraltar when that had become vacant.

There was unhappiness about the inclusion of St John's name but, given no one actually dreamt he would be appointed, it was approved. Amigo's name was added to the *terna*; but, by a bare majority, the Bishops elected to keep Fenton's name at the head of the list. Bourne had swung the meeting, but his highly personal approach was not something to rely on too often. He presented the new *terna* to Propaganda and continued to fret while Rome took another two months to consider the matter. Yet he had his way. On 1 March 1904 Pius X confirmed Peter Amigo's appointment as Bishop of Southwark.

Bourne expended enormous energy in achieving this result. He had bridges to mend with the Roman Curia and the English hierarchy if he were to gain his future objectives. Relations with the majority of the Southwark Chapter were irretrievably damaged. And for what end? The appointment of the man who, once his closest collaborator, was to become the greatest thorn in his flesh for more than a generation.

*'A veritable campaign of slander'*³⁷

The other internal Church matter which caused Bourne great anxiety during his early years in Westminster also related to the Diocese of Southwark. Unlike the controversy surrounding Amigo's appointment, however, this dispute was conducted largely in the full glare of Media publicity. Oldmeadow was, therefore, obliged to refer to the incident in the chapter of his biography headed, 'The Strange Case of "Mr A."' Oldmeadow exonerates the Archbishop as the innocent victim of a Modernist plot to democratise the Church by removing from the Bishop any control over ecclesiastical temporalities. The case was strange, but not quite that simple.

It all began early in 1906 when 'Mr A.' walked into the office of a newspaper editor, the Radical, Labouchere. The newspaper was the influential weekly *Truth*, whose metier was 'investigative journalism.' 'Mr A.' was William Reed Lewis, formerly British Consul in Algeria, now living in Dinard in northern France. Reed Lewis was 'reported to be a great busybody always interfering with other people's affairs. He is very friendly with the priests at Dinard ... He is in the habit of bringing over English priests from England to give missions and to preach to the many English who live permanently at Dinard.'[38] Reed Lewis wanted investigated alleged 'reckless speculation' of Church funds by English Bishops. *Truth* was happy to oblige. Greater publicity attached to the allegations by the fact that they were reproduced in the *Catholic Herald*. Then Ethelred Taunton was as willing as ever to forward any criticism of the Archbishop to the Vatican.

Reed Lewis and Taunton received their opportunity when a stockbroker named William Henry Bishop filed for bankruptcy on 23 December 1905. *Truth* gleefully relayed to its readers, 'It is well known that Mr Bishop had a considerable and influential Roman Catholic clientele; and the unfortunate part of the business is that representatives of at least one diocese are, in their official capacity, creditors of the estate for an enormous amount.'[39] Over several months *Truth* made many specific allegations, principally against Cahill and Bourne, but the gist of its criticism was: Bourne, when in Southwark, had entrusted the diocesan investments to a crook; he had failed to exercise the diligence expected of a trustee; he and Cahill indulged in speculative investments with Church money; and English bishops generally treated ecclesiastical goods as their private property, disregarding the terms of any trust deeds.

Bishop was in his seventies when the crash came. For over three decades he acted for the Diocese of Southwark. He had, in fact, also been declared bankrupt 46 years earlier, but had repaid his creditors and Bourne had no reason to know of this. He only knew that his predecessors 'had full confidence in Mr Bishop's capacity and integrity, that they employed him without hesitation as their stockbroker and ordinary financial adviser, and that he served them well. I had inherited and had reason to endorse their opinion, and I transmitted it in good faith to my successor, who in common with Mr Bishop's other clients had no reason to change it until his failure. No loss took place while I was Bishop of Southwark ... Mr Bishop failed in December 1905. I had ceased to be Bishop of Southwark in September 1903. From that date I have had neither control of, nor responsibility for, the administration of that diocese.'[40]

The greatest loss, estimated at £37,000, suffered by Southwark in respect of Bishop's failure related to the Dawes Trust. At their first meeting, the Trustees, including Bourne, had resolved to appoint Bishop as the Trust's financial adviser. The financial advice he gave was sound.

That was not the problem. 'Owing to the difficulty of obtaining the signatures of all the trustees as rapidly as the occasion often demanded, Mr Bishop was entrusted with a power of attorney' enabling him to deal with the investments. He did—on his own account. No one bothered to check that the share certificates were delivered, and Bishop covered his tracks by rendering false accounts. The alarm was raised at the end of October 1905 when a clerk informed Canon Murnane, who in turn told St John, the Financial Secretary. Bishop assured everyone that the clerk was lying, vindictive after his dismissal for drunkenness. Bourne maintained that 'steps were taken at once' to secure the Trust's investments, but it was too late. Bishop declared himself bankrupt. He noted again that all this happened in 1905. 'I left the Diocese in September 1903, and though technically still a trustee, I naturally took no further part.'[41] That, however, did not let the Archbishop off the hook. In English trust law there is no such thing as a 'technical' trustee. He remained a Trustee of the Dawes Trust with all the responsibilities and duties that entailed.

This was the most substantive allegation raised by *Truth*, but there were others. It claimed that Bourne followed Cahill's example in engaging in 'financial speculation,' resulting in significant losses.[42] The question of the Petworth Mission was raised again, it being alleged that Bourne simply set aside the benefactor's intentions to get his hands on the money.[43] No accounts were supposed to exist in respect of the massive sums spent on Westminster Cathedral.[44] *Truth* reproduced the observations of 'a layman' that, 'What Catholics most feel about the matter is the great want of judgment the Archbishop has shown in his financial administration while Bishop of Southwark ... The serious errors that have now come to light will have the effect of destroying all confidence on the part of the clergy and laity in his capacity for financial administration, and will seriously impair the flow of money for ecclesiastical purposes.' Bourne was able to rebut most of the specific allegations, but it was more difficult to dispel the general doubts engendered by this constant, anonymous criticism. The *Truth* articles themselves were contributing to the 'deep-seated feeling among the Catholic laity that ecclesiastical property ought to be protected against episcopal malversation.'[45]

Truth presented itself as performing a service to the Catholic community, regretting that the Catholic press was too much under episcopal control to act independently. Self-reform, the newspaper righteously declared, was simply not possible. 'One of the difficulties of the present situation is that as the English Bishops, the Archbishop himself not the least, are so deeply implicated in what has happened, no confidence is placed in their desire to grapple with the scandal. English Catholics are, therefore, looking to Rome for assistance in this matter ... As a matter of fact the Vatican authorities are pretty well aware of what has happened, and I believe that they have not been idle.'[46] And not just Rome, but the English Charity Commissioners. *Truth* knew what it was talking about, because this was part of a campaign coordinated by the newspaper, Reed Lewis and Taunton.

Other than a terse rebuttal in the letters pages of the *Tablet*, Bourne felt the best response was dignified silence.[47] This did not give his detractors the satisfaction they sought. They tried involving others whom they knew the Archbishop could not ignore. All this at the time when Bourne most needed to focus on the defence of Catholic schools in fighting the Education Bill before Parliament. Taunton wrote again to Cardinal Gotti. Claiming his only motivation was the desire 'to avoid scandal and damage to our holy religion,' he passed on [the erroneous] 'information that the State, through the Charity Commissioners, intend immediately to conduct a public enquiry into the administration of the trusts of the dioceses of Westminster, Southwark and Portsmouth.' He suggested that Propaganda should hold its own independent visitation to protect the interests of the Church.[48]

Simultaneously, Reed Lewis was active in London, taking himself off to the Charity Commissioners. Back in France he had the nerve to write to various Catholic peers telling them 'the Charity Commissioners have requested me to put unofficially before the Holy See their desire, that, if possible, this matter should be dealt with satisfactorily by the Ecclesiastical Authorities,' impertinently suggesting they might like to follow this up with their own letter to the Pope along the same lines.[49] Fortunately, Bourne sent his solicitor to the Charity Commissioners to check what had actually been said. He was given a rather different account. Reed Lewis was not, as he claimed, the authorised agent of the Charity Commissioners. Rather, they had told him that they felt the matter was one for the Church, not themselves. They specifically expressed their opinion that Bourne's action at Petworth did not constitute a breach of trust. The Commissioner concerned 'saw that after this conversation [Reed Lewis] appeared to go away satisfied and seemed to quite agree to what he had said.'[50]

A Little Local Difficulty

The Archbishop had countered the mischief in England, but Reed Lewis had also written to Cardinal Merry del Val in Rome. Receiving no reply to his first letter, he followed this up with a second, threatening to place the matter before the Charity Commission if he heard nothing in the next two weeks.[51] Merry del Val forwarded Reed Lewis's letter to Bourne, but his covering comments cannot have made easy reading. 'There is a feeling of real uneasiness on the part of a great many good and well-meaning Catholics, ecclesiastical and lay, in England as regard to this matter and that quite independently of those like Father Taunton and others who are actuated by a censurable spirit and with other objects in view. Your statements have not allayed that anxiety as yet, but I am unable to say whether that anxiety is well-founded. It certainly exists. If you think that the Holy See should take action, please tell me and suggest the form in which it would be advisable to proceed.'[52]

The Archbishop might ignore scurrilous articles in a dubious journal, but not this. The thought that he might not enjoy the full confidence of Rome mortified him. Under intense pressure as the Birrell Education Bill moved towards its climax, and away in Paris negotiating compensation from the French Government for confiscated bursaries, Bourne gave full vent to his wounded feelings. He quickly relayed the true position as it stood between Reed Lewis and the Charity Commissioners. He admitted that the question of tenure of ecclesiastical property needed reform. As it stood, it was a hangover from the days before the restoration of the hierarchy. 'It is a very difficult question, for the Church must be protected against the too great interference of the laity, and too much control from the State.' Now, however, was the wrong time to initiate reform, as any change would be viewed as an admission of guilt with respect to the allegations that had been made.

Bourne then expressed what he thought was really at stake. 'This is only part of a very much larger question. As soon as I was nominated to Westminster, a steady movement of opposition was set on foot in England to discredit me in England and still more in Rome. It was said openly at the outset that, although the Holy Father had been induced by Propaganda to make me Archbishop, care would be taken to prevent any other mark of Pontifical favour being bestowed upon me. The great object of these opponents has been 1) to show that Propaganda made a great mistake in proposing me to the Holy Father for Westminster, 2) to prevent the Holy See ever showing me any sign of satisfaction or approbation.'

He detailed the rumours he believed to be circulating about himself. That Merry del Val 'was strongly opposed to my nomination and very hostile to me personally.' That Gasquet would be made a cardinal in preference to himself. That, theologically, he was an 'obscurantist' and, then, a Modernist. That he did not enjoy good relations with other members of the hierarchy. The approach to the Charity Commissioners was a ploy to induce his resignation and that of the Bishops of Portsmouth and Southwark. His approach was unconventional, but heartfelt. 'If my word is accepted and I do possess the confidence of the Holy See, I appeal to the Holy Father, through your Eminence, to make this abundantly and undeniably clear, and to vindicate me in the face of my enemies. I have a right to make this appeal. The Holy See has placed me in a position of very great difficulty and responsibility contrary to my own wish and desire. I have done my best.'[53] He followed this up with another letter from Paris two days later. He was convinced 'that there is an organised conspiracy to do me injury in England and in Rome.'[54]

Who was behind this 'organised conspiracy'? Bourne was clear that 'the leaders of the cabal' were Southwark priests whom he had to discipline while their ordinary. 'They hate me and they will never forgive me.' There is little evidence for this. He was on firmer ground, however, when he identified Fr Ethelred Taunton as one of his enemies.[55] Why should Taunton have been so motivated? Undoubtedly, he was a restless spirit. Ordained for the Oblates of St Charles, he left three years later, having contracted unauthorised debts. Given a parish in Westminster, he again ran up debts he was unable to pay. He took up writing and drifted first to Bruges and then to Rome. Cardinal Gotti had asked whether Taunton should be granted faculties to function as a priest in Rome. Bourne's response was firm: 'He possesses neither my trust nor that of the hierarchy. To accord him a sign of Pontifical favour would be to cause embarrassment and perhaps scandal.'[56] Bourne also refused the *imprimatur* to the work on canon law Taunton intended dedicating to Pius X. It is clear why the two men were opposed.

It is also clear that Reed Lewis and Taunton were working in conjunction. As one made allegations in London, the other ensured that they were brought to the attention of the Vatican. Bourne convinced himself, however, that behind them both lay Abbot Gasquet.[57] Unwisely, Bourne confronted him with his suspicion before he had firm evidence. Gasquet professed indignation. The only connection with Reed Lewis to which he admitted was having instructed his wife.[58] Nothing can be proved. It is likely that Gasquet engaged in gossip rather than 'organised conspiracy,' but he might have kept better connections than Taunton and Reed Lewis.

Merry del Val's response to Bourne's outburst was predictable: Get a grip! He lectured the Archbishop, 'Surely you must realise that, by the very fact that I sent *you* Mr Lewis' letter and asked *you* to propose if necessary what you thought best. I do not see what better proof you could have of the trust and confidence which you enjoy; nor do I see that the Holy See has ever done anything which could indicate a want of confidence in you. As to the malicious or foolish reports which you enumerate, really they are beneath contempt and are of the kind which every man in a high and responsible position must expect and be ready to disregard.'[59] Insecurity was the cause of Bourne's hyper-sensitivity.

Reed Lewis contacted Merry del Val again in May 1907, announcing his intention of prosecuting Bourne for breaching the terms of the Dawes Trust. The Archbishop's solicitors had already advised him that any member of the public could petition the Attorney-General to bring an action for breach of a charitable trust, and also that Bourne and the other Trustees probably were in breach of trust for their failure to supervise the actions of Bishop and, therefore, had a liability to make good the loss.[60] Merry del Val, however, gave Reed Lewis no encouragement. He deprecated 'the impropriety of such a proceeding.' Bourne's explanations given five months earlier 'have satisfied the Holy See that there is no ground for this attack upon your good name. You may also inform Mr Reed Lewis that his action in persistently attempting to injure the position and reputation of the Bishops who enjoy the full confidence of the Holy See is unworthy of a Catholic and deserving of condemnation.'[61]

Bourne sent Reed Lewis a copy of Merry del Val's letter, and invited him to inspect the original should he wish.[62] He received the meekest of responses, 'I have no desire to verify its contents by reference to the original of H. E. Cardinal Merry del Val. I take this opportunity of congratulating Your Grace upon your enjoyment of the full confidence of the Holy See, which I trust you may merit for many years to come.'[63] It was the last time anything was heard of Mr Reed Lewis. (Perhaps Fr Taunton's death at this time was no coincidence.)

Archbishop Bourne was mistaken, however, if he thought that this was the last he had heard from either Church or State in respect of his financial administration of the Diocese of Southwark.

Notes

1. Ward, *Insurrection versus Resurrection*, p. 150.
2. Canon Brenan, Old Edmundians' AGM, 26 October 1903, *Tablet*, 31 October 1903, p. 713.
3. Tablet, 26 December 1903, pp. 1001–1002.
4. FAB, Pastoral Letter, 29 December 1903.
5. Bishop T. Wilkinson of Hexham & Newcastle to FAB, 1 January 1904, AAW, Bo. III/124/5.
6. FAB, Address at Salford, 21 September 1903, cited Oldmeadow, *Francis Cardinal Bourne*, i, p. 212.
7. Amigo to Moore, 8 October 1903, cited Clifton, *Amigo*, p. 13.
8. Oldmeadow, *Francis Cardinal Bourne*, i, p. 236.
9. FAB, Pastoral Letter, 29 December 1903.
10. FAB to Gotti, 11 October 1903, SCPF, 102/1904, f. 289, rr. 123–125.
11. FAB to Gotti, 16 September 1903, SCPF, 102/1904, f. 289, rr. 99–100.
12. FAB to Moore, 7 September 1903, SCPF, 102/1904, f. 289, r. 90.
13. FAB to Provost and Chapter of Southwark, 9 September 1903, AAW, Bo. III/56/1.
14. FAB to Gotti, 23 September 1903, SCPF, 102/1904, f. 289, rr. 105–106.
15. Canon Connelly [?] to FAB, 10 October 1903, AAW, Bo. III/56/8.
16. ACA, Lord Edmund Talbot to Norfolk, 24 August 1902.
17. Acta of Bishops' Meeting, Archbishop's House, 6 October 1903.
18. FAB to Gotti, 11 October 1903, SCPF, 102/1904, f. 289, rr. 123–125.
19. Amigo to Moore, 8 October 1903, cited Clifton, Amigo, pp. 13–14.
20. FAB to Gotti, 11 October 1903, SCPF, 102/1904, f. 289, rr. 123–125.
21. Canon O'Halloran to Norfolk, 30 October 1903, ACA.
22. Norfolk to O'Halloran, 1 November 1903 (copy) ACA.
23. Petition of Southwark Chapter to Propaganda, 16 November 1903, SCPF, 102/1904, f. 289, rr. 141–143.
24. O'Halloran to Moore, 13 November 1903, cited Clifton, *Amigo*, p. 14.
25. Memorandum of 'Certain Southwark Canons' to Gotti, 5 December 1903, SCPF, 102/1904, f. 289, rr. 162–167.
26. Gasquet to Fleming, 29 November 1903, cited Leslie, *Cardinal Gasquet*, p. 199.
27. Fleming to Gasquet, 16 February 1904, cited Leslie, *Cardinal Gasquet*, p. 87.
28. Merry del Val to FAB, 9 November 1903, AAW, Bo. IV/1/28a.
29. O'Halloran to Merry del Val, 30 December 1903, SCPF, 102/1904, f. 289, rr. 202–203.
30. FAB to Gotti, 4 November 1903, SCPF, 102/1904, f. 289, rr. 261–262.
31. Sir John Gilbert (1871–1934) was much involved in diocesan affairs in Southwark and Westminster. He was the first Catholic County Alderman of the London County

A Little Local Difficulty

Council 1910–1934 (representing the Municipal Reform Party), Vice-Chairman of the LCC 1917–1918 and Chairman 1920–1921. His chief work was in education and he was Chairman of the LCC Education Committee, on which he first served in 1908.

32. T. King to FAB, 21 December 1903, SCPF, 102/1904, f. 289, rr. 188–189.
33. Gasquet's Roman Diary, 1916, cited Leslie, *Cardinal Gasquet*, p. 246.
34. FAB to Gotti, 31 January 1904, SCPF, 102/1904, f. 289, rr. 222–223.
35. Gotti to FAB, 21 October 1903, AAW, Roman Letters VI/189.
36. Burton Diary, 22 December 1903, CDA.
37. FAB to Editor, *Tablet*, 6 October 1906.
38. J. Weld to FAB, 12 December 1906, AAW, Bo. III/124/2/44.
39. *Truth*, 28 March 1906, p. 750.
40. FAB to Editor, *Tablet*, 6 October 1906.
41. FAB, 'History of the Dawes Trust,' u/d [prepared on Amigo's behalf in 1907?], AAW, Bo. III/1/1; Clifton, *Amigo*, pp. 39–40.
42. *Truth*, 28 March 1906, p. 750; *Truth*, 2 May 1906.
43. *Truth*, 30 May 1906, p. 1297.
44. *Truth*, 17 October 1906, p. 923.
45. *Truth*, 30 May 1906, pp. 1296–1297.
46. *Truth*, 20 June 1906, p. 1492.
47. FAB to Amigo, 15 July 1906, SAA, Bourne Papers, Correspondence with Amigo.
48. Taunton to Gotti, 2 October 1906, SCPF, 102/1906, f. 354, r. 55.
49. W. Reed Lewis to Lord Denbigh, 7 November 1906, AAW, Bo. III/124/2.
50. Weld, memo, 28 November 1906, AAW, Bo. III/124/2/41.
51. Reed Lewis to Merry del Val, 28 November 1906, AAW, Bo. III/124/2/30.
52. Merry del Val to FAB, 1 December 1906, AAW, Bo. III/124/2/32.
53. FAB to Merry del Val, 6 December 1906 (copy), AAW, Bo. III/124/2/33.
54. FAB to Merry del Val, 8 December 1906, AAW, Bo. III/124/2/34.
55. FAB to Merry del Val, 6 December 1906 (copy), AAW, Bo. III/124/2/33.
56. FAB to Gotti, 20 April 1905 (draft), AAW, Roman Letters VI/272.
57. E. Fooks to FAB, 21 May 1906, AAW, Bo. III/124/2/4; Weld to FAB, 12 December 1906, AAW, Bo. III/124/2/44.
58. Gasquet to FAB, 10 January 1907, AAW, Bo. III/124/2/48.
59. Merry del Val to FAB, u/d, AAW, Bo. III/124/2/42.
60. Weld to FAB, 7 May 1907, AAW, Bo. III/124/2.
61. Merry del Val to FAB, 12 May 1907, AAW, Bo. III/124/2.
62. FAB to Reed Lewis, 20 May 1907, cited Oldmeadow, *Francis Cardinal Bourne*, i, pp. 322–323.
63. Reed Lewis to FAB, 17 June 1907, cited Oldmeadow, *Francis Cardinal Bourne*, i, p. 323.

Chapter 10

Education, Education, Education

The Background

Predicting in December 1903 education as the central issue of his time in Westminster, Bourne spoke more accurately than he could have known. The schools question, specifically what we now call 'faith schools,' was the controversy of the moment. It went back a long time. The education of her children was the Catholic Church's priority. Without being formed in the faith, the Church knew that poor Irish Catholics were unlikely to persevere in the practise of their religion in a hostile environment. The provision of schools took precedence over all else. The newly re-established hierarchy had decreed: 'No congregation should be allowed to remain without its schools … Indeed, wherever there may seem to be an opening for a new mission, we should prefer the erection of a school, so arranged as to serve temporarily for a chapel, to that of a church without one … For the building raised of living and chosen stones, the spiritual sanctuary of the Church, is of far greater importance than the temple made by hands.'[1]

Having spent so much of his own priesthood teaching, Bourne shared this priority with a passion. Through three decades of educational crises and proposals, he never wavered from the principle of Catholic education by Catholic teachers in Catholic schools for Catholic children. 'If there is one thing that stands out clearly, it is that any religious organisation that neglects the religious teaching of its children is bound very soon to lose vast numbers of its members, and gradually to fall away altogether.'[2] This was not to happen on his watch.

When the post-Reformation Church began the provision of education in earnest, schools were the exclusive concern of the churches, charity and private enterprise. The State was a latecomer in the field, making little effort to provide or regulate schools until the Forster Education Act of 1870. To supplement the voluntary sector, new school boards were to maintain schools paid for out of the rates.

From that point money and religion were contentious issues, poisoning any attempt at educational reform. As elementary education was made compulsory, places at board schools became free and the State paid for secular teacher training colleges. The voluntary sector found it increasingly difficult to compete. Catholics, in particular, had no endowments to fall back upon, and were forced to rely on fees and house to house collections to pay for their schools.

The Liberals were always more sympathetic to Protestant Nonconformity; their 'Cowper-Temple' clause prevented the teaching at public expense of religious education distinctive to any particular denomination. The Liberals maintained that the majority of parents 'would like their children to be taught the simple elementary religious truths—the fatherhood of God, the responsibilities of man, and a future state.'[3] The content of religious instruction in board schools was determined by what would give offence to no one, rather than what anyone actually believed: 'the religion of nobody taught by anybody and paid for by everybody.'

Fine, replied Catholics, if this satisfied Protestant parents, let them have their board schools. But it could never be sufficient for Catholics. This 'simple Bible teaching' said nothing of the divinity of Christ and, therefore, the nature of His authority. It failed to mention that He established a visible Church competent to teach in matters of faith and morals with that same authority. There was no reference to the sacramental system by which we are given access to the very life of God. By all means let the Protestant majority have religious education acceptable to them, but in equity, allow Catholics the same right to educate their children according to their own religious convictions. When his coreligionists were inclined to a greater stridency, Bourne always appreciated this appeal to reason and fairness was most calculated to advance the Catholic case with his fellow countrymen. 'An equitable solution is to be found not in ignoring, but in recognising in full, the religious differences of the country ... With regard to the provision of elementary schools, let all Englishmen alike stand on an equal footing before the law.'[4]

There was considerable divergence among voluntary schools, of which Catholic schools constituted less than 10%. They, some Anglicans and a tiny number of Jewish schools maintained 'the religious atmosphere theory' of education. For a believer, faith informed every aspect of life; it was not possible to compartmentalise education. By contrast, many Anglicans, as well as the nondenominational schools in the voluntary sector, were willing to restrict specific religious education to certain school hours—or to teach it out of school hours altogether to those children whose parents required it. Bourne and the Catholic Church knew this was incompatible with orthodox Christianity. 'The conscience of England would not accept schools from which religion was absolutely banished and therefore he put aside the solution which proposed purely secular instruction ... In religious teaching they must speak of God, of His governance of men; they must say something about the history of His dealings with mankind, and at once they were in the domain of dogma. Leave that out, and what religion was left?'[5]

These were the underlying disputes. Demand for educational reform grew with the increasing realisation that England was losing her economic advantage in the world. There was administrative chaos as the Board of Education attempted to correspond with 2,500 school boards and 20,000 schools.[6] Financial considerations compelled the voluntary sector to contemplate change. They simply could not compete with schools funded by the ratepayer. Their premises were often inadequate; their teachers were paid significantly less; standards were frequently lower, and the gap was increasing. Attempts to legislate for reform were opposed by the voluntary sector simply because they could not afford to implement them. Catholics alone struggled heroically to open more schools in the period, but overall the voluntary sector was in decline. By 1902 1,400 (mainly Anglican) voluntary schools had been transferred to the State sector. While voluntary schools still accounted for 71% of schools, many were small village schools and, for the first time, the State educated the majority of English children.[7]

Some Catholics wanted to preserve absolute independence at any cost, but successive Archbishops of Westminster realised the impracticality of such a policy. Catholics paid rates too. Why shouldn't their money be spent on schools for their children rather than simply financing education acceptable to Protestant parents? In return for public funding, Manning and Vaughan were happy to concede a right of inspection in secular subjects to ensure the State was receiving value for money. While capitation grants from central government were available to denominational schools, they were insufficient. It was estimated that prior to 1902 Catholics had spent £4 million building schools in England, of which only £60,000 came from the public purse.[8]

The catalyst for change came as the 1900 General Election returned a large Conservative majority committed to educational reform. Steered through Parliament by Arthur Balfour against determined Nonconformist opposition, the Education Bill maintained the dual system of voluntary and State schools while removing the worst of the financial inequalities. Much complexity was swept away by making local education authorities (county councils and county boroughs) responsible for all public elementary education in their area, both the provided (board) schools and the secular education in the non-provided (voluntary) schools. Non-provided schools were run by six school managers, four appointed by the Church, two by the local education authority. These managers had the power to appoint and dismiss teachers, and to determine the nature of religious instruction. (Parents were free to withdraw their children from such teaching in non-provided schools.) Local education authorities now paid for teachers' salaries, equipment and other running expenses in all schools. In non-provided schools, the Church had still to provide the site and school buildings as well as paying for the capital expenses of structural repairs and any 'alterations and improvements reasonably required' by the local authority.

It was not the perfect solution. Catholics pointed out that they were still left to pay the capital expenses of their own schools as well as paying through the rates their share of the same expenses of provided schools. There were concerns regarding the application of the new legislation by local authorities hostile to denominational education in general and Catholic education in particular.

The 1902 Education Act was before Parliament longer than any previous piece of legislation in history. The Catholic Church kept a watching brief over the proceedings. With Cardinal Vaughan ill, Bourne, as the only other diocesan bishop in London, coordinated much of the Catholic response. It prepared him for future battles. He frequently chaired the Committee established for this purpose. He corresponded with his brother bishops, clergy and laity. [9] In Vaughan's absence, he spoke powerfully on the Catholic position. He was realistic about the potential difficulties, he acknowledged that the Act was but 'an instalment of justice,' but welcomed the advantages it brought. 'In itself it is a gain to us; but it may be administered to our detriment ... We gladly recognise that the Legislature of the country has made a great effort to give us a fuller measure of justice than we enjoyed before ... We might fairly claim to have our schools, not only maintained, but provided, at the public cost … But knowing well the difficulties which beset the Government, and profoundly convinced of the absolute necessity of our schools wherever we have Catholic children to occupy them, we have declared our readiness to continue to build schools for ourselves … The settlement of the question is not absolutely equitable … Having accepted it, we must do our best to carry this agreement loyally into effect.'[10]

Cares and Anxieties

The 1902 Act gave Catholic schools a legitimate place in the national educational system. It gave Catholic teachers a proper salary. It relieved the Church of the crushing burden of the running costs of schools. Bourne never allowed his fellow Catholics to forget what they had gained. He maintained that it was madness to seek to return to the pre-1902 situation. 'We are making a great mistake in attributing to the Acts of 1902 and 1903 the special difficulties which some of us feel very keenly at the present moment. The causes are much further back.'[11]

Those special difficulties became immediately apparent. Nonconformists—close to their high water mark in terms of political influence—hated the new legislation with a passion. Led by men such as the Baptist, John Clifford, they alleged that they were being asked to pay personally for lessons in idolatry and superstition, ignoring, of course, the fact that central government had already been subsidising denominational education and that Catholics, through their taxes and rates, were paying for many things they found personally uncongenial. Such is life in a parliamentary democracy. But 'Rome on the rates' was a catching slogan to arouse Protestant indignation.

The Conservative Government and the churches could have ridden out Clifford's rhetoric, accompanied, as it was, by passive resistance, the non-payment of rates. In Methodist and Baptist strongholds such as Wales and West Yorkshire, local authorities attempted to frustrate the new Act at every turn. Applications for new Catholic schools were rejected, resources were awarded unevenly; the management of non-provided schools was made unnecessarily difficult. Given time and firm direction, these irritations could have been overcome, but the Conservative Government tore itself apart on tariff reform and other issues. A newly-resurgent Liberal Party was committed to repealing the Tory educational reforms. The political tide turned in 1904 with the Progressives (Liberals) winning control of the London County Council, which proceeded to condemn or require hugely expensive alterations to virtually all Catholic schools inspected. It further threatened to pay teachers giving religious instruction in non-provided schools less than teachers in provided schools.[12] Everyone knew the assault on the 1902 Act would intensify with the election of a Liberal Government.

Faced by an impending crisis, Bourne acted calmly and pragmatically. He asked the Duke of Norfolk to consult interested parties and submit proposals to the Bishops to ensure the Catholic position was coordinated and most forcefully represented to the Board of Education.[13] Norfolk reported back quickly. There was a rationalisation of existing structures. Each Diocese was to have just one education committee, a Voluntary Schools Association. At the national level, the old Catholic Poor Schools Committee was reorganised as the Catholic Education Council, chaired by Norfolk, its remit extended to cover all aspects of Catholic primary and secondary education.[14] It was to consist of three members from each diocese, one appointed by the Bishop, two by the Association. It was aimed at 'focussing the views of local bodies and ensuring uniform and united action.'[15]

Bourne's greatest contribution, however, displayed from the outset, was his political acumen. The 1902 Act was passed by a Conservative Government, and it was the Liberals who threatened its repeal. Yet Bourne did not make the mistake, as others urged, of launching an all out assault on the Liberals and throwing in the Church's lot exclusively with the Tories. He was roundly criticised by Norfolk for not instructing voters at the General Election along these lines: 'I find everywhere a feeling of something like dismay at what is regarded as the inadequacy of the Bishops' advice in regard to the elections. It seems to be felt that it is universally accepted that the result of the elections is most critical for our schools, that the nonconformists are openly preparing their attack, and that the Irish voters are urged by their political leaders to support the Party from whom that attack will come … I have not heard a single opinion expressed that the Bishops have risen to the occasion, on the contrary I hear it said that they have thrown cold water on any enthusiasm and activity.'[16] Bourne was unmoved. He knew better than to tie himself to a spent political force. He also realised that Tory support for denominational education owed more to its Anglican links than sympathy for the Catholic plight. Willing to work with the Church of England where their interests coincided, Bourne knew that this would not always be the case and he was determined to preserve Catholic freedom of action.

He had another factor to contend with. The vast majority of Catholic voters were Irish. Could he reasonably ask them to subordinate their desire for Irish Home Rule by voting for a Unionist party more likely to defend Catholic schools in England? There were English priests and politicians (and Irish Bishops) who thought so, but there was no guarantee that the Bishops could have delivered the Catholic vote for the Conservative Party—nor, if they could, that this would have altered the overwhelming defeat the Party suffered. Bourne's pragmatism crucially kept open his lines of communication with the Irish Parliamentary Party, and did not close the door to negotiations with the Liberals. For this, the Church owed him a great debt of gratitude.

Bourne had the good sense to see that the Liberal Party in 1906 was not a monolithic structure, but a coalition of interests. A remnant of Whig grandees was allied to Protestant Nonconformists, but also to Liberal Imperialists, trades unionists, intellectuals and economic and social liberals. Not all were uniformly hostile to Catholic education. Bourne saw divisions in the Liberal position and skilfully exploited them—as he could not have done had he followed Norfolk's advice and instructed his flock to vote Conservative.

In October 1903, Sir Henry Campbell-Bannerman committed his Party to the repeal of the 1902 Education Act, but simultaneously admitted 'that Catholics in this matter of their schools were entitled to separate treatment.'[17] There was a certain political calculation by the Liberals—they had no wish to alienate any vote unnecessarily—but also a genuine appreciation that the position of Catholic schools built with the pennies of poor Irish Catholics for their own children was different from the privileged position of the Established Church whose rural schools Nonconformists were compelled to attend for lack of an alternative. When the following March David Lloyd George launched a fierce Commons attack on the 1902 Act, Bourne did not resort to pulpit denunciations. He quietly arranged to meet Lloyd George, although on his own terms and leaving Lloyd George in no doubt 'that no concordat could be agreed to by Catholics which interfered with existing rights as to teachers.'[18]

Bourne spoke privately with the Liberals and their Irish allies, but backed it up with strong public rhetoric. He warned Yorkshire Catholics that it would be 'a very sad thing' if the Liberal Party 'after a magnificent political history should be committing itself to a policy which, as far as Catholics were able to understand it, was utterly destructive of Catholic schools.'[19] In Newcastle he hinted at Catholic electoral influence. Catholics must maintain their 'policy by the voting power they had at their command. He therefore urged upon them the necessity for complete organisation.'[20] Organisation was something Bourne was good at. In the 1906 General Election the Bishops arranged for the following question to be put to candidates: 'Will you, if returned to Parliament, resist any interference with the right of Catholic parents, at present secured by law, to have their children educated in the elementary schools of the country, in conformity with their conscientious religious convictions?'[21] Catholics could see at a glance a candidate's attitude towards their schools. Bourne arranged for the information to be stored nationally to prevent any post-election forgetfulness by MPs. In his own Diocese he used the Catholic Association to put the question and publish the candidates' replies. Beyond this Bourne simply exhorted 'fervent prayer.' Knowing that he would shortly be dealing with a Government of a very different political hue, he did not want to bring unnecessary baggage to future negotiations. He forbade his priests to make reference to the General Election from the pulpit or to attend political meetings.[22]

'A damned bad Bill!'

1906 was one of the watershed elections of the twentieth century. The Liberals and their Labour allies won 429 Commons seats, the Conservatives a mere 158 and the Irish Nationalists 83. Such a crushing victory seemed to justify Norfolk's criticism of the Bishops. It also made look rather foolish those Irish Nationalists who had loftily assured Catholic voters that they could vote for the Liberals (and Home Rule) with impunity, relying on the Irish Party, holding the balance of power in Westminster, to defend denominational education. John Redmond, the Irish Party leader, had not been alone in exhibiting such confidence. 'I do not share in the remotest degree the fears of those who think that a Liberal Government if returned to power would instantly attack the interest of the Catholic schools in Great Britain ... We need have no fear of the interests of the Irish Catholics of Great Britain. Any attempt to injure those religious interests of our people by any Liberal Government would mean their instant defeat by us, or at any rate it would mean our bitter opposition.'²³ The Irish Party miscalculated spectacularly, and was roundly criticised by certain Irish Bishops in consequence. Bourne, more wisely, refused to do so.

Catholic schools appeared to be at the mercy of a hostile Government determined to revoke the relative privileges conceded little more than three years earlier. There were more Protestant Nonconformist MPs in Parliament than at any time since Cromwell. Those MPs, overwhelmingly Liberal, expected a legislative programme to reflect their demands. In this they were not always subtle. 'After the Wilderness the Promised Land. And we have entered Canaan at last.'²⁴ No wonder that the *Tablet* predicted gloomily as a certainty that Catholics would be robbed of the right to appoint teachers and to give satisfactory religious instruction in their own primary schools.²⁵

It was an oversimplification, however, to attribute to the Liberal Government and Cabinet, a united and consistent opposition to Catholic schools. Bourne appreciated the more complex reality. There was no popular support for an exclusively secular system of national education. Yes, vocal and influential Nonconformists, led by Dr Clifford, demanded that all schools receiving State aid be run along lines acceptable to them: 'There shall be one and only one type of public school for children of the State, one and only one type of State training for the members of the teaching profession.'²⁶ The Nonconformist conscience would permit neither Catholic teaching nor Catholic teachers in the State system. And Clifford had powerful backers. One Liberal MP (admittedly the Catholic, Hilaire Belloc) alleged that the Government's educational policy had been forced upon it 'by a handful of wealthy Nonconformists ... the little group of Nonconformist capitalists who notoriously govern the Liberal newspapers and have financed so many of the Radical candidates.'²⁷

Clifford's rhetoric was mimicked in the election campaign by Liberal politicians such as Augustine Birrell, the Education Minister and himself a Nonconformist. In the constituencies he told supporters what they wanted to hear. 'He longed to see one kind of public elementary school for the whole country, and to abolish the unreal distinction between what were called board, and what used to be called voluntary schools ... He hoped that the Liberals would soon be in a position to carry out the principle that public control must go with public money.'²⁸

Privately, however, most Liberal ministers, Birrell included, were not anti-Catholic bigots. Bourne was almost bemused by the new Prime

Minister's candid pragmatism. 'I particularly recall the day when I saw Sir Henry Campbell-Bannerman—a most charming person—who received me with every kindness and consideration ... I pointed out to him that the Government would inflict serious injury on the most sacred interests of the Catholic Church. He replied very simply: "We have been put into power by the Nonconformists, and we must produce legislation that will satisfy the Nonconformists. If you, by your efforts, can bring about a change in public opinion, then we shall be quite prepared to alter our present attitude."'[29]

It is difficult now to appreciate that perhaps the greatest division in Edwardian England was between 'Church' (meaning, of course, the Church of England) and 'Chapel.' Politically, Anglican privilege may no longer have amounted to much, but we should never under-estimate the extent to which, socially, it rankled in the daily lives of ordinary people. Perhaps because they too had suffered from Anglican privilege, Irish Catholic MPs sympathised with Protestant Nonconformist grievances. They simply pointed out the incongruity of making Catholics pay for remedying this. Tim Healy put it succinctly: 'What the Nonconformists resented most was that in school they should bow to the vicar's wife, and that they were not taken on excursions organised by the parson. Yet why propose, because of the jarrings of Protestant opinion, to deprive every child who was not Protestant of religious instruction?'[30] A colleague was similarly perceptive, 'There is no real hostility to our schools; it is the ascendancy of the Anglicans that is assailed; and we have no interest in defending that.'[31]

Of 14,082 non-provided schools, only 1,063 were Catholic. (Unlike many Catholics, Bourne never made the mistake of over-estimating their position and consequent influence.) Of the remaining schools, just 13 were Jewish, 450 were Wesleyan and 739 of no particular denomination. The overwhelming majority, 11,817, were Anglican.[32] Catholic schools were mainly in urban areas, built by poor Irish Catholics for their own children. By contrast, most Anglican schools were small village schools where many of the children were not from Anglican families. Non-Anglicans deeply resented having to send their children to a Church of England school because there was no other school in the locality.

A new Education Bill was announced in the King's Speech when Parliament met in February 1906. The Liberal difficulty was how to legislate against the latter type of school without destroying the former. There was a widespread perception that the Liberals did indeed wish to distinguish the two types of school, the *Times* reporting it 'probable that Roman Catholic and Jewish schools will be given special treatment.'[33] That alarmed Dr Clifford: 'There is an uneasy feeling on our part that the noise being made by a certain section will be likely to affect the Government plans, namely, to allow Catholic schools, State supported, to remain in the Catholic atmosphere, and staffed by Catholic teachers, and this without any control on the part of the State.'[34]

When Bishop Burton of Clifton opened his evening paper on 9 April, he did not like what he read. 'Birrell brought in his Education Bill at 3 o'clock—a damned bad bill! We must hope that it will be wrecked, or chucked out by the Lords.'[35] Not everyone shared his view. The *Times* 'felt that the Government have gone out of their way to minimise Roman Catholic opposition, a development well calculated to accentuate the Nonconformist suspicions of the Bill.'[36]

Perhaps the 1906 Education Bill sought to reconcile the irreconcilable. On the one hand, it proposed to abolish the dual system and establish just one class of public elementary schools. Local authorities were empowered to take over non-provided schools and appoint all teachers. Teachers could not be appointed on the basis of their religious belief. 'No catechism or religious formula distinctive of any religious denomination shall be taught in the school'[37] at the public expense. So far the Nonconformist agenda was met. Yet Birrell revealed an additional intention. 'The object of the Bill was to establish, in rural districts at any rate, an undenominational kind of religious teaching acceptable to the great mass of the Protestants of this country.'[38] The Anglican educational monopoly in the countryside was to be swept away, while urban Catholic schools were to be afforded a measure of protection. How was this to be achieved as a matter of legislative drafting? Lord Robert Cecil warned the Government 'it was not easy to run with the Nonconformist hare and hunt with the Catholic hounds.'[39]

The Bill attempted to distinguish two types of non-provided school. Clause 3 covered run-of-the-mill Anglican schools. In these schools regular teachers were prohibited from giving any denominational education. This might be given by others, but its provision was severely circumscribed. Clause 4 sought to legislate for Catholic and Jewish schools, and possibly a minority of High Church Anglican schools. In these schools the local authority *might* grant 'extended facilities' to permit denominational education at all times and *might* allow ordinary teachers to give such instruction.

These extended facilities could only be granted in urban areas with populations over 5,000 where requested by 80% of parents.

The attempt to help Catholics was obvious—so were the potential problems. The Church would lose her right to appoint teachers—Catholic doctrine might be taught by those who did not believe what they were teaching. Catholics too had rural schools. Many Catholic schools admitted non-Catholic pupils—just 21% of parents could deprive a school of its Catholic character. And, even where these stringent conditions were met, there was no guarantee that the local authority would actually permit Catholic religious instruction. Recent experience of municipal belligerence made Catholics shudder for the future of their schools.

Introducing the legislation, Birrell had at least the decency to acknowledge the dilemma. 'The conscience clause does not meet the necessities, real or supposed, of these [Catholic and Jewish] cases. All minorities must suffer. It is the badge of their tribe ... As to the Roman Catholic schools, a man must have the heart of a nether millstone who is not deeply touched by the enormous sacrifices the Roman Catholics of this country have made to provide for the education and religious needs of their fellow-believers. They are cut off from much that once, at all events, they were fairly entitled to consider their own—cathedrals and splendid foundations, for instance. They have had cast upon them the obligation of looking after hundreds of thousands of poor Irish folks' children, whose fathers or grandfathers were driven out of Ireland and compelled to come to England under the pressure of circumstances which no man in this House, whatever his party, could hold them responsible for.'[40]

The Archbishops of Canterbury and York listened from the Peers' Gallery as the Bill was introduced in the Commons. Clifford and Bourne were in the Distinguished Strangers' Gallery. Afterwards, Bourne was spotted consulting the Irish MPs, Redmond and Healy, in the parliamentary lobby. What did he make of the legislation?

In fact, it came as no surprise. He had spent the preceding weeks actively and wisely. Two months earlier, Bourne had been able to tell his brother Bishops, 'For some weeks past I have been in confidential communication, direct and indirect, with members of the Government in reference to the Education Question, and I have availed myself of these opportunities to make clear our anxiety and our attitude concerning the whole matter. There is every disposition to listen to what we have to say, but the policy outlined is full of danger to our schools.'[41] Birrell had already communicated the provisions designed to assist Catholics to Bourne over dinner before the Bill's introduction.[42]

In coordinating the Catholic response, the Archbishop was ably assisted by Mgr William Brown,[43] who had experience with the old London Schools Board and the Southwark Diocesan Association. Bourne's moderation allowed Brown access to put the Catholic case to Birrell shortly after his appointment as Education Minister in December 1905 and again after the General Election. Bourne wrote to the Bishops in early February. (Despite later claims that he kept them in the dark in his dealings with the Government, the archives clearly show that he informed the Bishops of all relevant developments and offered to call meetings as they wished.) 'There is no idea of separate treatment: it is regarded as absolutely impossible even if acceptable to us. The Cabinet has not yet considered the question, and the actual Bill will probably not be presented until just before the Easter recess. Under these circumstances, if the situation remains unaltered, I do not propose to ask the Bishops to meet before Low Week, unless the majority of our colleagues desire me to summon a meeting. As soon as Parliament meets I will be in communication with Mr John Redmond, as I did last year, in order that he may clearly understand the points which arouse anxiety.'[44] The Bishops agreed with Bourne's reasoned approached, but found it difficult to rein in priests seeking more vocal opposition.

Communication with Redmond was Bourne's preferred method of contact with the Government. The Catholic Education Council, chaired by Norfolk, was the Bishops' official organ. Although Norfolk was punctilious to a fault and generously championed the Church's cause in public life, Bourne did not find relations with the Duke easy. Norfolk would have been horrified by the suggestion, but Bourne regarded him as condescending and arrogating to himself a role beyond that delegated. He wrote to Norfolk quite sharply: 'I have, as you know, been the means of giving to the Education Committee a power of initiative and of work and a responsibility much greater than my predecessors cared to confide to the Schools Committee ... It must always remain essentially an advisory body, the actual decision belonging to the Bishops alone.'[45] The Catholic Education Council was hampered by political divisions; Irish Nationalists refused to share a room with Norfolk and other Unionists.[46] It was a matter of public knowledge that they disagreed in their reaction to the Government's proposals. 'As for the Catholics, they are, no doubt, somewhat divided. The more moderate party are represented by the Irish Nationalists and Archbishop Bourne. Many of them are convinced that it would be unwise of their communion to reject a plan which guarantees the maintenance of their schools.'[47]

The Irish Parliamentary Party was entirely independent of the English Bishops. Always respecting that independence, Bourne dealt with its leaders from a position of equality. He avoided the mistake of his predecessor, who had appeared high-handed in his communications with respect to the 1902 Education Act—with a predictably poor response. Contacting Redmond, Bourne displayed every possible courtesy, leaving the politician to suggest a time and venue. The reply was immediate and favourable. Redmond offered to call at Archbishop's House the following day, bringing with him John Dillon. Redmond was completely won over by Bourne. 'He did not ask or expect the Irish Party to adopt an irreconcilable attitude and said the only hope was that by persuasion and finesse we might accomplish something. He said our action in supporting the Liberals in General Election was providential. If we had acted otherwise we would now be powerless. He promised to consult us on everything.' Bourne accepted popular control of Catholic schools as inevitable if they were to receive State aid, but he hoped to secure a *guarantee* of Catholic religious instruction where requested by the majority of parents.[48]

The mutual understanding of Bourne and the Nationalists is apparent even when they disagreed on specific details. One Irish MP assured the Archbishop at the outset that, while his Party was 'most anxious to cooperate,' it was 'desirable that the Party should maintain freedom of action in all matters.'[49] Thus, when Bourne gently suggested that the establishment of a Welsh Council be opposed—on the grounds it would be controlled by Nonconformists inimical to Catholic education—Redmond politely reminded him 'that it would be utterly impossible' for Nationalists to resist proposals for regional autonomy.[50] Similarly, Bourne warned Redmond, courteously but very firmly, to back off when, fearing Norfolk's influence, he expressed his misgivings over the new Catholic Federation.[51] Recognising their own legitimate spheres of influence, Bourne and the Irish Party cooperated effectively in all that was essential.

The Irish Nationalists were not the Archbishop's only means of communication with the Government. Catholics had welcomed the inclusion in the Liberal Cabinet of the elder statesman, the convert Marquess of Ripon. Hilaire Belloc was a Catholic MP with whom Bourne also had contact and who shared his moderation and quiet optimism. Bourne came in for considerable criticism (including from Bishops) for liaising with Belloc, especially when he voted for the Bill's Second Reading,[52] but it gave him an insight into the internal state of the Liberal Party he would otherwise have lacked. 'The Cabinet is sharply divided and the Liberal majority vaguely divided upon our claims. A mere opposition (which non-Catholics will not understand) will unite both sections of the Liberal Party and will lead to common action, though not in unison, in the Cabinet. Amendments which appear slight, but which are really vital, will strengthen that part of the Cabinet which desires to do us justice and will instruct that half of the majority that wishes us no ill.'[53]

That 'mere opposition' to which Belloc objected was most apparent in the northern industrial cities. Even before the Bill's publication, there were Catholic demonstrations, 60,000 men protesting at Liverpool, large crowds at Manchester and elsewhere. Bishop Casartelli of Salford and other Northerners had little time for Bourne's persuasion and finesse. When the legislation was introduced, there was nothing nuanced in Casartelli's response: 'I don't see a single redeeming feature in it.'[54]

Bourne enlisted modern technology to the cause, visiting the Gramophone Company to record a statement on Catholic education to be played at public meetings across the country.[55] He also resorted to more conventional means with his pre-Lenten Pastoral Letter. Bishop Cahill was not alone in his praise: 'I have read your pastoral with genuine admiration. It is like all your pronouncements so calm and moderate, yet unflinching and forcible.'[56] The tone was eminently reasonable. 'The present Ministry declare that it is their earnest desire to arrive at a definite, permanent and just settlement of the difficulties which have hampered and retarded the educational progress of the country for so many years, and to redress and remove all grievances connected therewith. It is a noble and most praiseworthy object, and we heartily welcome these declarations ... We shall approach the proposals of the Ministry in no captious or distrustful spirit ... What, then, is our claim? A Catholic Education, and not a Protestant Education, whether the latter be expressed in its simplest or in its most highly developed terms. A Catholic Education implies three things: Catholic Schools, Catholic Teachers, effective Catholic oversight of all that pertains to religious teaching and influence.' But Bourne hinted at other consequences should rational argument prove insufficient. 'A powerful party has been exposed to obloquy and disaster because it was thought by some to violate conscientious claims. We Catholics have no quarrel with any political party; we desire none. If a quarrel comes, it will be because it has been forced upon us. But if our claims are disregarded, if our appeal for consideration is set aside, let no one imagine that a final settlement has been reached. We shall be bound in conscience to use to the uttermost every legitimate means of resistance which we possess.' Divine assistance was sought through prayer and Exposition of the Blessed Sacrament throughout the Diocese.[57]

Meeting on 25 April, the Bishops agreed that the Bill must be resisted and authorised the publication of Bourne's statement giving their reasons. These were essentially threefold:

> Because the Bill gives to local authorities the right of control of religious teaching in public elementary schools ...
>
> Because while generous provision is made for the children of those parents who are able conscientiously to accept for their children what is styled 'simple Bible teaching,' the provision made for the children of those who conscientiously regard such teaching as not only inadequate, but absolutely unacceptable, is quite insufficient, and inflicts on such parents a very grievous civil liability solely upon the grounds of their conscientious religious convictions.
>
> Because of a concern that endowments given for the purposes of Catholic education could be confiscated and used for other purposes.

The proposed protection of Clause 4 was, they felt, 'wholly illusory as a safeguard for the protection of religious interests.'[58]

Bourne lost no time. He met Redmond the next day to agree tactics as to the Second Reading of the Bill and was able to announce to the Catholic Truth Society AGM his 'well-founded confidence that in this defence of our educational rights we shall have the unswerving and constant support of those who, in the House of Commons, are the representatives of Catholic Ireland.'[59] Bourne's careful solicitude for the Irish Party leaders had paid off. But those leaders also deserve great credit for their principled stand. It was not popular among all their supporters, one of whom wrote, 'I sincerely hope your party is not going to put the Home Rule clock back another 25 years over the Education Bill.'[60] Redmond countered such criticism: he was fighting for an issue which mattered profoundly to Irish Catholics living in England without jeopardising Home Rule. 'We were bound so to conduct this contest as to reduce to a minimum the risk of injury to the political movement [for Home Rule], and, therefore, from the first, we separated ourselves from the Duke of Norfolk and his friends. We followed our own line; we followed our own policy.'[61]

The Archbishop had not favoured the tactics of those Northern clerics who had called their people out in protest the moment the Liberals declared their intention to legislate for educational reform—not because he was opposed to a display of strength, when such was necessary, but rather because he objected to opposition for its own sake. In fact, he supported 'a great public meeting of the Catholics of London'—but only once they 'had an opportunity of knowing and considering the definite proposals of the Government regarding our Schools.'[62] Bourne prudently judged the moment for that pressure to be applied was after Easter—when the proposals were in the public domain, and prior to the crucial negotiations during the Bill's Committee stage.

A mass rally was to be staged in the Albert Hall on the evening of 5 May, just two days before the Bill's Second Commons Reading. Bourne liaised closely with John Gilbert to ensure maximum attendance and impact. Westminster and Southwark priests were asked to cooperate to produce 'the largest and most representative gathering of the Catholics of London which has yet been held.'[63] It was not to disappoint. Catholic Londoners turned out in force—unlike the North—women as well as men. Speakers addressed an estimated 40,000 in the overflow meetings in the surrounding streets.

In the Albert Hall itself, the 12,000 ticket-holders pledged themselves 'to resist to the uttermost the Education Bill as a violation alike of religious equality, common justice and civic equality.' That was never in doubt, but what most impressed the Press and neutral observers was the manner in which the meeting was conducted. The platform was full of prominent Catholics—the Bishops, Catholic members of both Houses of Parliament, Norfolk and the Irish Nationalists for once being prepared to bury their differences. Bourne spoke briefly but to great effect. 'Our concern on this occasion, let it be well understood, is solely for our Catholic schools. It is the duty of the Government to realise the justice of our position and so to modify its proposals that our schools may definitely retain their Catholic character ... The Catholic Church now stands opposed to His Majesty's Ministers only because they fail to safeguard our Catholic schools: in other matters she is not called upon to intervene.'⁶⁴ He was followed by only one other cleric, Mgr Brown.

The Archbishop avoided the pitfalls of clericalism and partisanship. There were high-ranking Conservatives who advised a different course. 'The Albert Hall meeting would have been a failure if I had submitted to the influence which these partisans tried to exert upon me.'⁶⁵ Fortunately, Bourne was not intimidated. A Liberal MP was impressed by the result. 'The audience was entirely composed of laity. I hardly saw one priest ... the phrases which we use, they used; the sentiments which we applauded, they set out for applause. They all declared they were Liberals; the meeting also declared itself Liberal ... If the Anglicans had been holding such a meeting, they would have crowded the hall with clergy, and the Bishops would have done practically all the speaking. Archbishop Bourne was wiser. He has made the form of his appeal—whatever we may say of the spirit—entirely democratic; and it was for the poor man's schools that he pleaded.'⁶⁶ Robert Morant was Secretary of the Board of Education, the civil servant responsible for drafting the 1902 Act and now required to undo its provisions by new political masters. He was equally impressed. 'I felt the Meeting the *best* and most earnest that I have ever attended. And I have been at those of all the different sections of opinion since 1901. To have seen the Duke of Norfolk and John Redmond walk up together and sit together, and to hear Your Grace's successive references to them received with practically *equal* cheers, showed unmistakably that you were leading a religious not a political campaign, and that there was sincerity in the unity. Both of these points being, I am sure, the keynotes that Your Grace must have been desirous of striking. Again thanking you for your courtesy, which I will repay as best I may by transmitting to my chiefs my impressions of the gathering last night.'⁶⁷

The *Standard* predicted 'that, after this expression of Roman Catholic opinion, the Bill has no chance of passing into law in its present form.'⁶⁸ The Archbishop may not have shared this confidence, but in organising the meeting he had displayed remarkable skill. The Government was left in no doubt that the appeal to reason was backed up by the will and ability to mobilise a mass movement transcending social and political divides. The response was immediate and positive. Through the intermediary of Lord Ripon, Birrell offered amendments designed to allay fears regarding Catholic educational endowments. Ripon himself congratulated the Archbishop on his speech as 'a model of moderation and discretion.'⁶⁹

As the Bill entered its Committee stage on 21 May, Bourne continued the dual approach of strong public utterances with a willingness to negotiate privately. In the face of some opposition, he had already secured the Bishops' agreement to a policy of 'promoting substantial amendments in the interest of the Catholic Schools' as opposed to simple 'obstruction.'[70] The Archbishop and the Watching Committee of the Catholic Education Committee worked closely with the Irish Nationalists to secure amendments aimed at saving most Catholic schools. Bourne forwarded a whole series of numbered slips to Redmond giving instructions as to how this objective might be achieved.[71] Typically, he wrote, 'I send you some suggestions. We are all very much concerned about some of the proposed amendments.'[72] At the same time he asked Brown to give the Irish all the necessary information to assist their parliamentary campaign.[73]

Not all Catholics appreciated the subtleties of the Archbishop's approach. He had to dampen the enthusiasm of those who called for another monster rally in Hyde Park coming swiftly on the heels of the Albert Hall meeting.[74] To be effective, he realised such tactics could only be employed sparingly. Other Catholics—supported by Ripon and Lloyd George in the Cabinet—urged a return to the pre-1902 situation, contracting out of the State system altogether. Bourne had no time for such utopian solutions. He knew in the long run this constituted financial suicide. However bad the terms offered by Birrell, Catholics had 'a very natural aversion to starvation.'[75]

Redmond placed Bourne's argument before the Commons. 'The power of contracting schools out of the Act was one of which he altogether disapproved. This would mean semi-starvation to the many schools about which he was concerned ... Contracting-out would mean inefficient and half-starved schools, and badly paid teachers.'[76] Redmond's close partnership with Bourne limited the potential damage and confusion that might have been wreaked by Catholics unilaterally pursuing their own policies. When Canon Rooney requested Nationalist support for contracting out, Redmond's response was unequivocal: 'I may say I am, and have been, acting all through in this matter in consultation with the Archbishop of Westminster.'[77] Bourne pointed out the political facts of life to the Bishop of Hexham & Newcastle: 'I have heard with some surprise, and considerable regret, that Canon Rooney and one or two other priests from your Lordship's diocese have without any reference to me or to the Catholic Education Council approached Mr John Redmond with a request to adopt a policy which certainly has never been approved by the hierarchy or recommended by the Council ... Canon Rooney must really bear in mind that it is not a question of what we shall accept but of what we may be able to obtain, and that the situation is one of extreme delicacy.'[78]

June saw frantic letters and interviews between Bourne, Ripon, the Nationalists and Birrell. Redmond and Dillon met the Prime Minister again, but, typically, found he had not mastered his brief, when he 'said that there would be no difficulty about [the appointment of] teachers, but subsequently modified this.'[79] At times the Government came tantalisingly close to satisfying Catholics concerns. On the floor of the House Birrell 'repeated his assurance that under [Clause 4] it was the intention of the Government that there should be the same sort of religious instruction, and the same sort of teachers, as at present in all the schools to which the clause applies.'[80] Bourne was sufficiently astute not to rely upon ministerial assurances but to hold out for statutory guarantees. And the devil lay in the drafting. How to meet legitimate Catholic grievances without making a nonsense of the whole proposal of educational reform?

No agreement had been reached by the end of the Committee stage in July. Bourne's analysis of the situation was realistic: 'Unless there be fundamental amendments, there will be open war on the part of the Catholic Body. We have done our best to be conciliatory, and the Ministry has forced us into this attitude of uncompromising hostility to their proposals. I think the more this line is taken publicly and privately, the better will be the chance of our persuading fair-minded men to see the justice of our position and to treat us equitably.'[81] At the Third Commons Reading on 30 July the Government had a majority of 192. A final settlement may have proved elusive thus far, but, as they returned home for the summer recess, Bourne graciously acknowledged the contribution of the Irish Party. 'Before you leave London I desire to express to you once more, and through you to your colleagues, my sincere and hearty thanks for the earnest and able efforts that you have been making during the past months in defence of the interests of our schools.'[82]

As Parliament returned in the autumn, Bourne continued to choose his words with great care, but his tone differed from the spring. 'The Government is approaching very near the dividing line, and unless they are very careful they are going to make a distinct attack on the consciences of Catholic parents, and, if that attack is made, it shall be resisted, and not only resisted, but it shall be overcome.'[83] He was reflecting the line adopted by the hierarchy in the preceding month. 'The clear, simple and perfectly just claims, which we put forth last Lent on behalf of our Catholics schools, have been disregarded and rejected by his Majesty's Ministers and by the House of Commons ... In the case of about half of our schools all public aid is refused, though rates will still be demanded of us ... These schools will be starved to death by the action of the Liberal Government, in defiance of all principles to which it owes its appellation. Then in the areas where, under these circumstances, no Catholic public elementary school can any longer exist, Catholic parents may be left under compulsion of the law to send their children to non-Catholic schools in opposition to the dictates of their conscience. The Government is thereby creating a situation of peculiar difficulty and delicacy, in which Catholics may be obliged to disregard a law which is manifestly unjust, and to obey rather the law of God, which no Legislature has the right to abrogate or set aside. In those schools in which it may, according to the provisions of the Bill, be possible to teach Catholic doctrine to Catholic children, no guarantee whatever is given that the teachers shall be Catholic. We are told to trust the goodwill and fairness of the local authorities. Such assurances are unworthy of serious consideration.' The Bishops noted, 'Our public appeal now lies to the House of Lords, and we call upon members of that House to prevent the injustice which is contemplated.'[84]

As the Bill passed to the Lords for its Third Reading there it appeared that Bourne's preference for compromise had failed and conflict was inevitable. On both sides there were those who relished the prospect of constitutional conflict between the Liberal Commons and the Tory Lords. At the King's request, a cross-party conference (attended by the Archbishop of Canterbury) sought, and failed, to achieve a settlement on the basis of mutual concessions.

Bourne was anxious to avoid denominational education becoming the subject matter of such a conflict, being wise enough to realise that the democratically-elected chamber was bound to prevail. Nevertheless, Catholics were obliged to seek protection from anyone in a position to offer it. They wrote to peers asking them to 'support either the rejection of the Bill, or the passing of such amendments as shall protect the religious liberties of parents and to ensure to all types of schools, whether denominational or undenominational, an equal share of public money.'[85]

Balfour and the Conservatives put the political ball back into the Government's court. Rather than reject the Bill outright, the Lords amended it beyond recognition. Local authorities would be obliged to ensure denominational teaching in Clause 4 schools. The Clause 4 provisions would be extended to rural schools. Only a bare majority of parents was required to ensure the provision of denominational education. And on the controversial matter of the appointment of teachers parents were to be given a veto over local authority appointments. It was all Catholics could hope for—and, politically, complete fantasy. But in those days prior to the Parliament Act, the Lords possessed an absolute veto on legislation and as early as mid-November, the Minister for Education had to admit 'that the Bill as amended is already an impossible Bill.' At the same time, however, he still seemed to proffer an olive branch to Catholics, commenting, 'I should not be sorry to see even Clause 4 amended in some particulars where, I think, the Roman Catholics and Jews still have some grievances.'[86]

The Catholic waters were muddied by two developments as the Archbishop struggled to maintain order on his side as the battle entered its final stage. Firstly, Norfolk led the Catholic peers into the division lobbies *against* the Lords' amendments. Norfolk justified himself by stating his belief that the Lords' amendments had 'not gone far enough.' Anything less than a statutory right to the appointment of teachers was entirely unsatisfactory.[87]

Norfolk also managed to wrong foot Bourne by leading a deputation of (mainly Northern) Catholic Education Council members to meet Lord Lansdowne, Tory leader in the Lords, on 29 November. In the name of 'the Catholics of England' they urged the Lords to 'stand by their amendments.' Redmond was not best pleased that he had not been consulted. It 'was a great mistake,' he maintained, and queered the Nationalists' pitch, if the cause of Catholic education was seen to be allied to Tory reaction.[88] Greatly embarrassed, Bourne had to admit that he 'was not informed of the proposed deputation until all the arrangements had been made. I knew nothing of it when I saw you on Monday ... The deputation on Thursday was forced on by people in the North and did not originate in London.'[89] (It is less clear whether Mgr Brown had been complicit in the arrangements. He was certainly more sanguine about its possible effect: 'there has been so much clamour in the North that nothing was being done to support the Lords. Indeed without the knowledge of our support Lansdowne would not have gone as far as he did. I have seen enough of politics to realise that one is most valued as a friend when one shows signs of becoming an enemy. I am convinced that had the peers merely moved a few mild amendments these would have been swept away with contempt—as it is there must be a deal.'[90]) Bourne, however, retained his preference for quiet negotiation. He and Redmond succeeded in scotching a second proposed delegation, this time to the Prime Minister.[91]

This was the highly charged and confused background against which Bourne summoned the Bishops to meet on 4 December to determine their policy, having first asked Redmond for his understanding as to how matters now stood.[92] After meeting the Archbishop the preceding day, Redmond and Dillon went on to an interview with Campbell-Bannerman and Birrell on 27 November. The Irish found that meeting 'very satisfactory.' For the first time, the Government countenanced meaningful concessions. They promised to reduce the majority of parents required to invoke the Clause 4 provisions from 80% to 75%. The Government seemed prepared to accept the Lords' amendment that Clause 4 schools should no longer be restricted to urban areas. Redmond was a little less precise—probably because Government thinking on the matter was far from formed—on the next point. 'On the question of the appointment of teachers the impression left upon my mind was that they would be willing to agree to the parents' committee having a consultative voice in the matter, but saw the gravest difficulty in giving them a veto. We made the claim that our amendment as proposed in Committee on the bill (of which I think Your Grace has a copy) should be accepted to the effect that no teacher should be appointed without the "concurrence" of the Parents' committee.' The Irish leader informed the Archbishop that he had told the Prime Minister that, provided they 'were completely satisfied upon these points and some minor ones ... we would be prepared on behalf of the Irish Party to support the Bill.' Redmond had the good sense to add that they might be talking about a hypothetical situation. If Lords and Commons persisted in their standoff, there was no agreed legislation to enact.[93] But at least Bourne was appraised of the political landscape.

What happened at the Bishops' Meeting on 4 December? The Archbishop passed on details of Redmond's negotiations. The Bishops were divided in their views. There were 'two or three in favour of wrecking the Bill,' but Bourne carried the remainder with him in his view 'that if we got the terms for which we were negotiating they would be well out of it and that the proper policy would be to facilitate its passage.'[94] The Bishops did not go as far as endorsing the Irish Party in their proposed support of the Government. Instead, they resolved, 'That Mr Redmond be informed confidentially that acceptance by the Government of the amendments outlined by him appears to the Bishops to be sufficient to justify Catholics in not actively insisting on the withdrawal of the Bill, not because such amendments make it satisfactory, but because it seems the safer course in the current very critical situation: but that they consider it vitally important that efforts should be made to render possible the provision of new Catholic schools.'[95]

And with that Bourne left for Paris for six days, leaving educational matters in the hands of Mgr Brown. Bourne himself was concerned with negotiating compensation from a French anti-clerical government for confiscated English clerical bursaries. He was also concerned at exactly this time by the threatened prosecution by the Charity Commissioners—a matter in which Rome was also now showing an interest. Nevertheless, even from France, the Archbishop kept abreast of developments at Westminster as is clear from a letter he wrote to Ripon on 8 December. Ripon forwarded this to the Education Minister advising that they should not 'lose this chance of a settlement with the R.C.s ... Putting aside all other considerations we do not want to lose their votes at elections if it can be avoided.'[96]

Bourne returned to London on 10 December in the midst of the Commons debate of the Lords' amendments. There were unfortunate altercations on the floor of the House (later continued in the letters pages of the Press) between Dillon and Norfolk's brother, Lord Edmund Talbot. The former alleged the Catholic peers were committed to a simple wrecking policy, the latter suggested the Irish had sold the pass on Catholic education. The Nationalists, however, continued their negotiations even as the debate was in progress. On 12 December Redmond assured the Archbishop, 'Today, after the Cabinet meeting, I had an interview with Mr Birrell and he gave me a positive assurance that in the event of a compromise being made—as he thought probable—the Government would agree to make part of that compromise *all* the amendments mentioned in my last letter to your Grace including the one making the concurrence of the parents' Committee a condition precedent to the appointment of teachers in Clause 4 schools. I gathered also that they would agree to 2/3 instead of 4/5 and they also propose to agree to amendments on the subject of new schools.'[97]

Education, Education, Education

That evening all save two of the Irish Party voted with the Government and against the Lords' amendments. The Tory Press and many English Catholics were quick to allege unprincipled political expediency. 'In their anxiety to promote Home Rule, the Irish members have left the business of defending their Church to the House of Lords.'[98] The Bishop of Limerick was even more vehement. 'I could not believe it within the bounds of possibility that they would do what they have done ... Let those who have taken their choice between the Catholic Bishops of England and Mr Birrell justify, if they can, before the Irish race throughout the world their discreditable vote ... The Irish Party, by a vote which will never be forgiven, rat upon themselves and forswear their own profession.'[99]

It was entirely understandable that those ignorant of the concessions gained from the Government should feel so passionately when it appeared the Nationalists had thrown over the cause of Catholic schools. However, Bourne stood by Redmond, revealing to the Bishop of Limerick the confidential negotiations which had been taking place. He also personally assured Redmond of his own gratitude at 'a long and most friendly and satisfactory interview' on 17 December.[100] This was followed up by a letter in the *Times*: 'Knowing as I do the negotiations which have taken place, I am satisfied that you have done your best to deal with a very delicate and critical situation.'[101]

On 20 December the Government withdrew the Education Bill. After an eight month battle, despite a massive Commons majority, it had been unable to secure its passage through Parliament. Bourne was to maintain that the Bill's final demise was due to the wrecking policy of Balfour, as well to the Bishop of Manchester and other Anglicans opposed to any compromise seen to concede 'some poor satisfaction to the *Romanists*.'[102]

A Ducal Spat

No one was under any illusions. 'The destruction of the Education Bill gives us not peace, but a respite in our struggle for the safety of our schools.'[103] The Nonconformists were furious at the failure of this flagship piece of legislation. Yet, even if it only provided a respite until the next onslaught, one would have expected universal relief among Catholics. Against all the odds, it appeared that they had won—at least for the moment. Some did express their appreciation to the Archbishop. Canon Tynan of Salford wrote, 'Now that the Education Bill is cleared away may I on behalf of this Governing Body be permitted to thank your Grace for the great patience and judicious *lead* given to us all in this crisis through which we have all gone?'[104] Not everyone shared this satisfaction. Bourne received an unpleasant surprise as he opened his post after Christmas.

The Duke of Norfolk was still smarting from what he felt to be 'the extraordinary action taken by the Irish Members in deciding to vote against all the Amendments *en bloc* which we had carried in the Lords.'[105] (He conveniently forgot that he and the Catholic peers had also voted against the same amendments, albeit for very different reasons.) He caught sight of the Archbishop's letter to Redmond in the *Times*. In the *Tablet* he read Redmond's Commons speech explaining the Irish Party's reasons for the voting the way it did. 'It was not without the very gravest deliberation and consideration, and it was not without consultation with those best entitled to speak on behalf of the Catholic body in this country, that we came to the conclusion that in the interests of the Catholic schools it would be unwise for the Catholic representatives in this House to make themselves in any way responsible for the wrecking of this measure. The Government has gone a long way to meet us … I am glad to be able to state that, in taking this course we acted, not only in consultation with, but with the concurrence of the responsible heads of the Catholic Church in England.'[106]

Norfolk's blood was up, he put pen to paper and there followed the most almighty row between the head of the Catholic Church in England and its senior layman. There was nothing he could do directly to influence the Irish Party, but Norfolk was determined to make his anger known. He was aggrieved that the Bishops in general, and Bourne in particular, had chosen to work more closely with Irish politicians than with the Catholic Education Council (i.e. himself). Norfolk sought an 'episcopal denial' of Redmond's statement that he had acted with 'the concurrence of the Bishops.' The implication was that, if not forthcoming, then Bourne had failed to keep him informed (or even misled him) over recent weeks.[107]

Bourne was not about to accept a lecture on the leadership of the Church, even from England's premier peer. Norfolk had copied his letter to each of the English Bishops. Bourne resented this. If the Duke had a complaint against the Archbishop, he was told that he should have communicated this privately.[108] At the best of times Bourne disliked Catholic divisions being aired publicly. Norfolk's circular letter allowed Bishops like Casartelli and Brindle to re-visit their own misgivings about Bourne's conciliatory policy. In an acrimonious exchange of correspondence, Duke and Archbishop disputed each other's version of the events of the previous five weeks.[109]

Where did the truth lie? Was Redmond correct to maintain that, in voting with the Government on 20 December 1906, he was acting 'with the concurrence' of the English Bishops? Had Bourne, deliberately or unintentionally, misled Norfolk and unfairly bypassed him in his capacity as chairman of the Catholic Education Council? Writing over thirty years later, Oldmeadow gave the benefit of the doubt to the Duke, whose action in voting against the Lord's amendments was described as having 'the full approval of the Bishops and the Education Council.' The Irish Party vote, by contrast, was an 'apparent right-about-face' and 'a puzzle to Catholics.'[110] When Bourne himself was more disillusioned with the Liberal Government, a few years later he appeared to distance himself and the Bishops from the Nationalists. He maintained that it was 'positively misleading' to assert that in December 1906 the Irish leaders had 'succeeded in obtaining from the Government an arrangement which the Bishops were prepared to accept as a solution of the problem.' He went on to deny 'that the Government has ever proposed, or that any one of any party has ever succeeded in obtaining, an arrangement which the Bishops could have conscientiously have accepted as a settlement of this question.' Yes, he had gladly borne 'public testimony to the tact and skill which Mr Redmond showed at that very critical moment, but I cannot allow a meaning to be read into my words which they do not, and were never intended to contain.' [111] While strictly correct, the Archbishop's own comments were inclined to mislead. A careful reading of contemporary accounts gives a rather different interpretation.

Bourne reminded Norfolk that the Bishops' 'position was made clear from the outset last spring. While cordially disliking the Bill, and asserting its fundamental injustice and protesting against it, we determined to abstain from anything in the nature of obstruction or aimless wrecking, and to work steadily for specific amendments.'[112] Having received Norfolk's letter, Bishop Burton chipped in with his own version of events. He too accurately described the 'undisputed facts' that the Catholic Education Council was 'the natural and undisputed adviser of the Bishops' and that the Irish Party had 'not been wont to communicate with the C. E. Council.' (He left unspoken any blame that might accrue to Norfolk for this state of affairs.) Burton proceeded to state that, of course, the Bishops would communicate with the Irish Party as being the only significant body in the Commons consistently sympathetic to their case. To the extent that those communications were confidential 'the Bishops cannot with propriety refer these to the C. E. Council, or to anyone else.' However, the fact the Bishops and the Irish Party were in contact in December was 'a matter of common knowledge' and Burton expressed surprise that Norfolk 'after all that has transpired, would appear to be still uninformed of the fact.'[113]

But what of Norfolk's specific allegation that, when questioned, the Archbishop had denied that 'the Bishops had assented to' the Irish Party voting with the Government?[114] And the further grievance that the lay English Catholic leaders had been kept in the dark on this apparent *volte-face*?

Bourne denied withholding information from Norfolk. When Redmond and Dillon first learned of the Government's willingness to offer concessions 'I communicated all that I knew to Your Grace in no way concealing the direction towards which my own judgment inclined.' On returning from France 'on two occasions by word of mouth, and once by letter, I informed your Grace of the progress of negotiations which were leading to results beyond my hope or expectations.'[115] Norfolk did not dispute this. He admitted that on 12 December Mgr Brown had told him 'that the Bishops had sanctioned the Irish Members abstaining from opposing the Bill provided certain concessions could be obtained from the Government.' However, he claimed that later that same evening Bourne had told him that there was no agreement between the Bishops and the Irish leaders. 'You at once assured me that this was not the case, that all that had happened was that the Irish Members had themselves come to the Bishops and asked whether in the opinion of the Bishops their conduct would be regarded as sinful if, provided they could obtain certain concessions from the Government, they decided to offer no further opposition to the Bill.'[116]

It is impossible to know exactly what Bourne said that evening. He responded to the Duke's charge simply by saying, 'I fear that we can hardly come to an understanding regarding recent events, as your remembrance even of our conversations is not in complete accord with mine.'[117] Probably the Archbishop had given a less than full account of his dealings with the Irish, partly because he regarded these as confidential, partly because he was only too aware of the antagonism between Norfolk and the Nationalists and also because he himself did not feel comfortable in his dealings with Norfolk. For the latter reason, both men bear some responsibility.

On the wider question of whether Redmond had acted with the Bishops' concurrence, Bourne was more forthcoming. He had known as early as 30 November that Redmond intended to lead his MPs into the Government lobbies if they could secure the amendments which seemed to be on offer. The Bishops on 4 December phrased their position more negatively than positively: the amendments meant that Catholics were justified in not actively insisting on the withdrawal of the Bill. Redmond was certainly entitled to say that he always acted in 'consultation' with the Bishops. Bishop Burton wanted to draw the line there. He told Norfolk, 'When you quote the Irish leader as stating that he acted "with the concurrence of the Bishops," you are quoting a statement which would seem to me to sin by excess. The Bishops cannot be accurately described as "having concurred" with his action... [They] consented to leave the Irish Party unfettered, but carefully abstained from bestowing explicit sanction upon their action.'[118]

That reflected the situation on 4 December. But the political situation was fluid and fast moving. Negotiations between the Nationalists and the Government, and contact between the Nationalists and the Church, continued right up to the final Commons vote—and beyond. Bourne correctly described the position in a memorandum prepared for the Bishops. 'On 4 December we could only give hesitating consent to Mr Redmond's negotiations. By 20 December he was entitled to say he had acted with *my concurrence*, for, step by step, consulting me at every stage, he had with no ordinary skill definitely won practically all that we had asked him to work for last spring.'[119] Strictly speaking, therefore, Redmond had acted with the concurrence of Bourne, rather than the Bishops as a whole, but the distinction is meaningless. The hierarchy could not be assembled to debate every twist and turn in this protracted contest. In this matter they were represented by Bourne as Archbishop of Westminster.

Bourne might have left matters there. He had exonerated and acknowledged his debt to the Nationalists. He thanked Norfolk and Talbot for their personal 'kindness and consideration.' He might have recognised Norfolk's valid point that it was the peers' intervention which allowed the Irish to extract concessions from the Government—nothing similar had been forthcoming when they acted alone during the summer months. He might have dwelt on the desirability of the actual result, and waved aside any further differences as the unfortunate consequence of genuine misunderstandings.

But Bourne did not leave matters there. He proceeded to give the benefit of his views on the conduct of Norfolk and his political allies. 'While Mr Redmond was loyally consulting me at every critical moment, my opinion and legitimate influence were neither sought nor considered as far as other Catholic representatives were concerned ... I was not consulted as to the action to be taken at the critical moments by the Catholic Peers: they went their own way. At the most critical moment of all a deputation was promoted to Lord Lansdowne. I was not informed of it until all the arrangements had been made, and I had to undo the mischief which was thereby wrought, as best I could. This deputation was the first evidence of want of unity among Catholics. My advice was not sought before Lord Edmund's speech of 11 December ... Mr Dillon's speech, which I regretted, was the direct outcome of Lord Edmund's words uttered without any previous consultation with me ... Then came necessarily Mr Dillon's rejoinder with its further unnecessary and premature disclosures.'[120]

Coming after the Bill had been withdrawn, Bourne's outburst might be considered unnecessary and ungracious. The Duke of Norfolk was not accustomed to being lectured—even by an Archbishop. Perhaps it was no bad thing that he was on this occasion. John Dillon posed the question—and gave the solution—which represented the Archbishop's mind exactly: 'How can the future of the Catholic schools be rendered safe in this country if you allow any person or persons with the best of motives to identify the cause of the Catholic schools of Great Britain with the cause of reaction and Toryism? ... There is only one way in which you can save the Catholic schools and that is by a broad, frank appeal to the sense of justice and fairness of the English people.'[121] Bourne had chosen the better, and safer, part, recognising that the defence of Catholic interests in twentieth-century Britain could no longer be left exclusively to Conservative peers.

The McKenna Bills

It is unfortunate that Catholics were divided in their moment of victory, but that was the sad fact of life acknowledged by Redmond. 'I deeply regret that the Bill, with these great concessions in it, was not carried into law. In that matter we have differed from the Duke of Norfolk and his friends. They thought it better to wreck the Bill ... Well, the Duke of Norfolk and his friends had their way, and the Bill was wrecked, and today what is the position? The Catholic schools in England are now face to face with a very uncertain future.'[122]

The Government's intention did not remain uncertain for long. A new Minister, Reginald McKenna, introduced the Education (Special Religious Instruction) Bill on 26 February 1907. There was no pretence at educational reform. The measure was aimed solely at pacifying the radical Nonconformists. The Bill had the advantage of brevity over its predecessor. It comprised a single clause drafted, to thwart the Lords' veto, as a financial measure. To allow Nonconformist passive resisters to resume payment of their rates with an easy conscience, any non-provided school wishing to give denominational religious instruction was required to refund the local authority the cost of that instruction, estimated at 1/15 of the amount of teachers' salaries. Any school not refunding the local authority within six months would be excluded from the national educational system and any share of public funds.

The Catholic outcry against this 'new penal law' was immediate. The *Tablet* declared it monstrous that, 'We are thus to be made to pay for our Catholic instruction three times over—through our school buildings, through our contribution to the rates, and, if this Bill passes, through the payment of a fifteenth of the salaries of our teachers.'[123] The Bishops emphatically condemned a 'fragrantly unjust' Bill 'because, while compelling Catholics to pay for a form of religious teaching which was directly opposed to their conscientious convictions, it deprived them of all public aid in giving to their children that teaching which their conscience claimed.'[124]

Bourne and Redmond resumed their earlier partnership, the Archbishop asking the Nationalists to maintain a watching brief. Redmond promised to send a copy of the Bill to Archbishop's House and to keep Bourne 'fully posted as to anything that may occur.' The Nationalists forced a division the moment the Bill was introduced in the Commons so that the Government was in no doubt as to their position.[125] As in the preceding year, the Archbishop's initial response was rational argument and organisation. 'Their duty was to show as clearly as possible to their fellow countrymen that that Bill was radically unjust. For that purpose it would be necessary to set forth in the clearest possible terms what the Catholic Church was already spending on the education of her children, while those who were supporting the measure were giving practically nothing at all, except in so far as contributions were forced from them by the rate and tax collectors. They wanted statistics. These were being prepared.'[126]

But Catholics had also learnt lessons in political strategy from the Nonconformists. They had witnessed the effectiveness of the campaign of non-payment of rates. The nation at large, and the Liberal Party in particular, had been impressed by the example of otherwise respectable citizens prepared to go to prison and to have their property seized rather than suffer an alleged violation to their religious conscience. Very well, two could play at that game. At least the Nonconformists under the 1902 Act had their own schools to which they might send their children at the public expense—save in 'single school areas,' where Catholics sympathised with their grievance and supported reform. McKenna wished to deprive Catholics of the equivalent opportunity.

At their Low Week meeting the Bishops requested Bourne to travel to Rome to discuss the legality of Catholic passive resistance.[127] Here was this most proper of men exploring the possibility of law-breaking—such was the injustice of the Government's proposals. He put the case to Cardinal Gotti in the most balanced manner. Having built and kept their schools in good order, Catholics were now faced with their loss and closure were public funding to be withdrawn. At the same time 'Catholics and Anglicans will be obliged to pay for religious instruction which only the Nonconformists accept.' Bourne thought a Catholic campaign of non-payment of rates would succeed because, although not numerous, they were highly organised. However, most Anglicans would not support such a move and he acknowledged it would 'be a new departure for Catholics, placing them in open opposition to the law.' The question he posed was whether the English Bishops might encourage or permit passive resistance or whether it was 'contrary to the moral law.'[128] It is intriguing to speculate on Rome's answer. There is no record of any. This might be because the political situation in England had changed again.

On 1 June McKenna told Liberals in Newcastle that he was dissatisfied with his own Bill, which he regarded as 'nothing more than a temporary expedient ... I tell you frankly I hate the principle of allowing one set of persons to obtain by a money payment the right to give denominational instruction to children in our schools ... if you ask me whether I would rather have that Bill embodying the principle which I hate, or another Bill which would put our whole educational system upon a satisfactory basis, I should say, Away with this little one; give me a big one.'[129] Two days later the Prime Minister announced that the Bill was to be withdrawn, citing pressure of parliamentary time.

This was no cause for rejoicing among Catholics. Here was a Minister of Education, publicly professing hatred of faith schools, committed to a more comprehensive bill in the next parliamentary session. 'We are a Protestant nation and further legislation would be introduced ... The Government will not be false to its pledges. The Liberal Government will carry out its policy; and though, in carrying out that policy, we be brought into violent conflict with the House of Lords, we will undertake that fight too. We call with confidence on every Liberal in the country to support us in our action.'[130]

Bourne and the Catholic Church were prepared to negotiate with or, if necessary, to oppose, the Government concerning their various educational bills. They accepted the need to convince public opinion and to engage fully in the parliamentary process. However, what lost the Government all respect in Catholic eyes was its decision to circumvent the normal democratic processes. Having failed twice in Parliament, the Government now sought to impose its will through administrative regulations issued at the whim of the Minister of Education. Catholics were doubly infuriated.

The 1902 Education Act applied only to elementary schools. Through Regulations issued in May 1907 McKenna introduced draconian conditions for denominational secondary schools to receive public funding. There must be no requirement that governors, teachers or pupils should be Catholic; the local authority was to appoint the majority of governors and thereby control the school; specific religious instruction could only be given if demanded by a majority of parents in writing; and 25% of places had to be made available free of charge to pupils from public elementary schools. For two years some leniency was shown, but from 1909 the full rigour of the Regulations was enforced. As John Gilbert complained, 'without reference to Parliament, the Government had succeeded in carrying out, with regard to secondary schools, what it had failed to carry out by legislation with regard to elementary schools.'[131]

The Regulations killed the expansion of Catholic secondary education. Time and again, Bourne protested against the injustice. He approached the Government 'both personally and through other persons, in order to see whether it would still be possible to set on foot a Catholic Secondary School acceptable to Catholic parents—i.e., under Catholic management, with Catholic teachers in all cases when they are necessary on Catholic principles—and at the same time act in compliance with [the Regulations], and so secure the Government grant. I am obliged to confess that all my endeavours have failed, and I am forced to the conclusion that [the Regulations have] rendered impossible the existence of any Catholic Secondary School unless it can be financed independently of aid from public sources.'[132] It took a decade and a change of Government for redress to be obtained.

Potentially even more drastic were the 'Regulations for the Training of Teachers' announced by McKenna on 10 July 1907 to come into effect three weeks later. Having failed so far in its assault on Catholic schools, the Government sought to turn off the supply of Catholic teachers. Encouraged by successive Governments, the Church had built teaching training colleges at its own expense, while the Government paid for the actual training. No longer—unless the college was prepared to accept any applicant regardless of faith. Catholic doctrine could only be taught to those whose parents submitted a written request. The building of new colleges would not be permitted. If a training college was found to have favoured a Catholic applicant, it was fined £100 for the first offence, closed on the second.

Redmond was scathing: 'Nothing could be said for the candour or courage of a Government which intended to crush denominational institutions in this country, not by introducing a Bill but by the issue of a couple of pamphlets without any notice whatsoever to the people of the country.'[133]

On 25 July Bourne led a delegation of Catholic peers, MPs, clergy and laity to meet the Prime Minister and Education Minister. Again, Campbell-Bannerman expressed sympathy but revealed his ignorance of the impact of the Regulations. Recognising that rational argument was achieving nothing, the Archbishop told McKenna to his face that Catholics would ignore the Regulations.[134] It was the right approach. Confronted, the bully backed down. Nothing was said officially, but the Regulations were a dead letter in respect of Catholic colleges.

As Catholics awaited McKenna's second attempt at legislation the political rhetoric was menacing. 'Two years ago the Government had stretched the patience of their own supporters by their concessions. They were not going to repeat that experiment. The Education Bill to be introduced early in the next Session would be a short Bill, a simple Bill and a drastic Bill!'[135] Bourne was not intimidated. He continued to appeal to the reason of his fellow countrymen and to encourage his fellow Catholics. 'At the present moment the political outlook, in so far as Catholic education is concerned, is gloomy to a certain extent, but I always maintain that it is not as gloomy as it was two years ago. Then we had to fight a new Government flushed with victory and with an enormous majority. That Government has learned a few lessons, and they know that if they are not very careful that more lessons will be taught them ... they are well aware that in any proposals they make they will have to take into account not only the Nonconformist conscience but the Catholic conscience.'[136]

Characteristically, Bourne remained calm under provocation. Some Catholics clamoured for a more confrontational approach. He knew this was not the way for an unpopular minority to proceed; he was more likely to be listened to if he spoke infrequently, in full possession of the facts. 'No one can say what the future may bring forth ... Some people thought there ought to be a pronouncement. I do not think it well to discuss hypothetical cases; I do not think any pronouncement necessary. A few days after I met you here on the last occasion, I had to speak on the Education question in the North of England. There is not anything new to say now ... If it is made a matter of party politics, and if any arrangement is proposed to the House of Commons which will entail upon Catholics a burden greater than they can bear, then it will be persecution, and we intend to resist it with all our might.'[137] The same the following month: 'I prefer that we here at the very centre of things should wait to criticise until we know exactly the facts we may be called upon to criticise.'[138]

The Archbishop was in the Commons gallery again as McKenna introduced his second Education Bill on 24 February 1908. It differed from Birrell's Bill in not attempting to include all schools in one national unified system through considerable flexibility. For McKenna, any school not falling within the prescripts of his rigid system was well off out of it.

The traditional Nonconformist grievance about having to attend the Anglican village school was to be addressed by the compulsory transfer of all non-provided schools in single-school areas (some 8,000 of them) to full local authority control. In other areas non-provided schools had a choice. They might be surrendered to the local authority and lose their denominational character—or they could opt out and lose their right to be funded from the rates. Grudgingly, McKenna would allow them a *per capita* grant from the Treasury—provided the schools met all conditions laid down by the Board of Education.

Bourne's response was predictable and cogent. 'If it be a fact that this system will satisfy the Protestant national conscience, so let it be. All we can say is, "It won't do for us." We are citizens in the same way everybody else is; we have to pay rates and taxes like everybody else. We are Catholics, and we are not Protestants, and your national Protestant system is absolutely useless to us, and in no sense an adequate return for our compulsory contribution to the educational funds of this country ... Is this a genuine attempt to meet the position of our Catholic schools, or is it a covert attempt to starve them out of existence? ... Is the grant sufficient to do two things—to provide us with equally good schools, because we can never consent again to an inferior type of education for our children; still more, is it adequate to give us equally good teachers, because we can never consent to engage teachers at starvation wages.'[139]

Catholic opposition to the Bill benefited from the Archbishop's attention. McKenna offered schools contracting out of the national system an annual Treasury grant to a maximum of £2.7.0 for each child. Bourne commissioned Charles Russell to establish the exact cost of educating a Catholic child. He was able to tell McKenna this amounted to £2.13.9.[140] In London it came to £3.10.0. As John Gilbert pointed out the proposed Treasury grant was 'totally inadequate' and itself not guaranteed. 'There is nothing in the Bill to prevent the Board of Education giving Catholic schools only 10s. a head.'[141] Having access to these statistics allowed Bourne to challenge effectively any Government claim to be acting fairly.

Bourne approached the principle of contracting out with caution. He distinguished the different senses in which different people used the same term. He was fundamentally opposed to contracting out if this meant the exclusion of Catholic schools from their rightful place in the national educational system. However, if contracting out was used more narrowly to refer to schools remaining within the national system while being funded by Treasury rather than local authority rates then, he argued, 'our criticism must be more cautious.'[142] On reflection, Bourne favoured contracting out in this second sense—and persuaded the other Bishops of its merits. 'The national system of Education can perfectly well have two branches—the rate-aided and the non-rate-aided.'[143]

Catholics were still squaring up for a massive battle. They did not know whether the principle of contracting out would be conceded on an acceptable basis nor the amount of any grant and any conditions attached. And they were prepared to fight alone. The Bishops held aloof from a proposed round table conference 'because our position is so clear that all know it; we can surrender nothing.'[144] Bourne cannily recognised the limitations of being identified with the Anglicans, whose 'battle is not so much for religious teaching as for the social and political predominance of the Establishment, and this is certainly not our concern. Their leaders might at any moment compromise on a basis which would mean disaster to us ... We can fight our own way without unreliable or compromising allies.'[145]

But, suddenly, the Government became much more desultory in pursuit of its objective. In April 1908 the dying Campbell-Bannerman was replaced as Premier by Herbert Asquith. He had no love for the Catholic Church, but his pragmatism was shared by the Wesleyan, Walter Runciman, who became Education Minister in the consequent Cabinet reshuffle. Political events in the country further encouraged compromise. The Liberals no longer enjoyed the overwhelming popularity which had swept them to power in 1906. Having lost control of the London County Council, parliamentary by-elections also went against them. Winston Churchill attributed his defeat in Manchester North West to 'the sudden and organised transference of between four and five hundred Catholic votes, always hitherto regarded as an integral part of Liberal strength in Manchester, to the Protectionist side, upon grounds quite unconnected with the main issues.'[146] Bishop Casartelli and the Irish Nationalist leaders had urged their people to vote against the Government specifically because of the threat to the schools. The Liberals came to appreciate that they had to take the Catholic opposition seriously.

It was something of a puzzle that in May 1908 the Government permitted the Education Bill to go to a Second Commons Reading, which, of course, they won comfortably. The *Tablet* speculated that this was either because 'they feel it necessary to do something to keep their Nonconformist supporters in good humour or that the negotiations for the proposed conference have failed. A third alternative is that the debate is to be entered upon by the Government as a sort of fishing expedition to see what suggestions they catch in the way of fresh suggestions towards a possible compromise.'[147] Asquith revealed his hand the following month. 'If the Government do not push on to its further stages at this moment our Educational Bill it is because we not only hope, but believe, that there are at work pacifying and reconciling forces which, if time be given, may work out a solid and lasting settlement.'[148]

The Runciman Bill

Mgr Brown maintained that Birrell had failed 'due to the haste with which his Bill was drawn.'[149] Runciman was determined to avoid the same mistake. Laws would only be passed once an agreed position had been achieved. Runciman worked patiently through the summer and autumn of 1908. He hoped that most Anglican schools would be transferred to local authority control, with the possibility of facilities for specific religious instruction on a voluntary basis. He had already acknowledged that Catholics constituted a special case. 'In the Roman Catholic schools it would be an outrage on the feelings of the parents to have a child taught by Protestant teachers.'[150] Again, they would be offered the option of contracting out in return for Treasury grants.

Catholics were placed in a dilemma. Should they enter into negotiations with Runciman at this point? Norfolk had gleaned from Archbishop Davidson of Canterbury that the Government was anxious to compromise and wanted a general conference of interested parties. On the one hand, were such a conference to fail, as Norfolk thought very likely, Catholics would be blamed for that failure. On the other hand, if Catholics held aloof, they might find themselves presented with an unpalatable *fait accompli*. Bourne continued to provide information showing the amount Catholics required to make good any loss from rate aid were they to contract out, but, he maintained, it was not necessary to enter more general discussions. The Minister 'knew and I knew perfectly well that until he had squared the Anglicans it was no use speaking to us, because the whole arrangement depended upon that.'[151]

For a moment it appeared that Bourne had miscalculated. On 19 November Asquith announced that McKenna's second Bill was to be withdrawn, and a new Bill introduced proposals which were 'the outcome of prolonged communication in various [non-Catholic] quarters.'[152] It appeared that the Catholic Bishops had been excluded from any substantive input and were left ineffectively protesting 'that they are unable to find in the present proposals of the Government any real settlement of the educational difficulties of the country.'[153]

In fact, Bourne had calculated far better than anyone else. Just as it appeared there was an agreement with the Church of England and the

Nonconformists, the whole edifice unravelled. As the Government attempted to rush legislation through Parliament, Archbishop Davidson withdrew Anglican consent on the grounds that there was not, after all, a financial agreement with the Government. Suddenly everyone engaged in recriminations. Some Anglicans accused Davidson of surrender, looking enviously at the contracting out provisions aimed at Catholics. Many Nonconformists felt betrayed in that denominational teaching would still be permitted in State schools. Catholics felt aggrieved that they were still being asked to pay twice over for aspects of elementary education.

Asquith announced to the Commons on 4 December that, 'The conditions of an agreed settlement no longer existed ... The Government had no option but to withdraw the Bill.'[154] It is difficult to understand how the Government found itself in this position given its self-proclaimed intention to enact non-contentious legislation. Bourne's statement to Runciman the preceding month appeared justified, 'You will not expect me at this moment (the Bill was not yet printed) to express a definite opinion, but it is only fair to you to say that I can hardly discern in your proposals a basis of permanent settlement as far as we are concerned.'[155] It was political opportunism, but perhaps the Leader of the Opposition was correct when he lectured the Government, 'A Bill which is unworkable from the Roman Catholic point of view carries within it the seeds of destruction.'[156] Bourne understood that, and saved the Catholic Church a good deal of unnecessary opprobrium in the circumstances surrounding the demise of Runciman's Bill.

Nor was he entirely negative. For good measure, he advised the Government on how a permanent settlement might be achieved. 'It seemed to him clearly that four types of schools ought to satisfy the British public. They had first of all the type of school in which simple Bible instruction was given ... There were special schools needed no doubt for [the High] Anglicans ... Then there were themselves ... Then there were the Jewish community, who should have their schools ... If there was to be justice and equality, a sensible Government ought to furnish, equip and maintain schools of these different types to satisfy the legitimate needs of the people of England.'[157]

A Government elected with Nonconformist votes was not about to legislate at the behest of a Roman Catholic prelate. Speaking to that constituency, it could still make ominous noises about denominational education. 'It is due to no fault of ours that those for whom you speak are disappointed and labour under a sense of real and serious grievance; and, for our part, I can say that, if no opportunity arises for dealing effectively with the subject in this Parliament, we cannot in the next—if we are returned to power—allow the present injustices and the limitations or absence of popular control to continue to deface our educational system.'[158] The danger, however, had passed. Two tied elections in 1910 meant that, even after the Lords' veto was removed, the Liberals held office only at the goodwill of Redmond's Nationalists. The *Tablet* exulted, 'All Catholics, whether Unionists or Radicals, may unite in common rejoicing. Whatever happens, the schools are saved for the lifetime of the current Parliament ... Dr Clifford, and the policy of persecution he stands for, has been overwhelmingly defeated.'[159]

Catholic schools emerged largely unscathed from what could have potentially become the fiercest persecution of modern times from a Government with a massive Commons majority. Many factors contributed to this: opposition by peers and Anglicans; the fact that the 1906 election result did not necessarily constitute a clear mandate for the destruction of denominational education. But Bourne's role should not be under-estimated. For three critical years, he judged the political mood with superb accuracy. He knew when and how to present a display of Catholic force and resolve. He knew equally well when to keep silent and to prefer quiet diplomacy. He knew how to appeal to the fair-mindedness of ordinary Englishmen. He resisted intemperate calls for an undiscriminating assault on the Government which would have provided its more radical members with the desired excuse to label the Catholic Church as a bastion of Tory reaction to be attacked and defeated. His use of the Irish Nationalists was controversial in some quarters, but precisely the right strategy in the circumstances. Far more than they appreciate the continued existence of Catholic schools today owes much to the leadership of this calm and clear-headed Archbishop.

Fisher's Proposals

The Liberals proposed further legislation after 1910 but, lacking a consensus, got nowhere. When educational reform was next seriously mooted, the political situation was unrecognisable from that of 1906. In 1917 Nonconformism was still a force to be reckoned with, but its influence was much reduced. The country had 15 years' experience of the 1902 Act—which had proved itself largely effective. An awareness of wartime deficiencies meant legislative proposals were motivated more by a genuine desire for reform than the wish to settle old sectarian scores. In December 1916 Lloyd George had become Prime Minister of a Conservative-dominated coalition, pledged to a more efficient prosecution of the First World War. Its professed confidence in the ability of the expert brought to office a new type of Education Minister.

H. A. L. Fisher was an Oxford history don, Vice-Chancellor of Sheffield University, an educationalist, an expert. He was someone with whom, from the outset, Bourne felt he could do business. The feeling was reciprocated. There are many more references in Fisher's diary to meetings with Bourne than with the Anglicans. Fisher was always available to the Archbishop of Westminster, whereas he 'discouraged' the Archbishop of Canterbury from sending delegations. He approached Bourne objectively. His assessment of Bourne after his death is, therefore, of some value. 'Let me tell you how much I came to respect and admire Cardinal Bourne ... I always felt his integrity, strength and intelligent appreciation of views other than his own and of the difficulties with which we were confronted.'[160]

In his education estimates placed before Parliament in April 1917 and in a draft Education Bill submitted to the War Cabinet the following month, Fisher advanced a far-sighted vision for reform. The school-leaving age was to be raised from 12 to 14; there were to be compulsory continuation schools to be attended by those up to the age of 18 for at least 8 hours each week for 40 weeks of the year; the provision of nursery and secondary education was to be expanded; salaries, training and school inspection were to be improved.

Fisher met with Bourne on 6 June before the introduction of the Bill. He assured the Archbishop 'that it was the intention of the Bill to leave all matters affecting denominational Schools as far as possible in the same position as they stand at present.'[161] He 'hoped to pass [this] new measure without arousing religious difficulties, and then later to meet them in private conference so as to reach agreement by consent.'[162] Fisher was quite clear as to his intention: firstly, to achieve educational reform within the dual system and to avoid controversy; subsequently, to attempt to remove the religious question by negotiation.

Bourne promptly disappeared from the scene for the better part of three months as a result of the serious illness brought on by the bitter conflict with his brother Bishops earlier that spring. His attitude to Fisher's proposals is likely to have been that of the *Tablet*: 'Regarded from a point of view purely educational, and from that of the wellbeing of the children, its principles are assured of a warm welcome ... In his attempts to meet these complaints and demands and to do something to remedy them, Mr Fisher has shown courage and vision, and will have behind him a strong body of support ... For a first step, however right the direction may be, it may be thought that the Bill goes too far ... There are other difficulties in the way connected with the financial burdens it will impose.'[163] This concern about increased financial outlay on the part of the Church was a perennial problem, and gave Catholics a reputation as obstructionists when it came to educational reform. But Bourne was convinced that Fisher meant no harm to denominational education and, together with the Catholic teaching profession, was prepared to give the new Education Bill a wide measure of support.

Returning from convalescence, he discovered that his attitude was not shared by many Bishops and Northern Catholics. When the Bishops met on 25 September 1917 Bourne was not inclined to take any action. Eventually it was agreed that he would write to Fisher.[164] 'I find that widespread anxiety and apprehension have already been created by many of the provisions of your Bill. The Bishops heartily welcome the purely educational reforms that you propose but they note with regret the controversial element the Bill contains. Many of its provisions seem quite inconsistent with the repeated declaration of the Government that controversial matters of party policy should not be legislated for pending the end of the war.' Specifically, it was objected that local authorities were given too many powers over denominational schools, Catholic parents might be compelled to send their children to non-Catholic schools; there was no right of appeal against decisions of the Board of Education.[165] A Standing Committee, comprising the four Archbishops and Catholic MPs, was established to watch the progress of the Bill.[166]

Opposition to the Bill lacked the unity and coherence which characterised the Catholic position in 1906. 'They wanted one settled policy. One could not pick up any of the Catholic papers without realising that the Catholic body was not properly organised upon this very educational Bill. There was one policy and another policy advocated.'[167] Many blamed Bourne. He simply did not share the vehemence of his Northern colleagues. Archbishop Whiteside of Liverpool was normally to be counted among the moderates—but not on this occasion. 'I am convinced that a number of its provisions and the whole spirit of the Bill are such that they make the Bill quite unacceptable to the Catholic body. I am equally convinced that if the powers granted by the Bill to the Board of Education and to the local education authorities become the law of the land, it will mean the gradual extinction of the Catholic and of the non-provided schools of the country ... You will ask what is to be the means of defeating this Bill ... : passive resistance on a gigantic scale.'[168]

Bourne did not see it that way. He trusted Fisher's assurances. He accepted aspects of the proposals were problematic for Catholics—either in principle or in practice (usually on financial grounds). He preferred to rely on information given privately behind the scenes. 'Mr Fisher's Bill can make no progress unless and until the Government can find Parliamentary time for it, and I am assured by Lord Edmund Talbot, in strict confidence of course, that it will be very difficult to find such time this session. He also assures me definitely that there can be no urgency in the matter or any ground for real anxiety at present. It seems to me that it would be a waste of time to summon the standing committee until there is something definite to place before it.'[169]

The suggestion that he enjoyed access to privileged information not available to them further infuriated the other Bishops. (In fact, Bourne's information was correct. Fisher's first Bill was withdrawn in December 1917, and its successor in February 1918, so amendments might be incorporated.) The Northern Bishops became increasingly forthright in their criticism. 'It is due to our people that some declaration on the Bill should be made ... We can only judge Mr Fisher's intentions, not by his views privately conveyed, but by his Bill. Our Catholics want an authoritative judgment on its face value. We cannot put them off by telling them that Your Eminence is going to have an interview with Mr Fisher next month.'[170]

These sentiments were forwarded to Rome. The Bishop of Salford told Gasquet that in September 1917 the Bill had been condemned by all the Bishops, who 'wanted to issue a pronouncement, as all our clergy and people were anxiously expecting us to do. But the Cardinal simply blocked us; he insisted on his own private negotiations with Fisher.'[171] This was presented to the Pope, who even adopted Casartelli's phraseology in a wounding letter sent to the Cardinal. 'We are told that public opinion in England, especially among Catholics, is very much engaged by the Fisher Bill, which, if approved in its current form, would be the ruin of denominational schools. We have similarly been told that at the last Bishops' Conference, the priests and people awaited new and rousing guidance from their pastors ... This guidance was lacking.'[172]

Was this fair? Bourne had suffered from protracted periods of ill health at this time. His relations with the rest of the hierarchy were damaged by their spectacular row over diocesan divisions in the spring of 1917. This should not have been allowed, however, to affect the Catholic position *vis-à-vis* the Government's educational policy. Nor is there any real evidence that, by themselves, these factors did that. Bourne was always offended by the suggestion that he failed to consult his brother Bishops. On this issue, as others, there is plenty of evidence that he was willing to meet and receive their views. The Bishops were more justified, however, when they complained that their views were not taken into account. Bourne listened, but he was quite prepared to take a different course of action if he felt circumstances justified it. And he believed that to be so in his dealings with Fisher.

He put up a spirited defence of his action to the Pope, giving a more objective account than Casartelli. Bourne held that Fisher's proposals 'contained some very worthwhile reforms and that only the details harmed denominational schools.' He had acted with the unanimous agreement of the other Bishops in writing 'a private but official letter in the name of the whole hierarchy,' to which Fisher replied by saying that 'his proposal had been badly put together, that he was ready to modify it.' This Bourne communicated to the Bishops, allowing Whiteside to take matters forward with Fisher in Bourne's absence. Whiteside himself 'said publicly that the concerns had been dispelled, and that Mr Fisher was really our friend.' Bourne made reference to amendments already conceded, and others they hoped to secure. He then made the valid point, that had Catholics simply condemned Fisher's proposals 'without distinguishing the reforms as a whole and the administrative details, our enemies would have strongly attacked us saying the Catholics, and only the Catholics, were the enemies of educational reform, because there is plenty of support for Mr Fisher's reforms, even among the supporters of denominational schools.' He concluded by regretting that Casartelli was unduly influenced by extremists in the Salford Catholic Federation.[173] As so often, Rome agreed with the last prelate who had spoken. Bourne cannot have been entirely mollified by the Cardinal Secretary of State's reply assuring him that the Pope 'approves fully of your wise manner of action in this delicate circumstance.'[174]

Although a little more effort and charm might have been expended convincing them of the fact, Bourne appreciated more than other Bishops that they were no longer fighting the battles of 1906. He was also deeply conscious of the effect upon national opinion (so soon after the Dublin Easter Rising) were Catholics to organise 'passive resistance on a gigantic scale' as the outcome of the First World War hung in the balance. Casartelli might mock Bourne for 'donning a gas-helmet at the front' in France and 'lunching with General Haig,'[175] but, of the two Bishops, there is no doubt which was closer to the national mood—and the average Catholic soldier in the trenches. Another change since 1906 was the emergence of an articulate professional body representing Catholic teachers. Casartelli resented the support they gave the proposals. 'The Catholic opponents of the Bill are entitled to their views, but they must surely give some little credit for discrimination and knowledge to those of their co-religionists who have refused to be stampeded into futile and unreasonable hostility and to see the cloven hoof in every attempt to better the education of the country.' Then, Bourne was not as isolated among the hierarchy as the Bishop of Salford suggested. Bishop Ward of Brentwood wrote, 'Personally I am exceedingly pleased that no drastic step has been taken in opposition to the Bill.'[176] Bishop Dunn of Nottingham agreed with Bourne that specifically Catholic questions such as denominational education should not be pressed in the 1918 General Election.[177]

Earlier educational battles had focused on the elementary schools, but McKenna's administrative regulations preventing public money being used for new secondary schools continued to rankle deeply with Catholics. After a 'very satisfactory' interview with the Cardinal, Fisher promised 'to use personal influence to get the secondary regulations changed.'[178] A year later new regulations were introduced offering substantive redress. A grievance was ended 'which has long proved an obstacle in the way of Catholic secondary education ... For this we owe a debt of gratitude ... to the educational broadmindedness and determination to do justice of Mr Fisher.'[179] Within three years the number of Catholic secondary schools receiving public funding increased by 50%.[180] However much others disapproved, the Cardinal's quiet diplomacy produced results.

Where it did not, Bourne was prepared to use other means. Fisher's second Education Bill incorporated certain points favourable to Catholics, but concerns remained as to whether parents would be forced to send children to non-Catholic schools and whether denominational secondary and continuation schools would receive equality of funding. Bourne invited the hierarchy to Archbishop's House on 8 February 1918 to discuss these matters. His approach is discernible in the statement produced by that meeting: 'It is the constant desire of the Bishops to cooperate by every means in their power in all projects for the real educational progress of the country, and it is with the purpose of being able to make that cooperation as close and cordial as possible that they feel it necessary to call attention to the need of further amendment.'[181] At the same time the publication of the Bishops' 18 Points contained in that statement gave Catholics in the country the guidance they sought. Bourne lamented the loss of the Irish MPs, but he used others, such as Sir Mark Sykes, to ensure Catholic interests were represented in the Commons.

As the Bill neared the end of its parliamentary procedure without the amendments the Bishops sought, Bourne did not allow his close relationship with Fisher to prevent firmer action being taken. He saw the failure to make public funds available for Catholic continuation schools as a 'manifestly unfair departure from Fisher's original pledge to respect the 1902 dual system. This 'made his Bill highly contentious' and, therefore, a breach of the wartime party political truce.[182] The Cardinal called a meeting of the Bishops on 5 July 1918 which agreed to make a private appeal to both Lloyd George and Fisher. In the event of an unsatisfactory answer, the Cardinal 'was empowered to take the extreme step of calling on the Cabinet to withdraw the Bill.'[183]

Bourne saw Fisher later that same day, but failed to achieve any further concession.[184] A letter to the Prime Minister led to Lloyd George's intervention; the Education Minister met the Cardinal and Lord Edmund Talbot again. Fisher declined once more to offer public funding for Catholic continuation schools, but instead suggested a conscience clause which meant Catholic parents did not have to send their children to non-Catholic schools. Talbot thought 'we have every reason to be satisfied with this.' He congratulated Bourne on his statesmanlike approach. 'I am, however, very glad Your Eminence wrote as you did to the Prime Minister. If things should not work out as I anticipate, then your letter, voicing the views of the Bishops, could be used in great effect in demanding reform, and with none the less force because Your Eminence and their Lordships refrained from giving public expression to your views at a moment of great national strain.'[185]

And, with this conscience clause, Fisher's Bill received the Royal Assent on 8 August 1918. Could more have been obtained had Bourne adopted a more aggressive policy? It seems unlikely. After all, 'the many meetings of protest against the Bill' in the North of England failed to ensure that Catholics gained all their demands. Bourne was more realistic in his assessment of what the Government and the country would tolerate in time of war. The *Tablet* expressed significant satisfaction with the measure in its final form.[186] (In fact, Catholics suffered no practical discrimination under the Act. The economic downturn after the First World War led to the Government dropping Fisher's innovation of continuation schools.)

Fisher always intended to implement reform in two stages. Having secured the 1918 Act, he began in autumn 1919 to sound out interested parties on the 'possible basis for a national settlement of the religious question.'[187] He met with Anglicans and Nonconformists, but found Archbishop Davidson reluctant to commit himself until the views of the Catholics were known. Fisher met Bourne on 27 January 1920 to discuss the religious settlement when, he thought, the Cardinal 'seems inclined to take it, but reserved judgment.'[188]

In March the Education Minister outlined his desired basis of agreement. He pondered: 'Was it possible to adopt as a first principle that the appointment, promotion and dismissal of all teachers in public elementary schools should be in the hands of the local education authority?' In return for the free use of non-provided school premises, the local authority would maintain those premises. The local authority would also be obliged to provide the specific religious instruction desired by parents 'in school hours by teachers suitable and willing to give it,' subject to the parent's right to withdraw their child from such instruction.[189] It is a little puzzling if Fisher thought Catholics would ever consent to participate in a national system on this basis.

He had already met with their representatives on 12 February. 'Bishop Bidwell, Monsignor Brown and Gilbert of the LCC meet me on the proposals for religious peace which they say will be unacceptable to the Catholics.'[190] That can hardly have come as a surprise. Catholics were not going to surrender the education of their children to teachers who did not believe what they were teaching. The public response was unambiguous. Brown was adamant, 'It is nothing more or less than a knife to the throat of Catholic schools. You pass into the hands of the butcher. He may cut your throat today or tomorrow, but cut it he most certainly will.'[191] The *Tablet* held there was no guarantee of a specifically Catholic education, doubting 'that the right of entry into Council schools [to give religious instruction] is any sufficient compensation for the surrender he invites us to make.'[192]

As with the earlier negotiations with Fisher, Bourne was absent again for three months—through illness and then business in Rome. Amigo fretted that something needed to be done, and wrote to Ilsely and Whiteside asking them to convene the hierarchy in Bourne's absence.[193] But Ilsley was also unwell and Whiteside disputed the urgency on the matter.

In May the Catholic Education Council condemned Fisher's proposals. The hierarchy agreed to publish the Council's resolutions, and, when his views were sought, Bourne made no difficulty about this. 'Letter only just received. Have not seen resolution. Gladly approve any action you think necessary.'[194] Those resolutions formed the basis of the Bishops' declaration: 'There exists in the country a large number of parents who earnestly desire for their children an education based on definite religious faith and principle ... it would be an injustice to deprive them of it ... There is also in the country a large number of teachers with definite religious convictions, who deem it an honour and a privilege to teach in schools of the character just described ... It is fully admitted that there are many parents and teachers who have quite other views ... Mr Fisher's proposals fail completely to recognise the sharp distinction that exists between these two categories of parents and teachers ... We call upon all our Catholic organisations to take every opportunity of placing the real issue clearly before the country. We feel satisfied that Mr Fisher has at heart the true educational progress of the nation, and that he will welcome the fullest discussion of his proposals.'[195]

Those proposals were contained in a Bill introduced by the Conservative MP Thomas Davies on 1 November 1921. Once more Bourne was criticised for not leading a more vigorous defence of the schools. Once more his attitude appeared justified by the outcome of events. He refused to rush into unnecessary pronouncements. He pointed out that this was only a private Member's Bill. 'An "agreed Bill" was a measure put forward without any opposition. If that should happen the whole situation would be changed. But, that is not going to happen! ... Therefore he was not at all alarmed about this Bill.'[196] Bourne's leadership was based on a more accurate assessment of the situation than his critics. As he had predicted, the conferences between Anglicans and Nonconformists 'ultimately came to an inconclusive termination, as no agreement could be reached on the precise nature of the *definite* religious teaching to be given in the schools ... The Davies Bill was at no time a real danger. The Coalition Government then in power would not have run the risk of endeavouring to carry such a measure into law without the certainty of practical agreement ... Our attitude was well known from the beginning, and would have been manifested still more clearly had there been any real necessity so to declare it.'[197]

The attempt to abolish the dual system by consensus came to an end with the replacement of Lloyd George's Coalition Government by Bonar Law's Conservative Ministry in November 1922. Even more effectively it was killed off by the Geddes Axe and the financial retrenchment that followed the post-War boom. Catholic schools had not only survived, but, as Bourne stated, the mood of the greater part of the nation was now far more sympathetic. Denominational education would be a part of the national educational system for many years to come.

Trevelyan's Bills

The 1926 Hadow Report recommended the separation of secondary and elementary schools. Again, the Catholic response was largely based on financial considerations. They opposed the suggestion unless public money was given them to build new schools. There were also fears that the connection between the priest and the children of his parish would be lost.

In discussing the implementation of the Hadow Report, Bourne found the Education Minister, Lord Eustace Percy, amenable and lost no opportunity to praise him. But, although Percy talked favourably about parental rights and equal funding for denominational schools, some Catholics queried, a little unfairly, the tangible results. There was unease at Bourne's speech at the Albert Hall on the eve of the 1929 Election. 'One Party [ie the Conservatives] had already almost fully accepted our claims to equal treatment as between "provided" and "non-provided" schools ... One party has answered our questions very frankly and very fully, and if you analyse these answers you will see that the party has adopted in the main the principles for which Catholics stand. They have given definite promises and pledges, foreshadowing real sympathetic treatment of the vital matters which affect Catholic schools. The other parties, as far as their leaders are concerned, appear to be—and I regret to state the fact—singularly shy and reticent.'¹⁹⁸ In the past Bourne had been criticised for not giving a clear lead to voters. Now he backed a loser. Amigo expressed a general concern, 'I fear that H E will have little or no influence with the present Government as they don't trust him. He was too much for Eustace Percy.'¹⁹⁹

That Labour Government had been in office less than two months when Sir Charles Trevleyan, the Education Minister, announced proposals to raise the school-leaving age to 15. The familiar routine was repeated: reform was tabled; public funds were not available for the required expansion of non-provided schools; therefore Catholics opposed reform. It was not only Catholics who opposed, however, and Trevelyan was obliged to re-think.

Before introducing a Second Education Bill, Trevelyan approached the Cardinal. Both showed a disposition to flexibility. The Government offered public funding to help Catholic schools comply with the proposals. In return, the Church was asked to surrender her right to appoint teachers—subject to a veto on religious grounds. The Bishops considered whether the proposal 'infringed any Catholic educational principle.' The majority thought that it did not, but the sacrifice of such an important right required clarification of the gains accruing to Catholic schools and sufficient guarantees as to retention of their Catholic identity.²⁰⁰ Trevelyan thanked Bourne for his 'spirit of accommodation,'²⁰¹ and continued negotiations with him, other church leaders, education authorities and teachers.

In spring 1930 Trevelyan published his White Paper, the basis of draft legislation. The clarification and guarantees sought by the Church were lacking. In the *Tablet's* opinion, it was Runciman and Fisher all over again. 'What object Sir Charles Trevelyan had in publishing the paper, when apparently he had secured agreement with nobody, passes our comprehension.'²⁰² There was frustration that Treasury grants were to be available to provided schools with no strings attached, while non-provided schools had to comply with stringent conditions; any grants were available only for existing, not future, schools; there were concerns whether the Church had an adequate veto over teachers' appointments.

Bourne got to work with his auxiliary, Bishop Manuel Bidwell. His underlying policy had not changed in a generation. He made it clear that the Church's attitude was not one of hostile obstruction, but a desire for amendments which might form the basis of 'a satisfactory national settlement.'²⁰³ At their request, Bidwell addressed a gathering of 126 Labour MPs in the Commons in May 1930. A few days later he and the Cardinal met with three Catholic Labour MPs. Bourne 'pointed out that the Bill in its present form was quite unacceptable to Catholics, for while control of the teacher might be a matter for discussion in a scheme for a satisfactory national settlement, no question of control could be considered in return for a restricted and temporary grant offered in the present Bill.' He urged the MPs to seek specific amendments. While Trevelyan was prepared to concede minor points, he would not give way on the fundamental issue of the control of teachers.²⁰⁴ Catholics were urged to contact their MPs pressing the case for equal treatment of both types of school. 150,000 Catholics demonstrated in Liverpool, urged on by Archbishop Downey: 'I ask you, men and women of the North, to rise up in your might and reject this Bill as an insidious attack on the Faith that is dearer to us than life itself!'²⁰⁵

A supposedly agreed piece of legislation proved to be nothing of the kind. Almost 100 amendments were proposed. Labour MPs were unhappy about the amount of maintenance allowances and the suggestion of means-testing. Some Conservatives opposed any increase in the school-leaving age. Some Nonconformists were still unreconciled to the principle of Church schools receiving public money. At the end of June the Press announced that the Bill was to be withdrawn. Bourne rejected the claim that it was the fault of Catholics. Trevelyan had, he maintained, insisted on the public control of teachers before a permanent, equitable settlement had been agreed. 'The Bill failed because the Government would not see the obvious issue, and it is not fair to attach responsibility to Catholics.' He also felt raising the school-leaving age and obliging Catholics to pay for school extensions was simply a means of transferring to others the cost of reducing the number of unemployed.²⁰⁶

A third attempt to raise the school-leaving age in the autumn of 1930 received the same Catholic response. 'The Bishops re-affirmed their resolution of 14 November 1929 that they "are of opinion that any grant given to provided schools to enable them to meet the requirements of the Board of Education should in equity be given also to the non-provided schools." They moreover declared their constant willingness to consider different methods of appointment of Catholic teachers, if the proposals of the Government should justify them doing so.'²⁰⁷ Bourne, Bishop Mostyn and the MPs, John Scurr and Francis Blundell, represented

Catholics at an Education Conference on 13–14 January 1931. A surprising degree of consensus emerged. Public funds would pay for 50–75% of works required by the current legislation; local authorities could pay for up to 100% of future improvements; teachers were to be appointed and dismissed by the local authority; a variety of arrangements were permitted to give the Church protection in respect of teachers giving religious instruction. With the exception of the Nonconformists, all attending the Conference 'thought that these proposals could be presented to their various interests with a likelihood of acceptance.'[208]

Many thought this the most propitious moment between 1902 and 1944 to achieve a general educational settlement. However, once again a settlement proved elusive. This time it appeared Catholics might be culpable. John Scurr had already tabled an amendment postponing the implementation of Trevelyan's Third Education Bill until legislation was enacted providing for the payment from public funds of the costs incurred by non-provided schools in meeting the Bill's requirements. Regardless of the optimism existing after the Conference, Scurr allowed his amendment to proceed. With the support of all 35 Labour Catholic MPs, it was passed, effectively wrecking the Bill. Even although the Bill still completed its Third Commons Reading, the Lords took the Government's defeat on the Scurr amendment as its cue to throw out the Bill on 18 February, specifically stating, possibly disingenuously, they were helping Catholics in the process.

What was going on? Were Catholics reneging on their position—or at least not allowing further negotiations the opportunity to succeed? The praise of the *Tablet*, his own support for Scurr after his ostracism by the Labour Party, suggests that Bourne approved his parliamentary tactics. He was certainly not about to concede Catholic responsibility for the debacle. The *Tablet* alleged it was the Government who altered its stance after the Conference, taking back guarantees offered in connection with the appointment of teachers. Lord FitzAlan (the former Lord Edmund Talbot) liaised closely with the Cardinal on matters of public policy. His statement suggests that Catholics were not out to wreck the legislation. Rather, FitzAlan pleaded for delay, 'expressing bewilderment that the Government were proceeding with the Bill without allowing the [Lords] to see the details of the Supplementary Bill [giving public funding to non-provided schools] which had to follow … Why, in the circumstances, Lord Ponsonby, who was in charge of the Bill, persisted in forcing a division, we cannot appreciate.'²⁰⁹ The Cardinal sought to spread the blame even wider. 'To my mind, the Conservative leadership of the House of Lords on the occasion of the recent Education Bill was deplorably inefficient, and it was unredeemed by any efficient Anglican action. A great opportunity of establishing a just principle was lost by political manoeuvring.'²¹⁰

He was right on the latter point. There were to be no further educational developments of significance in his lifetime. Trevelyan resigned shortly after the Bill's defeat. The general financial crisis which overtook the country meant there was precious little public funding available for any type of school. By the end of the year the Labour Government was replaced by a National Government committed to austerity. The Trevelyan Bill ended in a muddle from which no one emerges with particular credit. Once again, however, it must be queried whether genuine consensus had been achieved on the details of the proposals, and one has to wonder whether the legislation would have survived the financial and political upheavals of the following months.

Schools in General—and a Proposal in Particular

Bourne made one contribution to the educational debates of his day which looks like text book Thatcherism. He genuinely thought he might have achieved the resolution of the religious difficulties surrounding education with the voucher scheme he announced at the Manchester Catholic Congress of 1926 and which he continued to pursue over the coming years.

The genesis of the proposal might have been suggestions made during the debate surrounding the 1908 Education Bill. The Press had advocated adopting the position of certain Canadian provinces whereby rates were allocated towards the funding of schools according to the wish of the ratepayer. At first, Bourne and Redmond were enthusiastic. Bourne told Catholics in Leeds, 'Give us the Canadian system. Let us allocate our rates. Relieve us from the obligation of paying for schools which we can never use, and then we shall not ask you for very much in the way of Government grant.'²¹¹ However, both he and the Government seemed to have come quickly to appreciate that 'there were serious technical difficulties in doing so.'²¹² However, Bourne never forgot the underlying principle.

Bourne claimed to approach an old problem from a new perspective. Instead of starting with the State or the school, paramount importance should be given to the child and parental rights. Every parent unable to pay for private education should be given a voucher equivalent to the average amount it cost to educate a child locally. That voucher could be used at the parent's school of choice, provided or non-provided. Leaving the parent to choose removed the acrimony from the political debate. The State's interest was protected by a right of inspection. Ancillary advantages would be increased parental interest in education and the encouragement of competition between schools.[213]

The scheme might have had a greater chance of success in the 1920s than in the 1980s, when the State's role in education was more firmly embedded in the national consciousness. But at the time many Catholics felt that the suggestion was being sprung upon them without consultation.[214] The hierarchy conceded that Bourne's plan 'would not be unacceptable to them'—hardly a ringing endorsement.[215] Elsewhere there was a similar lack of enthusiasm. It was urged that the scheme was impractical on financial and administrative grounds. Bourne felt that he had produced the statistics to counter these arguments, but no one was listening. Even Lord Eustace Percy respectfully told him to go away and draft his 'suggestion in the form of a statement of the principle to which legislation should seek to conform.'[216]

Perhaps it was an idea before its time, perhaps the Cardinal was too radical. In any event, there was no interest in such an overhaul of the educational system which presumably was perceived to be for the sole benefit of denominational schools.

More generally, it was sometimes said that the Church under Bourne concentrated too exclusively on elementary schools; secondary education did not make the advances it ought in this period. No one disputed the facts, or the need for massive improvement. In 1923 across England there were '1,115 grant-aided secondary schools, of which only 66 are Catholic schools. But of these 66 Catholic schools—and this is the deplorable and distressing fact—only 14 were for boys.'[217] Secondary education in the State sector was still in the early stages of its development. The proposals put forward by Fisher and the Hadow Report only gained full acceptance in Butler's 1944 Education Act. Nevertheless, Catholic children, especially boys, were clearly at a significant disadvantage even at this stage.

It is unfair, however, to attribute responsibility to Bourne. Of course the Church gave priority to her elementary schools. When the vast majority of her children were in elementary schools, and the very existence of those schools sometimes in doubt, it is unrealistic to expect attention to be focused on secondary education. Where were the resources to come from? McKenna's Regulations had deprived Catholic secondary schools of public funding. Bourne strove long and, ultimately, successfully to overturn them.

Bourne certainly acknowledged the problem. 'Many more such secondary schools are needed. In no direction is still further progress more urgent.'[218] Couldn't he have promoted this more actively? He identified the catalyst for secondary education as 'a prime mover,' by which he usually meant an energetic priest on the ground—rather than the Bishop or the Diocese.[219] This might surprise us, but education was viewed as primarily a local affair, even by Catholic educationalists keen to develop secondary schools. The solution was seen to lie in the hands of the local deanery, priests and people.[220] One can only criticise Bourne for being a man of his time.

The other general criticism levelled was the failure to achieve a satisfactory permanent resolution of the whole educational problem. Some contemporaries and historians have felt the Church might have received a better deal by accepting the proposals of Birrell, Fisher or Trevelyan than she was doing under the 1902 Act or was to do under the 1944 Act. There is no substantive evidence to suggest that this is the case. Nor do we know that agreements were in fact obtainable in 1906, 1920 or 1931. Too often 'agreed' proposals were published before acceptance had been gained for the detailed provisions. It was not only Catholics who found the proposals difficult and who held out against them. Education Ministers so often appeared to be attempting to reconcile the irreconcilable. Time and again, Bourne showed himself willing to compromise—but not at any cost. He was a realist. It is worth repeating his words of 1906. What his contemporaries and posterity 'must really bear in mind that it is not a question of what we shall accept but of what we may be able to obtain, and that the situation is one of extreme delicacy.'[221]

In that situation of extreme delicacy Bourne achieved his objective—the continued existence of Catholic schools. That was not a foregone conclusion. To a large measure due to his skill and tact, often in the face of the opposition of both governments and some Catholics, those schools remained an integral part of the national educational system receiving public funding. It is a situation which many overseas Catholics viewed with considerable envy.

Of course, a place in the national system had to be balanced against the overriding need for the schools to remain genuinely Catholic. All Bourne's efforts were conducted with this in mind. He stated this at its most basic in 1929 and speaks as urgently to us today: 'What is it to be a Christian? It is to know and believe that Jesus Christ is truly God as well as truly man; that He came into and lived in the world to teach men to know God and to know themselves, and to fulfil their duty to God and to their fellow creatures. Are these things, which are quite fundamental to Christianity, being definitely taught not as mere theory or possible explanation but as facts accepted by all Christians, with which it is their duty to bring their lives in harmony? Is the duty of prayer and dependence on God definitely taught as the outcome of these facts of Christianity? For to make of a boy or a girl a Christian it is not enough to speak of Christ as the best and the wisest of men. He is not a Christian who does not accept Christ as God, however much he may admire and respect, and even accept His teaching in all other things. A Moslem or a pagan can do so equally, but does not thereby become a Christian.'[222]

Universities

Bourne's interest in university education pre-dated his time in Westminster. As Rector of Wonersh and Bishop of Southwark, he felt that all seminarians should firstly be formed as priests in the seminary, then the brightest should pursue a university degree to qualify them to teach in seminary and to address 'the intellectual needs of the day.'[223] He was happy for student priests to undertake further studies either at a Catholic university overseas or at the English universities, given Rome's decision in 1895 to permit Catholic students to attend non-Catholic universities, subject to certain conditions.

Bourne maintained that the clergy should be educated to 'the same level' as the laity.[224] When, thanks to the Duke of Norfolk's generosity, St Edmund's House for clerical students was opened in Cambridge in 1896, Bourne asked that Southwark students might be included as potential beneficiaries. Norfolk did more than that; he placed Bourne on the Board of St Edmund's.[225] Bourne arranged with the University of London for his seminarians to study for their external degrees while at Wonersh.

Bourne was anxious that Catholics should not simply be passive recipients of what the existing English universities had to offer. Rather, he wanted Catholics to contribute to the intellectual life of the nation.

'They ought in the near future to furnish to the Catholic Church in this country the men and women still so greatly needed, who will have the knowledge, zeal, and capacity enabling them to act as leaders, and to take their place in due course in the local and national life of the country ... Intellectual culture, reinforced and enhanced by sound Catholic faith, life, and practice, will be invaluable assets for the well-being of the nation.'[226] He saw the return of the Dominicans to Oxford with the opening of Blackfriars in 1921 as a first step in this process.[227]

With Catholics allowed to study at Oxford and Cambridge, the Cardinal recognised that the establishment of an exclusively Catholic university in England was probably a non-starter. Very well, he appealed, let there be a Catholic faculty at Oxford or Cambridge—preferably both—to allow clerical and lay students to obtain pontifical degrees in Theology, Philosophy and Canon Law. He invited a benefactor to come forward to endow such a faculty with £100,000 to buy land, build lecture halls and fund lectureships. Let the lecturers be 'the best men that we possess—seculars or regulars—without restriction to any particular order or congregation.'[228] It was not to be, but no one can accuse Cardinal Bourne of not entertaining and encouraging high aspirations.

Notes

1. Catholic Hierarchy, Oscott, 1852.
2. FAB, Hampstead, 29 October 1916, *Tablet*, 4 November 1916, p. 600.
3. A. Birrell, Bristol North election campaign, 2 January 1906, *Tablet*, 6 January 1906, p. 34.
4. FAB, CTS Conference, Birmingham, 26 September 1904, *Times*, 1 October 1904, pp. 523–525.
5. FAB, CTS Conference, Newport, 22 September 1902, *Tablet*, 27 September 1902, pp. 501–502.
6. J. Murphy, *Church, State and Schools in Britain, 1800–1970* (London: Routledge & Kegan Paul, 1971), p. 84.
7. *Ibid.*, p. 88.
8. Oldmeadow, *Francis Cardinal Bourne*, i, p. 273.
9. FAB to Norfolk, 22 May 1906, AAW, Bo. I/126; AAW, Bo. IV/19.
10. FAB, Pastoral Letter, 29 December 1903.
11. FAB, CTS Annual Conference, Blackburn, 25 September 1905, *Tablet*, 30 September 1905, p. 558.
12. *Tablet*, 22 April 1905, p. 601; 27 May 1905, p. 801.
13. FAB to Norfolk, 6 December 1904, AAW, Bo. I/126.

14 Minutes of Bishops' Meeting, 14 February 1905.
15 *Tablet*, 1 April 1905, p. 481.
16 Norfolk to FAB, 3 January 1906, AAW, Bo. V/14a.
17 *Tablet*, 24 October 1903, p. 648.
18 ACA, Talbot to Norfolk, 3 April 1904.
19 FAB, Leeds Town Hall, 5 August 1905, *Tablet*, 12 August 1905, p. 265.
20 FAB, Newcastle Town Hall, 29 June 1905, *Tablet*, 8 July 1905, p. 66.
21 Hierarchy's Letter to Clergy, 19 December 1905.
22 FAB, Circular to Westminster Clergy, 26 December 1905.
23 J. Redmond, MP, Manchester, 19 March 1904, *Tablet*, 26 March 1904, p. 500.
24 Methodist Sunday School General Secretary, *Sunday School Journal*, (1906), cited Moore, *Pitmen, Preachers and Politics*, p. 107.
25 Editorial, *Tablet*, 3 February 1906, p. 161.
26 Dr Clifford, letter to the *Daily News*, 1906, cited Oldmeadow, *Francis Cardinal Bourne*, i, p. 281.
27 Editorial, *Tablet*, 14 July 1906, p. 45.
28 Birrell, Towcester, 20 January 1906, *Tablet*, 27 January 1906, p. 150.
29 FAB, Edinburgh, 17 June 1931, *Tablet*, 20 June 1931, pp. 826–827.
30 T. Healy, MP in a pre-1906 conversation with Lloyd George and Rev. H. Price Hughes.
31 T. P. O'Connor to Redmond, 28 January 1906, cited D. W. Miller, *Church, State & Nation in Ireland, 1898–1921* (Pittsburgh: University of Pittsburgh Press, 1973), p. 149.
32 *Tablet*, 3 February 1906, p. 157.
33 *Times*, 6 February 1906.
34 Clifford, *Morning Post*, March 1906.
35 Burton, Diary, 9 April 1906, CDA.
36 *Times*, 10 April 1906.
37 Birrell, Commons, 9 April 1906, *Tablet*, 14 April 1906, p. 591.
38 Birrell, Committee Stage, Commons, 3 July 1906, *Tablet*, 7 July 1906, p. 2.
39 Third Reading, 12 December 1906, *Tablet*, 15 December 1906, p. 919.
40 Birrell, Commons, 9 April 1906, *Tablet*, 14 April 1906, p. 592.
41 FAB to hierarchy, 7 February 1906, AAW, Bo. V/14a.
42 Redmond to J. Dillon, 3 April 1906 (copy), NLI, RP, MS 15,182/10.
43 A Scottish convert, who was appointed Amigo's Vicar-General in 1904 and Auxiliary Bishop of Southwark in 1924.
44 FAB to hierarchy, 7 February 1906, AAW, Bo. V/14a.
45 FAB to Norfolk, 22 May 1906, AAW, Bo. I/126.
46 H. A. L. Fisher. Diary, 5 July 1918, OUL, 9/109.
47 *Daily News*, April 1906.

48 Redmond Memorandum, 'Interview with Archb. Bourne,' 16 February 1906, NLI, RP, MS 15,172.
49 J. Boland, MP, to FAB, 10 May 1905, AAW, Bo. I/126.
50 FAB to Redmond, 15 July 1906; Redmond to FAB, 16 July 1906 (copy), NLI, RP, MS 15,172.
51 Redmond to FAB, 4 December 1906 (copy); FAB to Redmond, 8 December 1906, NLI, RP, MS 15,172.
52 G. Lane Fox to FAB, 14 May 1906, AAW, Bo. V/14d.
53 H. Belloc to FAB, 16 April 1906, AAW, Bo. V/14d.
54 Bishop L. Casartelli, *Manchester Guardian*, April 1906.
55 *Tablet*, 20 January 1906, p. 106.
56 Cahill to FAB, 13 February 1906, AAW, Bo. V/14a.
57 FAB Pastoral, Quinquagesima Sunday 1906.
58 Acta, Bishops' Meeting, 25 April 1906, AAW, Bo. V/14a.
59 FAB at CTS AGM, Cathedral Hall, 26 April 1906, *Times*, 27 April 1906.
60 E. Foulkes to Redmond, 5 May 1906, NLI, RP, MS 15,246/6.
61 Redmond to United Irish League, Liverpool, 17 March 1907, *Tablet*, 23 March 1907, p. 470.
62 FAB to Organising Committee, 23 March 1906, AAW, Bo. V/14a.
63 Circular, Organising Committee to Clergy of Westminster and Southwark, 3 April 1906.
64 FAB, Opening Speech, Albert Hall, 5 May 1906.
65 FAB to Norfolk, 6 January 1907 (copy), AAW, Bo. I/178/12.
66 *Daily News*, cited Oldmeadow, *Francis Cardinal Bourne*, i, p. 301.
67 R. Morant to FAB, 6 May 1906, AAW, Bo. V/14a.
68 Cited *Tablet*, 12 May 1906, p. 755.
69 Ripon to FAB, 7 May 1906, AAW, Bo. V/14a.
70 Minutes of Meeting of the Bishops, 14 May 1906, AAW, Bo. V/14d.
71 NLI, RP, MS 15,172.
72 FAB to Redmond, 24 June 1906, NLI, RP, MS 15,172.
73 Brown to Redmond, 10 May 1906, NLI, RP, MS 15,172.
74 Brown speech to Catholic League of South London, 30 May 1906, *Tablet*, 2 June 1906, p. 863.
75 FAB to Redmond, 15 June 06, NLI, RP, MS 15,172.
76 Redmond, Commons, 25 June 1906, *Tablet*, p. 1031.
77 Redmond to Canon Rooney, 22 May 1906, (copy), NLI, RP, MS 15,246/6.
78 FAB to Wilkinson, 27 May 1906 (draft), AAW, Bo. V/14d.
79 FAB memo, 19 June 1906, AAW, Bo. V, 14d.
80 *Tablet*, 19 May 1906, p. 762.
81 FAB to Redmond, 9 July 1906, NLI, RP, MS 15,172.

82 FAB to Redmond, 1 August 1906, RP, NLI, MS 15,172.
83 FAB, Harrow Road, 26 October 1906, *Tablet*, 3 November 1906, p. 714.
84 Joint Pastoral, 21 September 1906.
85 Circular, T. W. Hunter, Secretary of Westminster Diocesan Association of Voluntary Schools to Peers, 3 November 1906.
86 Editorial, *Tablet*, 17 November 1906, p. 761.
87 Norfolk, Third Reading in Lords, 6 December 1906, *Tablet*, 15 December 1906, p. 955.
88 Redmond to FAB, 30 November 1906, AAW, Bo. V/14c/76.
89 FAB to Redmond, 1 December 1906, NLI, RP, MS 15,172.
90 Brown to FAB, 1 December 1906, AAW, Bo. V/14c/77.
91 FAB to Redmond, 1 December 1906, NLI, RP, MS 15,172; Redmond to FAB, 2 December 1906, AAW, Bo. V/14c/82; Redmond to Birrell, 2 December 1906 (copy), NLI, RP, MS 15,169/1.
92 FAB to Redmond, 29 November 1906, NLI, RP, MS 15,172.
93 Redmond to FAB, 30 November 1906, AAW, Bo. V/14c/75.
94 Redmond to Dillon, 17 December 1906 (copy), NLI, RP, MS 15,182/13.
95 'Confidential' Bishops' Resolution, 4 December 1906, AAW, Bo. V/14c/83.
96 Ripon to Birrell, 10 December 1906, PRO, Ed. 24/111, file B.11, cited Miller, *Church, State & Nation in Ireland, 1898–1921*, p. 169.
97 Redmond to FAB, 12 December 1906, AAW, Bo. V/14c/89.
98 *Times*, 13 December 1906.
99 Bishop O'Dwyer, *Tablet*, 15 December 1906.
100 Redmond to Dillon, 17 December 1906 (copy), NLI, RP, MS 15,182/13.
101 FAB to Redmond, *Times*, 24 December 1906.
102 FAB to Norfolk, 6 January 1907 (copy), AAW, Bo. I/178/12.
103 Editorial, *Tablet*, 29 December 1906, p. 1001.
104 Canon Tynan to FAB, 21 December 1906, AAW, Bo. V/14c/103.
105 Norfolk to FAB, 2 January 1907, AAW, Bo. I/178/1.
106 Redmond, Commons, 20 December 1906, *Tablet*, 29 December 1906, p. 1031.
107 Norfolk to FAB, 2 January 1907, AAW, Bo. I/178/1; Norfolk to FAB and hierarchy, 2 January 1907, AAW, Bo. I/178/1.
108 FAB to Norfolk, 3 January 1907 (copy), AAW, Bo. I/178/3.
109 FAB to Norfolk, 6 January 1907 (copy), AAW, Bo. I/178/12; FAB to Norfolk, 10 January 1907, AAW, Bo. I/178/16; Norfolk to FAB, 12 January 1907, AAW, Bo. I/178/17; FAB to Norfolk, 18 January 1907 (copy), AAW, Bo. I/178/18.
110 Oldmeadow, *Francis Cardinal Bourne*, i, pp. 307–308.
111 FAB, CTS Annual Conference, Manchester, 20 September 1909, *Tablet*, 25 September 1909, p. 484.
112 FAB to Norfolk, 6 January 1907 (copy), AAW, Bo. I/178/12.
113 Burton to Norfolk, 3 January 1907, (copy), AAW, Bo. I/178/8.

114 Norfolk to FAB, 2 January 1907, AAW, Bo. I/178/1.
115 FAB to Norfolk, 6 January 1907 (copy), AAW, Bo. I/178/12.
116 Norfolk to FAB, 12 January 1907, AAW, Bo. I/178/17.
117 FAB to Norfolk, 18 January 1907 (copy), AAW, Bo. I/178/18.
118 Burton to Norfolk, 3 January 1907, (copy), AAW, Bo. I/178/8.
119 FAB memo to Ilsley, Burton and Casartelli, u/d [January 1907], AAW, Bo. I/178/11.
120 FAB to Norfolk, 6 January 1907 (copy), AAW, Bo. I/178/12.
121 Dillon, Wolverhampton, 17 March 1907, *Tablet*, 23 March 1907, p. 471.
122 Redmond to United Irish League, Liverpool, 17 March 1907, *Tablet*, 23 March 1907, p. 471.
123 Editorial, *Tablet*, 9 March 1907, p. 361.
124 Acta, Bishops' Meeting, 10 April 1907.
125 FAB to Redmond, 24 February 1907, NLI, RP, MS 15,172; Redmond to FAB, 26 February 1907 (copy), NLI, RP, MS 15,172.
126 FAB, CTS AGM, 12 April 1907, *Times*, 13 April 1907.
127 Acta, Bishops' Meeting, 11 April 1907.
128 FAB to Gotti, 25 April 1907, SCPF, 102/1907, f. 398, r. 86 et seq.
129 McKenna to Newcastle Liberals, 1 June 1907, *Tablet*, 8 June 1907, pp. 911–912.
130 McKenna, cited Oldmeadow, *Francis Cardinal Bourne*, i, p. 334.
131 Gilbert to WCF, 17 September 1911, *Tablet*, 23 September 1911, p. 512.
132 FAB, National Catholic Congress, Newcastle, 4 August 1911, *Tablet*, 12 August 1911, p. 244.
133 Redmond, Commons, *Tablet*, 20 July 1907, p. 102.
134 *Tablet*, 27 July 1907, pp. 130–131.
135 H. A. Asquith, Speech to Lancaster Liberals, *Tablet*, 18 January 1908, p. 84.
136 FAB, Spitalfields, 29 November 1907, *Tablet*, 7 December 1907, p. 911.
137 FAB, Highgate, 18 January 1908, *Tablet*, 25 January 1908, p. 150.
138 FAB, Hampstead Catholic Federation, 11 February 1908, *Tablet*, 15 February 1908, p. 262.
139 FAB, Leeds Catholic Federation, 25 February 1908, *Tablet*, 29 February 1908, p. 340.
140 Charles Russell to McKenna, 29 November 1907, AAW, Bo. I/181.
141 Gilbert to FAB, 6 March 1908, AAW, Bo. I/181.
142 FAB to Norfolk, 22 March 1908 (copy), AAW, Bo. V/14b.
143 Acta, Bishops' Meeting, 28 April 1908.
144 *Ibid.*
145 FAB to Norfolk, 22 March 1908 (copy), AAW, Bo. V/14b.
146 W. S. Churchill, cited *Tablet*, 2 May 1908, p. 713.
147 *Tablet*, 16 May 1908, p. 789.
148 Asquith, National Liberal Club dinner, 12 June 1908, *Tablet*, 20 June 1908, p. 989.

149 Brown to Burton, 31 December 1906, CDA, Burton Correspondence, 1905–06.
150 Runciman, Commons, 19 May 1908, *Tablet*, 23 May 1908, p. 801.
151 FAB, Catholic Education Council, 24 November 1908.
152 Asquith, Commons, 19 November 1908, *Tablet*, 21 November 1908, p. 799.
153 Hierarchy Meeting, 25 November 1908, *Times*, 26 November 1908.
154 Asquith, Commons, 4 December 1908, *Tablet*, 12 December 1908, p. 918.
155 FAB to Runciman, 19 November 1908, cited FAB, Clifton, 7 December 1908, *Tablet*, 12 December 1908, p. 951.
156 Balfour, Commons, 4 December 1908, *Tablet*, 12 December 1908, p. 918.
157 FAB, Clifton, 7 December 1908, *Tablet*, 12 December 1908, p. 952.
158 Asquith to Free Church General Committee, 27 October 1909, cited *Tablet*, 6 November 1909, p. 745.
159 Editorial, *Tablet*, 29 January 1910, p. 161.
160 Fisher to Lord FitzAlan, 1935, cited Oldmeadow, *Francis Cardinal Bourne*, ii, p. 145.
161 Fisher to FAB, 16 October 1917, AAW, Bo. I/16.
162 FAB Memo, AAW, Bo. V, 25a.
163 Editorial, *Tablet*, 25 August 1917, pp. 229–230.
164 Amigo to Ilsley, 28 September 1917, BAA, D3952.
165 FAB to Fisher, 26 September 1917 (copy), AAW, Bo. V/25a.
166 Acta of Meeting of the Bishops, 25 September 1917.
167 WCF Council Meeting, 7 January 1918, *Tablet*, 12 Jan 18, p. 52.
168 Whiteside to Catholic Young Men's Societies, September 1917, *Tablet*, 6 October 1917, p. 434.
169 FAB to Ilsley, 15 October 1917, AAW, Bo. V/25a.
170 Whiteside to FAB, 19 October 1917, AAW, Bo. V/25a.
171 Casartelli to Gasquet, 10 November 1917, DAA, Gasquet, 889.
172 Benedict XV to FAB, 20 January 1918, AAW, Roman Letters, Misc./99.
173 FAB to Benedict XV, 29 January 1918 (copy), AAW, Roman Letters, Misc./99.
174 Cardinal Gasparri to FAB, 24 February 1918, AAW, Roman Letters, Misc./99.
175 Casartelli to Whiteside, 6 November 1917, SDA, Casartelli Letters, 4501–4600, Box 162; Casartelli to Gasquet, 10 November 1917, DAA, Gasquet, 889.
176 B. Ward to FAB, 24 July 1918, AAW, Bo. V/25d.
177 T. Dunn to FAB, 19 November 1918, NotDA, Dunn, G02.01.
178 Fisher Diary, 7 March 1918, OUL, 9/71.
179 *Tablet*, 27 September 1919, p. 391.
180 FAB, National Catholic Congress, Birmingham, 3 August 1923, *Tablet*, 11 August 1923, p. 165.
181 *Tablet*, 16 February 1918, p. 205.
182 FAB memo, u/d, AAW, Bo. V/25d.
183 Acta of Meeting of the Bishops, 5 July 1918.

184 Fisher, Diary, 5 July 1918, OUL, 9/109.
185 Talbot to FAB, 20 July 1918, (copy), NotDA, Dunn, G02.01.
186 *Tablet*, 27 July 1918, pp. 97–100.
187 Fisher, Diary, 13 November 1919, OUL, 14/96.
188 Fisher, Diary, 27 January 1920, OUL, 14/107.
189 Fisher, Kingsway Hall, 27 March 1920, *Tablet*, 3 April 1920, p. 462.
190 Fisher, Diary, 12 February 1920, OUL, 14/111.
191 Brown to Catholic League of South London, 12 April 1920, *Tablet*, 17 April 1920, p. 532.
192 *Tablet*, 1 May 1920, p. 589.
193 Amigo to Ilsley, 29 March 1920, BAA, D4351a; Amigo to Whiteside, 7 April 1920, (draft), SAA, cited Clifton, *Amigo*, pp. 94–95.
194 FAB to Ilsley, 24 May 1920, telegram, BAA, D4398.
195 Bishops' Declaration, *Tablet*, 26 June 1920, p. 846.
196 FAB, WCF AGM, 27 November 1921, *Tablet*, 3 December 1921, p. 720.
197 FAB, National Catholic Congress, Birmingham, 3 August 1923, *Tablet*, 11 August 1923, pp. 164–165.
198 FAB, Albert Hall rally, 25 May 1929, *Tablet*, 1 June 1929, p. 750.
199 Amigo to Downey, 30 October 1929 (copy), SAA, Amigo Papers, Correspondence with Bishops, cited K. Aspden, *Fortress Church: The English Roman Catholic Bishops and Politics 1903–63* (Leominster: Gracewing, 2002), p. 178.
200 Acta, Bishops' Meeting, 22 January 1930, AAW, Hi. II/139/2(a).
201 Sir Charles Trevelyan to FAB, 24 January 1930 (copy), AAW, Bishops' Papers, V/1.
202 *Tablet*, 10 May 1930, p. 627.
203 Memo approved by FAB, 7 June 1930, AAW, Hi. II/72.
204 *Ibid*.
205 Downey, Liverpool, 22 June 1930, cited *Tablet*, 28 June 1930, p. 865.
206 FAB, Waltham Cross, 18 October 1930, *Times*, 20 October 1930.
207 Resolution of Bishops' Meeting, 12 November 1930, AAW, Hi. II/139/2(a).
208 *Tablet*, 31 January 1931, p. 149.
209 *Tablet*, 28 February 1931, p. 282.
210 FAB, Edinburgh, 17 June 1931, *Tablet*, 20 June 1931, p. 826.
211 FAB to Leeds Catholic Federation, 25 February 1908, *Tablet*, 29 February 1908, p. 340.
212 FAB, Hanwell, 7 March 1908, *Tablet*, 14 March 1908, p. 432.
213 FAB, National Catholic Congress, Manchester, 24 September 1926, *Tablet*, 2 October 1926, p. 438.
214 L. Fairfield to Editor, *Times*, 3 November 1929.
215 Acta of Bishops' Meeting, 10 April 1929.
216 Lord Eustace Percy to FAB, 24 October 1929, AAW, Bo. IV/20/14e.

[217] Canon Driscoll, 'Our Lack of Grant-Aided Secondary Schools for Boys,' *Tablet*, 8 September 1923, p. 294.
[218] FAB, 'The Church's Opportunity,' *The Clergy Review*, February 1931, p. 122.
[219] FAB, Finchley Grammar School, 15 June 1929, *Tablet*, 22 June 1929, p. 851.
[220] Driscoll, 'Our Lack of Grant-Aided Secondary Schools for Boys,' *Tablet*, 8 September 1923, pp. 295–296.
[221] FAB to Bishop of Hexham & Newcastle, 27 May 1906 (draft), AAW, Bo. V/14d.
[222] FAB, Address to National Catholic Congress, Royal Albert Hall, Sept 29, "Is the education of England, of the people of England, really Christian today?" cited Oldmeadow, *Francis Cardinal Bourne*, ii, p. 295.
[223] FAB, Trinity Sunday Pastoral Letter, *Tablet*, 13 June 1903, p. 952.
[224] FAB, Silver Jubilee of St Edmund's House, Cambridge, 17 November 1921, *Tablet*, 26 November 1921, p. 699.
[225] FAB to Norfolk, 5 December 1897; FAB to Norfolk, 10 December 1897; ACA.
[226] FAB, National Catholic Congress, Birmingham, 3 August 1923, *Tablet*, pp. 166–167.
[227] FAB, Laying of foundation stone at Blackfriars, 15 August 1921, *Tablet*, 20 August 1921, pp. 252–253.
[228] FAB, National Catholic Congress, Birmingham, 3 August 1923, *Tablet*, pp. 166–167.

Chapter 11

The Forbidden Procession

The Nineteenth International Eucharistic Congress

In September 1908 Archbishop Bourne declined Walter Runciman's invitation to discuss educational matters on the ground that Catholics had been 'wounded to the quick' by the Government's recent action.[1] He was referring to the Eucharistic Congress held in London earlier that month. The behaviour of Asquith's Ministry had, in his opinion, constituted a profound insult to Jesus Christ present in the Blessed Sacrament, an outrage compounded by the fact that it was suffered in London before thousands of Catholics gathered from across the world.

The International Eucharistic Congress started in Lille in 1881. It became an annual event, hosted by a different city each year, attracting hundreds of thousands of clergy and laity, and gaining papal recognition. The object was

> to make people know, and love, and serve Our Lord Jesus Christ in the most adorable sacrament of the altar by the solemn functions and meetings which they organise, and to work towards the extension of Christ's social kingdom over the world. This end is reached :—During the Congresses (1) By prayer, solemn Masses, general Communions, adoration of the Blessed Sacrament, and specially by the final manifestation of faith, which is made as solemnly and as publicly as possible, so that it should constitute a national act of reparation ... [2]

With the increasing Catholic population, the *Times* noted that 'open air processions in honour of the Blessed Sacrament have of late become a rather familiar spectacle in this country on Sunday afternoons during the summer months, and are viewed with interest and respect by the general public.'[3] What was proposed now, however, was on an altogether different scale.

London, as the capital city of the British Empire, had been asked to host the Eucharistic Congress before. In 1903 the request was declined due to Cardinal Vaughan's ill health. Bourne was first asked to consider it in 1904, 'but refused, believing that Westminster was not ready for the honour.' The basic external structure of the Cathedral had only just been completed. The Archbishop wished it to be in a more complete form before hosting such an event. By 1908 two things had persuaded Bourne that London was now prepared to receive the Nineteenth Eucharistic Congress. The first was the success of the massive Albert Hall rally of May 1906. Bourne asked the same man, John Gilbert, to coordinate the organisation of the Congress. Secondly, Bourne had attended the Metz Congress of 1907, carefully noting how the event was conducted.[4] Interestingly, the occupying German authorities suspended legislation prohibiting Blessed Sacrament processions for the duration of the Congress.

Bourne hoped that the London Congress would awaken in the hearts and minds of all Catholics a renewed faith and love for Jesus present in the Blessed Sacrament, and serve as a reminder to the nation at large that long period when such a belief united all Englishmen with the whole of Christendom.[5]

Not everyone shared his enthusiasm. Extreme Protestant opinion was already inflamed by Edward VII's presence earlier that year at St James's, Spanish Place for the Requiem Mass for the King of Portugal. They feared the growing influence of Anglo-Catholicism as subversive of the reformed faith in England; now overt idolatry was to be welcomed at the heart of this Protestant nation. And it was not just Protestants who were opposed. Rome received the occasional anonymous letter. One maliciously attributed motives of vanity to Bourne. He wished, the writer claimed, to compete with the Pan-Anglican Synod being held around the same time and to further his ambition to be created a cardinal. Less easy to discount was the suggestion that the Congress would constitute an unnecessary and dangerous provocation. 'It must not be forgotten that this is a Protestant, albeit a free, country, and there is deep down in the heart of the English people an intense hatred of the Catholic Faith, which only needs arousing to be a storm that will overwhelm us. We are a small body that ought to work quietly and earnestly, instead of which we make a noise, empty and futile for the most part, out of all proportion to our numbers and influence.'[6]

That was very much a minority opinion among Catholics, however. As the Congress approached, they shared their Archbishop's pride that

The Forbidden Procession

Catholicism was once more at the heart of public life in England. Pius X sent the first Papal Legate to this country since Cardinal Pole 350 years earlier. The dignified and impressive Vincent, Cardinal Vannutelli was received with great warmth by the crowds gathered on 8 September at Charing Cross for his welcome by Bourne and the Duke of Norfolk. As he entered Archbishop's House the following afternoon, the papal flag was unfurled; above Westminster Cathedral another papal flag flew alongside the Union Jack. The Congress formally began that evening with the Papal Legate's solemn reception in the Cathedral.

The next four days were filled with liturgical celebrations and conferences aimed at furthering Eucharistic devotion. In addition to Vannutelli, six other Cardinals were present: the curial Cardinal Mathieu and the Archbishops of Armagh, Baltimore, Malines, Milan and Toledo. There were 120 archbishops, bishops and abbots in attendance, and almost 2,000 priests. The crowds exceeded all expectations. The Legate described it as a veritable 'Congress of the Nations.' Every day Pontifical High Mass was sung in the Cathedral. More exotically, the first Byzantine liturgy ever seen in England was celebrated by Eastern Rite Catholics. Exquisite attention was paid to the vestments and chant, an iconastasis erected in the Cathedral sanctuary. After daily Mass the participants divided into English- and French-speaking sections for theological, historical and devotional papers delivered in various locations in central London. The Church had hired the Albert Hall for the duration. Each evening great numbers gathered. On the Friday it is estimated that 7–8,000 Catholics were received by the Papal Legate within the space of two hours; others left disappointed. On the Saturday, it was the turn of 20,000 children—their procession up the Embankment was delayed for two hours by the crowds in Parliament Square for Winston Churchill's wedding. On Saturday evening the Albert Hall was packed again for the meeting of Catholic men.[7]

The edition of the *Tablet* which appeared on Saturday, 12 September manifested a legitimate pride:

> Up to the hour of our going to press everything connected with the Eucharistic Congress has gone off as well and as smoothly as even the most enthusiastic of us could desire. The only difficulties have been those which form the necessary penalty of any success which passes anticipation. The Cathedral was not vast enough, and the halls were too few and not great enough, for the crowds

that thronged to their gates. The supply of medals ran short almost before the Congress was opened, and there were moments when even the official guide books were hard to obtain. But it is not too soon to say that from all the points of view that matter the London Congress is an assured and overwhelming success.[8]

'This d---d procession'

'Up to the hour of our going to press.' The final event of the Congress was also to be its climax: the great outdoor procession of the Blessed Sacrament. It was estimated that 75,000 attended the final day's proceedings. In the event, it is thought the number was approximately double. With no indoor venue capable of holding anywhere near this number, the Archbishop determined, as was the custom at Eucharistic Congresses, that the greatest number possible should see the Papal Legate and adore their Eucharistic Lord in an outdoor procession.

The procession was planned with great care, the route devised by the Archbishop and the Cathedral authorities acting in conjunction with the Metropolitan Police. Main streets were avoided to ensure minimum disruption. Technically, it was argued, such a procession breached s.26 of the Catholic Emancipation Act, 1829, which forbade any Roman Catholic cleric 'to exercise any of the rites or ceremonies of the Roman Catholic religion, or wear the habits of his Order, save within the usual places of worship of the Roman Catholic religion, or in private houses.' But no one regarded this legislation as operative. 'Public processions of the Blessed Sacrament have for years past been common in all parts of the country, and in many places they are of annual occurrence. No one has interfered or objected ... all knew that the living practice was better than the dead statute.' When Protestants had appealed to the Government to prevent a Catholic procession in the preceding decade the Home Secretary had told them he had no intention of intervening. The Home Secretary at that time? One Herbert Asquith, the current Prime Minister.[9] The Catholic authorities were completely open about their intentions, publishing the full programme, including the Blessed Sacrament procession, in the national Press two months in advance.[10]

Protestant extremists, led by John Kensit, pledged that the procession should not pass peacefully. He boasted that, if the Sacred Host was carried through the streets of London, 'it would have been brought to the ground.'[11] But only on Monday, 7 September did the Protestant Alliance

The Forbidden Procession

write to Sir Edward Henry, the Metropolitan Police Commissioner, requesting that he cancel the illegal procession. They had also written to Edward VII, staying with Lord Crewe in Nottinghamshire. His host noted: 'The King has taken this d---d procession greatly to heart; and asked me to say that he was "greatly cut up about it"—a rather curious phrase ... He has received dozens of letters from enraged Protestants, who compare him disadvantageously with his revered mother, now with God, and hint that his ultimate destination may be directed elsewhere.'[12] The King telegraphed Asquith and the Home Secretary, Herbert Gladstone, 'in considerable anxiety' asking them to have the procession banned.

The machinery of the British Government was paralysed by the fact that everyone who mattered was on holiday at the time. The Home Secretary was no help to anyone. He wrote initially to the Prime Minister (both of them were on country estates in Scotland): 'Police confident they can preserve order. Difficult to say we anticipate breach of the peace. Procession not in main thoroughfares. Troup [the relevant Home Office official] against interference and on the whole I agree with him.'[13] His subsequent advice was inadequate and inconsistent. The following day he felt, 'Nothing but overwhelming force of police will prevent serious disorder.'[14] Two days later he had changed his mind again: 'Troup reports that police find no reason to fear riot and thinks himself that the chance of serious disturbance is very small.'[15]

No wonder the Prime Minister resolved to handle the matter himself. That Asquith had no natural sympathy for Catholicism is evident when he spoke of 'this gang of foreign cardinals taking advantage of our hospitality to parade their idolatries through the streets of London: a thing without precedent since the days of Bloody Mary.'[16] But he was also naturally tolerant. He had no wished to be bounced into a repressive stance by a minority of Protestant bigots, deploring 'the demand for revival of obsolete enactments.' He faced a predicament. The King required action, action he himself was loath to take, but he was not in a position to reveal the royal motivation for such action. (Edward VII's involvement was denied at the time, his private secretary claiming six weeks later that 'the King never interferes with processions in London or elsewhere; and that there is no truth in the statement to which you refer that His Majesty interfered in regard to the one in question.'[17])

Asquith attempted to manage matters quietly, using Lord Ripon, the only Catholic in the Cabinet, as an intermediary. At 5 pm on 9 September—just four days before the scheduled procession—a telegram from the Prime Minister arrived at Ripon's Studley Royal estate in Yorkshire. 'In circumstances would urge you strongly to use your influence to secure abandonment of public procession which is contrary to letter of law and provocative to Protestant sentiment.'[18] Ripon had only twenty minutes to catch the evening post. He obliged the Prime Minister by forwarding the telegram to the Archbishop; but he was not happy. Ripon felt strongly that Bourne

> and the Cardinals and indeed all the Catholics in this country will have a very just ground of complaint that no intimation should have been given to them that the Government wished the Procession to be stopped. What has Herbert Gladstone been about to have allowed things to go so far and then to stop the Procession passes belief. Under all the circumstances I feel it a great humiliation to have had to make such a communication at the last moment.

He ended by telling Asquith that he did not know how Bourne would react.[19]

'Not abandoned but modified'

Bourne might have cravenly called off the procession in its entirety. Or he might have refused to accede to a purely private request. If he had taken the former course of action, he would have been forcefully disowned by many fellow Catholics. Had he taken the latter, he would have been burdened with the responsibility of any violence which may have ensued. In fact, he took neither course. This bombshell arrived on his desk on the first morning of the Eucharist Congress, the largest Catholic event in England by far since the Reformation. One way or another, it seemed that the Congress would be overshadowed by a shameful dispute with the Government. The pressure was immense.

His response to Asquith was calm, measured and forceful. He pointed out that the arrangements had been publicised well in advance and

> made in full concurrence with the wishes of the police authorities. It is impossible for me consistently with my own honour to countermand this Procession, unless I am able to say in the most public manner that I do so in compliance with a formal request from you as Prime Minister of England ... Are you prepared to

> do this [invoke anti-Catholic legislation] at the bidding of a few bigoted persons, who would fain treat us as a sect to be tolerated merely on certain conditions? This is a position we cannot accept: we claim equality with all sections of our fellow-countrymen ... Are you prepared at this the last moment—without one single word of previous warning—when special trains have been ordered from the country, and thousands of poor people have paid their fares to come to London on Sunday, when the Press of the whole world is watching the Congress, to put to dishonour not only myself, but the Catholic Bishops of the whole Empire, and to make us avow before our colleagues from the United States and from every quarter of the globe that the hospitality of the capital of the Empire is not what they supposed it to be, and that your Ministry is unable to face the threats of a few fanatical persons? On behalf of my Catholic people and of those of the whole Empire, I claim the fullest liberty for the Procession on Sunday, and if there be any dangers of which I am unaware, I claim such a measure of police protection as will ensure due consideration for our honoured guests and for the Mysteries of our Religion ... If, however, I receive before midnight tomorrow, Friday, your formal request, as Prime Minister, for the abandonment of the Procession, all the arrangements shall be countermanded, and I shall give the fullest publicity in order that my own action may be amply vindicated.[20]

Bourne eloquently asserted the right of Catholics to equality of treatment before the law. If that equality was not granted, then Asquith must accept public responsibility for it. Faced down by the Archbishop, the Prime Minister had little choice. He formally requested that the procession be called off. Bourne replied, 'Having considered your communication, have decided to abandon ceremonial of which you question the legality provided that you authorise me to state publicly that I do so at your request.'[21] That authorisation was given.

The Archbishop had dealt skilfully with the Government, maintaining throughout the moral high ground. It would require greater skill and courage to sell his message to thousands of expectant Catholics. He chose to do so most dramatically at the great Albert Hall rally the night before the procession was due to take place.

> Thousands of Irishmen 'agin' the Government' were in that throng; most of the men had already become embittered towards the Liberal Premier by five years of hostility to Catholic schools. It is hard to imagine a more difficult moment in the life of Francis

Bourne. If he had been 'a leader pushed on from behind,' instead of a leader who leads, he could have had that mighty throng leaping to its feet and shouting for joy at the simple words 'We shall stick to the procession' ... The young Archbishop had a different message to give: a message so unwelcome that murmurs, and even outcries, interrupted the first clauses of his announcement. But his moral courage was accompanied by such a mien of cool and decisive leadership that he turned away the storm.[22]

Calmly he delivered his message. He revealed the correspondence which had taken place between himself and the Prime Minister. He announced there was to be no outdoor procession with the Blessed Sacrament. For a brief moment there was silence as his audience struggled to digest the news. And then they gave vent to their feelings. Fr Vincent McNabb recalled, 'It is a fearful experience to hear twelve thousand men hiss. I do not want to hear it again in life.'[23] 'Thrice after having made his composed statement of Mr Asquith's interference in regard to the procession of the following day, did the Archbishop have to recall his wayward flock to be still; but in the end the example of his own composure and his own quiet and dignified acceptance of a considerable disappointment, was followed.'[24]

The disappointment was considerable, but not complete. Bourne's final communication to Asquith had been very carefully phrased. The Government had alleged that it was the 'ceremonial' aspect of the procession that was in contravention of the law. Very well, the 'ceremonial' aspect would be abandoned—but the procession would go ahead—simply without the Blessed Sacrament being carried in the street. Tens of thousands of poor people had already bought their railway tickets. They were not to be failed. 'We owe it to the firmness and prudence of the Archbishop that the procession was not abandoned but modified.'[25]

At 4 pm on the following afternoon the procession left the Cathedral along the defined route. 800 altar servers in cassock and cotta preceded canons in their purple and red finery, a phalanx of abbots, bishops and archbishops with their chaplains, the Cardinal Legate resplendent in the scarlet *cappa magna* with a guard of honour of eight peers of the realm, the other Cardinals, finally Archbishop Bourne headed an endless line of priests of every diocese and order. The vast crowds, who had previously entertained themselves with hymn-singing, cheered the procession along its way.[26]

Some admitted to a certain nervousness. Bishop Burton confided to his diary, 'Walked in the Procession amidst wildly enthusiastic scenes: some booing at two cross-ways by ill-visaged roughs. Glad to get back into the Cathedral.'[27] Eye witnesses disputed the likelihood of a disturbance, especially had the Blessed Sacrament been carried. At two or three points Protestant protesters tried to disrupt the procession; they were held back by the police and hundreds of Catholic stewards. Some maintained this was a typical London crowd, and that the cheering Catholics regarded with pity, rather than anger, the protestors whom they vastly outnumbered. However, Mgr William Brown shared Burton's anxiety. 'There were some ugly rushes at various points of the route as the modified Procession passed, and some foreign ecclesiastics near me were in a state of terror. I was apprehensive of violence, because I knew a good many Irishmen in the Procession had short pokers up their sleeves, and had the crowd attacked there would have been bloodshed and perhaps even fatalities. A short poker with a heavy knob is a deadly weapon, and blows scattered left and right in a scrimmage could easily have cracked skulls.'[28]

Once the participants returned to the Cathedral, the Blessed Sacrament was processed indoors with perfect legality. Finally, the Cardinal Legate ascended the Cathedral balcony before a densely-packed crowd. The *O salutaris hostia* and *Tantum ergo* were sung; bugles sounded as Benediction was given. (With an eye to asserting continuity with the pre-Reformation Church, the Archbishop had borrowed from the Belgian shrine of Hal a monstrance given by the youthful Henry VIII.) 'Then a strange thing happened. The silent, awe-struck reverence changed with one accord and electric suddenness into a mighty, startling shout of adoration, different in tone and character to the other cheers. There was emotion in its sound and prayer. It was a spontaneous greeting to Jesus Christ in the Blessed Sacrament. It was a splendid if unconventional act of faith.'[29] The Nineteenth Eucharistic Congress drew to a triumphant, if unanticipated, conclusion.

There were consequences—not least for the politicians. The Press, even that section not inclined to sympathy with the Catholic Church, was almost universally critical of the Government. The Tory *Telegraph* found the Government's 'conduct throughout this lamentable business inexcusably weak and inconceivably foolish.'[30] Elsewhere it was felt that, 'Had Mr Asquith desired to do Protestantism a disservice, he has been eminently successful. The action of the Government has given the English

Romanists an opportunity of exhibiting themselves in an attitude which must command general respect and sympathy ... The Protestants have gained their point, but the honours of war and the moral victory are with the Catholics.'[31] Two weeks later Ripon resigned from the Government, alleging ill health. The King was furious with Gladstone's weak performance at the Home Office and wanted him gone.[32] Asquith protected his friend for a while, but he was removed the following year. A by-election in Newcastle at the end of September resulted in the loss of a Liberal seat, blamed upon the protest votes of 3,000 Irish Catholics.

In future the Government was more circumspect and courteous in its dealings with the Church. In 1910 allegations were raised with Winston Churchill, then Home Secretary, as to the legality of the rites for the consecration of Westminster Cathedral. Churchill's letter to Bourne was a model of rectitude and consideration, asking the Archbishop to call to discuss the matter at a time convenient to him. 'I do not, of course, in any way, accept or endorse the allegation that the proposed ceremony is illegal, and I am most anxious that nothing should occur to interfere with the performance of fitting ceremonies in connection with the consecration of your great and beautiful Cathedral. But, as your Grace is well aware, difficult questions arose on a recent occasion of a similar character, and I venture to hope that, if I have an opportunity of discussing the matter with you, it may be possible to avoid re-opening these questions and at the same time to give the police assistance and protection which you will probably desire.' Bourne duly visited Churchill and explained that the consecration of a cathedral did not involve a Blessed Sacrament procession. 'Churchill promised full assistance, saying that he would have given it even if Host had been carried. Asked me to treat interview as confidential as far as possible.'[33] Lessons had been learnt.

The Archbishop emerged from the controversy with a reputation hugely enhanced.

> It is hardly too much to say that the last few days have shown the Archbishop of Westminster to his people ... The crisis came and it found the Man ... we saw the simplicity and directness of speech, we saw the rare judgment and a high courage ... This fuller knowledge can hardly fail to result in some strengthening of those bonds of loyalty and affection which, by happy tradition, have for so long united the Archbishops of the See of Westminster and their flock.[34]

That came from the Church's inhouse journal, but similar praise was repeated across the board. Wilfrid Ward spoke for the English Church as a whole at a surprise reception for Bourne organised by prominent laymen: 'The eyes of the whole English public were at that moment on us, and there has been but one opinion as the firmness, tact and dignity with which your Grace met the situation and sustained the position of leader of the English Catholic body.'[35]

Despite his considerable victories in the educational crises, there had been a feeling until this point that perhaps Bourne had not quite settled into his office, that he had not yet found his place in public life, that he had not entirely connected with his people. Perhaps some retained a suspicion that there was substance in the allegations of financial irregularity and incompetence. After the Congress Cahill could express his optimism that critical tongues would be checked. 'I do thank God with all my heart. The *cold* stone has been rolled away; let us hope for ever.'[36] It was felt that the events of Congress 'have helped to hasten the [cardinatial] Hat to Westminster.'[37] Certainly, Rome shared the appreciation shown to Bourne. Merry del Val wrote,

> I hasten to congratulate you with all my heart upon the admirable way in which you have handled the matter under very difficult circumstances. Your letter to the Prime Minister is excellent; nothing could be better ... You have known how to turn that disappointment to good account and you have strengthened the position of the Church in England. The whole Congress has been an immense and remarkable success, and under God that is chiefly due to your efforts and ability ... I know that the Holy Father feels as I do.[38]

But it was at home that the most important results accrued. One tangible benefit was the confidence to hold each year national Catholic Congresses, which became a defining feature in the life of the English Church before the First World War.

> Along with the many other blessings that the Eucharistic Congress brought us from God it has taught us most important lessons, and, not the least among them, a greater consciousness of the position which the Catholics of England hold in the eyes of their brethren throughout the world, and of the consequent very weighty responsibilities which rest upon them.[39]

It allowed the Archbishop to re-define his relationship with his flock:

This Congress has culminated in complete success ... It has united the Catholics of England, and, if I may believe you, has helped me to gain that which is so important to one in my position—your complete confidence. Catholics have, in some sort, to take their bishops on faith :- you have had to take me on faith, and if it has ever been difficult for you to understand any actions of mine, you will believe me when I say, and I think I do not misjudge myself, that I have always acted, as I acted on Friday and Saturday, with only one aim in view—the interests of the Church ... I cannot help thinking that even in Mr Asquith's intervention we may trace also the intervention of Divine Providence. Mr Asquith has been one of the promoters of the success of the Congress, if only because Catholics in their disappointment were brought into keener sympathy one with another than they had been even in their joy, and because it gave to them the occasion for a demonstration of loyalty to the Holy See.[40]

Notes

1. FAB to Runciman, 24 September 1908, copy, AAW, Bo. I/181.
2. 'The Eucharistic Congresses: by a Member of the Committee,' *WCC*, (1908), pp. 84–85.
3. *Times*, 4 September 1908.
4. FAB, Archbishop's House reception, 16 September 1908, cited *The Story of the Congress* (London: Burns & Oates, 1908), pp. 95–96; FAB, 7 April 1921, *Tablet*, 16 April 1921, p. 499.
5. FAB, Pastoral Letter, 15 August 1908.
6. Anon., SCPF, 102/1908, f. 443, r. 555.
7. *Report of the Nineteenth Eucharistic Congress* (London: Sands and Co, 1909); Oldmeadow, *Francis Cardinal Bourne*, i, pp. 369–374.
8. *Tablet*, 12 September 1908, p. 404.
9. Editorial, *Tablet*, 19 September 1908, p. 441.
10. *Times*, 17 July 1908.
11. J. Kensit, Caxton Hall, 13 September 1908, cited *Report of the Nineteenth Eucharistic Congress*, p. 616.
12. Crewe to Asquith, 6 September 1908, cited R. Jenkins, *Asquith* (London: Collins, 1964), p. 190.
13. Gladstone to Asquith, 9 September 1908, cited Jenkins, *Asquith*, p. 191.
14. Gladstone to Asquith, 10 September 1908, OLU, Asquith MSS. 20/109.
15. Gladstone to Asquith, 12 September 1908, OUL, Asquith 20/141.
16. Asquith to Crewe, 10 September 1908, cited Jenkins, *Asquith*, p. 191.

17 *Times*, 4 November 1908.
18 Asquith to Ripon, 9 September 1908, AAW, Bo. III/124/7.
19 Ripon to Asquith, 9 September 1908, OUL, Asquith MSS. 20/107.
20 FAB to Asquith, 10 September 1908, (copy), AAW, Bo. III/124/7.
21 FAB to Asquith, 11 September 1908, cited *Report of the Nineteenth Eucharistic Congress*, p. 542.
22 'Francis, Cardinal Bourne: By one who knows him,' *Tablet*, 9 June 1934, pp. 720–721.
23 V. McNabb, OP, *Catholic Times*, cited *The Story of the Congress*, p. 54.
24 *The Story of the Congress*, p. 55.
25 Editorial, *Tablet*, 26 September 1908, p. 481.
26 *Report of the Nineteenth Eucharistic Congress*, pp. 597–600.
27 Burton, Diary, Sunday, 13 September 1908, CDA.
28 Brown, *Through Windows of Memory*, p. 139.
29 *Tablet*, 19 September 1908.
30 *Daily Telegraph*, 14 September 1908.
31 *Truth*, 16 September 1908.
32 Crewe to Asquith, 16 September 1908, OUL, Asquith MSS. 20.
33 Churchill to FAB, 11 March 1910, (annotated by FAB, 16 March 1910), AAW, Bo. V/40c.
34 Editorial, *Tablet*, 19 September 1908, pp. 441–442.
35 W. Ward, 16 September 1908, cited *The Story of the Congress*, p. 94.
36 Cahill to FAB, 14 September 1908, AAW, Bo. III/124/7.
37 *The Story of the Congress*, p. 122.
38 Merry del Val to FAB, 16 September 1908, AAW, Bo. III/124/7.
39 FAB, CTS Annual Conference, Manchester, 20 September 1909, FAB, *Congress Addresses* (London: Burns, Oates & Washbourne Ltd, 1929).
40 FAB, Archbishop's House Reception, 16 September 1908, cited *The Story of the Congress*, pp. 96–97.

Chapter 12

'No Narrow Mind'

Modernism

The theological crisis of the late nineteenth and early twentieth centuries was that of Modernism. Depending on one's perspective, it was either the attempt to present afresh the Catholic faith to a modern world by engaging with developments in science and the arts, or the substitution of a man-made religion for divinely-revealed truths. Pius X and Merry del Val had no doubts. Enthusiastically assisted by his Cardinal Secretary of State, the Pope sought to eradicate the evils of Modernism from the Church. Modernism was condemned by the 1907 Decree *Lamentabili* and Encyclical *Pascendi*. On which side of the line did Francis Bourne fall?

The charge of theological 'obscurantism' levelled against Bourne on his appointment to Westminster was bizarre, and impossible to sustain.[1] However, it was an accusation—together with that to the contrary—about which the Archbishop was still sensitive three years later. Bourne was neither a brilliant nor an original intellect, but he appreciated the need for Catholic scholarship to engage with the contemporary world. Preaching at a priest's Requiem Mass in 1902, he might well have been describing his own position. 'His was no narrow mind. In a day like our own, when so many new problems have arisen, when theories once held as almost sacred are seen to be not even matter of Catholic tradition, he was fully alive to the needs of the time, and could face and discuss such questions without on the one hand being carried away by the latest theory, or on the other denouncing as heterodox those who were not able to accept the explanations and theories of his own student days. Because of the same theological basis of his training he could consider and weigh new theories without fear, and without for a moment losing the complete self-possession of his mind.'[2]

Bourne's stance was largely determined by the 'theological basis' of his own formation. When it might have suited to have trimmed his views and vocabulary during the turbulent years of the Modernist crisis, he remained loyal to all that he had learnt from his Sulpician professor, the Abbé Hogan. 'As regards the ascertained doctrines of the Catholic faith, modern criticism, fairly conducted, cannot weaken them. They rest ultimately on the authority of the Church ... Far from shunning inquiry in their regard, the true believer invites it.'[3]

Wonersh: 'A hotbed of Modernist thinking'

Some argued that the young Bishop of Southwark had allowed Sulpician thought too much leeway at Wonersh to the detriment of the orthodoxy of his seminarians and priests. That is the criticism of Amigo's biographer. 'By 1900, it was a hotbed of Modernist thinking. Some of the professors appointed to Wonersh were trained at St Sulpice and introduced Modernist thought into their lectures. The most noteworthy example of this was Fr Charles Dessoulavy.'[4]

Is the accusation true? Certainly, there were rumours to that effect. Charged with providing him with the substance of these rumours, the Jesuit, Fr Daniel Considine, told Bourne that it was 'alleged that "advanced" views were well known to be held by some of the professors at Wonersh, and that some of their pupils held and afterwards preached the same doctrines on leaving the Seminary. [Bourne] himself, although not a Modernist, was considered to be in sympathy with a freer discussion of Biblical subjects and Christian Antiquities.'[5] However, many of these claims were made much later in the context of different ecclesiastical and personal battles. His successor as Rector, Joseph Butt, maintained that rumours of Modernism were circulated for 'purely vindictive' motives and that when Bourne was translated from Southwark to Westminster he 'left the Seminary entirely free from any such taint.'[6] Butt confronted Merry del Val in 1909, wanting to make 'it clear that the Archbishop could not possibly be implicated,' given his direct involvement in Wonersh had ceased some eleven years earlier.[7] Merry del Val admitted that he *might* 'have alluded to accusations against Wonersh. He plainly showed that he had believed the accusations to some extent because he tried to justify them at first saying several had apostatized, etc, and, when I denied this flatly, he kept saying that the place was full of Tyrell's works, etc.'[8]

Cardinal Gotti assured Butt that no formal accusations of Modernism at Wonersh had been received by Propaganda.[9] Bishop Amigo angrily rejected suggestions that he was the source of the rumours. He referred to the report, required by the Encyclical *Pascendi*, he had commissioned the preceding autumn from Abbot Bergh of Ramsgate 'in which he distinctly refuted the accusation of Modernism in the Seminary.'[10] Butt himself denied that he had sought the removal of Dessoulavy and another professor on the grounds of Modernism.[11]

Does the matter rest there? Not entirely. In 1909 Amigo denied having delated Bourne to Merry del Val for encouraging Modernism at Wonersh. However, he admitted that such reports had been circulating in Rome for at least 1 ½ years. Two years later Amigo did make comments remarkably similar to those he had earlier denied. 'It was this Philosophy Professor [Dessoulavy] who caused the mischief. Loisy and Tyrrell were widely read and encouraged, but not by Mgr Butt. At the time *Pascendi* had not been published and these two authors had not been condemned. The Archbishop was in sympathy with the movement at the very first, but never realised the harm it did till after the Encyclical *Pascendi*.'[12]

A memorandum by a Wonersh professor paints a similar picture:

> There existed a decided clique in the Seniors which seems to have been styled the 'Tyrrellites', who quoted Fr Tyrrell as a panacea for every conceivable evil, who argued against scholasticism and who seem to have adopted Fr Tyrrell as their patron saint (this is the language which existed about them at that time). I knew that certain questions were being discussed which would only disturb one's peace of soul and I was anxious not to hear any such arguments. I heard remarks such as … 'all truth is relative'… Now, some of the arguments I quote from merely *one* student, others are from two or three students who made casual remarks … It was the age of argument at Wonersh.[13]

In 1900 Wilfrid Ward relayed to his wife an account he had received from a seminary professor: 'He says that the *only* writer who does [the seminarians] any good and enables them to take an interest in theology is Tyrrell. He says that apart from Tyrrell the general attitude is fear of thinking at *all* on dogma, and consequently a total lack of interest in it. He says if Tyrrell were generally suspect it would be a most serious thing for the young theologians and priests.'[14] Ward doesn't identify the seminary, but given he lived in the Diocese of Southwark, it may well have been Wonersh.

To establish Wonersh as a Tridentine seminary distinct from its English counterparts, Bourne staffed it with foreign professors and alumni who had completed further studies overseas. Most had studied at St

Sulpice, which by the first decade of the twentieth century was regarded as a hotbed of heresy by the Integrists in the Roman Curia.[15] There is no evidence that Bourne himself ever challenged any doctrinal position of the Church. He told his flock, 'A Christianity that rejects the miraculous and the supernatural ceases to be Christian in any true sense.'[16] However, he wanted his students to receive a formation equipping them to deal with contemporary questions, he wanted them to be inspired, not simply to learn by rote. Loisy and Tyrrell seemed to give just that inspiration, an apparent answer to Protestant liberalism and modern scepticism. We may take it as reasonably certain that Bourne did encourage their study at Wonersh. In doing so, he failed to appreciate the fundamental flaws in their work—but then so did most orthodox Catholics at this point. Neither Loisy nor Tyrrell were overtly undermining Catholic dogma in 1900, and it is unfair to castigate Bourne in 1900 for not anticipating their subsequent defection from the faith.

'An ailing little soul': Loisy[17]

The Anglican historian of Catholic Modernism, Alec Vidler, thought the lay theologian Baron Friedrich von Hügel 'the chief engineer of the Modernist movement. He made it his business to seek out potential Modernists, to stimulate and encourage them in their intellectual pursuits, and to introduce them to one another's work.'[18] That assessment is contested, but von Hügel operated an impressive network of international contacts. His own cosmopolitan credentials were impeccable, born in Tuscany of an Austrian diplomat father and Scottish mother, his early years spent in Belgium before settling in England, where he married Lady Mary Herbert.

As soon as Bourne was appointed to Westminster, von Hügel engineered an interview with him. He had high hopes of recruiting the new Archbishop as a defender of liberal Catholic scholarship. He came away encouraged, 'Talked about Hogan, Mignot, Touzard, Semeira, Duchesne, Biblical Commission, Tyrell's *Oil and Wine*.'[19] It was not simply a social call. He wanted a specific service from Bourne, and to that end wished to introduce him to his friend, Eudoxee-Irénée Mignot, Archbishop of Albi, an isolated standard-bearer for liberal Catholicism among the French hierarchy and another former pupil of Hogan. Von Hügel wanted Bourne to call on Mignot on his return from collecting the pallium in Rome. That did not prove possible,[20] but the Baron arranged Mignot's visit to Archbishop's House the following summer.

Von Hügel was seeking help for another friend, Fr Alfred Loisy. The Modernist storm was coming to a head in France, and Loisy was at the centre of that storm. There are those who judge Loisy 'the most impressive, because the most learned, subtle and eloquent, of the Modernist leaders. As a biblical scholar he was among the most brilliant of his day.'[21] Based on the widespread admissions contained in his memoirs published three decades later, Loisy justified every fear Pius X entertained about Modernism. He confessed, 'Historically speaking, I did not admit that Christ founded the Church or the Sacraments; I professed that dogmas formed themselves gradually, and that they were not unchangeable; and it was the same for ecclesiastical authority which I conceived of as a ministry of human education without allowing it and absolute and unlimited right on the intelligence and conscience of the believers.' And again, 'Christ has even less importance in my religion than he has in that of the liberal Protestants; for I attach little importance to the revelation of God the Father for which they honour Jesus. If I am anything in religion, it is more pantheist-positivist-humanitarian than Christian.'[22]

Why did two Archbishops—indeed why did von Hügel—involve themselves in defending a man who had clearly lost his Christian faith? Because it was not apparent at this stage. Loisy wrote, 'It is no less than high time to provide for the needs of intelligent people.'[23] His writings seemed to some to do exactly that. In his *L'Évangile et L'Église* published in 1902, Loisy appeared to provide a convincing Catholic response to the liberal Protestant claims of Adolf Harnack that the divinity of Christ was only a later construction of the Church. He seemed to prove continuity between the Gospel and the Church. However, 'the book was in fact a gigantic and successful hoax.'[24] Loisy's brilliance in attacking Harnack was apparent, but his stance was not necessarily fundamentally different. Purporting to base his case firmly in the Tradition of the Church, Loisy too separated the Christ of faith from the historical Christ, effectively undermining the objective basis for faith. Loisy was subtle. It was often difficult to distinguish his own views from those of Harnack. George Tyrrell recognised that Loisy was less interested in establishing the divinity of Christ and the authority of the Church than showing whether these could be demonstrated from the Gospel using the historical-critical method.[25] After an initially enthusiastic response, Catholic critics claimed that Loisy 'has not merely rescinded from revealed doctrine, but has in many instances denied it.'[26] He claimed to have been misunderstood. The book was condemned by Cardinal Richard of Paris. It was feared that Rome would take even sterner measures.

Von Hügel enlisted the assistance of Mignot and Bourne. *L'Évangile et L'Église* and four more of Loisy's books were condemned by the Holy Office and placed on the Index at the end of 1903. Communicating the decision to the Archbishop of Paris, Merry del Val declared the books to be 'full of the gravest errors concerning the primitive revelation, the authenticity of the facts and teachings of the Gospels, the Divinity and the Science of Christ, the Resurrection, the Divine institution of the Church and the Sacraments; and that the Holy Father has been deeply afflicted and greatly disturbed by the disastrous effects such works are calculated to produce.'[27] It was rumoured that Bourne 'was supposed to have joined in a petition of the Archbishop of Albi (?) to the Holy See that Loisy might not be condemned because his influence was on the whole stimulating to Catholic ecclesiastical studies and students.'[28] There is no evidence for this, but, through von Hügel and Mignot, the Archbishop of Westminster did advise Loisy on a form of submission which would be acceptable to the ecclesiastical authorities.[29] Von Hügel himself was probably not aware of the full extent of Loisy's scepticism at this point, but he had a better idea than Bourne. He argued, therefore, that the Archbishop had better let matters drop given 'the moral impossibility of a *sincere* submission without any kind of reserve as to historical method and conscience.'[30]

'A great name': Newman

Loisy's condemnation particularly concerned the English Church given his use of Newman's theory of the development of doctrine. There was a flurry of activity in the spring of 1904 to prevent Newman's simultaneous condemnation. Not only was it feared that Rome would pronounce on an erroneous interpretation of Newman, but also that any such pronouncement would have disastrous implications in England, stemming the tide of potential converts who sought to follow in Newman's steps. The defence of the great English theologian produced some unlikely allies. Bourne endeavoured to discover the state of play in the Vatican.[31] Gasquet and Norfolk lobbied Merry del Val, and elicited a favourable response:

'It is obviously an iniquitous intervention on the part of those in England who are anxious to bolster Loisy's errors with a great name.'[32]

At the opening of the Birmingham Oratory Church Bourne returned to Newman's defence and re-stated his own position. Three years on the Archbishop's message was a little more nuanced; there was an appreciation of the havoc wrought by foreign 'interpreters.' He warned,

> We must be very jealous of his name ... We must be on our guard not to force his teaching into a shape he would disavow. The danger is greater among those to whom his language is not their mother tongue, and who are ever prone to build up a logical system, even though they have to piece together the foundations as best they may. Cardinal Newman did not aim at a system in this sense, and while we may cling with reverent affection to his own teaching, that very reverence will inspire us with a wholesome dread of some of his interpreters. Moments may come in which it may be necessary to disavow such commentators lest their interpretations be accepted for his doctrine, and our great English teacher be held responsible for their imaginings. The danger is not fantastic, for those in other countries who do not know his writings, and are acquainted only with these self-constituted interpreters, are led to fear that unconsciously and without intention he may have been the precursor of theories which to them seem very dangerous to the faith and traditions of the Church ... He looked back through the ages of the Church that he might never depart from her traditions. He looked forward to the new issues that he might see how they could be harmonised with the old teaching and its actual presentment. He neither rejected new statements because they were new, nor accepted them because of their novelty, but he weighed them all in the light of Divine Truth, in a spirit of humble, quiet, trustful prayer.

Bourne never claimed intellectual parity with Newman, but saw himself as heir to that same approach of utter fidelity to the Church's Tradition combined with a willingness 'to convey the old unchanging message in new words and a fresh setting acceptable to the Englishmen of his day.'[33] Bourne might be criticised for his initial failure to appreciate sufficiently the severity of the Modernist threat, but the tradition of Newman, the teaching of Hogan and his own temperament protected him from the greatest weakness of Modernism, intellectual pride. Bourne too drew his strength from 'a spirit of humble, quiet, trustful prayer.'

'A highly nervous, eccentric and erratic person': Tyrell

Modernism was most prevalent in France and Italy. The energy of the English Church was expended on ministry to poor Irish Catholics; intellectual speculation was a luxury for the few. The only home-grown Modernist of international repute was the Jesuit, George Tyrrell—and Bourne was quick to point out that this 'one notorious exponent of Modernism [was] more strictly an Irishman.' He reminded Merry del Val that Tyrrell had 'never occupied any position of trust or responsibility' and was widely recognised 'here to be a highly nervous, eccentric and erratic person.'[34]

Tyrrell was a convert. His preaching at Farm Street, his spiritual direction and early devotional writings impressed many. Maisie Ward felt that had he been content with these accomplishments he might have been judged a great spiritual guide. She ascribes his downfall to his introduction by von Hügel to modern German philosophy, biblical criticism and Loisy.[35] Venturing into fields for which he was not fully prepared, his presentation of the faith was based less on its objective historicity and more on subjective experience and its perceived moral value.

In 'retirement' from Farm Street, he wrote extensively, including in 1903, *Lex Orandi*. He argued, 'Certain historical facts enter into our creed as matters of faith. Precisely as historical facts they concern the historian and must be criticised by his methods. But as matters of faith they must be determined by the criterion of faith, i.e. by their proved religious values as universally effectual of spiritual progress; as implications of the spirit of Christian charity and sanctity; as selected by the exigiencies of the development of the inner life of the soul."[36] As the book was published in Roehampton, Bourne was approached, as Bishop of Southwark, for his *imprimatur*. *Lex Orandi* had already been approved by the Jesuits' own censors and was passed to another Jesuit at Farm Street for the *nihil obstat*. Bourne, therefore, granted his *imprimatur*, presumably as a formality. Three years later, in the light of Tyrrell's later works, a priest correspondent invited him to withdraw that *imprimatur* on the grounds that, 'The evil of the book lies in this that while it does not directly attack the Faith, it still teaches that we need not trouble ourselves about the *truth of the facts* of revelation, but only consider the *moral teaching* of the statements found in the Bible.' Bourne was not panicked by the continuing furore into an immediate revocation of the *imprimatur*, and noted: '*Imprimatur* was granted in usual manner on the recommendation of thoroughly competent censors. His Grace will, however, willingly consider any official complaint that you may wish to make.'[37]

Tyrrell invited condemnation. Expelled from the Jesuits in 1906, he provided a satirical commentary on the Encyclical *Pascendi* for the *Times* and the *Giornale d'Italia*. The *Tablet* was horrified. 'He not only refuses obedience to the teachings of the Holy Father, but uses language in regard to the Encyclical little short of insult against his Holiness.'[38] Nor was Merry del Val impressed. 'Tyrrell is carrying on his scandalous rebellion and is proclaimed abroad as one of the leaders of the school, and perhaps the chief one ... Tyrrell has many more correspondents and sympathisers than is generally believed.'[39] Tyrrell rejected scholasticism: 'The Modernist is no blind worshipper of present culture. He knows it is a medley of good and evil, and needs careful criticism and discrimination. But he believes that, on the whole, it stands for gain rather than loss; and that its new and true values must be absorbed into the Catholic organism if the latter is to live.'[40] Maude Petre's biography shows that by the time of his death, Tyrrell had repudiated the Catholic faith. He denied the authority of Trent and the First Vatican Council, and rejected papal infallibility. He wrote in January 1909, 'Houtin and Loisy are right; the Christianity of the future will consist of mysticism and charity, and possibly the Eucharist in its primitive form as the outward bond. I desire no better.'[41]

Tyrrell's was the only name brought before the Westminster Council of Vigilance.[42] Despite Merry del Val's views, Bourne did not condemn Tyrrell. He felt no formal requirement to do so: Tyrrell was resident in Southwark, not Westminster. It was Amigo who gave effect to the Holy Office decision to deprive Tyrrell of the sacraments and Amigo who refused Tyrrell a Catholic burial in July 1909 on the grounds he showed 'no evidence at all' of retracting his views. Tyrrell's friends felt that the Archbishop of Westminster would have acted differently. 'With your surmise regarding Bourne, I quite agree. When the Bishop of Southwark had refused, he was bound to refuse also, but had he had the business in his own hands he would have found a way of satisfying both parties.'[43] Bourne was motivated by compassion for a man suffering from Bright's Disease. Tyrrell's family were full of praise for the Archbishop. 'Nothing could have been nicer and more sympathetic than he was.'[44] Three years after Tyrrell's death, and in the midst of his own troubles in Rome, Bourne was still sufficiently interested in Tyrrell to request a copy of Maud Petre's newly-published biography at the earliest opportunity.[45]

The Archbishop was consulted about possible disciplinary action against Petre, von Hügel and others for their role in organising and attending Tyrrell's funeral in an Anglican graveyard. His response was not the one hoped for by Merry del Val. It showed a realistic assessment of his compatriots' willingness to take the side of the underdog. 'It is always dangerous to arouse in England the morbid unreasonable sympathy which people so readily give every wrong-doer whatever the nature of his crime.' To make his advice more palatable in Rome, he added, there was no point in creating 'martyrs for a cause.'[46]

With Maude Petre too, Bourne's attitude was one of paternal advice rather than outright condemnation despite the fact some felt that hers was the dominant influence on Tyrrell.[47] She was not, however, inclined to accept paternal advice. In 1907 Bourne followed Abbot Bergh's recommendation and refused his *imprimatur* to her *Through the Letter to the Spirit*. She went ahead and published anyway, sending the Archbishop a copy. His reply was firm but gentle, 'I am bound to say that you ought not to have published it, and that it is your duty as a loyal Catholic to withdraw it without delay. I do not question your good intentions, but I most earnestly implore you not to hesitate in taking the course which, for your own sake and in the interest of souls, I am obliged to urge upon you.'[48] Bourne took no further action against her, although she was denied the sacraments across the Thames in Southwark.

'Our leader': von Hügel

'I cannot make out, my dear sir, whether you are a [theological] Liberal or not; I incline to think *not*.'[49] Others did not share Ward's uncertainty. Maud Petre wrote, 'He was undoubtedly our leader through all the first stages of the Modernist Movement and his influence extended over at least four countries. He was our centre, our link with others whom we did not personally know. He diffused our writings and extolled our efforts; while criticising our shortcomings.'[50] Von Hügel was an enigma even to his friends. He knew every Modernist imaginable. Tyrrell was his confessor. Somewhat after the event, it is true, he wrote, 'You might think that my love for Loisy and Tyrrell, and my persistent admiration for some of their older books, mean that I am with them in their Immanentism, etc., which is not at all the case.'[51] His Biblical criticism put him firmly in the Modernist camp refuting the Biblical Commission's conclusions regarding Mosaic authorship of the Pentateuch and the apostle's author-

'No Narrow Mind'

ship of the Fourth Gospel, which he interpreted largely symbolically.[52] His Christology too was distinctly Modernist. He wrote to Loisy that he was unable to subscribe to the Encyclical *Pascendi*—as a layman, he was not required to do so.[53] Loisy's publication of his letters betrayed the fact that von Hügel shared many of his views.

And yet at the same time something distinguished von Hügel. Partly, it was character; there was nothing of intellectual pride or arrogance about him. Evelyn Underhill could reminisce, 'He is the most wonderful personality I have ever known—so saintly, so trustful, sane and tolerant.'[54] Von Hügel's concern was to re-connect theology with prayer and a sense of the mystical. In doing so, he never lost his belief in the objective content of faith and the transcendence of God. There was nothing false about his deep devotional and sacramental life. He was, thus, something of a mystery to his contemporaries. Perhaps Maisie Ward came closest to defining him: 'One great difficulty arises from the fact that there are quite simply two von Hügels. One is tempted at times to the undue simplification of describing them as the von Hügel of faith and the von Hügel of history!'[55]

After his advice had been sought on Loisy's condemnation, Bourne had little significant direct contact with von Hügel. Nevertheless, von Hügel benefited from the benign regime in Westminster. His biographer pondered whether Bourne 'was not pressed by Rome to take some action'[56] against him. Given Merry del Val's hawk-like surveillance of his adopted country for any sign of deviancy from orthodoxy, von Hügel was always going to feature on the ecclesiastical radar. The Secretary of State wrote to the Archbishop in 1906 referring to the criticism of him, that he 'ought to prevent the *Tablet* appearing to show sympathy and almost support in favour of writers of unorthodox views, because the *Tablet* is still more or less considered as the authorised organ of Archbishop's House, and it is a pity that men like von Hügel, W. Ward and others of more or less questionable orthodoxy should be allowed to pass as the authorised spokesmen of the Catholic Church.'[57] Bourne chose to ignore the Vatican. In 1924 von Hügel's daughter was able to reassure her father with the Cardinal's comment to her: 'I have never got him into trouble and I never will.'[58]

Why was Bourne so reluctant to take action, however symbolic, against von Hügel when this would obviously have been well received in Rome? Partly, perhaps, it was stubbornness, a resentment against being told how to act on his own patch. Partly, it was courage—the determination to do what he thought right regardless of any opprobrium this might entail for himself. And one suspects the Archbishop had a great deal of sympathy with von Hügel's stated aim 'to gain for the Catholic and Roman Church at least a place of respect and honour, and so far as possible one of formal and complete acceptation, among men of learning in England.'[59] The Baron's desire for personal sanctification would similarly have impressed Bourne. 'In the midst of these dangers, in the presence of these intellectual difficulties which to some are so very real, we must listen to the voice of the Holy Ghost in our hearts; we must be men of prayer.'[60]

'Ward who is so unsafe'

Bourne stood in a different relationship to Wilfrid Ward than to the other suspected Modernists of the period. As Archbishop of Westminster he was proprietor of the *Dublin Review*, of which Ward was editor from 1905 until his death in 1916. Bourne was bound to take note of his editor's theological stance. Ward was not a professional theologian, but a journalist and author, writing biographies of Wiseman and Newman. From a wealthy convert family, his connections were further extended through marriage to a niece of the Duke of Norfolk, whose political conservatism Ward shared. In theological matters, however, he was more liberal: 'The work of the adaptation of theology to the exigencies of the times has already effectively begun; though it may need a time of freedom from agitation and from the repression which follows its development.'[61]

Bourne already admired Ward's writing before his appointment to Westminster[62] and 'was very proud' to secure his services as editor of the *Dublin Review*.[63] Ward used his Fitzalan Howard connections to secure an interview with Merry del Val before taking up the editorship and felt able, therefore, to assure to the Archbishop, 'I talked to Cardinal Merry del Val about the *Dublin* and he seemed quite satisfied with the line I propose to take. It came at the end of a long discussion on other subjects, and he did not commit himself to any very definite opinions, but he seemed perfectly satisfied and said not one word expressing any doubt or anxiety on the subject.'[64] Bourne appreciated better than Ward Merry del Val's capacity to keep his own counsel and to distinguish between social niceties and theological judgments. Although Norfolk was to suggest again the possibility of seeking private advice from Merry del Val,[65] the Cardinal Secretary of State was far less sympathetic than the Duke and his nephew realised. They would have been surprised to learn what Merry del Val really thought: Wilfrid Ward 'is so unsafe. He is an acrobat and performs the trick of teaching or insinuating unsound doctrine and of wriggling out of them within twenty-four hours, and then tells everybody that all that is Newman. Poor Newman.'[66]

Ward's daughter appreciated the complexity of the Archbishop's position better than her father. 'Cardinal Bourne ... would give occasional criticism, sometimes with a little acerbity, but he steadily supported Wilfrid's editorship of the *Dublin Review* and his other intellectual work, and carried on for the whole Catholic Church in England a policy of encouragement of intellectual effort and discouragement of recriminations and attacks made in the name of orthodoxy ... While he sympathised with Wilfrid's intellectual position to a large extent (he was, after all, a pupil of Hogan and Le Hir), yet he felt on his side that my father did not enter sufficiently into the difficulties of a ruler and all the other interests he had to consider besides the purely intellectual.'[67] In the circumstances, Bourne gave Ward great latitude of editorial independence and showed him every consideration.

Bourne passed on to Ward criticisms of his articles which appeared in the *Dublin Review* in the autumn of 1907, urging only a more rounded treatment of 'these very debatable questions.'[68] Ward mistook the Archbishop's motivation, and Bourne had to elaborate:

> In pure friendliness and simple consideration for you I sent on the criticisms which had reached me on your articles. Neither to you nor to anyone have I passed judgment on those articles or their critics. It seemed right that you should know what was going on, and have the opportunity, if you wished it, of preparing a statement, calm and impersonal, which could be given to those of your critics who had made themselves known to me. My only thought was to give you such an opportunity for your sake ... Quite unnecessarily, as it appears to me, you write as though *I* were perturbed by these criticisms, and almost identified with them, or at least in proximate danger of such identification ... Of course, if you prefer it, I will in future keep all criticisms of the *Dublin* to myself, but you will realise that your ignorance of them will not prevent their having effect in regions where I may be able to exercise little influence in your favour.[69]

The Archbishop was criticised for alleged leniency in his handling of Ward. Archbishop Bagshawe, former Bishop of Nottingham, was unimpressed with his Metropolitan, 'You have not, I think, taken the same serious view of them that is taken by myself and others, which makes us desirous of a final settlement.'[70] Bagshawe's associate, Mgr Croke Robinson was even more outspoken, denouncing Ward's writings to the Archbishop as 'scandalous and offensive.'[71] Still Bourne took no action, beyond advising (together with Norfolk) that Ward get Bishop Hedley to write to Rome in support of his articles—which is precisely what happened.

Bourne also sought to defuse the situation when Cardinal Rampolla, Secretary of the Holy Office, required Ward to delete the final chapter of his Wiseman biography. Bourne pointed out the legal difficulties with compliance (ownership of the book rested with a non-Catholic publisher), engaged the support of Cardinal Mercier and repeatedly assured Rome of Ward's willingness to comply with its strictures. 'I can assure your Eminence that Mr Ward is in all things an obedient son of the Church, full of loyalty and good will.'[72] Even when Ward was not always willing to be guided, Bourne continued to counsel prudence. In dealing with the Vatican, there was nothing to be gained in attempting to have the last word; there were occasions when it was better just to let a matter drop.[73] Eventually, Ward followed the advice of Bourne and Mercier: the next edition of the Wiseman biography appeared without the final chapter.

The publication of *Pascendi* provided another potential flashpoint between Ward and Rome. His initial reading caused him sorrow and anger, believing, as he did (and as Tyrrell proclaimed in the *Times*), that the Encyclical condemned not only contemporary errors, but also much of Newman's thought. Subsequent discussion with theologians persuaded him that this was not the case. However, Ward felt the *Tablet's* treatment of the Encyclical superficial, evading the difficult issues it raised. He determined, therefore, to write his own commentary for the *Dublin Review*. He appreciated the risk he ran, and asked the Archbishop for a theological adviser to guide him. Bourne gave him Ward's friend, Fr Manuel Bidwell, Chancellor of Westminster. Ward submitted the article to Bidwell, who 'had evidently seen the Archbishop, and I think fought my battle. The article is now passed with some changes—but not serious ones.'[74] Ward escaped censure by Rome.

Not that Bourne was above criticising Ward. Simultaneously with writing his own article on *Pascendi*, Ward rejected another which he had commissioned from the Bishop of Limerick. The Bishop defended Newman against implicit condemnation, but Ward felt that he adopted too much the language and tone of the Encyclical and failed to appreciate the difficulties it caused some lay Catholics. Bourne was irritated—not least because it was rumoured that he personally had rejected the Bishop's article. He asked Ward to reflect on the nature of the *Review*, reminding him that he was the editor and not the proprietor. The Archbishop gave him a choice. 'You have asked for and been allowed a greater liberty of control of the *Review* than is usual when the Editor is not at the same time the Proprietor. I do not wish to lessen this liberty.' Ward ought to give space to a wider range of theological and philosophical opinion. Alternatively, if he was determined to prefer 'that particular school of thought which has your sympathy,' then he had to make it clear that those views were his personally, and not those of the Archbishop.[75] Hardly an unreasonable request. Von Hügel and Ward's more liberal friends might goad him that his position was 'equivocal' and that he was 'under the thumb of the Archbishop,'[76] but Bourne himself declared he would not intervene provided Ward remained 'within the bounds of Catholic orthodoxy.'[77] For his part, Ward wrote to the *Tablet* exonerating the Archbishop from responsibility for the omission of the Bishop of Limerick's article.

Bourne displayed courage in not jettisoning Ward in difficult times. Their relationship was not always easy. His daughter readily concedes that, in part, this was due to her father's lack of prudence and diplomacy—and a certain coolness on the part of the Archbishop. One senses, however, that Bourne essentially shared his editor's position when Ward wrote, 'I happen to be in contact with many earnest thinkers who feel deeply that the infidel movement can only be stemmed by the reconciliation of Christian faith with what is sound in modern thought and science and research, and that the Catholic Church alone can be strong enough to resist the tide ... To effect this reconciliation successfully free discussion is necessary.'[78] Maisie Ward was writing thirty years after the crisis to defend her father's reputation. Nevertheless, what she says about Bourne is verified by others, 'The Archbishop refused to undertake a campaign of denunciation and heresy-hunting. An interesting letter from Abbé Dimnet described him as "using very much the same language" as my father "in the presence of the Vicar-General Thomas and a secretary of Cardinal Richard's."'[79]

Pastorals and Encyclicals

Even before Bourne's arrival in Westminster intellectual controversies were making themselves felt in the life of the English Church. Cardinal Vaughan was no academic and had little time for those whose theories unsettled the faithful. He had no hesitation in condemning their position, known under its earlier title of 'Liberal Catholicism.' It was felt, especially in Rome, that press criticism of the Church required a response. This came at the end of 1900 in the form of a Joint Pastoral from the English hierarchy, 'The Church and Liberal Catholicism.' Although the Pastoral bore the signatures of the hierarchy, including Bourne's, it was reported that the real authorship lay with Merry del Val and Jesuits in Rome. Intriguingly, Ward believed that at least two of the Bishops signed the Pastoral while disagreeing with its contents, for fear of giving scandal if they did not.[80] Was one of these Bourne? He would have had no difficulty rejecting the substitution of 'the principle of private judgment for the principle of obedience to religious authority' and any attempt to democratise the Church, but the tone and tenor of the Pastoral were not his personally. Nor, given the line he subsequently took as Archbishop, is it clear whether he agreed the errors condemned had 'taken deep root in England.'[81]

Maisie Ward thought the Pastoral opportune. 'It was entirely necessary that those who were running into danger should remember before it was too late that Christ had left a deposit of revealed truth to His Church, which was empowered infallibly to teach and guard. The existence of the *Ecclesia docens* did seem by some to be set aside and human opinion put in place of divine revelation.'[82] Nevertheless, she conceded that the Pastoral was entirely negative in content, not giving Catholics the guidance they required as to how they might loyally serve the truth. The Pastoral proved an early skirmish in a wider conflict.

The temperature in Rome continued to rise after the election of Pius X. One of von Hügel's correspondents wrote late in 1906 of 'the burning question of "Modernism," the new two-edged sword with which our old men can kill whomsoever they like among us. The Pope's head and heart are full of zeal against the new heretics, and bursts with it ... Rome is swarming with spies watching the "Modernists." To be a friend to suspected people is a crime.'[83] The storm broke with the publication of two papal documents the following year. In July 1907 the *Tablet* welcomed *Lamentabili*, 'The Decree comes appositely ... It comes in time to warn those to whom "Modernism" is yet little more than a name, an attractive name, it is true—that certain of its tendencies are as dangerous as some of its already enunciated conclusions are false.'[84]

The Magisterium's comprehensive response to Modernism was, however, contained in the Encyclical, *Pascendi*, which appeared in September 1907. Everyone acknowledged that prior to the publication of *Pascendi* there was confusion as to what actually constituted Modernism. Was it the desire to save Catholic scholarship from discredit by engaging with modern thought and research on disputed questions, not least in the field of biblical criticism? Or was it the attempt—more or less consciously, in good faith or otherwise—to adapt the faith to modern sensibilities, substituting human experience for revealed truth? 'The Modernists had no text book. The Encyclical gave them one, and then proceeded to condemn it.'[85]

Pascendi was certainly strong on condemnation: 56 pages of a total of 66. The language too was strong. The Modernists were people who were 'thoroughly imbued with the poisonous doctrines taught by the enemies of the Church, and lost to all sense of modesty, put themselves forward as reformers of the Church.' Modernism itself was 'the synthesis of all heresies.' The Encyclical saw a concerted conspiracy. 'It is one of the cleverest devices of the Modernists (as they are commonly and rightly called) to present their doctrines without order and systematic arrangement, in a scattered and disjointed manner, so as to make it appear as if their minds were in doubt or hesitation, whereas in reality they are quite fixed and steadfast.'[86]

Tyrrell maintained that *Pascendi* travestied the Modernist position.[87] Certainly, there was little evidence for a conscious, coordinated plot; most who found themselves condemned were working in good faith, sincerely believing they were advancing the cause of Catholicism. There were a few like Loisy, holding themselves out as Catholics, while privately having lost their faith. That is not to say, however, that *Pascendi* was unnecessary. 'Nothing short of an intervention of authority could have saved the situation. Authority intervened, killed Modernism inside the Church, and cleared the path for the full revival of Catholic thought ... This period was undoubtedly one of chastisement even for some Catholic thinkers of undoubted loyalty.'[88] Writing in the late 1930s, Maisie Ward's optimism concerning the definitive demise of Modernism is questionable, but her basic assessment is fair. Too many Catholic theologians were subconsciously stumbling towards an implicit denial of the faith. In seeking to establish the academic credentials of their belief, they were sometimes overeager to accept uncritically the provisional results of liberal Protestant research. There was an excessive willingness to emphasize the human, to downplay the divine. Many Modernists might have been personally very devout—but take away the content of divine revelation, the divine institution of the Church and the sacraments—on what was their devotion founded? 'The

Modernists claimed that Catholic thought needed reviving—and no doubt it did. But did anything they wrote do much to revive it?'[89]

Pascendi mandated various solutions for combating Modernism. There was to be a return to Scholastic philosophy. Censorship was to be tightened. Suspect books and periodicals were to be removed from the seminaries. Modernists were not allowed to teach or hold positions of authority. Diocesan Councils of Vigilance were to be established 'to watch more carefully for every trace and sign of Modernism.'[90] In addition in 1910 Pius X required priests to take an anti-Modernist oath.

The Westminster diocesan journal reassured its readers, 'Happily the number of Catholics in this country who have manifested Modernist tendencies is comparatively insignificant, and few, if any, of them have acquired any established reputation for learning.'[91] This was the line followed by most English Bishops: they welcomed the Encyclical, but, given the problem did not really exist in England, there was little more to be said and done. Merry del Val disagreed, taking issue with the English Bishops' address to the Holy Father. 'There is one sentence which does not come very opportunely just now, I mean where it is said there is little or nothing of Modernism among English Catholics ... Though there are not many English Modernists, there is a quite sufficient number of them, of different grades, in proportion to the comparatively limited number of English Catholics, clerical or lay, who are in a position to discuss such matters, half tinkered converts, etc. Hence, though the address is excellent in itself and its true meaning, it would be better not to publish it.'[92]

Bourne did not let the matter drop. Knowing Merry del Val was unlikely to agree, he reiterated his assessment that the situation in England was more healthy and nuanced than the Secretary of State would have others believe, 'In using the word *paucissimos* we, the Bishops, wished to testify to a fact that we believed would bring joy and consolation to the heart of the Holy Father. And we used the word because honestly with the special knowledge which we have as to the condition of England, we consider it to represent the reality ... A *very* few in England have been infected with the deadly errors condemned in the Encyclical. A considerably larger number have had a vague sympathy for the persons, rather than the doctrines with which they have had little real acquaintance, of certain leading Modernists almost entirely foreigners, and this sympathy has been often taken as affecting the doctrines and not the persons. A certain number have adopted opinions, some legitimate and others erroneous but not in the gravest degree, of the Modernists. All these, with very few exceptions, being quite loyal to the Holy See, have changed anything that was faulty in their attitudes as soon as they realised the true character of Modernism.'[93] (Bourne was playing with fire to suggest to Merry del Val that Modernists might have 'legitimate' opinions!)

Gasquet informed Bourne of the state of affairs in Rome. 'Here the situation is very curious indeed but not by any means pleasant. There are more rumours and reports about everybody and everything than I remember before. Suspicions as to the leanings of this and that person to dangerous opinions: reports that "Rome" has directed this dismissal of this or that proposal: all these things are in the air and it is by no means pleasant.'[94] The Archbishop was determined that there should be no such atmosphere of suspicion, recrimination and denunciation in England— because he genuinely judged it unnecessary. What he had told Merry del Val privately, he repeated publicly. 'At one moment we had intended to address you more fully on this subject, but we feel there is no need to do so. The few at home who had embraced the fundamental errors condemned by the Holy Father, have by their subsequent letters made manifest their real spirit, and have by their own acts utterly destroyed such influence as they may once have possessed over the minds of loyal Catholics. Those, a larger number, who had evinced sympathy with the persons, rather than with the doctrines, of certain among the Modernistic writers, and were thereby in danger of ultimately adopting even their intellectual position, have been warned in time of the dangers of the path into which their steps were straying. Those who, unconscious of the final consequences of teachings which had attracted them, were inclined to accept conclusions which were covertly connected with the extreme Modernistic doctrines, have had their eyes opened ... On this account, trusting to that purity of faith and loyalty of obedience which are traditional among you, we feel that we are not called upon to dwell at greater length on this sad and painful subject.'[95]

Contrast this with the language and tone of the Pastoral issued south of the Thames just three months earlier. 'We, as loyal and devoted Catholics, lovingly accept the Encyclical, and at a time when the teaching of the Catholic Church is attacked, we gladly profess our faith as against the errors of Modernism ... We cannot permit to scholars the right to remodel Christian doctrine, and turn it, as they have sought to do, into a broad and liberal Protestantism.'[96]

'My fullest sympathy'

Bourne's public utterances were accompanied by genuine compassion for individuals who found themselves in conscientious difficulties. This applied not only to notorious Modernists, but also to priests of his own Diocese.

Almost the first pastoral case with which the Archbishop dealt on his arrival in Westminster concerned St George Mivart, a convert biologist who sought to reconcile Darwin's theory of evolution with Catholic doctrine. Mivart accepted evolution as it applied to the physical sphere, while maintaining the direct creation of the soul. It was, however, his theological musings which brought him into serious trouble with Rome, downplaying the traditional Catholic understanding of hell and arguing for the possibility of 'happiness in hell.' Mivart initially submitted to the Holy Office's condemnation, but withdrew that submission when he felt Catholics were being prevented from accepting the findings of scientific research, proceeding to make rash public comments on papal infallibility. When Mivart refused to retract his position, Vaughan denied him a Catholic burial when he died in 1900. It was a decision with which the Bishop of Southwark disagreed. 'I well remember, some years ago, how angry he was at Cardinal Vaughan's action in the case of Mivart.'[97]

Mivart had been ill for some time before his death. His family produced medical evidence that the illness had adversely affected his judgment. While Vaughan procrastinated on the family's plea to allow a subsequent Catholic burial, Bourne permitted this within weeks of his appointment as Archbishop. The widow wrote to him, 'You have filled my heart with gratitude in giving permission for my beloved husband to have a Christian burial ... Your name will be for ever blessed and loved for this noble act.'[98]

The Archbishop always found time to deal personally with his priests troubled by intellectual difficulties. Fr Cecil Burns was a lecturer at St Edmund's. Bourne wanted him to teach Thomistic philosophy, and spent time helping the priest reconcile his 'private opinions,' so that Burns subsequently wrote, 'Your great kindness at our last interview gives me the greatest confidence in hoping for your continued blessing and approval.'[99] In 1911 Mgr Poyer informed the Archbishop of his difficulty in taking the anti-Modernist oath. Bourne broke off from his work to reply immediately to Poyer.

> Your letter now received is the first intimation that I have received from any one that you have been passing through so serious a

> mental crisis, and I deeply regret that you have never mentioned the matter to me personally. I know not if I could have helped you, but certainly you would have had my fullest sympathy. And the knowledge of your difficulties would have made clearer to me many things which perplexed me in your attitude. I trust that you will come and see me and speak with all frankness ... I beg Our Lord to guide and comfort you and I will not forget you at the altar.[100]

Poyer's experience was the same as that of Burns: 'A thousand thanks for your sweetness and goodness yesterday. I shall never forget it and how I wish I had come to you before!'[101]

Bourne did not enjoy a good 'success rate.' Burns subsequently declined a parish appointment and told the Archbishop that he wanted 'no further connection with Ecclesiastical Authority.'[102] He left the Church in 1908 and became a distinguished academic in the Universities of London and Glasgow. Poyer still felt unable to take the anti-Modernist oath. Bourne wanted to maintain contact, and offered to find him a position in Canada.[103] (Why theological opinions problematic in England should be acceptable in far-flung parts of the Empire is not immediately apparent.) But Poyer declined the offer, leaving the Church to marry in 1911. No one can doubt, however, Bourne's heartfelt attempt to be a true father to his priests.

'Leanings towards Modernism'

Returning to the original question—was Bourne a Modernist? That term was used in a variety of different senses, being applied both to those who obstinately upheld a heretical position and also to those who sought a genuinely Catholic response to the various issues raised by modern learning and which needed to be addressed. Bourne was no Modernist in the first sense. As a seminarian, priest, seminary rector and bishop he consistently advocated engaging with contemporary culture, and continued to do so even when such views were far from popular in Rome.

As Bishop of Southwark, Bourne lent his patronage to liberal scholarship. The *Weekly Register* was a Catholic journal, begun by Manning and not favoured by Vaughan, which published the work of Tyrrell and his friends. When the *Weekly Register* ran into financial difficulties, Tyrrell insisted it be kept in existence as a counterweight to the *Tablet*, a journal *'professedly* Newmanian in its tone and tactics and views.'[104] It was to be reorganised as a monthly, and Bourne, with Hedley and Gasquet, was happy to give at least moral support. 'I do not wish to refuse any encouragement to the *Monthly Register*, that my name can give, as I wish it heartily every success, but I fear that I can only be a *very very* occasional contributor. The work of my diocese is always increasing, and leaves me little leisure for study or writing.'[105] His name appeared, with those of Gasquet, Wilfrid Ward, Bernard Ward and others, on the circular urging attendance at a meeting at Norfolk House to promote the venture. 'There is a strong feeling in the minds of many Catholics that it is of the utmost importance to our body that we should possess a periodical—probably, at least at first, of a monthly character—absolutely abreast of the religious, ethical and social movements of the day. Such a journal should be imbued with the Catholic spirit, and devoted to the interests of the Church.'[106] Despite the eirenic overtures, the contributors were mainly of a particular hue—von Hügel, Loisy and Duchesne were all approached. 'Despite these efforts the *Monthly Register* went the way of its predecessor in a very short time' and 'died from lack of support.'[107]

Bourne was not a trimmer. In the immediate aftermath of *Pascendi* he was not afraid to state that his views were unchanged. 'Subjects and methods of study will surely pass through vicissitude. What is done today will be criticised, and criticism will be a spur to greater effort. All these things must come to pass; they are the conditions of advancement and success.'[108]

He used his influence to mitigate the severity of some of the harsher anti-Modernist measures and rhetoric. 'He deprecated most earnestly the reckless flinging about of epithets that one sometimes heard. It was not Catholic, it was contrary to the spirit of the Catholic Church and most contrary to the spirit of charity. No such words as he had heard uttered should be uttered without most absolute proof.'[109] Bourne asked Pius X for permission to allow periodicals in the English seminaries so that seminarians might be able to read the *Dublin Review*.[110] He established in December 1907 a Council of Vigilance for Westminster but it was claimed that it 'rarely meets, and does no business, and that no effort has been made to deal in any other way with what is (alleged to be) a present danger.'[111]

Did Bourne underestimate the dangers of the crisis, and thereby justify the rumours of 'leanings towards Modernism' which Fr Considine reported? His sympathies clearly lay with a wide degree of openness in Catholic thought; he had a surprising degree of contact with those suspect in the eyes of Rome. He was able to distinguish degrees of legitimacy in the 'Modernist' position. In common with many others, he failed to see initially where the work of Loisy and Tyrrell was leading. Yet, at the same time, even before *Pascendi*, he could acknowledge the existence of dangers—and suggest sensible solutions. He warned of 'a danger of long-standing, which has ever existed to some extent, but which at the present time is especially acute:

> I mean the seeming conflict between old truth, and that which may be regarded as new knowledge. What is to be our attitude ... ? Neither headlong acceptance of the new teaching, nor panic at its approach. We have to consider it calmly, to place it firmly in juxtaposition to the received teaching, to wait for the living voice of the Holy Spirit to tell us definitely what we may accept, and what we must reject. And let us not be afraid that those who guide the teaching of the Church will speak too soon, or too late, hastily or imprudently; for the guidance of God is over them.[112]

Bourne's response to the Modernist crisis was fundamentally Catholic, and compassionate. He was largely at one with Wilfrid Ward, who 'condemned Modernism, but he considered that each Modernist's *conscience* was an affair for himself, for God, and for no one else.'[113]

'The brighter ecclesiastical atmosphere'

With the election of Pope Benedict XV on 3 September 1914 Bourne found himself more in tune with papal thinking on intellectual issues. Pope Benedict issued his first Encyclical within two months. He renewed the condemnation of Modernism in so far as it denied the content of revelation, but his tone differed massively from that of his predecessor. In fact, it is far more similar to Bourne's 1908 Pastoral. 'It is our will that Catholics should abstain from certain appellations which have recently been brought into use to distinguish one group of Catholics from another. They are to be avoided not only as "profane novelties of words," out of harmony with both truth and justice, but also because they give great trouble and confusion among Catholics.'[114]

Bourne led the English Church wisely and prudently through particularly testing times. No wonder he could later write with undisguised relief to Ward's widow, 'God has not spared him to these days in which the brighter ecclesiastical atmosphere associated with the new Pontificate would have rendered so much easier the task which he had taken in hand. But his merit will be greater because the work was more difficult ... The first declaration of the present Holy Father brought solace to many minds and has had far-reaching effects.'[115]

Notes

1. *Tablet*, 29 August 1903, p. 321.
2. FAB, homily at Requiem for Fr Robert Butler, 5 November 1902, cited FAB, *Occasional Sermons* (London: Sheed & Ward, 1930), p. 14.
3. Hogan, *Clerical Studies*, p. 168.
4. Clifton, *A History of the Archdiocese of Southwark*, p. 55.
5. D. Considine, SJ, to FAB, 8 June 1911, AAW, Bo. III/124/5.
6. Butt to Bidwell, 10 March 1911, AAW, Bo. IV/11/20.
7. Butt to Cahill, 17 May 1909, AAW, Bo. IV/11/1.
8. Butt to Cahill, 18 May 1909, AAW, Bo. IV/11/2.
9. Butt to Cahill, 19 May 1909, AAW, Bo. IV/11/3.
10. Amigo to Cahill, 28 May 1909 (copy), AAW, Bo. IV/11/10.
11. Butt to Bidwell, 10 March 1911, AAW, Bo. IV/11/20.
12. Amigo, 13 February 1911, SAA, cited S. Finnegan, *In Hope of Harvest: The Story of St John's Seminary* (Wonersh: The Wonersh Press, 2011), p. 129.
13. Corbishley to Doubleday, 6 January 1912, SAA, Wonersh, 1904–36.
14. W. Ward to J. Ward, 1900, cited M. Ward, *Insurrection versus Resurrection*, p. 221.
15. Burton, Diary, 29 November 1905, CDA.
16. FAB, Easter Day homily, 23 March 1913, *Times*, 24 March 1913.
17. Loisy, *Mémoires*, i, p. 209 cited de la Bedoyère, *The Life of Baron von Hügel*, p. 73.
18. A. Vidler, *A Variety of Catholic Modernists* (Cambridge: Cambridge University Press, 1970), p. 113.
19. von Hügel, Diary, cited de la Bedoyère, *The Life of Baron von Hügel*, p. 153.
20. Mignot to von Hügel, 29 November 1903, SAUL, von Hügel Papers, ms 2800.
21. B. Reardon, *Roman Catholic Modernism* (London: A. & C. Black, 1970), p. 16.
22. Loisy, *Mémoires*, ii, pp. 168, 397 cited de la Bedoyère, *The Life of Baron von Hügel*, pp. 143, 35.
23. Loisy, *Autour d'un Petit Livre*, (1903), cited Reardon, *Roman Catholic Modernism*, p. 104.
24. Ward, *Insurrection versus Resurrection*, p. 162.
25. *Ibid.*, p. 171.
26. Rome correspondent, *Tablet*, 4 April 1903, p. 534.
27. *Tablet*, 2 January 1904, p. 18.
28. Considine to FAB, 8 June 1911, AAW, Bo. III/124/5.
29. de la Bedoyère, *The Life of Baron von Hügel*, pp. 159, 162.
30. von Hügel to Ward, 10 March 1904, SAUL, Ward Family Papers, ms 38347/VII/143/140.
31. FAB to Ward, 19 March 1904, SAUL, Ward Family Papers, ms 38347/VII/43/1/2.
32. Merry del Val to Norfolk, 1904, ACA.

33   FAB, Opening of Oratory Church, Birmingham, 9 October 1906, *Tablet*, 13 October 1906, p. 582.
34   FAB to Merry del Val, 7 December 1907, (copy), AAW, Roman Letters, VII/111.
35   Ward, *Insurrection versus Resurrection*, p. 187.
36   G. Tyrrell, SJ, *Lex Orandi* (1903), cited, Reardon, *Roman Catholic Modernism*, p. 136.
37   R. Colley, SJ, to FAB, 20 August 1903, AAW, Bo. I/32 [annotated by FAB]; Fr F. J. Clayton to FAB, 25 February 1906, AAW, Bo. I/32 [annotated by FAB].
38   *Tablet*, 5 October 1907, p. 533.
39   Merry del Val to FAB, 17 October 1907, AAW, Roman Letters, VII/111.
40   Tyrrell, *Medievalism: A Reply to Cardinal Mercier*, (1908), cited Reardon, *Roman Catholic Modernism*, pp. 165–166.
41   *Tablet*, 23 November 1912, p. 807.
42   FAB to Merry del Val, 7 December 1907, (copy), AAW, Roman Letters, VII/111.
43   C. Dessouvaly to von Hügel, 30 July 1909, SAUL, von Hügel Papers, ms 2390, Location 8/I/1.
44   W. Tyrrell to J. Ward, 12 April 1906, SAUL, Ward Family Papers, ms 38347/VII/295/2.
45   FAB to Jackman, 30 November 1912, AAW, Bo. I/18.
46   FAB to Merry del Val, 15 August 1909, AAW, Bo. III/124/5.
47   Cahill to FAB, u/d, 1909, AAW, Bo. I/32.
48   FAB to M. Petre, 20 December 1907, AAW, Bo. I/32.
49   Ward, *William George Ward and the Catholic Revival*, cited de la Bedoyère, *The Life of Baron von Hügel*, p. 35.
50   M. Petre, *My Way of Faith* (1937), p. 256.
51   von Hügel, 1921, *Selected Letters*, p. 344, cited de la Bedoyère, *The Life of Baron von Hügel*, p. 239.
52   de la Bedoyère, *The Life of Baron von Hügel*, pp. 186–187, 190.
53   *Ibid.*, p. 195.
54   Evelyn Underhill, cited *Ibid.*, p. xii.
55   Ward, *Insurrection versus Resurrection*, p. 489.
56   de la Bedoyère, *The Life of Baron von Hügel*, p. 275.
57   Merry del Val to FAB, u/d [December 1906], AAW, Bo. III/124/2/42.
58   de la Bedoyère, *The Life of Baron von Hügel*, p. 354.
59   von Hügel to Loisy, cited *Mémoires*, ii, pp. 41–42, cited de la Bedoyère, *The Life of Baron von Hügel*, p. 134.
60   FAB, London Oratory, St. Philip's Day 1906, *Tablet*, 2 June 1906, p. 863.
61   Ward, 'Liberalism and Intransigence,' *The Nineteenth Century*, xlvii, June 1900, p. 971.
62   Norfolk to Ward, 12 October 1902, SAUL, Ward Family Papers, ms 38347/VII/222/1/84.

63 von Hügel to Ward, 18 April 1905, SAUL, Ward Family Papers, ms 38347/VII/143/147.
64 Ward to FAB, 7 January 1905, copy, SAUL, Ward Family Papers, ms 38347/VII/43/3/1.
65 Norfolk to Ward, 3 August 1907, SAUL, Ward Family Papers, ms 38347/VII/43/2.
66 Merry del Val to Broadhead, 17 January 1908, UCA, Broadhead Papers, OS/J/11.
67 Ward, *Insurrection versus Resurrection*, pp. 150–151.
68 FAB to Ward, 11 November 1906, SAUL, Ward Family Papers, ms 38347/VII/43/1/3.
69 FAB to Ward, 31 July 1907, SAUL, Ward Family Papers, ms 38347/VII/43/1/6.
70 Archbishop Bagshawe to FAB, 15 August 1907 (copy), SAUL, Ward Family Papers, ms 38347/VII/12.
71 Mgr Croke Robinson to FAB, 29 August 1907, copy, SAUL, Ward Family Papers, ms 38347/VII/43/4/2.
72 FAB to Cardinal Rampolla, 26 January 1910 & 27 February 1910 (copies), SAUL, Ward Family Papers, ms 38347/IV/J(4i & ii).
73 Cardinal Mercier to Ward, 2 May 1911, SAUL, Ward Family Papers, ms 38347/VII/203/1/12; FAB to Ward, 6 May 1911, SAUL, Ward Family Papers, ms 38347/VII/43/1/13.
74 Ward to Norfolk, 30 November 1907, cited Ward, *Insurrection versus Resurrection*, pp. 288–289.
75 FAB to Ward, 26 January 1908, SAUL, Ward Family Papers, ms 38347/VII/43/1/9.
76 B. Clutton to Ward, 23 February 1908, SAUL, Ward Family Papers, ms 38347/VII/68/1.
77 FAB to Ward, 26 January 1908, SAUL, Ward Family Papers, ms 38347/VII/43/1/9.
78 Ward, draft memorandum prepared for Rampolla, 1910, cited Ward, *Insurrection versus Resurrection*, p. 323.
79 Ward, *Insurrection versus Resurrection*, pp. 302–303.
80 R. O'Neil, MHM, *Cardinal Herbert Vaughan* (Tunbridge Wells: Burns & Oates, 1995), pp. 417–418.
81 Joint Pastoral, 'The Church and Liberal Catholicism,' 29 December 1900.
82 Ward, *Insurrection versus Resurrection*, p. 136.
83 Fr Genocchi, OP, to von Hügel, 5 November 1906, cited Bedoyère, *The Life of Baron von Hügel*, p. 181.
84 Editorial, *Tablet*, 27 July 1907, p. 122.
85 Ward, *Insurrection versus Resurrection*, p. 260.
86 Pope Pius X, *Pascendi Dominici Gregis*, 8 September 1907.
87 G. Tyrrell, *Christianity at the Crossroads* (London, 1913), p. 3.
88 Ward, *Insurrection versus Resurrection*, p. 254.
89 *Ibid.*, p. 178.
90 *Pascendi.*

91 Editorial, *WCC*, November 1907, p. 7.
92 Merry del Val to FAB, 17 October 1907, AAW, Roman Letters, VII/111.
93 FAB to Merry del Val, 7 December 1907, (copy), AAW, Roman Letters, VII/111.
94 Gasquet to FAB, 10 January 1908, AAW, Roman Letters VII/109 (loose).
95 FAB, Pastoral Letter, 1 March 1908.
96 Amigo, Advent Pastoral Letter 1907.
97 Dessouvaly to von Hügel, 30 July 1909, SAUL, von Hügel Papers, ms 2390, Location 8/I/1.
98 M. A. Mivart to FAB, 19 January 1904, AAW, Bo. I/85/5.
99 C. Burns to FAB, 30 July 1906, AAW, Bo. III/46/1.
100 FAB to Mgr Poyer, 16 May 1911, AAW, Bo. III/47/11.
101 Poyer to FAB, 18 May 1911, AAW, Bo. III/47/12.
102 Burns to FAB, 13 January 1908, AAW, Bo. III/46/8.
103 FAB to Poyer, 28 May 1911, AAW, Bo. III/47/15.
104 Tyrrell to Ward, 1901, cited Ward, *Insurrection versus Resurrection*, p. 145.
105 FAB to F. Ley, 13 March 1902 (copy), SAUL, Ley Papers, ms 36363/61.
106 Circular, FAB, Gasquet, B. Ward, W. Ward & others to Ley & others, 30 October 1902, SAUL, Ley Papers, ms 36363/76.
107 Ward, *Insurrection versus Resurrection*, pp. 146, 185.
108 FAB address at Ushaw Centenary, July 1908, cited *Cardinal Bourne: A Record of the Sayings and Doings* (London: Burns & Oates, 1911), p. 85.
109 FAB address to the inaugural general meeting of the CWL, 19 December 1907, *Tablet*, 28 December 1907, p. 1020.
110 FAG to Norfolk, 11 January 1911, SAUL, Ward Family Papers, ms 38347/VII/109/2/2.
111 Considine to FAB, 8 June 1911, AAW, Bo. III/124/5.
112 FAB, London Oratory, St Philip's Day 1906, *Tablet*, 2 June 1906, pp. 862–863.
113 Ward, *Insurrection versus Resurrection*, p. 300.
114 Pope Benedict XV, *Ad Beatissimi*, 1 November 1914.
115 FAB to J. Ward, 10 February 1918, cited Ward, *Insurrection versus Resurrection*, p. 517.

Chapter 13

The Red Hat

To date every Archbishop of Westminster has been created a Cardinal of the Holy Roman Church. The expectation is that 'the red hat' goes with the job. Of the ten Archbishops so honoured, a number were made cardinals within a matter of months of their appointment to Westminster. Only Manning had to wait longer than Bourne's eight years. It was a delay which Bourne felt keenly. Why was he made to wait?

Liberalising in Theology?

Was it because the Archbishop was suspected of Modernist tendencies? Amigo's biographer thinks there may be substance in this. 'One story current at the time which was still going the rounds a few years ago, was that Bishop Amigo had accused Archbishop Bourne of fostering Modernism at the Seminary. Also that this report was responsible for the long delay before Archbishop Bourne received the honour of the cardinalate.'[1]

In 1906 Bourne was fretting that from the moment of his appointment to Westminster 'a steady movement of opposition was set on foot to discredit me in England and still more in Rome.' He complained to Merry del Val that his opponents aimed 'to prevent the Holy See ever showing me any sign of satisfaction or approbation.' To this end they had circulated various rumours, including that he was "liberalising" in theology and that "Abbot Gasquet would be called to the Cardinalate in my place".'[2] Bourne's nerves were frayed by the 1906 Education Bill crisis—not helped by his being in Paris temporarily removed from the scene of parliamentary negotiations. Merry del Val was not the man to write to in a tone of self-pity. The Secretary of State told Bourne quite abruptly to ignore the petty stories which circulate around anyone in authority. If he aimed to put the Archbishop's mind at rest, he failed. While he dismissed the other rumours, he mentioned that Bourne had been criticised for exercising insufficient control over the *Tablet* which seemed 'to show sympathy and almost support in favour of writers of unorthodox views' such as von Hügel and Ward. 'But I do not think that anybody has said that *you* personally were liberalising, and the criticism has not gone very far when you have not been asked to explain by Propaganda.'³ That is insufficient reason to think that Modernism had cost Bourne the red hat, and nothing further was said publicly for another 2½ years.

At a meeting in London on 14 May 1909 Bishop Cahill heard a piece of clerical gossip. Dom Bede Camm had created a great stir in Archbishop's House by telling the Cathedral clergy that 'the Archbishop was known to be favourable to advanced opinions.' He went on to say that Fr Denis Sheil, whose sister was married to a cousin of Merry del Val, had learnt that the 'great cordiality' previously existing between Bourne and Merry del Val was now at end because of a letter written by Amigo to Rome complaining about Modernism in Wonersh and seeking advice on the closure of the Seminary. 'Finally he said Archbishop Bourne would never be made Cardinal while Pius X lived.'

People respected Bourne's integrity and competence, but he lacked the warmth and charisma—not qualities necessarily expected of early twentieth-century Catholic prelates—to inspire affection in a wider audience. Only a very few came to know him intimately. Those who did were usually fiercely loyal. Cahill was one of the inner circle determined to protect his friend at all costs, realising that Bourne 'could hardly defend himself effectively if he were supposed to be fighting for the Cardinalate.'⁴ Cahill shared his information with another of Bourne's supporters, Mgr Joseph Butt, whose presence in Rome as Vice-Rector of the Beda College allowed him to pursue the veracity of the allegations. Butt went immediately to Merry del Val, who revealed little. Butt felt the true source of the rumours was not Southwark, but Birmingham, where there was ongoing resentment at Wonersh's role in the ending of the Central Seminary experiment. Butt felt Amigo was 'truly innocent' although he may have 'said various silly things and full use is made of these.'⁵ Butt proposed to continue quietly talking to people in Rome to elicit further information and to put a stop to the calumnies which were circulating. On reflection Butt thought stories about Modernism in Wonersh unlikely to account for the delay in the Archbishop being made Cardinal. They required certainty before confronting Merry del Val directly.⁶

Unfortunately, Cahill lacked Butt's prudence. He wrote to the Archbishop, who was in the Iberian Peninsula, 'I have made up my mind to go for [Amigo]. I will let him begin, and then I will tell him that I am glad he has given me the opportunity, and pour out what is in my mind.'⁷

In the event, Cahill did not even wait for Amigo to begin, and launched a furious attack on the Bishop of Southwark. Sparing no detail, he pointed out the likely consequences of Amigo's alleged delation. If Bourne was thought 'to be favourable to Modernist views, this is, if one remembers the Encyclical, not far from saying he is a *fautor* of heresy. If so he will have incurred excommunication specially reserved to the Holy See.' When he saw him, Cahill thought the Archbishop

> overwhelmed by the accusation. I know him well enough to be sure that if he is convinced that these accusations are entertained in Rome, he will argue that Rome has no confidence in him, and that he is discredited; and when he arrives at that stage he will hardly hesitate to resign everything. He has now for some years been attacked. Only last November I received a newspaper cutting purporting to come as a telegram from Rome, and saying this very thing that he was to lose the Cardinal's hat because he did not deal firmly with Modernism. I made inquiries in Rome, and I was satisfied that the paragraph did not originate in Rome. We have been asking in vain what is at the bottom of these reports, who is the real author. Now a definitive statement is made giving the groundwork of the reports and coupling your name with it.[8]

Cahill would have done well to have checked the basis of his 'definitive statement' first. (Subsequently, both Camm and Sheil adamantly denied the statements attributed to them.) Amigo was indignant, rebuking Cahill for choosing

> to accept on the authority of Westminster Cathedral gossip such a gross charge against me ... The whole tone of your letter conveys the impression to me that you and some other bishops believe that I have been mean enough to write to Cardinal Merry del Val what would be most detrimental to the Archbishop and altogether false ... I am sorry that anybody should pain the Archbishop by such reports, but I think I have even more reason to be angry because my name has been associated with such a charge. It is a very great pity that Mgr Butt should have been to Cardinal Merry del Val, but, as he has been, I shall write to the Cardinal denying the statements attributed to me.[9]

Butt was horrified by Cahill's letter. He thought Amigo had 'every right to resent' the allegations. Butt was forced to have another embarrassing interview with Merry del Val, attempting to explain the fractious behaviour of the English Bishops and having to admit there were those who sought to attack Bourne by fastening upon him 'a vague sort of reputation of being favourable to Modernism.' Merry del Val acted very decently in the circumstances. He assured Butt that no one had run to him to tell tales about the Archbishop since the death of Ethelred Taunton. Butt urged patience on Bourne. 'There is not a jot of evidence to show that *anyone* here lacks confidence in you; on the contrary everything points the other way ... The one thing that might be disastrous at the moment is to make a stir ... The Bishops of Portsmouth and Southwark are the only two people at all likely to complicate matters, and I think it would be wise to try and calm down the former, and as far as possible to make the latter feel he is safe for the moment from any trouble here.'[10] Bourne eventually asked Cahill to write to Amigo absolving him of any responsibility for the allegations, but displayed no concern at Cahill's tactics. 'I trust that your letter will have made our good friend in Southwark realise the danger of his unguarded and reckless talk.'[11]

Undoubtedly, Merry del Val would have preferred Bourne to have taken a more forceful line on Modernism—and he held tremendous sway with the Pope—but there is no firm evidence that the Archbishop's theological opinions in any way contributed to the delay in his being made a Cardinal. Archbishop Mercier of Malines maintained a similar position to Bourne's—he was initially prepared to offer Tyrrell a place in his diocese, he advised Ward in his difficulties with Rome—but this did not prevent him being raised to the Sacred College in 1907. There must have been other reasons.

'We don't know'

Butt's advice was unfailingly wise and prudent. The Archbishop would have done well to prefer it to Cahill's speculation and paranoia. 'We don't know ... we don't know ... we don't know.' The Rector of the Beda knew that, when it wished, the Roman Curia kept its secrets well, and there was little point on speculating on ulterior motives. It was possible 'that *present* antics in Southwark' might be having an effect. Rome was distinctly unimpressed by the growing animosity between Bourne and Amigo. But it was not certain that this was the cause of the delay. There was some problem with the Patriarch of Lisbon, who might be using his influence adversely against Westminster. Again, it was not certain. And where did Merry del Val actually stand in all of this? He was 'inscrutable.'

'We must be *certain* of the Secretary's *present* hostility and *certain that it is blocking the way*, before we can safely deliver a direct attack.'[12]

The Archbishop was often his own worst enemy. Not being an 'Old Roman,' he seemed oblivious to Vatican etiquette. He could be terribly Anglo-Saxon: standing on his rights, lecturing others on the merits of his case. It was not well received by clerics accustomed to diplomatic niceties and ecclesiastical face-saving protocol. Bourne was not above giving the Pope himself the benefit of his mind when he felt he—or the British Empire—had received insufficient consideration. A case in point was Edward VII's funeral when Bourne requested permission for a Mass for the King to be said, despite being in the Octave of Pentecost. Permission was refused. The Archbishop communicated his irritation to both Merry del Val and Pius X: such an 'apparent want of sympathy on the part of Catholics in a national sorrow would, I am certain, have most serious results.'[13] Bourne learnt from Fr David Fleming how his comments had been received. 'I have been informed indirectly *but on the very best authority* that your letter of 29 May to his Holiness *was most displeasing to him.*'[14] Rome found Bourne difficult to deal with but, fortunately for his sake, by the time of Pius X the red hat was no longer awarded simply at the papal whim.

'Unspeakably painful'

Bourne was sensitive to criticism at the best of times. When he felt that the delay in being made a Cardinal might be due the Holy See's lack of confidence in his orthodoxy or abilities, his sensitivity knew no bounds.

It was not helped by constant speculation by the Roman correspondents of the secular and Catholic Press. Bourne was not even enthroned at Westminster before the *Tablet* reported, 'It is not improbable that the first Consistory of Pius X will be held some time in December, though nothing definite has been fixed yet on the matter ... The elevation of Mgr Bourne is also considered likely.'[15] Thereafter, Bourne had to read baseless stories concerning his probable elevation every few months. In November 1905 the *Times* reported, 'At the Vatican it is now considered as most probable that the fifth Cardinal to be appointed at the next Consistory will be Dr Bourne, Archbishop of Westminster.'[16] The *Tablet* had to respond, 'During the week a great many correspondents have announced, with varying degrees of assurance, that the Archbishop of Westminster is to be made a Cardinal at the next Consistory. The reports in question have no foundation.'[17] And so it went on for eight years—to the great detriment of the Archbishop's equanimity.

The speculation died down at times, and again approached a crescendo. Journalists and prelates assured themselves that the London Eucharistic Congress of 1908 was bound to bring papal recognition. An anonymous correspondent to Propaganda maliciously implied the very reason for the Congress was 'as a piece of window-dressing for the furtherance of a much desired end.'[18] But more friendly voices also thought that Bourne's successful handling of the Congress would be rewarded by Rome. The Papal Legate had not even left the country before Cahill was writing to the Archbishop, 'I think you must soon go to the hatter, the sooner you know the better, for then the enemies will be baulked.'[19] And he was raising his friend's expectations again later that same week. 'The *Daily Mail* has a paragraph from Rome that the red hat is to come to you as a reward, and that you are to be notified. May it be true this time.'[20] Mgr Mignot, Archbishop of Albi, might be thought a more authoritative source in such matters than the Rothermere Press. He wrote unhesitatingly to von Hügel, 'Mgr Bourne has conducted himself so well in this matter that the Pope will make him Cardinal.'[21]

When 1908 passed by and 1909 also began to slip away with no reliable news, the Archbishop's anxieties re-surfaced with a vengeance. Bourne always disavowed motives of personal ambition. There is little reason to doubt him. Beneath the insistence on due honour to ecclesiastical office, he lived a genuinely humble life. It was the thought that Rome had been prejudiced against him, the belief that the English Church and the capital city of the British Empire were being snubbed that discomforted him. Hence his susceptibility to the Cathedral gossip on Modernist leanings which caused him to write to Cahill,

> should there be any serious intention of disregarding Westminster I would ask you to intervene by a letter to [Merry del Val] ... The dignity in itself is nothing—but the manifest confidence of the Holy See is of extreme importance. Any omission now after the Congress would certainly be regarded as an expression of no-confidence and of disavowal, and the effect on my public position would be most grave. To me personally such clear absence of confidence would be unspeakably painful.[22]

'Not bound by precedent'

There was much contemporary—and subsequent—conjecture as to the reason why Bourne was made to wait. It might all be very much simpler than any of the theories advanced. Amidst all the groundless journalistic chatter, there were occasionally observations based on fact. A year after Bourne's arrival in Westminster the *Tablet*'s Rome correspondent noted,

> Death has ... dealt lightly with the Sacred College, for since the accession of Pius X, only two Cardinals have died and two have been created. The Sacred College is, therefore, only six short of its full number. In reality, however, all the seats in the Sacred College are never filled ... It is not at all probable at the present moment that any prelate of the English-speaking world will be raised to the purple this time.[23]

A commonsense and accurate comment.

The same correspondent made a similarly pertinent remark two years later.

> In less than three years no fewer than twelve Cardinals have died, while only six have been added to the Sacred College by Pius X. The Holy Father has already shown in a general way that he does not consider himself very rigorously bound by precedent in the creation of new Cardinals. He has not even bestowed the purple upon his own successor, the Patriarch of Venice, or on the Archbishop of Florence, although these sees were 'cardinatial' before his accession.[24]

Cardinals tended to be old men in the habit of dying frequently. Consistories at which their successors were appointed had, therefore, become a regular occurrence in the life of the Church. Under Pius IX and Leo XIII it was normal for a Consistory to be held every year, or at least every other year. Pius X felt no such compunction in observing this pattern. In a sudden burst of activity he created eleven new Cardinals in the two Consistories of 1907, but then followed the longest gap between Consistories at any time between the Fall of the Temporal Power and the Second World War. Various explanations were advanced—a desire for economy, Pius X's antipathy towards numerous curial Cardinals resident in Rome, diplomatic tensions with Austria and Portugal. Whatever the reason, one need not assume hostility towards the Archbishop of Westminster to explain why he was not made a Cardinal at an earlier date.

'A great surprise'[25]

When no Consistory had been announced by the summer of 1911 it was felt that the Church would have to wait until at least 1912 before any new Cardinals were created. Perhaps it was the deaths of a further three that persuaded the Holy Father that their numbers ought to be replenished. Gasquet wrote to Fr Fleming in early November, 'Well wonders will never cease! The surprise Consistory came as a bomb to all.'[26] The Archbishop had had word from Merry del Val just a few days previously, 'I have great pleasure in informing you that our Holy Father Pope Pius X has decided to confer upon you the eminent dignity of a Cardinal of the Holy Roman Church.'[27]

The Pope more than made up for so long a wait by creating nineteen new Cardinals. Again, a cursory glance at the list of names suggests there had been no particular prejudice against Bourne. He was still the youngest of the new Cardinals. The Archbishop of New York had had to wait a year longer for his red hat. The Pope also took the opportunity to affect the greatest change to the English Church since the restoration of the hierarchy sixty years earlier. England & Wales was to be divided into three provinces, Liverpool and Birmingham were to join Westminster as metropolitan sees.

The new Archbishop of Liverpool offered his congratulations. 'It will effectively clear away a cloud of misrepresentations that has gathered around Your Grace, and which must have caused you pain. One in your position could bear anything except the disfavour of the Holy See. Thank God, then, that all that is now gone.'[28] Not that one had a hint of that from the secular Press, which was fulsome in its tributes.

> Cardinal Bourne is, before all things, an administrator ... A singularly well-balanced mind, a disciplined, well-tempered will, a clear, cool judgment, and an unflagging zeal, behind a grave and calm exterior, are the instruments with which Cardinal Bourne bodies forth the ideals, practical, coherent and consistent, which form his universe of thought. Man of action, he is something of a recluse. Easy of access and simple, he lives much apart ... His little, simple exhortations at the time of his visitations show where his heart is placed ... He has proved efficient. That is his distinction.[29]

The *Times* vied with the *Telegraph* in its praise, speaking of

> his successful efforts to bind the Catholics of this province more closely together. In fact, never were English Catholics more united

than they are today ... Here and there through the work of the devoted pastor, the statesman and the leader of men has stood revealed ... His friends know him as a man singularly clear-headed and capable, with remarkable powers of concentration enabling him to grasp at once every side of a complex question and go straight to the issue involved. They know too that behind the quiet manner lies the immense strength which comes of entire singleness of aim. Rather silent than otherwise, he never speaks but to good purpose.[30]

The Archbishop travelled to Rome in late November. His old friend Mother Stuart described the *biglietto* ceremony—a polite fiction by which the recipient is formally notified of his impending dignity. The ceremony took place at the English College, where Bourne stayed. The *biglietto* 'was brought by the Chamberlain of the Cardinal Secretary of State who made his way through the crowd, mostly the English colony, but some of all nations, and a host of ecclesiastics. At the appointed moment the Archbishop appeared at a curtained door and met him, received the *biglietto* and handed it to—I think—Bishop Stanley to read aloud, received congratulations and returned thanks in Italian; then the messenger sped away in his hurried flight for the rest of his thirteen visits, and [the Archbishop] made his way to the top of the reception room, where, standing very suitably under a statue of Our Lady and a painting of St George on horseback, he made his discourse in English, and one could have heard a pin drop.'[31]

No wonder. Bourne's address was extraordinarily personal and poignant, referring to those 'unspeakably painful' moments the protracted anticipation had caused him. 'My gratitude to the Holy Father for his condescension towards me would be very inadequately told were I to leave unmentioned all that it means to me personally ... I have striven for the last eight years to discharge that duty to the extent of my power; I do not think that I have consciously failed therein. Yet all the time there were possibilities, nay probabilities, of misconception when perchance other voices, less informed, less authorised, and, therefore, less responsible, were endeavouring to convey information in all good faith, but not quite in the same guise. If then today the Sovereign Pontiff, in his exceeding kindness, is pleased to bestow upon me this, the highest token of his trust and confidence, may I not take it as a most consoling proof that my words and actions, perhaps even my silence, and, above all, my motives have not been misunderstood? The assurance of that confidence is the most precious gift that could be bestowed on me, while its absence would, indeed, make my burden almost too heavy to bear.'³²

Three days later the new Cardinal received the red hat from the hands of Pius X. Always ready to embrace modern technology, he alone arrived at the Vatican by motor car; the others preferring the traditional horse and carriage. There was then the business of taking possession of his titular church. He was particularly gratified by the choice of Santa Pudenziana. Not only was it one of the most ancient Roman churches, it had also been Cardinal Wiseman's titular. Christmas was spent with Mother Stuart in Malta.

It was late January 1912, therefore, when Cardinal Bourne returned to England. Before the public reception at Westminster Cathedral, he especially asked to spend the two previous nights at St Mary's, Clapham, the church of his baptism and ordination, so full of 'precious memories.'³³ After this brief period of seclusion, he was greeted by all the pomp the Archdiocese of Westminster could muster.

> The Cardinal crosses the threshold of his Cathedral, pauses in the vestibule, divests himself of his red mozetta, and assumes the brilliant red *cappa magna* of watered silk ... The Provost puts on his mitre and his Eminence takes his place beneath a silken canopy of white and gold. Again the organ peals, and the choir far away in the apse intone the *Sacerdos et Pontifex*.³⁴

After eight years no one was left in any doubt that England once more had a Prince of the Church in her midst.

Notes

1. Clifton, *Amigo*, p. 24.
2. FAB to Merry del Val, 6 December 1906 (copy), AAW, Bo. III/124/2/33.
3. Merry del Val to FAB, u/d [December 1906], AAW, Bo. III/124/2/42.
4. Cahill to Amigo, 24 May 1909, SAA, Wonersh, Addl. Material, 1934–1970, 52.
5. Butt to Cahill, 18 May 1909, AAW, Bo. IV/11/2.
6. Butt to Cahill, 25 May 1909, AAW, Bo. IV/11/11.
7. Cahill to FAB, 23 May 1909, AAW, Bo. IV/11/8.
8. Cahill to Amigo, 24 May 1909, SAA, Wonersh, Addl. Material, 1934–1970, 52.
9. Amigo to Cahill, 28 May 1909 (copy), AAW, Bo. IV/11/10.
10. Butt to FAB, 2 June 1909, AAW, Bo. IV/11/14.
11. FAB to Cahill, 15 & 7 June 1909, PDA A/6–04–16.

12. Butt to Cahill, 25 May 1909, AAW, Bo. IV/11/11.
13. FAB to Merry del Val, 13 May 1910 (copy), AAW, Bo. I/123; FAB to Pius X, 29 May 1910 (draft), AAW, Bo. I/123.
14. Fleming to FAB, 18 June 1910, AAW, Bo. I/123.
15. *Tablet*, 17 October 1903, p. 614.
16. *Times*, 5 November 1905.
17. *Tablet*, 18 November 1905, p. 810.
18. Anon., SCPF, 102/1908, f. 443, r. 555.
19. Cahill to FAB, 14 September 1908, AAW, Bo. III/124/7.
20. Cahill to FAB, 19 September 1908, AAW, Bo. III/124/7.
21. Mignot to von Hügel, 4 December 1908, SAUL, von Hügel Papers, ms 2819.
22. FAB to Cahill, 16 May 1909, PDA, A/6–04–16.
23. Rome correspondent, *Tablet*, 8 October 1904, p. 573.
24. Rome Correspondent, *Tablet*, 5 May 1906, p. 694.
25. Rome Correspondent, 29 October 1911, *Tablet*, 4 November 1911, p. 733.
26. Gasquet to Fleming, 4 November 1911, cited Leslie, *Cardinal Gasquet*, p. 201.
27. Merry del Val to FAB, 25 October 1911, AAW, Bo. IV/1/3a.
28. Whiteside to FAB, 31 October 1911, AAW, Bo. V/81c.
29. *Daily Telegraph*, 30 October 1911.
30. *Times*, 30 October 1911.
31. Stuart to Roehampton community, 25 November 1911, cited M. Monahan, *Life and Letters of Janet Erskine Stuart* (London: Longmans, Green and Co, 1922), p. 338.
32. FAB address at the *biglietto* ceremony, 27 November 1911, *Tablet*, 2 December 1911, p. 895.
33. FAB to Fr Stebbing, 12 January 1912, AAW, Bo. IV/20/19.
34. V. Wareing, 'The Cardinal's Home-Coming,' *WCC*, February 1912, p. 40.

1. *Francis Bourne in (?) 1869*

2.   *Seminary superior, aged 28*

3. *The first love: St John's Seminary, Wonersh*

4. *Southwark: friend and foe*
Canon Edward St John

4. Southwark: friend and foe
Bishop Peter Amigo

5. The Roman Curia
Cardinal Merry del Val

5. *The Roman Curia*
Cardinal Gasquet

6. *Archbishop Bourne, 1908*

7. *The new Cardinal, November 1911*

8. *A Cardinal at War*
Visiting the Fleet, 1916

8. *A Cardinal at War*

With the Dublin Fusiliers at the Western Front, 1917

9. *Cardinal Bourne in 1924*

10. *Cardinal Mercier*

11. *Centenary of Catholic Emancipation, September 1929*

12. *At Folkestone, April 1934*

13. *Golden Jubilee of priesthood*
On the balcony of Archbishop's House

13. *Golden Jubilee of priesthood
Outside the Cathedral*

14. The burial place: the Galilee Chapel, St Edmund's College, Ware

Chapter 14

'Trouble and Sadness'[1]

'Mgr Amigo, whom I believed I knew intimately'[2]

Westminster and Southwark priests of a certain generation tend to know only one thing about Cardinal Bourne and Bishop Amigo: the two men did not get along. For the better part of thirty years that was a massive understatement. But it was not ever thus.

Bourne made a huge effort (and expended considerable goodwill at home and in Rome) to ensure Amigo's appointment to Southwark. He was entirely transparent as to his motivation. 'He had desired Dr Amigo to be his successor in Southwark, because he believed that he of all men would continue and develop his work.'[3] He never let Amigo forget the fact. 'I beseech you to be on your guard against any action which would injure Bishop Butt's work for the maintenance and continuity of which alone, I procured your appointment as my successor in Southwark, at a cost to myself which evidently you are unable to appreciate.'[4]

Several years later, in the midst of appeals and recriminations, Bourne analysed the underlying source of the friction with his successor. 'Having been made bishop at 35, I always had against me certain older priests to whom my nomination was very disagreeable. Mgr Amigo was consecrated on 25 March 1904, and immediately these priests, believing (with reason) that he could be influenced by fear and flattery, told him that his nomination was also very unpopular, but that he could rapidly make himself popular by detaching himself completely from me, and freeing himself from my influence.'[5] Even if 'certain older priests' had determined to turn Amigo against him, they did not succeed in doing so immediately. The Archbishop had earlier reminisced, 'In the beginning he often consulted me, and I advised him as best I could.'[6]

An example of more harmonious relations was the 1906 Catholic Truth Society Conference held at Brighton. Bourne wrote to Amigo in advance assuring him he was 'most anxious to help you personally in any way that I can.' However, he proceeded to raise a difficulty. The

Archbishop felt, 'considering the position which the Canons of Southwark created for me at the time of my translation—an action which they have never retracted or justified—I cannot take part in such a public demonstration in the diocese, unless the situation has been made quite regular.'[7] The more magnanimous option would have been to have put the incident firmly in the past. However, it is indicative of the Archbishop's sensitivities that he proposed to absent himself from the only event that approximated to a national Catholic conference at the time the education crisis approached its climax—because of an unrelated quarrel with some of the Southwark Chapter three years earlier. Fortunately, Amigo smoothed ruffled feathers and secured an invitation, not only in his own name, but also that of the Chapter and clergy of Southwark, which assuaged Bourne's wounded self-esteem. He wrote in response, 'You may count on me, therefore, for the inaugural address at the Conference and for such other help as my presence may afford.'[8]

'Your own child'

Bourne again placed their breakdown in relations at too early a date when he wrote to Amigo in 1908, 'The experience of the last four years has been painful in the extreme to me, and I do wish that you could bring yourself to follow in these matters the very happy precedent established by Bishop Butt to which I steadfastly adhered.'[9] There is no evidence of any serious dispute between the two men until the very end of 1906. Given the emotional energy the Archbishop had invested in Wonersh, it is not surprising that the first, and arguably the most serious, breach involved the Seminary.

At the beginning, regarding the Seminary too there was agreement and cooperation. In his first Pastoral, the new Bishop of Southwark wrote regarding priestly formation, 'We have to carry on the work of our predecessors.'[10] A few weeks later Amigo invited Fr Burton of St Edmund's, Ware to give the retreat to the Juniors at Wonersh. 'It will also give you an insight into what the Archbishop has done for the formation of priests.'[11] Amigo wrote to his predecessor asking 'whether you would like to assist at the High Mass on St John's Day's. I certainly should like to see you at the Seminary on that day, and it would be a great pleasure to all to have you on the sanctuary. Do remember that you must always look upon St John's as your own child, and that you will be welcome there at all times.'[12] Possibly a trifle over effusive, the invitation appeared innocuous. Amigo was justifiably pained and surprised by Bourne's refusal. 'You must realise how well nigh impossible it is for me to go the Seminary at all now that I know that it was by your direction, and not by oversight, that I received no invitation to the Clergy Reunion last summer. It has pained me deeply to think that you could consent to an act of discourtesy at the bidding of men who, whatever their merits may be, cannot possess a greater claim to your consideration than I possess.'[13] Amigo could only point out that no offence had been intended. The Clergy Reunion was an internal Southwark affair.[14]

Wonersh was not the happiest of places, and it was inevitable that some incident there would produce a major clash between the Archbishop and his successor. There was not long to wait. Wonersh was still largely staffed with Bourne's appointees. The Rector and Head of the Seniors was Mgr Joseph Butt, the Regent of the Juniors was Fr Thomas Hooley. This dual structure was a potential cause of friction. Both Butt and Hooley were Bourne loyalists, but of very different temperaments. Hooley was the self-appointed guardian of Bourne's memory; his stridency irritated most of the staff. 'Fr Hooley was always maintaining that the Senior discipline was *hopeless* under Mgr Butt and that things were always in a very bad state. Fr Hooley in his earnestness and zeal insisted on small rules and restrictions very strictly (as laid down by Cardinal Bourne in the beginning) and to the letter, so much so that I think he was inclined to be very narrow-minded and to comprehend no other opinion than his own. Everyone who *questioned* the legality, propriety or utility of any Junior custom was wrong in doing so in Fr Hooley's opinion. Thus when many Juniors became Seniors and no longer observed many of the Junior restrictions, Fr Hooley thought that all his work was being frustrated if these were not insisted upon on the Senior side, and as he often tried to push Mgr Butt and was always pointing out what he considered as breaches of discipline, it is not altogether surprising that he soon became odious in the eyes of the Seniors ... Everybody knew that he was continually trying to get Mgr Butt to fall in with his views.'[15]

Butt was diffident, neither a disciplinarian nor a manager of men. He was also self-deprecating and lacking in ambition. Within weeks of Amigo's appointment as Bishop, the Rector was writing to him about staff meetings at the Seminary. 'I have no means of knowing whether it is I myself that am the difficulty, or whether it is something else that might be altered. I fear it is the former, because, whatever we may discuss, our meetings always resolve themselves into an attack on me in some form or another.'¹⁶ Matters deteriorated and it was only a question of whether Butt or Hooley left Wonersh first.

Having visited the Seminary early in 1907, Amigo discussed the problem with Bourne on 25 March. Despite the unpleasantness at St John's, Butt at this point was unwilling to resign until Bourne persuaded him to do so at a meeting the following day. Bourne was surprised and pleased to find Amigo held such a high opinion of Hooley. The Archbishop wished to ensure continuity at Wonersh through staff he himself had chosen and formed. He was utterly opposed to an outsider as Rector, pressing Amigo to appoint Hooley immediately as Butt's successor. Amigo agreed to this at his meeting with the Archbishop—and then immediately regretted his promise. 'I felt ready to do so, not through being convinced, but because it had come upon me so suddenly and I had not had time to think. I have great admiration for Dr Hooley and I think that he will in time make a capital Rector, but the more I thought about it after our interview the more I felt that time had not come.' At a further meeting on 16 April, Amigo attempted to meet Bourne's implacable opposition to an external appointment by persuading Butt to stay on for the moment. Amigo would consider appointing Hooley as Rector after a few years.

Bourne then went to Rome and Amigo to Bruges. In their absence Butt held another staff meeting at Wonersh 'and found that all of them felt that things could not go on as they were.' Consequently, Butt's letter of resignation awaited Amigo's return. Amigo believed his course of action clear. 'Now that the change has to be made, I feel that I cannot put Dr Hooley on as Rector. He is not equal to it. He realises himself the strong opposition he would have in house and outside. A splendid man like him after two or three years on the mission or with extra study, would make an excellent head, but I cannot conscientiously appoint him at present. The staff is dead against him ... The only reason for hesitation is your objection.'¹⁷

Bourne was furious, telling Amigo to regard their friendship as ended.¹⁸ He considered that he had persuaded Butt to resign on a false premise. His anger increased when Amigo appointed a non-Wonersh priest, Fr Arthur Doubleday, as Rector—even although Doubleday sought Bourne's counsel before accepting. The Archbishop wrote to Amigo, 'Now that you have definitely disregarded my advice about the Seminary, may I make one last and very earnest request. I will not trouble you further about the matter. I implore you to be very careful how you interfere with the working of the Seminary. The system there has been built up as the result of very long and patient care. It is a delicate organism which may be very easily disorganised, even quite unintentionally, by anyone who does not fully understand it. To reconstitute it or to remould it would be a very difficult task.'[19]

Bourne was deeply pained by anything he felt detrimental to the character and future of Wonersh, which was largely his creation. Amigo had protested that the appointment of an outsider need not necessarily result in change, but change did occur. Some changes had already been implemented as economies dictated. Doubleday introduced more. He relaxed restrictions, official spiritual direction was abolished, staff and seminarians lived a more separate existence. New staff were appointed who had not been trained at Wonersh themselves.[20] These reforms did militate against the Sulpician spirit. But St John's was the Southwark diocesan seminary, not Bourne's personal fiefdom. Amigo had made an over-hasty promise to Bourne which ought not to have been given. It was for Amigo, as Bishop of Southwark, to make decisions affecting Wonersh. In Westminster Bourne had no hesitation in overturning his predecessors' policies on seminary education. However distressing he might find it, Amigo had the same right in Southwark.

Having given him the benefit of his mind, Bourne had told Amigo he would leave matters there. He failed to do so. Pettily, he withdrew permission for Fr Burton to preach the Junior retreat at Wonersh that year.[21] A few months later Doubleday sought Amigo's advice, 'Will you tell me whether I am to invite the Archbishop for St John's Day? I leave the matter to you entirely. I am not going to be small, even though smallness is one of the rights of a schoolmaster.'[22] Bourne was invited, but refused to attend. He continued to care deeply about the Seminary, but he ought to have accepted it was no longer his responsibility. Instead, he wrote, 'If he would only put things right in the Seminary I could forgive him everything else. It is very hard to see a work of the supreme importance being ruined.'[23]

Against this context, it is easy to see why the allegations of Modernism at Wonersh which Amigo reputedly made to Merry del Val in 1909 were so keenly felt. The vehement reactions on all sides were determined by more than theological opinions. It was rumoured that, partly on the grounds of Modernist tendencies, partly due to financial constraints, Amigo was considering closing Wonersh. (Something Amigo strongly denied.) Bourne sought to take advantage and used his former Vicar-General in Southwark as an intermediary to negotiate for the transfer of the Wonersh Seniors to St Edmund's. Nothing came of the proposal.[24]

Mother Janet Stuart, attempting to mediate between the Archbishop and the Bishop, appreciated that Wonersh lay at the heart of their disagreements. She wrote to Amigo, 'It must be so discouraging and perplexing to your young priests and students at the Seminary to see the spectre of something between them and the Archbishop who is known to be devoted to St John's ... My Lord, if you sent him a special and urgent invitation, say, to give a retreat, or to be with you at the gathering of the clergy ... I feel certain that his Grace would fall in with your wishes if he possibly could ... Without some direct step on your part I do not believe, my Lord, that the preliminary impression can be removed that your Lordship does not really wish the Archbishop to go to St John's ... Perhaps it would be heroic in your Lordship to make the effort, as you said it would be heroic in him to go, but—why not, my Lord, when the good of the clergy is at stake?'[25] Despite her best efforts, it was to be another eleven years before Bourne set foot in Wonersh again.

'The first cause of friction'

When it came to the initial breach concerning Wonersh, Bourne was obviously at fault. He and Amigo were two Bishops independently responsible for their respective dioceses. The Archbishop had no right to expect his wishes to be implemented in Southwark nor to express himself to Amigo in the way he did. In other areas, however, as the dispute became increasingly bitter, culpability is more equally shared. The Archbishop was forgetting Wonersh when he later wrote that matters relating to the governance of Southwark were 'the first cause of friction' between himself and Amigo.[26] They did, however, have much wider implications for the Church generally than squabbles over the Seminary.

Bourne might have thought that he had heard the last of allegations relating to his financial administration of Southwark when *Truth* dropped its campaign and Mr Reed Lewis meekly accepted that the Archbishop enjoyed the Holy See's full confidence. Not a bit of it. Those allegations had begun with the bankruptcy of William Bishop in December 1905. It took two years for Bishop's affairs to be investigated.

Westminster and Southwark cooperated in rebutting the accusations made by *Truth*. Bourne advised Amigo, 'All those whose judgment carries weight consider that it is best to ignore *Truth*. Those who are behind these attacks are neither honest nor truthful ... However if you think it necessary to make any statement, it should be done through a solicitor. No bishop or priest should deal with such a paper as *Truth*.'[27] He praised Southwark's action, 'Canon St John tells me that it is proposed that Counsel should be employed to force Mr Bishop to declare himself truthfully tomorrow, and so make it clear that the Dawes Trustees have acted well within their trust and have in no way indulged in foolish speculation. I think this an excellent idea.'[28] While he pointed out that he was no longer Bishop of Southwark at the time the losses were suffered, the Archbishop was careful to exonerate his successor from any blame.[29] Bourne worked closely with Southwark's diocesan solicitor.

With the investigation of Bishop's affairs complete, the Charity Commissioners advised the Attorney-General in January 1908 that there had been a breach of trust in connection with the Dawes Trust because the Trustees had allowed Bishop to retain the securities for too long a period. The Attorney-General intended bringing proceedings against the Trustees (including Bourne and Amigo) until pressure was brought to bear, pointing out the wider damage the Church would suffer. The Southwark debt stood at £300,000 and few were willing to lend to the Diocese.[30] The Attorney-General was persuaded not to bring an action only on the basis of the Charity Commissioners' Scheme for the Dawes Trust. Three lay Trustees were appointed immediately; the Commissioners had to approve any future changes; the Trustees' investment powers were restricted.[31] Amigo admitted to Rome, 'This fact demonstrates the lack of trust in the diocesan administrators.'[32]

On 15 December 1908 Amigo took the eminently sensible step of appointing a Commission of three priests and seven laymen under the Duke of Norfolk's chairmanship 'to investigate the general financial position of the Diocese, to have access to all accounts and documents and the assistance if necessary of Chartered Accountants. To ascertain the cause of excess of expenditure over income and to make such recommendations as they think fit.'[33] Everyone accepted this as a very proper course of action. The accountants quickly assured Norfolk, 'We have made a preliminary examination of the accounts of the Diocese ... The books have been carefully kept, and they contain all the information necessary to enable us to report to you.'[34]

St John was requested to draw up a statement of account for the accountants. However, it was felt that this did not reflect the true value of diocesan properties. On further examination the accountants felt obliged to devalue the properties in the financial books.[35] The scope of the Commission's work became more wide-ranging. Bourne was surprised to learn that the Commission was investigating his actions regarding the parish endowment of Petworth, given he had the Holy See's approval and the Charity Commissioners had said the matter did not concern them. Nevertheless, he cooperated, providing a statement of the relevant circumstances.[36]

As the Commission's work continued, Bourne became increasingly suspicious. It is not the case, as Amigo later told Merry del Val, that, 'The Archbishop objected to ... my appointing a Commission to help in getting in money.'[37] Rather, he maintained that the Commission's purpose had fundamentally changed. 'Very shortly it was discovered that the Commission was in reality an enquiry into the conduct of Canon St John as financial adviser of the late Bishop Butt and the present Archbishop.'[38] Bourne challenged Amigo in the autumn of 1909. He claimed that the Bishop of Southwark answered he 'had intended the Commission merely as a basis for an appeal for funds, and that its scope had been unlawfully extended by Mgr Brown and Canon St John. I spoke to them both on the subject, and also to the Duke of Norfolk, and all declared to me most emphatically that they had kept strictly within your Lordship's terms of reference, which they quoted to me. I am obliged, therefore, to hold your Lordship responsible, before God and to myself, for the grave outrage committed on the memory of Bishop Butt, and on me your predecessor, and on Canon St John, the faithful servant of us both.'[39]

From January 1910 the Archbishop agreed to sign Southwark trust deeds and documents only 'as soon as he has been fully informed of the proceedings of the Commission of Enquiry appointed by [Amigo] to investigate the financial condition of [his] Diocese.'[40] Bourne felt the Commission was being manipulated by his enemies in Southwark and 'that my administration of the Diocese of Southwark was being subjected to criticism of an exceedingly unfair character.'[41] Was there any basis to his fear? When it eventually reported in November 1910, the Commission displayed no particular interest in historical matters. But Amigo's own

'Trouble and Sadness'

Vicar-General, Mgr Brown, admitted the Archbishop had a point. There were two members of the Commission who were looking to extend its scope. He also felt that Amigo had made a tactical mistake in not producing the documentation the Archbishop requested.[42]

Amigo consulted a barrister who advised that the Archbishop was 'becoming a trifle too overbearing and dictatorial.'[43] One Bishop had no right to require from another documentation and information relating to the other's Diocese, even when the first was a former Bishop of that Diocese. However, Bourne was also writing to Amigo in a second capacity. He offered in April 1910 to retire as a Trustee of the Dawes Trust once he had been provided with 'a statement of the annual income in the various years since the Trust was constituted.'[44] Not only was Bourne entitled to this information, as a Trustee he was legally required to satisfy himself as to the position of the trust fund and that the arrangements made with respect to his successor were appropriate. Failure to do so would have been a breach of trust. Amigo was wrong in not facilitating Bourne's legitimate requests as a Trustee.

Of course, this all begs the question—what was Bourne doing as a Trustee of Southwark trusts more than six years after he ceased to be the diocesan Bishop? The original answer was simple enough. The legal documentation to effect the retirement of one trustee and appoint his successor cost money—and money was in short supply in Southwark. In addition, much of the trust property was mortgaged; a change of trustee required the mortgagee's consent—again money, time and potential complications. With respect to the Southwark Trusts, Amigo wrote to Bourne, 'I know that you consented to remain on simply to help me and I am most grateful to you for it.'[45] One understands why Bourne remained a Southwark Trustee after 1903, but one feels that he and Amigo were badly advised. It proved a very false economy.

The opportunity to effect the necessary changes arose in the summer of 1906. As *Truth* was casting around its allegations as to financial mismanagement in the Church, the Southwark diocesan solicitor, Edward Fooks, suggested that the Archbishop might wish to retire as a Trustee 'to save yourself trouble in the future.' Amigo wrote to him, 'I should not like your having more trouble on my account. I shall be very pleased if you agree to stay on, but if you decided to give it up I shall quite understand.'[46] Bourne replied immediately, 'I consented to remain only because [Bishop Amigo] wished me to do so, I now formally resign my place as one of the Trustees of that Fund.'⁴⁷ His resignation was accepted at the Trustees' meeting on 14 August. How much subsequent trouble would have been saved had legal effect been given to the Archbishop's wish at that point.

One can appreciate Bourne's 'extreme astonishment' when he heard from Fooks three years later telling him he was still a Trustee. It required a deed of retirement to release the Archbishop as a Trustee, and this had never been drawn up. Whose fault was this? Bourne had communicated his wish to retire to St John, as the diocesan treasurer. St John had instructed Fooks to draft the legal documentation but 'subsequently, at the instance of one or other of the Trustees, he was told to suspend the work which was already begun and he never received instructions to complete it. Believing myself no longer a Trustee I have not sought to know what was being done in the recent critical transactions ... I have never once received notice or Agenda of any meeting of the Fund.'⁴⁸ Bourne was right to be angry. Southwark had exposed him to a further three years of potential liabilities while depriving him of the information required to fulfil his fiduciary duties—and this in the immediate aftermath of the losses resulting from the Bishop bankruptcy. However regrettable, this did not justify the Archbishop in refusing to sign documentation for reasons unconnected to the Trusts.

'Cast away as useless'

Relations between Bourne and Amigo were already low. In the Archbishop's opinion 'the whole situation has been enormously aggravated by the Bishop's action towards Canon St John ... The whole series of events must be taken together.'⁴⁹ It became impossible to separate disputes over the financial administration of Southwark from the personality of St John. Bourne, Amigo and St John went back a long way. They had been personal friends—perhaps going back to seminary days at St Edmund's. Years later Bourne told Amigo, 'It was very largely due to [St John's] friendship with, and confidence in, you, that you were invited to join the Diocese of Southwark and eventually became its Bishop.'⁵⁰

As Bishop of Southwark, Bourne inherited the services of St John, who from ordination in 1887 had been Bishop Butt's secretary and treasurer. That connection alone assured St John's reputation in Bourne's eyes. St John was a convert, the nephew of Newman's friend. A late vocation, he had worked for five years as a bank clerk. On the strength of that experience, and having acted as bursar while still a student at St Edmund's, he was accredited with a certain financial acumen. No one ever questioned St John's commitment or good faith. There were differing views of his financial abilities. Bourne maintained that he was a 'great success' as treasurer and the means of securing many substantial donations for the Diocese.[51] Others—increasingly Amigo—did not share that assessment. Even the Westminster diocesan solicitor confided, 'I have my doubts about St John. I think that the Archbishop overrated him.'[52] Bourne may not always have been the best judge of character, yet he was nothing but loyal to those who served him faithfully.

St John worked for Southwark in a financial capacity, but his heart was in the provision of care and accommodation for destitute children through the Rescue Society. Into this work he poured his leisure time and his personal resources. It began with his realisation 'that a very large number of Catholic boys were homeless on the streets of London, exposed to great danger both to their religion and morality.' Starting in a disused carpenter's shop in Blackfriars in 1889 he set up his first Home 'fully determined that, with God's help, he would never turn away a homeless lad from his door.' A new Catholic Boys' Home was opened by the Cathedral in 1900.[53] Despite mounting debts, Bourne gave St John unconditional support.

Amigo's doubts about St John were aroused following Bishop's bankruptcy and the loss sustained by the Dawes Trust which 'brought discredit upon the financial administration here. I did not sacrifice Canon St John then, but I determined to take away part of his work, as I felt he had too much in hand.' Amigo claimed the clergy lacked confidence in St John, who surrounded himself 'by the wrong sort of laymen.'[54] Little or no action was taken, however, until the Charity Commissioners' threat of proceedings two years later provoked a flurry of activity.

Even then much of the practical responsibility in connection with Norfolk's Commission remained with St John. It was not until the revaluation of diocesan property investments that St John felt he was being sidelined. At first he was inclined to reduce his workload. He wrote to a co-Trustee, 'There has been a good deal of opposition of late to the work I am engaged in and I think a new hand might improve matters. I have no intention of leaving the Rescue Society but I do think the time has come for some other priest to gradually take over the work from me.'[55] He was surprised when Amigo took him at his word. 'Canon St John has not been happy. He does not like my insisting on separating all Rescue Work with its Institutions from Bishop's House and he does not think me firm enough with the clergy. I have always assured him that I fully trusted him and that I recognise how self-sacrificing and hard-working he has been. I cannot however have continual comparison with the firmness of the late administration and threats of going, so that when on 25 February he answered that he wanted to go, I accepted.'[56]

Having resigned as diocesan treasurer, St John continued his work with the Rescue Society for a further few months, but, brooding on perceived injustices, he decided that he wanted out altogether. In June 1909 he resigned from the Rescue Society. He did not go alone. Fr Cooksey resigned as the Society's Chaplain—'in view of [the Bishop's] actions over the last few months'—Thomas King resigned as Secretary and John Gilbert and a Mr Richardson from the Finance Committee.[57] Amigo publicly praised St John's 'zeal and devotedness,'[58] but privately he was fuming. When St John asked for a year's leave of absence from the Diocese, Amigo replied that three months was quite long enough.[59] On reflection, St John decided to remain quietly in Southwark until the Norfolk Commission published its findings.

St John suspected foul play, maintaining that the Commission's deliberations were being spun out until he was no longer in a position to challenge them. He raised his misgivings with the Duke. 'The Report was passed unanimously at the last meeting in December ... Mgr Brown told me the week before last when I met him on other business that he had sent the proofs to the Accountant with only "a few verbal alterations" yet it now appears with three pages of new and misleading matter ... It must have been evident to all members who attended the first meetings of the Commission that Mgr Brown was exceedingly hostile to the last two administrations during the first few months of its sittings ... It was equally clear to me that he was determined since last July that no report should come out until I had been removed from all access to accounts and evidence. I have stated many times that my dismissal during the sitting of the Commission made it impossible for me to do public work in the Diocese until the Report was out, yet it has been most cleverly delayed for seven months.'[60] To Amigo St John was even more forthright. 'It is with the deepest regret that I have to say that after the fullest deliberation in the presence of God, I feel bound to state that your Lordship's action in reversing so many of the works of your predecessor is sinful and I cannot take any part in it.'[61]

Bourne now became intransigent regarding the Southwark Trust Deeds sent to him. 'The Archbishop refuses to sign unless he sees all the minutes and papers of the Commission'[62]—his fears, no doubt, fed by St John. In April 1910 Bourne met with Amigo and agreed to sign certain Southwark documents 'because I hoped that you would at last act justly towards Canon St John.'[63] St John was the cause of the final breakdown in relations between the Archbishop and Bishop. Without explaining his authority for doing so, Bourne challenged the validity of a proposed meeting of the Southwark Rescue Society, and protested again against St John's exclusion.[64] Amigo's response was predictable. 'I have made up my mind that as he and his friends left me in the lurch last June, I am not going to ask them to work for the Society any more.'[65]

Bourne protested against Amigo's 'relentless persecution' of St John. Yet however badly he felt St John had been treated, Bourne put himself in the wrong by linking this to his willingness to sign Southwark Trust Deeds. But that is what he did. 'When an honourable arrangement has been reached I shall be pleased to discuss any other matters of business with you.'[66] Amigo gave the only response open to a self-respecting Bishop, 'I must protest as strongly as I can against your attempt to coerce me in my dealings with one of my priests by blocking the business affairs of my diocese. The responsibility of my conduct towards Canon St John is mine, and—forgive me for saying so—mine alone, and I should be false to myself and my charge as Bishop if I endured for a moment any dictation or interference as between the Canon—so long as he is under my jurisdiction—and myself except that of the Holy See.'[67] It was now virtually impossible for the two prelates to resolve their differences by themselves.

By 1911 St John was living with Bourne in Westminster until the Bishop of Liverpool offered him the chaplaincy of Walton Jail, a position he fulfilled conscientiously until retirement in 1925. Even in old age the Canon remained a source of contention between Westminster and Southwark. Having become involved in the cause of Catholic emigration to Canada, Bourne proposed him in 1929 as the Westminster provincial representative on the Emigration Society—to be vetoed by Amigo. Old quarrels had lost little of their bitterness. The Archbishop was still prepared to berate Amigo, '[St John] was prepared to give you, and actually gave to you, the same loyal, self-sacrificing, straightforward service which he had given to your predecessors. Yet after a few years he was cast away as useless, in circumstances which were a grievous hurt to his feelings and good name. For this grave wrong no reparation has ever been made as far as I am aware.'[68]

'A direct and public insult'[69]

If Bourne and Amigo appeared irreparably divided by 1910, they were capable of yet deeper acrimony. Their disagreement concerning Wonersh and the administration of Southwark were known to a number of the clergy and a handful of influential laity in the two Dioceses. The next incident was laid open to public gaze, to the horror of the reserved and correct Bourne. This time the blame is unambiguously attributable to Amigo.

When Bourne's creation as Cardinal was announced, Amigo graciously put aside their personal differences, and wrote magnanimously in his Advent Pastoral Letter, 'Among the eighteen new Cardinals there is one who is intimately associated with Southwark, above all, as first rector of St John's Seminary, and as fifth bishop of the diocese. We heartily congratulate him, and we rejoice at his elevation to the Sacred College.'[70] Amigo offered, with the Southwark Chapter, to greet the Cardinal at Dover or Folkestone on his return to England. He arranged for the Southwark Chapter to draw up an address of congratulation and there was talk of a reception by Wonersh alumni. Writing from Rome, Bourne waived the offer of a reception committee at the Channel, wishing to spare them the winter cold. Instead, he preferred 'to receive the address which you so kindly propose to present to me, at Archbishop's House on some day quite convenient to your Lordship, when, perhaps you and your Chapter could give me to pleasure of staying to luncheon after the presentation of the address.'[71] The honour bestowed on Bourne might, after all, be the means of affecting their reconciliation.

It was not to be. Bourne received no response to his letter. As he was created Cardinal, it was simultaneously announced that England was to be divided into three ecclesiastical provinces. The division of existing Dioceses was mooted. It was rumoured that a new Diocese of Brighton was to be created, and that the South London portion of Southwark was to be absorbed by Westminster. There was understandable anxiety and indignation south of the Thames. No one took the trouble of actually

'Trouble and Sadness'

asking him, but Bourne was blamed as instigator of the scheme. Although he denied the allegation, 'the feeling has been freely expressed that his Eminence is in some degree responsible for it.' To his mortification, the Press announced 'that the addresses of welcome which Cardinal Bourne had agreed to accept from the Bishop, the Chapter and Clergy, and from the Convents of the Diocese of Southwark, have been abandoned.'[72]

In early January 1912 Mgr Brown presided over large protest meetings. A resolution was proposed and unanimously agreed: 'The members of the Catholic League of South London, representing the laity of many parishes, humbly approach the Holy Father ... and earnestly implore him not to sever their connection with the Diocese of Southwark, to which they are so deeply attached, nor to deprive them of their beloved and apostolic Bishop, nor take away from them their venerable Cathedral Church of St George.' At another meeting a petition to the Holy See was discussed; John Gilbert protested to Merry del Val that he was prevented from putting forward the alternative point of view. A petition against the separation of South London from the Diocese of Southwark was also circulated among the clergy. [73]

The proposal for a congratulatory address to the Cardinal was Amigo's initiative. It was publicised—as was its withdrawal. Bourne's reaction was entirely predictable. 'The last ten months have been, as far as London is concerned, the most painful in my life, on account of his attitude towards me since my elevation to the Cardinalate. My return home on such occasion was a unique moment in my life, and it was used by him and his advisers to offer me the most direct insult in their power.'[74] Amigo assured Bourne several times that he had nothing to do with stopping the address.[75] That is difficult to accept. He seems to have approved the Chapter's withdrawal of their address and supported the clergy petition—to the extent of accusing the only six priests who refused to sign of personal disloyalty to him.[76]

Oldmeadow wrote, 'This affront practically made his old See of Southwark the one diocese in England which Cardinal Bourne could not publicly enter.'[77] Oldmeadow's qualification is important. Unofficially, Southwark was divided, with Bourne loyalists extending hospitality to their former Bishop. Thus, an informal celebration was hosted by Southwark rebels in May 1912 at St. Bede's, Clapham Park, where Fr Thomas Hooley was parish priest. 'It was the first visit since his elevation to the Cardinalate to his birthplace, and the reception of his Eminence by the congregation of the parish and a number of Catholics from other parts of South London was of a most enthusiastic character. There was a large congregation present at the High Mass, which was celebrated by the Very Rev Canon St John.'[78]

When friends tried to mediate between Bourne and Amigo, they found that the Cardinal's resentment at his usage by Southwark at this time high on his expanding list of grievances. 'You will understand that I cannot pay an official visit to Southwark until some *amende* is made for the strange treatment which I then received. The least I can ask for is that I should receive a letter signed by the Bishop and his Vicar General, and also on behalf of the Chapter, expressing their regret.'[79] It was not a concession Amigo was prepared to entertain.[80]

'Send it up to Rome'

The Norfolk Commission reported to Amigo on 30 November 1910. Its findings scarcely justified Bourne and St John's fears of a witch hunt against the previous regime. It concluded that the Diocese's assets significantly exceeded its liabilities, but there were difficulties with liquidity and expenditure exceeding income. Rejecting cuts to the Seminary and the Rescue Society, the Commission proposed the same solution Bourne had advanced a decade earlier—the parishes had to produce a greater income. The Commission cleared the Dawes Trustees of misapplication of trust funds. They then turned their attention to the role of St John. 'With regard to the accounts of the Diocese, your Commission find that they have been kept in a clear and regular manner, and they gladly bear witness to the promptitude and lucidity with which all necessary information has been supplied, and the unimpeachable evidence of the ability, zeal and devotion of the late Diocesan Treasurer.' Concluding with a recommendation of future annual audits and a prohibition on investment in residential property, the Commission hardly seemed to merit the antagonism aroused.

Bourne was still refusing to sign Southwark Trust Deeds. Amigo admitted that the document in question was insignificant, but the principle was not.[81] Contemplating an appeal to the Holy See as early as April 1910, one of his Canons counselled him, '[Bourne] is a hard fighter, but when that fails, he can be a gentle diplomat. The danger is that if he consents to sign the documents, and says a few soft words, your heart will melt and your resolution to make things clear in Rome fail you.'[82] The

'Trouble and Sadness'

Bishop received the same advice from his barrister, 'Why not write an ultimatum and, if that fails, send the whole case up to Rome—and the sooner the better, I say.'[83]

Still Amigo hesitated, appreciating the gravity of such a step. Before doing so, he sounded out Merry del Val, telling of his troubles with the Seminary, the Norfolk Commission, St John and the Trust Deeds.[84] The Secretary of State's advice was unequivocal, 'What you say is astonishing and I cannot express my surprise in words. It seems incredible. As it is probable that the Holy See will have eventually to act in the matter, it is *essential* that you should have the facts and documents clearly put before Cardinal De Lai ... I fail to see where your position is at fault, but of course if the matter is to be discussed here, there will have to be the *audi alteram partem*. I am sorry you are having all this trouble.'[85] Amigo secured a considerable tactical advantage by submitting his side of the case to Merry del Val first. It was always to be that much more difficult now for Bourne to have his claims accepted in Rome.

Amigo 'sent up the whole case' to Cardinal De Lai of the Consistorial Congregation. On 7 October 1910 De Lai instructed Bourne to resign from the Southwark Trusts and to leave Amigo free in the administration of his Diocese. The Archbishop made the perfectly valid point that, as a matter of English law, he was obliged to satisfy himself that the proposed arrangements were in order before retiring as a Trustee. He was on less firm ground, however, when he alleged that Amigo intended to commit 'illegal' acts. He argued that Amigo risked putting him 'in a very dangerous situation with respect to the civil law.' Bourne was offended that he had not been allowed to make his own representations. 'In your letter your Eminence seems to judge me already according to Mgr Amigo's charge. I pray you suspend judgment until I have the time to show a completely different side of the question.'[86]

Bourne left Westminster for Rome on 21 November and was gone for the better part of two months. On arrival he wrote to Bishop Cotter, Cahill's successor in Portsmouth, 'Our friend in Southwark has been making complaints to the Holy See against me, and that is the main reason of my coming here at present. I do not think that there will be much difficulty in dealing with the matter.'[87] At first Bourne's confidence appeared well placed. He told De Lai that he was perfectly happy to retire from all Trusts, except the Ellis Trust, where his appointment had been personal and not as Bishop of Southwark. The problems with the Dawes

Trust and Modernism at Wonersh both related to the period after his transfer to Westminster. St John was only being used as a scapegoat by those too cowardly to attack Bourne himself. The nature of the difficulty was twofold: the weakness of the Diocese of Southwark and the character of its Bishop.[88] De Lai was persuaded that Amigo was the problem. When Bishop Graham retired from Plymouth, De Lai attempted to transfer Amigo there. The Bishop of Southwark was having none of it.[89]

Rome next attempted to resolve the dispute by sending Fr Alexis Lépicier[90] to London to attempt a mutually acceptable solution. Lépicier was a Frenchman, but with an intimate knowledge of both Westminster and Southwark. He was to consult with Bidwell and Brown as representatives of their respective Dioceses, but he also established cordial relations with Bourne and came to share his perspective at an early stage, arousing suspicions south of the River.

From the beginning of Lépicier's mission, Rome had in mind the creation of two new ecclesiastical provinces in England, possibly seeing two additional archbishops as a counterweight to Bourne. Thus, the proposal in August 1911 was:

1. That Mgr Bourne retires from the Southwark trusts without conditions or requiring special and unnecessary declarations from the Bishop; since his zeal and capacity is unquestioned.
2. That the Diocese of Brighton is erected immediately ... [Amigo was to be the administrator of the new Diocese until Southwark's debts were repaid.]
3. The erection of two new Provinces of Liverpool and Birmingham.

Lépicier was to communicate this confidentially to Bourne, Amigo, Ilsley and Whiteside so that they could decide how best to implement the Pope's wishes.[91]

Bourne expressed himself delighted. 'Now that the Holy See has given me in the amplest terms the assurances and declaration which the Bishop of Southwark has persistently refused me, I am able to retire honourably from the trusteeship of the properties belonging to that diocese with which I am still connected, and I desire to do so without delay.'[92] His retirement from the Southwark Trusts did not proceed as quickly as he hoped; he was not entirely to blame in the matter. A mortgagee was trying to foreclose on the church in Eastbourne, and even Bourne's own Chancellor argued that his immediate withdrawal from all Southwark

Trusts would precipitate a crisis of financial confidence in Southwark.[93] The Southwark diocesan solicitor enquired whether the Cardinal would be prepared to resign from the Trusts without being released from his liabilities to the mortgagees.[94] Surely one of the least attractive propositions ever put to an Archbishop of Westminster.

Bourne viewed Rome's proposals of August 1911 as a complete package. His mistake was his failure to insist on their simultaneous implementation. The new archdioceses of Liverpool and Birmingham were created by Apostolic Letter dated 28 October 1911. The announcement was made at the same time as that of Bourne's creation as Cardinal. However, Southwark's financial weakness was used (with justification) to delay the second proposal. Little had been achieved, therefore, in resolving the differences between Bourne and Amigo.

The Cardinal felt that he had gained little when he received reports from Southwark laymen such as Thomas King. According to King, Brown had 'addressed those present as to why the Bishop had gone to Rome and stated most emphatically that the cause of the trouble was due to the fact that the Bishop having reported to the Holy See that Your Eminence was responsible for the losses in connection with the Dawes Fund, Your Eminence had been ordered by the Holy See to refund the money lost; that Your Eminence had stated you were unable to do this unless you took over the management of the diocese of Southwark.'[95] To all the old arguments was added the new controversy of the very future of the Diocese of Southwark, and the Cardinal's intentions in that regard. Matters again ground to a halt. 'I cannot proceed with any other business. The allegations must be substantiated or withdrawn.'[96]

The Holy See involved other members of the English hierarchy in the hope of brokering a settlement between Westminster and Southwark. Early in 1912 Bourne, Amigo, Ilsley, Whiteside, Hedley and Bishop Keating of Northampton were appointed, together with four lay counsellors, to consider both the financial issues and the question of diocesan divisions.[97] Their meeting in February dissolved into an 'unseemly and unilluminating wrangle.' No minutes were taken and the Vatican refused to accept a verbal report. On 13 May 1912 Rome re-appointed the Commission of six Bishops, Abbot Bergh of Ramsgate acting as secretary.

Prior to the second hearing Keating travelled to Rome to establish at firsthand what exactly Merry del Val and De Lai expected of the Commission. 'The preponderating desire of the Holy See is that the dispute between the Cardinal and the Bishop of Southwark should be settled *by us*, extra-judicially, but in such thorough fashion that the Holy See can issue a final mandate on the subject when the report is presented ... So now we are bound to get to the bottom of this trouble in all its details and find a way out for the Holy Father ... We are not asked or expected to apportion praise or blame for past quarrels, but to make the Bishop of Southwark master in his own house without exposing the Cardinal unjustly to financial liabilities in respect of trusts over which he is allowed no control.' Rome also expected the Commission to report on the feasibility of the division of Southwark. Keating thought it wise that the four impartial members of the Commission meet first to attempt a compromise settlement which might be presented to Bourne and Amigo.[98]

When the Commission met at Westminster on 3 July, progress seemed surprisingly smooth, at least regarding the Trusts. Bourne said, in view of the various allegations circulating, he had received legal advice to the effect that he should 'withhold his signature to any further documents until he received from the Bishop of Southwark a letter which His Eminence could at his discretion make public, by which as official representative of the Diocese, he officially and formally exempted His Eminence from all charges of maladministration of the funds of the Diocese. The Bishop of Southwark, at the urgent request of the other members of the Commission, agreed to draw up such a document, and circulate it for the approval of the Commission.' On this basis, the Cardinal agreed to sign such Southwark documents as were presented to him.[99] The Bishops managed to kick the subject of diocesan division into the long grass. There was a 'need for going beyond the accountants' figures.' This would require a 'small sub-committee of experts, who could refer to ledgers, inspect properties, etc.' Sufficient time should be allowed for a fund-raising campaign in Southwark to bear fruit. Appointing Canon St John and Mgr Brown to the sub-committee, together with Canon Glancey, the Birmingham diocesan treasurer, did not bode well for harmonious relations or a speedy conclusion.[100] A further meeting of the Commission on 3 October found the sub-committee unable to agree as to the financial state of the Diocese of Southwark.[101]

Bourne and Amigo took it upon themselves to visit Rome to press their respective cases in person. They were gone for several weeks. Fortunes fluctuated. In early November Bourne thought his objective gained. De Lai accepted Amigo's transfer from London as the only means of permanently resolving the dispute. Amigo was to be the Bishop of a new Diocese of Brighton, Bourne was to give up the rural parts of Westminster and be compensated by South London. Westminster would assume the responsibility for Southwark's debts 'to save the situation from the bankruptcy.' Having secured his aims, the Cardinal thought it wiser to retire from Rome and asked Bidwell to come out to represent his interests.[102]

Bourne knew that Amigo would object. Being transferred from Southwark to a rump Diocese was a very public humiliation. However, the tables were turned almost immediately. Amigo had two very powerful backers. The Duke of Norfolk thought it folly to spend money establishing a new Diocese when the urgent need was to reduce Southwark's debts. Bourne acknowledged Norfolk's opposition was problematic; Rome is 'evidently anxious to avoid offending him.'[103] Even more conclusive was the opposition of Merry del Val, who objected to any instant settlement being imposed on Southwark. Given his influence with Pius X, Merry del Val's views were likely to prevail.

Bidwell's inaction did not reflect well on him. He was the consummate Church bureaucrat, who wriggled to escape the approaching dilemma. (He was not popular with his fellow clergy, one of whom remarked that he could never look at Bidwell 'without thinking that his head was exactly like an egg, and longing for a spoon to crack it with.'[104]) Asked by his Archbishop to represent him in Rome, Bidwell judged his chances of success slim. He was reluctant to be seen opposing Merry del Val, his former employer at the Secretariat of State. He placed his predicament before Lépicier: 'Could I, of all men, place myself in this position of apparent antagonism to the Secretary of State? And yet how could I disclaim any intention of opposing his wishes without appearing disloyal to my Archbishop?'[105] Once again, Bourne was let down by someone in whom he had reposed his trust. Bidwell chose disloyalty to his Archbishop, and ignored the summons to travel to Rome.

The situation rapidly slipped through Bourne's fingers. Before leaving Rome he had audiences with both the Pope and Merry del Val. The latter he did not find 'helpful or sympathetic.' He attributed Rome's new preference for indefinite postponement to the intervention of the Secretary of State.[106] Frustrated, suffering from flu and at risk of seriously irritating the Pope, the Cardinal withdrew to fret on the French Riviera.[107]

The dispute between Bourne and Amigo, and De Lai's proposed solution, came before the Cardinals of the Consistorial Congregation on

12 December 1912. They opted, as Bourne had foreseen, for delay—effectively a victory for Amigo, who was left in undisturbed possession of Southwark. The Cardinal felt the defeat deeply. 'It seems to me very serious that no notice whatever is taken of the very painful situation in London, and I am left absolutely without any practical advice as to the course I ought to pursue … In my own diocese I have no difficulty and there is real peace and harmony: it is on the other side of the Thames that difficulties are raised, and I am treated as undeserving of any consideration.'[108] Amigo might have replied that the solution was for Bourne to remain on the northern bank of the Thames.

Why did Bourne lose? He was not well served by advisers such as Bidwell. Brown, acting for Amigo, showed far greater loyalty to his Bishop. Then, while the Cardinal was able to convince men such as Lépicier of the merits of his case, he failed to take the time and effort to charm the really significant players such as Merry del Val and Norfolk. It reflected his failure to see the necessity of basic social skills in daily intercourse. 'I have endeavoured to remain silent, while others have talked very freely, with the result inevitably my attitude has been misrepresented to my detriment. It is not my way to enter into this war of tongues, and the talkers, therefore, have the field to themselves.'[109] It was not enough to recognise that his reticence told against him; he should have done something about it. And when he did speak, it was with an abruptness to which Rome was unaccustomed. As matters drew to a head, he lacked even the semblance of subtlety in his dealings with the Secretary of State. 'I made it plain that I had been patient under great provocation, and that I considered myself entitled to prompt and adequate protection.'[110] Bourne presented his case badly in Rome, but essentially the difficulty was personal feeling which had led him to fight the wrong battle. Save in the most exceptional of circumstances, Rome will always uphold the rights of a Bishop in his own Diocese, and that is what happened here.

'A better state of things'?

A ruling from Rome would not of itself effect personal reconciliation between Bourne and Amigo. The initial causes of Amigo's appeal became generally subsumed into a much wider dispute about the creation of new Dioceses. That involved the whole English hierarchy and will be dealt with separately in the next chapter.

'Trouble and Sadness'

When asked to mediate, Bishop Keating expressed bewilderment. 'To me, personally, the subject in dispute is extremely vague.'[111] With his greater involvement, Mgr Brown, might have been able to enlighten him. 'What strikes me about the whole affair is that *au fond* the trouble is really personal, not official or administrative. Both the Cardinal and the Bishop are men who feel personal grievances acutely and anything that seems to arise from the official difficulties speedily becomes one of a personal nature.'[112]

Various brave souls undertook to reconcile the Cardinal and the Bishop. Abbot Bergh made the effort while he accompanied the two to Rome in 1912. He abandoned the attempt as impossible. The next to try, for the avoidance of scandal, was Fr Hopper, a Southwark priest and intimate of the Cardinal from their time at St Edmund's. He wanted the past to 'be effectively buried' to move on to 'a better state of things.' The Cardinal showed he had forgotten and forgiven little as his conversation with Hopper ranged over 'the Trust Deeds, the Seminary, the treatment of the clergy educated by H. E., Canon St John, Bp Butt, the traditional hostility of Southwark, etc.' He was prepared to accept an invitation to Southwark only upon the receipt of a letter signed by Amigo, his Vicar-General and Chapter expressing their regret at the withdrawal of the congratulatory address on his being created a Cardinal and acknowledging that he was not responsible for the proposed division of Southwark. Amigo felt unable to make such a statement.[113] Mother Stuart urged Amigo to issue, and Bourne to accept, a public invitation to some major event in Southwark.[114] Again, the two men's stubbornness precluded any settlement.

His perceived exclusion from Southwark caused the Cardinal the greatest pain. There was the 'question as to whether or not I am ever to visit the many friends that I have in the Diocese of Southwark. It is evident that Bishop Amigo takes offence if I appear in his Diocese, for whatever he may say to me, he has made complaints about this matter in Rome ... Forty-two years of my life were closely connected with that part of England ... Am I on account of his extraordinary character to be debarred from the freedom of action which every other Bishop in the country may exercise without criticism?'[115] Invited by Amigo to open a novena at Southwark Cathedral in 1915, the Cardinal considered this an inadequate occasion to mark his re-emergence into his former Diocese. 'Four years ago you did me a very personal wrong. That I have forgiven from my heart, though I can never forget it. But your Lordship must not forget that the public affronts then offered to me in my ecclesiastical character still remain without reparation of any kind.'[116]

The showdown with the entire hierarchy on the question of diocesan divisions no doubt helped persuade Bourne that he would never entirely 'win' his battle with Amigo, and relations did begin to thaw a little. The consecration of Mgr Doubleday, the former Wonersh Rector, as Bishop of Brentwood in 1920 was the occasion for a partial mending of the rift. 'For the first time I was able to visit my old cathedral of Southwark, and in circumstances that were in every way fitting and suitable. This has done a great deal of good and has enabled many, who previously had feared to do so, to show their real sentiments of affection and loyalty. It is hoped later on to arrange some similar opportunity for a visit to the Seminary at Wonersh which I have not seen for thirteen years.'[117] That visit to the Seminary duly occurred.

Relations between the Cardinal and the Bishop would never return to their pre-1906 warmth. Tempers could still flare and incidents could still provoke harsh words. When Amigo took up the plight of a brother Bishop in 1920 he received a sharp rebuke. 'I regret to refer to your discourtesy to me yesterday … Your Lordship manifested both by your words and manner that you did not accept my word; and when I pointedly put the question to you, you declined to do so. There could hardly be a graver discourtesy. I hope that you were not conscious of the insinuation conveyed in the last words you said just before you took leave of me.'[118] Again, the fault was not altogether on one side. Amigo asked the Wonersh Rector to notify him if Cardinal Bourne was ever to visit the Seminary; he made no such stipulation about visits from Cardinal Gasquet.[119]

'Too human a love'?

With hindsight, the dispute between Bourne and Amigo was inevitable. Bourne failed to detach himself from Southwark, practically and emotionally, on his transfer to Westminster. On his departure, he wrote to the Diocese, 'We shall not be very far away, and the affectionate memory of these years will not pass from our mind and our heart, and, amid the still larger cares which God is entrusting to us, we shall never fail to watch with the deepest interest the growth, the progress and the development which are characteristic of the great diocese of Southwark.'[120] With Bourne, this was not just an aspiration, but a very real expectation. Even Oldmeadow acknowledged 'the one great blunder of Francis Bourne's

'Trouble and Sadness'

career—a blunder which brought sorrow and difficulty to the very end of his life. Like many another tragical blunder, this blunder of Francis Bourne's was well meant ... [He hoped the two Dioceses] would display for the edification of all London an example of mutual help and fraternal unity.'[121]

Bourne must bear the greater and original part of the blame, but Amigo was culpable too. A skilled political operator, he revelled in enlarging the sphere of conflict and drawing in other combatants. Once secure in Southwark, he enjoyed baiting Bourne. The wily old Latin knew how to create maximum embarrassment, how to provoke the publicly stiff and sensitive Cardinal. Canon Fuller recalled one such incident at the hierarchy's lunch at St Edmund's in 1929 to mark the centenary of Catholic Emancipation. Amigo sat on the Cardinal's right; the seminarians noted they seldom spoke. After lunch Bourne rose first and gave out the predictable platitudes about the Church's progress over the preceding century. When Amigo rose to speak, everyone held their breath; he relished the moment. 'I am very pleased to be here. I believe that this is my first invitation to St Edmund's since I became Bishop of Southwark.' There was silence; Bourne studied his plate. Amigo went out of his way to mention diocesan differences. There were a number of bursaries, of little value, paid by the French government as compensation for the loss of Douai. Originally, paid to the London District, they should have been shared between all the successor Dioceses; in practice, they were kept by Westminster. 'I've often wondered what happened to those bursaries which used to be paid to the London District in the old days.' Finally, Amigo referred to the Cardinal's position as *primus inter pares*, laying special emphasis on the latter.[122] Bourne's enjoyment of the occasion was ruined.

Yet the relationship between the two men was seldom predictable. Amigo took time out from his appeal to Rome to write to his adversary, 'Let me congratulate you on the Golden Jubilee of your birth and I wish you most heartily many happy returns on your birthday and I have not forgotten you in my Mass today. I cannot agree with you about your actions over the Trust Deeds of Southwark and supporting Canon St John against me, but differences of opinion do not affect my friendship towards you. Yours affectionately, Peter.'[123] It worked the other way too. A couple of years later the Cardinal wrote to the Bishop of Southwark, 'May I offer you my very sincere and heartfelt good wishes and congratulations on your attainment of the twenty-fifth anniversary of your ordination to the Priesthood. I give you an almost daily Memento at the Altar, and on Tuesday I will offer my Mass for you.'[124] It is as though one is witnessing the bickering of an ageing couple.

Every cleric attracts the attention of those with special sensitivities and the clearly deranged. Amigo must have thought he was dealing with just such a person when he received a letter signed by 'A Poor Sinner.' One wonders, however, whether she might not just have had some genuine inspiration when she wrote, 'May I add to what I have already said, that Our Lord told me a year ago, that the Cardinal had been in fault in formerly loving you with too human a love and it was necessary this chastisement should fall upon him, to correct this but now that His Eminence will love you only in God, will your Lordship not love him thus, also?'[125]

The dispute between Bourne and Amigo was protracted and often far from edifying. It is not surprising that it alternately amused and scandalised those priests and laity who learnt of it. However, Bourne must not be viewed through the prism of Amigo. The scope and consequences of his life and ministry are of far greater significance.

Notes

1. FAB to Cardinal De Lai, 13 October 1910, AAW, Bo. III/124/8/3.
2. *Ibid.*
3. FAB, speech following Amigo's consecration, 25 March 1904, *Times* cited Clifton, *Amigo*, p. 19.
4. FAB to Amigo, May 1907, SAA, cited Clifton, *Amigo*, p. 38.
5. Memorandum presented by FAB to Pius X, 3 December 1912, AAW, Bo. IV/4/9.
6. FAB to De Lai, 13 October 1910 (copy), AAW, Bo. III/124/8/2.
7. FAB to Amigo, 15 July 1906, SAA, Bourne Papers, Letters to Amigo.
8. FAB to Amigo, 2 August 1906, SAA, Bourne Papers, Letters to Amigo.
9. FAB to Amigo, 10 October 1908, SAA, Bourne Papers, Letters to Amigo.
10. Amigo, Pastoral Letter, Trinity Sunday, 1904.
11. Amigo to Fr Burton, 9 September 1904, AAW, SEC XIV/25/57.
12. Amigo to FAB, 17 December 1906, AAW, Bo. III/2/1.
13. FAB to Amigo (draft), 19 December 1906, AAW, Bo. III/2/2.
14. Amigo to FAB, 20 December 1906, AAW, Bo. III/2/3.
15. Corbishley to Doubleday, 6 January 1912, SAA, Wonersh, 1904–36.
16. Butt to Amigo, 15 April 1904, SAA cited Finnegan, *In Hope of Harvest*, p. 104.

'Trouble and Sadness'

17 Amigo to FAB, 8 May 1907, SAA, Wonersh, Addl Material, 1904–1970.
18 FAB to Amigo, 9 May 1907, cited Clifton, *Amigo*, p. 38.
19 FAB to Amigo (draft), 29 May 1907, AAW, Bo. III/2/4.
20 Finnegan, *In Hope of Harvest*, pp. 123–124.
21 Doubleday to Amigo, 25 September 1907, SAA, Wonersh, Addl. Materials, 1904–1970/37.
22 Doubleday to Amigo, 1 December 1907, SAA, cited Finnegan, *In Hope of Harvest*, p. 127.
23 FAB to Cahill, 13 January 1909, PDA A/6–04–16.
24 Butt to Amigo, 18 May 1909, SAA, Wonersh, Addl. Materials 1904–1970/51; Ward to Burton, 8 September 1909, AAW, SEC XIV/15A/41.
25 Stuart to Amigo, 6 October 1909, SAA, Amigo, Consistorial I/55.
26 'Dawes Trust—Archbishop's Statement,' February 1911, AAW, Bo. III/1/14.
27 FAB to Amigo, 15 July 1906, SAA, Bourne Papers, Correspondence with Amigo.
28 FAB to Amigo, 31 July 1906, SAA, Bourne Correspondence.
29 FAB letter to *Tablet*, 6 October 1906, cited Oldmeadow, *Francis Cardinal Bourne*, i, p. 316.
30 Clifton, *Amigo*, p. 40.
31 Memorandum by Southwark diocesan solicitors, 12 April 1910, AAW, Bo. III/1/10.
32 Amigo statement prepared for De Lai, 4 May 1910, SAA, Amigo Papers, Consistorial I/120.
33 Cited Clifton, *Amigo*, p. 41.
34 Messrs Herman Lescher Stevens & Co to Norfolk, 16 January 1909 (copy) SAA, Amigo/Consistorial Dossier I/36a.
35 Clifton, *Amigo*, p. 41.
36 FAB memorandum on the Mensal Benefice of Petworth, early 1909, AAW, Bo. III/124/1.
37 Amigo to Merry del Val, 28 July 1910 (copy), SAA, Amigo Papers, Consistorial I/150.
38 'Dawes Trust–Archbishop's Statement,' February 1911, AAW, Bo. III/1/14.
39 FAB to Amigo, 26 January 1910 (copy), AAW, Bo. III/124/1.
40 FAB to Amigo, 31 January 1910, SAA, Amigo, Consistorial I/78.
41 FAB memorandum, u/d [spring 1912?], AAW, Bo. III/124/1.
42 Brown to Amigo, 24 March 1910, SAA, Amigo Papers, Consistorial I/109.
43 Stokes to Amigo, 10 March 1910, SAA, Amigo Papers, Consistorial I/97.
44 FAB to Amigo, 9 April 1910, SAA, Amigo Papers, Consistorial I/115.
45 Amigo to FAB, 3 August 1906, AAW, Bo. III/1/4.
46 *Ibid.*
47 FAB to St John, 5 August 1906, AAW, Bo. III/1/5.
48 FAB to Amigo, 19 February 1909, AAW, Bo. III/1/6.

49 FAB to Fooks, 3 August 1910, AAW, Bo. III/124/1.
50 FAB to Amigo, 3 November 1929, SAA, Bourne Papers, Letters to Amigo.
51 FAB to Gotti, 11 October 1903, SCPF, 102/1904, f. 289, rr. 123–125; FAB letter to *Tablet*, 6 October 1906, cited Oldmeadow, *Francis Cardinal Bourne*, i, p. 317.
52 Weld to Bidwell, 17 March 1911, AAW, Bo. III/1/21.
53 B. Bogan, *The Great Link* (London: Burns & Oates, 1948), pp. 309–310; *WCC*, July 1934, pp. 127–129.
54 Amigo to Merry del Val, 28 July 1910 (copy), SAA, Amigo Papers, Consistorial I/150.
55 St John to Mr Wellesley, 6 June 1908, SAA, Amigo Papers, Consistorial Dossier/10.
56 Amigo to Canon Scannell, 13 March 1909, SAA, Amigo Papers, Consistorial Dossier/28a.
57 Resignations, 30 June 1909, SAA, Amigo Papers, Consistorial I/43–48.
58 Amigo letter to Diocese cited *Tablet*, 10 July 1909, p. 66.
59 St John to Amigo, 28 June 1909; Amigo to St. John, 29 June 1909, SAA, Amigo Papers, Consistorial I/39.
60 St John to Norfolk, 14 February 1910 (copy), SAA, Amigo, Consistorial I/82.
61 St John to Amigo, 19 December 1909, SAA, Amigo Papers, Consistorial I/63.
62 Amigo to Norfolk, 20 February 1910 (copy), SAA, Amigo Papers, Consistorial I/84.
63 FAB to Amigo, 12 July 1910, SAA, Amigo Papers, Consistorial I/133.
64 FAB to Amigo, 24 June 1910, SAA, Amigo Papers, Consistorial I/125.
65 Amigo to FAB, 26 June 1910 (copy), SAA, Amigo Papers, Consistorial I/128.
66 FAB to Amigo, 12 July 1910, SAA, Amigo Papers, Consistorial I/133.
67 Amigo to FAB, 15 July 1910 (copy), SAA, Amigo Papers, Consistorial I/137.
68 FAB to Amigo, 3 November 1929, SAA, Bourne Papers, Letters to Amigo.
69 FAB memorandum, AAW, Bo. III/2/24.
70 Amigo, Advent Pastoral 1911, *Tablet*, 16 December 1911, p. 993.
71 FAB to Amigo, 6 December 1911, SAA, Bourne Papers, Letters to Amigo; *Tablet*, 16 December 1911, p. 993.
72 *South London Press*, 19 January 1912.
73 *Tablet*, 13 January 1912, p. 64; *South London Press*, 19 January 1912; Gilbert to Merry del Val, 15 February 1912 (copy), AAW, Bo. III/124/3.
74 FAB to Hedley, 26 November 1912 (copy), AAW, Bo. IV/4/7.
75 Amigo to Ilsley, 9 January 1913, BAA, D2831.
76 Clifton, *Amigo*, p. 45.
77 Oldmeadow, *Francis Cardinal Bourne*, ii, p. 77.
78 *Tablet*, 1 June 12, p. 868.
79 FAB to Fr Hopper, 9 January 1913, AAW, Bo. III/2/30.
80 Amigo to Ilsley, 9 January 1913, BAA, D2831.
81 Stokes to Amigo, 19 July 1910, SAA, Amigo Papers, Consistorial I/143.

82   O'Halloran to Amigo, 10 April 1910, SAA, Amigo Papers, Consistorial I/116.
83   Stokes to Amigo, 19 July 1910, SAA, Amigo Papers, Consistorial I/143.
84   Amigo to Merry del Val, 28 July 1910 (copy), SAA, Amigo Papers, Consistorial I/150.
85   Merry del Val to Amigo, 1 August 1910, SAA, Amigo Papers, Consistorial I/152.
86   FAB to De Lai, 13 October 1910 (copy), AAW, Bo. III/124/8/2.
87   FAB to W. Cotter, 25 November 1910, AAW, Bo. III/8.
88   FAB, draft memorandum, 5 March 1911, AAW, Bo. III/1/23.
89   De Lai to FAB, 9 February 1911, AAW, Bo. III/124/8/3.
90   Fr Alexis Lépicier (1863–1936) entered the Servite Order as a novice in the Fulham Road in 1878, and studied at St Thomas' Seminary, Hammersmith, St Sulpice and Propaganda. Ordained at Fulham Road in 1885, he was Master of Novices at the Servite Priory, Bognor Regis (1890–1892). He was a member of the faculty at Propaganda (1892–1913), Rector of the Servite College, Rome (1895–1913), Procurator of the Order (1901–1913) and Prior General of the Servite Order (1913–1920). Lépicier acted as adviser to numerous Congregations. He was appointed Archbishop in 1924 and Cardinal in 1927. Sharing a Sulpician formation and a passion for ecclesiastical education, Bourne came to depend on Lépicier in his dealings with Rome.
91   De Lai to Lépicier, 7 August 1911, AAW, Bo. III/6/6.
92   FAB to P. Witham, 4 October 1911 (copy), AAW, Bo. III/124/1.
93   Bidwell to Lépicier, 13 December 1911, AGOSM, Lépicier Papers.
94   Fooks to Weld, 19 March 1912, AAW, Bo. III/124/1.
95   T. King to FAB, 16 April 1912, AAW, Bo. III/1/27.
96   FAB to Joseph Weld, 22 May 1912 (copy), AAW, Bo. III/124/1.
97   Clifton, *Amigo*, p. 45.
98   Keating to Whiteside (copy), 10 June 1912, NorDA, FV.6.
99   Memorandum [by Whiteside?], AAW, Bo. III/1/30.
100 Keating to Merry del Val, 8 July 12 (copy), NorDA, FV.6.
101 FAB to De Lai, 3 October 1912 (copy), AAW, Bo. III/124/3.
102 FAB to Bidwell, 15 November 1912 (copy), AAW, Bo. III/124/8.
103 *Ibid.*
104 M. Ward, *Unfinished Business* (London: Sheed and Ward, 1964), p. 99.
105 Bidwell to Lépicier, 18 November 1912, AGOSM, Lépicier Papers.
106 FAB to Bidwell, 21 November 1912 (copy), AAW, Bo. III/124/8.
107 Amigo to Ilsley, 4 December 1912, BAA, D2793.
108 FAB to Lépicier, AGOSM, Lépicier Papers.
109 FAB to Norfolk, 26 December 1912 (copy), AAW, Bo. III/124/3.
110 FAB to Bidwell, 21 November 1912 (copy), AAW, Bo. III/124/8.
111 Keating to Whiteside, 10 June 1912 (copy), NorDA, FV.6.
112 Brown to Lépicier, 21 November 1912, AGOSM, Lépicier Papers.

[113] Amigo to Ilsley, 9 January 1913, BAA, D2831; Hopper to Amigo, 9 January 1913, SAA, Bourne Papers, Letters to Amigo.
[114] Stuart to Amigo, 4 March 1913, SAA, Bourne Papers, Letters to Amigo.
[115] FAB to Lépicier, [December 1912?], AGOSM, Lépicier Papers.
[116] FAB to Amigo, 26 December 1915, SAA, Bourne Papers, Letters to Amigo.
[117] FAB to Lépicier, 14 August 1920, AGOSM, Lépicier Papers.
[118] FAB to Amigo, 11 February 1920, SAA, Bourne Papers, Letters to Amigo.
[119] P. Hallett to FAB, 31 August 1929, AAW, Bo. III/124/5.
[120] FAB farewell letter to Southwark, *Tablet*, 10 October 1903, p. 582.
[121] Oldmeadow, *Francis Cardinal Bourne*, i, p. 232.
[122] Fuller, interview, 7 November 2001.
[123] Amigo to FAB, 21 March 1911, AAW, Bo. III/2.
[124] FAB to Amigo, 23 February 1913 (copy), AAW, Bo. III/2/32.
[125] 'A poor sinner,' [Rosa Josephine Gosling] to Amigo, 28 February 1914, SAA, Bourne Papers, Letters to Amigo.

Chapter 15

'How good and how pleasant it is, when brothers live in unity'[1]

'My confidence in the Archbishop has not abated'[2]

Young, unknown and inexperienced: even the English hierarchy greeted Bourne's appointment to Westminster with surprise. Eyebrows were further raised by his vehement insistence that Amigo succeed him in Southwark. Yet, basically, there was a fund of goodwill towards the new Archbishop from among his brother Bishops. There was widespread admiration for his handling of the education crisis and the problem of the procession at the 1908 Eucharistic Congress. Bishop Hedley was often called upon to speak on behalf of the English Bishops. He did so at the dinner following the consecration of Westminster Cathedral. At the time no one would have seriously disputed the praise reserved for the Archbishop. Hedley 'gave expression to the feelings of high and deep appreciation with which he and all his colleagues regarded his Grace's conduct of public affairs. In conclusion he begged the Archbishop to be assured that he would always find them ready to come to his side whenever he thought well to summon them.'[3] That readiness was not to survive long.

'To augment the number of Dioceses'

For six years from 1911 the English hierarchy was preoccupied with the proposal to create new Dioceses. Even after 1917 there were periodic rumblings for the remainder of Bourne's life. Given the context of his dispute with Amigo, Bourne was usually blamed as the instigator of the proposal. But the matter had a far longer history.

The ancient Catholic hierarchy of England was destroyed by Elizabeth I. Tentative steps towards restoration were taken in the reign of James II, when the country was entrusted to first one, then four, Vicars-Apostolic, who were basically missionary Bishops. Against local advice, Rome increased their number to eight in 1840 with a view to the normalisation of ecclesiastical governance, which occurred in 1850. The Vicars-Apostolic suggested their existing eight Districts simply be converted into eight Dioceses, to be subdivided at some future point as they decided. Rome, however, wanted more Dioceses immediately and decreed thirteen Dioceses in 1850 'to forestall later disputes among the Bishops.'[4] Yet more were contemplated. In restoring the hierarchy, Pius IX looked forward to a 'fresh increase in Catholicism. And therefore We desire at present to reserve it to Us and Our successors to divide this Province still further and to augment the number of Dioceses, as necessity may arise.'[5]

Rome's fears about the English Bishops' reluctance to increase the number of Dioceses were justified. In the next sixty years only three new Dioceses were created—proportionally, a significantly smaller increase than that of the Catholic population. The Bishops countered that the Church in England was desperately poor; it lacked the resources to support more Bishops and new diocesan structures.

'The unfortunate division of this important city'[6]

From 1688 the capital had been under the single jurisdiction of the Vicar-Apostolic of the London District. In determining new diocesan boundaries in 1850 arguments were advanced for and against the division of London. Wiseman, the last Vicar-Apostolic of the London District, strongly opposed division. The Cardinals in Rome, however, wished to stress continuity with the medieval Church. They knew that before the Reformation the Thames constituted the diocesan boundary—although the population on the South Bank at the time was insignificant. Bourne later maintained that, 'In 1850 it was fully expected that the Archbishop would have jurisdiction over the whole of London. To the very great surprise and disappointment of Cardinal Wiseman, it was decided otherwise to the immense harm of religion.'[7] Westminster and Southwark were divided in 1850, albeit that for a further year Wiseman also administered Southwark. During that time he continued to reside at St George's, Southwark, Pugin's cathedral then being the only truly impressive Catholic church in London.

Bourne argued forcefully for the unification of London as one Diocese—under his authority. 'It is the only radical solution of difficulties which were acute under Cardinal Wiseman, generally latent but sometimes acute under Cardinal Manning, and have been made intolerable now. Cardinal Manning complained bitterly of the division of the control in London, and always deplored it.'[8] On the death of Bishop Grant, it was rumoured that Manning had sought to unite London under his jurisdiction.[9]

There were valid arguments for unification, but the suspicion remained that Bourne was motivated by personal considerations: the removal of Amigo. There is no evidence that Bourne contemplated reorganisation prior to the spring of 1911. Indeed, Amigo and Gasquet cited against him a letter he had written to Rome as Bishop of Southwark in 1901 when he claimed it was 'practically impossible ever to divide the Diocese.' However, they neglected to quote the parts of that same letter which might have been used as evidence for just such an action. 'The Diocese of Southwark becomes more and more overwhelmed by the expansion each year of the city of London ... These thousands of new homes form part of the city of London ... While the bishop is young and in good health, he can endure the enormous amount of work, but should he be elderly or sick, it would be necessary for him to retire in favour of someone stronger, or to have an auxiliary.'[10] Or, one is tempted to add, to ask for the Diocese to be reduced to a more manageable size.

Where did the scheme originate? The conviction that Bourne himself had formulated the project led the Southwark Chapter to withdraw their congratulatory address after Bourne's elevation to the Sacred College—to his fury and mortification. The Cardinal always denied this. Amigo expressed himself perplexed when Bourne told him at the end of 1911 'that he had nothing to do with the suggestion of South London being joined to Westminster.'[11] Bourne was nothing but consistent. For over a decade he maintained his position that he was in no way responsible for the proposal. He asserted his innocence to Pius X, Cardinal De Lai, Fr Lépicier and Mgr Bidwell, even in memoranda to himself. Given the list includes those in a position to know and those whom did not require convincing, it is difficult to accept that Bourne was not telling the truth.

Not that many believed him. One of his priests wrote,

> If the Cardinal is not already aware of what people are saying and thinking I think he ought to be told how widespread and practically universal is the opinion that he engineered the whole of the South London idea, and that it was only stopped at the eleventh hour ... As far as I can gather Southwark as a whole is completely alienated and rendered hostile, and even in Westminster people will not believe but that the Cardinal has just failed to pull off a *coup d'état*. On this side of the Thames we don't care, but on the other feeling

has been strongly aroused. It has got beyond the stage of a personal matter—on which this Cardinal might suffer in silence just as his predecessor did. I am writing as I do because I firmly believe the interests of the Church require that the Cardinal should speak out—boldly and *angrily* and repudiate the insinuation.[12]

If not Bourne, then who did conceive the idea? The Cardinal insisted that the suggestion was initiated by Rome. That is supported by those who ought to have known the truth of the matter. At an audience with Benedict XV, Lépicier explained 'how the thought of uniting London under one and the same jurisdiction emanated originally from the Consistorial Congregation itself, a proof of this being the delegation papers given me in 1911. This made an impression upon the Holy Father but it is strange that some people should have represented to him the matter differently from what is the reality.'[13] The Cardinal's secretary confirmed this. 'So true is it that the unification of London scheme originated in Rome that I remember well the day the Cardinal got the letter proposing it and how indignant he was, considering it for the moment a hopeless solution of the difficulties in question. And it was only subsequently that he came to realise its wisdom and accepted *Rome's* point of view. And then to find the truth is so twisted that they would have it that it is his scheme! It is really too bad. It is indeed providential you were given the opportunity of disabusing the Holy Father.'[14]

In sending Lépicier to reconcile Bourne and Amigo, De Lai had proposed in May 1911 not only the creation of two new Archdioceses, but also the unification of London. Essex and Hertfordshire would be separated from Westminster to form a new Diocese; in return, South London would be transferred from Southwark to Westminster.[15] Two questions, however, remain. Why had accounts of the possible unification of London been current in England for at least two months prior to Lépicier receiving these instructions? Is it likely that the Roman Curia had the interest or the knowledge to specify proposals for new English provinces and Dioceses giving some detail as to potential boundaries and sees? The suspicion remains that, in presenting such a proposal, Rome was simply lending its authority to suggestions originating in England.

There is conclusive evidence to acquit Bourne of the charge. The first time he mentions the scheme is in March 1911 in a letter to his Chancellor, Bidwell. Having no reason to dissemble his true feelings and involvement, he wrote, 'The new idea was quite unanticipated by me and startled and distressed me.'[16] Did the idea originate from someone else in the Church in England? Fr Clifton suggests Canon St John; his dealings with the London County Council had convinced him of the necessity for the Catholic Church in the capital to speak with one voice.[17] That, however, was clearly not the case. It would credit St John with an originality he displays nowhere else. Bourne disclosed to Bidwell, 'I mentioned the matter in confidence to Canon St John. He too was startled at so drastic a proposal.'[18]

If the idea of uniting South London to Westminster did arise in England rather than Rome, the indicators point to Bidwell. Bourne's letter of March 1911 is his first reference to 'the new idea.' He is not announcing it, however, to Bidwell; it presupposes he already knows. Amigo's suspicions were moving in the same direction. He knew Bidwell had visited Rome just prior to this, and speculates that he had used the opportunity to suggest the unification of London.[19] Fr Arthur Hinsley wrote in March 1911 to Doubleday at Wonersh that Bidwell 'had been in touch with the Holy See with a view to Westminster absorbing Southwark.'[20] Is it possible that Bourne's own Chancellor would have made such a radical suggestion in Rome without first discussing the matter with him? Bidwell's actions during Amigo's appeal certainly show him capable of acting independently from, and even contrary to, his Archbishop's wishes. A former member of the Roman Curia—he had worked at the Secretariat of State—Bidwell would have known whom to approach in the Vatican and how best to articulate discreetly such a plan. That Bidwell was intimately involved in these issues is demonstrated by the fact that when Lépicier was sent to England, it was to consult Bidwell (and Brown representing Southwark).[21] Finally, we have Bidwell's own testimony. 'If anything, I feel more convinced than the Archbishop himself of the importance of getting the matter settled as soon as possible, for I am convinced that the present arrangement according to which London is divided between two dioceses will not work in the most favourable of circumstances and is simply disastrous in the present circumstances.'[22]

We can, therefore, with some confidence accept Bourne's assertion that he did not initiate the scheme. The unification proposal did not arise initially because of any evaluation of the change on its own merits. It was an attempt to resolve a dispute between two Bishops. One Southwark benefactor mused whether Bourne might suggest that 'Amigo should be created Archbishop of Darlington and sent off to the Philippines, *because he speaks Spanish*.'[23] Brown took the matter a little more seriously, but saw it in the same light. 'To me it seems useless trouble and vexation to have all kinds of elaborate plans for dividing Southwark and other dioceses which are really only devices for trying to remove one Bishop who is obnoxious to another.' Bourne and Amigo lived less than two miles apart. Incapable of cooperation, the solution was advanced of significantly increasing that distance. After Amigo declined a transfer to Plymouth, the London plan was formulated. Brown felt it failed to address the underlying problems, especially if Amigo 'stood in the eyes of the world as a disgraced and discredited man. Even the present plan of a Diocese of Sussex and Bishop Amigo perhaps as Bishop would not affect the real issue—the personal trouble would still continue—probably more acutely—if they were not first reconciled. The world would still know they were not friendly.'[24]

As a former Bishop of Southwark, Bourne's initial response to the proposal was not favourable. He told Norfolk that when Rome asked him in spring 1911 'whether I would be willing to take over South London, I strongly opposed the idea. But when the matter was urged and I had time to reflect more carefully, I felt bound in conscience not to refuse the additional burden if the Holy See eventually desires to place it upon me.'[25] Amigo's consequent removal from London enabled him to do so with some enthusiasm. Not that he blinded himself to the 'grave reasons against allowing the diocese of Southwark to disappear altogether.' For historical, sentimental and legal reasons, Bourne urged that Southwark should not lose completely its separate identity and institutions. He would govern South London as 'Bishop of Southwark' rather than Archbishop of Westminster, St George's would be his co-cathedral and the Southwark Chapter would remain as an honorary association. Yet there would be one body of clergy and one curia serving London north and south of the Thames.[26]

Having reconciled himself to the change, Bourne set about justifying it. With his episcopal experience on both sides of the River, he reflected that he was the man to implement this reform.[27] He urged his reasons on De Lai.

> I must draw to your Eminence's attention again the very grave and continued inconvenience caused by the division of the city of London in two dioceses with two Ordinaries entirely independent of each other ... I am also persuaded that this division which places the wealthier districts in one diocese and the poorer in another is the fundamental cause of the financial difficulties of the diocese

'How good and how pleasant it is, when brothers live in unity'

of Southwark, which wishes to rival the diocese of Westminster without the necessary resources.[28]

De Lai did not require convincing. Unification was part of his idea in May 1911 to solve the dispute between Bourne and Amigo. The latter would be given the new Diocese of Brighton, which De Lai suggested as the centre of a new southern Province.[29] (Bourne had no wish to see Amigo as a rival Archbishop, and nothing further is heard of the proposal.) Lépicier was charged with working out a scheme of settlement to give effect to this. In July 1911 Bourne was more than satisfied with the progress being made.[30] His confidence appeared justified when in the following month De Lai announced the Holy Father's wishes, including his desire 'that the diocese of Brighton is erected immediately.' Lépicier was to communicate this confidentially to Bourne and Amigo, and to Ilsley and Whiteside as the new Archbishops of Birmingham and Liverpool.[31]

What went wrong? Bourne argued that 'the change must be made rapidly and decisively, or the difficulties will be enormous.'[32] He could not have spoken more accurately. The Consistorial Congregation had already decided to create a new Diocese of Brighton. This was to be incorporated in the Bull, *Si qua est*, signed at the end of October 1911. 'Then at the last moment, regarding the creation of the diocese of Brighton, Mgr Amigo raised a new difficulty due to the gravity of Southwark's financial problems.'[33] Rome failed to expedite matters. Because the proposal to unify London arose out of, and was unavoidably entwined with, the larger dispute between Bourne and Amigo, diocesan division became part of the brief entrusted to the Commission of English Bishops appointed by the Holy See to find a solution. Bourne and Rome had previously seen all aspects of any resolution being implemented simultaneously. The Bishops managed to present diocesan restructuring as 'a secondary matter' to be investigated only after the Cardinal's withdrawal from the Southwark Trusts.[34] The Commission succeeded in postponing the creation of a new Diocese of Brighton, stating it to be a financial problem, requiring detailed expert analysis.[35]

It was argued that Southwark's debts made it unfeasible to detach the wealthier county of Sussex, leaving the crushing liabilities with the poorer districts of South London. Various remedies were suggested: leaving Amigo to administer both Dioceses until the level of debt was significantly reduced; a fundraising appeal. All were orientated to the medium to longer term. Keating pleaded with Merry del Val, 'It is imperative that sufficient time should be given for this appeal to bear adequate fruit before any division of the Diocese of Southwark takes place.'[36] Through procrastination the Bishops ensured the impetus was lost in discussions over financial minutiae. These matters were being debated in July 1912. Bourne should have cut through all the peripheral issues and dealt with the principle. Yes, the Southwark debt problem was real and grave. Very well, Westminster would assume responsibility for all the assets and liabilities of South London, giving Amigo a clean slate in Brighton. That is, in fact, what the Cardinal did suggest—but only to his own Chancellor and only in November 1912. By that time Rome was about to decide against him.[37]

The Cardinal admitted that he was not certain that this plan had ever been put to Amigo.[38] This was not Bourne's fault. De Lai had told him in the winter of 1911–12 'not to enter into discussion with Mgr Amigo, and to leave it to the Holy See to find a solution.'[39] Partly in deference to De Lai, partly due to personal disinclination, Bourne made no particular effort to advance forcefully the case for the unification of London with those whose opinions mattered most. Simultaneously, Amigo was winning the argument with the likes of Norfolk and Merry del Val. Whether Amigo always fought fairly is not altogether certain. He told Keating that, 'All the debts will be on my shoulders, and the chances of paying them cut away from me.'[40] De Lai had assured him three months earlier this was not to be the case.[41] With Bourne considering himself bound to silence, Amigo had the field to himself. It was no good for Bourne to complain, 'It is clear that it is Cardinal Merry del Val—influenced by sympathy for the other side, and by the opposition of Norfolk—who is thus working for the delay.'[42] The result was exactly that—Rome decided in December 1912 that the unification of London was to be delayed.

Bourne took the Vatican at its word. Immediately after the decision he spoke to Norfolk about 'the *postponement* of the changes which the Holy See had proposed, *and still contemplates.*'[43] When Archbishop Ilsley fell seriously ill in the autumn of 1913, Amigo was terrified that Bourne would engineer his transfer to Birmingham and then effect the unification of London.[44] Rome had sufficiently impressed upon the Cardinal in 1912 that Amigo was to be left undisturbed in his Diocese so the unification of London did not feature in his various proposals for diocesan restructuring advanced during the First World War. Not that he had modified

'How good and how pleasant it is, when brothers live in unity'

in any way his belief in this 'much needed and much desired' remedy.[45] He even rehearsed again his arguments for such a move. The creation of the London County Council in 1888 had united local government north and south of the River; the Church ought to speak to the civil authority with a single voice. The multiplication of bridges and trams meant the Thames no longer constituted a significant physical boundary. Westminster Cathedral was viewed by many in South London as their spiritual home and was easily accessible to them. 'Thus the divided ecclesiastical jurisdiction becomes ever more anomalous.'[46] The Cardinal was, however, speaking to himself.

The suggestion never went entirely away. Amigo's greater sympathy for Irish independence and its controversial expression had Bourne's secretary writing to Rome. 'Many of these situations, incomprehensible to the ordinary Englishman, would be avoided by having London as one ecclesiastical entity. Much misunderstanding on the part of Catholics and non-Catholics alike would be avoided if the one diocese for London policy could be carried out ... Such instances of tactlessness as I have described will certainly tend to bring the Catholic Church into disrepute and cause the man in the street to identify the Church not so much with Rome as with Ireland.'[47] Lépicier needed no convincing of the merits of his former recommendation. He took the matter to Benedict XV, but was told that there was nothing doing while the unification of London represented the 'individual wish of [Bourne] against the general mind of the Bishops of England and of the Consistorial Congregation in Rome.'[48]

Bourne might be criticised for wilful stubbornness in pursuing an idea which was never going to be adopted. That is not, however, entirely fair. A number of English Bishops came to realise that Rome was not exactly consistent on the issue. Vacancies in Birmingham and Liverpool in spring 1921 gave the opportunity for Amigo to be moved with his honour intact. There was a further reorganisation of local government in London. This, the Cardinal urged, was the ideal moment to incorporate South London into Westminster.[49] The Pope replied 'emphatically that the unification of London is, in principle, an accomplished fact—the only question now open being that of the opportunity.'[50] Benedict XV appeared to further encourage Bourne in this direction. 'He promised in my farewell audience that everything would be done to bring about the long desired result, and that I would hear about it as soon as possible. Since then I have heard nothing and I was beginning to be anxious lest some unexpected hitch might have arisen ... As far as ordinary administration is concerned we could take over at once.'[51] Bourne's lack of a Roman training meant he failed to appreciate that the Vatican tended not to deal in resounding negatives; senior prelates were expected to be able to read between the lines.

The Consistorial Congregation had, in fact, already determined on 14 April 1921 against unification so long as Amigo wished to stay in Southwark.[52] In very Roman fashion, Archbishop Cerretti of the Secretariat of State 'clarified' matters for Bourne. 'I spoke to the Holy Father again about the last decision of the Consistorial Congregation, and he wishes me to assure you that the question is decided definitely in principle. However, it is necessary to wait for the Diocese of Southwark to become vacant before putting the decision into execution. I may add in confidence that the Bishop in question before having been asked if he would accept an archbishopric wrote to say he would never leave his Diocese under any circumstances.'[53] This did not prevent Bourne pressing Pius XI to reconsider the matter as late as 1934. In the twenty-first century the Thames appears a very permanent ecclesiastical boundary.

'Such an upheaval'

The Bishops most directly affected were told in the summer of 1911 that Rome had decided that England would be divided into three ecclesiastical Provinces. The remaining Bishops officially learnt of the proposal at the hierarchy's meeting in October. Bishop Burton noted, 'This Consistorial Congregation seems bent on doing what they deem best for the Province, so that we may witness such an upheaval among us as has not taken place since 1850.'[54] The upheaval did not just concern the creation of two new Archbishops. Rumours abounded of extensive diocesan reorganisation.

When the English hierarchy was restored in 1850 it provoked a surge of anti-Catholic feeling; many Catholics doubted the wisdom of the action. There was no such outcry against Pius X's document, *Si Qua Est*. 'Catholic England has welcomed the division with three Provinces, and is hopeful of its effects in the future, and Protestant England which is the country generally has not shown any hostility.'[55] Reaction to the suggestion of the creation of new Dioceses was a good deal more mixed.

What brought about the suggestion? Amigo had no doubts. 'I fear that it was the Cardinal himself who set this question of divisions going ... I am sorry that because he objects to me my Diocese and other Dioceses in England should suffer.'[56] He was right. Bourne took up the cause of

'How good and how pleasant it is, when brothers live in unity'

wholesale diocesan reorganisation 'in order that the suggested change in Southwark not be an isolated fact (which might bear personal significance) but part of a larger scheme.'[57] To be fair, although he attributed the initiative to Rome rather than himself, the Cardinal never disguised what he believed to be genesis of the idea. Addressing the hierarchy in fraught circumstances in 1917, he gave his account of the history of the matter. 'It was apparent that the whole scheme originated in the Southwark troubles and is the fruit of the long quarrels between Southwark and Westminster.'[58]

The creation of a Diocese of Brighton was fundamental to the proposal to resolve the dispute between Bourne and Amigo. Various suggestions were made for other changes. In 1911 these crystallised around a new Diocese of Cambridge to be formed by removing from Northampton the counties of Norfolk, Suffolk, Cambridgeshire and Huntingdonshire. Northampton was to be compensated by the transfer of Oxfordshire from Birmingham. Had they been adopted, Bourne's projects would have had added colour to the bench of Bishops. He had Robert Hugh Benson, the convert son of the Archbishop of Canterbury, novelist, preacher and dabbler in the occult, lined up for Cambridge.[59] Bourne later proposed Bede Jarrett, the impressive Dominican Provincial, as Bishop of a Diocese of Northampton which would include Oxford, while the scholar Charles Duchemin[60] was put forward for Cambridge.[61]

What was the rationale for the reorganisation? With these initial proposals it often seemed to consist of the Cardinal and others poring over maps, deciding that certain Dioceses were too large and advancing what they felt were more logical configurations.[62] Amigo discovered that Rome's approach was no more sophisticated. 'Last night I saw Cardinal Merry del Val. He had a Catholic Directory map on his table, and pointed out to me the absurdity of having Oxfordshire in Birmingham. He certainly would be in favour of yielding to our Cardinal in this.'[63]

The Archbishop of Birmingham and the Bishop of Northampton complained that they were not consulted about the dismemberment of their Dioceses.[64] Amigo told Keating he thought that the Cardinal was in Rome seeking the creation of new Dioceses and telling the Vatican 'that it is no use consulting the Bishops as each Bishop like a parish priest simply thinks of his own part, not taking a wide outlook.'[65] That was precisely what he was doing.

For Bourne this was just part of a wider vision to invigorate Catholic life in England, a vision he shared on his return to Westminster in January

1912. 'The recent erection of new Provinces; the possible eventual creation of new Dioceses; the division of existing parishes or missionary districts; the multiplication of churches, and presbyteries and schools; no one of these things can be brought about without sacrifice in many different forms. For Bishops and clergy and faithful there is the sacrifice of most legitimate and natural sentiment, when old ties have to be broken and new relations have to be formed ... Then thoughts of material concern make their own call for sacrifice. Human prudence and generous abandonment to God's care easily come into conflict ... But generous alms-giving has never failed in the past; it will not be wanting in the future as God brings home to the heart and conscience of our people the fact that we are entering on a new phase of the efforts of the Catholic Church in this country.'[66] The Cardinal had convinced himself that an immediate increase in the number of Dioceses was desired by Rome and would serve the cause of the conversion of England. His fears were justified that other Bishops might not view matters in this light and simply fight to maintain the integrity of their own Diocese, but he ought to have appreciated that Rome was unlikely to act to the prejudice of an incumbent Bishop without at least consulting him.

Keating was one of the first to discover that Rome blew hot and cold with respect to these proposals. Having made representations against changes to Northampton, he was inclined to rest there and implicitly criticised Amigo's continued agitation in Rome and at home. 'I have done my duty to my Diocese, so far as I was allowed. Beyond that, I have a strong disinclination to meddle with ecclesiastical "wires." I do not say this in condemnation of others. I can quite realise that a Bishop is bound to act vigorously when the very existence of his Diocese is threatened. But, in the interests of the Church, I do feel that, like the European Powers, we ought to try to confine, not extend, the area of unrest.'[67]

Appointed by Rome to the commission on diocesan reorganisation, Keating took his duties seriously and prepared to discharge them in a business-like manner. Imagine his surprise, therefore, when Keating approached de Lai and Merry del Val in person in the summer of 1912 and they indicated such reorganisation hardly concerned them at all. The proposed division of his own Diocese was to be laid aside. The two Cardinals also assured him that any future divisions would not be undertaken at the instance of one individual but only following consideration by the English hierarchy as a whole or at least a representative episcopal commission. Keating reported back to his brother Bishops that Rome simply wanted to see the dispute between Bourne and Amigo settled.[68]

Had the Vatican stuck consistently to this approach, it would have saved itself and the English hierarchy a huge amount of trouble and unhappiness. Discussing the matter a decade later, Bourne was rightly aggrieved. 'I am, and will always be, persuaded that in this matter the action of the Holy See towards me was, evidently unintentionally, neither fair nor open. It created for me a false and extraordinarily difficult situation that I would have otherwise avoided.'[69] He had been led to believe in 1911 that the creation of three ecclesiastical Provinces was only one part of a plan which included the unification of London and the multiplication of Dioceses. Yet, at the first sign of opposition, Rome prevaricated on the second and third parts of the plan. The Cardinal felt himself deprived both of a settlement of his dispute with Amigo and the means of a giving impetus to the growth of Catholic life in the nation.

And it really was prevarication on the part of Rome. Bourne was back in the Eternal City in the spring of 1914 and diocesan reorganisation was discussed again in some depth. Rome agreed that the Cardinal should raise the matter in his keynote speech at the Catholic Congress in Cardiff in July.[70] There was deep personal antipathy between Bourne and Merry del Val, but they shared the conviction that the moment had to be seized, that a bold project might yield much in terms of the long held aspiration for the conversion of England. The Cardinal Secretary of State believed, 'Catholic evangelisation in England ... [is] deficient or stagnant in many parts.'[71] Thus, he assured Bourne that he would produce confirmation that his Cardiff speech represented Rome's desire regarding diocesan division.[72]

Bourne addressed the Catholic Congress on the Church's role in the national life and the imperative of missionary activity. He knew he was stirring up a hornet's nest among some of his brother Bishops, but believed he had Rome's backing, when he expounded the implications of *Si qua est*. 'The words of the Bull are as follows: "Moreover, in this new constitution of the Dioceses of England we have reserved to ourselves certain other matters to be later determined, as shall seem opportune, or experience and the good of souls shall suggest." And in the letter giving communication of the Bull the Cardinal Secretary of the Consistorial Congregation informed me that the other matters to which allusion had thus been made were *paulisper dilata*—postponed only for a while. This, then, is the goal set before our zeal and generosity by the Holy See: to hasten as quickly as we may the erection in this country of new centres of episcopal influence, first in the form of apostolic vicariates where no other course is possible, and then of fully constituted diocesan Sees ... It is fully understood that there is not a diocese in this country overburdened with resources; that subdivision of existing diocesan funds, especially those which furnish support to the Bishops and their administrative staffs, would be in almost every case quite impossible; and that, therefore, new funds must be built up in order to render the erection of new Sees prudently possible.'[73]

Merry del Val honoured his agreement with Bourne. The desired letter was ready and waiting, and duly published in the *Tablet* on 25 July. 'The important address which Your Eminence delivered at Cardiff on 10 July has deeply interested the Holy Father, and he wishes me to assure you that he has read it with very great pleasure. His Holiness's attention has been more particularly drawn to what Your Eminence has pointed out in connection with the Bull *Si qua est* and the development of the Catholic Church in England. Your Eminence has put forward the mind of the Holy See and the ultimate object in view when the new ecclesiastical Provinces were erected nearly three years ago. As you have rightly stated, all over the world, "a wise and gradual growth of the episcopate means in every case greater earnestness among the children of the Church, greater activity of zeal, and a rapid increase in the number of those who accept her teaching." The Holy See is confident that the same methods cannot fail to promote constant and far-reaching progress in the life of the Church in England, and lead to the salvation of the thousands who are seeking for light and grace, and who are at present beyond the reach of those who can minister to them. Difficulties and obstacles obviously exist and others may arise before the goal can be reached, but the Holy Father trusts that the zeal and generosity of English Catholics will find the means of overcoming them, and thus develop the admirable work which their forefathers have accomplished since the restoration of the hierarchy, and which they themselves have carried on so nobly to this day.'[74]

Bourne must have congratulated himself. He had prepared the ground well and secured a decisive victory. Diocesan multiplication having been so clearly expressed as the mind of the Holy Father, a duty of loyalty laid upon them, how could the English Bishops possibly continue to resist?

'How good and how pleasant it is, when brothers live in unity'

A month later the outbreak of World War I and the death of Pope Pius X changed everyone's calculations.

'An opportunity now in England'[75]

Most would have presumed that the War would have postponed any consideration of internal and administrative changes. Yet within fourteen months of the outbreak of hostilities, the Cardinal had resumed his campaign. He enlisted the help of his former ally, Fr Lépicier, whom he regarded 'as a sort of "godfather" of all projects for the progress of the Church in England.'[76]

Bourne acknowledged that his promotion of diocesan reorganisation might appear inopportune, but enumerated reasons why this was not, in fact, the case. The War, he argued, had changed everything, including 'a real religious awakening and men's minds are turning more than ever to the Catholic Church.' This was noted by others. The sheer awfulness of trench warfare inclined men's minds to eternal realities. For the first time vast numbers of Englishmen were transported to Catholic countries such as France and Belgium, thrown alongside Catholic soldiers and chaplains. Residual prejudice faded. The Cardinal may well have been correct in urging that, ironically, it was easier to raise funds in wartime than in peace. 'There is a great wave of charity across the country.' The Catholic working classes in the industrial heartlands were benefiting from full employment and higher wages.[77] Bourne asked Lépicier to impress on Rome that 'we have an opportunity now in England which must be met during the War in order to prepare for the future when our chance of doing good to our fellow countrymen will be such as the past never provided.'[78]

Recognising, nevertheless, Bishops were concerned about the financial implications of division, the Cardinal believed that he had the solution. No Bishop would be compelled to part with diocesan funds. Rather than create new Dioceses immediately, Vicariates would be erected. A Vicar-General could live modestly in a parish without the expense of a cathedral and full curia. The faithful would have the incentive of raising an endowment of £10,000 knowing the creation of a new Diocese was imminent.

The Cardinal was anxious to advance the cause of the Catholic faith in England at an auspicious moment. He may well have been correct that the multiplication of Dioceses was a means of achieving this, increasing the Catholic presence on the ground, calling the faithful to greater effort.

Yet his motives were mixed. In addition to the possibility of removing Amigo from London, there was also a spirit of competition with the Anglicans. Pastoral zeal in the Church of England saw the erection of eleven new Anglican dioceses between the 1880s and 1920s. Bourne did not wish to be left behind. Nor was he above exploiting perceived Anglican weaknesses, the disestablishment of the Anglican Church in Wales, the lack of an Anglican bishop in Cambridge.

A willing accomplice in the Cardinal's project, recognising in it 'a whole system of measures intended for spreading the Faith,'[79] Lépicier took the proposals to the Pope. Unsurprisingly, he found Benedict XV unacquainted with the finer detail of the constitution *Si qua est* and English diocesan boundaries. Of course he made sympathetic noises about a scheme designed to promote the Catholic faith in England, but he also made issued a significant *caveat* to which Bourne and Lépicier ought to have paid greater attention, the difficulty 'of dividing a Diocese while its occupant is living.' In his enthusiasm, Lépicier glossed over this. 'We may well believe that this difficulty will vanish away in the presence of the greater good which is expected from the much desired adjustment of the Dioceses.'[80] Wishful thinking!

Bourne did not enter the fray unprepared. Rome was unwilling to divide a Diocese against the wishes of an incumbent bishop. Very well; Nottingham was vacant. Let the opportunity be taken to reform a geographically unwieldy Diocese through the creation of a new Vicariate of Lincoln comprising Lincolnshire and Rutland. Other Bishops were unwilling to contemplate division. Very well; Cardinal Bourne would lead by example, offering to separate Essex from his own Diocese of Westminster—an offer initially made conditional on the simultaneous creation of vicariates in Lincoln and Sussex. A further tactical advantage arose when Bishop Hedley asked for Wales to be created an independent Province with its centre in Cardiff; a request to which the Archbishop of Birmingham, within whose Province it currently fell, acceded. (Amigo demonstrated his obstructionism by lecturing Ilsley: 'Your suggestion about dividing Newport was very unfortunate and the result seems to have been to give Wales an Archbishop. I am very sorry that your Province is thus cut down.'[81] What concern was this to Southwark?)

Cardinal Bourne wasted no time in pressing home the points made by Lépicier. He was in Rome in early December 1915 seeing Benedict XV and Cardinal De Lai. Both he and the Vatican were at fault. Bourne

'How good and how pleasant it is, when brothers live in unity'

still did not appreciate Rome's *modus operandi*; the Vatican failed to recognise the English Cardinal did not do nuance. He returned to London shortly before Christmas under a significant misapprehension. Bourne had raised the matter twice with the Pope. After the second audience, he noted 'Full understanding on all points.' The impression left by De Lai was even more misleading. 'In the evening took leave of Card. De Lai who … promised repeatedly that all the other matters should be carried through at once (Vicariates, Cardiff, Bidwell), if possible before the New Year. We parted most affectionately and in complete agreement.'[82]

No sooner was Bourne back in England than the project began to unravel—or, at least, those elements which most keenly concerned him. The Pope did create a separate Province of Wales in February 1916. The *Tablet* presented this as 'the first fruits' of the Cardinal's policy announced at Cardiff in July 1914.[83] The opportunity to divide Nottingham was effectively lost with the appointment of a new Bishop, even although Thomas Dunn was a Westminster priest and the Brief appointing him reserved to the Holy See the right to create a separate Diocese of Lincoln. Initially, Dunn was not hostile, telling the Cardinal, 'Personally, I have no objection to the proposal of division.'[84]

More ominous, however, was the fretting of the Bishop of Southwark, who was 'much disturbed by the evidence of Cardinal Bourne's activity in Rome' and threatened to go out there himself.[85] In fact, Amigo had friends in Rome acting on his behalf. On 25 January De Lai visited Gasquet, asking him to set down his 'views as to a scheme for division suggested by Cardinal Bourne.'[86] It seemed to De Lai the most natural way to proceed. Why not seek the views of another Englishman, an Englishman who had the advantage of being resident in Rome and a fellow curial Cardinal[87]? Far easier, it seemed, than trying to correspond across war-torn Europe. De Lai was right to consult, but he looked in the wrong place. Gasquet might pose as a benevolent umpire, but was, in fact, far from impartial. He lacked any official standing to speak for the English hierarchy. The Bishops might complain about Bourne's tendency to do business in Rome without consulting them, but Gasquet was no more transparent.

The Consistorial Congregation met in early March. They favoured the Lincoln proposal in principle, but had questions of detail. Essex and Sussex posed greater difficulties. Southwark's financial woes were raised once more.[88] Amigo had muddied the waters by suggesting a Diocese of Essex-Kent based in Greenwich. Bourne was dismissive. Such a proposal further fragmented London. 'As the bird flies Essex and Kent are very close. But as bishops do not have wings, and do not yet travel by plane, they must, to go from one to the other, either cross the Thames by boat ... or go into central London by train ... The project is impractical and would expose the Church to ridicule.'[89] There was a momentum for change in Rome, but Gasquet used his presence and position to stall matters. 'I had an audience of the Pope. The Holy Father spoke at length about the proposed divisions of the English Dioceses which Cardinal de Lai so urges. I begged him to get the opinion of the Bishops on the general question and on the lines of the division. Finally he said he would adopt my advice.'[90]

Sensing his cherished hopes slipping away, the Cardinal attempted to kick start matters. He dropped his condition that Essex should only be separated from Westminster in the event of the other new Dioceses being created, urging this now occur 'without delay' with Mgr Bernard Ward as the first Bishop.[91] Bourne left London for Rome on 27 November 1916. He was to be away for four months. Ostensibly, his motive was to attend the Consistory creating new cardinals. In reality, he was trying to breathe new life into the plans for diocesan division. He left a lengthy memorandum with the Consistorial Congregation arguing for Dioceses of Essex, Kent, Cambridge and Lincoln. Oxfordshire, he proposed again, should be given to Northampton once there was a vacancy at Birmingham. Herefordshire was to be moved from the Welsh Province to Birmingham, ideally as a separate Benedictine Diocese based at Belmont Abbey. Liverpool too ought to be split with a new Diocese of Preston, while Hexham and Newcastle was also in need of division. The Cardinal sought a Bull effecting these changes accompanied by a letter from the Pope encouraging a spirit of generosity from English Catholics.[92]

On 11 December Bourne was named a member of the Consistorial Congregation, the Vatican department responsible for approving his proposals. The appointment caused consternation in England. 'Several of the Bishops are alarmed at the nomination of Card. B. to the Consistorial. I hope it does not mean mischief ahead!'[93] Gasquet's explanation that it was intended simply as a consolation prize for Bourne not achieving his wish in this and other matters did not entirely soothe episcopal nerves.[94] Keating still feared 'he may succeed in rushing his hobby horse without the opinion of other bishops being heard.'[95]

'How good and how pleasant it is, when brothers live in unity'

The insistence with which Bourne pressed his case at every opportunity with Benedict XV and De Lai was almost counterproductive. Others were equally active—with greater success. A prolific correspondent, Amigo succeeded in arousing in Keating, Ilsley, Casartelli and Dunn a similar distrust of the Cardinal's actions, and a determination to thwart them. Casartelli wished there was 'some way by which the remaining 15 diocesans outside Westminster can make themselves heard.'[96] They feared they would be presented with a *fait accompli* at their Low Week meeting. With others, Casartelli wrote to Gasquet seeking his 'powerful protection in face of such dangers.'[97] It appealed to Gasquet to act as protector to the English Bishops. But Bourne saw Gasquet as the obstacle to other plans too and vented his frustration, charging him with dishonourable motives. The curial Cardinal confided to his diary: 'According to him I having been his *rival* for the See of Westminster have always been the centre of opposition.'[98] The accusation had substance.

Whatever his motivation, Gasquet was certainly powerful, enjoying unlimited access to the Pope, whom he persuaded to defer any decision until after the War and a proper consultation of the Bishops.[99] Being personable and on the ground, Gasquet was able to glean valuable information. '[De Lai] told me that the subject of the division of the English dioceses was actually again coming up before the Consistorial but promised to let me have the papers for me to give my views privately.'[100] Forewarned was forearmed. Gasquet took himself off to the Cardinal Secretary of State, who assured him 'that he will block the discussion by asking the Congregation to declare it impossible during the war and until the English bishops have been consulted.'[101] Merry del Val implemented exactly that policy Gasquet had recommended to the Pope five weeks earlier. To be certain, Gasquet wrote a long letter to Benedict XV on 'the state of unrest which exists in England' quoting the complaints of Southwark, Salford, Nottingham, Northampton and Portsmouth.[102]

Merry del Val remained an enigma to the English Bishops. Amigo and Casartelli were surprised given his earlier support for diocesan division. While in Rome Casartelli 'spoke very frankly [to Merry del Val] about the whole question; he listened, but he did not commit himself to any definite expression of his own policy. On the other hand, I have more than once heard Card. Bourne say that he believed M. d. V. had some dislike against him and worked against him; so I doubt if they cooperate. It is very obscure.'[103]

Bourne's opponents were jubilant. Bishop McIntyre, Rector of the English College, wrote, '[His Eminence] asked the authorities to put him on the Consistorial hoping thereby to pilot his schemes through. But he has been sadly deceived. We were too active for him; and just before the general meeting on Thursday last, some friend must have given a hint that there would be no thoroughfare, for he withdrew his bill to avoid rejection.'[104]

That, one would have thought, was the end of the affair. Cardinal Bourne would return to Westminster and turn his mind to other matters. Yet he was nothing if not persistent and the Roman Curia nothing if not inconsistent. On 20 February 1917 De Lai gave Bourne the news he had been hoping for all along.

> I have the honour to tell Your Eminence that I have sent the letters to the three Bishops of Southwark, Northampton and Nottingham according to the agreed plan for the creation of the three dioceses of Kent, Cambridge and Lincoln. I hope that they will obtain the desired effect. I have also given instructions for the programme for the bull for the creation of the diocese of Essex. At the same time I am pleased to tell Your Eminence that the Holy Father has approved the choice of Mgr Bernard Ward to govern the new diocese.[105]

De Lai's letters to Amigo, Keating and Dunn were subtly different. The creation of new Dioceses was presented as the mind of Rome, but at the same time they were assured no action would be taken until after consultation and adequate funds raised.[106] No wonder there was confusion, frustration and anger.

'Some very strong speaking'

Understandably, the English Bishops felt they were being heard by neither Cardinal Bourne nor the Vatican. The solution had to lie in their own hands. Amigo and Keating believed 'that the question of projected divisions should be dealt with in Low Week. It is for us all to act and not simply for one.'[107] But Amigo was not prepared to wait that long. Westminster was the Province most affected by the proposals, so he wrote to his fellow suffragans, Nottingham, Northampton and Portsmouth, asking them to meet on 7 March. (Whiteside declined Casartelli's request for a similar meeting of the Liverpool Province.) The Westminster suffragans took two decisions. They agreed a courteous but firm response to De Lai: 'None of us agree to any change during the war and we think

'How good and how pleasant it is, when brothers live in unity'

that, though dioceses will eventually have to be divided, the process must be gradual ... to have Vicariates again in England is a retrograde movement ...The Bishops as a Body have never been consulted in this most important matter and your Eminence will probably find that they are against such proposals, knowing the real condition of England at present.'[108] They also asked the Archbishops of Birmingham, Liverpool and Cardiff to convene a meeting of all the Bishops, ostensibly to discuss National Service and the possible conscription of seminarians. Amigo was delighted when Ilsley summoned his brethren to meet at Oscott on 15 March.

That meeting resolved to send the following telegram to the Pope: 'The Archbishops and Bishops of England and Wales assembled at Oscott wish to express their strong conviction that the sub-divisions of the dioceses of this country will be detrimental to religion in England, and beg the Holy Father not to allow even the first step to be taken in such an undertaking until the Hierarchy of England have been heard.'[109] For the first time the English Bishops had been able to act in concert. Yet their pressing need to keep Gasquet abreast of all that had occurred hardly suggests a mature independence. Dunn related how the 'temper of the meeting was a most painful one. It almost amounts to scandal, and it is a grievous pity that the Cardinal of Westminster should *despise* all the other Bishops in the land ... just at a time when it is so important that we should all be working in harmony together! I'm not *angry* with him, but I am unutterably saddened. Can't you muzzle him!'[110] Amigo's letter smacked more of triumphalism. 'The Bishops are fairly stirred up now and Low Week will be lively ... for the first time the Archbishop of Westminster finds himself with all the other Bishops opposed to him.'[111] Whereas Casartelli delighted in telling Gasquet, 'I think it would have been a revelation to H. E. of Westminster if he could have heard all that was said and written!'[112]

In Rome Bourne was blissfully unaware of the firestorm awaiting him back home. He enquired gently of Cotter of the proceedings of the Westminster suffragans.[113] (Feeling that he was being asked to inform on his brother Bishops, Portsmouth did not reply.[114]) Bourne went so far as to advise Amigo there was no difficulty with the Oscott resolution being discussed at the Low Week meeting the following month.[115] Yet, at the same time, to prevent a precedent being established, he wrote to Amigo and Ilsley reminding them that he alone had the right to call a meeting of the Westminster suffragans and the national hierarchy, but assuring them that, had they only asked, he would have willingly done everything possible to facilitate such meetings in his absence.[116] Scarcely a justification for Dunn's denunciation of the 'whole attitude of HE has seen fit to take up—treating Bishops, as he treats everyone else, as so much dirt under his feet.'[117]

The Cardinal believed he could afford to be sanguine. As he was denounced by the Bishops in England, the creation of the new Diocese of Essex was being rapidly implemented in Rome. With no other Bishop prejudiced by the proposal, he and Bernard Ward fine-tuned the detail, eventually agreeing on Brentwood as the diocesan seat. The Diocese was formally erected on 22 March and, following the Cardinal's return to England, Ward consecrated Bishop on 10 April. Amigo was sour and patronising, explaining to Ward 'that though there is great irritation among us about the way in which the new diocese has been created none of us have anything against him personally. I told him that I was glad that he was being made a Bishop but that I strongly objected to his having such a diocese.'[118]

What really irritated the English Bishops, however, was Benedict XV's letter to the Cardinal on the creation of the new Diocese. As it appeared in the *Tablet*, it amounted to unqualified approval of Bourne's policy by the supreme authority. Assurances from Gasquet, Merry del Val, De Lai, the Holy Father himself, seemed worthless. There it was in print: 'An appeal from the Holy Father to the English Bishops for a further sub-division of dioceses.' 'Willingly and joyfully, as We have already said, We have accepted this proposal and carried it into effect. In truth, the division of a too numerous flock between two shepherds will enable each of them more easily and more carefully to feed the sheep committed to him and to devote himself to leading back to the Chief Shepherd the wanderers who were without the fold of Christ. And would that others also of the English Episcopate might see their way to imitate the excellent example you have set! For the size of the territory assigned to them is so great that the strength of one man is hardly equal to the task of governing it; so that thoroughly efficacious pastoral vigilance is sometimes lacking to the faithful, while conversions among those in error are possibly too infrequent. We are indeed aware that for some their poverty presents a difficulty in the way of an increase in the number of dioceses. But the remarkable and eager generosity of the English Catholics inspires Us with the certain hope that this obstacle may be easily overcome.'[119]

'How good and how pleasant it is, when brothers live in unity'

The Cardinal left Rome the day that letter was written. He travelled via Paray-le-Monial, where he joined other Allied ecclesiastical leaders in placing their national flags in the Sacred Heart chapel, and Boulogne, where he visited the Army camps. He had little idea of the reaction awaiting him back home. This should be viewed in the wider context. Britain had been at war for 2½ years. There were massive and mounting casualties. The people lacked the decisive military and naval victories they had been promised. A mounting sense of frustration had led to the political coup of December 1916 with the peace time Prime Minister Asquith being ousted by Lloyd George.

Against this backdrop the English Bishops aired their own grievances, getting a little carried away with their use of military imagery. Thus, for the Bishop of Northampton, the Cardinal was an 'autocrat of the most Prussian type, who consults no one but himself and wishes to stifle all opinion opposed to his own.'[120] The same Bishop discussed the tactics to be adopted at the Low Week meeting of the hierarchy scheduled for 17–18 April. 'The main point to be hammered into H.E. at our Low Week meeting is the *personal* matter of his going to Rome behind our backs and engineering projects affecting our dioceses which he knows to be opposed to our wishes. However excellent, in his own eyes, his motives may be, his underhand methods are detestable, and injurious to peace and harmonious working. It will not be pleasant hearing for him; but severe things have to be said; and we must have the courage to say them.'[121] Bishops who normally accepted Bourne's hospitality at Archbishop's House for the Low Week meeting chose to stay elsewhere.

Publication of the Pope's letter had raised the stakes. Amigo was alarmed. 'I am afraid of some of Bishops, especially Birmingham, thinking that after the letter it will be disrespectful to the Holy See to take any strong line. It will be my duty to disabuse Birmingham of such an idea.'[122] The sense that they would be opposing the Pope's personal wishes did indeed convince some to withdraw their opposition. Plymouth for one chose to reconsider: 'The letter H.E. the Cardinal has sent us quite changes the point of view. The Holy Father has chosen this way to ask us to do what has been done in Westminster and has practically appealed to each Bishop. Under these circumstances I have written to say that I am willing to further his wishes, and therefore must set aside the long and lucid document to which we gave our signatures.'[123]

Amigo's animus against Bourne was such that he was not about to be deflected from his purpose now. He massaged Gasquet's sense of self-importance. 'I feel certain that all of us are grateful to your Eminence for your most kind interest in the matter which so vitally affects the interests of this country. It is most important for us that you are in Rome and able to explain the true state of the case to the Holy See.'[124] And he relayed Gasquet's counsel to his brother Bishops 'that if we the Bishops remain united and act together nothing more will be heard about divisions for a long time to come.'[125] Gasquet got to work in Rome. Amigo and, simultaneously, the other Westminster suffragans wrote to the Cardinal to protest their right to meet in his absence. 'As Ordinaries, we are responsible to the Holy See, and to the Holy See alone. When we need counsel, or the support of joint action, we are free to seek such counsel or support from our fellow bishops, whether within or outside our own Province, without leave or even reference to any Metropolitan. Should the encroachments of the Metropolitan himself give cause to our anxiety, it is as lawful as it is natural for the suffragans to concert common measures for resisting him.'[126]

Armed with confidences from Gasquet, the English Bishops convinced themselves that the Pope required their protection. 'The whole affair is distressing and dis-edifying. But our unanimity is the strongest proof that none of us are contending for personal advantage or spleen, but for a most important principle which it is *our duty* to defend to the last trench. Under ordinary circumstances we should defer implicitly to the least suggestion of the Holy See, even though we were doubtful of its wisdom. But the circumstances are *not* ordinary. We know that this letter has been extorted from the Pope against his will, and it is clear from the contents that the matter has been foisted upon him by Cardinal Bourne. Therefore we shall serve the Holy See, not by allowing the Pope to be made a tool of to work a great and mischievous injustice, but by regarding the letter as a "general sentiment," which he does not expect or even wish to be put into practice at present ... I feel confident that the Roman authorities *look to us* to relieve them from the pressure brought to bear upon them.'[127] Benedict XV might have been thoroughly wearied by English squabbling, but one wonders whether he saw himself as similarly threatened by Cardinal Bourne.

Bourne himself professed to be mystified by all this episcopal agitation. 'I suppose that next week will reveal to us the thoughts of many minds. At present they are to me quite inexplicable.'[128]

'How good and how pleasant it is, when brothers live in unity'

And so the Bishops met at Westminster on 17 April. On the Agenda were 'the proposals of the Holy See for the creation of new Dioceses of Rochester, Cambridge and Lincoln.'[129] The minutes of the meeting were a masterpiece of bureaucratic reticence and understatement.

> There was a discussion as to the proposals of the Holy See for the division of certain dioceses; and also, in connection with this, on the conditions necessary in order to call a meeting of the Bishops of a Province in the absence of the Archbishop of Westminster. The Cardinal Archbishop then gave a full account of the negotiations with the Holy See, beginning with the year 1901, which ultimately led to the proposals for dividing certain dioceses which had been put forward during the last few weeks. The Archbishop of Liverpool pointed out that the Bishops had already sent to Rome their reasons for dissenting, which had been agreed to by all the Bishops … It was agreed, therefore, that the matter should rest there for the present.[130]

What actually happened? On 12 April Gasquet went to see Merry del Val and wrote to the Pope. Four days later he wrote gleefully, 'I received from the Holy Father today a letter in reply to mine sent on Friday morning. It is absolutely satisfactory in every way.'[131] Using official diplomatic channels, Gasquet telegrammed Amigo immediately. Its receipt elicited jubilation. 'I am more grateful still for the most important telegram which came this morning in time for the Meeting. It came in most usefully, and I thought your Eminence meant it to be so, as your sending it through the British Mission showed.'[132]

Various Bishops kept diaries and recorded their recollections of the Low Week proceedings. 'A tense half hour of questioning and explaining: Northampton, Nottingham, *et aliquot alii*, spoke very straight.'[133] 'Rather painful; some very strong speaking; especially by Card. B., Northampton and Southwark. Very strained feelings!'[134] The Cardinal used the Pope's letter as an appeal to the Bishops' loyalty to acquiesce in the matter of diocesan division. The Bishop of Plymouth indicated his willingness to do so. Others may have been prepared to do likewise.

Amigo decided it was time to show his hand. 'At that moment I thought that I had better just read your telegram.'[135] Yes, Cardinal Bourne had worked hard to obtain his letter from the Pope. Yes, he had employed that letter to best effect to support his case for diocesan division. Did that really justify the outcry of his opponents, opponents who, ironically, were happy to use exactly the same methods to further their ends? Yet again the Vatican gave succour to the most recent plaintiff. And now Gasquet had the field to himself. Supported by Merry del Val, he was almost guaranteed success. That took the following form:

> Following telegram from Cardinal Gasquet have just received letter from Holy Father reaffirming that no diocese will be touched without full free consent of its own Bishop. Denying *Tablet* translation. Word 'queant' purposely chosen to express material possibility not mere willingness: regretting false interpretation of his letter as appeal to bishops for immediate divisions which it is not.[136]

It all turned on the use of the Latin word *queant* in Benedict's letter to Cardinal Bourne. The *Tablet* had translated it as 'the English Episcopate *might see their way*' to follow the Cardinal's example. The Pope now said he had intended to convey his wish that 'the English Episcopate *might find themselves in a position*' to do this. A specific request for action was downgraded to a vague aspiration that the circumstances might change. Read in the context of the papal letter as a whole, this one word did not alter too much. However, sprung on the Cardinal in a heated and hostile meeting, it took on a very complexion. Amigo alleged that his rival had wilfully and misleadingly modified the Pope's letter to English Catholics; he was not to be trusted. The allegation stuck and Bourne was forced to back down.

Liverpool, Salford and Northampton drafted a statement for the *Tablet* giving a revised translation of the papal letter. The meeting resumed the following day. The Cardinal was no longer in 'defiant mood'[137] and Ilsley took the initiative. The Bishops agreed to petition Rome 'to postpone the consideration of all the projects of sub-dividing dioceses in England until after the war. They further petitioned the Holy See that before It thinks good to make new proposals in this matter, It will allow the whole English Episcopate to be heard on the future general policy of dividing dioceses in England, as well as allowing each Bishop who is affected to be heard as to any proposed sub-division of his own diocese. The Cardinal Archbishop promised to transmit this resolution to the Holy See.'[138] He, in turn, gave an account of the push for diocesan division, maintaining that previously he had been bound to keep confidences, acting throughout only as 'the mouthpiece of the Holy See'[139]—a plausible, but partial, reading of affairs. The Cardinal also deprecated the suggestion that the Bishops send two of their number to act as their delegates in Rome.[140]

'How good and how pleasant it is, when brothers live in unity'

(In the event, the Bishops failed to implement their earlier resolution to this effect, and, to his regret, Amigo initially travelled to Rome alone.)

The Bishops were left assessing the consequences of their confrontation with the head of the hierarchy. The Archbishop of Liverpool viewed the whole sorry episode in the traditional narrative of intrigue and counter-intrigue:

> It is not easy to gauge the effect of the Low Week Meeting. I am certain that the Oscott telegram, followed by the Oscott memorandum, has proved a bomb-shell at Rome. It has also shown the Cardinal that the Hierarchy can be articulate, in spite of himself and in opposition to him. I think and hope that this has been an eye-opener to him. Moreover it has been a revelation to him that we have friends at Court, who can have access to the Holy Father, and express our views.[141]

The Bishop of Northampton took a more comprehensive approach. Bourne had no fiercer critic than Keating, but he possessed the integrity to admit that the Cardinal was not solely to blame. In doing so, he provided a rare critique of the Roman authorities, who

> even now, hardly seem to recognise their own share in the trouble. First in the *Si qua* and [De Lai's] covering letter; then in Card. Merry's own letter expressly written to strengthen Cardinal B's hand when he sprung his schemes upon us at the Cardiff Congress; now, a third time, when he is armed against us by a letter of the Holy Father which has appeared in the *Tablet* and elsewhere; Rome has left nothing undone to give him public backing, and to silence our opposition as far as possible. Several of us have exposed the situation frankly both to Card. de Lai and to Card. Merry himself.[142]

As a Church historian, Ward was aware of precedents. In the 1840 division of Districts and the creation of the Vicariate of Wales in 1895, Rome had also acted over the heads of the Bishops concerned. 'So at least, the grievance is not a new one.'[143]

But the bad blood between Bourne and many of the hierarchy continued. Keating challenged the Low Week minutes, claiming that the Cardinal had promised not just to transmit the Bishops' resolution to Rome, but also to make his own the Bishops' policy regarding diocesan division. Ward, who had taken the minutes, bridled at Keating's allegation that inaccuracy was due either to Ward's ignorance or the Cardinal's censorship. 'I certainly did not understand the Cardinal to say that he would himself adopt the resolutions of the Bishops. He has never talked or written in that sense ... if I may say so, I should be slow to think that his Eminence should have acted as you imply with respect to the Acta.'[144]

What was the Cardinal's response to the crushing defeat of his cherished project? According to Amigo, he had written to the Pope, 'complaining how the Bishops had misunderstood him in spite of his good intentions and that he threatened to resign.'[145] This is not substantiated elsewhere. The Cardinal himself recalled simply that he had advised the Pope, in the face of such opposition, 'the only prudent course was to give way to their request that nothing further should be done during the war.'[146] At least one of his brethren took pity on him. The Bishop of Plymouth wrote to the Bishop of Nottingham, 'I am sorry about this Roman trouble. No matter how things may have come about I felt deeply sorry for the Cardinal and the imminent danger of his parting company with nearly all the Episcopate. His story was a very sad and touching one, and all the more so as no response was given. He seemed so much *alone* that one would have stood with him anyhow—a man cornered in his own house. Do all you can my dear Lord to soften the asperities ... After all the suspicion the Cardinal made a gallant fight all along the line.'[147]

For a while, defeat took its toll, as the Cardinal did not hesitate to point out to Keating. 'I need not disguise the fact that Low Week was an intensely painful experience to me, and had much to do with my recent illness.'[148] Pressure forced the Cardinal to retire to his Hertfordshire country home for several weeks from June 1917. Unusually, he dwelt on the past, taking the opportunity to produce several pages of autobiographical notes as if conceding, in his mid-fifties, that his career was over. This period of retrospection was not to last.

'A veritable obsession'[149]

The Cardinal persisted. Others deemed his attitude obstinate and perverse. A month before the War ended, concerned that Catholics were getting left behind the Anglicans in the creation of new dioceses, he was writing again to Lépicier. 'Brentwood is a complete success, fully constituted in less than a year with Chapter erected and endowment, etc complete. The same thing might be accomplished quite as easily elsewhere with good will and a little energy. The laity certainly approve of the policy.'[150] Foreign affairs temporarily distracted him following the Armistice.

'How good and how pleasant it is, when brothers live in unity'

Initially, it was far from evident that Brentwood was 'a complete success.' There was much early friction. Ward, a Westminster priest, originally inclined to support the Cardinal in his conflict with the hierarchy. He came to revise his position. There was quibbling about the diocesan seat: the Cardinal did not favour a third Bishop resident in London. Meanwhile Ward complained that he was expected to run Brentwood without funds while Westminster reserved to itself certain Church institutions located in Essex. Direct negotiations with Westminster having failed, Ward resorted to more traditional ecclesiastical procedure: he laid his problems before Gasquet in Rome. Gasquet in turn forwarded his letter of complaint to De Lai. Cardinal Bourne did not want Rome involved. Ward reported back to Gasquet, 'Something must have been happening of which I am not acquainted in detail, for Cardinal Bourne seems now to wish to arrange matters in the sense desired; though his advisers continue to make difficulties and matters are moving very slowly.'[151]

The Cardinal protested that his 'only object was to give the fullest independence and autonomy ... to the Diocese of Brentwood.'[152] Were that the case, then he lacked political acumen. If Brentwood was to have been a persuasive argument for his policy, then he should have acted more expeditiously and generously. The Cardinal did not see it that way. In peacetime, he mused to himself that 'the multiplication of Bishoprics in England' were one of the two main works remaining before him and that 'future development must be along the lines' of Brentwood.[153]

Personal experience prompted the Cardinal to return to the subject. A motor journey through Lincolnshire convinced him that the Diocese of Nottingham was indeed too large, and he raised again the question of division with Dunn. The Benedictines and Capuchins were mooted as possible custodians of a new Diocesan of Lincoln. The religious orders were not enthusiastic.[154]

The death or resignation of a Bishop produced anxiety in the life of a Diocese. Would the Cardinal urge this as the moment to effect division? He made the attempt on a number of occasions. Ilsley's retirement and Whiteside's death in January 1921 appeared to give the Cardinal the free hand he craved. Lépicier's services were enlisted once more. 'I hope you may find it possible to bring to the notice of the Holy Father how the present is an ideal time for making changes and new dioceses in England & Wales. Never before and never again I venture to say will the matter be so easy.'¹⁵⁵ Only Amigo's refusal to contemplate promotion and removal from Southwark frustrated possible restructuring.

With the exception of Brentwood, Bourne's sole success was announced to an unsuspecting Church in November 1924. There had been rumours about the division of Liverpool at the time of Whiteside's death.[156] To the surprise and irritation of his successor, Archbishop Keating, translated from Northampton, a new Diocese of Lancaster was created, taking the northern parts of Liverpool and the westerly counties of Hexham and Newcastle.

A further preoccupation was for Dioceses at Oxford and Cambridge. Bishop Cary-Elwes received a letter from the Cardinal in 1923 asking him to reconsider the 1917 proposal to separate Cambridge from Northampton. The scheme had impressive backers. 'You must forgive me, if in what I am about to write I seem to be interfering. But the thought, that I ought to place before you what has long been in my mind, has come to me in such a way that I believe it to be from Our Lord Himself, and that I should be disobeying Him were I not to write.' However, Our Lord had not communicated a similar desire to the Bishop of Northampton.[157] The Cardinal returned to the subject over the years. Oxford was to be taken from Birmingham and added to the truncated Northampton. Bede Jarrett, Charles Duchemin and Alban Goodier, the Jesuit Archbishop of Bombay, were variously suggested as Bishops for these university sees. Save for the ever loyal Lépicier, no one in Rome was listening. 'The situation at Oxford and Cambridge continually troubles me. Everyone knows that Protestantism declines there, and Communism is on the increase. Despite my repeated representations, the Holy See apparently does not see the necessity of increasing there the influence of the Catholic Church, which alone can confront the threat.'[158]

There was a certain stubborn logic to the Cardinal's thinking: more Provinces, followed by more Dioceses, followed by more parishes. 'At the summit of all ecclesiastical progress is the intensive action of the hierarchical government of the Church. This was the mind of Pius X when by the Apostolic Letter *Si qua est*, issued in 1911, he created two new Provinces, with the avowed object of thereby rendering easier an increase in the number of Episcopal Sees, a policy already abundantly justified by results in the two instances where it has been actually carried into effect. All the world over—and our Anglican friends have shown themselves fully aware of this fact—a prudent multiplication of episcopal

'How good and how pleasant it is, when brothers live in unity'

centres means rapidly augmented progress. Next in order must come the setting up of new parishes.'[159]

He may well have been right. This was a time of opportunity for the Catholic Church in England and Wales. Numbers were growing. In a world changed by war and agnosticism, residual anti-Catholicism was declining. Protestant difficulties were creating an ecclesiological vacuum. In these circumstances the Cardinal 'urged that we must be prepared for expansion.'[160] In the early twentieth century new Dioceses did not entail bloated bureaucracies. If their claim to be successors to the apostles was taken seriously, energetic Bishops on the ground could have given the necessary impetus to Catholic growth. Brentwood and Lancaster went on to become successful Dioceses.

Archbishop Whiteside wrote knowingly to the newly-appointed Ward, 'The fact of the matter is that the progress of the Church in England is to a great extent a money question, as every Bishop very soon finds out.'[161] Having none of the experience of a financially-pressed parish priest, Bourne may have underestimated such mundane necessities. But perhaps he possessed more of the apostolic and evangelical spirit.

Bourne lacked not imagination, but political realism. He failed to accept that Rome would not impose his schemes on reluctant incumbent Bishops. (To be fair, his persistence was frequently encouraged by Roman ambiguity.) He failed to counter the concealed influence of Gasquet and others in the Vatican. Most damningly, he failed to persuade his brother Bishops, and hardly attempted to do so. He was let down by his temperamental inclination to act alone rather than to collaborate with others.

The issue poisoned relations between the hierarchy for two decades. On the day of Bourne's death, his eventual successor wrote to his arch-rival in generous terms, 'May we all meet in heaven where there will be no question of divisions but unending peace and unbroken friendship.'[162]

The Primate of England & Wales

For sixty years England and Wales constituted one ecclesiastical Province. The creation of two additional Archbishops in 1911—and a fourth in 1916 with the creation of the Welsh Province—raised new questions as to the relations between the Provinces and their respective Archbishops. No one seriously disputed that some form of recognition be accorded to the Archbishop of Westminster. Since 1850 he had been the sole Archbishop in England & Wales. There were occasions when the Church needed to speak to the secular authority with one voice. It was natural that its spokesman should be the Metropolitan of the capital city of the British Empire. But how exactly was he to relate to his archiepiscopal brethren, to his own suffragans? What weight need he accord to their views?

As always, Bourne had decided opinions coloured by his desire to demonstrate the continuity between the contemporary Catholic Church and the pre-Reformation Church. He expressed these views to Rome immediately the proposal to create new Provinces was communicated to him.

> The following conditions seem absolutely necessary to me. The Archbishop of Westminster should have the title of "Primate of England and Wales" ... The Archbishop of Canterbury has retained the ancient title of 'Primate of All England.' ... The Catholic archbishop, the first in the country, should not have a less honourable title than those of the Anglican prelates.[163]

The Apostolic Letter, *Si Qua est*, did accord certain privileges to Westminster. He was to be the perpetual president (*praeses perpetuus*) of the episcopal meetings of England and Wales; he enjoyed precedence over the other two Archbishops with the right to use the throne, pallium and cross anywhere in the country; and he was given certain rights to represent the English and Welsh Bishops before the Government.[164]

The document said nothing, however, about the title of Primate. The Cardinal was determined this should be conferred. He felt it practically a *fait accompli*, as he wrote back to Jackman from Rome in November 1912, 'You cannot speak of Primacy until it has been granted. In this again I believe that Card. M. del Val is the *only* opponent.'[165] Merry del Val may have been the only opponent in Rome, but he was a powerful one and he seems to have been supported from England by the Duke of Norfolk. Even in Rome the ramifications of the dispute with Amigo were felt, such that, having been initially favourable, the Pope later 'said that he could not possibly allow such a title as he had heard that, contrary to my assertion, it would give great offence to the Bishops in England who were entirely opposed to my having such a title.' Instead the matter was referred to the Consistorial Congregation.

The Cardinal sought assistance from Bishop Hedley. He urged the historical associations. 'I do not wish to treat the matter as a personal one. I should indeed be glad of the title as a closer link with Ss Augustine, Anselm, Thomas, Edmund, etc. whose memory is constantly before me.

'How good and how pleasant it is, when brothers live in unity'

But I think it would be a real calamity if this title, so greatly reverenced in England, were definitely abandoned to the Anglicans. And this will certainly be the case if it be not speedily resumed by us.' Westminster ought clearly to assume the position which Canterbury once held.[166]

Hedley duly obliged, circulating a petition among the English Bishops that the primatial title be granted. Some lacked enthusiasm. Keating could not see the point: it was purely honorific; no such position existed in other newly-created hierarchies; the Cardinal had received such powers as he required under the 1911 constitution. Nevertheless, 'if the Bishops are strongly in favour of it, I wish to unite with the rest in the petition. Unanimity is my foible just at the present.'[167] The majority signed the petition. Once again, it was Amigo who frustrated the Cardinal's wishes. Ilsley had favoured granting the title. Amigo wrote to him, saying he himself was refusing to sign the petition. Swearing Ilsley to confidence, Amigo mentioned that he had it on good authority that the Pope himself and Merry del Val opposed the request.[168] Ilsley was easily swayed. Believing he was fulfilling Rome's wishes, he wrote to Merry del Val. 'Considering the arbitrary line of action he has taken and displayed so notably in his recent contentions with the Bishop of Southwark, I fear that his nomination as Primate would only open the door further to more arbitrary action and further friction. On this account far from supporting the petition I feel constrained to oppose it.'[169] The opposition of an English Archbishop effectively killed the proposal.

Cardinal Bourne never forgot the slight or accepted the rejection. The *Tablet* was viewed as his mouthpiece. Writing thirty years later on his seventieth birthday, there was no pretence at subtlety.

> In England there is no Catholic Bishop with the official title of Primate. But the already illustrious See of Westminster has practically been primatial from its foundation ... the fact of his residence in the capital city of the British Empire further establishes him in a virtual Primacy ... The Catholic Primate—we will call him so, for convenience ... Cardinal Bourne's memorable success as Catholic Primate ... his five-and-twenty years as Primate.[170]

Standing Committee

The question of the Primacy was largely an honorific one. The day to day dealings of the English hierarchy were not. One has significant sympathy for Bourne. Often his attempts at diocesan restructuring were the immediate cause of the bitter disputes characterising episcopal relations in the early twentieth century, but it is clear they were often the expression of much more enduring and deep-seated frictions. In their more rational moments, the Cardinal's opponents conceded this. Unfortunately, there was no consensus for a solution.

The underlying problem was how the other Bishops, who were largely autonomous and answerable only to Rome, were to relate to the Archbishop of Westminster both in the internal life of the English Church and in their contact with third parties. The dispute with Amigo and diocesan division brought the matter to the fore again, but the dilemma was an old one. It was the relationship between Westminster and other Dioceses, between London and the provinces. Amigo, scarcely a disinterested party, put the issue thus: 'whether England is to have an Episcopate or simply "a shining planet with many insignificant satellites around."'[171]

The constitution *Si qua est* addressed the issue. Westminster was to 'represent before the supreme civil authority the entire body of Bishops of England and Wales, always, however, after having consulted all the Bishops, the opinion of the majority of whom he is always to follow.'[172] But what consultation was to occur? Was the position the same when the Bishops were dealing, not with the supreme civil authority, but the Apostolic See? Keating, at least, appreciated that this was a historic problem and much turned on the interpretation of the Apostolic Letter. "Westminster has *always* been somewhat autocratic. The outline of a better system is sketched in *Si Qua est*, especially in the phrase "*semper tamen auditis omnibus Episcopis quorum maioris partis sententias sequi debet*." This will serve as a *fulcrum* for lifting the weight of precedent. But steady pressure will be more effective than a jolt!'[173]

The Oscott meeting of March 1917 was a watershed. The Bishops surprised themselves by acting in concert without the leadership of Westminster. It surprised and pained the Cardinal too. In his convalescence, he spoke from the heart.

> I have spared neither trouble nor expense to do my duty to the Hierarchy; that I have in my relations with the Bishops on no single occasion failed to observe the precedents left me by my Predecessors; that I have invariably given to them all the information that it was my duty to impart to them; that I have requested meetings for purposes of consultation more frequently than any other Archbishop of Westminster. It was, therefore, a very bitter

surprise to find some of my brethren under the impression either that I had acted, or that I intended to act, in a way of which they might legitimately complain. My life is necessarily a very isolated one. I can open my mind to the Bishops only when they give me the opportunity of doing so. There is certainly nothing that I need and prize more than their sympathy and co-operation. I have never consciously done anything to warrant a lessening of their confidence in me.[174]

It was not just in connection with diocesan division that certain Bishops felt national coordination was required. Education was a perennial concern. 'We are already developing separate "provincial" policies, and in some matters, e.g. education, this process may become serious.'[175] The experience of total war also produced a tendency to centralisation previously resisted by the English. Voices were raised for the creation of some platform in the Church to give consistent and permanent expression on matters such as conscription and military chaplains. 'There ought to be some means of arranging for a Standing Committee of the Bishops in England of the nature of the one in Ireland. The Secretary should be the person to communicate with the Holy See instead of the officials of Archbishop's House. I am thinking of proposing this in Low Week.'[176] Amigo was not the only Bishop to support the proposal. But their Lordships had had enough conflict for one meeting. In the face of strong opposition from the Cardinal, the suggestion was shelved.[177]

Despite the existence of similar bodies in other English-speaking countries, Bourne never warmed to the idea of a Standing Committee. There was a highly personal element to his opposition. Unfortunately, it was Amigo who raised the matter again in 1921. The Cardinal responded,

> I am profoundly convinced that it would mean a fundamental, unnecessary and disastrous alteration in the relations and traditions which have characterised the Episcopate in England for at least seventy years. If the matter is pressed it must raise definitely the question of the confidence that my brethren place in me. I am unable to believe that any one of my colleagues would desire to revive the very painful discussions of 1917, which were the direct cause of the serious breakdown in my health from which I have only recently wholly recovered.[178]

Scarcely a mature and exhaustive analysis of the proposition. It served Bourne's purpose, however; the item was dropped from the agenda.

In the early twentieth century and today, the matter remains complex and contentious. Those at the time spoke of the need for a 'Standing Committee.' Today we would speak of an Episcopal Conference. Our Lord appointed individual men apostles—not committees. In a modern world of instant communications cooperation and coordination are essential. But when does this become excessive bureaucracy or abnegation of individual responsibility?

Some saw immediately the benefits of a Standing Committee. 'At present each bishop is a law unto himself, and though no doubt this tells for the good of the Church of England, much confusion and wasted energy would be avoided if there were centralised discussion and decision.'[179] But there were those among Bourne's critics who shared his suspicions in this regard. The Bishop of Clifton was one. 'My own view is that as each bishop is meant to be and is "an independent unit," the less we have of meetings, except where common counsel is imperatively needed, the better.'[180]

The situation was further complicated by Rome's ambivalence towards the cooperation of Bishops at the local level. Bishop Dunn discovered that the Vatican's preferred solution was for disputes and uncertainties to be referred directly to the highest authority. He was told in audience by Benedict XV 'that nothing could possibly be more advantageous for diocesan administration than that local Ordinaries should be in continual communication with him. He said that in a short personal interview more could be done than in months of correspondence and he added, significantly, that there would be less possibility of misunderstandings. He told me to let this desire be made known to the Bishops.'[181]

The traditional autonomy of the Bishop under the Holy See continued throughout Bourne's long tenure at Westminster. That principle was examined and revised immediately by his successor. 'At the first meeting of the bishops [Arthur Hinsley] presided over, it was resolved that the bishops would now meet three times a year instead of one and that a standing committee consisting of the four archbishops should be instituted "to deal with matters of emergency."'[182] But it was only in the post-Conciliar Church of the late twentieth century that collegiality really took hold.

'An autocracy'[183]

Was the English hierarchy completely dysfunctional under Bourne's leadership? Comments in episcopal correspondence suggest this. Northern Bishops especially resented Bourne's preference for discreet diplomacy, whereas they would have had mass demonstrations and open confrontation with the Government. So Salford could write to Liverpool on educational matters, 'To my mind it is little less than an insult to the whole bench of Bishops. We are practically told, like troublesome children, to keep quiet and not to interfere.'[184] Casartelli's frustration and invective merely mounted with the disputes over diocesan division. 'For the last few years, our hierarchical system has gone to pieces. Our Westminster meetings are a farce. We are gagged, and everything is decided and done without us or in spite of us. I am not the only bishop who feels like this.'[185]

Frequent complaints were levelled by his brother Bishops that Bourne discouraged discussion and was inclined to act without consultation. That was his preferred mode of action. By upbringing and temperament, he was reserved and distant save to an intimate few. A more expansive character might have been able to bring others along with him. Yet this was still the early twentieth century. Being 'a team player' was not a job specification for a Bishop. As his more objectively-minded critics conceded, and as archival evidence bears out, the Cardinal consulted on routine matters at least as frequently as his predecessors in Westminster.

One has to remember also the personal factors at play. Most of these men had known each other since boyhood. Many of them had been together at Ware and Ushaw. Men like Amigo and Casartelli were strong characters in small scenarios, never reluctant to engage in controversy. Longstanding resentments could erupt, but occasionally reconciliation could blossom too. So, when the Cardinal gave him his opening, Bishop Cotter was only too eager to drop his guard, 'Life is too short to allow a misunderstanding to interfere with or mar a friendship which I genuinely value and desire to possess and again I thank Your Eminence for so kindly enabling me to explain my action.'[186]

Only one member of the hierarchy described himself as Bourne's 'intimate friend.'[187] That was Bishop Cahill. While his zeal could exceed his prudence, Cahill was unfailingly loyal to Bourne. The two frequently stayed with each other. While detained in Rome, Bourne relied on Cahill for news of the Bishops' Low Week Meeting.[188] After Cahill's early death in 1910, there was no other diocesan Bishop he could look to for similar support. It is telling that divisions within the hierarchy really began after that date.

Archbishop of Westminster for three decades, Bourne could have expected to have had a far greater influence on the composition of the English hierarchy. That was the other Bishops' fear when in December 1916 he was appointed to the Consistorial Congregation, the Vatican department with oversight for the appointment of bishops. Again, however, his diffidence as to the niceties of Roman procedure, meant he achieved little. (Coupled to this was the longevity of the occupants of the sees of Liverpool, Birmingham and Southwark.) The claim the Cardinal sought subservience on the part of his brother Bishops is belied by those he wished to see advanced: men like Bede Jarrett, Alban Goodier and Robert Hugh Benson. His stated aim was to see men of spiritual stature and learning, in both the secular and theological spheres. He would have done himself and the harmony of the English Church a service, had he overcome his own diffidence and managed the Roman system to achieve such an outcome.

All told, Bourne's relations with the hierarchy constituted neither the happiest nor the most edifying legacy of his time in office.

Notes

1. Ps 133.
2. Burton, Diary, 17 May 1910, CDA.
3. Hedley, Dinner for hierarchy at Consecration of Westminster Cathedral, 28 June 1910, *Tablet*, 2 July 1910, p. 8.
4. G. Albion, 'The Restoration of the Hierarchy, 1850' in Beck (ed.), *The English Catholics 1850–1950*, p. 93.
5. Cited Albion, 'The Restoration of the Hierarchy, 1850,' p. 112.
6. FAB to De Lai, 30 November 1917, AAW, Hi. II/179.
7. FAB memorandum [draft for that presented to Consistorial on 23 December 1916?], AAW, Bo. III/12/4.
8. FAB, 'Memorandum for the consideration of Fr Lépicier,' 1911, AAW, Bo. III/6/21.
9. Southwark correspondent, *Tablet*, 18 March 1871, p. 339.
10. FAB to Ledochowski, 28 March 1901, SCPF, 102/1901, f. 211, r. 450.
11. Amigo to Ilsley, 18 January 1912, BAA, D2466.
12. Dunn [to Jackman?], 19 January 1912, AAW, Bo. I/122.
13. Lépicier to Jackman, 21 November 1920, AGOSM, Lépicier Papers.
14. Jackman to Lépicier, 30 November 1920, AGOSM, Lépicier Papers.
15. De Lai to Lépicier, 15 May 1911, AAW, Bo. III/6/3.
16. FAB to Bidwell, 28 March 1911 (copy), AAW, Bo. III/124/8.
17. Clifton, *Amigo*, p. 44.

'How good and how pleasant it is, when brothers live in unity'

18   FAB to Bidwell, 28 March 1911 (copy), AAW, Bo. III/124/8.
19   Amigo to Ilsley, 18 January 1912, BAA, D2466.
20   Clifton, *Amigo*, p. 44.
21   De Lai to FAB, 15 May 1911, AAW, Bo. III/6/1.
22   Bidwell to Merry del Val, u/d [November 1912?] (copy), AAW, Bo. III/124/8.
23   C. Robertson to Lépicier, 19 January 1912, AGOSM, Lépicier Papers. Robertson (of the eponymous jam) was a wealthy convert who also gave generously to the Archdiocese of Birmingham and the Servite Order.
24   Brown to Lépicier, 21 November 1912, AGOSM, Lépicier Papers.
25   FAB to Norfolk, 3 January 1912 (copy), AAW, Bo. III/124/3.
26   FAB, 'Memorandum for the consideration of Fr Lépicier,' 1911, AAW, Bo. III/6/21.
27   FAB to Bidwell, 28 March 1911 (copy), AAW, Bo. III/124/8.
28   FAB to De Lai, 1912 (draft), AAW, Hi. II/179.
29   De Lai to Lépicier, 15 May 1911, AAW, Bo. III/6/3.
30   FAB to Stuart, 11 July 1911, GASSH, Rome.
31   De Lai to Lépicier, 7 August 1911, AAW, Bo. III/6/6.
32   FAB to Bidwell, 28 March 1911 (copy), AAW, Bo. III/124/8.
33   De Lai to Lépicier, 25 September 1911, AAW, Bo. III/6/6.
34   Keating to Whiteside, 10 June 1912 (copy), NorDA, FV.6; Keating, notes of interviews with De Lai and Merry del Val, u/d [summer 1912], NorDA, FV.6.
35   FAB to De Lai, 7 July 1912, AAW, Bo. III/1/32.
36   Keating to Merry del Val, 8 July 1912 (copy), NorDA, FV.6.
37   FAB to Bidwell, 15 November 1912 (copy), AAW, Bo. III/124/8.
38   *Ibid.*
39   FAB, memorandum presented to Pius X, 3 December 1912, AAW, Bo. IV/4/9.
40   Amigo to Keating, 17 December 1911, NorDA, FV.5.
41   De Lai to Lépicier, 25 September 1911, AAW, Bo. III/6/6.
42   FAB to Jackman, 4 November 1912, AAW, Bo. I/18.
43   FAB to Norfolk, 26 December 1912 (copy), AAW, Bo. III/124/3. (My italics.)
44   McIntyre to Amigo, 15 November 1913, cited McInally, *Edward Ilsley*, p. 331.
45   FAB to Lépicier, 22 October 1915 (copy), AAW, Bo. III/124/8.
46   FAB memorandum, [Draft for that presented to Consistorial on 23 December 1916?], AAW, Bo. III/12/4.
47   Jackman to Lépicier, 28 October 1920, AGOSM, Lépicier Papers.
48   Lépicier to Jackman, 21 November 1920, AGOSM, Lépicier Papers.
49   Jackman to Lépicier, u/d [early 1921], AGOSM, Lépicier Papers; Amigo to M. Glancey, 28 January 1921, cited McInally, *Edward Ilsley*, p. 367; Amigo to Gasquet, 16 March 1921, DAA, Gasquet, 917A; Brown to Gasquet, 22 April 1921, DAA, Gasquet, 917A.
50   Lépicier to FAB, 20 April 1921, AAW, Bo. III/12.

51 FAB to Lépicier, 24 April 1921, AGOSM, Lépicier Papers.
52 De Lai to FAB, 25 April 1921, AAW, Bo. III/12.
53 Archbishop Cerretti to FAB, 3 June 1921, AAW, Bo. III/10/51.
54 Burton, Diary, 12 October 1911, CDA.
55 Robertson to Lépicier, 22 November 1911, AGOSM, Lépicier Papers.
56 Amigo to Keating, 19 December 1911, NorDA, FV.5.
57 FAB memorandum, 1915, AAW, Bo. III/10/9.
58 Burton, Diary, 17 April 1917, CDA.
59 R. Watt, *Robert Hugh Benson: Captain in God's Army* (London: Burns & Oates, 1918), p. 64.
60 Mgr Charles Duchemin (1886–1965) was Rector of the Beda College (1928–1961).
61 FAB to unknown recipient, 29 May 1932, AAW, Bo. III/10/58; FAB to Cardinal Rossi, 7 January 1933 (copy), AAW, Bo. IV/4/43.
62 Bidwell's notes of meeting presided over by Lépicier, 1911, AAW, Bo. III/6/25.
63 Amigo to Ilsley, 11 January 1912, cited McInally, *Edward Ilsley*, p. 322.
64 Ilsley to Amigo, 7 January 1912, BAA, cited McInally, *Edward Ilsley*, p. 322.
65 Amigo to Keating, 17 December 1911, NorDA, FV.5.
66 FAB, Address, 21 January 1912, *Tablet*, 27 January 1912, p. 132.
67 Keating to Browne (copy), 8 January 1912, NorDA, FV.6.
68 Keating's notes of interviews with de Lai and Merry del Val, u/d (summer 1912); Keating to Whiteside (copy), 10 June 1912, NorDA, FV.6.
69 FAB to unspecified Cardinal, 1 July 1921 (copy), AAW, Bo. III/9/6.
70 FAB, Enthronement of Bishop Ward, Brentwood, 7 November 1917, *Tablet*, 10 November 1917, p. 597.
71 Merry del Val to Gasquet, 2 July 1912?, DAA, Gasquet Papers, File 882, cited Aspden, *Fortress Church*, p. 111.
72 Merry del Val to FAB, 27 June 1914, AAW, Bo. III/10/4.
73 FAB, National Catholic Congress, Cardiff, 10 July 1914, *Tablet*, 18 July 1914, pp. 84–85.
74 Merry del Val to FAB, 14 July 1914, AAW, Roman Letters, VIII/91.
75 FAB memorandum, [Draft for that presented to Consistorial on 23 December 1916?], AAW, Bo. III/12/4.
76 FAB to Lépicier, 22 October 1915 (copy), AAW, Bo. III/124/8.
77 FAB memorandum, AAW, Bo. III/12/4.
78 FAB to Lépicier, 21 April 1916 (copy), AAW, Bo. III/10/28.
79 Lépicier to FAB, 18 November 1915, AAW, Bo. III/10/7.
80 Lépicier to FAB, 22 November 1915, AAW, Bo. III/10/8.
81 Amigo to Ilsley, 10 February 1916, BAA, D3536.
82 FAB memorandum, 6–12 December 1915, AAW, Bo. IV/3/5a.
83 *Tablet*, 12 February 1916, p. 200.

'How good and how pleasant it is, when brothers live in unity'

84 Dunn to FAB, 18 May 1916, AAW, Bo. III/10/29.
85 F. Sheehan to Gasquet, 15 January 1916, DAA, Gasquet Papers, 917A.
86 Gasquet, Diary, 25 January 1916, cited Leslie, *Cardinal Gasquet*, p. 246.
87 Gasquet had been created a Cardinal on 25 May 1914.
88 De Lai to FAB, 6 March 1916, AAW, Bo. III/10/20.
89 'Notes on the Essex-Kent Project,' u/d [under cover of FAB's letter to De Lai of 16 March 1916], AAW, Bo. III/10/23a.
90 Gasquet, Diary, 2 July 1916, cited Leslie, *Cardinal Gasquet*, p. 248.
91 FAB to Lépicier, 21 April 1916 (copy), AAW, Bo. III/10/28.
92 FAB memorandum [draft for that presented to Consistorial on 23 December 1916], AAW, Bo. III/12/4.
93 Casartelli to Gasquet, 12 January 1917, DAA, Gasquet, 889.
94 Amigo to Gasquet, 17 January 1917, DAA, Gasquet, 917A.
95 Keating to Gasquet, 28 January 1917, DAA, Gasquet, 889.
96 Casartelli to Amigo, 8 December 1916, SDA, Casartelli Letters, 4001–4100, Box 161.
97 Casartelli to Gasquet, 6 December 1916, SDA, Casartelli Letters, 4001–4100, Box 161.
98 Gasquet, Diary, 20 January 1917, DAA, Gasquet, 902.
99 Gasquet, Diary, 30 December 1916, cited Leslie, *Cardinal Gasquet*, p. 250.
100 Gasquet, Diary, 30 January 1917, DAA, Gasquet, 902.
101 Gasquet, Diary, 3 February 1917, DAA, Gasquet, 902.
102 Gasquet, Diary, 6 Feb 1917, DAA, Gasquet, 902.
103 Casartelli to Keating, 23 February 1917, NorDA, FV.1.
104 McIntyre to Amigo, 9 February 1917, SAA, cited McNally, *Edward Ilsley*, p. 342.
105 De Lai to FAB, 20 February 1917, AAW, Roman Letters, Misc./93.
106 De Lai to Amigo (copy), 20 February 1917, NotDA, Dunn, G03.03.
107 Amigo to Whiteside, 23 February 1917, LAA, 52 V A/51.
108 Amigo, Dunn, Keating and Cotter to De Lai, translated u/d copy for Gasquet, DAA, Gasquet, 917A.
109 Acta of Oscott Meeting, 15 March 1917, NotDA, Dunn, G03.03.
110 Dunn to Gasquet, 15 March 1917, DAA, Gasquet, File 864, cited Aspden, *Fortress Church*, p. 112.
111 Amigo to Gasquet, 16 March 1917, DAA, Gasquet, 917A.
112 Casartelli to Gasquet, 19 March 1917, DAA, Gasquet, 889.
113 FAB to Cotter, 15 March 1917 (copy), BDA, A1.
114 Cotter to FAB, 12 February 1920, AAW, Bo. III/124/8.
115 Amigo to Gasquet, 19 March 1917, DAA, Gasquet, 917A.
116 FAB to Amigo, 22 March 1917, cited Amigo to Gasquet, 2 April 1917, DAA, Gasquet, 917A; FAB to Ilsley, 22 March 1917, (copy), AAW.

[117] Dunn to Amigo, 30 March 1917, SAA, cited Aspden, *Fortress Church*, p. 113.
[118] Amigo to Gasquet, 2 April 1917, DAA, Gasquet, 917A.
[119] Benedict XV to FAB, 22 March 1917, tr. *Tablet*, 7 April 1917, p. 432.
[120] Keating to Amigo, 31 March 1917, SAA, cited Aspden, *Fortress Church*, pp. 113–114.
[121] Keating to Dunn, 29 March 1917, NotDA, Dunn, G03.03.
[122] Amigo to Gasquet, 12 April 1917, DAA, Gasquet, 917A.
[123] Bishop Kiely of Plymouth to Ilsley, 12 April 1917, BAA, D3840.
[124] Amigo to Gasquet, 2 April 1917, DAA, Gasquet, 917A.
[125] Amigo to Dunn, 2 April 1917, NotDA, G03.03.
[126] Keating, Dunn and Cotter to FAB, 10 April 1917, AAW, Bo. III/124/8.
[127] Keating to Ilsley (copy), 11 April 1917, NorDA, FV.1.
[128] FAB to Ward, 14 April 1917, BDA, A1.
[129] Amigo to Gasquet, 5 April 1917, DAA, Gasquet, 917A.
[130] Acta of the Annual Meeting of the Bishops, 17 April 1917.
[131] Gasquet, Diary, 16 April 1917, DAA, Gasquet, 902.
[132] Amigo to Gasquet, 17 April 1917, DAA, Gasquet, 917A.
[133] Burton, Diary, 17 April 1917, CDA.
[134] Casartelli, Diary, 17 April 1917, SDA.
[135] Amigo to Gasquet, 17 April 1917, DAA, Gasquet, 917A.
[136] Telegram from Salis, British Minister to the Vatican, to Amigo, 18 April 1917, (copy), NotDA, Dunn, G03.03.
[137] Burton, Diary, 18 April 1917, CDA.
[138] Acta of Annual Meeting of the Bishops, 18 April 1917.
[139] Keating to Amigo (copy), 21 April 1917, NorDA, FV.1.
[140] Casartelli to Merry del Val, 22 April 1917 (copy), SDA, Casartelli Letters, 4201–4300, Box 161.
[141] Whiteside to Dunn, 28 April 1917, NotDA, Dunn, G03.
[142] Keating to Casartelli (copy), 26 April 1917, NorDA, FV.1.
[143] Ward to Keating, 28 May 1917 (copy), BDA, A1.
[144] Keating to Ward, 19 May 1917, BDA, A1; Ward to Keating, 21 May 1917 (copy), BDA, A1.
[145] Amigo to Gasquet, 22 May 1917, DAA, Gasquet, 917A.
[146] FAB to Lépicier, 2 October 1918, AGOSM, Lépicier Papers.
[147] Keily to Dunn, 7 May 1917, NotDA, Dunn, G03.03.
[148] FAB to Keating, 7 July 1917, NorDA, FV.1.
[149] Casartelli to Keating, 18 November 1917, NorDA, FV.1.
[150] FAB to Lépicier, 2 October 1918, AGOSM, Lépicier Papers.
[151] Ward to Gasquet, 1 July 1918, DAA, Gasquet, 889. The division of funds was not finally settled until the 1920s, the case being decided by Rome.
[152] FAB to Ward, 1 March 1918, BDA, D2/a/1.

153 FAB notebook, 29 March 1920, cited Oldmeadow, *Francis Cardinal Bourne*, ii, p. 169.
154 FAB to Dunn, 27 September 1920, NotDA, Dunn, G03.03; FAB to Dunn, 26 October 1920, NotDA, Dunn, G03.03; Dunn to Capuchin Provincial, 4 November 1930, AAW, Bo. I/14.
155 Jackman to Lépicier, u/d early 1921, AGOSM, Lépicier Papers.
156 Amigo to Gasquet, 16 March 1921, DAA, Gasquet, 917A.
157 FAB to Bishop Cary-Elwes, 7 October 1923, AAW, Bo. I/14; Cary-Elwes to FAB, 8 October 1923, AAW, Bo. I/14.
158 FAB to Rossi, 9 July 1933 (copy), AAW, Bo. IV/4/45.
159 FAB, 'The Church's Opportunity,' *Clergy Review*, February 1931, pp. 120–121.
160 FAB Memorandum, Division of Dioceses: '*Status quaestionis,*' 21 April 1925, AAW, Bo. I/14.
161 Whiteside to Ward, 27 December 1917, BDA, D2/b/Liverpool.
162 Hinsley to Amigo, 1 January 1935, SAA, Amigo Papers, Correspondence with Hinsley, C4, cited Aspen, *Fortress Church*, p. 185.
163 FAB to De Lai, 21 August 1911 (copy), AAW, Bo. III/6/7.
164 Pius X, *Si Qua est*, 28 October 1911, *Tablet* translation, 18 November 1911, p. 803.
165 FAB to Jackman, 11 November 1912, AAW, Bo. I/18.
166 FAB to Hedley, 1 December 1912 (copy), AAW, Bo. IV/4/8.
167 Keating to unnamed recipient (copy), 6 December 1912, NorDA, FV.6.
168 Amigo to Ilsley, 12 December 1912, BAA, D2801.
169 Ilsley to Merry del Val, 8 January 1913, draft, BAA, cited McInally, p. 321.
170 Editorial, *Tablet*, 28 March 1931, pp. 417–418.
171 Amigo to Gasquet, 5 April 1917, DAA, Gasquet, 917A.
172 Pius X, *Si Qua est*, 28 October 1911, *Tablet* translation, 18 November 1911, p. 803.
173 Keating to Browne (copy), 8 January 1912, NorDA, FV.6.
174 FAB to Keating, 7 July 1917, NorDA, FV.1.
175 Casartelli to Gasquet, 6 December 1916 (copy), SaDA, cited Aspden, *Fortress Church*, p. 117.
176 Amigo to Gasquet, 15 February 1917, DAA, Gasquet, 917A.
177 Acta of the Annual Meeting of the Bishops, 18 April 1917.
178 FAB to Amigo, 20 March 1921, AAW, Bo. I/14.
179 Doubleday to Dunn, 29 March 1920, NotDA, Dunn, G.03.02.17, cited Aspden, *Fortress Church*, p. 117.
180 Burton, Diary, 18 April 1917, CDA.
181 Dunn to Whiteside, 4 July 1917, NotDA, Dunn, G03.03.
182 *Acta*, Meeting of Hierarchy, 1 May 1935, AAW, cited Aspden, *Fortress Church*, p. 202.
183 Casartelli to Gasquet, 10 November 1917, DAA, Gasquet, 889.
184 Casartelli to Whiteside, 14 March 1912, SDA, Casartelli Letters, 1401–1500, Box 158.

[185] Casartelli to Whiteside, 6 November 1917, SDA, Casartelli Letters, 4501–4600, Box 162.
[186] Cotter to FAB, 12 February 1920, AAW, Bo. III/124/8.
[187] Cahill to Gotti, u/d, SCPF, 102/1904, f. 289, rr. 54–55.
[188] FAB to Amigo, [1903?], SAA, Amigo Papers, Letters Pre-1904.

Chapter 16

A Cardinal at War

'These times of sadness'

His contemporaries noted that Cardinal Bourne seemed more at ease on the battlefields of the First World War than in meetings with his brother Bishops back home. War played to his strengths at a time when the Church required a quiet administrator who inspired confidence, spoke of spiritual realities and did not doubt the justice of his country's cause.

The First World War caused few difficulties of loyalty for British Catholics. There was regret that Austro-Hungary was an enemy power, but, otherwise, the balance of power neatly matched confessional divides. Allied to France and Italy, England was fighting for the cause of Catholic Belgium and, later, Poland. The Allies were resisting Protestant Prussian militarism and the Muslim Ottomans. The entry of a British Christian army into Jerusalem seemed to justify those who viewed this conflict as a crusade. The Cardinal was a patriotic Englishman, but not given to jingoist excess. One English Bishop confided to his diary on New Year's Eve 1916, 'God send us a happy New Year and the smashing of Prussia!'[1] That was not Bourne's way. He recognised claims above the purely national. Writing during the Boer War, he defined Catholics as 'children of the kingdom of earth of the Prince of Peace.' 'The present condition of the world, the constant possibility of terrific wars, the jealousy and distrust existing between the great Powers of the earth, all these things are at variance with the instincts of Christianity.'[2]

Summer 1914 found the Cardinal, like his fellow countrymen, engaged in normal peacetime activities, sublimely unaware of the impending catastrophic slaughter. In July 1914 he was outlining his plans for diocesan division to the Catholic Congress in Cardiff. On the day war was declared, he was presiding at the annual meeting of the Catholic Prisoners' Aid Society at Archbishop's House.

His response was immediate, but measured. He had regarded the prospect of war with horror, encouraging ecumenical exchanges between the two countries and writing, 'In these days of "Dreadnoughts" and quick-firing guns of enormously destructive power, the effect of a war between two first-class powers such as England and Germany would be too awful to contemplate.'[3]

Issued the day after the declaration of War the Cardinal's Pastoral Letter displayed a concern for the spiritual state of his subjects and a remarkable realism. There was no mention of victory, no patriotic hyperbole. Given the national mood, his words were considered and courageous.

> War is in truth one of the greatest material evils that the world can see, but our Divine Master has warned us that it is an evil for which we must be prepared ... War is at the same time a reminder of sin, for without the sin of individuals and of nations enmities and consequent hostilities would not exist. It is, then, in a spirit of humble penitence that we must approach the Altar of the Lord ... We have so many things for which to beseech His clemency. In the first place that He may give to the Empire a lasting peace and security: then that He may comfort and strengthen all those whose days must now be spent in constant and often unrelieved anxiety for the men who are periling their lives in the defence of King and Country: and, again, for the numberless souls who will be hurriedly called into the presence of their Maker with scanty opportunity of preparation for that summons.[4]

Words were matched by action. No one could accuse the Cardinal of failing in his support for the War effort. His personal standing, and that of the Church, increased accordingly. As Amigo left Southwark for Ireland on vacation, the Cardinal urged his clergy to cancel their holidays and to return if they were away. 'Our people will need all the encouragement that the presence of the priest can give in these times of sadness.'[5] Immediately, he offered the Red Cross use of the Catholic hospital at Dollis Hill.[6]

The Cardinal's direction to the Catholic Women's League at the outbreak of War was direct: 'I am at my post; you ought to be at yours.'[7] And he gave them work to do: nursing, making clothing for the wounded and replacing their menfolk in domestic service. Within a month they were housing 3,000 Belgian refugees. But perhaps the CWL's most important contribution to the War effort were their 'Huts' for servicemen in England and overseas, providing not just material comfort and recreation, but also attending to their spiritual needs. Makeshift accommodation was opened by Westminster Cathedral for Catholic servicemen on leave. By the end of the War more than 100,000 of them had slept on the premises and two million meals had been served.[8] The Cathedral crypt served as an air raid shelter.

Less publicly, the Cardinal was occupied in investigating the status of prisoners of war, ensuring their spiritual needs were met—often at the Vatican's request.[9] His services were frequently sought as mediator between the Vatican and the British Government on the subject of prisoners of war and German missions within the British Empire. Knowing the relief of enemy combatants in time of war was not a popular issue, the Cardinal quietly accepted the additional work, enlisting the help of his own priests.

> It is important that the clergy should be continually on the alert to ascertain the existence of, and then regularly to visit, the many hospitals, detention camps, etc., which are being set up all over the country ... I am particularly anxious that every religious consolation should be given by the clergy to the Catholic 'enemy aliens' who may be interned within their districts.[10]

Occasionally, the Cardinal was called upon to intervene at a more international level. Thus, he received a request from the Archbishop of Cologne, via the Vatican, that Allied air attacks might be suspended to allow the traditional Corpus Christi procession to take place in safety. Bourne took the matter immediately to Downing Street. It says much for the respect with which the Cardinal was held by the Prime Minister (a Welsh Nonconformist) that the desired assurance was forthcoming within twenty-four hours.[11]

Bourne was no pacifist. Even in the pre-War years, he advocated military training in schools and compulsory military service for the young male population generally.[12] While in November 1914 he presided at a WCF meeting which called on all Catholics to recognise the urgent need to answer the call to military service,[13] the Cardinal was reluctant to act as the Government's recruiting officer. The Archbishop of Glasgow had fewer inhibitions, and Bishop Hedley wrote, 'The country is in grave danger, and anyone who neglects to help when he can help, violates the cardinal precept of Justice, and is, to a greater or lesser degree, guilty in the sight of God.'[14] The Cardinal was more circumspect; he preferred to entrust the intrinsic justice of the Allied cause to the individual's conscience.[15] Asked by the Government to assist with recruitment in Quebec, he wisely suggested the matter be referred to a French bishop.[16]

Far more importantly, Cardinal Bourne addressed the moral and spiritual concerns of his flock. He began in the pages of the London Press, reminding them of the just war theory, which permits Christians to support and participate in armed conflict provided certain conditions are satisfied.[17] From the outset, the Cardinal gave Catholic servicemen the comfort of knowing that they were engaged in a conflict with justice on their side. Speaking to recruits from Lancashire in the second month of the War, Bourne reassured them, 'You could not have a nobler cause to defend ... In this war every reasonable man, who had tried to understand the real issues at stake ... can only give one answer.'[18] He never wavered in his belief, preaching in the same vein in the first days of peace. 'The invasion of Belgium by Germany, with no kind of justification, in defiance of every law alike, human and divine, is one of the greatest, if not actually the greatest, crime that mankind has ever witnessed. It was a coldly conceived, long planned, and most deliberate violation of justice.'[19]

Churchmen of all denominations spoke out against the perceived decadence of Edwardian society. Bishop Casartelli saw the Great War as divine punishment for sin and lack of faith. Bourne occasionally used similar language. More often, however, he spoke in terms of purification. Again and again, he returned to the theme of the War as a prolonged period of Lent, when unsought suffering might, if accepted in a Christian spirit of self-sacrifice, produce healing and moral regeneration. He referred back to the education crisis. Implicitly in England, explicitly by anti-clerical regimes in Europe, governments had impeded Christian teaching. 'Thus children have passed in thousands, year after year, into their place in life without any true or accurate knowledge of what Christianity really means. Today we reap the consequences, and it has needed the mighty scourge of war to bring back men's minds to the thought of those things.'[20]

He developed his views in a Pastoral Letter in the early months of the War.

> The Lenten spirit which the present War is impressing upon the nations is intended to raise up to God a people imbued with newly awakened ideals ... Young men who seemed careless, frivolous, selfish—sinful, too, perhaps—have in thousands risen to a new consciousness of the real sense and purpose of their lives. By their

actions they have proclaimed their belief that there is another more valuable life beyond the grave ... A latent spirit of heroism; a deep sense of duty; a strong love of Empire and country; a readiness to sacrifice comfort and ease; a willingness to give up even life itself ... all these qualities have made themselves manifest in a degree few would have expected. It would seem to be according to the Divine Providence that our country should still have a far-spreading mission to fulfil.[21]

Commentators felt the Cardinal was fully justified in speaking thus. The Jesuit, Charles Plater, following exhaustive research and writing after the War, claimed, 'Not one clear case appears in all the reports and letters in which a Catholic soldier has been unsettled in his belief in God by the War.'[22] Faced with the horrors of trench warfare, Catholics at least seemed inclined not to blame God, but human sinfulness. Everywhere people noted a return to the practice of the faith. The Archbishop of Westminster reflected and helped articulate the beliefs of his people.

His contribution was not limited, however, to homilising, pastoral letters and promoting the war effort from the safety of Archbishop's House. The Cardinal was most appreciated by Catholic servicemen for his personal encouragement in simple, direct advice they could easily comprehend. Throughout the War, he toured army camps in England, paid a number of visits to the Western Front and became the first Cardinal since the Reformation to pay an official visit to the Fleet. The provision of chaplains for Irish soldiers was to cause a certain amount of acrimony between the English and Irish hierarchies. But it was Bourne, rather than their own Bishops, who actually visited and encouraged those Irish Catholics training in England, embarking for France and serving at the Front, assuring them of the justice of their cause and urging their spiritual preparedness.

On 25 January 1915 the Cardinal, with the approval and assistance of the military authorities, made a twelve day visit to France, visiting the Front and army hospitals, addressing regiments with a significant number of Catholics and meeting the military chaplains. His plainspoken counsel was appreciated by men who would shortly confront the ultimate realities of life and death.

> You will soon take your place in the ranks of those who have so nobly fought. You are going to face death as they have done. Some will be taken, others will be left, and God alone knows who will remain to return home to his kith and kin. When death is near it will be

> comparatively easy for you to keep free from sin and at peace with God your Maker. But in these days of preparation, when even the possibility of death still seems far off, you are exposed to special dangers and temptations against which I would very earnestly warn you ... May God be with you all ... May He watch over and guide you and bless you; give you courage in the fight.[23]

Closer to the trenches Bourne showed himself impervious to personal danger when the Germans started shelling the locality; his Army hosts were more nervous, refusing to allow him to advance further into the danger zone.[24]

In August 1916 the Cardinal spent two Sundays with the Royal Navy, including a visit to the Grand Fleet at Scapa Flow. Acquainting himself as far as possible with every aspect of the sailor's life, again he concentrated on spiritual realities. Mass was celebrated and Confirmation conferred. He encouraged his co-religionists in their patriotic duty, but reminded them of even greater duties. 'He urged them to live lives nearer to God's wishes, and reminded them that prayer for victory, important as it undoubtedly was, was not so important as a life so in accordance with the Divine Will as to be worthy of victory.'[25] There was a similar message for the British sailors he visited on their ships off the Italian coast in January the following year.

> The Cardinal exhorted each and everyone to be true to his religion in every thought, word and action ... He begged them all to use every opportunity they got of approaching the Sacraments ... and in this connection the Cardinal reminded them what delight it gave to an anxious father or mother or wife or sister to read in their letters home that they had recently been to Confession, etc.[26]

Against the backdrop of total war, episcopal arguments about diocesan division seem very petty. They led some Bishops, however, to express sarcastic suspicion about the Cardinal's wartime activities. Casartelli wrote to Gasquet that Bourne would be far better employed back home than 'at the Front lunching with General Haig.'[27] Such jibes were unworthy. The voice of the pastor is more evident in the Cardinal's account of his visit to the British fleet in Italy: 'Last Sunday ... I celebrated Mass and spoke to [the British Catholic sailors] as a father can speak who is given the opportunity of seeing his children who are facing danger.'[28]

'At the end of our resources'

The wave of enthusiasm for the War which swept the nation in August 1914 was reflected in the Catholic Church. Within two weeks of the declaration of hostilities with Germany over 100 priests had applied to serve as military chaplains. The *Tablet* announced that no further applications were required.[29]

Those applications were submitted to Cardinal Bourne, assisted by Mgr Bidwell as Secretary of the Chaplains' Department. Bourne had taken with him from Southwark charge of army chaplains, while the Archbishop of Westminster was already the superior for the small number of Catholic naval chaplains. At the request of both the Vatican and the British Government, and after consultation with the hierarchy, these arrangements had been formalised in 1906. As a result the Cardinal was effectively Bishop to the Forces. Thus, candidates applied to Westminster with the permission of their bishop or superior. Bidwell recorded their details and, when the War Office required another chaplain, he presented the candidate. Having passed a medical, the priest was told directly of his commissioning date and where he was to report, and given instructions as to pay, kit and portable altar.

Reflecting the number of Irishmen serving the Crown, Catholics were proportionally over-represented in the peacetime army. It is estimated that one in seven soldiers were Catholic at the outbreak of War. Some 400,000 Catholics served in the British Army during the course of hostilities. However, just seven priests crossed the Channel with the British Expeditionary Force in August 1914. By late September the number attached to the British Army in France was still only twelve. Complaints from Irish soldiers appeared in the Press that they had not heard Mass since leaving home and that the sacraments were not being administered to the wounded and dying. Lord Edmund Talbot asked questions in the Commons, but was told that the provision of Catholic chaplains was not a priority for Lord Kitchener, Secretary of State for War. [30] That response was not good enough for the Cardinal, frustrated that his volunteers were not being deployed. His repeated representations to the Prime Minister ensured the War Office agreed to send to the Front such Catholic chaplains as might be required.[31] While logistical difficulties would always remain, the Cardinal had no further grounds to criticise the lack of cooperation of the British military authorities, who allowed a higher ratio of Catholic chaplains to soldiers than it did for Protestants. Rather, the Church would struggle to meet the increasing demand of the War Office as the local commanders realised the value of Catholic military chaplains.

Relations with the Admiralty were not initially as smooth. At the outbreak of War, there were even fewer Catholic naval chaplains. By the end of 1914 there were still just eleven, of whom only one was serving on board ship as opposed to 233 Anglicans. Bourne acknowledged the 'less satisfactory' situation regarding the Navy, but also the practical problems. 'It is a very difficult question, for it would be practically impossible and certainly not desirable to have ships exclusively for Catholics and, where they are scattered, there must be many vessels in which R. C.s are very few.'[32] Of course, this did little to satisfy those sailors who might be months at sea without recourse to the sacraments nor the Irish Parliamentary Party and the Press who championed their cause.

The spiritual welfare of sailors was felt to be further prejudiced by a residual anti-Catholicism (largely absent in the Army) among senior naval personnel. The Benedictine Fr Weld-Blundell sought Bourne's help when the Admiralty opposed the celebration of Mass on board ship in contravention of assurances given by Winston Churchill, First Lord of the Admiralty, that every facility was being offered to Catholic naval chaplains.[33] But perhaps it was 'agitation on the subject in Ireland'[34] that brought the matter to a head. Protests on behalf of Catholic sailors by the Irish bishops in January 1915 led to a meeting the following month between Bourne, the Bishop of Waterford and Redmond on the one hand and Churchill on the other. The Cardinal noted that Churchill approached the matter 'in no ungenerous manner,' and the situation gradually improved to the position where there were 31 Catholic naval chaplains by the end of the War.[35]

Bidwell acknowledged at the outset the distinction between the forces serving overseas and those stationed at home. The Archbishop of Westminster was responsible for all full-time military chaplains, wherever they were based. However, many barracks in the UK lacked a full-time chaplain. Their responsibility fell on the local bishop and clergy. While the War Office empowered commanding officers to appoint Catholic chaplains, the hierarchy were unaware of troop movements and many commanding officers, albeit inadvertently, failed to request a chaplain.[36] The Cardinal, of course, had no jurisdiction over local priests outside his own Diocese, but he attempted to coordinate matters, asking his brother Bishops for their assistance so that full-time chaplains might be appointed to serve camps which were too far from a Catholic church to allow the local clergy to minister to the troops. 'You would render me a great service if you would kindly let me know of any camp situated in your Diocese where no Catholic chaplain has been appointed.'[37]

After Bourne's intervention with the Prime Minister, the number of Catholic chaplains serving at the Front increased rapidly. At the outbreak of the War, Catholics were permitted a chaplain to every division sent overseas and three chaplains for the military hospitals. In November 1914 the War Office authorised a Catholic chaplain for every Irish regiment or battalion which was predominantly Catholic. The War Office also offered its 'sympathetic consideration' to any request to increase the number of hospital chaplains. From this point, the Church struggled to fill its allocated quota. Immediately, a further 16 chaplains were required and Cardinal Bourne turned to Cardinal Logue of Armagh to supply half of these.[38]

Bourne was acutely conscious of allegations in the Irish Press that the spiritual needs of Irish Catholic soldiers were not being met. This criticism was picked up by the *Catholic Herald* in England, and circulated in Rome and the US. The Cardinal did not deny the problem, but felt such criticism unhelpful. 'In dealing with the Chaplain question there has been from across the sea much, often unfair and inaccurate criticism of the Government, which only makes negotiation more difficult, and, at the same time, a reluctance to give the help which would have been most valued.'[39]

By June 1915 there were 225 full time Catholic chaplains, but a further 45 were required immediately. Bourne sought help. 'I hope that Ireland will come to my assistance, for practically all the priests in England have been called up already.'[40] In January 1916 the Senior Chaplain on Salisbury Plain wrote to the Cardinal detailing the extreme lack of spiritual provision for soldiers in camps and those departing for the Front. Bourne forwarded the report to Cardinal Logue and pleaded with him. 'England has provided more than 270 [chaplains]—my own Diocese has given 35 and we are really at the end of our resources. Can your Eminence in your charity obtain no more help from Ireland which so far has given no more than 60?'[41] Logue appealed to Catholic Ireland. 'There is grave reason to fear that many of our young Catholic countrymen, who may be called upon to face death at any moment, may be deprived of those aids which rob death of its terrors. Surely no higher or holier call could appeal to the zeal of a priest than the call to bring the consolation of holy religion to those brave men who are hourly exposed to imminent peril of their lives.'⁴² A year later Logue alleged 'a great scarcity of priests in Ireland.'⁴³

As the shortage of chaplains grew increasingly acute, there was increasing acrimony across the Irish Sea. Some in Ireland and among his detractors at home blamed the incompetence of Bourne and Bidwell, and their unwillingness to hand over responsibility in this matter. Some of this was simply petty and personal. It is difficult to avoid the impression that Amigo and Gasquet used real grievances to further their wider campaign against Bourne. On the other hand English lay Catholics cast aspersions against the Irish hierarchy. 'We are grateful for the appeals … made by his Eminence Cardinal Logue; but we respectfully submit that circumstances seem to show that these appeals have not met with an adequate response, and that some further effort is needed, and at once.'⁴⁴ Mgr William Keatinge was more impartial. 'How miserably our English (and Irish) bishops have failed, in this war, to rise to the occasion. They can't see beyond the petty wants of their diocese.'⁴⁵

The thought of Catholic soldiers dying without the spiritual comforts they desired was heart rending. The anguish it produced made contemporaries say some harsh things. There is no reason to doubt the hard work put in by Cardinal Bourne and his deputies, nor the sacrifices made in his own Diocese. When the Anglican Diocese of London had 2% of its clergy acting as military chaplains, 'the proportion of chaplains given by the Diocese of Westminster is one in six of the secular clergy.'⁴⁶ Even his most cherished project, the diocesan seminary, was pared to the minimum to provide more chaplains for the Front.⁴⁷

What was the reality? Everyone admitted initial failings due to the War Office's obstruction and the time taken to adjust to the experience of total war. Thereafter, judgments were mixed. An English Jesuit chaplain wrote home at Christmas 1914, 'For the first three months of the War the supply of chaplains was inadequate. Now, thanks to the efforts of our Cardinal Archbishop, we are very well provided, at least in our division … but we have met regiments that had not seen an English-speaking priest since the beginning of the War.'⁴⁸ Another chaplain told of the canvas church at the base at Rouen equipped with altar, rails, pulpit, harmonium and confessionals where there were six Sunday Masses, daily Mass, Confessions and Benediction. 'This is so different from the South African War! No British Catholic soldier may have the least fear of living or dying without the Sacraments, and when enquiry is made in response to the letter of some responsible person at home to whom a soldier has written and told his tale of how he has seen neither priest nor sacraments for months, it is invariably found that he has lived almost next door to priest and church for months and never had the interest nor care to put his head inside the door.'[49]

Once again, Mgr Keatinge probably gave a fairer assessment. He rejected claims of disorganisation and a failure to distribute chaplains appropriately. Nevertheless, he admitted the sheer shortage of chaplains 'means that, even with the best distribution of our limited numbers, men have to die without the Sacraments. Our establishment is also to be increased in the near future, but that will not be of any use unless we can get the priests to fill the posts.'[50]

Catholics were not the only chaplains in the First World War. Anglicans too experienced organisational problems and difficulties in recruiting chaplains, leading to calls for the conscription of clergy.[51] Some Anglicans, clergy and officers, looked enviously at the pastoral care, sacramental ministry and spiritual authority of Catholic chaplains untroubled by the doctrinal difficulties which beset the Anglican Communion. One wrote, 'It makes me despair of the Church of England. Rome makes no mistakes. We have no fewer than five Roman priests in our division for barely 400 R.C.s, and at the present only six C of E chaplains. Frantic appeals for more make no difference.'[52]

In an age of total war without the advantage of instant communications, there were bound to be failings in the provision of military chaplains. For most of the War the Church could provide only three quarters of the Catholic chaplains requested by the War Office. Tragically, this meant that there were those who died without the ministrations of a priest, without the grace of the sacraments. Acknowledging this, however, the achievements are extraordinary. By the end of the War 651 Catholic chaplains ministered to the 6% of the British Army which was Catholic—as opposed to 1,985 Anglicans ministering to the 70% who were Church of England.[53] Thirty-six had given their lives in the course of the War.[54] Contact between priests and men was often easier than in civilian life. Many Catholics returned to the practice of the faith, and the dying and wounded invariably sought the sacraments.[55] It is estimated that there were 40,000 conversions during the War in France alone.[56] The testimony of the servicemen is compelling. 'Of the devotion of the Catholic chaplains I hardly like to speak. It is wonderful. But I do complain of the shortage of chaplains. It is unfair to those at the front, both chaplains and men.'⁵⁷

Bourne was criticised for a shortage of chaplains and lapses in organisation. When one views similar problems in other denominations, it is difficult to know to what extent, if any, he was personally culpable. But if he is criticised, then it is only fair that he takes some share of the credit for the effort and organisation which allowed hundreds of Catholic chaplains to minister so effectively on the ground.

Episcopus Castriensis

Some argued that the Archbishop of Westminster's role as ecclesiastical superior of military chaplains was anomalous. Germany, Austria, Spain and Italy all had military bishops appointed specifically as ordinary with full jurisdiction over chaplains. Each of those countries, however, had large Catholic populations. With just a handful of Catholic chaplains, the appointment of a military bishop, an *Episcopus Castriensis*, in peacetime Britain made no sense. As the number of chaplains soared after the outbreak of war, representations were made for structural reorganisation. Motivations varied. Some chaplains looked back nostalgically to the situation existing prior to the Boer War, wanting to return to a position where their superior was 'one of their own.' Amigo and others saw an opportunity to clip the Cardinal's wings. Others argued that there were now significantly more priests serving as chaplains than in any British diocese; therefore, it was only right that they should have their own bishop devoted exclusively to chaplaincy matters. Whatever the reasons advanced, Bourne rejected them firmly.

His opponents implied that it was only Bourne and Bidwell, in addition to heavy diocesan duties, attempting to organise hundreds of Catholic chaplains across the globe, causing unnecessary delay and disorganisation. However, Bourne appointed senior chaplains to organise the distribution of chaplains locally, and made Fr Stephen Rawlinson OSB his Vicar-General with responsibility for the Armies in France. There is no suggestion from the military authorities that they found this system inefficient. Quite the contrary. While always requiring more chaplains, the War Office, with no particular axe to grind, noted, 'These arrangements have worked quite smoothly.'⁵⁸ The Admiralty agreed. 'The present arrangement with the Cardinal Archbishop of Westminster, which has been established for a long time, has worked well and there is nothing to complain of from the point of view of the War Office and the military forces generally.'[59]

The impetus for change began in Ireland. When Bourne accepted responsibility for military chaplains across the British Empire, he carefully excluded those chaplains stationed in Ireland, who fell under the remit of the Irish hierarchy. But Westminster did have charge of Irish soldiers and sailors serving in the British forces outside the 32 counties and the Irish chaplains caring for them. With Ireland a part of the United Kingdom, the arrangement did not appear unusual. However, as complaints arrived of Irishmen deprived of spiritual sustenance, pressure mounted for this responsibility to be transferred to the Irish bishops. There is no evidence that Cardinal Bourne treated the Irish hierarchy with anything other than courtesy and respect, but that was not how it was presented in Rome by those always eager to interpret matters to his detriment. Gasquet felt 'the Irish Bishops objected to being *bossed* from Westminster.'[60] Cardinal Logue expressed legitimate Irish feelings less pejoratively. 'More of our priests, especially suited to the work of a chaplain, would join up if the nomination of senior chaplains should concern the bishops of Ireland.'[61]

The Irish hierarchy made its views known in Rome not only directly, but also through the Irish College, the Irish Press and their compatriots in the US. It seems to have been at their instigation, as well as being part of a wider scheme to appoint military bishops in all combatant countries that Cardinal Gasparri, the Cardinal Secretary of State, raised in August 1915 the proposal to nominate a bishop as Chaplain General to the British naval and military forces. He had in mind William Brown, Amigo's Vicar-General in Southwark. The views of the British Government were sought.[62]

No progress was made until Cardinal Bourne arrived in Rome in December 1915. In audiences and dicastries he put his case for chaplains to remain under Westminster's supervision. Once again the Vatican agreed with the last prelate to visit. Benedict XV assured him 'that there had been a complete misunderstanding regarding the question raised by the Consistorial regarding the Army and Navy.' Bourne explained the existing system to Mgr Pacelli (the future Pius XII) who expressed 'his warm admiration.' A further audience with the Holy Father resulted in a 'full understanding on all points,'[63] and allowed Bourne to write to the British Minister to the Vatican, 'I have now been able to discuss fully with all here in Rome ... the project submitted to Your Excellency last August

... I am able to assure Your Excellency that it is not now intended to proceed further with that project.'[64]

It was the same situation as with diocesan division. Bourne felt that he had secured his objectives while visiting Rome, only to discover back home that Rome was inclined to back his opponents. It is true that the Cardinal did not do subtlety, but the Vatican was at fault in allowing him to labour under a misapprehension. The question of the appointment of a military bishop was about to become less nuanced.

The Pope and the Curia again made use of Gasquet as the English Cardinal resident in Rome. It would have been better had they dealt with Bourne directly. Instead, Cardinal De Lai shared with Gasquet Bourne's protests against Rome's proposal. The Holy Father requested Gasquet to write to Bourne 'as a friend' to drop his opposition.[65] They asked the wrong man. Gasquet fulfilled his obligation and wrote diplomatically to Bourne, intimating that it was the wish of the highest authority that a military bishop be appointed and that he would be well advised 'to cultivate peace all round and to refrain from raising difficult issues.'[66] Bourne was ill disposed to take lectures from the man plotting with Amigo to thwart him. He fired off a typically abrupt response which Gasquet interpreted for the Pope's benefit, further undermining Bourne's reputation in Rome. Gasquet had gone some way to securing his objective. 'The Holy Father was very vexed at the attitude of opposition to everything taken up by Cardinal Bourne. He is apparently determined on a change but whether now or after the War I cannot say.'[67]

Simultaneously, back in London, Amigo was at work, trying to persuade the military authorities to express their support for restructuring. They were having none of it, displaying a professionalism and impartiality lacking in Rome. 'From the War Office point of view the present arrangement was satisfactory enough and that they did not like to say that it was unsatisfactory and thus offend the Westminster Authorities.'[68] The War Office and Admiralty displayed a very proper neutrality, carefully refraining from expressing any opinion as to Church politics—provided a steady stream of chaplains was forthcoming.

Never the diplomat, Bourne was outmanoeuvred by the Irish-Southwark-Benedictine alliance arrayed against him. Supplied with evidence as to the inadequacies of the current regime, Gasquet 'immediately took it to Cardinal Merry del Val for use at the Consistorial meeting which is to come off immediately at which Cardinal Bourne is going to make a supreme effort to keep things as they are.'⁶⁹ Gasquet was appointed to the special commission to investigate the question. In this capacity, he was able to see Bourne's case. 'He attacks me personally for having given my opinion against his view. According to him I having been his *rival* for the See of Westminster have always been the centre of opposition, not so much actually as listening to others.' Whether Bourne was wise to commit his opinion to writing, the evidence certainly supports him. Gasquet was equally intemperate in his views. 'The basis of Cardinal Bourne's position would appear to be that things should be left as they are, to increase *his* position in regard to England and in fact the British Empire in place of the *Consistorial*. This is the real danger.'⁷⁰

Bourne thought he had neutralised the threat by having himself appointed as an observer to the Special Commission. Once again, however, Gasquet was able to square Merry del Val and other cardinals in advance of the meeting on 25 January 1917 and delay any real discussion of the issue until after Bourne's departure. Not surprisingly, the result went against Westminster.⁷¹

Faced with defeat, Bourne offered to concede what the Irish Bishops had sought two years earlier, namely Logue receiving equivalent powers to his own in respect of Irish chaplains. The 'result would be Westminster remains unchanged, as defined by Propaganda decree … , Armagh gets Home Rule with full responsibility for Ireland.'⁷² While this might have been the practical solution, it did not satisfy Bourne's enemies in Rome and England who wanted to see him stripped of all power in chaplaincy matters. The Vatican would not act without the British Government's agreement and, therefore, Bourne tried to persuade the Foreign Office 'to say that *they have confidence in me and my proposals*.'⁷³ Once again, the Government reaffirmed its policy of allowing the Church to decide on purely ecclesiastical matters. Bourne then sought unsuccessfully to have Bidwell named as the military bishop. All this came to a head simultaneously with the dispute over diocesan division at the Low Week meeting of the hierarchy in 1917. Amigo gave one last stir to an explosive situation. 'I told the Bishops at Oscott that it was high time we stopped Bidwell or even the Cardinal acting for all … It is indeed high time that we had an *Episcopus Castriensis*.'⁷⁴

Amigo did not speak for the whole hierarchy. Asked by the Pope, Dunn 'gave it as my opinion that the *status quo* should not be in any way modified or changed at the present time but that after the War the whole question should be reconsidered.'⁷⁵ However, his defeat on diocesan division and subsequent illness left the Cardinal in no mood to continue his opposition. A military bishop was finally appointed in October 1917. In typically Roman fashion Bidwell was appointed an auxiliary bishop of Westminster as a face-saving device for Bourne.

Gasquet and Amigo largely achieved the desired humiliation of Bourne. It was a pyrrhic victory. The new military bishop was Mgr William Keatinge, educated at Downside under Gasquet and former Senior Catholic Chaplain in France. He was appointed on 30 October 1917 Titular Bishop of Metellopolis, Vicar Apostolic for the British Military. (The Royal Navy remained under Bourne's jurisdiction.) Keatinge was not consecrated, by Cardinal De Lai, until 25 February 1918 at the English College Chapel, Rome with less than nine months of the War remaining. It is uncertain how much changed, for better or worse, following his appointment. Amigo was 'delighted' by his 'victory,' but foresaw the danger. 'In all probability Keatinge will be full of enthusiasm and go about a good deal. Meantime in London questions will need settling. If Keatinge has not a very good representative in the War Office these may be referred to Westminster as before and Bidwell will take the matters in hand.'⁷⁶ When the number of chaplains reduced dramatically in peacetime, it is telling that their supervision reverted to one of the Westminster auxiliaries.⁷⁷

What Amigo categorised as an attempt to regain influence, the Cardinal would have expressed as a simple acknowledgement of practical realties. There were occasions when the presence and authority of the Archbishop of Westminster, resident in London, were required in negotiations with the Government. 'Cardinal Bourne treats the War Office from outside and with full independence ... One may see the advantages of the method ... An Army Bishop, being subordinate to the War Office, would simply have been left to chafe.'⁷⁸ The Cardinal's contention was borne out by the Anglican experience. Although they appointed a Bishop for the Troops in France in 1915, Lambeth Palace still found it necessary to assume increasing responsibility for coordination and liaison between bishops and Government departments with respect to the provision of Anglican chaplains.⁷⁹

Perhaps a similar solution should have been adopted by the Catholics: official relations with the Government being retained by Westminster, while a bishop acceptable to the Irish was appointed for the troops on the ground. Indeed, Australia and New Zealand both sent (diocesan) bishops to the Front. Interested only in the practical results of a particular system, Bourne characteristically refused to adopt policies principally aimed at improving public relations, even when the intended audience was as important as the Irish hierarchy and potential Irish chaplains. All parties to the dispute would have argued vehemently that they held their position for the sole purpose of ameliorating the condition of ordinary Catholic servicemen. Nevertheless, a great deal of time and effort was wasted which might have been more effectively expended elsewhere.

Conscription

Britain's proud boast was that, unlike Germany, her Army consisted entirely of volunteers. However, as the carnage of the trenches continued, that position became increasingly untenable. As 1915 progressed it became probable that Britain too would be forced to introduce conscription. There was concern for the situation of priests and seminarians, partly due to the incompatibility of armed service with the clerical state, but also because, under canon law of the time, having killed a man, or simply having lost a limb, was an impediment to ordination.

Cardinal Bourne met with Lord Derby, the Director-General for Recruiting, in September 1915 to seek Government reassurances. Derby promised that priests would be exempted, but could give no such guarantees for seminarians. In fact, he agreed to include in the draft legislation the exemption suggested by the Cardinal: 'Catholic priests and students who have already entered on their professional studies in immediate preparation for the priesthood.'[80] This exempted major seminarians, those already studying philosophy and theology, but not minor seminarians still engaged in general studies, although, of course, most of these were too young to be called up. The numbers involved were approximately 200 diocesan seminarians and 400 non-ordained members of religious orders. The hierarchy gladly sanctioned the Cardinal to continue negotiations with the Government on its behalf.[81]

When the Military Services Act was passed in January 1916, it appeared that seminarians were still at risk. Unmarried men between the ages of 16 and 40 were liable for military service. The only relevant exemption was for 'Men in holy orders or regular ministers of any religious denomination.' With the Medical Corps full, it seemed as if seminarians would be compelled to fight. The Cardinal wrote to the Pope explaining the true position. 'I have succeeded in obtaining from our Government a complete exemption for our seminarians and members of religious orders and institutes from the effects of the new law on compulsory military service. This exemption will be achieved by administrative direction of the Minister for War. Thus, we avoid debate in Parliament and all publicity in the Press.'[82] Bourne's preference for private negotiation had proved successful, attaining his aim and avoiding public imputations of lack of patriotism. When the hierarchy and religious superiors appreciated what had been gained, they were fulsome in their praise of the Cardinal.

The Church was not permitted to relax for long. One year later the need for manpower meant the scope of conscription was being extended, and the War Office proposed ending the previous concession. Although in Rome, the Cardinal was kept fully informed of developments by telegraphs from Bidwell. He wrote immediately to the Prime Minister explaining the Catholic position: the number of seminarians was only sufficient to meet the bare minimum need for priests, canon law prescribed the length of their studies and British priests were required to replace enemy aliens.[83] Again, Bourne sought to protect seminarians while doing everything possible to prevent the Church appearing unpatriotic.[84]

Fortunately, the Church had friends at the War Office who appreciated the value of Catholic chaplains and who were prepared to restrain the activities of recruiting officers. Bidwell and Amigo used their contacts with Sir Reginald Brade, Under-Secretary at the War Office, who proposed an acceptable compromise. The 150 or so seminarians at risk of conscription equated roughly to the shortfall of Catholic chaplains. The seminarians would not be called up provided, on ordination, they became Army chaplains or freed up another priest to do so.[85] The Cardinal immediately accepted the offer,[86] although Amigo complained of Bidwell's role in the negotiations.[87]

Bidwell was to be kept busy visiting the War Office to release seminarians and religious called up by overzealous recruiting officers.[88] However, official regard for the Cardinal and the desire for a continuing supply of chaplains, meant the principle of non-combative roles for the clergy was maintained throughout the War.

'The Shepherd and Teacher of the whole flock': Pope Benedict XV

Pope Pius X died on 20 August 1914. Two days later Cardinal Bourne was on his way to Rome for the Conclave to elect his successor. Given

A Cardinal at War

Europe was at war, the atmosphere among members of the Sacred College was remarkably friendly. Bourne described his experience. 'Cardinals at the Conclave may have their meals in their rooms; but most of us preferred to eat together. We each had our strong national feelings; yet not one of us made allusion to the War. Each of us knew that his supreme task was to choose a successor of St Peter. So we met and talked in total peace and harmony: and our work was done in three days ... so closely were we under the influence of the Holy Spirit.'[89] On 3 September the Cardinals elected Giacomo Della Chiesa, the Archbishop of Bologna, as Pope Benedict XV. It was an unusually sensitive election. A protégé of Leo XIII and Cardinal Rampolla, Della Chiesa was perceived as a Francophile, but Austro-Hungarian cardinals defied their government to vote for him. Cardinal Bourne was to spend the next four years interpreting and defending the Pope's actions to wartime Britain, while himself not averse to (more or less) private criticism of the Holy Father.

Britain was at a disadvantage at the beginning of the War. As a Protestant power she had seen no need to maintain diplomatic relations with the Vatican. Likewise, anti-clerical France. Prussia, Bavaria and Austria had the field, therefore, to themselves. There was felt to be a pro-Austrian bias in the Roman Curia given the desire to support the last unequivocally Catholic power in Europe and the hope that Austria would be sympathetic to the restoration of the Papal States. As an unabashed patriot resident in Rome, Gasquet fretted at the perceived handicap under which his country laboured. 'It is impossible to understand the mentality of the general run of Roman ecclesiastics. They are absurdly pro-German and believe every German story. The German representatives at the Vatican have been preparing the ground for a couple of years.'[90]

Gasquet was not prepared to allow this imbalance to continue. From the outset he and the Duke of Norfolk pressed for British diplomatic representation at the Vatican. They were pushing at an open door with the Government conscious of the need to represent its own actions at the Holy See, not least due to the many Catholics spread across the British Empire. Cardinal Bourne was simply kept abreast of the negotiations which led to the establishment of a British Mission by the end of the year, led first by Sir Henry Howard and later by Count de Salis. (Possibly with an eye to British public opinion, it was a unilateral act with no nuncio being received at the Court of St James. This left the Cardinal in an ambiguous position, variously recognised and rejected as the Holy See's representative in

London.) Gasquet, at least, was delighted by the British Mission's arrival in Rome, while noting the corresponding anger of the Irish College.[91]

Among the British population generally, and not a few Catholics, the Pope's wartime position was misinterpreted. Convinced of the justice of their own cause, the British expected the Vatican's outright denunciation of the Central Powers, preferably accompanied by the excommunication of all Catholics serving in the German army. Cardinal Bourne had to correct these misconceptions. He did so forcefully in a homily subsequently published as a CTS pamphlet.

> The whole of this criticism is based on the fallacy that no protest is of any value unless it be shouted on the housetops and published in the daily papers ... Because the Holy Father, in accordance with the traditions of the Holy See, has followed the traditional methods, and made his protest in the way most likely to have its effect ... they think he has not spoken at all ... The Holy Father is the Shepherd and Teacher of the whole flock, of every nation, without exception. He has to consider every nation alike. While we know, and can have no doubt in this country, of the terrible things that have been wrought, especially in Belgium, we must never forget that similar accusations, hardly less in gravity, have been made—I do not pronounce on their truth, because I have no means of doing so—in the most circumstantial way against one of our allies, namely Russia, about its treatment of the Galician Poles. If the Holy Father is to speak publicly in condemnation, all these questions must come before him if he is not to fail in that duty of justice and impartiality which is his special prerogative.[92]

In fact, Benedict XV did condemn the German invasion of Belgium in January 1915 only to be labelled by the German Press as 'the French Pope.' Pope Benedict sought to prevent the escalation of hostilities and Italy's entry into the War. In addition to his genuine aversion to further loss of life, he was concerned both by domestic instability within Italy and the extra strain placed on the Austro-Hungarian Empire. Unsuccessfully, he counselled Emperor Franz-Josef to make territorial concessions to Italy.[93]

Even at the time the Vatican was alarmed by the Treaty of Rome between Britain, France, Russia and Italy which preceded Italy's entry into the War. Signed by the British Foreign Secretary on 26 April 1915 it gave Tsarist Russia and the Orthodox Church the former church of Santa Sophia in Istanbul, encouraging their pretensions in the Balkans and the eastern Mediterranean. This was as nothing, however, compared to the papal displeasure when the Bolsheviks published the secret provisions of the Treaty in autumn 1917, revealing Britain's support for Italy in excluding the Holy See from future peace talks.

Bourne was left to pick up the pieces. Fresh from a papal audience, Gasquet relayed the Holy Father's impressions.

> That England, with a Minister to the Holy See, should agree with Italy to exclude the Pope from all questions of the War appears incredible. The Count de Salis has been kept in the dark and knew nothing of this secret plot ... I do not know what you can do I am sure ... As a matter of pure politics, I don't understand our diplomats, for this kind of thing throws people here into the arms of Germany ... [The Pope] was frankly astonished at England which he had always considered honest and straight forward, but as he says this secret treaty explains many things.[94]

Amigo seems to have organised the parliamentary question asked by the Irish Parliamentary Party. Replying for the Government, Lord Robert Cecil denied any intention of prejudicing the Holy See; rather, the Allies' sole purpose was that only belligerent powers should participate in any peace conference.[95] Privately, he admitted that the clause did apply exclusively to the Vatican.[96] Typically, Bourne preferred private diplomacy, and secured an interview with Arthur Balfour. He received neither a convincing explanation nor a sincere apology. The Foreign Secretary deeply regretted the clause and its drafting. He felt that it had been included without adequate attention. He repeated Cecil's questionable assertion that it was not aimed exclusively against the Holy See. He added the common disclaimer of the politician: this was the work of the previous administration. One does not feel the Cardinal pushed the Foreign Secretary too hard. He concluded by assuring the Pope, 'Mr Balfour's own attitude towards the Holy See is not only correct but very well disposed. He understands perfectly the attitude imposed on the Holy See by the spiritual interests of all nations, and he deplores the unjust criticisms objecting to this attitude.'[97]

The furore concerning the Treaty of Rome occurred as relations between Britain and the Holy See, and between the English Catholic Church and the Vatican, were at their most strained. Since the beginning of the War Benedict XV occupied himself in humanitarian work, calling on the cooperation of local hierarchies. In conjunction with the Swiss government, he laboured tirelessly for the material and spiritual well-being of prisoners of war, making enquiries regarding missing persons, forwarding correspondence and aiding repatriation. He virtually bankrupted the Vatican in the process.[98] No one objected to these activities of the Pope. The situation changed when he sought a peaceful resolution of the War.

The Pope's appeal for a truce for the first Christmas of the War was ignored. In the summer of 1915 he appealed to the nations to settle their differences at the negotiating table.[99] He returned to the subject at the end of the year. 'It is absolutely necessary that the belligerents on either side should make concessions on some points and on others give up advantages that had been hoped for; and each must make such concessions with good grace, even at the cost of certain sacrifices, so as to save themselves from the awful responsibility before God and men of the continuation of this unparalleled butchery.'[100] No one was listening to the voice of reason and reconciliation. When the possibility of a separate peace with Austria-Hungary was mooted in the spring of 1917, Cardinal Bourne warned the Pope not to involve himself, at the risk of offending the British Government.[101]

The Pope's general strategy was to work for peace on the basis of the *status quo* existing prior to August 1914. This found its greatest expression in the Pope's Peace Note of August 1917. His stated objectives were 'to maintain an absolute impartiality towards all the belligerents ... ; to endeavour continually to do the utmost good to all without distinction ... ; ... to omit nothing, as far as in Our power lies, to contribute to hasten the end of this calamity by trying to bring the peoples and their leaders to more moderate resolutions in the discussion of means that will secure a "just and lasting peace."'[102] Specifically, the Pope requested the 'simultaneous and reciprocal diminution of armaments,' the reciprocal renunciation of war indemnities, the evacuation and restoration of all occupied territories (Belgium, northern France and the former German colonies) and the examination 'in a conciliatory spirit' of outstanding territorial disputes (Trent, Alsace-Lorraine, Armenia, the Balkans and Poland).[103]

The Peace Note was sent to all belligerent powers. Only Catholic Austria was sympathetic. Believing military victory possible, the Germans had no interest in negotiating. Both France and Italy were opposed to granting any role of mediation to the Vatican, the latter also determined to wrest territory from the Austrians. The British Government merely acknowledged receipt of the Note, which the *Times* disparagingly dismissed as a 'German Peace Move.' Six months later Cardinal Bourne informed the Foreign Office of the Holy See's irritation at the lack of any substantive response.[104] President Wilson of the United States upheld the need to defeat German militarism if there was to be a lasting peace. But at least he had the courtesy to reply to the Vatican at length. There was a significant similarity between Pope Benedict's Peace Note and his own 'Fourteen Points' issued the following January.[105]

The Peace Note placed British Catholics in a dilemma. Were they loyal to the Pope or to their own Government? The overwhelming majority had no hesitation. National interests won out. In a letter to the *Manchester Guardian* Casartelli distanced British Catholics from the papal initiative. While rejecting the more scandalous utterances of the British Press, Bishop Keating followed suit. 'The words of His Holiness were addressed, not to the Church, but to the secular powers. They were not to be regarded as a doctrinal exposition, but as a diplomatic effort. An English Catholic, therefore, was free to form his own opinion without any violation of his obedience. He could follow the leading of his own individuality, and could identify himself with his Government's policy.'[106] Gasquet put to the Pope himself the real objection to the Peace Note. 'I told him that what had hurt the feelings of the Allies was the way the note apparently put both parties on a level for wrong doing.'[107] Overwhelmingly, the British hierarchy identified themselves as partisans rather than proponents of peace.

Cardinal Bourne shared that view but with greater nuances. He attempted to maintain three incompatible positions. Firstly, the Peace Note was to be received with 'courtesy and respect'—and then, practically, ignored. Secondly, it was argued implausibly 'that the hopes of the Holy Father are identical with the aims of the Allies.' Finally, the Note was to be rejected because only military victory would secure a lasting peace.[108]

English Catholics were not used to hearing their leaders disagree with the Pope, so the Cardinal set out the reality of the situation for his flock. Defending the Pope against the gross Media slurs of German or Austrian bias, Bourne pointed out that the Peace Note was not a matter covered by papal infallibility.

> I am quite certain that the day will come when we are able to look back on these things more calmly, when men will recognise that it is the voice of the Sovereign Pontiff that has compelled all the belligerent nations to face certain aspects of this contest which are being lost sight of ... to protest against the attempts which have

> been made, notably by one of the evening papers, to misrepresent entirely the whole attitude of the Holy See in the matter … We are perfectly free, everyone of us, whether Catholic or not, to differ from any statement contained in that Papal document.[109]

While he could appreciate the complexities of the papal position and Benedict's sincere desire for peace as the universal pastor, there was ultimately no mistaking Bourne's own position. 'The Pope has proposed that all belligerents should come to a compromise. No! We demand the total triumph of right over wrong. We do not want a peace which will bring no more than a truce or an armistice between two wars. There may be in our land some people who want peace at any price, but they have no following among us. We English Catholics are fully behind our war leaders.'[110] Whether those were the words of a Christian leader can be debated, but they certainly placed Bourne in the mainstream of his fellow countrymen.

There came a point when even the Vatican could no longer able to ignore the calumnies of the British Press. Fleet Street blamed the Pope's Peace Note for Italian defeats by the Austrians in 1917. The *Morning Post* alleged that the Vatican was accepting German bribes and Italian priests had demoralised their troops by maintaining that a better peace would be obtainable were the Pope, rather than the Italian king, their temporal ruler.

Cardinal Gasparri contacted the Archbishop of Westminster, requiring redress. 'Such an article cannot be allowed to pass unnoticed. Therefore, I ask Your Eminence to ensure a reply is published, in the same paper, if possible.'[111] Bourne secured an interview with the *Morning Post* the following week, but rather detracted from his denials of Vatican bias by letting it be known he was acting on Gasparri's instructions.[112] When the *Morning Post* failed to withdraw its accusations, merely re-defining them as 'observations,' the Cardinal was stung to take further action. This time he wrote a comprehensive letter effectively demonstrating the paper's lack of substantive evidence. It was an eloquent defence of Pope Benedict. 'As for the Note itself, it is hated as much by the Prussian military caste, with whom is our essential quarrel, as by any Englishman or Frenchman; and no candid person can say it would be a "German Peace" under which the Flemish littoral would belong to an independent Belgium and under which Alsace and Lorraine would settle their own future.' It was a strong case to anyone approaching the matter impartially. He concluded forcefully, 'You say that your appeal is to the

Ten Commandments. So is mine. And I remember that one of them is "Thou shalt not bear false witness."'[113] Bourne at his best.

He continued to round on 'the meaner writers' in the Press, accusing the *Morning Star*, *Globe* and *National Review* of being either 'wilfully misleading' or 'guilty of criminal recklessness' in ascribing a pro-German bias to the Vatican. The Cardinal pointed out, with references to Bismarck's persecution of Catholics in the 1870s, the Pope had to be sensitive to 'the spiritual interests of Catholics' in Germany, Austria and Turkey. The Press ought to appreciate that the Holy See had to act diplomatically and impartially as it was not in the business of producing simplistic slogans for the less intelligent elements of the popular Media.[114]

In 2005 Josef Ratzinger took the name Benedict, partly in recognition of Benedict XV's role as a Pope of peace. Contemporaries, including most Catholics, failed to appreciate his tireless efforts to end the slaughter of the First World War. A decade on, however, Cardinal Bourne was prepared to pay tribute where it was due.

> He had been much and very unfairly criticised during the Great War, equally by both sides in that prolonged contest. Now men began to see at last how wonderfully and unflinchingly he had maintained the traditional international and supra-national position of the Holy See ... had the voice of Benedict XV been listened to, the war would have ended much sooner, with more durable terms of peace, and in conditions even of a financial order more reasonable and possible than those which were ultimately laid down.[115]

Peace: 'Not the greatest gift'

Pacifism was an unpopular cause in the country at large and the Catholic Church in particular during the First World War. Not just strict conscientious objectors, but those who favoured a negotiated settlement received no support from the Bishops. The Bishops' displeasure extended to the Guild of the Pope's Peace, a small group 'open to all Catholics who were prepared for peace as promoted by the Pope.'[116] Unlike other members of the hierarchy, Bourne refrained from public condemnation of pacifists and conscientious objectors. However, his reticence seems to have been based simply upon prudence, starving them of the oxygen of publicity.

Thus, when the CTS published the Guild's work in its *Catholic Book Notes* in April 1916, Cardinal Bourne set to work behind the scenes. He had the Duke of Norfolk write to the CTS Secretary with the desired effect:

an expression of regret in the *Tablet*.[117] Speaking in Italy, the Cardinal belittled the significance of the British pacifists. They were, he claimed, a group without influence or numbers, living 'in the world of metaphysics.'[118]

As the War entered its fifth year, Cardinal Bourne urged the nation not to lose its resolve. There was the danger, he maintained, of 'our being tempted to think that peace is worth having at any price, that terms must be made anyhow and in any manner; and we have to ask God today that He may continue to steel the courage of the nation and fortify our resolution so that no peace may be accepted which is not right and true and just.' Those who had disturbed the international peace had to be conclusively defeated so that they were in no position to do so again.[119]

The Cardinal returned to the theme in the autumn of 1918, condemning those who were inclined to accept peace on basis of 'no indemnities and no annexations.' 'Be not misled ... Peace is *not* the greatest gift God can bestow, unless peace be founded upon justice. Be not carried away by formulae such as no indemnities and no annexations. But justice may call for them. Peace without justice is not worth the having.'[120] His words brought angry letters, and the accusation that he was no Christian. But Bourne was not one to flinch in the face of criticism. He repeated his case. 'We are entitled to full and adequate reparations for the injuries and wrongs so wantonly, so unjustly, so unnecessarily inflicted upon us and our Allies by those, who for their own ends, provoked this awful struggle. We are entitled—nay, it is our duty—to take all lawful means to render remote and impossible the renewal of such unjust provocation ... The task before the Allied nations is to mingle justice rightly with charity.'[121] The immediate criticism subsided with the Allied victory, but one is left with the impression that the Cardinal was rather stronger on justice than charity.

As he had done at the outbreak of hostilities, Cardinal Bourne sounded a note of caution in the midst of the victory celebrations. 'There will be, inevitably, a long period of transition, trying to the individual and to the community, testing the patience, the courage and the temper of the nation as profoundly as the war itself has done.'[122] Yes, on the National Day of Thanksgiving he thanked God for 'victory granted to a righteous cause,' but he was far from certain that underlying lessons had been learnt. It was almost as if he could see two decades into the future. 'Human nature is still the same: the old passions and sins may easily revive and may work among conquerors and conquered the old prolific evils which ultimately give rise to civil contests and to wars of nations. The world is not at rest.'[123] Bourne expressed grave reservations as to the chances of the Versailles Peace Conference achieving a lasting peace when it turned its back on Christian principles.[124] Closer to home, he identified the situation in Ireland and 'the menace of class warfare' as 'portents of danger.'[125]

Yet at the same time Cardinal Bourne rightly sensed that something had changed in England. Catholics remained a small minority. But, whereas previously they had been merely tolerated, by 1918 there was an increased interest in and respect for their faith. The English people 'are impressed with a new sense of the reality of religion. They observe its effectiveness in the face of death and danger; its power to heal, tranquillise and uplift; the definiteness and uniformity of Catholic teaching. In England, too, many have adopted Catholic emblems, beliefs and practices which before the war would probably have repelled them. The message of war-shrines, crucifixes and rosaries, finds an echo in the heart of a people, a stirring, it may be, of the old Catholic tradition, never wholly obliterated. Belief in the efficacy of prayers for the dead is becoming more frequent; and it is dawning on many that their choice must be between the religion of Catholics and no religion at all.'[126]

England was entering an uncertain world in the inter-war years. But it seemed that English Catholics could be quietly confident in a leader willing and able to make a significant contribution to the new order.

Notes

1. Burton, Diary, Sunday, 31 December 1916, CDA.
2. FAB, Lenten Pastoral, *Tablet*, 25 February 1899, p. 312.
3. *WCC*, July 1909, p. 183.
4. FAB, Pastoral Letter, 5 August 1914.
5. FAB, Circular to Clergy, 10 August 1914.
6. *Tablet*, 8 August 1914, p. 205.
7. M. Fletcher, *O, Call Back Yesterday* (Ware: Old Hall Press, 2000), p. 134.
8. *Times*, 2 June 1919.
9. AAW, Bo. V/42d.
10. FAB, Circular to Clergy, 25 July 1915.
11. FAB to Lloyd George, 27 May 1918 (copy), AAW, Bo. IV/4/24; Lloyd George to FAB, 28 May 1918, AAW, Bo. IV/4/27.
12. *Times*, 1 April 1913.
13. *Times*, 24 November 1914 cited J. Davies, '"War is a Scourge": The First Year of the

Great War 1914–1915: Catholics and Pastoral Guidance' in *Recusant History*, 30,3 (2011), p. 488.
14 Hedley, *Catholic Federationist*, January 1915, cited M. Snape, 'British Catholicism and the British Army in the First World War,' *Recusant History*, 26 (2002), p. 323.
15 FAB, Address to Irish troops, Farnborough, 14 November 1915, *Tablet*, 20 November 1915, p. 670.
16 W. Long to FAB, 21 April 1917 [annotated comments 23 May 1917], AAW, Bo. V/50c.
17 Oldmeadow, *Francis Cardinal Bourne*, ii, p. 107.
18 FAB to Lancashire recruits, *Tablet*, 24 October 1914, p. 583.
19 FAB, Homily for St. Albert's Day Mass for Belgians, Westminster Cathedral, 15 November 1918, cited FAB, *Occasional Sermons*, pp. 84–85.
20 FAB, Pastoral Letter, 27 February 1916.
21 FAB, Pastoral Letter, 7 February 1915.
22 C. Plater, SJ, *Catholic Soldiers*, p. 9, cited Snape, 'British Catholicism and the British Army in the First World War,' p. 344.
23 FAB addressing Catholic troops at Rouen, 3 February 1915, *Tablet*, 13 February 1915, p. 208.
24 *Sketch*, February 1915.
25 'The Cardinal Archbishop's Visit to the Fleet, August, 1916,' *WCC*, September 1916, p. 167.
26 FAB, Address to Catholic sailors off Taranto, 27 January 1917, *Tablet*, 17 February 1917, p. 212.
27 Casartelli to Gasquet, 10 November 1917, DAA, Gasquet 889.
28 FAB, Interview with *Corriere d'Italia*, cited *Tablet*, 17 February 1917, p. 217.
29 *Tablet*, 22 August 1914, p. 284.
30 *Tablet*, 26 September 1914, pp. 437, 443.
31 FAB to Hierarchy, 5 November 1914, AAW, Bo. I/16.
32 FAB to Gasquet, 26 February 1915, DAA, Gasquet, 889.
33 O. Weld-Blundell, OSB, to FAB, 13 November 1914, AAW, cited Johnstone & Hagerty, *The Cross on the Sword*, p. 60.
34 FAB to Gasquet, 26 February 1915, DAA, Gasquet, 889.
35 Johnstone & Hagerty, *The Cross on the Sword*, p. 53; FAB, 17 March 1915, *Tablet*, 20 March 1915, p. 370.
36 Bidwell to W. Keatinge, 26 September 1914, cited Johnstone & Hagerty, *The Cross on the Sword*, p. 91.
37 FAB to Hierarchy, 5 November 1914, AAW, Bo. I/16.
38 War Office to Redmond, *New York Freeman's Journal*, 24 November 1914, cited Johnstone & Hagerty, *The Cross on the Sword*, pp. 87–88.
39 FAB to Gasquet, 22 January 1915, DAA, Gasquet, 889.
40 FAB to Redmond, 25 June 1915, NLI, RP, MS 15,172.

41 FAB to Logue, 1916, cited Johnstone & Hagerty, *The Cross on the Sword*, p. 95.
42 Logue, *Irish Catholic*, cited *Tablet*, 19 August 1916, p. 240.
43 Logue, *The Irish Catholic*, 21 March 1917, cited Johnstone & Hagerty, *The Cross on the Sword*, p. 186
44 'A Memorial to the Irish Hierarchy on the question of the Shortage of Catholic Army Chaplains,' *Tablet*, 17 March 1917, p. 342.
45 Keatinge to Rawlinson, 2 July 1917, Rawlinson MSS, DAA, cited Johnstone & Hagerty, *The Cross on the Sword*, p. 96.
46 FAB, *Times*, 25 April 1918.
47 *Edmundian*, July 1917.
48 *Tablet*, 26 December 1914, p. 865.
49 W. Forrest, SAA, cited Johnstone & Hagerty, *The Cross on the Sword*, p. 111.
50 Keatinge, *Tablet*, 28 October 1916, p. 567.
51 Bell, *Randall Davidson*, p. 848.
52 J. Bickersteth, June 1917, cited Snape, 'British Catholicism and the British Army in the First World War,' p. 337.
53 Snape, 'British Catholicism and the British Army in the First World War,' p. 337.
54 Johnstone & Hagerty, *The Cross on the Sword*, p. 174.
55 Snape, 'British Catholicism and the British Army in the First World War,' p. 348.
56 Johnstone & Hagerty, *The Cross on the Sword*, p. 109.
57 'Exile' to Editor, *Tablet*, 24 March 1917, p. 381.
58 Covering note by A. Strange, u/d, 1915, PRO, WO 32/5634.
59 Memorandum, Sir Graham Greene, Admiralty, 9 September 1915, WO 32/5634.
60 Gasquet, Diary, 22 March 1916, cited Leslie, *Cardinal Gasquet*, p. 246.
61 Logue to Benedict XV, February 1916, AAA, Logue Papers, cited Johnstone & Hagerty, *The Cross on the Sword*, p. 182.
62 Sir Henry Howard to Sir Edward Grey, 18 August 1915, WO 32/5634.
63 FAB memorandum, 6–12 December 1915, AAW, Bo. IV/3/5a.
64 FAB to Sir Henry Howard, 12 December 1915, AAW, Chaplains Correspondence, cited Johnstone & Hagerty, *The Cross on the Sword*, p. 181.
65 Gasquet, Diary, 27 March & 28 April 1916, cited Leslie, *Cardinal Gasquet*, pp. 246, 247.
66 Gasquet to FAB, (draft), u/d, DAA, Gasquet, 917A.
67 Gasquet, Diary, 25 May 1916, cited Leslie, *Cardinal Gasquet*, p. 248.
68 Amigo to Logue, 14 July 1916, SAA, Chaplains' Correspondence, cited Johnstone & Hagerty, *The Cross on the Sword*, p. 181.
69 Gasquet, Diary, 8 January 1917, DAA, Gasquet, 902.
70 Gasquet, Diary, 20 January 1917, DAA, Gasquet, 902.
71 Gasquet, Diary, 23 & 25 January 1917, DAA, Gasquet, 902.
72 FAB to Bidwell, 5 February 1917, AAW, Chaplains' Correspondence, cited Johnstone & Hagerty, *The Cross on the Sword*, p. 182.

73 FAB to Bidwell, 13 February 1917, (copy), AAW, Bo. III/124/8.
74 Amigo to Gasquet, 5 April 1917, DAA, Gasquet, 917A.
75 Dunn to Whiteside, 4 July 1917, NotDA, Dunn, G03.03.
76 Amigo to Gasquet, 5 March 1918, DAA, Gasquet, 917A.
77 Sir Charles Wingfield to Sir John Simon, 1934 Annual Report, 12 January 1935, cited T. E. Hachey (ed.), *Anglo-Vatican Relations, 1914–1939: Confidential Annual Reports of the British Ministers to the Holy See* (Boston: Hall & Co, 1972), p. 266.
78 Mgr Vanneufville, *Le Correspondant*, December 1917, cited *Tablet*, 26 January 1918, pp. 125–126.
79 Bell, *Randall Davidson*, pp. 848–849.
80 Lord Derby to FAB, 30 October 1915, AAW, Bo. V/27b.
81 Minutes of Bishops' Meeting, 17 January 1916.
82 FAB to Benedict XV, 26 January 1916 (draft), AAW, Bo. V/27a.
83 FAB to Lloyd George, 22 January 1917 (draft), AAW, Bo. V/27a.
84 FAB to Bidwell, 3 February 1917 (copy), AAW, Bo. V/27a.
85 Brade to Bidwell, 19 February 1917, AAW, Bo. V/27a.
86 FAB to Bidwell, 20 February 1917 (copy), AAW, Bo. V/27a.
87 Amigo to Whiteside, 20 February 1917, LAA, 52 V A/50; 23 February 1917, LAA, 52 V A/51.
88 Bidwell to FAB, 14 March 1917, AAW, Bo. V/27a.
89 FAB addressing alumni of St Charles's, 3 October 1914, cited Oldmeadow, *Francis Cardinal Bourne*, ii, pp. 103–104.
90 Gasquet to FAB, 3 November 1914, AAW, Bo. IV/4/11.
91 Gasquet to FAB, 22 January 1915, AAW, Bo. IV/4/12.
92 FAB homily, Brook Green, 30 May 1915, *Tablet*, 5 June 1915, pp. 730–731.
93 J. Pollard, *The Unknown Pope* (London: Geoffrey Chapman, 1999), p. 97.
94 Gasquet to FAB, 2 December 1917, AAW, Hi. II/168.
95 Parliamentary debate, 6 December 1917, *Daily Telegraph*, 7 December 1917.
96 Amigo to FAB, 30 December 1917, AAW, Hi. II/168.
97 FAB to Benedict XV, 14 December 1917 (copy), AAW, Bo. IV/4/22.
98 Pollard, *The Unknown Pope*, pp. 113, 116.
99 *Ibid.*, pp. 113, 117.
100 Benedict XV address to Consistory, 6 December 1915, *Tablet*, 11 December 1915, p. 759.
101 Pollard, *The Unknown Pope*, p. 123.
102 Benedict XV, Peace Note, cited H. Rope, *Benedict XV* (London: The Catholic Book Club, 1940), p. 128.
103 Pollard, *The Unknown Pope*, p. 126.
104 E. Drummond, Foreign Office, to Talbot, 5 February 1918, AAW, Bo. V/50c.
105 Pollard, *The Unknown Pope*, pp. 127–128.

106. Keating, Homily, 6 September 1917, *Tablet*, 22 September 1917, p. 381.
107. Gasquet, Diary, 9 October 1917, DAA, Gasquet, 902.
108. Editorial, *Tablet*, 18 August 1917, p. 196.
109. FAB, Golders Green, 14 October 1917, *Tablet*, 20 October 1917, p. 511.
110. FAB, cited A. Rhodes, *The Power of Rome in the Twentieth Century*, p. 242.
111. Gasparri to FAB, 25 November 1917, AAW, Roman Letters, Misc./97.
112. FAB interview, *Morning Post*, 5 December 1917.
113. FAB, *Morning Post*, 7 December 1917.
114. FAB, 'The War and the Holy See,' *WCC*, January 1918, pp. 3–5.
115. FAB, Speech, Archbishop's House, 12 February 1928, *Tablet*, 18 February 1928, p. 213.
116. Youssef Taouk, 'The Guild of the Pope's Peace: A British Peace Movement in the First World War,' *Recusant History*, 29 (2008), p. 254.
117. FAB to Norfolk, 16 April 1916, ACA cited Taouk, 'The Guild of the Pope's Peace,' p. 256.
118. FAB, Interview with *Corriere d'Italia*, cited *Tablet*, 17 February 1917, p. 218.
119. FAB, Woodchester, 4 August 1918, *Tablet*, 24 August 1918, p. 212.
120. FAB, Kensington, 8 September 1918, *Tablet*, 14 September 1918, p. 292.
121. FAB, *Observer*, 10 November 1918.
122. FAB, 'The Duty of Catholics at the Dawn of Peace, *WCC*, December 1918, pp.223–224.
123. FAB, Westminster Cathedral, July 1919, cited Oldmeadow, *Francis Cardinal Bourne*, ii, p. 116.
124. FAB, Liverpool, 27 May 1919, *Tablet*, 31 May 1919, p. 667.
125. FAB, Westminster Cathedral, July 1919, cited Oldmeadow, *Francis Cardinal Bourne*, ii, p. 117.
126. FAB, Pastoral Letter, *The Nation's Crisis*, 27 January 1918.

Chapter 17

On the International Stage

'All that concerns international dealings'

By virtue of his family and education Cardinal Bourne avoided narrow insularity. Yet when appointed Archbishop of Westminster he was virtually unknown overseas. After his death his former secretary wrote with justification, 'His influence abroad was very great. He made English Catholicism a vital factor in international life.'[1]

The Archbishop of the capital city of the British Empire would always be exposed to international affairs, especially during and in the aftermath of the First World War. Bourne positively embraced the role. In Westminster he developed a taste for travel and each year spent several weeks overseas. In addition to lengthy stays in Rome, he travelled extensively in Europe and beyond. The Jesuit, Cyril Martindale, found him a welcome exception to the average English Bishop, who had no interest in Catholic affairs overseas. Bourne, in turn, entrusted the drafting of statements on international matters to Martindale.[2]

Bourne's approach to international affairs was typified by his relationship to the Catholic Council for International Relations. Inaugurated in 1923, it sought to promote 'the Peace of Christ' and 'to build up a well instructed Catholic conscience *at home* on all that concerns international dealings [through publications, lectures, study circles and conferences].' The thinking was rather more joined up than with some Catholic bodies in subsequent generations. Although its specific remit was international matters, the Council also promoted general Catholic doctrine and concerns, such as the Church's teaching on education and birth control.[3]

The Cardinal gave the Council his wholehearted backing while always willing to administer a sharp rebuke if he felt it was overstepping its brief. He welcomed its formation, seeing the Council as 'a continuation of the efforts which he had started many years ago, and were more than ever necessary now, to bring international relations more into line with Christian International Law.'[4] As its President, Bourne chaired the

Council's meetings and was in constant contact with its secretary, John Eppstein. He attended the international conference organised in Oxford in August 1925. He urged Catholic colleges and schools to involve themselves to prepare 'their students to take an intelligent interest in its far-reaching activities as they grow up to manhood and womanhood.'[5]

By the standards of the day, the Cardinal was relatively relaxed about lay Catholic initiatives, but he was also aware of their limitations. Eppstein was an idealist and an enthusiast of the type of which the pragmatic Cardinal was deeply suspicious. He reminded Eppstein of the need for the hierarchy's consent and that the Council was 'to be regarded as a body for the purposes of study and for informing the Catholic mind, not for public or executive action.'[6] Bourne deprecated petitioning the Government on matters, such as the submission of all international disputes to arbitration, which he felt fell outside the Church's competence.[7] His patience with Eppstein and Martindale finally snapped when he wrote in November 1925, you 'must really let me go my own way and at my own pace. Rushing things always leads to disaster. I feel that I have done all that I can do, ought to do, and am prepared to do for the present, in the matter of the new Catholic International Confederation.'[8]

'An ill-advised intrusion'[9]

The risk of misinterpretation or unpopularity never prevented the Cardinal from venturing statements on foreign affairs. In his early days at Westminster, he courted controversy as much on his international, as his national, pronouncements.

At the 1906 CTS Conference Bourne condemned the French Government's persecution of the Church and religious orders. His remarks were also aimed at 'public opinion in England [which] is scarcely doing justice to France today.'[10] For his pains, the Archbishop was told by the *Times* not to meddle in another country's domestic affairs. It was not advice he was inclined to accept, then or subsequently, and he set out his reasons for intervention. Noting that the *Times* was scarcely averse to criticising the internal policies of other countries, he upheld the moral duty to intervene. 'To Catholics worthy of the name spiritual interests are of more concern than material interests ... I think most certainly we have the right to protest ... [The Catholic Church is not a national church.] It is a Church which is one organic whole, so that when one part, when one member, is suffering, the whole body is affected.'[11]

In 1909 Bourne again challenged the prejudices of liberal England on a sensitive issue where less courageous men would have remained silent. Appalling atrocities, involving the inhumane treatment of the native population, had been committed in the Belgian Congo when it was the personal property of King Leopold II. However, control of the Congo passed to the Belgian State in August 1908. A Congo Reform Association formed in London proceeded to attack the Belgian Government before it had had the opportunity to implement reforms and whipped up a fury of national indignation. Even Catholics supported the proposal for a British naval blockade of the Congo, and Norfolk advised Bourne 'you would do well to keep out of it. I think it would be most unfortunate if it could be supposed that religious sympathies [for Belgian Catholics] prevented our striving to mitigate a great wrong.'[12]

For the Archbishop, however, it was a matter of justice and he engaged in a public correspondence with Arthur Conan Doyle.[13] He felt that the Belgian Government deserved the opportunity to remedy the situation. He trusted the Belgian Bishops, who assured him that the accounts of atrocities were being exaggerated in order to serve the purposes of Protestant missionaries and British commercial interests. Norfolk was correct; Bourne's motives were misinterpreted. The Press decried the fact that the Catholic Church should hold itself aloof from a great humanitarian crusade.[14] Others, however, including the Belgian Interior Minister, thanked the Archbishop for his willingness to withstand domestic pressure and to articulate the sincere desire of the Belgian Government and people to effect reform. Casartelli was not normally a Bourne ally, but on this occasion he gave credit where it was due. 'Catholics owed a debt of gratitude to the Archbishop of Westminster for the admirable lead he had given them, and for his clear, statesmanlike definition of their position.'[15]

The Archbishop was not slow to point out the hypocrisy of the British establishment. The Portuguese Revolution of 1910 unleashed a sustained wave of well documented anti-clericalism. Bourne denounced the silence of the moral crusaders who had so recently criticised him. 'The British Press is almost entirely silent. The Portuguese Government are treated here with the greatest possible leniency. There are no Albert Hall meetings held in protest. The Established Church raises no outcry. The Nonconformists are silent. It is an example of how the persecutors of the Catholic Church are given the benefit of every doubt.'[16]

The next controversial intervention of the Archbishop saw the identity of his critics reversed. He was castigated by his French-speaking co-religionists and praised by British imperialists. The occasion was the 1910 Eucharistic Congress held in Montreal, the result of Bourne's suggestion made at the London Congress two years earlier.

Bourne had a busy schedule even before the Congress opened. Over 19 days he travelled 6,000 miles across Canada, through the prairies and Rockies to the Pacific. As he went, he preached in parishes and visited Catholic schools, hospitals and religious houses.[17] Although necessarily a cursory acquaintance with the country, it was sufficient for him to appreciate the great issue facing both the Dominion and the local Church, a problem of which Rome was fully aware. It was the linguistic divide at the heart of Canada. Catholicism had been the faith of French speakers, but immigration from Ireland and elsewhere had changed that. Within a decade the proportion of French-speaking Canadians had fallen from one half to one third. The use of French was now confined to Quebec and parts of Ontario. The vast expanses of the Canadian West, with a significant Catholic population, were entirely English speaking, but ecclesiastical appointments failed to reflect this. Without an Anglophone clergy, it was feared that these territories would be lost to the Church.[18] Whether it was wise for a visiting English Archbishop to raise the issue in the context of a Eucharistic Congress was another matter.

But Bourne did not hold back. Speaking in Montreal on 10 September 1910, he praised the French language as the medium in which Canada had first been evangelised, noting that English had been the language of Protestant sects. He then proceeded to lecture his hosts. 'Now the circumstances have changed vastly ... If the mighty nation that Canada is destined to become in the future is to be won for and held to the Catholic Church, this can only be done by making known to a great part of the Canadian people in succeeding generations the mysteries of our faith through the medium of our English speech ... God has allowed the English tongue to be widely spread over the civilised world, and it has acquired an influence which is ever growing. Until the English language, English habits of thought, English literature—in a word the entire English mentality—are brought into the service of the Catholic Church, the saving work of the Catholic Church is impeded and hampered.'[19]

The speech caused uproar. The federal government was delighted. One member wrote to Bourne, 'In the name of the English-speaking

Catholics of Canada, I beg to thank your Grace for the brave and timely words you spoke on Saturday night last in Notre Dame church.'[20] Equally predictably and not unreasonably, the French nationalist leader asked, 'What possible connection can there be between the cult of the Eucharist and the defence of the coasts of British Columbia?'[21] Bourne had anticipated the objection. 'I may seem to have wandered from the purpose of a Eucharistic Congress, which is to glorify and promote devotion to the Most Blessed Eucharist ... [Yet the day of unity of Canadians in the Catholic and Eucharistic faith] cannot dawn until the doctrines of the Catholic Church have been made known to every child of the Canadian nation in his own mother tongue, and are accepted and expressed by him in the language that he learnt from his mother's lips.'[22]

The Archbishop attempted to justify himself in the Press, alleging that he had been misunderstood by his French-speaking audience. He claimed that he had only asked for the English language to have that freedom of expression within the Catholic Church in Western Canada, which French enjoyed in the Eastern Provinces.[23] That is not quite what he had said in Montreal. There had been more than a hint of the manifest destiny of the English language in his original speech.

Most people would have drawn a discreet veil over the matter at that point and waited for the storm to blow over. Not Bourne. He returned to the subject before a less sensitive audience at the 1912 Catholic Congress in Norwich. Again, he claimed not to understand what all the fuss had been about and why people felt he was interfering in disputes which 'are not in any sense my personal concern.' He conceded nothing. 'Now, when nearly two years have passed, let me affirm again, for the satisfaction of all my critics, fair and unfair alike, that what I then said, I believed with all my heart; that I believe it now with, if possible, even greater intensity.' He maintained that a united Canada had a great destiny before it, but only religion, only the Catholic faith, had the capacity to unify Canada. For the sake of the nation, for the sake of the Church, he had addressed the burning issue of language in the hope that the English tongue might be purified and consecrated to the service of the faith.[24] He was entitled to hold such views. They might possibly have been correct. Yet it was surely wrong, discourteous and counter-productive to raise them so publicly in the context of a Congress dedicated to the honour of the Most Holy Eucharist.

Less controversially, the Cardinal advocated an independent Poland from the early stages of the War. Throughout the 1920s he urged the British to acquire a better knowledge of that country, partly because of the intrinsic rights of the Polish people, partly because geography made Poland 'Europe's bulwark against Bolshevik power in the Near East.'[25] He was thus popular with Poles even before his two visits in 1927 and 1929. 'We had heard that Cardinal Bourne well understands our position in the world, and that he was kind enough to point ... that this nation of nearly thirty millions has a right to live and occupy her proper place among the nations. Later on, when some of us were able to go to England to meet His Eminence personally, and speak with him about Polish matters, he would put questions about Poland and its independence with such great sympathy, with such great understanding of what we have felt in our hearts, that his conversation each time used very much to impress us.'[26]

'What is Cardinal Bourne doing in the East?'[27]

The two visits to Poland in the 1920s were not Cardinal Bourne's first time in Eastern Europe. Shortly after the War, he was in the Balkans as part of a three and a half month tour which took him across the Mediterranean to Egypt around the Levant to Turkey, Greece and beyond.

Having spent Christmas 1918 in Rome, he paid an official visit to the Catholics in the British Fleet at Taranto. In Egypt he made an exhaustive inspection of the Catholic schools, which educated 25,000 Egyptians. In Jerusalem he met the Grand Mufti, 'and men of every class and creed came to see me, Latins and Greeks, Melchites and Orthodox, Christians and Moslems.'[28] Having been accorded every courtesy by the British administrations in the Near East, he sailed out of Beirut on a Royal Naval warship. He revelled in the fact that, as the guest of the British High Commissioner, he was 'probably the first Cardinal to visit Constantinople since fall of the Byzantine Empire.'[29] Having visited the Greek Patriarchate, there was time for a trip to Santa Sophia, ostensibly to see for himself the building on which his own Cathedral was loosely based, but also with more weighty considerations to ponder. There were further inspections of British forces in Salonika and Adrianople before the Cardinal proceeded to the Balkans.

By late February 1919 he was in Sofia having audiences with King Boris II of Bulgaria. In Rumania royal trains and limousines were placed at his disposal, and he stayed at the Royal Palace in Bucharest as the guest of King Ferdinand. The last part of his journey was along the Danube on a ship sent by Admiral Troubridge. He was widely feted in Ljubljana and Belgrade, where he was visited by the Yugoslav Prime Minister and the Serbian Orthodox Metropolitan. His travels over, there were audiences with Pope Benedict in Rome, Arthur Balfour in Paris and, finally, George V at Buckingham Palace on 1 April. All this appealed enormously to Bourne's sense of the dignity of the office of Archbishop of Westminster, but it posed obvious questions. 'How came an Archbishop of Westminster to undertake, at such a time, so long a journey ... and was this journey an official one or an unofficial one?'[30] Fortunately, the Cardinal's desire to publicise his perceived achievements meant the mystery initially surrounding the tour was quickly dispelled.

'The primary reason of his journey to the East was that of visiting the Catholic naval chaplains, officers and men, whose immediate ecclesiastical superior he is as superior.'[31] Amigo commented sarcastically of the Cardinal's activities: 'In his Lenten Pastoral he speaks of Divine Providence entrusting him with his present occupations. He would find plenty to occupy him at home.'[32] One should not underestimate, however, the boost to morale given to British Catholics in otherwise forgotten outposts by the head of their own Church. He spoke to them in a language and with an honesty they appreciated. Warning of the need for patience and endurance in peace, as in war, he elicited a response from the ordinary soldier. '"Very encouraging, the Cardinal!" said more than one soldier to me afterwards, "but it's all right; he talked to us straight, and that's the best way." Really everyone was delighted with the Cardinal ... It still surprises me that a visit from one man could give so much pleasure.'[33]

Others quickly recognised the potential value of a British Cardinal in the region in the immediate aftermath of the Allied victory. 'It was suggested by those in authority that my journey might be turned to good account in other respects, and that my visit to countries in the East, where so many important questions have arisen, both political and ecclesiastical, would afford an opportunity of obtaining information that would be valuable to both civil and ecclesiastical rulers, in the consideration of the international situation which has arisen out of the War.'[34]

The War brought the British Empire territorial gains in the Middle East. There were those suspicious of the intentions of the new imperial masters. Under the Ottoman Turks, with the approval of the Holy See,

France had possessed the sole right to protect Christians in the Near East. The British and the Italians considered that right abnegated in the new world order.[35] The French were also concerned about their privileged position in Egyptian education. The Orthodox were nervous given their traditional protector, the Tsar, had been murdered and his regime overthrown. The Pope was anxious both about custody of the Holy Places and the possibility that Santa Sophia might be given to the Orthodox. Calls from the USA for an energetic Protestant proselytism of the Holy Land further alarmed vested interests. The Vatican had received (disputed) allegations that Anglicans were being favoured in Jerusalem to the detriment of Catholics.[36] What would be British policy?

Cardinal Bourne undertook his journey with the full knowledge and approval of the Vatican. He went as a high-ranking English Catholic with a mission to reassure. He began, ironically given his Montreal speech, with the French. At least he had learnt one lesson and this time addressed his audience in Cairo in their own tongue. He received a warm welcome, but objected to the description of England as a 'Protestant State.' 'I would rather say that our Government is "a Christian Government." ... I can, from my own experience, declare that under the influence of the Government of which I am proud to call myself a loyal subject, there is no cause to fear for the progress of religion or for the advancement of education. One may openly be a Catholic, a practising and even a militant Catholic.'[37] In Alexandria he reminded the French that it was England which had sheltered their priests during the Revolution and the anti-clericalism of the Third Republic.[38]

On his return the Cardinal rejected French accusations of anti-Catholic prejudice in the Holy Land. He asserted 'I could find no evidence of any unfair discrimination on religious or national grounds on the part of the British administrators. On the contrary, I satisfied myself that they were doing their best to overcome the necessary and inevitable obstacles which were delaying the reinstatement of various religious institutions.'[39] But he was not above citing French concern to place gentle pressure on British administrators in the Holy Land. Thus, he wrote to General Storrs, the Military Governor of Jerusalem, 'We are sure to be watched very closely by the French and on this account I am very anxious that there should be no unnecessary difficulties with regard to the erection of the hospice which will be necessary for the custodians of the Sanctuary at Gethsemane which the Franciscans, owing to your kind intervention, will now be able to erect.'[40]

Back in London the Cardinal saw the Conservative MP and former intelligence officer, Sir Samuel Hoare, about the future of Santa Sophia. Throughout his tour Bourne enjoyed good relations with the Orthodox. He suggested, therefore, that Constantine's basilica should be returned to Christian worship, Catholic, Orthodox and others having joint use, as at the Holy Sepulchre in Jerusalem.[41] Likely to be less well received by the Orthodox was his advice to the Holy Father to create a Latin Patriarchate of Constantinople. Of course, none of this was implemented. The Foreign and India Offices, conscious of the large Muslim population in the British Empire, vetoed Santa Sophia's return to the Church. The Vatican too seemed more relaxed with the prospect of Santa Sophia as a mosque than the centre of a rival Orthodox establishment.[42]

But if the Church was suspicious of the British, the reverse was also true. They found themselves in possession of lands with an entrenched European presence not necessarily well disposed to the new power. The Latin Patriarch of Jerusalem, an Italian, was considered anti-British. The British in Egypt were uncomfortable about the influence of a Catholic Church largely staffed by French and Italians. They too had expectations and an agenda. They wanted local support for the regime built up through the medium of English education and the appointment of British Catholic Bishops in the region.[43]

Ever the patriotic Englishman, Bourne was happy to concur. Too much so in the opinion of some. 'Perhaps he allowed himself to be too closely associated with the mind of the Government in all this. There is no doubt however that he was absolutely convinced of the Government's complete integrity.'[44] Following a meeting with the British High Commissioner in Cairo, the Cardinal wrote 'fully and confidentially' to both Cardinal Gasparri and the British Minister to the Vatican in support of the appointment of a British Bishop in Egypt.[45] In his discussions with the British-run Education Ministry, the Cardinal displayed a certain realism. It was simply impossible to find sufficient British Catholic nationals to replace foreign members of religious orders in Egypt. Currently, there was no English teaching order able to run Catholic boys' schools. 'With regard to girls' schools the difficulty of obtaining British teaching sisters would probably not be great.'[46]

What were the fruits of Cardinal Bourne's visit to the Near East? His enthusiasm for the imperial project clearly resonated with the British administrators. Sir Reginald Wingate wrote back to his masters in Whitehall, 'I am convinced the political effect of a British Cardinal's presence in this country has been excellent.'[47] The visit brought satisfaction to the Catholic community back home. Even Keating in Northampton could write, 'I beg to offer to you a cordial word of welcome and of congratulation. The mission entrusted to you, in all its circumstances of ecclesiastical and political import, has covered with glory the English Church as well as your Eminence's person.'[48] Amigo noted sourly, 'I am told that he is very pleased with the success of his visit to the East.'[49] In Rome Cardinal Billot was critical: "*ha fatto molto male nell'Oriente.*"[50] But this may simply reflect a Frenchman's prejudice.

The Cardinal's presence went some way to allay fears as the Government intended. Bourne consistently maintained 'that the extension of British influence was in no sense antagonistic to the Catholic religion—that, in a word, the Catholic Church is given fair play and free scope under the British Flag.'[51] His assertions were accepted because they were, on the whole, matched by the subsequent experience of local Christians. But elsewhere he raised expectations he could not fulfil. Others were not going to allow the British to have everything their own way. No sooner had Bourne left the Near East than he was followed in swift succession by Cardinals Giustini[52] and Dubois,[53] representing Italian and French interests respectively.

A year later the administration in Cairo expressed disappointment, 'The policy in regard to increasing British influence on the Roman Catholic community in Egypt has I am afraid failed. The Vatican are no doubt anxious not to antagonise the French Government at a moment when they are, I understand, renewing relations with Rome.'[54] If the Cardinal's visit led to no discernible permanent change in Egypt, the position was different in Palestine. Bourne consistently urged the need for an English-speaking Bishop 'in close contact with the Civil Governor ... having free access to the authorities.'[55] Mgr Godric Kean of Salford was appointed Auxiliary Bishop of the Latin Patriarchate of Jerusalem in 1924, and a handful of British subjects were ordained to serve the local Catholic population. The Cardinal enthusiastically endorsed plans for Maltese immigration in the Holy Land.[56] In the Catholic Women's League Bourne had an organisation willing and able to help implement his vision of the Catholic Church working in harmony with the British Empire for the good of humanity. Under his patronage, the CWL established the Bethlehem Settlement, founding schools teaching in English.[57]

The British and the Vatican had fewer interests in the Balkans and the Cardinal was, consequently, a freer agent to form his own opinions. He did so willingly, regardless of whether any ecclesiastical interests were at stake. He warmed immediately to the young Bulgarian king, whom he felt represented the best hope of stability against the Bolshevik threat. Accordingly, he pressed the Foreign Secretary to mitigate the terms to be imposed on Bulgaria, as one of the Central Powers, at the Peace Conference.[58] British diplomats thought Bourne's impressions necessarily superficial given his limited acquaintance with the countries he had visited, but conceded that he had understood the 'salient points' and did him the credit of forwarding his views to the Foreign Secretary.[59]

In Yugoslavia he promised the people that 'he would do all in his power to elucidate public opinion and the opinion of those who were shaping the future of Europe in respect to the newer and acute problems that troubled their national existence.'[60] He took to heart their fears of Italian designs against their new country. In Rome he lectured the Pope on the urgent need to fill vacant sees and counselled him to avoid 'any appearance of Italian sympathies at the Vatican.'[61]

Cardinal Bourne's tour had been undertaken to improve relations between the British Government and the Catholic Church in 'countries in which the problems of the future were likely to be specially acute.' He went 'to allay groundless fears, to dissipate misapprehensions, and to gather at first-hand information ... which would help Church and State to arrive ultimately at conclusions satisfactory to both alike.'[62] In furthering these objectives the Cardinal could indeed feel pleased with himself.

'Without the smallest anti-Jewish prejudice'[63]

More than any other place visited on his extended tour of 1918–19, it was Palestine which was to occupy Cardinal Bourne over the years ahead.

At a time when mild anti-Semitism was perfectly acceptable in English society, Bourne held remarkably enlightened views. English Jews always remembered that he stood up for those being massacred in the Russian pogroms. He spoke unequivocally at the Queen's Hall in January 1906. 'We desire to raise our voices with the voices of the oppressed so that the sound, if not heard in Russia, may be carried all over the world ... We ask for no privilege, no exceptional treatment of any kind, but equal rights of all before the law.'[64] Bourne's support was not limited to protest meetings. He wrote twice to Pius X urging him to do all he could to end the killing. Merry del Val replied that the Pope would act, but urged Bourne to moderate his fervour; Rome could not be seen to act at the bidding of the Chief Rabbi.[65] The Cardinal defended Russian Jews again in 1913, denouncing false accusations of ritual murder being used to justify renewed persecution. His support for the Chief Rabbi earned him the disapproval of the French Catholic Press.[66]

Something changed following the Cardinal's visit to Palestine in January 1919. He remained without any trace of racial prejudice. But he was deeply disturbed by what he had witnessed. In their desire to defend the Suez Canal on one flank and Middle Eastern oil pipelines on the other, the British had made irreconcilable promises to the French, Arabs and Jews which were to be the cause of great strife in the future. The Cardinal strongly objected to political Zionism, the attempt after the Balfour Declaration of November 1917 to create a National Jewish home or Jewish State in Palestine. He did so because he felt the practical consequences were profoundly unjust and destabilising.

The Cardinal found the situation in the Holy Land 'distinctly menacing.' The Jews arriving in Palestine were seeking not simply refuge, but domination. With their greater financial resources, they threatened to swamp Palestine. There were fears that both land and political control would pass into Jewish hands. Local Arabs resented Zionist policies such as positive discrimination in favour of the Hebrew language. 'This naturally aroused a fierce resistance on the part of the indigenous native Arab population, both Moslem and Christian.'[67] The Cardinal mused that the Allies had promoted the principle of 'self-determination' in the Peace Conference of Versailles; yet flouted that very principle in Palestine.[68] He queried why Christian armies had fought to oust the Ottomans from Jerusalem simply to hand it over to 'a new non-Christian power.'[69]

This was not just special pleading on behalf of Catholics. The Cardinal was genuinely concerned by the plight of all Arabs, Muslim and Christian, who had pleaded with him during his visit and who continued to write to him in Westminster. The Palestine Arab Delegation turned to him in autumn 1921, 'We call upon the help of all Christian communities in this our struggle to prevent this great calamity befalling us, which means our death as a free and independent people, and we have every hope that

Christendom will not fail us in this hour of need.'⁷⁰ Had Bourne had his way, their aspirations would have been met. For him the Palestine Mandate granted by the League of Nations to Britain had just one purpose: to 'lift up the Syrian [ie local Arab] population and teach them self-government.'⁷¹

Cardinal Bourne was deeply embarrassed by the fact that his own country was responsible for the original injustice, and this galvanised him to seek redress. He was extremely critical of Balfour for making such a disputed and dangerous promise. For his own part, he was unable to comprehend whether, in doing so, Balfour had been simply flippant or had genuinely failed to understand the import of his actions.⁷² In either event the Cardinal was determined immediately to bring 'to the attention of those concerned his profound conviction of the dangers and difficulties of this new policy.'⁷³

He meant what he said. When the Cardinal met Balfour in Paris, the Foreign Secretary professed himself 'really startled when I told him some of the facts concerning [Zionism].'⁷⁴ Bourne proceeded to take his concerns further, asking Talbot to pursue the matter with Lloyd George. The Prime Minister sought to pacify Bourne. 'He said he had no intention of [Zionism] being allowed to develop on the lines indicated and feared by you ... He knew Balfour had been vague and was more disposed to favour the Zionist movement than he was himself.'⁷⁵ The Cardinal might have been wise to wait until platitudes were translated into definite policies, but he was sufficiently encouraged to write to General Storrs in Jerusalem, 'I hope that you are keeping quite well and that Zionism is dead or at least moribund. I have done my best to hasten its demise.'⁷⁶

Of course, this was not the end of the story. Cardinal Bourne defended Sir Herbert Samuel as 'a very upright man' and counselled the British public against believing the slurs cast against him by 'some of our foreign friends, especially in Italy and France.'⁷⁷ Yet it was crucial that, in such a volatile situation, the British administration in Palestine was not only objective, but also seen to be so. Presumably, the *Tablet* had the Cardinal's authority to write, 'The situation of Sir Herbert Samuel has become impossible. In the circumstances now existing in Palestine, the British High Commissioner ought not to be a Jew. The chief officer of the British Executive ought not only to be impartial but high above suspicion. The Arabs know that the man who rules in the name of Great Britain is hailed by the Jews as "our Samuel."'⁷⁸

When it came to be ratified, the Vatican held no principled objection to the British Mandate in Palestine. But, as drafted, Rome felt that '(1) the Jews would have given them a privileged and preponderant position over Catholics and generally over other nationalities and religious confessions; and (2) the rights of Christian confessions and especially the Catholic confession would not be adequately safeguarded.'[79] Bourne was asked to negotiate with Lloyd George.[80] Whatever concessions he was promised 'for the protection of Catholic interests in Palestine' 'profoundly satisfied' the Pope.[81] The Vatican was mollified by the decision to appoint a Catholic as the Christian delegate on the Commission to determine the custody of the Holy Places.[82]

We are so accustomed to Middle Eastern conflict, to hostility between Jew and Arab, that we overlook quite how prescient the Cardinal was in this matter. Well into the 1920s he displayed a tremendous persistence on the subject of Zionism, raising it at every opportunity. He did so most notably at the CTS Conference in Leicester in 1921. He assured his audience he was no anti-Semite. 'I have no word to say against the Jews, as such. I have stood up for them on the public platform once before and claimed fair play and just treatment, but I feel quite certain that unless this question of Zionists is settled in a way that is fair and just to the immensely larger non-Jewish population of Palestine, there will be terrible trouble in the future.' Unusually for the Cardinal, he sounded an apocalyptic note. 'We are going to have terrible difficulties in Palestine, and England is going to have enormous difficulties with the other Christian countries of the world, unless this matter is satisfactorily cleared up.'[83]

Such was the surprise of the *Jewish Chronicle* at their former friend's vehemence that it assumed 'the outburst' did not represent his own views, but was dictated by 'a higher authority,' probably Gasparri, who resented British partiality to Zionism.[84] (At Bourne's death, the newspaper magnanimously preferred to overlook the speech and 'to remember only the qualities of a great man and a splendid religious leader.'[85]) The Latin Patriarch in Jerusalem read the Cardinal's mind more accurately and thanked him accordingly. 'In this sad plight we are the more grateful for the noble declarations of Your Eminence. We are sure that they are a true expression of the English soul whose instinct is justice. Whatever the future may have in store for them, the people of Palestine will never forget the noble stand made on behalf of their rights by one of England's most devoted and illustrious sons.'[86]

When the Cardinal returned to Palestine on pilgrimage in 1924 he noted the improved situation. 'There is no longer the same unwise insistence on an untenable domination on the part of the Zionist.'[87] He was not to live to see the intolerable pressure placed on the system by Jews fleeing Nazi persecution in the 1930s, nor the fulfilment of his prediction of widespread conflict.

The League of Nations

By 1917 many, including Catholic clergy, were turning their attention to the international order which would prevail after the War in the hope that killing and destruction on such a massive scale might be avoided in future. The Jesuits in particular felt that any such attempt had to be informed by the moral principles of the Catholic Church. Accordingly, Cardinal Bourne requested Fr Joseph Keating SJ to represent the Church on the Clergy Auxiliary Committee of the League of Nations Society. The Society sought 'the cooperation of the clergy to educate public opinion to discard war in favour of arbitration as a method of settling international disputes.'[88]

The Cardinal's attitude towards the League was absolutely consistent. He recognised that 'the only real effort so far to substitute mutual understanding for the clash of hostile nations is to be found in the League of Nations,'[89] and, therefore, gave the League his unfailing support. But not without reservations.

Unlike too many at the League of Nations, the Cardinal was no utopian. He readily acknowledged the League's successes, but also pointed to its failings. These were not, however, to prevent the involvement of Catholics in the League's work. 'If we wait until we have something that is perfect we shall have to wait for ever.'[90] The Cardinal was, of course, critical of the League when it appeared to adopt the Allied attitude towards the Holy See, denying and excluding its influence in the life of the international community. Catholics were uneasy about the obligation to commit member states to declare war in certain contingencies.[91] Even before the rise of Nazism, Bourne sounded a cautionary note about a racist tendency in certain quarters of the League. 'It is mixed up with the nonsense which is constantly talked about the superiority of what are strangely called Nordic nations over Latin races.'[92] By the standards of the day, the Cardinal was no clericalist. He turned down a request from the Archbishop of Canterbury to attend a conference while the League of Nations project was still in

371

embryonic form. He 'felt that statesmen and diplomats were alone competent to work out the details.' Laymen, not clerics, were the competent authority when it came to the practical management of international affairs. 'If a workable scheme can be devised it goes without saying that it will have the support of Catholics throughout the world.'[93]

Once the practical details had been worked out, the Cardinal fulfilled his promise. Together with the Archbishops of Canterbury and York, he accepted Lord Robert Cecil's invitation to become a Vice-President of the League of Nations Union. He offered Cecil all possible support. He wrote in similar terms to the secretary. 'So far as my own Diocese of Westminster is concerned I am most willing that the clergy should give the League of Nations Union every assistance in their power. I beg God to bless the purposes of the Union and to bring them success.'[94] He was happy to associate the Catholic Church with an appeal from other Christian leaders to the Prime Minister to support the League.[95]

The Cardinal called fellow Catholics to active involvement. (Indeed, the first Secretary of the League of Nations was a British Catholic, Sir Eric Drummond, later Earl of Perth.) Only through involvement could Catholics hope to shape the policies of the League. 'It would be a good thing for many Catholics to be members—of what is called the League of Nations' Union, because in that way they may be able to exercise the influence of which I speak.'[96]

At the end of his life the Cardinal saw with foreboding the threat posed by Nazi aggression. He acknowledged 'the League of Nations has indeed within it seeds of fundamental weakness.' He regretted the United States' refusal to join the League, and the inclusion in 1934 of Soviet Russia. 'Peace can only be founded on Christian principles, and the Russian Government has very forcibly overthrown those principles.' But this was not, in his opinion, a reason to disengage. 'It is the duty of all Catholics, by word and action, to give all the support they can to the League of Nations and to endeavour so to improve it as to make it a real and permanent instrument for the preservation of the peace of the world.'[97] Four years later—admittedly in a significantly different international situation—his successor adopted a different approach. Cardinal Hinsley resigned as Vice-President of the League of Nations Union because of its perceived partiality to the Spanish Republicans and its identification with the International Peace Campaign.[98]

Bourne was both a committed internationalist and a pragmatic realist. Offering unwavering support to the principles of the League of Nations, he could be fiercely independent of particular policies. He never accepted unconditionally the principle of 'self-determination.' (He knew only too well that the Allies ignored the principle when it clashed with their interests, as in Palestine and the South Tyrol.[99]) With an eye on India and the Empire, he slammed the principle in his 1921 Lenten Pastoral Letter. 'The foolish catchword "self-determination," ill-defined and wrongly interpreted, has always wrought untold harm in Europe, for it has led men to think that political frontiers may safely be made dependent solely on the racial unity and characteristics of peoples, without thought of the geographical, historical, social and economic conditions which so largely govern the uprising and delimitation and final constitution of the nations.'[100]

The Dictators

In the years immediately following the War Cardinal Bourne preached a message very different to that of certain European demagogues. 'At the present time there was a danger that the love of country might show itself in an exaggerated spirit of nationalism ... Men forgot that nations were inter-dependent ... All over Europe there was a real danger that the hatred engendered by the war might be maintained too long, and that men might attach so much importance to their own particular country and their own national aspirations that it might conflict with the law of brotherly love ... They must forgive and forget if the world was once more to be regenerated.'[101]

As a Cardinal of the Universal Church who loved his country, Bourne avoided the extremes of nationalism and internationalism which plagued the first half of the twentieth century. His Catholicism provided this sense of balance. He deliberately repeated his message to Italians whose homeland was wrought with tensions between their Catholic faith and Mussolini's Fascism. 'Nationalism and nationhood was a God-given right ... but nationality, although perfectly legitimate, was possessed of definite limitations, too often overlooked. A grave error was committed by the exponents of self-determination ... No nation could be self-determined, as the Providence of Almighty God determined all things, and nations were determined by circumstances connected with history, geography, economics, politics, dynasty and other factors, making "self" determination a fallacy. The reverse to nationalism was found among those who exploited internationalism and would sweep away all nationhood, which was quite impractical.'[102]

Long before Nazism made its presence felt on the international stage, the Church had to respond to the claims of Italian Fascism. As Bourne's mouthpiece, the *Tablet* had no truck with Fascism's appeal to patriotism or its assertion to be a bulwark against Socialism and Communism. Fascists were responsible for 'deplorable excesses, and naturally attracted to themselves numbers of undesirables who were spoiling for trouble ... Their methods so far are decidedly too dangerous to be maintained.' Because the Church stood apart from Fascism, her property and institutions suffered widespread outrages. These were detailed by the *Tablet*, which readily admitted that Catholics were not the only victims.[103] The Cardinal himself condemned Mussolini's restrictions on the freedom of the Church.[104] In this he was not always at one with other members of the hierarchy; Amigo was unequivocal in his public support for Mussolini and, later, Franco.

So much insidious nonsense has been spoken about 'Hitler's Pope' that Catholics instinctively feel that they must have something to be ashamed of. They should read the *Tablet* of the early 1930s. The Cardinal himself visited the Rhineland and Bavaria in 1930, but Hitler became German Chancellor only after Bourne's final illness effectively withdrew him from the international stage. Even before the Nazis came to power, however, the principal British Catholic journal—in stark contrast to the Rothermere Press—criticised each week the programme and action of Hitler's party. The threat was identified at an early stage. 'Nazism becomes more and more a menace to Germany, and therefore, to all Europe ... The Catholic Church in Germany will have difficulty in avoiding an open conflict with Nazism.'[105]

The *Tablet* appealed to British Catholics to support their co-religionists in the fight against Nazism and was in contact 'with Catholic priests and laity in several German centres, including Cologne, where a beginning of moral and intellectual cooperation with Englishmen has already been made.'[106] German pastoral letters and homilies were regularly quoted. 'It is impossible to concede the least licence to a party such as the National Socialists, which is in opposition to Catholic principles on most important points. The Church is in duty bound to enlighten the faithful in a most precise manner on the character of the National Socialist party, and to put her children on their guard against the menace to religion offered by that party. Our clergy have not only the right, but the duty of warning their flocks in this matter ... We grant that a rapid growth of Hitlerism in the Reich might create difficulties for Catholics, but we do not surrender our principles for the sake of a quiet life.'[107]

Even if not personally writing its editorials, the Cardinal at the very least tolerated the *Tablet's* policy and activities. In his own Diocese the *Cathedral Chronicle* was similarly strident in its condemnation of 'Hitler, the adversary of the Christian Ideal.'[108] It was not simply due to the threat to the Church that these two Catholic journals waged their honourable campaign. The *Tablet* also condemned the anti-Semitic rioting which accompanied the Nazi seizure of the Reichstag building in 1930.[109]

Unfortunately, Cardinal Bourne chose not to give public support to meetings protesting against the treatment of German Jews. There was no question of any sympathy for the Nazi regime. Rather he felt that Catholics had not received the support to which they were entitled. 'The Jews have not at any time raised any protest against the persecution of Catholics which has so recently taken place in Russia, Mexico and Spain.'[110] While the Cardinal's response should have been based on justice rather than reciprocity, Amigo gave exactly the same answer in Southwark.[111]

Bolshevism had been around for rather longer; its opposition to religion was more total and explicit. The Cardinal's denunciation of Soviet Russia was equally absolute: 'Moscow's is a diabolical movement against civilisation.'[112] He defended his right to criticise on the grounds that 'Moscow herself has given this matter an international complexion by proclaiming that her aim is to achieve revolutions, of an anti-God character, throughout the world and not only within her own frontiers.'[113] Nevertheless, whatever threat Communism posed to the Church and world peace, this did not justify support for the Nazis. 'Herr Hitler is not Europe's sole White Hope against Red Russia.'[114]

We can surmise that the Cardinal would have been no supporter of appeasement. His political judgment was too good, his assessment of human nature too accurate. These informed his response to calls for disarmament. He declined to participate in a 'Disarmament Week' in 1931, feeling it highly imprudent for Britain to disarm further when Russia refused to engage in the process.[115] The experience of the First World War did not justify recklessness with national security. 'Great as were the dangers of the War, they were now face to face with still graver dangers.'[116] He spoke similarly to the CCIR. 'It was the manifest duty of Catholics to pray and work for peace, but if disarmament was to take place it could only be on the assumption that the right of a nation to protect itself, by force of arms if necessary, should be safeguarded ... Could it be truly said at the present time that the League of Nations fully commanded the confidence of all nations and was in a position to settle international disputes and to guarantee security to any menaced nation? Would anyone undertake to say that the League of Nations was in a position to guarantee a disarmed France against hostile attack? Can we honestly say to the Poles that they are wrong in maintaining an army? Was it not true to say that Great Britain had already disarmed to the limit of safety?'[117] Eight years before World War II Bourne was closer to Winston Churchill than Neville Chamberlain.

'The Vatican: where incidentally he is not popular'[118]

Francis Bourne was a Roman Catholic who had no inhibitions in criticising Rome when he felt that justified, which was often. Normally his barbs were reserved for officials of the Roman Curia, but there were occasions when the Pope himself was treated to the full force of the Archbishop of Westminster's views. Temperament and education conditioned Bourne's attitude. His seminary years had not been spent in Rome, preparing him for the workings of the Holy See. He had no time for the Italian concept of *bella figura*, the concern for image and reputation. He was a blunt Anglo-Saxon for whom substance was everything. He preferred to correspond in French rather than Latin.[119] If he felt uncomfortable dealing with Rome, most Romans reciprocated. At his death the Anglican *Church Times* alleged that the Cardinal's fierce patriotism had made him '*persona ingrata* in Rome.'[120]

Bourne's first major clash with the Roman Curia concerned Edward VII's funeral in May 1910. He thought it perfectly natural that British Catholics should mark the day with a special Mass and sought permission from the Vatican.[121] Refusal—because the date fell within the Pentecost octave—caused him very great astonishment.[122] (Disingenuously, the Bishops announced that they had substituted Benediction for Mass for the convenience of their people.[123]) In the frankest terms, the Archbishop told the Pope of the potential damage the decision could cause in a Protestant nation.[124] Pius X was unaccustomed to being addressed with such candour. Bourne received a letter from Fr David Fleming, Gasquet's confidante: 'I have been informed indirectly *but on the very best authority* that your letter of 29 May to his Holiness *was most displeasing to him*.'[125] On every score Bourne was unimpressed, not least that his confidential letter to the Pope had been shown to Fleming. He aired his grievances to Merry del Val. 'I personally am with reason profoundly distrustful of [Fleming], and the Bishops who have had dealings with him share this feeling of distrust. It would on this account be very unfortunate were the Holy Office to employ him as a means of communication with the Bishops here or in matters that concern them.'[126] It was by no means an isolated incident.

Bourne had particularly bad relations with Cardinal Bisleti, Prefect of the Congregation for Catholic Education, and was furious when a book written by Fr John Vance, a lecturer at St Edmund's, Ware, was censured by the Holy Office. The Cardinal pointed out that Vance's book had received all the requisite local permissions. The Holy Office decree, he felt, was 'absolutely unjust.' Vance was simply caught up in a dispute between the Thomistic school of Louvain, which Vance followed, and that of Rome. The Cardinal objected most strongly to Rome's 'arbitrary' methods. Such a method of proceeding, Bourne maintained, did the Catholic Church no good. 'I write out of affection for the Holy Father who is made responsible for all these things, and out of devotion to the interests of the Church which suffer in a country like ours so terribly from methods quite alien to national instinct and sentiments.'[127]

Bourne and Bisleti crossed swords again over St Edmund's the following decade. The Englishman had no confidence in the Italian. 'Cardinal Bisleti has no personal knowledge of conditions outside Italy; he views everything through Italian spectacles and this makes him unjust to other nations.' The Archbishop of Westminster unburdened himself to Lépicier, now also a curial Cardinal, whose help he sought. 'While there has never been a greater reverence for the Apostolic Chair nor greater devotion to the person of the Pontiff, there is a growing want of confidence in the competence, wisdom and fairness of the Roman Congregations ... I have often been worried quite unnecessarily by the action of those Congregations. I cannot recall a single instance in which I have sought guidance or assistance and received the least real help. In real emergencies they evade the issues ... The excessive centralisation and *italianisation* of the Holy See—even to the extent of substituting Italian for Latin in official letters and in the daily work of the Congregations—is the great menace of the Church today.'[128] As a Frenchman, Lépicier was only too willing to confirm Bourne's view of the Vatican.[129]

Another spat with the Holy Office concerned a convert clergyman cousin of the Prime Minister, Stanley Baldwin, who was seeking Ordination. The Cardinal resented Rome's request for further information when he sought the necessary dispensations. 'It is equivalent to telling me that the Holy Office does not trust my judgment or believe my word. Naturally I do not ask for the dispensation without satisfying myself as to Mr Baldwin's history, qualifications, '*scientia competens*,' suitability for work in my diocese, etc., etc. Why then ask endless questions and treat me as though I was withholding information, or endeavouring to obtain a dispensation for one unworthy of it. If the Holy Office cannot trust me in a matter of this kind or accept my word, it is surely a waste of my time to continue sending in my application. I cannot believe that you have realised the nature of the letter sent to me or its implications. I regard it as a communication unworthy of the Holy See and offensive to me personally as a Bishop and a Cardinal.'[130]

It could legitimately be pointed out, as Gasquet attempted during the military chaplaincy dispute, that Bourne failed to make life easy for himself. As a Catholic Bishop, he was bound to have dealings with the Roman Curia. Why not simply accept, and accommodate, their manner of proceeding? More could be achieved through charm and contact than through constant conflict. Instead, Bourne had a reputation in Rome for being difficult.

There was a lighter side to all of this. Canon Reggie Fuller was a remarkable survivor, someone who knew Cardinal Bourne personally, was ordained by him in 1931 and lived almost another 80 years. He recalled with perfect clarity the Cardinal's attitude. 'He didn't care very much for the Curia in Rome. He tolerated the Curia—usually with a few cracks.' Fuller remembered an incident concerning bicycles at St Edmund's. Seminarians were issued with them given they were in the midst of the countryside. They cycled in the course of catechetical work and their duties with the SVP and the Legion of Mary, also visiting tea shops on their free day. The Congregation in Rome wrote to the Cardinal asking whether this permission was not a temptation to sin. The Cardinal chose to ignore their enquiry.[131]

Bourne's relations with Rome were typified by his dealings with the English College, the national seminary in Rome, which he felt characterised the Roman system. The College saw itself as the centre of English Catholic life in Rome, and it was, therefore, a considerable statement by the Cardinal when in the Eternal City to make his residence with the

Sulpicians or the Redemptorists. Bourne made himself unpopular in Rome by refusing to send seminarians to study there. But he had his reasons dating back to his time in Southwark. He told Cardinal Vaughan that he had 'a very strong objection to sending a youth of immature mind to pass so long a time as seven years in Rome according to the system in vogue at the English College.'[132] In addition to an inadequate formation, Bourne deprecated the failure to liaise with Bishops. 'If the authorities of the College would take the Bishops into their confidence, and pay some little attention to their wishes, there would be no difficulty in improving its condition.'[133] His correspondence with the Rector demonstrates his lack of confidence in the College's ability to consult the relevant Bishop on the most basic issues concerning his student's formation and welfare.[134]

Given these actions and comments, some might be inclined to claim him as a forerunner for a certain strain of Catholicism in the post-Conciliar Church in Britain. That would be a mistake. There is a crucial distinction. Cardinal Bourne was quite prepared to fulminate against practical decisions of the Vatican when he felt them to militate against the interests of the English Church, of which he, of course, was the better judge. Yet never at any time was there a hint of dissent in questions of the doctrine and discipline of the Church. In these matters he was at all times faithful to Christ and His Vicar.

On one important issue Cardinal Bourne's stance was approved by the Vatican. It concerned *the* Roman Question, the status of the Pope who had once been the temporal ruler of central Italy but who was now reduced to being 'the Prisoner of Vatican' after Italian unification and Garibaldi's storming of Rome in 1870. Bourne broached the subject in a major speech at the 1911 Catholic Congress in Newcastle.

The Archbishop waxed lyrical on the British fascination with Italian culture. He sympathised with the legitimate Italian desire for unification. But he insisted on the need for a just and permanent resolution of the situation of the Holy See. The independence of the Papacy, he said, could not be subject to 'a fluctuating Parliamentary majority.' Importantly, he avoided any reference to 'the Temporal Power,' with its implicit challenge to the legitimacy of the Italian State. Instead, Bourne spoke of 'the civil independence of the Pope.' 'There is no desire on the part of the Papacy for temporal dominion as such, there is no lust of territory ... So long as those spiritual things are duly and really and incontestably safeguarded, the extent of the civil independence which guarantees them is a matter of a very small account.' The Archbishop cited the examples of San Marino, Andorra and Monaco.[135] It all sounded so very reasonable. Who could object? Crucially, the Holy See itself did not object. Bourne noted, 'The *Osservatore Romano* has reproduced all that I said about the Holy See, so that evidently the line which I have taken is acceptable.'[136] (Was it coincidental that Bourne learnt ten weeks later that he was finally to be created a Cardinal?)

It was an idea whose moment had not yet come, but it was not forgotten. Just before the end of the War Bourne prevailed upon Cardinal Gibbons of Baltimore to raise with President Wilson the possibility of having the Roman Question placed on the table at the Peace Conference.[137]

On his way to the Near East, the Cardinal saw Benedict XV and Gasparri. Wishing to avoid any reference to the suggestion emanating from the Holy See, they wanted the British Cardinal to float publicly through the *Tablet* a definitive settlement of the dispute between the Papacy and the Kingdom of Italy. This was to be upon the basis of Bourne's Newcastle speech, laid out in more detail in a memorandum he had drawn up. The Holy See sought sovereignty over St. Peter's together with 'several thousands of acres of the land behind and north of the Vatican ... for the Offices needed for his administration of the Universal Church, and for the residence of the Cardinals in Curia and the other necessary officials.' The Italian State was to make a one off capital payment to the Holy See for the building of these offices. In return, the Holy See would formally renounce its claim to the remainder of the city of Rome, which it would recognise as the capital of a unified Italy. This arrangement would be endorsed by the Peace Conference at Versailles. Bourne asked Talbot to raise the proposal with the Foreign Secretary and to keep it to the fore of his mind.[138]

The *Tablet* duly ran its Article, 'The Pope and the Powers', on the opening day of the Peace Conference, but there was a reluctance in the British Government and elsewhere to advance the matter. Yet when the Lateran Treaty between the Holy See and Italy was signed in 1929, there was a remarkable similarity to the terms proposed by Cardinal Bourne in the preceding decade—only a rather smaller area being conceded to the Vatican. He spoke at length about the Lateran Treaty in his Easter Sunday homily, but made no reference to his own earlier attempts at reconciliation. 'One thing only is necessary for sovereignty—namely, to be absolutely *sui juris*—not to be the subject of another. This sovereignty may be rooted in a purely spiritual function ... But Peter and his successors, as mortal men, must have a foothold for their feet, a place in which to dwell, a territory in which to exercise the necessary and essential functions of their purely spiritual charge and sovereignty.' He rejoiced that the independence of the Pope had been secured.[139]

Sir Alec Randall was the Secretary to the British Mission to the Vatican in the late 1920s. He noted one peculiar feature of the arrangement. 'It was unilateral ... it was not necessary to have a Nuncio in London. Full diplomatic relations were adequately secured by the Minister in Rome, and if there happened to be any business which could not be transacted by him it could be handled in an informal way by the Cardinal Archbishop of Westminster (or his representative) who at one time was often to be seen in the Colonial Office, discussing missionary affairs.'[140] Bourne agreed with this assessment. At the time the British Mission was established, he pointed out 'to Mgr Pacelli the much stronger position that the Archbishop of a capital holds in dealing with a government than that held by a Nuncio who is debarred from using those political and parliamentary influences which the Archbishop can freely exercise.'[141]

Others were less certain. The Archbishop of Westminster might indeed know his way around Whitehall. But he was not a professional diplomat, and lacked diplomatic training. There was also a potential conflict of interest, especially when he was not in agreement with other members of the hierarchy. The Foreign Office picked up on this tension. 'The majority of Catholic Bishops in England would favour [the appointment of a Nuncio] since under the present circumstances the Archbishop of Westminster is inclined to arrogate to himself a primacy over the other Catholic Archbishops and Bishops to which he is not entitled.'[142]

The British Government was inconsistent. Rather than use the official diplomatic channels, Lloyd George specifically asked Bourne to communicate to the Pope news of the appointment of Lord FitzAlan (the former Lord Edmund Talbot) as Viceroy of Ireland because he was thought to be a more secure channel.[143] The Cardinal was understandably irritated, therefore, when the Labour Government initially refused to receive from his hands a copy of the newly ratified Lateran Treaty, asking that it be sent instead through the British Minister at the Vatican. He vented his frustration in a letter to the Foreign Secretary, 'From all previous Governments, I have received consideration on many similar occasions and I regret that there should be a break in a pleasant tradition. Although he holds no strictly diplomatic position, the Archbishop of Westminster does represent the Catholic Church in this country and is officially appointed by the Holy See to do so. Successive Governments have for nearly eighty years—and very notably in my own case—made use of his good offices in dealing with the Holy See, not, I believe, without mutual advantage.'[144]

FitzAlan's intervention led to a Government climb down in that instance, but the diplomatic status of the Archbishop of Westminster continued to be a minor irritant for the remainder of the Cardinal's life. His death and the appointment of a new British Minister to the Vatican allowed Amigo the opportunity to press for a change. The Holy See finally appointed its own accredited to representative to the Court of St James in 1938, relieving the Archbishop of Westminster of both a potential source of influence and of embarrassment.

Notes

[1] Jackman, 'Francis Cardinal Bourne,' *The Dublin Review*, April 1935, pp. 177–195.
[2] P. Caraman, SJ, *C. C. Martindale* (London: Longmans, 1967), p. 191.
[3] Lord Morris to the English hierarchy, 1 January 1926, AAW, Bo. V/64.
[4] Minutes of CCIR Meeting, 19 June 1924, AAW, Bo. V/64.
[5] FAB to Lord Campden, 5 February 1926, AAW, Bo. V/64.
[6] FAB to Eppstein, 24 March 1925 (copy), AAW, Bo. V/64.
[7] FAB to Eppstein, 11 July 1925 (copy), AAW, Bo. V/64.
[8] FAB to Martindale, 19 November 1925 (copy), AAW, Bo. V/64.
[9] *Times*, September 1906.
[10] FAB, CTS Conference, Brighton, 23 September 1906, *Tablet*, 29 September 1906, p. 484.
[11] FAB, Guild of Ransom Annual Reunion, 15 October 1906, *Tablet*, 20 October 1906, p. 623.
[12] Norfolk to FAB, 24 October 1909, AAW, Bo. III/5.
[13] FAB to A. Conan Doyle, 30 October 1909, cited *Tablet*, 6 November 1909, p. 742.
[14] *Westminster Gazette*, 5 November 1909.
[15] Casartelli, Homily, 28 November 1909, *Tablet*, 4 December 1909, p. 902.
[16] FAB, Speech, early 1911, cited Oldmeadow, *Francis Cardinal Bourne*, ii, p. 91.
[17] Editorial, *Tablet*, 17 September 1910, p. 441.
[18] Roman correspondent, *Tablet*, 18 June 1910, p. 973.
[19] FAB, Eucharistic Congress, Montreal, 10 September 1910, cited *Tablet*, 24 September 1910, pp. 514–515.
[20] C. Murphy, Secretariat of State, Ottawa, 12 September 1910, AAW, Bo. I/18.

21 M. Borassa, cited Meynell, *A Record of the Sayings and Doings of Francis, Fourth Archbishop of Westminster*, p. 114.
22 FAB, Eucharistic Congress, Montreal, 10 September 1910, cited *Tablet*, 24 September 1910, p. 515.
23 FAB, *Canadian Gazette*, 13 October 1910.
24 FAB, 'The Apostolate by Means of the English Language,' National Catholic Congress, Norwich, 2 August 1912, *Tablet*, 10 August 1912, p. 203.
25 FAB, Newman Association, Oxford, 11 June 1927, *Tablet*, 25 June 1927, p. 846.
26 E. Dabrowski, *Tablet*, 4 June 1927, pp. 749–750.
27 Amigo to Gasquet, 27 February 1919, DAA, Gasquet, 917A.
28 FAB, National Congress, Liverpool, 30 July 1920, *Tablet*, 7 August 1920, p. 169.
29 *Tablet*, 22 February 1919, p. 205.
30 FAB, 'The Cardinal Archbishop on His Eastern Tour,' *WCC*, March 1920, pp. 44.
31 *WCC*, April 1919, pp. 66–67.
32 Amigo to Gasquet, 27 February 1919, DAA, Gasquet, 917A.
33 Press accounts of the tour cited by *WCC*, April 1919, p. 66.
34 FAB, *Times*, 11 April 1919.
35 A. Randall, *Vatican Assignment* (London: William Heinemann Ltd, 1956), p. 31.
36 Chief Political Officer, Egyptian Expeditionary Force, to Balfour, 30 September 1918, PRO, FO 141/667/6.
37 FAB, Address to Salesians, Cairo, 10 January 1919, *Tablet*, 8 February 1919, p. 166.
38 Oldmeadow, *Francis Cardinal Bourne*, ii, p. 146.
39 FAB to English Press, 1 April 1919 (copy), AAW, Bo. V/54.
40 FAB to General Storrs, 30 April 1919 (copy), AAW, Bo. V/54.
41 Sir Samuel Hoare to FAB, 1 May 1919, AAW, Bo. V/58g.
42 Pollard, *The Unknown Pope*, p. 198.
43 FO records (141/460/2); Sir Reginald Wingate to Foreign Office, 30 December 1918 (copy), PRO, FO/141/460/2.
44 Wheeler, 'The Archdiocese of Westminster, Beck (ed.), *The English Catholics 1850–1950*, p. 179.
45 Wingate to Foreign Office, 16 January 1919 (copy), PRO, FO/141/460/2.
46 Memorandum, P. F. Daniels, interview with FAB, 9 January 1919, PRO, FO/141/460/2.
47 Wingate to Foreign Office, 16 January 1919 (copy), PRO, FO/141/460/2.
48 Keating to FAB, 5 April 1919, AAW, Bo. IV/20/13c.
49 Amigo to Gasquet, 11 April 1919, DAA, Gasquet, 917A.
50 Burton, Diary, 21 May 1920, CDA.
51 *Times*, 11 April 1919.
52 Prefect for the Congregation for the Discipline of the Sacraments (1914–1920) and Papal Delegate to the Holy Land in 1919 for the seventh centenary of the visit of St Francis of Assisi.

53 Archbishop of Rouen (translated to Paris in December 1920); visited Constantinople in March 1920 for informal discussions with the Patriarch.
54 Minute of British Residency, Cairo, 11 December 1920, PRO, FO/141/460/2.
55 FAB, National Congress, Liverpool, 30 July 1920, *Tablet*, 7 August 1920, p. 169.
56 Admiral Calthorpe to Lord Methuen, Governor of Malta, 17 February 1919, *Daily Malta Chronicle*.
57 FAB, Address to CWL Bethlehem Settlement meeting, 18 February 1925, *Tablet*, 21 February 1925, p. 242.
58 FAB to Balfour, 26 February 1919 (copy), AAW, Bo. III/124/10.
59 Sir R. Roderick, Rome, to Balfour, 21 March 1919, PRO FO 608/30/12.
60 *Tablet*, 4 October 1919, p. 417.
61 FAB, Notes, Audience, 15 March 1919, AAW, Bo. III/124/8.
62 FAB, 'The Cardinal Archbishop on His Eastern Tour,' *WCC*, March 1920, p. 45.
63 FAB, National Congress, Liverpool, 30 July 1920, *Tablet*, 7 August 1920, pp. 169–171.
64 FAB, Queen's Hall, London, 8 January 1906, *Jewish World*, 12 January 1906.
65 Merry del Val to FAB, 6 December 1905, AAW, Bo. IV/4/3.
66 FAB to Chief Rabbi, 25 September 1913, cited *WCC*, December 1913, p. 313.
67 FAB, Easter Sunday Homily 1924, Westminster Cathedral, cited FAB, *Occasional Sermons*, p. 126.
68 FAB, National Catholic Congress, Liverpool, 30 July 1920, *Times*, 31 July 1920.
69 FAB, National Congress, Liverpool, 30 July 1920, *Tablet*, 7 August 1920, p. 169.
70 Palestine Arab Delegation to FAB, 6 October 1921, AAW, Bo. IV/14/3.
71 FAB, Bolton, 26 June 1922, Press cutting, PRO, FO, 141/667/6.
72 FAB, Bolton, 26 June 1922, *Tablet*, 1 July 1922, p. 22; FAB to CTS Conference, Leicester, 26 September 1921, *Jewish Chronicle*, 30 September 1921.
73 FAB, National Catholic Congress, Liverpool, 30 July 1920, *Times*, 31 July 1920.
74 FAB to Storrs, 30 April 1919 (copy), AAW, Bo. V/54.
75 Talbot to FAB, 24 February 1919, AAW, Bo. III/124/10.
76 FAB to Storrs, 30 April 19 (copy), AAW, Bo. V/54.
77 FAB to CTS Conference, Leicester, 26 September 1921, *Jewish Chronicle*, 30 September 1921.
78 Editorial, *Tablet*, 8 July 1922, p. 37.
79 Vatican Memorandum passed by Gasparri to Count de Salis, 4 June 1922, AAW, Bo. V/62.
80 Gasparri to FAB, 6 June 1922, AAW, Roman Letters IX/143.
81 Gasparri to FAB, 21 June 1922, AAW, Roman Letters IX/153.
82 *Tablet*, 22 July 1922, p. 98.
83 FAB to CTS Conference, Leicester, 26 September 1921, *Jewish Chronicle*, 30 September 1921.
84 *Jewish Chronicle*, 7 October 1921.

85   *Jewish Chronicle*, 4 January 1935.
86   Latin Patriarch of Jerusalem to FAB, 28 October 1921, AAW, Bo. IV/14/5.
87   FAB, *Messenger*, February 1925.
88   J. Keating, SJ, to FAB, 14 December 1917, AAW, V/57d.
89   FAB, CCIR meeting, Cathedral Hall, 24 November 1931, *Tablet*, 28 November 1931, p. 697.
90   FAB, CCIR & CWL meeting, Cathedral Hall, 30 March 1927, *Tablet*, 2 April 1927, p. 448.
91   FAB, Minutes of CCIR meeting, 19 June 1924, AAW, Bo. V/64.
92   FAB, Manchester, 25 September 1926, *Times*, 27 September 1926.
93   FAB to Davidson, 22 October 1918, cited *Tablet*, 2 November 1918, p. 487; FAB to Lord Robert Cecil, 27 July 1919 (copy), AAW, Bo.IV/20/23b.
94   FAB to Col. Fisher, Secretary, 30 September 1919 (copy), AAW, Bo. V/80.
95   FAB to Ramsay Macdonald, April 1924, *Tablet*, 17 May 1924, p. 659.
96   FAB, Manchester, 25 Sept 26, *Times*, 27 September 1926.
97   FAB, Lent Pastoral 1934; *WCC*, October 1934, p. 179.
98   *Times*, 16 December 1938.
99   FAB to the Foreign Office, 11 September 1919, ASV, Secretary of State, AA.EE.SS, Austria-Hungary, fasc. 565.
100 Lenten Pastoral Letter, 1921.
101 FAB, Newcastle Cathedral, 16 October 1921, *Tablet*, 22 October 1921, p. 530.
102 FAB, Italian Church, Clerkenwell, 13 November 1932, *Tablet*, 19 November 1932, p. 666.
103 Editorial, *Tablet*, 9 September 1922, p. 324; Editorial, *Tablet*, 19 April 1924, p. 519.
104 FAB, Address to Our Lady's Catechists, 12 July 1931, *Tablet*, 18 July 1931, p. 91.
105 *Tablet*, 11 October 1930, p. 470.
106 *Tablet*, 2 July 1932, p. 2.
107 Bishop of Mainz cited *Tablet*, 6 December 1930, p. 730.
108 *WCC*, November 1934, p. 202.
109 *Tablet*, 18 October 1930, p. 502.
110 Mgr Collings, FAB's private secretary, to Lord Denbigh, 31 March 1933, AAW, Hi 2/125.
111 Clifton, *Amigo*, p. 139.
112 FAB, Address to the Knights of St Columba, 3 November 1932, *Tablet*, 5 November 1932, p. 610.
113 FAB, Homily, St Mary's, Derby, *Tablet*, 29 March 1930, p. 425.
114 *Tablet*, 18 October 1930, p. 502.
115 FAB's Private Secretary to G. Bailey, Secretary National Council for Prevention of War, 6 January 1931, copy, AAW, Hi. II/66.
116 FAB, France, 17 September 1931, *Tablet*, 26 September 1931, p. 412.

117 FAB, Speech, CCIR meeting, 24 November 1931, *Morning Post*, 25 November 1931.
118 Sir George Ogilivie-Forbes, Despatch, 30 October 1930, cited Moloney, *Westminster, Whitehall and the Vatican*, p. 86.
119 Aspden, *Fortress Church*, p. 44.
120 Cited Oldmeadow, *Francis Cardinal Bourne*, ii, p. 343.
121 FAB to [De Lai?], 8 May 1910, draft, AAW, Bo. I/123.
122 FAB to Merry del Val, 13 May 1910, copy, AAW, Bo. I/123.
123 *Tablet*, 27 May 1910, p. 806.
124 FAB to Pius X, 29 May 1910, draft, AAW, Bo. I/123.
125 Fleming to FAB, 18 June 1910, AAW, Bo. I/123.
126 FAB to Merry del Val, 8 July 1910, copy, AAW, Bo. I/123.
127 FAB to Cerretti, 14 September 1919 (copy), AAW, Bo. III/124/6.
128 FAB to Lépicier, 30 December 1928, AAW, Bo. I/112.
129 Lépicier to FAB, 9 January 1929, AAW, Bo. I/112.
130 FAB to Mgr Canali, Holy Office, 3 November 1930, AAW, Roman Letters, Misc./115.
131 Interview, Fuller, 7 November 2001.
132 FAB to Vaughan, 7 March 1902, draft, AAW, Hi. II/49.
133 FAB to Fr Moriarty of the Roman Association, 28 July 1907, draft, AAW, Hi. II/49.
134 FAB to Bishop Giles, 5 March 1908, copy, AAW, Hi. II/49.
135 FAB, National Catholic Congress, Newcastle, 4 August 1911, cited FAB, *Congress Addresses*, pp. 42–58.
136 FAB to Stuart, 13 August 1911, GASSH, Rome.
137 FAB to Cardinal Gibbons, 12 October 1918, AAW, Bo. I/62; Gibbons to FAB, 12 December 1918, AAW, Bo. I/62.
138 FAB to [Bidwell?], 25 December 1918 (copy), AAW, Bo. I/62; Memorandum, 'The Roman Question—Settlement suggested by the Archbishop of Westminster,' AAW, Bo. I/62.
139 FAB, Homily, 'The Roman Question,' *WCC*, May 1929, p. 85.
140 Randall, *A Vatican Assignment*, pp. 15–16.
141 FAB memorandum, 6–12 December 1915, AAW, Bo. IV/3/5a.
142 Sir Charles Wingfield, British Minister to the Holy See, to Sir Robert Vansittart, Permanent Under-Secretary, 23 February 1935, cited Moloney, *Westminster, Whitehall and the Vatican*, p. 87.
143 Talbot to FAB, 31 March 1921, AAW, Bo. I/72; FAB to Cerretti, 31 March 1921 (copy), AAW, Bo. I/72.
144 FAB to Ramsay MacDonald, 11 June 1929, AAW, Bo. IV/20/1a; A. Henderson to FAB, 28 June 1929, AAW, Bo. IV/20/1c; FAB to Henderson, 29 June 1929, AAW, Bo. IV/20/1f.

Chapter 18

Ireland

'Irish Blood'

Listening to Cardinal Bourne's voice on gramophone recordings a century on, one is struck by two things. The pitch is surprisingly high for a man of sombre aspect and stout frame. Then there is an unmistakable Irish lilt—a legacy from his mother and aunt. (Years later he recalled fondly their 'soft Dublin accent.'[1]) His private secretary thought this was not the only trait inherited from his mother. 'There was no mistaking the fact that he had Irish blood, of which one symptom was a mixture of mildness and a quick temper.'[2] The Irish connection, however, amounted to little more substantial than this. Ellen Bourne left Dublin in adolescence. There was no family there with whom contact was maintained. The Cardinal himself visited Ireland probably no more than four times in his entire life. While he made periodic reference to his Irish ancestry as evidence of his affinity for that island, he needed to tread carefully. Others were to pour scorn on his claim to Irish sympathies.

When it came to political matters, the Cardinal's views derived as much from his father as his mother. Henry Bourne was sufficiently sympathetic to moderate Irish nationalism to have welcomed Gladstone's early electoral successes on the grounds that he had disestablished the Protestant Church of Ireland.[3] That sympathy was, however, as much sectarian as national. For Henry Bourne the Fenians were 'a set of vile rascals.'[4]

His private secretary claimed that the Cardinal 'persistently sympathised with Irish aspirations and supported Home Rule.'[5] He could appear very comfortable, however, with benevolent Tory Unionism. Like the rest of the English hierarchy, Bourne held out for a Catholic University for Ireland. Otherwise, by the end of the nineteenth century he was prepared to admit, 'Slowly, tardily, yet no longer, we trust, reluctantly, justice is being done to our brethren in that much-loved land.'[6] One wonders as to the congregation's reaction to his 1904 St. Patrick's Day homily. 'England and Ireland have been thrown providentially side by side, both doing a work together which neither alone could accomplish. We can proudly say that England, even more perhaps than Rome, by its world-wide influence makes for the general good of mankind. Union of the two races is necessary for the cause of God. United by the closest ties of blood equally with both races, I plead most earnestly for this union. He who strives to make them understand one another is surely doing God's work, while those who create, or foster, or perpetuate misunderstandings, are the enemies of Faith and Fatherland alike.'[7]

The Archbishop was criticised for travelling in the Papal Legate's party for the consecration of Armagh Cathedral in 1904—although this was at Cardinal Vannutelli's specific request. In doing so, he became an official guest of the Viceregal government of Dublin Castle and perforce distanced from the Irish hierarchy.[8] Speaking in Armagh, Bourne reverted to his desire to see the closer union of England and Ireland. On this occasion, however, he employed greater tact and clarity. What united them was faith and blood—a sentiment warmly applauded by his audience.[9]

The Tory Government hoped that economic prosperity combined with land and administrative reforms would satisfy Irish grievances—with the need for minimum political change. There is no evidence that Bourne fundamentally disagreed with this policy. But changing political fortunes in England and sustained opposition from within both the Unionist and Nationalist constituencies to a negotiated, consensual settlement meant that the Archbishop was denied the luxury of observing the solution of Ireland's problems as a benign bystander.

'I am a Home Ruler'

With little evidence from his initial public pronouncements, the Irish Parliamentary Party sensed that Bourne was more sympathetic to their objectives than his predecessor. Redmond was encouraged to hope: 'I may tell you, but of course in confidence, that I have some very great hope that he may be drawn more and more to identify himself with the aspirations of the Irish portion of his people.'[10] Bourne's willingness to treat the Irish parliamentary leaders as partners in the struggle for Catholic schools—rather than simply subjects to obey his directives—helped enormously. The Archbishop's conduct in the educational crisis promised to draw the English Catholic Church closer to the cause of Irish nationalism than ever before. An Irish Bishop acknowledged as much. 'Mgr Bourne has done more to promote unity and to win the affection of Irish Catholics by his noble letter to John Redmond thanking the Irish Leader for the services rendered to Catholic Education in England by the Irish Party than could be effected by any amount of speeches.'[11]

Of course, as the Irish Party recognised, they had to tread carefully. Bourne recoiled immediately from any suggestion that he was committing the Church in England to a particular political stance. He consistently forbade political meetings in Catholic schools or political fundraising outside Catholic churches. Ireland was not to be discussed at Catholic Congresses. The Archbishop explained that his approach was dictated by English Catholic divisions on Irish nationalism. Personally, however, 'the refusal in no way denotes any want of sympathy with our brethren in Ireland in their endeavours to realise their legitimate aspirations.'[12] Likewise, he reassured Redmond that the proposal for political collections outside churches, 'if carried into effect, would not have helped, but hindered, what I have so much at heart, a better and closer mutual understanding between the Catholics of Ireland and England.'[13]

Many years later Bourne was confronted by a Sinn Féin journalist at Hare Street. Having no appointment, the journalist's reception was far warmer than anticipated, even being given dinner and a bed for the night. The Cardinal articulated the journalist's unspoken thought, namely, that he was 'quite unsympathetic' to the Irish question. The Cardinal attempted to get the journalist to see matters from his perspective. 'I am an Archbishop in England, and in London at that; I have the interests of my own archdiocese to think of first and the interest of the Church in England second. I cannot afford to forget that, in any public statement I make. In Ireland, it is Ireland that counts. In England, it is not only Ireland but also England and the whole Empire … You have to expect a slightly different point of view on the Irish question from one whose duty it is to be English as well as Catholic and an Archbishop … In all things that concern Ireland alone I am for that solution commonly known as Dominion Home Rule.'[14] The journalist was won over by the Cardinal's candour and charm.

While the matter hung in the balance, however, Bourne had responded less directly to similar questions. 'I was sometimes asked in public company, very often guilelessly—occasionally, I fear, with a spite of malice—if I were a Home Ruler. I had one answer which often stood me in good stead, and expressed a profound conviction, which later events confirmed. I used to reply, "Yes, I am a Home Ruler—I want Home Rule for England." It seemed to me that so many matters, not really affecting England at all, were so constantly forced upon the attention of our legislators, that our own home concerns were frequently made dependant on issues which ought not to have affected them at all. To my mind, then and now, the recognition of Irish self-government means the bestowal of true self-government on England.'[15] The Cardinal was correct. Irish autonomy freed up Westminster to concentrate on issues this side of the Irish Sea. But such a response—'I want Home Rule for England'—sounded flippant, designed to avoid controversy. It cut little ice with his co-religionists engaged in what was, from their perspective, a just struggle to rid themselves of the colonial overlord.

Bourne's stance was, however, rather more considered than this throw away remark suggests. He elaborated on his position. 'The widest possible self-government for Ireland, and for Wales and Scotland too if they desire it, has for a great many years seemed to me the only possible solution of the many difficulties that confront us. When the whole Constitution was under consideration in 1910, I urged this conviction very strongly on the late Duke of Norfolk in the hope that, while there was yet time, the party with which he was associated would adopt this policy, which seemed to me a necessity of political salvation. Had they done so, their political adversaries could hardly have opposed it, and the history of the last six years would have been vastly different.'[16] His credibility would have been far greater had he urged this federal solution more publicly at the time.

It was not, however, simply a question of the Cardinal being wise after the event. He was pressing the policy privately with the wartime Colonial Secretary: 'Push on as rapidly as possible with the *Federal* solution, giving to Ireland not an exceptional position, but a place fully equal in all local and purely national matters to that of England, Wales and Scotland. This solution may not meet with any great gratitude in Ireland in the present circumstances, but it will put England right in the eyes of the United States, the Dominions, and the Continental countries, as being manifestly willing to give the only logical and possible self-government that Ireland can reasonably claim. As I mentioned to you it is the only solution that I am able to put trust in, and for many years I have hoped to see its realisation.'[17] Had the Cardinal communicated these feelings to Catholics in Ireland and England at the time, then he might have been spared much opprobrium and have been trusted to play a positive role in the resolution of Irish difficulties.

It was not just Bourne who displayed great wariness. Rome too was extremely circumspect. In the febrile days immediately preceding the First World War, Ireland was on the brink of civil war with both Unionists and Nationalists engaged in gun running and threatening insurrection. Yet there was no enthusiasm in the Vatican for Irish nationalism. Merry del Val wrote to Gasquet, 'You will have noticed our reticence and reserve in regard to the conflict in Ireland and you may be sure that we shall continue to be very cautious.'[18]

'This tragic farce in Dublin'[19]

Initially, it appeared that the War might provide the solution to Ireland's predicament where English and Irish politicians had so signally failed. Redmond generously pledged full Irish cooperation to the war effort. Vast numbers of Irish enrolled in the British Army. To many it seemed only logical and just that such support should be rewarded by the implementation of the Home Rule Bill already on the statute book, but suspended for the duration of the War. Even the carnage of the Western Front and Gallipoli did not diminish this underlying optimism. On 18 March 1916 the Cardinal celebrated a Requiem Mass for fallen Irish troops in a packed Westminster Cathedral. The following week the *Tablet*, referring to these 'new Days of Creation,' wrote gushingly about the end of old enmities. 'In one overwhelming ideal the two nations are at last one ... The seemingly unthinkable has taken thought ... A short space back and none could have braved the prediction that an English Queen should decorate an Irish leader [Redmond] with shamrock, or that an Irish leader should consent to be so decorated.'[20]

Five weeks later the Easter Rising occurred. Denied effective German support, largely limited to Dublin and beset with internal divisions, its failure was inevitable. Nevertheless, the occupation of public buildings, held against the British Army for the better part of a week, and the proclamation of an Irish Republic shocked the establishment. Popular support for the Rising at the time was extremely limited; Redmond categorically condemned it at Westminster. The *Tablet* had good cause to write the following week: 'Today the rebel leaders are disowned by everybody and everywhere ... Nationalist Ireland has been tried in a furnace, and what flaw in her armour has been revealed? The Syndicalists and the Sinn Féiners have come out into the open, and learned the value of German help and the measure of their own strength ... The movement collapsed of its own weakness, and because the sympathies of Nationalist Ireland were already enlisted on the side of law and order.'[21]

It was the British military authorities' use of martial law to attempt to destroy revolutionary nationalism once and for all which caused the mood to swing. In the midst of a total war for national survival, the Easter Rising was treated as treason and the insurgents dealt with accordingly. Yet the atmosphere of suspicion engendered by the large scale round up of suspects, the summary nature of the courts martial and the actual executions (albeit limited in number) succeeded in creating a sympathy for the insurgents and their objectives which the Rising itself had not.

Bourne kept his own counsel during the Rising, but he was to become implicated in its aftermath. Sir Roger Casement came from a Protestant Ascendancy family, although, as a child, his mother had him secretly baptised a Catholic. Orphaned, he was raised a Protestant by his father's family. Casement entered the British Consular Service and was knighted for his human rights work in the Belgian Congo and Latin America. Attracted to the nationalist cause, Casement had sought arms and recruits for the Rising in Germany. Put ashore by the Germans, and picked up almost immediately by the British, he was imprisoned in the Tower of London. Convicted of treason and sentenced to death, Casement asked to be reconciled to the Catholic Church. While the vast majority of English viewed Casement as a wartime traitor deserving the death penalty, various literary figures and churchmen sought his reprieve on humanitarian grounds. What would Bourne's response be?

The Cardinal was one of those made aware of the contents of Casement's 'black diaries.' The British Government used these revelations of his promiscuous homosexuality to silence pleas for clemency. The Cardinal recalled that he had been 'informed on the highest authority that [Casement's] moral life had been deplorable and that proof to this effect might be produced at his trial.'[22]

Following his sentencing, Casement was held at Pentonville Prison. The chaplain there, Fr Thomas Carey, sought the Cardinal's guidance, given the complexities of the situation and the notoriety of the prisoner. Casement was asked to sign the following formula: 'I, N. N., hereby publicly express my sincere repentance for all actions in my public or private life opposed to the law of God, and condemned as such by the Church and my sincere regret for the scandal they may have caused, and I further declare that I fully and unreservedly accept the authority and teaching of the Catholic Church in such matters.'[23] He refused, feeling this tantamount to a denial of his nationalist beliefs. 'If ever published, it would be interpreted as a confession on his part that he was guilty of violation of the law of God in his public life. And this he is not prepared to admit.'[24]

Bourne was vilified by Irish nationalists at the time and homosexual rights activists subsequently for supposedly withholding spiritual comforts from a condemned man. In 1920 an Irish journalist revived the accusation that, 'Cardinal Bourne refused the faculty for Casement's reception into the Church, on the ground that the condemned man would not sign a document in which he specifically repudiated and condemned anything in his public or private life that the Church condemned.' The story went that Fr Carey reconciled Casement to the Church in defiance of, or at least without reference to, the Cardinal.[25]

That is untrue. The Cardinal was unable to defend himself publicly in what touched so confidentially a dead man's conscience, although he recorded privately what had taken place four years earlier. He recalled that the first he heard about Casement wanting to become a Catholic 'was merely that he wished to belong to the religion of the majority of his countrymen.' Next Casement stipulated 'that he would consent to be confirmed only by an Irish Bishop.'[26] The Cardinal was quite justified, therefore, in investigating further whether his request was motivated more by nationalist politics than personal faith.

Casement was voluntarily seeking to become a Catholic. If his desire was genuine, he was freely accepting as a matter of faith the full teaching of the Church in doctrine and morality. The document tendered to Casement might have been drafted with the particular circumstances of his life in mind, but it was not an intolerable imposition designed to humiliate Casement. At the time, it was the uniform practice of the Church to require any baptised adult Christian seeking to become a Catholic to swear a written document abjuring heresy.

When Casement refused to sign, Bourne did not consider the matter closed. As events developed and the chances of a reprieve diminished, the Cardinal continued to advise the prison chaplain, 'If and when the eventuality of which you write is certain to take place, any confessor may deal with the matter *privately "in foro interno"* on his own responsibility.'[27] This was not the Cardinal washing his hands of a controversial case.

Rather, he took the only course of action which was both reasonable and compassionate. Casement could only become a Catholic if his faith and repentance of past sin were genuine. The only other person who could know this was Fr Carey, the priest responsible for Casement's thorough instruction. The Cardinal reminded Carey that, knowing the state of Casement's soul, he possessed the authority to take whatever action was necessary. Indeed, the Cardinal went beyond this. 'As soon as it became clear that he would not be reprieved, I sent two of my priests with the amplest faculties to receive his abjuration and to reconcile him to the Church, with a message that I would pray for him, that I wished him every grace and blessing of Almighty God and that I would offer my Mass for him on the day of his death.'[28] Any priest would have interpreted the Cardinal's note as an invitation to reconcile Casement *in extremis* provided he judged the requisite intention was there. Carey did exactly that. Casement was hung on 3 August 1916, having first made his peace with God, receiving absolution and Holy Communion.

'The Black and Tan Cardinal'?

The British Government tried to regain the initiative as Lloyd George attempted to broker a negotiated settlement on the basis of immediate Home Rule. Once more, Ulster proved a stumbling block. In the end Westminster could not even deliver on the limited measures to which the Irish Parliamentary Party's leadership had reluctantly agreed. Moderate nationalism was fatally weakened. An attempt to reach a settlement through a Convention representative of all Irishmen sitting in Dublin likewise failed through the intransigence of both the Ulster Unionists and Sinn Féin, the new power in the land. John Redmond's death signalled the end of a political era.

Preaching at Redmond's Requiem Mass in Westminster Cathedral on 8 March 1918 before Lloyd George and many of his Cabinet colleagues, the Cardinal's homily represented little more than wishful thinking.

> The eyes of the world are upon Ireland today. Friends and foes alike are watching to see the issue. Are the misunderstandings, the discords, the strifes of so many years at length to have an end? Is the one great outstanding menace to the well-being of the Empire to be removed? May the thought and the memory of John Redmond and his death be, as he would most certainly wish them

to be, a source of understanding and of union and unity to all Irishmen of every political faith and religious belief.[29]

The German offensive of March 1918 ensured there would be no immediate end to the strife in Ireland. The proposal to extend conscription to Ireland enflamed an already tense and radicalised situation. At a purely logical level, there was no reason why Ireland alone in the United Kingdom should be exempt from conscription. But, privately, and for pragmatic reasons, the Cardinal urged the Prime Minister against such a course of action before self-government was granted. It was simply not worth the effort. 'I venture to write to you on account of the persistent rumours that it is the purpose of the Government to announce their intention of applying conscription to Ireland without waiting for the result of the Convention and the carrying into effect of the conclusions at which it has arrived ... Half, if not more, of the value of any settlement will be lost if it be preceded by an attempt at conscription. I do most earnestly hope and pray that the Government will resolutely avoid the policy with which rumour now credits it. I write in no sense as a critic. No one can sympathise more sincerely with you than I do in the tremendously heavy burden of anxiety and responsibility that you have to carry, and you have my earnest prayers that you may have every guidance that you need.'[30] Lloyd George asked Bourne to visit him, but such a mild letter could never cause the Prime Minister to reverse his policy.

The Military Service Bill was passed. It did not introduce conscription immediately to Ireland but gave the Government the power to do so by Order in Council. It was the worst of both worlds. There was no influx of new recruits for the Army, while the British Government incurred all the opprobrium of the introduction of conscription on a hostile nation. The assessment of John Dillon, the new leader of the Parliamentary Party, was regrettably accurate: 'To hold conscription over Ireland like a sword of Damocles would poison every hope of an Irish settlement.'[31]

Bourne sought to mitigate the consequences of the legislation. He advised the Irish Chief Secretary: 'Give a *long* opportunity for voluntary enlistment before applying conscription, and then a *big* loophole on the plea of the need for agricultural labour. The tranquilising of Ireland is of more importance than even men for the Army.'[32] Long played to the Cardinal's sense of self-importance: 'Your Eminence has been always so ready to help His Majesty's Government that I venture to appeal to you for advice, counsel and, if happily it be possible, for active assistance ... I am writing to ask whether your Eminence would be willing to come and see me and have a general discussion upon the situation as a whole.'[33]

But the time for private discussion was over. Others were speaking loudly and clearly, starting with the Irish hierarchy. Conscription finally forced most Irish Bishops to accept Sinn Féin as a legitimate political force. The Bishops spoke out boldly: 'We consider that conscription, forced in this way upon Ireland (i.e., against the will of the Irish nation and in defiance of the protests of its leaders), is an oppressive and inhuman law, which the Irish people have a right to resist by all the means that are consonant with the law of God.'[34] The Declaration was interpreted by some in England as the Irish hierarchy sanctioning armed resistance to conscription. The result was what Bourne feared most: open dissension among Catholics.

The Declaration produced a series of anti-Catholic articles in the English Press which the Catholic Union took as their cue to censure the Irish Bishops in April 1918:

> The Catholic Union has viewed with the deepest regret the action which the Catholic Bishops of Ireland have deemed it necessary to take for resisting compulsory service in the present war, action which appears to support a movement for organised disobedience to the law … The Catholic Union cannot regard without serious misgivings any interference by ecclesiastical authority in questions which are purely temporal and political, and in no way connected with faith or morals.[35]

The Cardinal might regret the fact, but the genie was now out of the bottle and every controversialist in the English Catholic Church felt authorised to weigh in on the subject.

Genuine sympathy for the Irish was mixed with outrage at the audacity of English laymen in criticising Bishops pronouncing on the situation in their own country. Casartelli and the Salford Chapter led the way; they 'protested against the resolution of the Catholic Union which has been published, and repudiated the claim of that Union to represent English Catholics.'[36] Amigo followed: 'The Irish Bishops had been blamed for their recent action, partly because the situation in Ireland was not properly understood by some people in this country. The Bishops of Ireland are learned and holy men, and I, for one, will not presume to sit in judgment upon them. As a matter of fact, knowing them as I do, I am in agreement with them.'[37]

Ireland

The only person to remain silent was the Cardinal. When the English hierarchy met in May 1918 to consider the new Code of Canon Law, Bourne refused to allow any discussion of the Catholic Union's action. He likewise refused to sign a letter of protest, supported by most English Bishops.[38] Increasingly, the Cardinal was becoming publicly distanced from the rest of the hierarchy, if not on his actual views on the Irish crisis, then at least in his response to it. So when Lord Curzon made the unsubstantiated claim that Irish priests were threatening their people with eternal damnation unless they resisted conscription, there was consternation in England that it was left to a layman, the MP Mark Sykes to rebut the charge. He reminded the Commons, 'The reason why we have no law in Ireland now was that Sir Edward Carson challenged it. He entered into a covenant which imagined resistance to the law.'[39] In many ways, this statement came more effectively from an English layman, but that was not how Bourne's colleagues saw it. The Bishop of Nottingham wrote despairingly to Amigo, 'I fear we are, as a body, timorous rather than prudent ... Promptitude was vital and Mark Sykes came to the rescue of the Church. But where were the Bishops that a layman should have to speak for the Church!'[40]

The Armistice with Germany brought no respite for Ireland. The peacetime General Election produced an overwhelming Sinn Féin victory and the near elimination of the old Parliamentary Party. The victors shunned Westminster and set up their own Assembly of Ireland, Dáil Éireann, in Dublin in January 1919. A parallel system of government and justice was established. Attacks on the Army and Royal Irish Constabulary invited British reprisals, and Ireland was plunged, depending on one's perspective, into a war for independence or a state of anarchy and terrorism. Lloyd George's response was both political and military. He legislated for two Home Rule Parliaments in Dublin and Belfast—of no interest, of course, to Sinn Féin—but also countenanced brutal counter-terrorist measures, especially after the assassination attempt on the Viceroy, Lord French, in December 1919. For many, the actions of the Auxiliaries and 'the Black and Tans' were as ruthless and unprincipled as the IRA campaign itself.

Cardinal Bourne sought divine intervention for an end to the terror and killing. He told those gathered for the beatification of Oliver Plunkett, 'This is not the time nor the place, neither have we any mission, to discuss the political aspects of the question ... in union with our Irish brethren, and in deepest sympathy with them in the anguish of these terrible moments ... we desire to lift up our hearts to the Lord ... We desire ... to make it known to all our Catholic people in England that, in our judgment, there is no matter more urgently needing their united prayer than the prompt, speedy, just and permanent settlement of the destinies of our Irish brethren.'[41]

Others saw the need to combine prayer with action. Fr Charles Plater, SJ, established the Committee of British Catholics for Reconciliation. The emphasis, however, was more on reconciliation between British Catholics than between the hostile parties in Ireland. Plater wrote,

> If it were not for the aggravation of the Irish question the masses of Catholic workers in this country would be a solid conservative force. As it is, their support is largely given to extremist elements ... If the Catholic Irish in this country were convinced that their English co-religionists had true sympathy with Ireland there would be far more Catholic unity in this country and Catholic organisation would be immensely facilitated. [I propose] that an attempt be made to get Catholics in England of all parties, Unionists and self-determinationists, to join together and support the movement for peace and reconciliation ... The basis is to recognise that Ireland and England should negotiate as equals on their mutual relations.[42]

A Memorial would be circulated, studiously avoiding all partisanship and reference to violence, which could be signed by Catholics of all shades of opinion.

The idea appealed to Bourne. 'I like Fr Plater's suggestion very much. The matter is indeed most urgent and I approve of you taking with him the steps that he indicates. May God, through the intercession of our Blessed Lady, help and guide you. Please let me know how it all develops. If this question could only be settled the progress of the Church would be immensely accelerated.'[43] The Memorial was published at the end of October 1920, pressing for reconciliation on the basis of self-governing Dominion status. Copies were sent to Lloyd George and the Irish hierarchy. While approving the Memorandum, the Archbishop of Liverpool withheld his signature, preferring it to be a lay initiative. The Cardinal was not asked to sign, although the organisers acknowledged that they had 'received at the very beginning of our efforts your commendation and good wishes.'[44]

Ireland

Bourne's life was made more difficult by the unwelcome arrival of an Irish Australian Archbishop and the death of an Irish hunger striker across the Thames. A former President of Maynooth, Archbishop Daniel Mannix of Melbourne was a noted controversialist, having led the campaign against conscription in Australia during the First World War. En route to Rome, Mannix toured the United States speaking passionately in favour of Irish independence. The British Government feared the presence of this turbulent priest in his home country. His ship intercepted by a destroyer, he was made to disembark in England and forbidden entry to Ireland. 'The greatest British naval victory since Jutland,'[45] the Archbishop remarked sardonically. The Cardinal was discomforted by rumours, originating he believed with the Archbishop himself, that he had colluded with the Government in Mannix's ban. 'It is extremely painful to me even to allude to so gross a calumny. Lest, however, the lie should go uncontradicted, I desire it to be known that neither directly nor indirectly was I consulted in any way on this matter.'[46] Not everyone sympathised with the Cardinal. Bishop Dunn 'couldn't help laughing over the recent disclaimer from [His Eminence] re Mannix.'[47]

Mannix took up residence in a Westminster convent. His discourtesy in not calling upon the Cardinal was noted.[48] But nor did Bourne inconvenience himself to seek the Australian's company. Others filled the gap. On 23 September 1920 the Irish-born Bishop of Portsmouth hosted a reception for Mannix at the Cannon Street Hotel attended by Amigo and 300 priests. The editor of the *Universe* described it as 'a Sinn Féin demonstration of the most violent kind.'[49] Bourne was furious that the reception had been organised in his Diocese without reference to him and that, in his opinion, he had been ridiculed by those present. Mannix only left London to undertake a widely-reported speaking tour of the North of England. There is, however, a hint of over-reaction in the Cardinal's plea to the Vatican.

> I now formally claim the protection of the Holy See against this Prelate who is stirring up strife and doing the Catholic Church in England enormous harm by his interference and his rash impudence. I would suggest that ... Archbishop Mannix be called to Rome as soon as possible, and that he be warned to abstain meanwhile from addressing public meetings.[50]

Simultaneously, the Cardinal was having to address, at least indirectly, the case of Terence MacSwiney, the Lord Mayor of Cork. In Brixton

Prison for possession of an RIC cipher and documents 'whose publication might cause disaffection,' MacSwiney went on hunger strike. Mannix visited him on a number of occasions and gave him the Last Rites. Amigo wrote to the Prime Minister, 'As Bishop of many Irish priests and people in the large Catholic diocese of Southwark, I ask clemency for Cork's Lord Mayor, who is dying in my diocese; resentment will be very bitter if he be allowed to die.'[51]

Others had qualms about intervening on MacSwiney's behalf. The Archbishop of Canterbury was generally sympathetic to those suffering as a result of the Irish Troubles.[52] He was not prepared, however, to intercede on behalf of a hunger striker. When IRA prisoners went on hunger strike in 1939 Bourne's successor in Westminster declared that their death would constitute suicide; they should be denied the sacraments and a Christian burial.[53] Contemporaries were less certain in 1920. For weeks, as MacSwiney lay starving to death, correspondents in the *Tablet* debated the morality of his action. The Cardinal and others sought guidance from Rome: 'A pronouncement by the Holy See on the ethics of hunger-striking seems urgently needed. I think that Cardinal Gasquet has already written to your Grace on this subject. The conflict of opinion among priests and theologians is doing untold harm.'[54] Once again, he did not receive the assistance to which he felt he was entitled. The matter was taken to the Pope, but no ruling was forthcoming.[55]

MacSwiney's sisters wrote to the English hierarchy asking them to demand his release. It appears that their intemperate letter to the Cardinal went unanswered. MacSwiney's family did not know the Archbishop of Westminster if they thought him likely 'to condemn the action of your Government,' which is equated with 'the evil forces of injustice and tyranny.'[56]

MacSwiney died on 25 October. His funeral rites were reported in the *Tablet*. 'The body of the Lord Mayor was conveyed on Wednesday evening to St. George's Cathedral, Southwark, where it rested on a catafalque before the high altar, covered with the Sinn Féin colours. On Thursday morning, when the Cathedral was densely crowded, Episcopal High Mass of Requiem was celebrated by the Bishop of Portsmouth in the presence of the Bishop of Southwark; the Archbishop of Melbourne was among those present.'[57] The account omitted to mention that the coffin was provided with an IRA guard of honour and the deceased had been clothed in his uniform as an IRA commandment.[58]

While Amigo had neither foreseen nor condoned these incidents, there was fury in Westminster. Both Cardinal and secretary vented their anger in Rome. Jackman wrote to Lépicier, 'According to Ojetti[59], if there is doubt as to whether a man has committed suicide or not, he may be allowed Christian burial but without any pomp or ceremony. In this case serious doubt exists, and the opinions are weighty on both sides, and yet all the pomp and ceremony possible was indulged in!! And why in London? Cork, one could understand.'[60] Jackman followed this up with a letter to the Unionist MP, William Hewins, asking him to write to Cardinal De Lai, pointing out how 'the Mass was exploited for flouting the authority of the land' and urging him to appoint 'English Bishops for English sees.'[61]

Cardinal Bourne was under pressure to condemn the proceedings at the funeral from Catholic laymen who failed to appreciate that he lacked jurisdiction in Southwark. He used the episode to illustrate the liabilities of ecclesiastical division in London. 'Action most harmful to the interests of religion and of the Catholic Church can thus take place at less than two miles from the door of the Archbishop of Westminster and he is powerless to interfere, while the world outside cannot understand this powerlessness and he has to keep silence.'[62]

Acting completely out of character, keeping silence was the one thing the Cardinal then proceeded not to do. His article in the *Times* on 12 November provoked an intense outburst. One of his own flock wrote: 'I have just been reading in the *Universe* your views on the chief political question of the day and cannot say how disappointed I am with it. The people of this country—Catholic and non-Catholic—are waiting for a lead and all they obtain from the former is no more than that to which Carson and his covenanters would subscribe!'[63] Kester Aspden judged, 'Bourne had shifted the main responsibility for the violence on to the IRA; to his critics he appeared an apologist for state violence.'[64] Is that a fair assessment?

Like Plater's Committee for Reconciliation, the Cardinal began by supporting 'the widest possible system of self-government' for Ireland— subject to defence considerations and retention of the link with the British Crown. Then he turned to the question of the current violence. He admitted 'the ghastly consequences' of the presence in Ireland of the British security forces. He continued, 'I feel convinced that the vast majority of those who live in England view the continued presence of these troops in Ireland with shame and a great desire for their withdrawal.' He failed to identify himself with this 'vast majority' and call personally for their withdrawal. But otherwise, up to this point, his statement was unexceptional. It would have been perfectly admissible for the Cardinal, like many Irish Bishops, to condemn the IRA atrocities, had he also condemned British reprisals.

Instead, he concentrated upon 'a secret, oath-bound association using assassination as its weapon; an association, therefore, to which no Catholic who is obedient to the Church can possibly belong.' (Challenged by the Bishop of Cork a few days later, he had to admit he could not substantiate that such an association was indeed 'oath-bound.'[65]) The Cardinal maintained that 'the real and legitimate Sinn Féin ... is at present apparently unable to control this murder gang.' He posited the question as to whether the deteriorating state of violence in Ireland was due to 'the unwelcome presence' of the British security forces or to Sinn Féin's inherent inability to control the forces of lawlessness.[66]

In itself, there was nothing objectionable to Irish nationalist sentiment in the Cardinal's statement. It was more the tone in which it was expressed—that of a detached observer personally unconnected to the matters he was addressing. Then also, what was left unsaid. Having referred to the security forces' unpopularity among the Irish people, the Cardinal failed to explain why this was so or whether he shared their sentiments. A London journal had its finger more surely on the pulse of humanitarian opinion than the Catholic Archbishop when it wrote, 'Englishmen, unfortunately, cannot control Sinn Féin outrages, and they can do nothing but denounce them, but they can and ought to control the acts of their own Executive, and they have a duty to insist that it shall not engage in a competition of murder and sabotage with its assailants.'[67] The Cardinal might have appreciated why his statement caused offence had he been closer to the Irish in his own Diocese or had he been better advised. It is disquieting that his Principal Secretary was simultaneously writing in the following terms: 'If only the Irish people and Irish bishops and priests would realise that however true their grievances now they are only the tools of Bolshevism who have found a wonderful fertile soil in Ireland.'[68]

Yet condemnation of the Cardinal's statement was not universal. It earned the praise of many high-minded English, which partially explains why peace took so long to achieve. The non-partisan Peace with Ireland Council thoroughly approved.[69] Its Chairman, Lord Henry Bentinck, asked Bourne to speak at their forthcoming meeting in the Albert Hall. However, he probably frightened the Cardinal by expressing his hope that they would 'make a very effective protest against the un-Christian, un-English policy of the present Government.'[70] Instead, Bourne reverted to his customary low profile role. He replied, 'I find it better in these things always to act in accordance with our traditional practice. I can help you in better ways than by appearing on the platform.'[71]

What caused the Cardinal to write to the *Times*? He concluded his article stating that he had placed his thoughts before the public 'at the urgent request of those who have asked me to set them forth.' Writing in the immediate aftermath of the Mannix and MacSwiney affairs, Bourne was convinced, 'Harm has been done to the Catholic cause that it may take years to undo.'[72] He was anxious lest English public opinion identify the Catholic Church with Irish republican terrorism. His perception was shared by Jackman: 'The Catholic laity are being put in a difficult position to defend the Cardinal's apparent inaction in face of what is tantamount to an act of open disloyalty taking place within a short distance of his own residence, and he, the acknowledged leader of the Catholics in England, makes no voice of protest.'[73] There were plenty of Establishment voices urging him to repudiate such associations. But, in acceding to their request and raising that 'voice of protest,' Bourne misjudged.

Sunday, 21 November 1920 witnessed the worst day of the Irish Troubles. It began in the early hours of the morning with the IRA's cold-blooded assassination of twelve British officers in their Dublin lodgings. That afternoon the security forces surrounded Croke Park, where 5,000 had gathered to watch a Gaelic football match. Intending to search the spectators, the RIC opened fire on the crowd, leaving 14 dead. That evening two IRA prisoners and a civilian held in Dublin Castle were shot dead, allegedly attempting to escape. There seemed no end to the bloodshed and killing.

MacSwiney's funeral at St George's Cathedral had proved contentious for Amigo. The events of 'Bloody Sunday' produced an equivalent scenario for Bourne. The bodies of the twelve murdered British officers were brought back to England. Three of them were Catholic. On 26 November their coffins were brought into Westminster Cathedral, where their Requiem Mass was celebrated in the Cardinal's presence. There was no logical reason why this should not have happened when the nine Protestant officers' funeral took place in Westminster Abbey. But, coming so soon after MacSwiney's funeral and the *Times* article, it was appearances which counted. The Cardinal's presence was perceived as partisan, another illustration of his lack of sympathy for the Irish nationalist cause. Those who held such a view would have felt further justified if they could have read the letter the Cardinal received from the Prime Minister conveying 'the very grateful thanks of His Majesty's Government for your courtesy in allowing last Friday's service to be held in your beautiful Cathedral and for the part you yourself took in the service.'[74]

It was the Catholic Union which again contributed the next phase of acrimony and strife. Having previously rebuked the Irish hierarchy, the Union now turned their ire on the Belgian Bishops. While the English hierarchy produced no corporate statement on Ireland's suffering, the Belgians addressed a joint Pastoral Letter to their Irish brethren. They were, in fact, balanced in their approach, expressing confidence in the fairness of the British Government, while expressing sympathy for the Irish: 'We range ourselves beside you to demand of that Government that an inquiry of unquestionable impartiality be set up with a view of strengthening the public conscience.'[75] Coming from the victims of recent German aggression, this was acutely embarrassing to the English. Yet Lord Walter Kerr of the Catholic Union told Cardinal Mercier that the Belgians were very much mistaken. 'There is no suppression of nationality in Ireland any more than there is oppression of religion, and on neither ground can sympathy with the Irish revolutionary movement be justly claimed from a free Catholic people like the Belgians.'[76]

Once more Bourne seems to have prevented the Union's condemnation by the hierarchy as a whole. But now individual Bishops were determined to speak out. Both Keating and Amigo wrote to the *Tablet*. The former was emphatic: 'Lest silence should be construed as consent, and the whole body of English Catholics should be committed to the views on the Irish tragedy expressed in their latest *motu proprio* by the Catholic Union, I ask space to repudiate, on my own behalf, specifically and emphatically the grave censure passed upon the Irish Bishops, who are infinitely better informed upon the facts of the case than their self-constituted critics, and who deserve all our sympathy and confidence.'[77]

Bourne's stock sank still lower when he refused to authorise a relief collection in England for Catholics driven from their work in the Belfast shipyards by Protestant mobs. The Cardinal may have suspected the impartiality of the White Cross, of which Michael Collins was a Trustee, but that was no excuse for inaction. When Casartelli urged that such a collection 'would go a long way to promote better feeling between Irish and English Catholics,'[78] Bourne replied lamely that they 'must be very careful to avoid anything that might appear to have a political complexion.'[79] Not a robust application of Gospel values. Archbishop's House was defensive. During Bourne's absence in Rome, one of his secretaries was interviewed. 'It has also been asked why the Cardinal has not ordered collections for the relief of distress in Ireland. The answer is that he has repeatedly declared himself willing to do so, if he receives a request to that effect from the Hierarchy of Ireland, who know the needs more accurately than anyone else.'[80]

What really irritated his brother Bishops was the fact that a number of Anglican Bishops were far more outspoken in their criticism of British reprisals. They simply could not understand why the Cardinal refused to speak out. Dunn had a tendency to temper his comments according to his audience, but, on this matter, his sentiments were shared by most of the Catholic hierarchy: 'I told His Eminence that it was a great shame that Canterbury and many other Protestant Bishops were speaking against reprisals and we should be dumb. He would not hear of any joint statement.'[81] Speaking in the Lords the Archbishop of Canterbury admitted the Sinn Féin outrages to be worse than the Black and Tan reprisals, but said that was not the basis on which a civilised country should set its standards of behaviour. 'You cannot justifiably punish wrongdoing by lawlessly doing the like. Not by calling in the Devil will you cast out devils or punish devilry.'[82] Davidson's querying of Government actions was not universally popular in England, but Amigo's Vicar-General greeted it with relief: 'I have recalled how you spoke out boldly against outrages in Ireland when few voices were raised in defence of the suffering people in the affected districts ... I have never hesitated to point out the value of your timely intervention—at a time when prominent persons in our own Church here were silent about the excesses.'[83]

To be compared unfavourably with the Anglican hierarchy in the defence of his Catholic co-religionists pained Bourne enormously. But even this did not represent the depths of the opprobrium into which he was to sink as a result of his conduct during the Irish Troubles.

The Cardinal's 1921 Lenten Pastoral began well enough: 'The tragedy of Ireland continues and becomes still more acute. Horror and outrage, in the form both of aggression and of repression, are reported day by day.' But once again he then obsessed exclusively about the 'murder gang' he had denounced three months earlier in the *Times*. 'In the midst of this welter and confusion I have grave reason to fear that some of my own flock, impelled by legitimate love of country and urgent longing for the realisation of lawful aspirations, are unwarily allowing themselves to become implicated, by active sympathy or, even, actual cooperation, in societies and organisations which are in opposition to the laws of God and of the Catholic Church.'[84] Then, extraordinarily, he required all Westminster priests to read from the pulpit Cardinal Manning's 1867 Pastoral Letter against Fenianism which spoke of the United Kingdom as 'one indivisible realm' as the result of divine Providence.

The letter was not well received. In one London parish 'a member of the congregation called out, "I protest as a Catholic and an Irishman against an Englishman attacking us. It is disgraceful!" Considerable excitement followed, and "Hear, hear!" was shouted from all parts of the church.'[85] The letters in the Archbishop's mailbag the following week were 'very abusive.'[86] One Catholic lady wrote from West London, 'Is Cardinal Bourne aware of the fact that the pulpit of the Roman Catholic Church is not there for a man holding the position he does in the Church to air his political views? Let Cardinal Bourne mind his own business. That he is English is very easy to note ... Perhaps [he] has forgotten that the greater number of Catholics in London are Irish and that if it were not for these poor Irish the number of Catholic churches in London would be very small indeed.'[87]

A more public denunciation was contained in the letter published in the *Times* from the Irish MP, Jeremiah MacVeagh. 'I desire as a Catholic to protest against his Eminence's action in "enjoining" the priests of the Archdiocese (the majority of whom do not share his political views) to read in all churches on Sunday a political manifesto ... I want to be told by Cardinal Bourne whether trust in the Coalition Government is a Catholic doctrine; and, if not, I want to know what right he has to have it promulgated from the pulpit in every church in his Archdiocese ... If he has a shred of sympathy with the Irish people in the agonies through which they are at present passing, he has succeeded in keeping it well under control; and I cannot recall that he uttered a word of condemnation or extended a helping hand when his co-religionists were being hunted from the factories, mills and workshops of Belfast for no other crime than that they worship God at the same altar as himself.'[88]

Ever the chameleon, the Bishop of Nottingham told the Cardinal how pleasing the idea of re-issuing Manning's Pastoral was to him, and had the same Pastoral read in his own Cathedral.[89] The Earl of Denbigh and the Editor of the *Tablet* quibbled at MacVeagh's misquoting of parts of the Cardinal's letter. But MacVeagh was far closer to ordinary Catholic sentiment in believing the Cardinal to be lacking any 'shred of sympathy with the Irish people.'

On 18 March 800 people met at London's Kingsway Hall to protest against the Cardinal's letter. Oldmeadow was dismissive. The meeting was almost exclusively of 'young people (men and women) of the clerk and shop assistant type ... They were nearly all Southwark.'[90] The diocesan journal, carrying an article entitled 'A Challenge to Episcopal Authority?' was more honest, recognising the exceptional nature of the gathering. The Cardinal was accused 'of taking a cowardly and unfair advantage of the pulpit to attack the Irish Catholic race upon a matter on which they are trying to secure their independence, and the meeting forwarded its resolution to the Pope[91]: "We, Irish Catholic residents in London, enter our emphatic protest against the action of Cardinal Bourne, in issuing a Pastoral Letter which openly sought to interfere with our legitimate political activities in support of our country's demand that its own political determination should be recognised and respected. We consider that that letter, which entered no protest against the continuous acts of unchristian brutality perpetrated by the English Government in Ireland, was written at the dictates of a bigoted anti-Irish coterie, and was intended to assist the present Coalition Government in their efforts to thwart the will of the Irish nation."'[92]

Bourne was in Rome at the time of the meeting. Gasquet and Merry del Val could be relied upon to promote British interests at the Vatican, and there were periodic rumours of a papal condemnation of Sinn Féin. However, Irish nationalism made itself heard in Rome through the Irish College and prominent Irish Americans. Amigo was in Rome in the first weeks of 1921 and gave his take on the Irish situation to the Pope and his Secretary of State, subsequently forwarding a copy of MacVeagh's letter. So when Benedict XV wrote to the Irish hierarchy in April, his tone was conciliatory. 'In the public strife which is taking place in your country, it is the deliberate counsel of the Holy See—a counsel consistently acted upon up to the present in similar circumstances—to take sides with neither of the contending parties.'[93]

Bourne had been told to adopt a similar approach during his time in Rome. He reported back to the Vatican, 'Acting on Cardinal Gasparri's wishes I have been doing what I could since I returned home. On this side there is no difficulty about conversations. The real difficulty is to find a man who can really "answer for and make himself responsible for the other side." Many have found an easy task in stirring up strife. Is there a single one who now has the power to quell it?'[94]

It is this 'encouragement' from Rome which may explain the Cardinal's changed stance at the Bishops' Low Week Meeting on 5–6 April. Amigo had tabled an item on the Agenda: 'Is it too late for a Joint Letter of sympathy with the Irish Hierarchy in their troubles?'[95] He must have expected a familiar response. Bourne agreed to a joint letter from the hierarchy calling for renewed prayers throughout May 'that a true, just, and lasting understanding may be established between the sister countries of England and Ireland.'[96] He had never been averse to seeking spiritual assistance to resolve Irish difficulties, but on this occasion he was prepared to go much further.

The Cardinal presented the Bishops with a letter he proposed writing to Lloyd George on their behalf and agreed to relay to Cardinal Logue details of their action, conveying 'the sympathy of the English Bishops with the Irish Bishops in this time of trial.'[97] Bourne sent his letter to the Prime Minister that same day:

> I need not tell you that [our Bishops] have been most gravely concerned about the condition of Ireland. They feel that the good name of England in other countries has been, and still is being, obscured by terrible happenings which it is impossible to explain or to justify. They desire me to impress upon you most earnestly that all ground should at once be removed from the definite charges which are so constantly being made of reprisals exercised by the forces of the Crown upon perfectly innocent persons. In this connection they are convinced that much could be done towards promoting a good understanding, and the restoration of law and order, were the auxiliary troops withdrawn without delay from Ireland. Every week is adding to the difficulties of the situation. The Bishops hope that the Government will immediately take such measures as may promptly lead to the permanent reconciliation which all men, whatever their political opinions may be, so greatly desire.[98]

At last Bourne, and the hierarchy jointly, had spoken publicly and unambiguously against the atrocities being committed in the name of the British Government. Even at this late stage objection was raised to the letter. The night before it was discussed by the Bishops, the Cardinal showed his letter to Lord Edmund Talbot, recently appointed Lord Lieutenant of Ireland. He advised the Cardinal to tone it down, dropping the call for the immediate withdrawal of the Black and Tans. He used the argument adopted earlier by the Cardinal himself: the Black and Tans 'cannot with safety be withdrawn at present and that things would become worse if they were.' Talbot insinuated that the Cardinal would be guilty of political naïveté were he to send the letter unamended. 'I am afraid many of those who really understand the present position will only say "Here's another instance of those who might be expected to know better simply showing ignorance of the situation."'[99]

Whether the letter had been dispatched before Talbot's written opinion arrived, or whether he simply chose to ignore that advice, the Cardinal did not back down. Lloyd George responded petulantly, taken aback by Bourne's abandonment of his previous compliance. 'The P.M. was rather annoyed at the letter from the Bishops. Said he was surprised and thought you and they would have realised the situation better. He wished you had asked him to come and meet the Bishops and let him explain things to them.'[100] There are worse things for an Archbishop of Westminster to endure than the irritation of a Prime Minister.

This was Bourne's final involvement in the Irish Troubles, which were resolved surprisingly swiftly—at least as far as the British Government was concerned. Lloyd George, while maintaining his publicly bellicose stance, was, in fact, already putting out feelers towards a possible settlement. He had no compunction in using 'loyal' Catholic Bishops as intermediaries. It was the Irish-born Archbishop Clune of Perth who initiated the negotiating process in December 1920. For all his caution, Bourne was obviously ruled out for the role, having gained himself the reputation among Irish republicans of being their inveterate opponent. After a number of false starts, real progress was finally made after George V's conciliatory speech at the opening of the Northern Irish Parliament on 22 June 1921. A truce between the British Government and the Irish republican forces finally came into effect the following month. Under the Anglo-Irish Treaty of 6 December 1921, the Irish Free State came into being on 6 December 1922 as a Dominion within the British Empire.

The bitterness engendered in the Troubles would not be forgotten in Bourne's lifetime. He visited Ireland briefly in 1931, meeting the Irish President, the Archbishop of Armagh and the Papal Nuncio. The following year Dublin hosted the International Eucharistic Congress, and Bourne wrote to the Nuncio seeking reassurance. He had heard rumours that the conventional 'courtesies and consideration' would be withheld from him, 'because I come from England.' Rather than be subjected to insult, the Cardinal offered to develop a 'diplomatic indisposition' and stay at home.[101] On the Nuncio's advice, Bourne did attend the Congress, which passed without incident. Yet clearly he remained the object of considerable suspicion in the eyes of many Irish.

'The son of an English father and an Irish mother'[102]

Cardinal Bourne was considered to be politically astute. Why did he get it so badly wrong in connection with Ireland? There were practical considerations. He was still bruised after his confrontation with the hierarchy over diocesan division in 1917, leaving him unwilling and unable to coordinate a joint response to any major issue. The Cardinal was also overseas for significant periods of the Irish Troubles. His four month absence in the Middle East and the Balkans possibly meant that he failed to appreciate fully the significance and severity of the difficulties at their outset. Combined with his prolonged travels, bouts of ill health in the early 1920s also affected his ability to respond to the crisis. But these factors only explain and excuse so much. Bourne claimed his mixed parentage gave him a particular insight into Anglo-Irish relations and a role to play in achieving 'a true and real understanding between the sister countries.'[103] Sadly, he signally failed to realise this.

In his magisterial overview of the early twentieth-century English Church, Kester Aspden concludes that Bourne's sympathy with Irish nationalist aspirations and empathy with Irish sufferings were inhibited by an exaggerated respect for the British political establishment.[104] This is only partially correct. The Cardinal had the wisdom to recognise that, as a small minority, Catholics could generally achieve more through quiet negotiation than patent opposition. But, when necessary, he was not afraid to ruffle official sensibilities. When he finally wrote to the Prime Minister to express the Bishops' protest against reprisals and to demand the withdrawal of the offending Crown forces, it was in terms which alarmed Talbot and angered Lloyd George.

On his own admission, a more important factor for Bourne was the unity of the Church. This overriding concern was something which long pre-dated the immediate Troubles. As early as 1905 he explained his

Ireland

thinking to an Irish Bishop. 'Bishops and clergy in England, owing to the necessary political divisions among Catholics here, must stand aloof from party politics, if they are to do their duty to the souls of all alike. It would be fatal to the influence of the Catholic Church in England were she to become identified in the popular mind, as the Nonconformists are, with any political organisations.'[105] In this respect he was consistent. In 1920 he was writing, 'It is well known how scrupulous the English Bishops have always hitherto been in avoiding any public utterances that might weaken their spiritual influence with the politically widely divergent members of their flock.'[106] In connection to Ireland, Bourne carried the principle to exaggerated lengths with unfortunate results.

The Cardinal's stance was also coloured by his sensitivity to English public opinion. Generally speaking, this was a good thing. He appreciated that if the conversion of England were to be a reality, then the Catholic Church had to reach beyond the Irish immigrant community. Correspondence with the Vatican in autumn 1920 shows this consideration to be uppermost in his mind. Jackman reflected the Cardinal's views, writing in the aftermath of the Mannix and MacSwiney incidents, 'With your knowledge of England and the English character you will readily see that two such instances of tactlessness as I have described will certainly tend to bring the Catholic Church into disrepute and cause the man in the street to identify the Church not so much with Rome as with Ireland.'[107] The Cardinal employed the same arguments the following month. Mannix's promotion of the nationalist cause in his speaking tour of the North of England was doing 'the greatest possible harm to the Church in England by identifying it in the public mind with the extreme party in Irish politics.'[108]

The Cardinal's reputation for prudence and political impartiality which normally served him so well, now became a liability. Aspden's assessment is accurate. 'Acutely conscious of the divisive nature of Irish politics, Bourne wanted to avoid committing the hierarchy to any position which could have been interpreted as partisan, although he failed to recognise that not acting could itself be interpreted as a partisan stance.'[109] A Bishop's highest duty is to be a prophetic voice for peace, truth and justice—regardless of any vested interests offended in the process. On this occasion, Bourne fell short. While there was no mention of Ireland in Bourne's Advent Pastoral of 1920, Amigo had no such inhibitions. 'While we unhesitatingly and in the strongest terms condemn the murder of innocent or even guilty men, ought we not as vigorously to deprecate the reprisals on the lives and property of our fellow citizens in Ireland by those employed to preserve law and order? ... To tolerate, much more to condone such deplorable acts is to sap the moral foundations of the Government and it is the duty of Bishop, priests and people to raise their voices in earnest protest against them. We must not sin against the law of God.'[110] The law of God was at issue, and Bourne was at fault in not raising his voice in protest.

Notes

[1] Stuart, 'Notes,' AAW, Bo. IV/1/27.
[2] Jackman, *Irish Catholic*, 13 June 1940.
[3] Henry Bourne to Harry Bourne, 19 November 1868, UCA, Bourne Family Papers, OS/K2/67.
[4] Henry Bourne to Harry Bourne, 5 December 1867, UCA, Bourne Family Papers, OS/K2/31.
[5] Jackman, *Irish Catholic*, 13 June 1940.
[6] FAB, Lenten Pastoral, 1899, *Tablet*, 25 February 1899, p. 312.
[7] FAB, St Patrick's, Soho Square, 17 March 1904, cited Meynell (ed.), *A Record of the Sayings and Doings of Francis, Fourth Archbishop of Westminster*, p. 56.
[8] Jackman, *Irish Catholic*, 13 June 1940.
[9] FAB, Armagh, 24 July 1904, *Tablet*, 30 July 1904, pp. 193–194.
[10] M. Moloney to Redmond, 22 March 1905, NLI, RP, MS 15,245/4.
[11] Dr Mangan, Bishop of Kerry, Rome, 1907, cited Oldmeadow, *Francis Cardinal Bourne*, i, p. 341.
[12] FAB to Bishop Patrick O'Donnell, Bishop of Raphoe, 7 February 1905 (copy), AAW, Bo. I/73.
[13] FAB to Redmond, 13 March 1907, NLI, RP, MS 15,172.
[14] FAB interview, *Chicago Tribune*, 1921.
[15] FAB, St Patrick's Day Banquet, Hotel Cecil, 17 March 1926, *WCC*, April 1926, p. 77.
[16] FAB, *Times*, 12 November 1920.
[17] FAB to W. H. Long, 17 May 1918 (copy), AAW, Bo. I/72.
[18] Merry del Val to Gasquet, 10 July 1914, cited Leslie, *Cardinal Gasquet*, p.190.
[19] Editorial, *Tablet*, 29 April 1916, p. 552.
[20] *Tablet*, 25 March 1916, p. 392.
[21] Editorial, *Tablet*, 6 May 1916, p. 584.
[22] FAB memorandum, 6 November 1920, AAW, Bo. III/5.
[23] AAW, Bo. III/5.
[24] T. Carey to FAB, 17 July 1916, AAW, Bo. III/5.

Ireland

25 Cited Oldmeadow, *Francis Cardinal Bourne*, ii, pp. 38–39.
26 FAB memorandum, 6 November 1920, AAW, Bo. III/5.
27 FAB to Carey, 22 July 1916, AAW, Bo. III/5.
28 FAB memorandum, 6 November 1920, AAW, Bo. III/5.
29 FAB, Westminster Cathedral, 8 March 1918, *Tablet*, 16 March 1918, p. 354.
30 FAB to Lloyd George, 5 April 1918 (draft), AAW, Bo. V/27b.
31 Dillon, House of Commons, 9 April 1918, *Tablet*, 13 April 1918, p. 471.
32 FAB to Long, 17 May 1918 (copy), AAW, Bo. I/72.
33 Long to FAB, 11 June 1918, AAW, Bo. I/72.
34 Declaration of Irish Hierarchy, April 1918 .
35 Resolutions of the Catholic Union, 30 April 1918, *Tablet*, 4 May 1918, p. 580.
36 *Tablet*, 4 May 1918, p. 592.
37 Amigo, Southwark Cathedral, 19 May 1918, *Tablet*, 25 May 1918, p. 686.
38 Aspden, *Fortress Church*, pp. 82–83.
39 M. Sykes, Commons, 25 June 1918, *Tablet*, 29 June 1918, p. 815.
40 Dunn to Amigo, 30 June 1918, NotDA, Dunn Papers, cited Aspden, *Fortress Church*, p. 84.
41 FAB, Westminster Cathedral, 17 June 1920, *Tablet*, 19 June 1920, p. 821.
42 Plater to E. Eyre, 31 August 1920, AAW, Bo. V/36a.
43 FAB to Eyre, 8 September 1920, AAW, Bo. V/36a.
44 H. Somerville to FAB, 20 0ctober 1920, AAW, Bo. V/36a.
45 Sheed, *The Church and I*, p. 43.
46 FAB to hierarchy, 6 November 1920, AAW, Bo. IV/20/9c.
47 Dunn to Amigo, 9 November 1920, SAA, cited Aspden, *Fortress Church*, p. 89.
48 Jackman to Lépicier, 28 October 1920, AGOSM, Lépicier Papers.
49 H. S. Dean to Jackman, 24 September 1920, AAW, Bo. V/36a.
50 FAB to Cerretti, 22 November 1920 (copy), AAW, Bo. IV/20/9l.
51 Amigo to Lloyd George, 5 September 1920, *Tablet*, 11 September 1920, p. 354.
52 Bell, *Randall Davidson*, p. 1058.
53 J. Hagerty, *Cardinal Hinsley* (Oxford: Family Publications, 2008), p. 340.
54 FAB to Cerretti, 26 September 1920 (copy), AAW, Bo. IV/20/9a.
55 Burton. Diary, 7 October 1920, CDA.
56 M. MacSwiney to FAB, u/d (copy), BAA, D4431.
57 *Tablet*, 30 October 1920, p. 576.
58 Clifton, *Amigo*, p. 77.
59 B. Ojetti, SJ, *Synopsis Rerum Moralium et Juris Pontifici* (Prato, 1904).
60 Jackman to Lépicier, 28 October 1920, AGOSM, Lépicier Papers.
61 Jackman to W. A. S. Hewins, 14 November 1920, SUL, Hewins, 76/247–248.
62 FAB to Cerretti, 4 November 1920 (copy), AAW, Bo. IV/4/34.

63 F. L. Head to FAB, 13 November 1920, AAW, Bo. V/87.
64 Aspden, *Fortress Church*, p. 93.
65 Bishop of Cork, *Times*, 15 November 1920; FAB, *Times*, 16 November 1920.
66 FAB, *Times*, 12 November 1920.
67 *Westminster Gazette*, 28 November 1920.
68 Jackman to Lépicier, 30 November 1920, AGOSM, Lépicier Papers.
69 B. Williams, Treasurer, Peace with Ireland Committee, to FAB, 12 November 1920, AAW, Bo. V/87.
70 Lord Henry Bentinck to FAB, 19 November 1920, AAW, Bo. V/87.
71 FAB to Bentinck, 22 November 1920 (copy), AAW, Bo. V/87.
72 FAB to Cerretti, 4 November 1920 (copy), AAW, Bo. IV/4/34.
73 Jackman to Lépicier, 10 November 1920, AGOSM, Lépicier Papers.
74 Lloyd George to FAB, 29 November 1920, AAW, Bo. V/36a.
75 Belgian Hierarchy, Joint Pastoral Letter, 7 November 1920.
76 Lord Walter Kerr to Mercier, 10 December 1920 (copy), AAW, Bo. V/87.
77 Keating to Editor, 13 December 1920, *Tablet*, 18 December 1920, p. 827.
78 Casartelli to FAB, 10 January 1921, AAW, Bo. V/36a.
79 FAB to Casartelli, 11 January 1921, AAW, Bo. V/36a.
80 *Evening Standard*, 26 February 1921.
81 Dunn to Amigo, 2 December 1920, SAA, cited Aspden, *Fortress Church*, p. 96.
82 Davidson, House of Lords, 22 February 1921, cited Bell, *Randall Davidson*, p. 1059.
83 Brown to Davidson, 11 December 1920, cited Bell, *Randall Davidson*, p. 1064.
84 FAB, Letter to Clergy, 6 February 1921.
85 *Tablet*, 19 February 1921, p. 242.
86 FAB to Dunn, 21 February 1921, NotDA, Dunn, G03.03.
87 K. Barnes to FAB, 15 February 1921, AAW, Bo. V/87.
88 J. MacVeagh to *Times*, 15 February 1921.
89 FAB to Dunn, 21 February 1921, NotDA, Dunn, G03.03; *Tablet*, 19 February 1921, p. 242.
90 Oldmeadow, Notes, 18 March 1921, AAW, Bo. V/87.
91 'A Challenge to Episcopal Authority?' *WCC*, April 1921, pp. 65–66.
92 *Catholic Herald*, 26 March 1921.
93 Benedict XV to Logue, 27 April 1921, *Tablet*, 28 May 1921, p. 698.
94 FAB to Cerretti, 31 March 1921 (copy), AAW, Bo. I/72.
95 Agenda for Low Week Meeting, 5–6 April 1921, AAW, Hi. II/139/2(a).
96 Joint Letter of Hierarchy, Low Week 1921.
97 Acta of Low Week Meeting, 6 April 21, AAW, Hi. II/139/2(a).
98 FAB to Lloyd George, 6 April 1921 (copy), AAW, Bo. V/36a.
99 Talbot to FAB, 6 April 1921, AAW, Bo. I/72.
100 Talbot to FAB, 9 April 1921, AAW, Bo. I/72.

Ireland

101 FAB to Nuncio in Dublin, 18 May 1932 (copy), AAW, Bo. I/72.
102 FAB, *Times*, 12 November 1920.
103 *Ibid.*
104 Aspden, *Fortress Church*, pp. 89, 98.
105 FAB to Bishop O'Donnell of Raphoe, 7 February 1905 (copy), AAW, Bo. I/73.
106 FAB to Cerretti, 22 November 1920 (copy), AAW, Bo. IV/20/91.
107 Jackman to Lépicier, 28 October 1920, AGOSM, Lépicier Papers.
108 FAB to Cerretti, 22 November 1920 (copy), AAW, Bo. IV/20/91.
109 Aspden, *Fortress Church*, p. 98.
110 Amigo, Advent Pastoral 1920.

Chapter 19

And at Home

The Imperial Crown of England

Although half Irish, Cardinal Bourne consistently identified himself as an Englishman. He frequently referred to the British Empire as an instrument of Divine Providence, for example, when speaking to the overseas contingents of Catholic soldiers in London for the coronation of George V. 'No power in the world is more fitted for the providential extension of the Catholic Church than that which has its symbol in the Imperial Crown of England.'[1] He eulogised Queen Victoria after her death as one 'possessed of so lofty a character and such high ideals ... against whose fair repute no true word could be uttered, whose character disarmed the calumniator, and whose life was ever giving an example of those domestic virtues upon which all society is built.'[2] Such adulation might raise eyebrows today; at the time it placed Bourne in the mainstream of British society. With great pride the Archbishop led Edward VII and Queen Alexandra to their seats on the sanctuary at St James's, Spanish Place in 1908 for the Requiem Mass for the assassinated King and Crown Prince of Portugal—the first reigning British monarch to attend Mass since the seventeenth century.

Love of country, and England's destiny, were themes Bourne expounded in good times and bad. After a series of defeats in the Boer War, he told the Catholics of Southwark, 'Patriotism with an Englishman was at the present moment a duty.'[3] British successes in the Middle East were not simply attributable to General Allenby and Lawrence of Arabia. 'By the mysterious workings of Divine Providence, the control of Palestine had fallen into the hands of the English people.'[4] Comprising many Irish nationalists, not all Catholics in England shared this imperialist fervour. The *Catholic Herald* questioned the Cardinal's Holy Land pilgrimage in 1924, alleging that he had gone merely to 'wave the Union Jack.'[5]

Cardinal Bourne's intense patriotism was, however, intrinsically bound up with his faith. England had a providential role to fulfil in spreading

Catholicism, but she had to be reminded of her own Catholic past. He lost no opportunity to point out that the Anglicans were interlopers, Catholics the legitimate heirs of English history. Thus, his homily on the 800th anniversary of Waverley Abbey:

> We, the Catholics of England, come here today as to a true spiritual home. We come not as strangers and foreigners, but as fellow citizens with those who once made this spot sacred by their unending prayers and by lives consecrated wholly to the service of God and of their fellow men. We are singing today the same old litanies in the identical ancient tongue. We are offering up the same sacrifice which day by day they offered in this place. We are using the same time-honoured chant ... We must never forget that this is all one continuous work. The Church in Britain, the Church of Augustine, the Church of our English Martyrs, the Church of our Second Spring, is the one same Church engaged always in the same identical work.[6]

'A mild contempt for party politics'

In a wireless tribute to the Cardinal after his death, Viscount FitzAlan made reference to his 'Christian patriotism,' which he combined with 'a mild contempt for party politics.'[7] During his long tenure at Westminster Bourne necessarily spent much time with politicians of all hues, yet he himself was not a political prelate. On the eve of the education crisis, he reminded priests, 'It is no part of the pastoral duty of the Bishops to interfere in what are generally called politics.'[8]

Cardinal Bourne once sketched out what he felt had been the general political predilections of Catholics in England in his lifetime.

> I can just remember, it is among my very earliest memories, when most Catholics were Liberals ... At the time of which I speak the dis-establishment of the Protestant Church in Ireland by Mr Gladstone had won the sympathy of many Catholics for the party of which he was leader. Some three years later, however, he very foolishly thought it well to attack the Church in connection with the decrees of the Vatican Council, and Catholics began to turn away from the Liberal Party. For many years the majority of English Catholics would, I think, have been found in the Conservative camp.

To Bourne's mind, however, the Conservatives were too close to the Anglicans for comfort.[9]

And at Home

Whereas Cardinal Vaughan had mixed socially with Tory grandees, Bourne eschewed any suggestion of party political preference. The Cardinal's impartiality was praised in a letter written to Rome by the Catholic great and the good in the 1920s. 'Some of the Bishops now ruling in this country, owing to their antecedents or political utterances, do not enjoy that position and prestige to which their sacred office should entitle them. It should be said that with certain exceptions (most notably our venerated Cardinal Archbishop) they have not that influence in the cities in which they dwell that should rightly belong to their high station.' They contrasted this to the time of Manning and called for 'English' Bishops who would not meddle in 'secular politics.'[10] Of course, this was code for Catholic aristocrats and Unionists saying they did not want low-born 'Irish' Bishops with nationalist sympathies.

There were occasions on which Bourne was accused of departing from that neutrality. During the education crisis one Catholic MP, incorrectly, told Lloyd George, 'Archbishop Bourne has declared war against us in England; and I gather from other quarters that he and the Tories are probably already in secret alliance. This will make it a very bitter fight—especially in Lancashire.'[11] Amigo subsequently criticised the Cardinal for being too close to Lloyd George. 'He is very friendly with Lloyd George but I am sorry that he trusts the Prime Minister who will use him without helping us.'[12] This was perhaps Bourne's greatest weakness. Without supporting their political platforms, he would openly display his approval for individual politicians for whom he felt a personal affinity. He was obviously charmed by Lloyd George, sharing his preference for informal contact and the use of experts, rather than more formal channels of debate. Cardinal Bourne worked well with the 1920s Conservative Education Minister, Lord Eustace Percy, but Amigo felt he had been unwise in the public praise he bestowed upon him. 'I fear that His Eminence will have little or no influence with the present [Labour] Government as they don't trust him. He was too much for Eustace Percy.'[13]

When it came to parties, rather than personalities, Bourne remained scrupulously fair. 'It was plain that a man could be a Conservative, a Unionist, a Liberal, a Radical or a Nationalist, and at the same time be a most excellent Catholic.'[14] Others would have had him modify his stance in the light of the threat to Catholic schools. It appeared probable at one moment. 'We came very near to [the position of a party being in direct opposition to the Church], for at that time constant and direct attacks were made by the Liberal Party against Catholic education.'[15] But the Archbishop refused to be swayed.

> Men, of equal merit as Catholics, have been and always will be Conservatives or Liberals … There is nothing in the teaching of the Catholic Church against this free choice … speaking as one who is neither a Conservative nor a Liberal, neither anti-Conservative nor anti-Liberal, and standing, from my official position, absolutely aside from mere party politics, it seems manifest that both parties have an equal love of, and an ardent desire for, the well-being of England … I welcome the presence of Catholics in both political parties.[16]

Catholics might vote for any mainstream political party, but party allegiance could not be unconditional. In 1907 the Archbishop identified two areas of public policy in respect of which Catholics must unite irrespective of party: the defence of Catholic schools and the repeal of anti-Catholic legislation.[17] Two decades on, he repeated this teaching,

> Catholics might belong to any party they chose. But they must bear in mind three things: First, that no man can go the whole way with his party; because every party was guided in this country by men who very often did not know, and certainly did not yet accept, all the principles of the Catholic Church. Secondly, Catholics must go straight, in obedience to the voice of conscience, and keep their party straight. Then, again—but he hoped this was a very far-off and improbable hypothesis—if it should be their party developed principles which were in opposition to those of their Church, it would be their duty to leave that party.[18]

Bourne was unswerving in his opposition to a Catholic Party as impractical and undesirable. Unlike some of his episcopal brethren, he was too much of a realist to sanction even the possibility. He knew that across the broad sweep of public life there was insufficient common ground between Catholics to effect a stable and permanent union. 'From time immemorial Catholics in England have been divided in their political allegiance, owing to the different standpoints from which they regard matters affecting the public good.'[19] Then Catholics in Britain were too few and too scattered to secure significant representation at Westminster. It was not the business of the Church to organise a political party; the attempt to do so could expose Catholics to dangerous risks. 'Once a Catholic Party was formed, the Church would be blamed for all the errors into which such a party would inevitably fall, sooner or later.'[20]

Instead, Bourne urged Catholics to work within the existing political parties on matters of general concern and with each other on specifically Catholic issues. He was sufficiently politically astute to realise that Catholics should not identify exclusively with any one of the existing political parties. 'It is clear that if we place our reliance upon either of the great parties we shall be disappointed, as we have been in the past.'[21] Or punished by their political rivals when they attained power. 'It was ... for the good of Catholics and for the good of the nation at large that Catholics should be well represented in all political parties.'[22] The Cardinal felt his policy justified. By the 1920s more Catholic MPs represented British constituencies than ever before.[23] Regardless of the party in power, there were always Catholic MPs in Government to make the Church's concerns heard. In 1931 German Catholics, although a far greater proportion of the population, felt British Catholics were much more effective in public life. This, the Cardinal attributed, to the avoidance of the mistake of a Catholic Party.[24]

This did not mean that Catholics should not take their faith into politics. Umbrella organisations aimed at uniting and channelling Catholic activity in the public sphere did not begin under Bourne, nor were they confined to the capital. His predecessor in Southwark, Bishop Butt, had established the Catholic League in South London in 1896. There were flourishing Catholic associations in Salford, Birmingham and elsewhere, yet such organisations attained a high level of effectiveness in the early years of Bourne's time at Westminster when Catholic interests were most threatened.

A competent administrator himself, Bourne encouraged other Catholics to organise. He reminded young Catholics in Liverpool what they were capable of

> by making the power of the Catholic vote felt at election time; by canvassing and urging voters to do their duty; by recalling the former pledges, fulfilled or broken of the candidates who offer themselves for re-election; by studying and printing and publishing the record for fairness or injustice of those who again solicit the popular suffrage ... Show an Englishman that he is making a mistake and committing an injustice, and in very many cases he will do his best to redress the wrong ... It is our duty then, the

duty of you all, to educate public opinion. Unless we do, we can do nothing ... All can effect much in their ordinary conversation. Some are able to write in the press and correct the mistakes which appear therein. A few may appear on public platforms.[25]

As the threat to the schools became critical, he extended the Catholic Association which already existed in his own Diocese to act as 'a rallying point' for all Catholics.[26] He explained what was happening. 'In Westminster Catholic Associations are being formed in every Borough of the County of London north of the Thames, and these, while retaining a very wide autonomy, will be maintained in unity and cooperation by a Federation Council embracing them all.' As the move to organise became more systematic and widespread, the Archbishop insisted on one overriding principle. 'In every case these organisations are characterised by the fact that they are essentially non-political, aiming solely at uniting Catholics, as such, in defence of their religion.'[27]

Federation and Union

At a meeting at Archbishop's House in autumn 1906 Archbishop Bourne announced his desire for greater cooperation between the Catholic Associations in his Diocese. There was to be a 'Catholic Federation.' The immediate objective was the defence of the schools, but it was envisaged that the Federation would be a permanent body with a wider remit. (Around the same time Casartelli founded a similar organisation with the same name in Salford.) From the beginning Bourne was President of the Westminster Catholic Federation, 'and from that time onward he never ceased to take a most kindly paternal interest in its progress ... He was ever ready to guide and advise in its multifarious forms of activities.'[28]

No sooner was the idea conceived than objections were raised. Redmond wrote to the Archbishop telling him that he regarded this as an unwelcome encroachment upon his territory. 'We would regard such a move as a hostile one to our own political organization and that I hold very strongly it would be most injurious to the Catholic cause.'[29] Bourne required Irish votes in the Commons to constitute a credible political bloc in the educational crisis. But he was not deterred. Defence of Catholic interests was the exclusive preserve of no one political party, Conservative, Liberal or Nationalist. He responded courteously, but robustly. 'There is no reason why this new organization should be regarded as antagonistic to any of the various political organisations which command the sympa-

And at Home

thies of Catholics in London. On the other hand to manifest hostility to it would certainly be regarded not only as an act of unfriendliness to London Catholics and to myself personally, but as a challenge to my authority as Archbishop.'[30]

It was not just the Irish who were put on notice. The Chairman of the new Federation 'thanked God for the distinguished leadership which Catholics had received from the Duke of Norfolk, but in these democratic days they must be led by committees and councils who had been elected on constitutional principles in every Catholic parish in London.'[31] The Federation represented a real, and largely successful, attempt to secure and maintain the political independence of the Archbishop of Westminster.

The Archbishop encouraged both clerical and lay participation. The Executive Committee comprised ten laymen and four priests, nominated in equal numbers by the Archbishop himself and the Committee of the Catholic Association. He was fortunate in his associates. A Liberal himself, the Committee chairman, Charles Russell, had the ear of the Government. The Committee secretary was W. P. Mara[32], a tireless and effective organiser. The Committee met each Friday evening at Archbishop's House, often under Bourne's presidency. The Archbishop called upon his parish priests to ensure the formation of Catholic Associations in the 18 London boroughs and ultimately in every parish in his Diocese. The objective was the effective organisation of Catholic electors 'for the representation and defence of Catholic interests.'[33] He was deeply conscious of the under representation of British Catholics at Westminster and in local government. A wider Federation Council was formed early in 1907 with the overwhelming majority of members elected by the local Associations. The Archbishop signalled both his respect for the independence of the Council members, and also his continuing support. 'He had sufficient confidence in them to know that they would do their best, and in matters of uncertainty they might refer to him.'[34]

Faced by the serious and sustained threat to Catholic schools, the WCF was remarkably successful in ensuring unity among Catholics and making the Catholic voice heard in the public arena. Branches were rapidly established in the London boroughs with 5,000 members. The Federation undertook much of the organisation of the popular demonstrations against the Government's educational proposals and the relentless pressure on politicians. Questions, prepared by the Committee and approved by the Archbishop, were put to parliamentary candidates by branch members. Replies were carefully collated so Catholics might vote with the benefit of full information and MPs might be reminded subsequently of pledges made.

As the danger to the schools receded, divisions emerged. By 1909 the purpose of the Federation was less apparent. Charles Russell was obviously addressing real controversies when he wrote that the Federation should only intervene in politics when questions vital to the Catholic interest were at stake.

> The question, however, arises, when are we to know when there is a vital question at stake? I respectfully submit that the only occasion when we can say that a vital question is at stake is when His Grace the Archbishop in his wisdom directs us ... I wish to see in the hands of the Hierarchy an efficient weapon which can at the proper time be used with deadly effect upon our opponents ... I do not want to see an organisation established whose name and power can be taken in vain and used by irresponsible groups.[35]

In 1911 Bourne felt obliged to remind the WCF 'that they were an advisory body and could not take "public executive action" until directed by the hierarchy.'[36] Generally, however, the Federation was ready enough to restrict itself to the kind of Catholic social and moral action acceptable to the hierarchy, allowing the Cardinal to adopt an attitude of distant paternal surveillance. He explained his general policy.

> On the one hand he should not seek to control their initiative, so as to take from them the power of thinking out and proposing what they felt to be really for the good of the diocese, and on the other they should be willing to accept loyally his guidance, though there were moments when he was not able to open fully out his mind or make them understand on what principles that guidance was based. He had always known them ready to accept any guidance he might give them in respect of carrying out the suggestions they made to him. That covered what he might call his experience of the work of the Federation ever since the beginning.[37]

Not all Federations were so docile. The Cardinal clashed with Casartelli over the efforts of the Salford Federation, and its Secretary, Thomas Burns, to develop a more overtly political role and establish a Catholic Party. To the Cardinal, this seemed suicidal. His attitude was justified by the resentment of ordinary Catholics who did not take kindly to perceived efforts to detach them from the Liberal or Labour parties. Nor did the

Cardinal appreciate being lectured by Burns, through the offices of Casartelli, on the error of his opposition to a Catholic Party. He wrote to the Bishop of Salford, 'I find Mr Burns an extraordinarily difficult person to deal with.'[38] Casartelli, with his detestation of Socialism, sided with Burns and his agitation for separate Catholic political representation. But he recognised he was on weak ground. 'We cannot allow a controversy with [His Eminence], the scandal and consequent trouble would be too great.'[39] With Casartelli's death in January 1925 this alternative vision of the purpose and function of a Catholic Federation was effectively ended. Bourne's prudence and pragmatism had won out.

Towards the end of his episcopacy a little life was breathed into the Federation by Pope Pius XI's call for 'Catholic Action,' the increased presence and activity of Catholics in the public sphere. Thomas Williams, Archbishop of Birmingham, took up the challenge in England. He explained his vision to the Cardinal. This was to be no incursion into the political realm or lay-led initiative. He envisaged rather a coordinated attempt 'to save our country from the consequences of irreligion and paganism ... Let us have the correct order about the Federation from the beginning, I mean that the Hierarchy ought to give directions, and these come down from headquarters.'[40] A sick man, bruised by his earlier encounters with obstreperous Northerners, the Cardinal agreed. 'We have some over-zealous indiscreet people who are rather tiresome.'[41] The response to Rome's request was familiar: the English were already doing this; no further action was required. 'You have read and you will have heard a great deal about what is called *"Catholic Action,"* and how our Holy Father has repeatedly insisted on the need of such Catholic Action in every diocese in the world.' 'Catholic Action has long been organised in this Diocese by the Westminster Catholic Federation. It will now be the renewed duty of all concerned to make the Federation as powerful and efficient as possible.'[42]

One of the Cardinal's last public acts was to open and bless the Federation's new offices near his Cathedral in the summer of 1934. It was no longer the force it had been a generation earlier—primarily because there was no equivalent threat to galvanise Catholics across the political spectrum. Instead, the Federation was involved at that moment in the formation of the 'Clean Film Movement' to promote public morality in the cinema.[43]

If the Federation was largely the preserve of middle and politically-aware working-class Catholics, then the Catholic Union of Great Britain represented another social stratum entirely. Established by the Duke of Norfolk in 1871, it comprised aristocrats, gentry and the upper middle classes whose professed principal aim was the repeal of the remaining anti-Catholic legislation. The Cardinal found the Union less amenable to episcopal guidance. With respect to Ireland and to British party politics, he was often left wondering whether the Union's primary motivation was the Catholic faith or narrow class interest. For their part, members of the Union viewed Bourne with a mixture of grudging respect for his competence and condescension for his humbler origins.

No one can accuse Bourne of undue deference to his social superiors. He had been Archbishop of Westminster for twenty years before he first addressed the Catholic Union. When he did, there was no veneer of diplomacy. He scolded the assembled grandees:

> The fact that the Catholic Union has not been in past days sufficiently in close contact with the members of Episcopate, and especially with the Archbishop who lives here in Westminster, in London, where the centre of the Union naturally is, has been a source of weakness ... It was said that anyone who wrote to [the Union's Secretary] to propose that the Catholic Union should do something, the reply invariably came back that he deeply regretted that that particular thing was outside the scope of the Union ... In taking public action which in any sort of way might involve the interest of the Catholic Church, [Catholic societies] should consult the Ecclesiastical Authority. It would not be right to conceal from them that the absence of these connecting links had sometimes been a cause of anxiety.[44]

Old Catholics and distinguished converts were served firmly with notice that they were living in a new and democratic age.

'Words of outrage'

The Catholic Emancipation Act of 1829, extending the vote to Catholics and allowing them to sit in the House of Commons, did not repeal all anti-Catholic legislation. What remained no longer constituted real persecution, but rather an irritant and, in some cases, a gratuitous insult to the faith. Catholics found most offensive the Royal Declaration the new monarch was required to make from the throne before the assembled Lords and Commons on the day he first met Parliament. Dating from the seventeenth century, it was a crude attempt to exclude Catholics from office. The king was required to reject the doctrine of transubstantiation and declare that 'invocation or adoration of the Virgin Mary or any other Saint, and the Sacrifice of the Mass as they are now used in the Church of Rome are superstitious and idolatrous.'[45] Catholics objected not to their sovereign affirming his Protestant faith, but to the fact that of the many faiths practised throughout the British Empire, theirs alone was singled out for attack and abuse.

When Bourne arrived at Westminster Catholics were still smarting from the offensive words uttered at the accession of Edward VII. As Bishop of Southwark, he had joined with the hierarchy in deploring the situation and seeking redress. 'As Guardians of the truths of Revelation, we venture earnestly to implore the Committee of the House of Lords, appointed to report on the Royal Declaration and Oath, to counsel the Legislature not to encroach upon the domain of theology by continuing to single out doctrines professed by the majority of Christians for denunciation by the Sovereign upon his accession to the throne.'[46]

Lord Salisbury's engrained Anglican conservatism, and a failure to agree an alternative, meant there was no change at the time. But the situation was clearly intolerable when the King-Emperor ruled over a British Empire with at least twelve million Catholic subjects, including Irish, Maltese and almost 50% of Canadians, whose House of Commons passed a resolution deploring the words their monarch was required to utter. The imperial dimension clinched the matter, a fact exploited by English Catholics. 'If the abomination had been repeated today, in the teeth of that solemn protest, and with every circumstance of deliberation, it is not too much to say that the bonds of the Empire would have been loosened.'[47]

Nevertheless, legislation had still to be enacted at Westminster, and Bourne maintained constant pressure for repeal. One of the four issues he identified in 1907 as requiring the consent of all Catholics was 'the repeal of the infamous enactment which compels every Sovereign on his accession to greet his Catholic subjects with words of outrage applied to their most hallowed beliefs.'[48] Impartial observers felt Bourne's dignified response to the unjust prohibition of the Eucharistic Procession in 1908 hastened the revision of the Royal Declaration.[49] That autumn Redmond introduced a Bill to that effect. Asquith acknowledged the iniquity of the situation, but a large parliamentary majority returned by Protestant Nonconformists led to further pragmatic procrastination. (After the indecisive Election of January 1910, Asquith was to become dependent on Irish Nationalist votes.)

The matter became critical again with Edward VII's death on 10 May 1910. Even before the King's death, Bourne wrote to the Prime Minister, playing the Empire card. He expressed 'the very earnest hope that some way may be found whereby the new Sovereign may be relieved from the necessity of uttering the words of a Declaration which is injurious to his own honour and truthfulness, and a grievous insult to every one of the millions of Catholics scattered throughout the British Empire. I have before me the words of strong and urgent protest uttered in Canada, in Malta, in India, in Ceylon, in Mauritius, in Australia, on the occasion when this Declaration was last spoken ... I need not refer to the protests often renewed throughout the British Isles.'[50] No more probably needed to be said, but nothing was left to chance. Lord Edmund Talbot was sent to gain assurances from the Liberal Government Ministers, and returned satisfied.[51] The Archbishop entrusted the Catholic case to Lord Braye in the Lords and Redmond in the Commons.

The Vatican's refusal to allow a Mass for the dead King caused an anxious moment and the fear of an anti-Catholic backlash. But concerns for imperial unity won the day. George V would not be required to insult his Catholic subjects at the outset of his reign. Parliament approved a new form of the Declaration, passed into law in August 1910, which satisfied all but the most bigoted Protestant: 'I ... declare that I am a faithful Protestant and that I will, according to the true intent of the enactments which secure the Protestant succession in the Throne of my Realm, uphold and maintain the said enactments to the best of my powers according to law.'[52] Unlikely to have much bearing upon Asquith, the Archbishop was gracious in his thanks: 'It is with great pleasure that I write to convey to you my own deep appreciation—heartily endorsed at a very large public meeting last night by all who are taking part in this our first National Catholic Congress—of the courage, determination and tact that you have shown in dealing with the question of the Accession Declaration. I am sure that our feelings will be shared by Catholics throughout the Empire.'[53]

Periodic attempts were made to repeal the remaining Catholic disabilities. Overturning the Act of Settlement to allow a Catholic to sit on the throne was a reform too far. But increasingly Catholics asked why one of their number should not be Lord Chancellor of England. Although not

And at Home

enforced, it grated that in the 1920s legislation was still on the statue book impeding gifts to religious houses and requiring religious orders to register to with the local J.P. and forbidding them to wear their habits outdoors. It was still illegal to ring Catholic church bells, external worship was prohibited and the provisions of the Emancipation Act could still be invoked against Catholic processions. An attempt in 1925 to make a clean sweep of these outstanding irritants foundered on the question of the Lord Chancellor. In his anachronistic capacity as 'Keeper of the King's Conscience,' it was argued that a Catholic could not advise a Protestant monarch.

A Roman Catholic Relief Bill was re-introduced the following year by Lord FitzAlan and two Tory MPs, the Catholic Francis Blundell and the Anglican Dennis Herbert. Having passed the initial parliamentary stages, the Cardinal wrote courteously, but firmly, to Stanley Baldwin. He wrote not as a supplicant seeking charity, but as an injured party entitled to redress, telling the Prime Minister the Bishops looked to him 'to see that this Bill passes into Law during the current session of Parliament. Trusting in the spirit of justice and the fairmindedness of H.M.'s Ministers and of the large majority of the House of Commons we have abstained from all public action in this matter, and it would be a grievous disappointment to all whom I represent, were this long over-due act of reparation to be again postponed. We do not ask for privileges but we do claim to have the same rights as the rest of Englishmen.'[54] The Cardinal's stance in the General Strike taking place at this time gave him additional reason to feel confident of the Government's support.

The Bill's success was not guaranteed. The Evangelical Home Secretary, Sir William Joynson Hicks, suggested the Government only provide facilities for the Bill if Catholics consented to the retention of restrictions against their outdoor processions. As in 1908 ultra-Protestants could still threaten legal sanctions against Blessed Sacrament processions. Bourne was having none of it. He allowed Catholic parliamentarians to head the public negotiations, but he resumed his direct correspondence with Baldwin.

> That our religious processions should continue to be subject to a law of exception instead of being brought definitely under the common law of the land affecting processions of all kinds, as we desire them and are fully justified in desiring them to be, will justly give rise to feeling and expressions of resentment and indignation most harmful to His Majesty's Government and to the good name

429

of England throughout the Empire ... In the interest of the Government and of England and of the Empire, no less than in that of those whom I represent, I venture to ask your very earnest attention for these most grave considerations.[55]

Baldwin had no special affinity for Catholics, but he could not ignore the Cardinal's appeal to the Englishman's sense of fair play and the imperial consequences if institutional prejudice was perceived to continue. Bourne's strategy of adopting Baldwin's language and sentiments as his own was successful. His desire to see the Woolsack opened up to Catholics had to be abandoned, but everything else was achieved. Baldwin was persuaded to face down his own Home Secretary. FitzAlan congratulated the Cardinal on his leadership. 'I do not think facilities would have been granted by the Government had it not been for Your Eminence's letter to the Prime Minister.'[56] In success, the Cardinal was as gracious as he had been over the Royal Declaration, thanking Baldwin 'for the very important personal part which you so kindly took in making possible and easy the passing into law of the "Catholic Relief Act." We know how difficult the matter would have been without your kind personal intervention.'[57]

'A Party to which a Catholic should not belong'[58]

The greatest change to the British political landscape during Bourne's lifetime was the eclipse of the Liberals by the Labour Party as the principal party of opposition to the Conservatives. The emergence of the Labour Party presented the Catholic Church with a dilemma. On the one hand the Church unequivocally condemned European Socialism for its repudiation of religion and private property. Even the British Labour Party initially inclined to a purely secular educational system.[59] On the other, working class Catholics in the industrial cities, who formed the vast majority of the faithful in this country, instinctively looked to the Labour Party to protect their economic interests.

Kester Aspden claims that the Catholic Bishops studiously disregarded the advance of the Labour Party until forced to do so by Casartelli and the Catholic Federation at the Low Week Meeting in 1917.[60] With respect to Bourne, and others, that is not correct.

As early as 1907 a Dr Mooney spoke at the CTS Conference in Preston in the presence of the Archbishop. He argued that, given the Labour Party's bye-election victories, Socialism could not simply be ignored. Catholics had to distinguish Socialism and social reform. Of

And at Home

course militant materialism must be confronted, but the situation was nuanced. 'It must not be lost sight of that the central principle of Socialism, the desire to even out the conditions of existence, to abolish poverty and its concomitant evils, is in some sense a challenge to us as Christians and as Catholics ... Catholics must be social reformers.'[61] This was Bourne's own line of argument.

For a generation Bourne was cautiously consistent. Socialism was one of the main subjects discussed at the 1909 CTS Conference in Manchester. Again, the Archbishop listened carefully to the speakers, assuring them that the Bishops were prepared to give considerable latitude to their discussions. He then set out his own views. He fully acknowledged and deplored the 'terrible social inequalities' which caused contemporaries to turn to Socialism. The Church had to meet 'Socialism in a constructive way,' and only 'the teaching of the Catholic Church' constituted 'a real bulwark' against the excesses of Socialist doctrine.[62] In his own Diocese he urged his clergy to study the Church's social teaching, especially relevant papal documents, so they might better instruct their people in these matters.[63]

Throughout, the Archbishop counselled against those who cast wild epithets at their political opponents. 'He supposed there was no other word used more carelessly and more inaccurately than "Socialistic."' For example, many accused Lloyd George of 'Socialism' because of the taxation and welfare measures contained in his Budgets. It was no business of the Catholic Bishops to opine on the economic wisdom of such policies, but they were certainly not 'Socialist' in the sense understood and condemned by the Church.[64]

Bourne was prepared to ask whether the British Labour was, in fact, a Socialist Party. The Church, and he himself, condemned Socialism when it denied the right to the private ownership of property, when it denied the parent's right to a religious education for their children and when it promoted class warfare. He was sufficiently realistic to appreciate that there were individuals within the Labour Party who were Socialists in the true sense of the word. Yet when the average Labour Party member called himself a 'Socialist,' the Archbishop was convinced that he meant little more than 'that he was in favour of social development, or social progress in some form or other.'[65]

The Archbishop evinced sympathy for the Socialists' sense of social justice. 'Though they did not think of the world to come, [they] had nevertheless to some extent the same object as the Church in so far as they were labouring to secure contentment in the present life. Catholics, therefore, who possessed the knowledge of Revelation, and who knew that contentment in this life was indeed part of God's plan, ought not to regard those who were opposed to them as necessarily their enemies.'[66] In the early twentieth century when Socialism was being roundly condemned by many European hierarchies, these were advanced views for a Catholic Archbishop. It is scarcely surprising, therefore, that he should find himself accused of being a Socialist.[67] In the 1924 General Election campaign, he was charged with having said 'that the views of the Labour Party in England approximated more nearly to Catholic principles than did those of any other party.' Bourne denied this, alleging errors in translation. (He had been speaking in French to a Dutch journalist.) But he continued to assert 'that the leaders of the Labour Party were unconsciously approximating towards Catholic views.'[68]

Needless to say, this did not go down well in certain quarters of the Catholic Church. The Tory grandees who were accustomed to influence under Cardinal Vaughan must have despaired at the new regime. But Bishop Casartelli was also virulently anti-Socialist, largely as a result of his experience of European politics. Both the Salford Catholic Federation and the Catholic Union sought episcopal condemnation of the Labour Party.

A public squabble erupted in the correspondence pages of the *Tablet* between the Catholic Social Guild, who maintained that membership of the Labour Party was perfectly permissible, and Thomas Burns as Secretary of the Catholic Trades Unionists. Burns was in no mood for compromise. 'We would prefer to disturb the Catholic surface of our time, disedifying as it may be to those who could cry peace where there is no peace, rather than be consenting parties to a propaganda which revives "Catholic Socialism" under unofficial approbation.'[69] The Bishops declined any involvement. They

> deprecate any pronouncement upon the controversy that has arisen between these parties on the subject of Socialism. They do not consider there is anything to pronounce upon. Their Lordships agree that no Catholic can consistently belong to any of the Socialist organisations, and consider it a distinct advantage that Catholic Trades Unionists have laid down for themselves that excellent prohibition without the intervention of the Bishops. The Catholic Social Guild on the other hand claims a certain latitude in discussing economic theories, misnamed Socialism, until those theories have been authoritatively

condemned. As the Bishops are not prepared to deal with these theories, the Catholic Social Guild will continue to enjoy this latitude it claims without their telling them so.[70]

Burns felt his moment had arrived in February 1918 as the Labour Party adopted its infamous Clause IV committing the Party to 'the common ownership of the means of production.' The Salford Federationists trumpeted, 'The Labour Party is now extinct and the Socialist Party of Great Britain is an accomplished fact ... The policy of permeation is finished. Catholics cannot permeate Protestantism, and they cannot permeate Socialism. They must stand outside both. The question remains, Shall we face facts?'[71] Their frustration mounted at the Bishops' continuing procrastination. Why could they not be more like the Dutch who had no truck with equivocation: 'Catholics! The choice is either for or against Christ, for or against your Holy Faith. The alternative is either Catholic or socialist: but to be a Catholic and a socialist at the same time is an impossibility.'[72] The Cardinal remained unmoved. 'Mr Burns causes a good deal of irritation ... [and appeared to] think that the Bishops must make pronouncements as and when he wishes.'[73]

The Catholic Union, with their impeccable connections, managed things more subtly. The Tory MP, Stuart Coats, expressed to Cardinal Gasquet his consternation at 'the attitude of the Catholic hierarchy in this country, with not a word of warning given to those hundreds of thousands of Catholic electors at the approach of the election, just when the Labour Party has finally announced itself as a definitely Socialist Party ... [He wished that] Catholics in this country can have some authoritative warning given them that they cannot support a Party by their votes which is pledged to Socialism.'[74]

Rome reacted cautiously, seeking the advice of Cardinal Bourne and the Bishops of Northampton, Southwark and Salford. The first three, for differing reasons, all opposed any condemnation of the Labour Party. Keating believed that such a move would be interpreted as the Church 'siding with the rich against the poor, and using her spiritual influence for political objects.'[75] Amigo was equally pragmatic. 'The Labour Party will probably be in power in a short time and ... it is for us to try and work with them ... it would be a profound mistake to condemn the Labour Party. Our own people consist mainly of the working class, and mostly in favour of the Labour Party, and they look upon it simply as a political party willing and ready to help them with their difficulties, whereas the others have promised much and done little for them.'[76]

Bourne consulted Canon Moyes[77] and sought to pronounce on the principles at stake. 'As to the Labour question, I feel convinced that any profound or really thorough examination of the theological issues involved would result in finding that many of the Socialistic prospects—whatever their economic value may be—are not contrary to faith or morals, and that it would be supremely imprudent, on the strength of them, to ban the Labour Party.'[78] Moyes was afraid 'the Catholic labouring man will have his religion put in antagonism to his political and professional interests and sympathies, resulting either in alienation from the Faith, or in ostracism in his Trade Union and the odium of disloyalty to his fellow workmen.' Moyes agreed with the Cardinal: this was not a matter of faith. 'A great deal of what people call "Socialism" is not forbidden by any law, natural or Divine. Neither is Socialism an inseparable whole, nor is the Labour Party committed to it as such.' He appreciated what was at stake. 'The matter seems one which may deeply affect the whole future of Catholicism in England. But I hope sincerely that Rome will not be pushed by these Northerners into saying undemocratic things which will have to be explained away afterwards.'[79] The preponderance of episcopal opinion encouraged Rome in its inclination to do nothing.

Burns continued to seek the censure of the Labour Party, the Bishops continued to avoid studiously any such thing. In 1921 Burns persuaded Catholic trade unionists to pass a resolution declaring that no Catholic could be a Socialist and that the British Labour Party was indeed a Socialist Party. The Cardinal simply commented laconically 'those who passed the resolution with regard to Catholics and the Labour Party do not adequately represent the Catholics of this country.'[80]

An inconclusive General Election led to Ramsay MacDonald's formation of the first (minority) Labour Government in January 1924. The Catholic Bishops were faced with a reality rather than a hypothesis. Divisions ran too deeply to allow them to speak collectively. However, in the summer of 1924 Cardinal Bourne spoke unequivocally in the Amsterdam interview referred to above. '"I assure you positively that our Labour Party's programme contains nothing which threatens religion. No doubt there are extremists among them; but the Party as such has nothing in common with the Socialists of the Continent ... Mr Macdonald is neither a materialist nor a Marxist, and one can say the same of the principal "Labour men." The Cardinal added that, without knowing it, the Party gets near, in certain respects to the social doctrine of Catholicism.'[81] Bourne repeated these views in East London early the following year.[82] There were Bishops who would have disagreed, but such a clear declaration effectively killed any possibility of the Church's condemnation of the Labour Party.

Whatever his personal relationship with Lord Eustace Percy in the outgoing ministry, the Cardinal had no principled objections to the second Labour administration either. With Casartelli no longer in Salford, he felt able to speak for the hierarchy as a whole. He wrote to a correspondent during the 1929 Election campaign, 'As far as the Labour Party in England is concerned the Bishops are of the opinion that it is not a Socialist party in the sense in which socialism is condemned by the Catholic Church.'[83] He used a keynote speech in the Albert Hall to make the same point more publicly, referring to 'the new Ministry, to which as representing the constituted authority of the country, I wish every success.'[84]

The Cardinal had to address the matter one final time. Pope Pius XI's 1931 Encyclical, *Quadragesimo Anno*, concerned the Church's social teaching. It included an unambiguous statement: 'No one can be at the same time a sincere Catholic and a true Socialist.' Bourne was adamant: there was no new principle at issue. 'Another question will now be asked me—"Has the Holy Father's Encyclical caused you to change your mind in any way?" On this point I am able to say that I see no reason whatever for changing my mind. On the contrary, I think that the Encyclical, if I understand it rightly, fully confirms what I have already said ... I think it will be generally admitted that very few members of the Labour Party in England would base their desire for Social Reform on the principles which His Holiness has so rightly and so strongly condemned.'[85] Westminster had spoken; the case was closed.

The Catholic Church's acceptance of the British Labour Party arguably represents Bourne's greatest contribution to the political and ecclesiastical life of the twentieth century, and deserves greater recognition. He was not the only Catholic Bishop to pursue this line, but his doing so consistently and from such an early stage as Archbishop of Westminster, proved conclusive. Unlike elsewhere in Europe, the Church would not be identified with reaction and privilege. Catholicism did not become the preserve of the middle and upper classes. Believing that the Church had their material, as well as spiritual, wellbeing at heart, working class Catholics continued to practise their faith until Vatican II and beyond. It was not just the Church which reaped the fruits of the Cardinal's wise tolerance. The steadying influence of so many Christian members, Catholic and Nonconformist, helped ensure the Labour Party remained, essentially, a social democratic, rather than a Socialist, party.

Notes

1. FAB, Westminster Cathedral, 1911, cited Meynell (ed.), *A Record of the Sayings and Doings of Francis, Fourth Archbishop of Westminster*, p. 140.
2. FAB, Pastoral Letter, January 1901, cited Oldmeadow, *Francis Cardinal Bourne*, i, p. 171.
3. FAB, Kingston, 14 December 1899, *Times*, 15 December 1899.
4. FAB, CWL AGM, 19 January 1925, *Tablet*, 24 January 1925, p. 117.
5. *Catholic Herald*, 23 February 1924.
6. FAB, Homily, Waverley Abbey, 18 July 1928, cited FAB, *Occasional Sermons*, pp. 151–156.
7. Fitzalan, Broadcast tribute to FAB, cited Oldmeadow, *Francis Cardinal Bourne*, ii, p. 343.
8. FAB, Ad clerum on behalf of the Bishops, 19 December 1905.
9. FAB, Speech on Encyclical, *Quadragesimo Anno*, AAW, Bo. IV/1/20.
10. U/d letter from Catholic Union to Gasquet—forwarded by FitzAlan under cover of his letter of 31 July 1923? DAA, Gasquet, 889.
11. T. P. O'Connor to Lloyd George, 25 September 1909, cited Aspden, *Fortress Church*, p. 28.
12. Amigo to Gasquet, 25 February 1920, DAA, Gasquet Papers, 917A.
13. Amigo to Downey, 30 October 1929 (copy), SAA, Amigo Papers, Correspondence with Bishops, cited Aspden, *Fortress Church*, p. 178.
14. FAB, Leeds Town Hall, 5 August 1905, *Tablet*, 12 August 1905, p. 264.
15. FAB, Premierland Hall, East London, 13 January 1925, *Tablet*, 17 January 1925, p. 73.
16. FAB, Address to Annual Catholic Reunion, Birmingham, 22 January 1907, *Tablet*, 26 January 1907, pp. 139–140.
17. Ibid.
18. FAB, Premierland Hall, East London, 13 January 1925, *Tablet*, 17 January 1925, p. 74.
19. FAB, Address to Annual Catholic Reunion, Birmingham, 22 January 1907, *Tablet*, 26 January 1907, p. 141.
20. FAB, Birmingham Catholic Congress, 4 August 1923, *Times*, 6 August 1923.
21. FAB, Address to Annual Catholic Reunion, Birmingham, 22 January 1907, *Tablet*,

26 January 1907, p. 141.
22 FAB, Leeds Town Hall, 5 August 1905, *Tablet*, 12 August 1905, p. 264.
23 FAB, Birmingham Catholic Congress, 4 August 1923, *Times*, 6 August 1923.
24 FAB, Cathedral Hall, 24 July 1931, *Times*, 25 July 1931.
25 FAB to Catholic Young Men's Societies, Liverpool, 4 December 1904, *Tablet*, p. 929.
26 FAB, Catholic Association Dinner, *Tablet*, 20 January 1906, p. 101.
27 FAB, Address to Annual Catholic Reunion, Birmingham, 22 January 1907, *Tablet*, 26 January 1907, p. 142.
28 H. A. Smith, 'The Late Cardinal and the WCF' *WCC*, April 1935, p. 59.
29 Redmond to FAB, 4 December 1906 (copy), NLI, RP, MS 15,172.
30 FAB to Redmond, 8 December 1906, NLI, RP, MS 15,172.
31 Russell, Catholic Association Dinner, Holborn, 15 January 1907, *Tablet*, 19 January 1907, p. 94.
32 William Mara, KSG, JP (1861–1949), a judge's clerk. He was active in the campaign for Catholic schools at the time of the 1906 Bill and served as Secretary of the WCF from its inception in 1906 until the late 1920s.
33 Westminster Catholic Associations' Federation Committee Rules, AAW Bo. I/25; Tablet, 22 December 1906, p. 981; FAB, Speech on 25th anniversary of Westminster Federation, 21 June 1931, *Tablet*, 27 June 1931, pp. 854–855.
34 *Tablet*, 2 February 1907, p. 184.
35 Russell, 'The Catholic Federation,' *WCC*, November 1909, pp. 317–318.
36 Catholic Times, 10 March 1911, cited Aspden, *Fortress Church*, p. 33.
37 FAB to WCF, 3 April 1916, *Tablet*, 8 April 1916, p. 478.
38 FAB to Casartelli, 7 September 1923, AAW, Bo. V/43d.
39 Casartelli, cited Aspden, *Fortress Church*, p. 154.
40 Archbishop T. Williams to FAB, 6 October 1933, AAW, Bo. I/25.
41 FAB to Williams, 10 October 1933, AAW, Bo. I/25.
42 FAB, Lenten Pastoral, 1934; Circular, FAB to Westminster clergy, 4 May 1934, AAW, Bo. I/25.
43 *WCC*, August 1934, p. 141; *WCC*, September 1934, p. 167.
44 FAB, Address to the Catholic Union, 22 March 1923, *Tablet*, 31 March 1923, p. 440.
45 Viscount Llandaff, 'The Royal Declaration,' *Report of the Nineteenth Eucharistic Congress*, pp. 50–51.
46 Vaughan and the English hierarchy, June 1901, *Tablet*, 13 July 1901, p. 73.
47 Editorial, *Tablet*, 2 July 1910, p. 5.
48 FAB, 'The Attitude of Catholics towards the Public Questions of the Day,' Birmingham, January 1907, *WCC*, March 1908, p. 74.
49 *The Spectator*, 19 September 1908, cited *Report of the Nineteenth Eucharistic Congress*, p. 634.

50 FAB to Asquith, 9 May 1910, AAW, Bo. I/44.
51 Talbot to FAB, 12 May 1910, AAW, Bo. I/44.
52 Cited Oldmeadow, *Francis Cardinal Bourne*, ii, p. 53.
53 FAB to Asquith, 1 August 1910, cited *Tablet*, 5 August 1910, p. 207.
54 FAB to S. Baldwin, 1 May 1926, copy, AAW, Bo. I/108.
55 FAB to Baldwin, 30 June 1926 (copy), AAW, Bo. I/108.
56 FitzAlan to FAB, 14 December 1926, AAW, Bo. I/108.
57 FAB to Baldwin, 25 January 1927, draft, AAW, Bo. I/108.
58 T. Burns, *Blackburn Weekly Telegraph*, 25 October 1919.
59 John Davies, 'Catholic Representatives in Parliament: The North West of England, 1918–1945,' in *Recusant History*, 26,2 (2002), pp. 364–365.
60 Aspden, *Fortress Church*, p. 62.
61 Dr Mooney, CTS Conference, Preston, 10 September 1907, *Tablet*, 14 September 1907, pp. 431–432.
62 FAB, CTS Conference, Manchester, 19 September 1909, *Tablet*, 25 September 1909, p. 509; 21 September 1909, *Tablet*, 25 September 1909, p. 513.
63 FAB, Allocution, Diocesan Synod, 13 October 1909.
64 FAB, National Catholic Congress, Leeds, 30 July 1910, *Tablet*, 6 August 1910, p. 220.
65 FAB, Premierland Hall, East London, 13 January 1925, *Tablet*, 17 January 1925, pp. 73–74.
66 FAB, Ampleforth, 12 June 1912, *Tablet*, 22 June 1912, p. 976.
67 FAB CSG meeting, 20 March 1912, *Tablet*, 30 March 1912, p. 492.
68 FAB, Premierland Hall, East London, 13 January 1925, *Tablet*, 17 January 1925, pp. 73–74.
69 Burns to the Editor, *Tablet*, 20 January 1917, p. 84.
70 Acta of Meeting of the Bishops, 17 April 1917.
71 *Catholic Federationist*, April 1918, pp. 2–3.
72 Joint Pastoral of Dutch hierarchy, 10 December 1918, *Tablet*, 1 February 1919, p. 123.
73 FAB to Casartelli, 20 May 1919, SDA, Catholic Federation File, cited Aspden, *Fortress Church*, p. 137.
74 S. Coats to FAG, 27 October 1918, DAA, Gasquet Papers, File 889, cited Aspden, *Fortress Church*, pp. 133–134.
75 Keating to Gasparri, 1919, NorDA, cited Aspden, *Fortress Church*, p. 135.
76 Amigo to Gasparri, cited Clifton, *Amigo*, p. 110.
77 Canon Theologian of Westminster.
78 Moyes to Jackman, u/d, AAW, Hi. II/128.
79 Moyes to Jackman, u/d, October/November 1919?, AAW, Hi. II/128.
80 Jackman to Eyre, 17 December 1921, AAW, Bo. V/43d.
81 *Nouvelles Religieuses*, 1 November 1924, translation of *De Tijd* interview, cited *Tablet*,

15 November 1924, p. 628.
82 FAB, Premierland Hall, East London, 13 January 1925, *Tablet*, 17 January 1925, pp. 73–74.
83 FAB to C. C. Longridge, 18 May 1929 (copy), AAW, Hi. II/128.
84 FAB, National Catholic Congress, Royal Albert Hall, 13 September 1929, cited FAB, *Congress Addresses*, p. 183.
85 FAB speech, Edinburgh, 17 June 1931, AAW, Bo. IV/1/20.

Chapter 20

To 'Guide Society Aright'

'Definite principles'

In addition to ministering the sacraments and governing the local Church, the Bishop's main duty is to teach the faith of Christ as passed down from the apostles. Cardinal Bourne wrote no doctrinal treatise. Yet in his pastoral letters, homilies and speeches for the better part of four decades, he consistently expounded and defended the teaching of the Catholic Church. In doing so, he reached a wider audience in more accessible terms.

Bourne was prescient in identifying moral and social issues as the overriding questions of his day. 'The main problems are these: the preservation of the Christian character of the mind of this country, and the safeguarding of the Christian morality of its people. In other words: are the English people to remain definitely Christian in their outlook upon life, and equally Christian in the conduct of their lives?' He appreciated, however, that the underlying cause of incipient secularism was doctrinal. The behaviour of the English people was determined by their belief—or lack of it. 'Is not England, then, in real danger of losing her Christian character which radically depends upon her acceptance of Jesus Christ as her Divine Lord and Saviour?'[1]

Although not immediately apparent to all contemporaries, Bourne saw that Protestantism in England had passed its high watermark. Not only was it unable to retain the allegiance of most Englishmen in terms of religious practice, but its internal divisions and inconsistencies made it increasingly unable to address convincingly the questions thrown up in the aftermath of the First World War. The Cardinal was convinced that 'the Catholic Church had a new work to do, or rather an old work in new conditions. It was becoming more and more clear every day that it was only the Catholic Church that could guide society aright; only the Catholic Church that, by its definite principles, could withstand the torrent of evils which must come upon this country if those tendencies prevailed.'[2] The Catholic Church was no longer a persecuted minority on the fringes of society. She was now centre stage with a vital task which no one else could perform. 'The Catholic Church gives a clear answer and affords a plain solution. Can she, as the second hundred years of her renewed freedom begin in our country, save, renew, and perpetuate the Christianity of England?'[3]

Cardinal Bourne was neither a brilliant theologian nor a great orator. But he had a grasp of what was truly important, and a conviction in expressing it, which appealed to Middle England. In the face of Protestant Modernism, one of his own priests urged him to make a robust defence of the divinity of Christ. 'God has given you that particular gift of style, which impresses the English public with a feeling of power joined to precision, of strength yet self-possession.'[4]

The Demon Drink

Bourne's first foray into the field of social and moral teaching as Archbishop of Westminster was on a traditional topic. Temperance had been one of Manning's great crusades. Initially, it seemed that his fervour was matched by his successor-but-one. In his first Westminster Pastoral Bourne wrote, 'There is an evil in our midst which probably overshadows all the rest ... We should be wanting in our duty were we not to speak to you ... of the havoc which is being wrought all around us by the abuse of strong drink ... It is, therefore, our duty, in so far as our opportunities permit, to take some part in the public efforts which are made to advance the cause of Temperance.'[5] It was not just words. The new Archbishop had already signed the public memorial on Temperance, declaring 'that public houses should be suppressed by public opinion, and that compensation should be granted to dispossessed publicans by the trade itself.'[6] He called his priests to a meeting at the Cathedral which resulted in the creation of a Temperance Committee 'to consider in what way it may be possible to promote Temperance work in the Archdiocese.'[7]

The experience of total war gave new impetus to the Temperance movement. The damage to the physical and moral health of servicemen, the loss to the war effort, galvanised churchmen in an early display of Christian unity. On 6 April 1915 the Cardinal joined the Archbishops of Canterbury and York and the President of Free Church Council in signing a statement urging nation to follow the King's lead and to abstain completely from alcohol for the duration of the War.[8]

Bourne played an active role in the Temperance Council of the Christian Churches of England and Wales established in the same year, presiding at its first AGM. At a meeting addressed by Archbishop Davidson and General Booth of the Salvation Army, the Cardinal condemned the effect alcohol abuse had on public order and the plight of women and children. He proposed the motion declaring 'the absolute necessity for legislation after the close of the War to defend the industry and home-life of the nation against intemperance.'[9] In the closing days of the War he spoke on behalf of the Temperance Committee before a Commons Committee, setting out its proposals for peacetime: limited licensing hours, a permanent licensing authority and the prohibition of the sale of alcohol to minors.[10]

The Cardinal's position on Temperance was more nuanced than that of some Protestants. Speaking both to churchmen and to Parliament, he emphasized strongly the need to provide alternative recreational activities to take the place of public houses. He also queried the veracity of some of the promotional material put out by the Temperance movement. He found many of the pamphlets 'which professed to treat of this problem from the scientific point of view ... utterly unconvincing.'[11] Such honesty and moderation won him few friends among the activists of the movement.

Some disliked the fact that the Cardinal favoured Temperance—and never prohibition. He was not a teetotaller, offering wine at his table at Archbishop's House and taking a glass or two himself.[12] Before agreeing to an Anglican Bishop's request to address a Temperance meeting, Bourne wanted to know the line it would take. 'If the campaign is to be directed against all forms of alcohol I fear that I cannot conscientiously take part in it.'[13] The Cardinal favoured education as the means of combating alcoholic excess, and had reservations about the desirability and effectiveness of legislation. He told MPs, 'There will always be a considerable number of persons who desire refreshment of an alcoholic character. They claim truthfully that they can and do use such refreshment in moderation. There is no law, human or divine, which may legitimately debar them permanently ... from the use of their liberty in this matter ... Legislation is not the cure for all the evils of the world, but wise law-making may remove obstacles which are insurmountable by purely voluntary effort.'[14]

Above all, the Cardinal was far too balanced to view the Christian virtue of temperance as a single issue campaign. Rather, it was applicable to life as a whole. 'He thought it a great loss to this movement that, in the English mind, temperance had come to be associated simply with matters connected with strong drink. Such an application lowered the whole aspect of the question. Temperance was one of the great moral virtues—it must regulate every appetite of human nature.'[15]

The Nation's Crisis

Cardinal Bourne saw the First World War as a defining moment for the Catholic Church in England. Residual anti-Catholicism was on the wane. Taken from their villages and slums, a generation of soldiers had fought in Catholic countries alongside Catholic colleagues and allies. No one could fault the Church's contribution to the war effort. The Cardinal was determined that the Church should make an even greater contribution to the national life in peacetime. (His tenacity in seeking diocesan division should be viewed from this perspective.) He identified a vacuum created by partisan infighting within the Church of England and the gradual collapse of Protestant confidence and credibility occasioned by liberal scholarship. He sought to manoeuvre the Church to assume the role he felt she was destined to fulfil.

The years immediately after the War saw a brief flowering of Catholic social teaching under the Cardinal's patronage, but his interest in social questions predates that time. Again, there were shades of Manning in the young Archbishop, who declared, 'The mission of the Church is first of all to the poor. Wherever she goes her longing is to bring consolation, light and help to those most in need.'[16] Bourne invited criticism in 1907 by lending his Cathedral pulpit for a series of homilies on Catholic social teaching by the Dominican, Fr Vincent McNabb, who was believed to hold advanced ideas.[17]

This teaching was to be expounded and disseminated more systematically by the Catholic Social Guild, established under the presidency of Mgr Henry Parkinson at the 1909 National Catholic Congress. Bourne welcomed its contribution and hoped it would 'render much assistance by giving to all Catholic social workers a clear knowledge of the principles that should guide them.'[18] Not all Catholics approved, fearful that the Church was meddling in politics of a radical persuasion. But the Cardinal always gave the Guild 'the greatest encouragement' and fought 'to secure fair play for it.'[19] Introducing a discussion on the question of a living wage, the Cardinal warned off the critics: 'The Catholic Social Guild was engaged in what was really very important pioneer work, and on that account he trusted that those who might not be able to accept the whole of the suggestions that were sometimes put forward by the Catholic Social Guild would not on that account be too hasty in condemning them. Their work was a very important one; and, as pioneers, they had a right to expect every sort of consideration from them, because it was only by a very frank discussion of these social problems that they could ultimately arrive at a proper solution.'[20]

In 1917 the Cardinal turned for help to the CSG, in the person of one of its founders, Fr Plater, to draft a pastoral letter on the social question. Bourne consulted others too, including the Unionist MP, William Hewins, who acted as his adviser on political affairs.[21] The Pastoral Letter, when it appeared in the first weeks of 1918, was widely promulgated. The Westminster Catholic Federation paid for it to be printed in full in the *Times*, *Daily Telegraph*, *Guardian* and regional papers. Published as *The Nation's Crisis*, it sold 25,000 copies.

The Cardinal recognised that the War had changed the world for ever. The Church had to address 'a new order of things, new social conditions, new relations between the different sections into which society is divided.' The Cardinal spoke directly to these new circumstances. 'During the War the minds of people have been profoundly altered. Dull acquiescence in social injustice has given way to active discontent. The very foundations of social and political life, of our economic system, of morals and religion, are being sharply scrutinised ... The army, for instance, is not only fighting, it is also thinking ... And the general effect of this on the young men who are the citizens of "after the War" is little short of revolutionary.'

The moment was propitious for Catholics. 'There can, we think, be no doubt at all as to the readiness of our countrymen to listen to the teachings of the Catholic Church if an opportunity can be given to them of knowing what that teaching is ... They are impressed with a new sense of the reality of religion. They observe its effectiveness in the face of danger and death ... Again, social reformers of every school are turning more and more to Catholic tradition for their inspiration.' The great social Encyclicals of Leo XIII had given Catholics a tremendous resource to be placed at the service of society as a whole. Bourne's tone was neither pessimistic nor condemnatory. The Church's task with respect to non-Christian social reformers was 'not to denounce them as impious revolutionaries, but to show them that the Catholic Church alone can purify and realise their aspirations. They simply do not know, for instance that Pope Leo XIII has denounced in terms as strong as they themselves are likely to use, the greed and self-seeking which have laid upon the working classes "a yoke little better than slavery itself."'

Merry del Val and the Catholic Union were unlikely to share Bourne's optimistic recognition of 'the true lineaments of the Christian spirit' in contemporary industrial unrest. The Cardinal spoke of 'its passion for fair treatment and for liberty; its resentment at bureaucratic interferences with family life; its desire for self-realisation and opportunities of education; above all, its conviction that persons are of more importance than property—these surely give us points of contact and promise a sympathetic response to our message.'

The Cardinal limited himself to generalisations. Nevertheless, at a time when his brother Bishops seemed to be speaking to an exclusively Catholic audience on issues which concerned only them or were denouncing the threat of Bolshevism, it was important that the Archbishop of Westminster was making overtures to those beyond the fold of the Church. 'When once people come to see that we share their aspirations they will be more ready to listen when we show them what those aspirations involve. They will learn to distrust the false prophets and specious theorists. They will understand how might is not right; how society is not a conglomeration of warring atoms, but a brotherhood; how the family, which is the bulwark of liberty, would be injured by the introduction of divorce or the weakening of parental authority; how property has its rights, however much those rights may have been exaggerated; that cordial cooperation among all classes of society is necessary if their ideals are to be realised ... If, then, it is true that there are many ears open to receive our voice should we Catholics remain apathetic at this critical moment? The opportunity may never come again.'

In terms of specific action, the Cardinal recommended the principles of the CSG. 'Much may be done by the formation of social study circles among Catholics of all classes. By this method, far more than attendance at occasional lectures or be desultory reading, the student obtains a real grasp of modern problems and the principles underlying them ... Such circles may well be organised among Catholic women also ... It is too much to expect a busy, overburdened priest to undertake in all cases the entire guidance of such study circles: but the clergy can encourage their formation and be ready to advise when occasion arises.'[22]

This was not simply a pious aspiration. One 'branch of the Westminster Catholic Federation has taken up the study of social questions in deference to the [Cardinal's] wishes. They authorised the parish priest to buy a large number of copies of some suitable CTS publications, to offer these to the congregation, to ask them to read the pamphlet carefully during the week and to meet in the sacristy on the following Sunday after Benediction for discussion of the pamphlet.'[23] The *Tablet* noted the existence of 150 CSG study groups endeavouring to ensure 'that Christian principles might be applied to modern conditions ... How much might be done at the deliberations of Trades Unions and Labour Conferences, Boards of Guardians and city councils, public meetings and citizens' associations, were Catholic minds more alert and Catholic tongues more ready ... At this moment people are ready to listen. If we delay, the mind of the nation may harden into materialism.'[24] An attempt was even made to introduce social teaching into the curriculum of Catholic schools.[25]

An unlikely source of praise for *The Nation's Crisis* was the Anglican Bishop of Birmingham, who wrote, 'I want to thank the Cardinal ... for the inspiring letter he has written, and I wish that from our own Church there could go forth more frequently the same kind of statesmanlike utterance.'[26]

The Cardinal produced a flow of pronouncements in the spirit of his Pastoral Letter. His secretary was puzzled why these failed to attract greater controversy, especially 'his short article in the Catholic newspaper, *America*, in which his Eminence stated that when a man accumulated so much wealth that he could no longer *personally* control it, he should be deprived of the surplus. I often wondered why this article ... did not give rise to furious controversy.'[27] There was a similar message for the English Press: 'The problem to be solved is to find a way of distributing the surplus wealth so that the poor man, manual labourer, or inferior clerk may have the additional remuneration he so urgently needs; and the rich man no longer receive the heaped-up increment which he in no sense requires and cannot efficiently control. The problem is international, as is the problem of obtaining a just peace. There are in the world two international forces, Christianity and Labour, to which will fall in large measure the task of solving these problems. Let these two forces come to a complete understanding, and they will be invincible.'[28] This was radical stuff coming from a Prince of the Church in the early twentieth century, but it is impossible to accuse Bourne of indifference to the concerns of labouring Catholics.

He spoke in similar terms to Glaswegian workers: 'We must never return to the days when workers were merely "hands," when their human interests were disregarded, and when the increase of production was held to be the sole aim of industrial life. The old political economy has been killed by the war, and we have to shape a new social and economic order. To that task must be devoted the best every one of us can give.'[29] He offered encouragement to workers in the Staffordshire Potteries: 'The first charge on any industry must be the provision of a living wage for all those who are engaged in it.'[30]

For Bourne, these were days of opportunity for the Catholic Church and the nation as a whole with the prospect of a more equitable society attained through education and the application of Catholic social teaching. Keating in Liverpool noted that Bourne 'has lately been saluted as a "cheerful Cardinal" in contrast with "a gloomy dean" [Dean Inge of St. Paul's].'[31] It was not only Anglicans, however, who were gloomy. Merry del Val found Bourne's optimism inexplicable. 'It seems to me strangely incongruous to speak of joy in these days ... the flood of evil on every side is very distressing and I am at a loss to understand what Cardinal Bourne means when he speaks as if the world were better after the war from a religious standpoint. I am afraid the evidence is all the other way at present and it is no good closing our eyes to the facts.'[32]

Bourne was not joyously espousing the rights of labour because he welcomed social revolution. On the contrary, he was motivated by an abhorrence of economic conflict and class warfare. This was his message at the Peace celebrations: 'Class warfare, whether in the form of seeking greater gain from the industry of others than may lawfully be claimed, or in the guise of claiming retribution for labour in excess of its rightful demands ... must bring upon the nation misfortune and disaster more far-reaching and irreparable than all the calamities of the recent War.'[33] He had already identified the means of avoiding such conflict:

> There can be little doubt that a violent class war can only be averted if public opinion is sufficiently educated to recognise what is right and just in the workers' demand and what is wrong or unreasonable. The ultimate issue will, in fact, rest with an educated public opinion ... Never was the necessity more imperative that earnest men, both of the working class and the moneyed class, should regard the situation not from the mere standpoint of a class or

individual advantage, but from the moral standpoint of justice and the common good.

The Cardinal realised that priests alone were unable to inculcate society with the tenets of Catholic social teaching. 'The social apostolate must be in very large measure a lay apostolate. The duty lies alike upon the Catholic worker and the Catholic employer; no intelligent Catholic is without responsibility in the matter.'[34]

Cardinal Bourne never lost his interest in social issues. In the last months of his life he was still championing the work of the CSG, urging it to establish a strong centre in London and to see the formation of Catholic undergraduates at the University of London as a priority.[35] But after the early 1920s the urgency and the enthusiasm were diminished. The Cardinal was too shrewd to be taken in by the utopianism of the Catholic Land Movement. He gave his provisional patronage to the 'Land Colony' founded in Buckinghamshire, but urged that the 'scheme should be in the hands of a competent farmer.'[36]

When the Cardinal turned his attention to the blight of mass unemployment in the wake of the Great Depression, like other Bishops, it was to deplore the deleterious effects of the dole upon a man's initiative rather than the economic hardship suffered. At Easter 1931 he voiced his concern that, 'Many are growing accustomed to live on the public funds, and thereby losing the old zest in self-supporting labour.'[37] Later that year he was praising the 'generosity' of welfare provision through unemployment insurance, which he claimed represented the application of the true principles of Catholic social teaching. At the same time, the Cardinal urged recipients to claim only in case of genuine need given the benefits came often from taxes paid by people not significantly wealthier than themselves.[38]

The Cardinal's proposed solutions to the massive social problems in this period look decidedly parochial and inadequate. He presided at the first meeting of the Catholic Fund for the Homeless and Destitute in 1932. The hostel it opened near Holland Park had given shelter to 152 men in eight months, but what was that by comparison to the thousands of unemployed arriving from the Midlands and the North in search of work?[39] He simply commended the pressing issue of the housing crisis to his clergy, asking 'them to give generously of their wise counsel and assistance whenever opportunity arises for them to do so.'[40] It was alleged that Bourne cancelled a conference on the housing question in 1934 because it might constitute implicit criticism of Sir John Gilbert's

Municipal Reform Party on the London County Council, from whom Bourne hoped for a better deal on Catholic schools than their Labour opponents.[41] Having previously asked for lay leadership, the Bishops refused to support a pilgrimage to Rome by the unemployed because they had not sought episcopal approval in advance.[42] Whether Bourne agreed with the views stated or not, he allowed the *Tablet* to carry an article disparaging the Jarrow Hunger March 'as got up under Moscow's orders and to advance Moscow's interests.'[43]

The ageing Cardinal was prepared to leave the larger social questions in the hands of the politicians and of God. He poured cold water on clerical initiatives to accept the challenge to Christian leaders thrown down by George Lansbury, the Labour Leader, to put into practice their preaching on helping the needy. Bourne asked, 'What can the "leaders of the Church" reasonably advise of a useful character concerning unemployment? They are not experts either in politics or economics, and the wisest heads are perplexed how to act. We have no reason to suspect that the Government is not doing its best. As far as the Catholic Church is concerned, all our organisations are, I believe, doing their best to relieve the existing distress. I am very reluctant to venture into questions in which I feel no competence.'[44] Instead, he urged spiritual remedies, promoting, for example, the Pope's day of prayer 'when millions upon millions of Catholics in every part of the world were praying for the betterment of that world, as well as making extra sacrifices by way of atonement.'[45]

What happened in the course of a decade to transform the Cardinal's reforming optimism into caution and inaction? Certainly, there was his experience of the General Strike of 1926. But his attitude to social questions was also influenced by the Catholic experience of COPEC.

COPEC

Cardinal Bourne might wish to position the Catholic Church to the centre of national life, but he was unable to ignore the inconvenient fact that Catholics constituted a small proportion of the population, their political significance further diminished after the departure of the Irish Members from Westminster in 1918.

That presented the Church with the unavoidable question framed by the *Tablet*.

> There is one line of cooperation to which some Catholics still hesitate to commit themselves: it is the line indicated by the

participation of Catholics in the interdenominational conference of social workers at Swanwick, and the interdenominational meeting at the recent conference of the Catholic Social Guild at Preston. There are Catholics to whom the word 'interdenominational' smells of heresy and religious compromise ... The practical question upon which cooperation rests is whether it is not better to secure some substantial recognition of Christian principles in the social and economic life of the nation, short of the full measure of Catholicism, than to allow the national system to fall into the hands of the secularist or the atheist? There surely can be little doubt as to the wiser policy; and the Catholic Social Guild, in adopting it, has given a lead which deserves a grateful recognition ... Two results have come of that policy. The Catholic Social Guild has been brought more closely into touch with the general feeling and sentiments of the social reform work carried on outside the Church, and thus has gained a more detailed knowledge of the general situation as regards the social problems which call for reform. That in itself is a gain. One of the greatest hindrances to Catholic influence and action hitherto is that as a body we have been too much isolated from general movements in the nation in which we might profitably have taken part, and consequently have lacked the knowledge which is necessary for effective action. The second result is the Catholicising influence which the Guild has already had upon the general programme of the interdenominational social workers.[46]

Many Bishops still resolutely opposed any such cooperation. It was, therefore, the Cardinal's tentative approval which permitted a new departure—at least in the short term. Cooperation in the less controversial area of temperance had established a precedent. In December 1919 Cardinal Bourne delegated Fr Charles Plater to represent him at a Mansion House conference called by the Lord Mayor of London with a view to 'promoting wholehearted cooperation between all classes to secure prosperity in industry and satisfactory conditions of life for workers.'[47]

It was Dr William Temple, the Anglican Bishop of Manchester, who conceived of a scheme on an altogether grander scale. He devised the Conference on Christian Politics, Economics and Citizenship (COPEC). The first conference was to be held in Birmingham in April 1924. Twelve commissions were established in 1920 to prepare reports.

The COPEC Secretary was a Miss Lucy Gardner, whose involvement in social work had already brought her into contact with the CSG. At

Plater's suggestion, she wrote to the Cardinal, informing him of the Conference and their desire 'to secure the help and cooperation of your Church.'[48] Bourne was sympathetic, allowing his name to go forward as a supporter of the Conference and appointing Fr Leslie Walker, another Jesuit at Campion Hall, Oxford, to represent him on the COPEC executive. The Jesuits of the time were not by definition advocates of every ecumenical and progressive cause. Before it began, Walker nearly derailed the very principle of Catholic participation. An early COPEC pamphlet spoke of the 'failure' of the Churches in social issues. Walker was apoplectic. 'To assent to such a statement is for a Catholic quite impossible. It would involve disloyalty to Christ who has promised that His Church should never fail in these matters.'[49] He sought the Cardinal's instructions on resignation. Dr Temple had to pour oil on troubled waters, admitting 'that it is really dangerous to speak of the Church as "failing," and there have been official utterances on the part of Rome.'[50] With a view to securing smoother cooperation in future, although Walker remained very much involved, the Cardinal wrote to the Bishop of Manchester telling him that he had 'entrusted any work connected with the Conference to our Catholic Social Guild.'[51]

The Conference was a considerable undertaking. 1,500 delegates were invited, including 800 representatives from the various Christian denominations. Of these, it was anticipated that 65 would be Catholic. The Cardinal was invited to speak. However, as he would be leading a national pilgrimage to the Holy Land, he suggested Archbishop Keating, almost the only other Catholic Bishop who displayed any enthusiasm for COPEC.[52] (Dunn made his views plain: '[My] impression has always been that COPEC was an organisation which Catholics ought to shun and ignore altogether.'[53])

Even Walker was unable to fault the subsequent proceedings. Catholics were represented on all but one of the commissions preparing reports, their comments were generally adopted and the COPEC executive was 'most anxious that all Catholics should take their full share in the Conference and in all that concerns it.'[54] Ominously, however, the Jesuit wrote to the Cardinal in December 1923 asking for a meeting early in the New Year to review the direction the Conference was taking.[55] Innocently, Bourne invited the Catholic representatives on the various commissions to Archbishop's House on 4 January 1924 so that they could 'consider together the attitude to be adopted on certain questions which have arisen.'[56]

Meanwhile Walker asked the Catholic representatives to prepare for the Cardinal statements of their experience. The results cast in doubt the very possibility of continued Catholic participation. Some representatives needed no coaxing to air their grievances. Ada Streeter was a CSG member who sat on the Property and Industry Commission. With the exception of a lone northern industrialist, she had no time for her colleagues. 'The majority of members are avowed Socialists of a more or less pronounced type and include representatives of the "intelligentsia" of the Labour Party, several Nonconformist Ministers, and some rather fanatic idealists who are looking for the realisation of the "Kingdom of God" in the reconstruction of society on a basis of egalitarianism.' Streeter was prepared to remain on the commission if she could issue a minority report based on Catholic social teaching, but the chairman was determined on a unanimous report, even if this had to be couched in meaningless platitudes. She concluded that 'the motive is *not* an unbiased enquiry into the social applications of Christian Doctrine, but a deliberate endeavour to clothe the *whole* programme of the Labour Party in the garb of the "Teaching of Jesus."' As evidence she produced notes from meetings calling for the nationalisation of land and equality of property.[57]

Francis Urquhart was the Dean of Balliol College, Oxford. His application to the COPEC project did not match that of Ada Streeter, but his conclusions were similar. He had already considered resignation from the Christianity and War Commission. 'The members are nearly all pacifists at heart and instead of a having a fruitful attempt to insist on sound principles in international relations, there will simply be a barren discussion on the wickedness of *all* war ... The whole thing is deplorably impractical—I am tempted to call it "amateur."'[58] For good measure, the Cardinal was made aware of the opposition of Archbishop McIntyre in whose Diocese the Conference was to be held.[59]

Bourne did not abandon his support for participation immediately, but consulted Abbot Bergh of Ramsgate. It was his advice which killed continued formal Catholic involvement. He concentrated less on the actual views expressed and the emerging impracticalities than on ecclesiological considerations. The Abbot noted COPEC treated 'Christianity and its social implications as a matter to be enquired into and decided by vote. It is assumed as common ground that the Church of Christ is not one but many; and on this supposition the work is planned. The sharing therein of Catholics appears thus precluded.' In this democratic process there was no place for the authoritative teaching office of the Catholic Church—hardly surprisingly given the overwhelmingly Protestant inspiration and membership of the project! Bergh did not dismiss COPEC out of hand, recognising that it was organised by 'men of goodwill.' 'Hence, it deserves sympathetic consideration and such help as Catholics can give it. In my humble opinion this can most properly be done, otherwise than by formally joining the association or movement organised on its present lines. The keeping in touch with the Conference, and especially the supplying of statements showing the Catholic attitude towards the matters discussed seem likely means of turning it to good.'[60]

In the event, due to Bourne's illness, the meeting on 4 January was chaired by his auxiliary, Bidwell. At issue was the fact that the Catholic representatives were unwilling to sign reports which did not reflect Church teaching. Opinion was surprisingly evenly divided as to the line of action to be taken, some favouring staying with the intention of further influencing the final reports, others wanted out. Put to the vote, six opted for resignation, five (including Walker) were for staying.[61] One wonders whether it might have gone the other way had the Cardinal been present. However, he felt obliged to accept Bidwell's recommendation to adopt the majority view. He wrote to the hierarchy and Fr Leo O'Hara SJ, the principal coordinator of the Catholic representatives together with Walker, that he was accepting the line indicated by Bergh: 'Catholics, while ready to give advice and information on the subjects considered by the Conference on Christianity, Politics, Economics and Citizenship, might not co-operate formally with it or in future participate in any of its activities.'[62] Keating was the only Bishop who argued that COPEC should be given the opportunity to respond to Catholic objections before formal withdrawal and the attendant publicity.[63]

The Cardinal chose not to publicise immediately the fact of the Catholic withdrawal—the *Tablet* made no reference to it for three months. The hawks were concerned that this might lead to a Catholic re-engagement with COPEC. Their concerns appeared justified by the encouragement Bourne gave Fr O'Hea to adopt a minimalist interpretation of the prohibition just a matter of days later. The Cardinal wrote, 'The occasional presence of Catholics, as benevolent outside well-wishers, on a COPEC platform does not present much difficulty; the danger consisted in service on committees being regarded as a close identification with the principles, or non-principles, of the organisation.'[64]

Fearing a quasi-official Catholic presence at the Conference, Archbishop McIntyre sought to pre-empt the situation. He and his suffragans produced a joint Pastoral Letter in February, directly attacking Catholic involvement in COPEC.

> There is at present great activity in promoting schemes for social betterment, and the cooperation of Catholics in the movement is being solicited. If these schemes concerned only social betterment, we would gladly respond to the appeal for cooperation; but the principles of social betterment actually being adopted are generally so steeped in religious theory as to be more pronouncedly religious than social ... All this is simply religious theory—and theory of a deadly kind. It means nothing less than that the visible, historic Catholic Church, with its clear, definite, dogmatic teaching, coming down through the ages, is now to be superseded by a new religious force, called 'our common Christianity,' and conducting to a veiled kingdom that 'needed discovering.' We have the gravest fears that this is nothing but Modernism in action, on a large scale; nor are our fears diminished in the least by the assurance that 'the Church of England had given a lead.'[65]

McIntyre was working on the (correct) assumption that one Catholic Bishop would not publicly attack the public pronouncement of another. The Cardinal might not like the Birmingham Pastoral, and its implicit criticism of his own position, but he would not override it. Even had he been minded to do so, McIntyre timed his Pastoral to appear when Bourne was travelling to the Holy Land. Thus, Walker and O'Hea attended the Conference in April simply as private individuals.

O'Hea waited four years before contacting the Cardinal with a new suggestion for interdenominational cooperation. The proposal was for the CSG to participate in a Social Council of the Churches. O'Hea emphasized that this 'Council is to be distinct from and independent of' COPEC, and was to avoid the former difficulties by steering 'well clear of theological doctrine.'[66] In the face of considerable episcopal opposition Bourne had invested significant personal energy and prestige in the earlier COPEC venture. He had been damaged by its failure to provide that platform for Catholicism in public life for which he had hoped. His changed attitude is explicable also by the acrimony surrounding the end of the Malines Conversations and Protestant unreliability in supporting traditional moral values. And so the Cardinal only offered O'Hea limited comfort. 'I find it increasingly difficult to cooperate with non-Catholics.

They have no definite principles and land us easily in false positions. I do not think we ought to become *members* of this new council, but you might do as the Americans do at Geneva and be benevolent observers ready to give help when you can legitimately do so.'[67]

'Real scandal to the Christian mind'

It was on matters of traditional Christian morality, rather than doctrinal questions or social teaching, that the Cardinal saw a widening gulf separate Catholics and Protestants in the years after the First World War. As late as 1917 the Cardinal had been able to unite with the Anglican Archbishops and Free Church leaders in opposing legislation designed to facilitate divorce. It was one of the last occasions that concerted action was possible. Whereas Bourne was continuing to mobilise Catholic priests and organisations in defence of marriage, by 1923 Archbishop Davidson was arguing for divorce in the House of Lords—if only on the limited grounds on adultery.[68] The Cardinal was under no illusion as to the logical consequence of this and had no inhibitions in voicing his frustration. 'The Church of England had allowed marriage to be a farce—a contract terminable at pleasure. It was no longer an indissoluble ordinance.'[69]

The great moral issue of the inter-war years was artificial contraception. In 1920 a resolution was passed: 'We utter an emphatic warning against the use of unnatural means for the avoidance of conception, together with the grave dangers—physical, moral, and religious—thereby incurred, and against the evils with which the extension of such use threatens the race. In opposition to the teaching which, under the name of science and religion encourages married people in the deliberate cultivation of sexual union as an end in itself, we steadfastly uphold what must always be regarded as the governing considerations of Christian marriage. One is the primary purpose for which marriage exists, namely the continuation of the race through the gift and heritage of children; the other is the paramount importance in married life of deliberate and thoughtful self-control.'[70] Words with which Cardinal Bourne could concur wholeheartedly, but, in fact, the mind of the 1920 Lambeth Conference. Within a decade everything would have changed.

We choose to forget the origins of the early twentieth-century birth prevention movement. Marie Stopes is now held up as a great protagonist of 'women's liberation;' the unsavoury company she kept is conveniently ignored. Much of the impetus for contraception was based on prevalent theories of racist eugenics and social engineering. A Professor E. W. McBride addressed the Neo-Malthusian and Birth Control Conference in 1922:

> The leaders who had studied eugenics had come to the conclusion that the only practical eugenic measure was birth control ... Our colonies wanted immigrants of courage, initiative and adaptability; and these qualities were not to be found among our lower classes ... If the practice of voluntary birth control became more widespread, then an enlightened public opinion would be formed, which would support measures of compulsory sterilisation against those who persisted in having families at the public expense.

The chairman of the meeting wanted to know 'what can be done about the less intelligent, and purely animal, nations who do not adopt birth control?'[71]

Before they had been formed by 'enlightened public opinion,' the working class—against whom such proposals were aimed—and, indeed, most Englishmen, rejected such ideas as morally repugnant. Bourne clearly and consistently enunciated their beliefs. Speaking to the National Council of Public Morality in 1919, he laid out basic, immutable principles. In limiting the size of family 'the only accepted method which is allowable is, first voluntary continence by mutual consent, and secondly, that life is so sacred a gift of Almighty God that any direct interference with that life, even in its pre-natal condition, is a grievous sin.'[72]

Marie Stopes opened the first birth control clinic in Britain in 1921 by. Almost immediately, Anglican support for the constant teaching of the Church began to crumble. When the physician, Lord Dawson, addressed the Church Congress in Birmingham in support of contraception, the secular Press noted that he 'fearlessly and plainly opposed the teachings of the Roman Church and the alleged teachings of the Anglican.'[73]

By contrast to the Anglican position at the time and the Catholic position nearly fifty years later in the wake of *Humane Vitae* (admittedly against far more powerful opposition), the Cardinal's response was confident and sure-footed. Challenged to public debate by Marie Stopes, he initially determined to deny the oxygen of publicity to such 'perverse views.' 'Any public discussion on "birth control" seems to him to be forbidden by the common law of decency.'[74]

When action became unavoidable, however, the Cardinal did not flinch. Responding to increasing Press coverage, in 1922 the CTS commissioned the Catholic doctor, Halliday Sutherland, to write a pamphlet, *Do Babies Build Slums?* He refuted the claim that large families caused poverty and exposed the risks to women's health associated with the use of artificial contraception. Instead, he advocated abstinence and natural family planning. The pamphlet was subsequently expanded into a book published by Harding & Moore Ltd. It included this passage: 'The poor are the natural victims of those who seek to make experiments on their fellows. In the midst of a London slum, a woman who is a Doctor of German Philosophy (Munich) has opened a birth control clinic where working women are instructed in a method of contraception described by Professor McIlroy as "the most harmful method of which I have had experience." (Proceeding of the Medico-Legal Society, 7 July 1921) It is truly amazing that this monstrous campaign of Birth Control should be tolerated by the Home Secretary. Charles Bradlaugh was condemned to jail for a less serious "crime."' Marie Stopes demanded that an apology be issued and the book withdrawn. When this was refused, she issued a writ for libel against author and publisher.

Anticipating the Catholic response four decades later, there were those who counselled silence in the face of controversy.[75] Bourne had no truck with such pusillanimity. He acknowledged that Sutherland had 'rendered a conspicuous service to national and Christian morality as well as to the teaching of the Catholic Church,' and urged the Catholic Union to give him every assistance in defending the libel action.[76] He felt that 'it would be monstrous were Dr Sutherland left in the lurch by his fellow Catholics.'[77] The Cardinal asked the Catholic Union to assemble a meeting of leading Catholics, whom he would address, encouraging them to fund Sutherland's legal expenses. Bourne personally found £500 of the costs.[78] These escalated as the case passed from one court to another, the Cardinal requesting parish collections so the Catholic case could continue to be heard.[79] In the first instance, Sutherland was vindicated—a verdict overturned by the Court of Appeal. Eventually, the Lords found in Sutherland's favour by a 4–1 majority.

In the Cardinal's eyes, the most disturbing aspect of the case was the revelation that Catholics were now left alone to defend traditional Christian morality. 'The other religious denominations of this country had been given full opportunities of assisting in this particular matter, and that they had not taken their part was, he considered, a dishonour to them.'[80] This hard fact was further emphasized by the 1930 Lambeth Conference, which overturned the previous Anglican position and accepted the use of artificial contraception in certain circumstances. The Cardinal recognised this as a watershed and denounced it as such.

> I know the intense surprise and real scandal to the Christian mind which has been caused at home and abroad by this abandonment of unbroken traditional Christian teaching ... Lest, therefore, any be led astray by this resolution of the Lambeth Conference, and placed, thereby, in danger of committing grievous sin, I now reaffirm the teaching of the Catholic Church on this subject, binding on the conscience of every man and of every woman. Any direct interference with the natural consequence of the marital relation, namely conception, whether within the marriage state, or outside it, is an unnatural vice, sinning against the nature which the Creator has bestowed upon us, and, therefore, grievously displeasing in His sight.[81]

With extraordinary prescience the Cardinal foresaw where events would lead should Christianity's teaching on the tempering of the passions be relaxed, namely the breaking of the inviolable link between the unitive and procreative aspects of the marital act. So he taught at the 1929 Catholic Congress: 'What in reality and in ultimate analysis is the ground of the demand for extended facilities for divorces, for birth prevention and the like? Simply that the instincts and the passions of which we have been speaking are entitled to self-gratification though, in seeking in it, they contravene Christian or even the natural law. For the self-control which Christianity has always taught, and which paganism upholds to a certain extent, the right to self-gratification is substituted ... Apparently [the apostles of birth prevention] do not see that the principles which underlie all their assertions and appeals lead logically and inevitably to the condoning and justification of every form of self-indulgence within or without the married state ... May not such self-gratification be sought with equal justification in every form of self-indulgence, for the old distinction between the natural and the unnatural can by such pleaders no longer be logically maintained ... I do not think that the people of this country are awake as yet to the inevitable consequences of the doctrines to which I have alluded.'[82]

If the British people were not awake to those inevitable consequences, no blame can be attached to Bourne. The moment the issue could no longer be ignored, he had Fr Thomas Williams, the future Archbishop of Birmingham, gather leading moral theologians and doctors with a view to making the Catholic position on birth control central to the Higher Studies Conference to be held in Oxford.[83] He wrote to the CWL at their request 'forcibly' re-stating the Church's teaching after reports certain priests were sanctioning birth control.[84] The CWL were staunch allies; committed to the advance of the role of women in society, they were ideally placed to promote Catholic moral teaching. The Cardinal encouraged the Catholic Federation to instigate criminal proceedings against Marie Stopes.[85] And there was another spat with Stopes in respect of a *Tablet* article in 1930. (On that occasion the matter was settled out of court with the issuing of an apology, but no payment of damages.)[86]

The Cardinal's involvement was not limited to legal proceedings and pulpit pronouncements. In 1928 he opened St Nicholas's Home in Highbury to allow unmarried mothers to keep their children.[87] If Marie Stopes is held out to be an apostle of the birth control movement, then Cardinal Bourne is entitled to be known as the apostle of the Pro-Life Movement.

Women and Children

Today such views would ensure Bourne's condemnation by secular society for being regressive in respect of women's issues. That is not how he was perceived—by men and women—in his own day. He was Archbishop of Westminster at the time of the suffragette movement. Characteristically, he said little, save for a denunciation of excesses, especially 'acts of violence to persons or property.' Yet, he happily conceded that Catholics were entitled to hold views either way on the issue of women's suffrage.[88] One suspects that, personally, he supported votes for women. Once they were enfranchised, he courted them as a force for good in public life. At the 1920 Catholic Congress in Liverpool the Cardinal appealed 'most eloquently ... to the women to use their powers for the common good, particularly in agitating to oppose wider divorce measures ... For the first time at a Congress of the kind in England the women's movement was approved and encouraged by high ecclesiastical dignitaries.'[89]

The Cardinal was entirely comfortable in dealing with women holding positions of responsibility, for example, in the CSG. Not all his contemporaries were. Across the River, Amigo gave no indication of support for the equal treatment of women in the public sphere. He used his Advent Pastoral of 1926 to question their position in the workplace. 'Freedom, too, is a good thing, but it is abused when cited by girls as an excuse for despising domestic work ... and [preferring] industrial work.'[90]

In one area especially Bourne consistently demonstrated his support for the public role of women in the Church. The influence, possibly the very existence, of the Catholic Women's League was due to his encouragement of its founder, Margaret Fletcher[91]. She wrote to the Archbishop in October 1906 setting out her vision for an organisation along the lines of those already existing in Germany, France, Italy and the USA. Its purpose consisted of 'utilising all the available power and influence of Catholic women in a nation, and opposing them to the de-Christianising influence of non-Christian women.'[92] After initially suggesting such work might be undertaken under the auspices of the Ladies of Charity, Bourne quickly grasped the potential of such an entity and gave it his unqualified backing.[93] He was actively involved in the formation of the first Committee and continued to read in detail all the reports of its sub-committees. At the beginning he had to defend the League against those who sought to portray it as 'political,' infringing upon the territory of established Catholic charities or 'encouraging "double-died Tories"'! Bourne came in for 'severe criticism;' but he was not to be deflected. 'He learned the lesson that once having made up one's mind on a project, it is best to go ahead, and so the CWL went ahead.'[94]

Bourne set out his wider views at the League's inaugural general meeting: 'Women at the present day undoubtedly exercised very great influence, and rightly exercised that influence ... Some kind of training was required ... As a rule they had no knowledge of the traditional philosophy of the Catholic Church, and that was one direction in which a League of this kind was able to render good service ... Then there were specific good works ... He would say plainly there was no antagonism of any kind between the promoters of the League to any existing Catholic works ... He had encouraged the League because he believed that it was his duty to encourage every good work that was proposed, unless, of course, he saw very definite reasons for refusal, and he trusted he would always do so ... A certain number of the proposers had been to speak to him with excellent schemes. He had encouraged them to speak very frankly ... And now today he was able, and glad to be able, to give the League much more definite approbation.'[95] When a Roman branch of the League was founded for expatriate ladies at his suggestion, Bourne found himself required to smooth ruffled clerical feathers in the Eternal City.[96]

What was the practical role of the League? Bourne explained. 'Whenever a difficult piece of work presented itself and he did not know to whom to confide it he had got into the habit of telephoning to the CWL—and never in vain.'[97] At the beginning it had been decided, in his opinion, wisely, 'that no very rigid constitutions should limit the scope of its energies and activities.'[98]

In 1919 Margaret Fletcher was surprised by the Cardinal's directive to proceed immediately to Prague. There was a real fear that in the new Czechoslovakia the Catholic Church faced persecution given its close identification with the former Habsburg regime. Travelling across war-torn Europe, Fletcher was puzzled as to what she could bring to the situation. But academic contacts gave her access to President Masaryk, whom she found sympathetic towards the expression of Catholicism in England and the United States. As a Catholic laywoman, she lectured in Prague on Church schools and the role of women in England, helping local Catholics recover their confidence by organising their first mass meeting after the War. To have worked through more establishment channels would have aroused suspicions of counter-revolutionary intentions. Bourne's unconventional use of the CWL was a stroke of genius.[99]

Catechesis for children attending non-Catholic schools was a role for which the Cardinal thought the League pre-eminently suited. And the need might one day be far greater. 'A day might come when home instruction will be the only means of teaching our children their Catechism. We may have grave difficulties with our schools in the future, they may be suppressed. I hope this will never happen, but if it ever does it would be on the mothers organised like this that we should have to rely. So I hope the Catholic Women's League will consider this project and adopt it.'[100] He later repeated the request, asking the League to train up a group known as 'Our Lady's Catechists' to teach the Catechism.[101]

As anticipated, the CWL functioned as 'a kind of information bureau.' It existed 'to direct into right and appropriate channels those Catholic women with leisure and ability who wished to help in many works then needing assistance, but who without some guidance scarcely knew where to direct their energies.'[102] By the time of its Silver Jubilee the League boasted 9,000 members. In addition to catechesis, its remit extended to the Catholic Girl Guides, international and emigration work, and the running of mothers' and girls' clubs. There was a Junior League and even a CWL settlement in Bethlehem.[103] One President of the League acknowledged that without the Cardinal's 'unfailing kindness,' 'the League would have had much more of an uphill fight than it has had, in fact I do not think it would now have been in existence.'[104]

Much of Bourne's clerical life was devoted to what we would describe as 'youth ministry.' Of course, this related mainly to seminary formation and the fight for Catholic schools. But those did not mark the limits of his concern for the young. For many, Bourne first came to national prominence for what was labelled his 'hooligans speech' of March 1901. At the Mansion House he attacked society's treatment of destitute youth, especially in the light of the local authority's attempt to close of St John's Home for Waifs in Southwark.[105]

Few today remember Bourne's contribution to the scouting movement. At one point it seemed that Catholics would have to remain apart from the enterprise. But Robert Baden-Powell wrote to Bourne seeking his advice on the draft constitution's clauses relating to religious observance and inviting him to join the Advisory Council.[106] The Archbishop accepted. In conversation with Baden-Powell he discovered 'that the suggestion had been put forward by some that perhaps the question of religious differences might be overcome by a new universal religion to embrace the Scouts of the whole world. To Sir Robert His Eminence replied that any attempt to do that would at once ruin his movement. He added that there must be no sort of intermingling of religions and the boys must be told to practise the religion in which they believed and had been brought up in. The Founder at once accepted his advice, and it was on that understanding that Catholics entered into the great Scout movement; that understanding had been loyally observed.'[107]

The risk of religious indifferentism overcome, Bourne zealously promoted the scouting movement at home and abroad. There was a troop of Westminster Scouts known as 'The Cardinal's Own,' which Baden-Powell agreed to review, while the Cardinal said Mass at the great international Jamboree held at Birkenhead in 1930. Another instance of his discerning and working with a movement closely identified with the spirit of the times, but without any compromise to Catholic principles.

Notes

1. FAB, National Catholic Congress, 13 September 1929, *Tablet*, 21 September 1929, p. 363.
2. FAB, Stamford Hill, 16 July 1919, *Tablet*, 26 July 1919, pp. 127–128.
3. FAB, National Catholic Congress, 13 September 1929, *Tablet*, 21 September 1929, p. 362.
4. Fr J. P. Arendzen to FAB, 29 September 1921, AAW, Bo. IV/21.
5. FAB, Pastoral Letter, 29 December 1903.
6. *Tablet*, 7 November 1903, p. 739.
7. FAB to London clergy, 23 February 1910, AAW, Bo. I/129; March 1910, AAW, Bo. I/129.
8. Bell, *Randall Davidson*, p. 749.
9. Conference of Temperance Council of the Christian Churches, 22 February 1916, AAW, Bo. I/129.
10. *Morning Post*, 8 November 1918.
11. FAB, Mansion House meeting of Temperance Council of the Christian Churches, 12 February 1923, *Tablet*, 17 February 1923, p. 234.
12. Oldmeadow, *Francis Cardinal Bourne*, ii, p. 194.
13. FAB to Bishop of Croydon, 5 December 1922, AAW, Bo. IV/20/11d.
14. FAB, Commons Committee, 7 November 1918, *Tablet*, 16 November 1918, p. 558.
15. FAB, Mansion House meeting of Temperance Council of the Christian Churches, 12 February 1923, *Tablet*, 17 February 1923, p. 234.
16. *FAB, Folkestone, 1907*, cited Meynell, *A Record of the Sayings and Doings of Francis, Fourth Archbishop of Westminster*, p. 139.
17. F. Valentine, OP, *Father Vincent McNabb* (London: Burns & Oates, 1955), p. 114.
18. FAB, National Catholic Congress, Leeds, 29 July 1910, *Tablet*, 6 August 1910, p. 206.
19. FAB, CSG AGM, Oxford, 15 August 1921, *Tablet*, 20 August 1921, p. 256.
20. FAB National Catholic Congress, Plymouth, 5 July 1913, *Tablet*, 12 July 1913, p. 55.
21. FAB to Hewins, 5 February 1918, SUL, Hewins Papers, 67/121.
22. FAB Pastoral Letter, 27 January 1918.
23. *Tablet*, 4 May 1918, p. 595.
24. Editorial, *Tablet*, 11 October 1919, p. 448.
25. FAB, 'Catholic Social Study,' *WCC*, May 1918, p. 85.
26. Bishop of Birmingham, Diocesan Magazine, March 1918.
27. Jackman, 'An Appreciation,' *Catholic Times*, 4 January 1935, p.2.
28. FAB, *Observer*, 10 November 1918.
29. FAB, Glasgow, *Leeds Mercury*, 15 October 1918.
30. FAB, Hanley, Staffordshire, 27 October 1919, *Tablet*, 1 November 1919, p. 564.

31   FWK address, 24 October 1921, LAA, Keating Papers, Series 7 IV A/8, cited Aspden, *Fortress Church*, p. 141n.
32   Merry del Val to Broadhead, 5 April 1920, UCA, cited Aspden, *Fortress Church*, p. 122.
33   FAB, Cathedral, National Day of Thanksgiving for Peace, 6 July 1919, *Tablet*, 12 July 1919, p. 54.
34   FAB, 'Catholic Social Study,' *WCC*, May 1918, pp. 82–83.
35   FAB, Address, CSG London rally, 27 May 1934, *Tablet*, 2 June 1934, p. 694.
36   B. Keating to FAB, 14 July 1931; W. J. Dutton & W. L. Coulton to FAB, 6 July 1932, AAW, Hi. II/129.
37   FAB, Easter Day homily, 5 April 1931, *Tablet*, 11 April 1931, p. 489.
38   FAB, Southend, 27 September 1931, *Tablet*, 3 October 1931, p. 446.
39   *Tablet*, 14 May 1932, p. 643.
40   FAB, Trinity Sunday Pastoral, 1934.
41   Aspden, *Fortress Church*, p. 180.
42   Acta, 4 July 1933, AAW, Hi. II/139/2(b).
43   *Tablet*, 5 November 1932, p. 589.
44   FAB to Fr Worsley, 12 November 1932, copy, AAW, Bourne Papers, Hi. II/223.
45   FAB, Poplar, 5 June 1932, *Tablet*, 11 June 1932, p. 768.
46   Editorial, *Tablet*, 13 April 1918, pp. 473–474.
47   *Times*, 1 December 1919.
48   L. Gardner to FAB, 22 December 1920, AAW, Bo. V/Misc.
49   L. Walker, SJ, to Gardner, 29 June 1921 (copy), AAW, Bo./Misc.
50   Walker to FAB, 3 July 1921, AAW, Bo./Misc.
51   FAB to W. Temple, 5 December 1922 (copy), AAW, Bo. V/76a.
52   Gardner to FAB, 19 March 1923, AAW, Bo. V/76a.
53   Dunn to FAB, 21 February 1925, AAW, Bo. 5/76a.
54   Walker to FAB, 12 March 1923, AAW, Bo. V/76a.
55   Walker to FAB, 12 December 1923, AAW, Bo.V/76a.
56   FAB circular, 18 December 1923 (copy), AAW, Bo. V/76a.
57   A. Streeter to FAB, 16 December 1923, AAW, Bourne Papers, Bo. V/76a.
58   F. Urquhart to FAB, 20 December 1923, AAW, Bourne Papers, Bo. V/76a.
59   Walker to FAB, 28 December 1923, AAW, Bo. V/76a.
60   Bergh to FAB, 28 December 1923, AAW, Bo. V/76a.
61   Notes of meeting, 4 January 1924, AAW, Bo. V/76a.
62   FAB circular to hierarchy, 7 January 1924, AAW, Bo. V/76a.
63   Keating to FAB, 19 January 1924, AAW, Bo. V/76a.
64   FAB to O'Hea, 21 January 1924, copy, AAW, Bo. V/76a.
65   McIntyre & Birmingham and suffragans, Joint Pastoral Letter, 12 February 1924.
66   O'Hea to FAB, 4 August 1927, AAW, Hi. II/103.

67 FAB to O'Hea, 6 August 1927, copy, AAW, Hi. II/103.
68 Davidson, House of Lords' Debate on Matrimonial Causes Bill, 26 June 1923.
69 FAB, Workington, 12 September 1926, *Tablet*, pp. 371–372.
70 *Report of Lambeth Conference, 1920* (London: SPCK, 1920), p. 44.
71 *Daily Telegraph*, 14 July 1922.
72 FAB, National Council of Public Morality, Lansdowne House, 23 May 1919, *Tablet*, 31 May 1919, p. 666.
73 *Evening Standard*, 15 October 1921.
74 FAB to McNabb, 22 October 1921, AAW, Bo. V/59; Jackman to M. Stopes, 17 November 1921, AAW, Bo. V/59.
75 Eyre to Jackman, 7 April 1922, AAW, Bo. V/59.
76 FAB to Franey, 15 May 1922, (copy), AAW, Bo. V/59.
77 Eyre to Jackman, 28 July 1922, AAW, Bo. V/59.
78 FAB to Sir Charles Russell, 4 January 1923, AAW, Bo. V/59.
79 *WCC*, January 1925, p. 19.
80 FAB to Catholic Confederation, 22 November 1924, *Tablet*, 29 November 1924, p. 701.
81 FAB, Homily, Swansea, 5 October 1930, AAW, Hi. II/16.
82 FAB, National Catholic Congress, Royal Albert Hall, 13 September 1929, *Tablet*, 21 September 1929, pp. 364–365.
83 Williams to Jackman, 5 July 1922, AAW, Bo. V/59.
84 Acta, Bishops' Meeting, 10 April 1923.
85 Eyre to Collings, 5 December 1927, AAW, Bo. V/43d.
86 Weld to FAB, 10 June 1931, AAW, Bo. I/13; Weld to FAB, 31 December 1931, AAW, Bo.I/13.
87 *Times*, 3 October 1928.
88 FAB, Pastoral Letter, 2 February 1913.
89 'Impressions of the Liverpool Congress,' *WCC*, September 1920, pp. 163–164.
90 Amigo, Pastoral Letter, Advent 1926.
91 Margaret Fletcher (1862–1943), the daughter of an Anglican clergyman, converted to Catholicism in 1897. She was an artist, journalist, proponent of women's education, rights and responsibilities, and Catholic lay leader.
92 M. Fletcher to FAB, 8 October 1906, AAW, Bo. I/30.
93 Fletcher, *O, Call Back Yesterday*, p. 111.
94 Fletcher to FAB, 28 November [1906?], AAW, Bo. I/30; Mary Talbot to FAB, 19 November 1906, AAW, Bo. I/30; FAB, Address, CWL Annual General Meeting, 23 November 1927, *Tablet*, 26 November 1927, p. 705.
95 FAB, Address, Inaugural general meeting, 19 December 1907, *Tablet*, 28 December 1907, p. 1020.
96 FAB, Rome, 20 October 1912, *Tablet*, 2 November 1912, p. 702.
97 *Ibid*.

98 FAB, CWL AGM, 19 October 1921, *Tablet*, 29 October 1921, p. 570.
99 Fletcher, *O, Call Back Yesterday*, pp. 140–154.
100 FAB, CWL AGM, Leeds, 7 March 1913, *Tablet*, 15 March 1913, p. 412.
101 FAB, CWL AGM, 13 December 1923, *Tablet*, 22 December 1923, p. 817.
102 FAB, CWL AGM, London, 19 November 1931, *Tablet*, 28 Nov 31, p. 706.
103 *Tablet*, 11 June 1932, p. 770.
104 M. Hope to FAB, 30 March ?, AAW, Bo. I/30.
105 Oldmeadow, *Francis Cardinal Bourne*, i, pp. 192–195.
106 R. Baden-Powell to FAB, 14 February 1910, AAW, Bo. I/17.
107 FAB, Address, Catholic Scout Guild dinner, 17 January 1929, *Tablet*, 26 January 1929, p. 116.

Chapter 21

Separated Brethren

The Strange Death of Protestant England

At the turn of the twentieth century England remained a Christian, and self-professedly Protestant, country. 60% of the population identified themselves as Anglican; 15% were Nonconformists; only 5% Catholic. However, Anglican numerical supremacy masked serious problems. For many, membership meant little more than baptism, marriage and funeral rites in the Established Church. Anglican weakness was particularly pronounced in London, the North and urban districts—precisely those areas in which Catholicism was growing. In an age of scepticism and scientific advance, its hold on the middle classes was diminishing. The Church of England was troubled by doubt and doctrinal dispute, which came to a head in 1917 with Hensley Henson's nomination as Bishop of Hereford—despite his acknowledged difficulties with belief in the Virgin Birth, the Resurrection and miracles.

Bourne's counterpart at Lambeth Palace for the greater part of his time at Westminster was Randall Davidson, Archbishop of Canterbury from January 1903 until his resignation in November 1928. The two men enjoyed, for the most part, civil, but cool, relations, moving, as they did, in very different circles. Davidson's background lay in Scottish Presbyterianism, but, as an Old Harrovian and Oxonian, his Establishment credentials were impeccable. He owed his preferment to royal favour, but possessed impressive intellectual and administrative gifts. Influential in public life, he was nevertheless a man of reserve and discretion.

As the Archbishop of Westminster was committing his intimate thoughts to paper in 1917, Davidson was similarly recording his own. He was the consummate Anglican, defining himself against both Anglo- and Roman Catholicism. He wished 'to assert in practice the thoughtful and deliberate comprehensiveness of the Church of England, as contrasted with the clear-cut lines and fences of demarcation which mark the rulings of the Church of Rome, and the corresponding, though quite different, rulings of protesting sects ... I am increasingly certain that the [High Church] rigorist attitude is a mistaken one, and that we rightly inculcate and use an elasticity in these matters—an elasticity which I have sought not only to condone, but even to encourage in certain credal matters.'[1] This latitudinarianism gave him little sympathy for Catholicism, which he thought 'exclusive and arrogant.'[2]

For his part, Bourne clearly recognised the decline of Protestantism. That was not a cause for rejoicing when it led, not to Catholicism, but to religious indifference. He analysed the underlying causes. Firstly, 'the want of definiteness in the religious teaching ... A second and more potent reason for this loss of influence was that those of whom he had spoken had not considered it necessary to give definite religious teaching to their children in the schools.'[3] He noted that within his own lifetime the Nonconformists had largely 'given up teaching religious faith or belief,' preferring, instead, social and charitable work.[4]

This lack of definite religious belief made dialogue difficult. The Archbishop of Westminster mused, 'Is there any body outside the Catholic Church which can say what it is that they believe, that is, what every member is bound to believe? In fact, in this country all belief becomes a matter of opinion.'[5] Of course, the Cardinal maintained unceasingly where truth might be found. 'The one and only purpose of the Catholic Church is to teach men the knowledge, love and service of their Lord and Saviour ... The Church accomplishes this purpose in a very simple way. She takes the words of her Founder in their natural and obvious sense, as He evidently meant them to be taken: and upon this she bases the whole of her teaching and worship. The Catholic Church is a primitive Church, a scriptural Church, an evangelical Church.'[6]

'Part and parcel of the State'

While under no illusion that Anglicanism was a result of the Erastian settlement of the Reformation, 'part and parcel of the State,' Bourne never underestimated its attraction for a significant proportion of Englishmen, embodying, as it did, their cherished values of 'nationality and respectability.'[7]

Much of his episcopate was spent refuting Anglican claims to continuity with the pre-Reformation Catholic Church in England. He lost no opportunity of asserting that the Catholic Church, through union with the successor of St Peter, her doctrine and liturgy, was the sole valid successor of the faith brought to these shores by St Augustine. The ultimate sacrifice paid by the English Martyrs for loyalty to the Pope and to the Mass was 'the complete disproof of that imaginary continuity to which some members of the Established Church laid claim.'[8]

The polemics became particularly shrill on occasion. 'How can Anglicans ever have the impertinence—I don't wish to be offensive—but how can they have the impertinence to tax us with being intruders and schismatical usurpers? We can claim, and we alone can claim, to stand in uncontested continuity with St Benet Biscop, with St Bede, with St Francis of Assisi and with the great saints.'[9] Perhaps because the Cardinal uttered these words in the North, Hensley Henson, now Bishop of Durham, entered the fray on behalf of the Church of England.

Bourne and Henson clashed again three years later. Marking the 1,300[th] anniversary of the conversion of Edwin of Northumbria and the founding of York Minster by St Paulinus, Archbishop Lang of York claimed unbroken succession of office between Paulinus and himself, maintaining they held 'the same Faith' and belonged to 'the same Church.' It was a challenge the Cardinal could not let pass. Sadly, he was ill-served by Oldmeadow's gratuitous insult that the Anglicans had no more right to York Minster 'than the Germans had to Belgium in 1914–1918.'[10]

Bourne chose to celebrate Easter 1927 at St Wilfrid's, York, solemnly processing through the city's streets. In his homily he responded to Anglican pretensions 'in the interest of truth.' One had only to examine their respective positions regarding the Mass, Our Lady and papal authority. 'I claim, then, that we, and we alone in England, who belong to the Latin Church, who call ourselves Catholics, and are styled by others "Roman Catholics," believe and worship as Edwin and Paulinus believed and worshipped.'[11] Henson replied in the pages of the *Times*, rebutting the necessity for membership of 'the Latin Church,' and making reference to the Orthodox to justify his contention that 'great branches of the Catholic Church stand outside the communion of Rome.'[12] Lang returned to his original claim of continuity, aiming a carefully calculated blow at Bourne. 'I think that on the side of the Roman Catholic Church there is now more willingness abroad than here in England to study and think and understand. Would Cardinal Mercier have spoken in the terms and tone of the sermon of Cardinal Bourne?'[13] Two months later the Cardinal repeated his arguments amid the ruins of Furness Abbey. Clearly, there was to be no meeting of minds.

'May they be led to seek unity'

When not engaged in polemics, Bourne could adopt a more balanced position towards non-Catholics. He never questioned the availability of grace and the possibility of salvation outside the Church. 'All could approach God by prayer and all should do so.'[14] He offered more hope and comfort than many of his contemporaries, writing, 'This is certain, that no man of really good will is ever rejected by his Maker, and that to every soul is offered *real opportunity* of salvation. None can be lost, whether within or without the visible Unity of the Church, except by his deliberate fault.'[15]

But he was deeply conscious of the difficulties faced by non-Catholics. 'You know the terrible contests and disagreements that are going on within the Established Church itself ... We cannot be indifferent to the struggle going on in their midst.' And he never doubted the solution. 'For them, too, we must pray that out of this turmoil God may bring peace, and that they may be led to seek unity where Jesus Christ has placed it, namely, in the Holy Roman Church.'[16] The Catholic Church in England had to be missionary. 'What is our work? In the first place it is for those who are already the children of the Holy Catholic Church that they may have near at hand all the helps that their Faith can give them. But our work is no less for you, my brethren, to whom as yet the light of the Catholic faith has not been given ... We come to you in the spirit of Augustine, which is the spirit of Jesus Christ, a spirit of gentleness, with no desire to be aggressive.'[17]

During Bourne's time at Westminster, the number of converts to Catholicism rose steadily from an annual figure of 6,500 prior to the War to almost double that figure by the 1920s. The Cardinal sought to encourage converts, arranging 'At Homes' at the Cathedral to introduce them to other Catholics that they might integrate more easily into the Church.[18] When the Duke of Marlborough sought to be received into the Church the Cardinal asked that all possible be done to resolve his matrimonial status.[19]

The convert, Charles Robertson, initially made St Charles's House, Begbroke Place near Oxford available to the Church in the hope that it would be used by secular clergy studying at the University. Never fully utilised as Robertson intended, it became instead in 1919 'a "clearing-house" for convert clergymen.' It met a pressing practical need: a place for them to live and an 'opportunity for quiet reflection in a Catholic atmosphere.'[20] Twelve convert clergy passed through the house in its first nine months. Yet it was difficult to attract public subscriptions and Robertson regretted that the hierarchy failed to give the project the support it deserved. Only Bourne, he felt, recognised its importance and responded accordingly. He thanked the Cardinal: 'I am very glad to think Your Eminence is *so* keen about it, and this should stimulate others to help in every possible way.'[21] Bourne arranged a grant of £1,000 from the Converts' Aid Society, of which he was President, and gave a personal contribution. The second warden of St Charles's House was a Westminster priest, Mgr Henry Barton Brown. When heavy debts led to the failure of the venture in Oxfordshire after just one year, Bourne arranged for Barton Brown to continue the work in a property at Hatfield in his own Diocese.[22]

In principle, the Cardinal was all in favour of converts. In practice, he did not always find relations with them easy. He found in convert clergy a highly-developed individualism which did not always lend itself to obedience to authority. 'There is sometimes an impression that they are quite sufficiently trained already, so far as their character is concerned. This is very rarely the case. They may be earnest and devout men, but almost always they are strongly attached to their own personal view and their personal will. They have never learnt adequately to obey, or to sacrifice their own wishes in the search after a higher good at the call of duty. If they are ordained, they will be prepared to perform acts of heroism if the work be of their seeking. They will refuse a very simple service if it be not entirely to their liking.'[23] He did not, therefore, favour ordination immediately after conversion, feeling they needed time to 'acquire the Catholic outlook.'[24]

This had produced a sharp disagreement with the Holy See in 1904 when it ordered the priestly ordination of Robert Hugh Benson, the convert son of the former Archbishop of Canterbury, in his first year of studies in Rome. Learning of Bourne's disapproval, Pius X reputedly smiled and asked, 'Who is Bishop of Rome?'[25] The Archbishop of Westminster persevered, however, and, through the offices of Merry del Val, obtained a ruling from the Pope 'that at least two years should elapse between the conversion of a Protestant clergyman and his ordination.'[26]

Evelyn Waugh was another troublesome convert, although his quarrel was primarily with Ernest Oldmeadow. In 1932 the *Tablet* condemned Waugh's novel *Black Mischief*, lamenting that any Catholic should have written such an immoral book, querying whether Waugh merited even to be called a Catholic. Waugh's friendship with Tom Driberg placed the columns of the *Daily Express* at his disposal to lampoon the *Tablet's* Editor. He acknowledged Oldmeadow's right to opine on the literary merits of his novel, but refused to accept any lecture in moral theology. Oldmeadow 'was in the position of a valet masquerading in his master's clothes. Long employment by a Prince of the Church has tempted him to ape his superiors, and, naturally enough, he gives an uncouth and impudent performance.'[27] A further attack in the *Tablet* the following year produced a letter of support for Waugh signed by prominent Catholic priests, literary figures and artists.

Waugh complained to the Cardinal,

> Your Eminence's patronage alone renders this base man considerable, and it is with the earnest petition, as much for the good name of the Faith as for the comfort of all intelligent English Catholics, that a scandalous misuse of your patronage may be corrected, that I ascribe myself, Your Eminence's very humble and obedient servant,
>
> Evelyn Waugh.[28]

He had a point. Bourne's retention of Oldmeadow at the *Tablet* did Catholicism few favours. Waugh was also disgruntled by Westminster's delay in his annulment proceedings. He had the opportunity to settle scores a generation later. In Ronald Knox's biography he alleged that Bourne was incapable 'of appreciating Ronald's potentialities, still less of directing his elusive temperament.' But at least Waugh had the grace to acknowledge the Cardinal's decision regarding Knox's formation: two years residence at the London Oratory, pursuing his own course of studies in the Oratory Library. 'It was a humane and, in many ways, a wise decision.'[29]

Bourne's wisdom and imagination were evident elsewhere too. Vernon Johnson was an exotic convert of the early twentieth century, an Anglo-Catholic religious and popular preacher. With Bourne, he shared a great devotion to St Thérèse of Lisieux, to whom he attributed his conversion. After his ordination in 1933 Johnson 'was sent for by Cardinal Bourne, who said to him, with a smile: "You're a freak! You'll be no good as a parish priest or a curate. I'm going to appoint you to Lower Edmonton, but directly under me. Whatever activities you engage in must be referred to me."'[30] Johnson was asked to help with the formation of late vocations, but given sufficient time to develop his ministry of preaching and apologetics. It was a flash of brilliance and humanity which is seldom recorded in the written evidence concerning Bourne, but which people frequently confirmed in their personal encounters with the man.

'To cooperate when cooperation is possible'

Despite the public controversies, Bourne displayed from the outset a surprising willingness to collaborate with non-Catholics in practical matters. He declared it his 'aim to cooperate when cooperation is possible, consistently with principle.'[31] For two decades he involved himself and his Church in various initiatives. Contemporaries remarked on the novelty of the joint conference in May 1906 when Anglican and Catholic Bishops sat together with Free Church leaders and the Duke of Norfolk to promote Sunday observance.[32] The Archbishop of Westminster added his name to a joint letter in the same cause.[33]

The Cardinal accepted the joint presidency, together the Archbishops of Canterbury and York, General Booth and John Clifford, of the Temperance Council of the Christian Churches of England and Wales when it was established in 1915, and presided at its first Annual General Meeting. He joined other Christian leaders in 1917 in signing a memorial opposing the extension of divorce. In 1919 a joint appeal was made to the nation during the railway strike. There was joint action in international affairs, urging support for the League of Nations and protesting against Soviet religious persecution. After the War Davidson and Bourne coordinated collections for the 'Save the Children Fund.' (In 1920 Davidson nominated Bourne for membership of the Athenaeum. Bourne responded by saying he hoped it would enable him 'to do something more for the causes we both have at heart.'[34])

Archbishop Whiteside of Liverpool supported the Cardinal in these initiatives. 'Catholics may co-operate with non-Catholics in promoting social and even moral amelioration of those amidst whom they live, as far as always without compromise of principle.'[35] However, the Bishop of Nottingham was more representative of the Catholic hierarchy when he expressed his discomfort concerning proposals for joint action on Temperance matters, 'I don't like the idea of going in with the heretics but it seems to be our only chance.'[36]

The Cardinal was even prepared to go beyond cooperation on practical issues, and at least countenance the discussion of areas of doctrinal difference. Wilfrid Ward was approached by the Bishop of Winchester in 1913 about the possibility of Catholics joining in 'a discussion among Christians of different denominations on matters of common interest to all who wish to uphold Christianity against modern disbelief.' Ward took the matter 'to the Cardinal who thought the scheme workable.' It was the opposition of the local Bishop, Cotter of Portsmouth, which appears to have put a stop to the proposal. But even then the Cardinal suggested Ward write to Cotter to seek to persuade him.[37]

Bourne's positive attitude to cooperation with non-Catholics did not survive. This was not primarily the increasing conservatism of an older man, but rather the result of bitter experience. COPEC had potentially represented the most significant Catholic involvement with other Christians to date, but it foundered on impossible utopianism, ambiguity and the increasing realisation that practical and doctrinal issues could not be separated. The Malines Conversations and the General Strike represented further setbacks to the cause of cooperation.

The Cardinal expressed his frustration.

> We are constantly being invited by non-Catholic fellow-countrymen to join in various societies and make united appeals on various matters of public interest. Formerly, say thirty years ago, it was a good deal easier to answer these appeals in the affirmative. Today one has to hesitate a good deal, and very often one is compelled reluctantly to say, 'It is impossible to cooperate, but one will be prepared to help as best one may, but independently.'[38]

As the twentieth century progressed, he felt that English Protestants were increasingly compromised by modernism and secularism. 'I regret to have observed how very apathetic the Church of England often appears in aiding those interests about which the Catholic Church is deeply concerned. We find very often, among our Anglican friends, a want of sympathy on moral questions such as birth prevention and divorce which astonishes us ... The same may be said of the school question.' The problem again was the lack of definite religious teaching outside the Catholic Church. 'Too often the appeal for joint action is not based on any definite principle but on a vague appeal to sentiment. It is not easy to see how such action is likely to render any real or lasting service to the national cause.'[39] And this is broadly where matters remained until the Second Vatican Council. Today Bourne's words once more seem very apposite.

Separated Brethren

Notes

1 Davidson, Notes, January 1917, cited Bell, *Randall Davidson*, pp. 795–796.
2 Davidson to Rev A. H. Mathew, 20 January 1908, cited Bell, *Randall Davidson*, p. 1018.
3 FAB, Newcastle, 26 May 1913, *Tablet*, 31 May 1913, p. 851.
4 FAB, Bolton, 24 June 1922, *Tablet*, 1 July 1922, p. 22.
5 FAB, Mansfield, 25 March 1925, *Tablet*, 28 March 1925, p. 424.
6 FAB, St Peter's, Hove, July 1927, cited Oldmeadow, *Francis Cardinal Bourne*, ii, p. 243.
7 FAB Address, 'The Apostolate by Means of the English Language,' Norwich Catholic Congress, 1912, p. 253, *WCC*, pp. 249–256.
8 FAB, 1928 Lenten Pastoral, *Times*, 20 February 1928.
9 FAB, Sunderland, 8 September 1924, *Tablet*, 13 September 1924, p. 339.
10 *Tablet*, 16 April 1927, p. 505.
11 FAB, Homily, St Wilfrid's York, 17 April 1927, *Tablet*, 23 April 1927, pp. 555–557.
12 H. Henson, *Times*, 20 April 1927.
13 C. Lang, *York Diocesan Gazette*, May 1927.
14 FAB, Ramsgate, 25 June 1901, *Tablet*, 6 July 1901.
15 FAB, 'The Catholic Apostolic Roman Church,' J. Marchant (ed.), *The Reunion of Christendom* (London: Cassell & Co, 1929), p. 19.
16 FAB, Lenten Pastoral, 1899, *Tablet*, 25 February 1899, p. 312.
17 FAB speech, Sittingbourne, 26 June 1901, *Tablet*, 6 July 1901, p. 28.
18 *WCC*, October 1925, p. 199.
19 FAB to Martindale, 28 April 1925, AAW, Bo. IV/6/2.
20 H. Hinde to FAB, 26 April 1919; Hinde to FAB, 8 September 1919, AAW, Bo. V/43a.
21 Robertson to FAB, 12 January 1920, AAW, Bo. V/43a.
22 J. Sharp, 'Oscott in Oxford: Lost Opportunity or Misguided Pipe Dream?' in *Recusant History*, 30,2 (2010), pp. 321–341.
23 FAB, *Ecclesiastical Training*, p. 59.
24 Jackman to Editor, *Times*, 27 November 1936.
25 Leslie, *Cardinal Gasquet*, p. 173.
26 Merry del Val to FAB, 22 October 1904, AAW, Bo. IV/4/2.
27 *Daily Express*, 11 September 1932.
28 'An Open Letter to His Eminence the Cardinal Archbishop of Westminster,' May 1933, printed privately but not published, cited S. Hastings, *Evelyn Waugh: A Biography* (London: Sinclair-Stevenson, 1994), pp. 283–284.
29 E. Waugh, *Ronald Knox* (London: Chapman & Hall, 1959), pp. 167–168.
30 'The Vernon We Knew' in *Sicut Parvuli*, XXXII, No. 1 (January 1970), p. 43.
31 FAB speech, Edinburgh, 17 June 1931, AAW, Bo. IV/1/20.

[32] Bell, *Randall Davidson*, p. 507.
[33] Editorial, *Tablet*, 12 January 1907, p. 45.
[34] FAB to Davidson, 4 February 1920, LPL, Davidson Papers 520, f. 345.
[35] Whiteside, Lenten Pastoral 1919, *Tablet*, 5 April 1919, pp. 126–127.
[36] Dunn to Amigo, 23 November 1918, SAA, cited Aspden, *Fortress Church*, p. 126.
[37] Ward to Cotter, 17 June 1913, cited Ward, *Insurrection versus Resurrection*, p. 436.
[38] FAB, Cambridge Summer School, 7 August 1932, *Tablet*, 20 August 1932, p. 246.
[39] FAB speech, Edinburgh, 17 June 1931, AAW, Bo. IV/1/20.

Chapter 22

Malines and Back

'The first streaks of that dawning day'

Much ink has been spilt over the Malines Conversations, reflecting both their contemporary controversy and a more recent preoccupation with ecumenism. The Conversations were a rare example of attempted reconciliation between Rome and Canterbury between the sixteenth and late twentieth centuries. The fact they occurred outside England, on Belgian soil, has meant that Cardinal Bourne's role has been underestimated. Viewed through the prism of his biographer's own prejudice, it was assumed that his attitude was overwhelmingly and consistently hostile. More recently, his involvement has been reassessed.

There were many strands in the thread which led to the Archiepiscopal Palace in Malines in December 1921. It began with the chance meeting of an English aristocrat and a French priest in Madeira in 1889. For half a century Viscount Halifax was the acknowledged lay leader of the Anglo-Catholic wing of Anglicanism. After his death the *Tablet* queried whether Halifax had really been seeking for the Church of England 'Reunion *with* Rome,' rather than 'Recognition *by* Rome,'[1] but unity was always an imperative. As early as 1880 Halifax wrote, 'There is one direction above all others towards which our eyes must be ever turning, in the hope that at last it may please God to allow us to see the first streaks of that dawning day which shall restore us to visible communion with the rest of the Latin Church, from which we have now been separated since the schism of the sixteenth century.'[2]

Fr Fernand Portal urged Halifax to act on his inclinations. A warm friendship developed between the two men, and a determination to make a new beginning in the quest for unity. Halifax outlined the approach he was to pursue a generation later, 'The first thing necessary is to get to know each other: the second that we really do want union with all our heart, and without making any sacrifices to the truth, to judge as leniently as possible all that has been said and done in the past or is being said and done now, by either side. Above all, many explanations are needed.'[3]

Portal came to England as Halifax's guest in 1894, visiting Anglo-Catholic parishes and religious communities, meeting the Archbishops of Canterbury and York. He was impressed by all he saw. However, another player in the later drama commented perceptively at the time. 'He has seen nothing but with Halifax's eyes.'[4] Foreign Catholics' unrealistic estimate of Anglo-Catholic significance within the Church of England was to be a fault line bedevilling future discussions. It allowed Portal to write, 'In England prejudices are disappearing, the Established Church asserts her independence of the civil authority, the influence of the Oxford Movement continues to grow, and the Church is recovering the fullness of the faith.' Anglicans encouraged by Portal's analysis would have done well, however, to pay more attention to his conclusion. 'The inevitable, providential end of this evolution is Rome.'[5]

Sympathetic audiences with Leo XIII appeared to justify the optimism of Halifax and Portal. The papal letter, *Ad Anglos*, asking the English people to pray for reunion, was favourably received. However, rather than the informal conferences Halifax and Portal envisaged, Rome set up a commission to examine the validity of Anglican orders. English Catholics under Vaughan, working with Merry del Val, were accused of procuring the negative ruling contained in the 1896 Bull, *Apostolicae Curae*. All immediate hope of reunion was dashed. Portal's superiors ordered him to abandon work in this field.

The First World War was to effect a permanent change of attitude. The Anglican establishment argued that 'the War and its horrors, waged as it was between so-called Christian nations, drove home the truth with the shock of a sudden awakening. Men in all Communions began to think of the reunion of Christendom, not as a laudable ambition or a beautiful dream, but as an imperative necessity.'[6] The enforced proximity of men of differing backgrounds and creeds had produced a lessening of prejudice and suspicion. Personal relations established between Catholic and Anglican chaplains 'were often of the pleasantest character and led to a greatly increased knowledge and understanding of each other's position.'[7]

The impetus for unity *within* English-speaking Protestantism sprang from the 1910 World Missionary Conference held in Edinburgh. Many desired to overcome divisions impeding missionary activity and to expand such cooperation as already existed. The Edinburgh Conference encouraged those, especially American Episcopalians, who in the aftermath of the War organised a Pan-Christian Conference in Geneva to promote unity. Benedict XV stood aloof, but wished them well.[8] The attitude of English Catholics was much cooler. The closest Canon Moyes could bring himself to approve of such developments was to remark, 'Even partial reunion among the sects would be at least a homage to the ideal of unity.'[9] Keating in Northampton, progressive in other matters, re-stated the traditional line. 'For us, reunion means one thing only—the recantation of the heresies of the Reformation, and the return of our country to the Papal allegiance. The new movement has no practical interest for us than the realisation of our age-old and cherished aspiration, the conversion of England.'[10]

When 252 Anglican Bishops gathered for the 1920 Lambeth Conference, reunion headed the agenda. The Conference set out its vision—so different to that of most Catholics. 'It is not by reducing the different groups of Christians to uniformity, but by rightly using their diversity, that the Church can become all things to all men.'[11] The Conference charged a Reunion Committee under Archbishop Cosmo Lang to devise practical proposals. His was the idea to issue *An Appeal to All Christian People*, and his was the most influential hand in its drafting. The *Appeal* proposed reunion on the basis of the acceptance of Scripture, the Nicene Creed, the sacraments of Baptism and the Eucharist, and a common ministry, including episcopacy. Within this framework considerable latitude would be permitted regarding forms of worship. Local Anglican provinces were encouraged to invite other Christians to discuss how these proposals might be implemented.[12]

The Committee acknowledged that any scheme for reunion was incomplete without 'the great Latin Church of the West.' It recognised positive developments: the establishment by religious orders of Catholic houses of study in Oxford, their participation in theological discussions and cooperation in social questions. 'Should the Church of Rome at any time desire to discuss conditions of reunion we shall be ready to welcome such discussions.'[13] Nevertheless, the authors of the *Appeal*, aware of official Catholic teaching, felt that practically, in the West, they were only addressing other Protestants. Their scepticism as to the likelihood of Catholic engagement seemed justified by Bourne's judgment: 'It was difficult logically to see how these various people could address God in unity when some might accept, and others reject, the doctrine of the Trinity; some might believe, and others disbelieve, in the fact of the Incarnation ...

The point was, "Is there or is there not a divinely revealed body of facts, committed by God to His Church?" ... In his honest opinion the religious result of the Lambeth Conference ... must ultimately be the deterioration, if not the destruction, of the Christian religion in this country.'[14]

Outside England, however, other Catholics interested themselves in Christian unity. Cardinal Mercier enjoyed enormous international prestige for his wartime leadership of the Belgian people. Bourne was unstinting in his praise, 'The name of Cardinal Mercier ... will rank for ever with those of the greatest pastors who are enshrined in the annals of Christendom. Unfaltering in confidence, dauntless in courage, unswerving in the teaching of the truth, relentless in his pursuit of injustice even in high places, he has shown himself the true spiritual shepherd of the Belgian people.'[15]

Mercier noted the changes effected by the War. 'The painful awareness of disunity which the War has caused in men's hearts is at present arousing, among men of different religious confessions, a keen desire for unity.' Touring the United States in 1919 to thank the American people for their wartime support, he came into contact with non-Catholic theologians desiring reunion. He met Episcopalian Bishops, whom he addressed as 'brothers in the Christian Faith,' drawing a papal request for clarification. Mercier assured the Pope of his orthodoxy. He had after all declined an invitation to the Pan-Christian Conference, 'saying that Catholics are no longer in search of unity seeing that they are in sure possession of it.'

But Mercier did not allow matters to rest there. 'Does not charity demand that we make it easier for those souls in search of unity to find the way to the true Church of Our Lord Jesus Christ? ... I offer to make such an attempt. Having first requested the prayers of those around me for a special intention of Your Holiness, I would try to invite to Malines, *one after the other*, groups of the theologians of each of the principal dissident churches, in particular the Anglican and the Orthodox. I would keep them for a number of days—put them in contact with a Catholic theologian of sound doctrine and a loving heart. In the intimacy of a tête-à-tête the penetration of souls can, with the grace of God, be much deeper.'[16] The Pope ignored the suggestion.

It was at this point that Portal felt the censures of the 1890s sufficiently distant to justify another attempt at reunion. He wrote to Mercier asking him to consider the Lambeth *Appeal* as an invitation to engage actively in such work. Portal himself was encouraged when one of those responsible for drafting the *Appeal* assured him that the Anglican Bishops would be prepared to submit to 're-ordination' if the cause of reunion required it.[17] Aware of Mercier's sympathy, Davidson had sent him copies of the Report of the Lambeth Conference and its *Appeal*. The response was effusive. 'May God hearken to the prayers we continually offer for the union of all Christian believers, and crown with success your efforts to attain their goal.'[18]

So many paths appeared to converge on Malines that a reminder is needed that simultaneously other approaches were being pursued. At the end of October 1920 Cardinal Bourne received a letter from Fr Leslie Walker SJ, who had just received a visit from a Dr. Cowie, President of the (Anglican) Federation of Catholic Laity, who had expressed deep unease at developments within the Church of England. His constituency viewed the Lambeth Conference as a step in the direction of Nonconformity. This fear was corroborated by the Bishop of Chelmsford's suggestion that Anglo-Catholics be expelled from Anglicanism. If Rome could sanction a Uniate Church, Cowie felt that several hundred clergy and their people 'would embrace the offer.' The concessions sought were a married clergy and a vernacular liturgy. The Cardinal was asked to submit the proposal to Rome.[19]

The proposal elicited the Cardinal's 'deep and sympathetic interest.' Unfortunately, he entrusted the matter to his Canon Theologian, the rigid and unimaginative Moyes. While assuring the Anglicans that their request would 'be met in the full spirit of apostolic charity,' Moyes outlined his understanding of reunion in such chilling terms as to deter all but the most hardened enquirer. 'In order to enter into communion with the Catholic Church it is required not merely that they should be in *agreement* with her doctrines, but that they should unite with us in *submission* to her authority.' Anglo-Catholics were required to acknowledge that they stood in no different position to Rome as Calvinists and all adherents of the ancient heresies. Moyes had no sympathy for a Uniate Church. 'It would mean a dilution of Catholic western discipline and would work for invidious comparison and confusion ... tending to weaken and discredit Catholicism at a time when its unity and cohesion are needed more than ever in its battle against disbelief.' Far better, he argued, that they were received into the Catholic mainstream.[20]

Walker did not demur from these conclusions, but it was an opportunity lost due to a lack of creative orthodoxy on the part of English Catholics. Walker mentioned his meeting in South London with thirty

Anglican clergy of the 'Free Catholic Movement' and High Churchmen in Cambridge who were similarly unsettled by the direction taken by Anglicanism. He felt 'there are multitudinous signs that the Holy Spirit is working wondrously among our separated brethren.' Something might have been achieved, but the moment passed. Bourne saw no reason to appraise Rome of developments. It allowed Frank Weston, Anglican Bishop of Zanzibar, to persuade doubters that, after all, their future might lie within the Church of England. [21]

'Close and intimate contact'[22]

Halifax and Portal arrived in Malines on 19 October 1921. Asked to host a series of informal meetings between Anglicans and Catholics, the Belgian Cardinal expressed surprise. His visitors argued that if such preliminary talks progressed to formal negotiations, then England might well be a more appropriate venue. Initially, however, to escape the prejudice of centuries, a neutral location was preferable. Mercier accepted 'this conclusion: either it was good for the conversations to take place outside England, at Malines or elsewhere, or they would not take place at all.' Were sufficient progress made he would transfer responsibility to the English Catholic hierarchy to negotiate, with a papal mandate, with the Anglican authorities.[23]

In what capacity did Halifax go to Malines? Before travelling, he approached Davidson, placing the Anglicans in a dilemma. They respected Halifax's social standing and personal sanctity, but they did not trust him. 'His zeal outruns his discretion, and as an agent he would be certain to commit his principals in ways that might be difficult afterwards to justify.' Yet to rebuff Halifax would have called into question the sincerity of the Lambeth Conference's professed desire for unity with Rome. Anglican politics dictated the response, given many were 'suspicious about the *Appeal* because it seems to be moving entirely in the Protestant direction.'[24] Davidson furnished Halifax with a carefully-nuanced letter to present to Mercier.

> Lord Halifax does not go in any sense as an ambassador or formal representative of the Church of England ... Anything that he says therefore would be an expression of his personal opinion rather than an authoritative statement of the position or the endeavours of the Church of England in its corporate capacity. I cannot but think however that you would find a conversation with him

consonant with the thought expressed in Your Eminence's letter to me of 21 May, and of the visions set forth in the Lambeth Conference *Appeal*.[25]

Sufficient to convey sympathy and goodwill, while leaving open the possibility of disowning anything said. The status of the conferences and their participants was to be a continuing source of ambiguity.

Thus began the Malines Conversations, a series of five conferences between Anglicans and Catholics held over five years. The First Conversation between 6 and 8 December 1921 was attended by the Anglicans, Halifax, Dr Walter Frere, Superior of the Community of the Resurrection, and Dr Armitage Robinson, Dean of Wells and patristic scholar; the Catholics attending were Portal, Mercier and his Vicar-General and successor, Mgr Van Roey. The participants agreed to start with less contentious issues with a view to building up trust and goodwill. Nevertheless, the conversation was wide-ranging, covering dogma, authority, sacraments and Scripture. The Anglicans admitted the need to regularise the question of their orders in the eyes of Rome and the Orthodox, if reunion were ever to be attained.

What was said was almost less important than the fact that the meeting occurred harmoniously. Mercier was honest but hopeful. 'Obviously, the disagreement of both sides on several fundamental questions was notorious; we all knew that. But we also knew that if truth has its rights, charity has its duties ... No doubt the warming of hearts towards one another is not unity in Faith, but it certainly prepares the way ... For the whole world, I would not one of our severed brethren should have the right to say that he knocked trustfully at the door of a Roman Catholic Bishop, and that this Roman Catholic Bishop refused to open it.'[26]

Robinson also regarded their meeting 'as a token of hope,' but sounded a note of realism. 'If I seemed to be a drag on the enthusiasm of our generous and saintly friend Lord Halifax, it was because I am convinced that no good can come from any presentation of our position which would not be accepted by the central body of our Churchmen.'[27] English Catholics were far more aware of the difficulty. The *Tablet's* intentions might not have been constructive, but it raised a crucial point, 'Which of your divisions do you want us to unite with? We cannot conscientiously be expected to unite with all three!'[28] Fr Francis Woodlock observed, 'The Bishops of Durham and Manchester should have accompanied the group that went to Malines to confer with Cardinal Mercier. The conferences might have broken up sooner; but they would not have accomplished less.'[29] His fellow Jesuit, Walker, sought to enlighten Mercier. 'The strength of the Protestant party within the Anglican Church is still sufficiently great to make the issue [of reunion] very doubtful ... Mr Bell [Davidson's chaplain] agrees with me here, and assures me of what is evident to anyone living in this country, namely that private individuals do not represent the Church for which they speak, but are almost invariably eccentric in one direction or another.'[30]

The participants agreed that their discussions were to be regarded as confidential. Halifax reported back to Lambeth and Mercier to Rome, but no effort was made to inform Westminster of developments. Cardinal Gasparri wrote reassuringly to Mercier: Pius XI 'authorises your Eminence to say to the Anglicans that the Holy See approves and encourages your conversations and prays with all his heart that the good God will bless them.' Mercier duly communicated the message to Lambeth.[31]

The Second Conversation took place fifteen months later. Mercier was surprised that the Anglicans wished to discuss practicalities before attaining doctrinal agreement. A married clergy and the retention of Anglican rites and customs were conditions for reunion. Also discussed were the future position of the English Catholic hierarchy and how the principle of the Pope's universal jurisdiction might be preserved while allowing the Anglican hierarchy the widest possible autonomy. Davidson wrote to Mercier of his alarm that reunion seemed to be taken as an accomplished fact. It was unfair 'that I should encourage further discussion upon subordinate administrative possibilities without expressing my conviction that such a doctrine of papal authority is not one to which the adherence of the Church of England could be obtained. I say this simply for clearness' sake, and not as meaning that I desire these conversations to end.'[32]

The Archbishop of Canterbury nominated for the Third Conversation on 7–8 November 1923 Bishop Gore of Oxford and the church historian, Dr Beresford Kidd. Although Gore was no friend of Roman Catholicism, the inclusion of these two did nothing to give Evangelical and Liberal Anglicanism a voice at Malines. Two more Catholics also attended: the French church historians, Mgr Pierre Batiffol and Fr Hippolyte Hemmer. Halifax had objected to the English Jesuits as too conservative. (It was a little strange, and ultimately not helpful, that the Anglicans were allowed to choose Catholic participants as well as their own.) The Dominicans were viewed as more sympathetic, but Halifax vetoed Fr Jarrett because of his views on Anglican orders, while Fr McNabb's superiors refused him permission to attend. This glaring omission of any English Catholic was highly unfortunate. It gave credence to the charge that Anglicanism was being considered by foreign Catholics lacking any practical understanding or experience. At Davidson's request the Third Conversation concentrated on the Petrine ministry. While recognising the principle, there was no agreement as to its practical application. Nevertheless, the two new Anglicans expressed themselves pleased at the reception accorded them by Mercier.

After the Third Conversation the context changed dramatically. Despite the secrecy agreed at the outset, knowledge of the existence of the talks inevitably leaked out. Davidson felt it prudent to make a public acknowledgement in a letter to Anglican archbishops at Christmas 1923. He defended his position to Convocation. While upholding the principles of the Reformation, he maintained, 'Personal intercourse is of the very highest value for the better understanding of matters of faith or opinion whereon people are in disagreement, however wide or fundamental the disagreement may be. To me the quenching of smoking flax by stamping out of an endeavour to discuss, thus privately, our differences would, I say it unhesitatingly, have seemed to be a sin against God.'[33]

At the same time Mercier revealed in a Pastoral Letter, 'For more than two years I have been in close and intimate contact with a few prominent Anglicans, for whom I feel a deep regard and sincere affection ... Our discussions were in no sense "negotiations." To negotiate, it is necessary to hold a mandate, and neither on one side nor on the other were we invested with a mandate. And I, for my part, had asked for no such commission; it was enough to know that I was acting in agreement with the supreme Authority, blessed and encouraged by It.'[34]

'Our war against the English Catholics'[35]

There were those, particularly the survivors of the 1890s controversy over Anglican orders, determined to end the Malines Conversations at any cost. They were supported by the English hierarchy, the English Jesuits and the English Catholic Press. Now matters were out in the open, they no longer felt themselves constrained. But it was not just Catholics who were troubled. The Church of England was in the throes of internal crisis relating to proposed revisions to the Book of Common Prayer. The revelation of contact with Rome, however unofficial, further inflamed passions. George V wrote to Davidson expressing unease 'about these interviews with Cardinal Mercier.'[36]

The delayed Fourth Conversation on 19–20 May 1925, therefore, took place in a more charged atmosphere. The subject matter once more was the papacy and the episcopacy. Other papers had been circulated to participants in advance. On the second day, however, Mercier delivered unexpectedly a lengthy paper, 'The Anglican Church, united, not absorbed,' commissioned from the Benedictine canonist, Dom Lambert Beauduin. The Anglicans were to have a married clergy and their own liturgy. The Archbishop of Canterbury would be created Patriarch of a Uniate Church with the right to nominate Bishops independently of Rome. Canon law was not to apply to England and the existing English Catholic hierarchy was to be suppressed. In such a febrile situation, these were proposals too far. There was no subsequent discussion. While both sets of participants were surprised at the disciplinary concessions offered, there was no equivalent compromise on doctrinal differences.

All concerned agreed one further meeting was required to approve the process for drawing up reports of all that had occurred in the preceding five years—followed by a lengthy interval for reflection. A Fifth Conversation was planned for January 1926. In the event it did not take place due to Mercier's death from cancer that month. When the participants reassembled in October 1926 Portal too was dead. Those deaths and the various controversies in the interim made it apparent that there were to be no further Conversations at Malines.

'Altogether sympathetic'

What role did Bourne play in all of this? It suited the purposes of his biographer to maintain that the English Cardinal was deliberately kept in the dark at the outset and, when he discovered the truth concerning this Continental charade, he consistently opposed it. Such an interpretation is not supported by the facts.

There were certainly those keen to exclude the English Catholics. Before Halifax even approached Mercier, the Archbishop of York wrote to Canterbury, 'I do not think that we need be susceptible about the Romans in this country. They are not a national or regional self-governing Church.'[37] That contention had its own logic. Davidson's position transcended the purely national and, therefore, he might expect to relate to the Pope rather than an English Archbishop. Yet such a proposal was highly questionable when the impending talks concerned England above all else.

Halifax's expectation of support from Westminster was not high. Although coloured by hindsight, his biographer records: 'To Halifax the villains of the piece were Cardinal Bourne and those behind him … He bore Cardinal Bourne no grudge … The man was wrong, short-sighted, altogether lacking Mercier's large-hearted charity; but all the same he could not help like him.'[38] However, at the suggestion of his Foreign Office friend Stephen Gaselee, Halifax paid a visit to Cardinal Bourne at the end of November 1921. Such a step, he thought, was 'necessary.'[39]

In fact, Halifax was pleasantly surprised. 'I told [Cardinal Bourne] we had seen Cardinal Mercier and talked with him on the subject of the reunion of the Churches, etc. etc. "Ah! Cardinal Mercier," he said, "I know him well and have a great regard for him; we were at Louvain together. He is a great man, a most distinguished personality with strong influence. I am *very glad* that you have seen him." My visit was a complete success. I was entirely satisfied on departing and asked his permission to come and see him after my return from Malines and to tell him everything that had been said, and also, as I hoped, to ask for his good services to help in every possible way to bring about such conferences as Leo XIII discussed in 1894. The Cardinal was altogether sympathetic and I am sure you are going to be as satisfied as I am.'[40]

When Dr Frere disclosed this information in his account of the Conversations published in 1935, Oldmeadow accused him of 'a grave misstatement.' Acknowledging the fact of the visit, Oldmeadow alleged the statement that Halifax had informed the Cardinal of the imminent Conference in Malines was 'untrue,' and this was indicative of the 'suspicious disdain' with which Bourne was continuously treated by the Anglican participants. Out of courtesy or a desire to avoid controversy, Frere meekly accepted that he might have been misinformed.[41] Oldmeadow, of course, lacked access to Halifax's contemporary account of the meeting contained in his letter to Portal cited above, but nor did he have substantive grounds for implying that Halifax had misled the Cardinal.

Halifax had promised to report back to Bourne after the First Conversation. A great deal of misunderstanding and unpleasantness might have been avoided had he done so. This was almost certainly nothing more than an unfortunate oversight. Oldmeadow, of course, was not so generous. He maintained that, with the exception of one letter at the end of 1923—when, in any event, the existence of the Conversations was made public to the world—Bourne was treated by Mercier 'as if he did not exist.' Oldmeadow based his assertion on the heated correspondence which passed between the two Cardinals subsequently. Bourne complained, 'The Archbishop of Canterbury has been given the fullest information of the proceedings at Malines—I have been excluded from all such knowledge and thereby a grave wrong has been done both to me and to the interests of the Catholic Church in England.'[42] Rather than challenge the assertion, Mercier over hastily sought to defend the behaviour imputed to him, 'Your Eminence gave me no testimony of sympathy, no word of encouragement.'[43] In the petulant attempt to justify themselves, both men made factual errors concerning the events of 1922–23.

Bourne knew—and approved—of the First Conversation and subsequent developments much earlier than Oldmeadow indicated. (To be fair, however, no evidence for this exists in the Westminster Archives.) After a period of quiet, a flurry of activity seems to have been initiated by Cardinal Gasparri communicating Pius XI's approval of the Conversations to Mercier on 25 November 1922. It may well be, however, that Bourne was already aware of what had occurred at that first conference. The fact that the Archbishop of Canterbury's Chaplain, George Bell, had been meeting with the Jesuit, Leslie Walker, in April 1922 is itself an indication that contact between English Catholics and Anglicans was not quite as unusual as we might be led to believe. Bell inferred that Walker had no actual knowledge of Malines, but, talking of initiatives towards reunion, Walker let slip something of interest. 'He said that he had gathered that Lord Halifax had been making independent movements of his own and had talked on the subject with Cardinal Bourne at Mrs Wilfrid Ward's house.'[44] What transpired between Halifax and Bourne on that occasion we shall probably never know.

We do know that the two corresponded in September 1922 concerning Halifax's publication of Mercier's works. Bourne highlighted differences in ecclesiology between Catholics and Anglicans. Nevertheless, he told Halifax, 'I have read with much interest what you have just written, and I rejoice that you have given to the English-speaking world the authoritative words of Cardinal Mercier.' If the Anglicans were able to accept Mercier's understanding on ecclesiology 'then indeed a Conference such as you suggest would be most useful, and with God's blessing do immense good.' Halifax expressed his gratitude for Bourne's kindness.[45] Scarcely the language of enmity and suspicion. This relationship of mutual goodwill continued. On 27 November 1922 Halifax 'saw Cardinal Bourne for some time and found him most kind and sympathetic.'[46]

Prompted by papal approval, Mercier finally wrote to Bourne at this point—a year earlier than claimed by Oldmeadow. Given his contact with Halifax, the contents of Mercier's letter would have come as no surprise. Having supplied details of the First Conversation, Mercier continued,

> If our next meeting takes place it will also remain a private one. But the Holy Father knows it is desired by the Archbishop of Canterbury, and Your Eminence can see the terms in which the Holy See has approved it and is willing to encourage it. I recommend this humble effort of charity to the prayers of Your Eminence. I need not say that I should be deeply grateful for any advice and suggestions that you would like to give me. Living in daily contact with the Anglican Church you will be able to help me with information and clarification from which I should be very happy to profit.[47]

Nothing he read caused Bourne undue concern. In his reply there was no trace of hostility, only a realism which Mercier would have done well to heed. 'I think these informal conferences may well be encouraged, though in my opinion it will be *a very long time* before anything definite can emerge from them.' Responding to Mercier's request for advice, Bourne gave his assessment of Halifax. 'While I have the highest respect for his entire good faith and excellent intentions, I am convinced that he is far from clear as to his own standpoint. He has always been very vague and inconsistent. Moreover, he represents only an infinitesimal group of Anglicans.'[48] There was nothing objectionable there. Most Anglicans would have concurred wholeheartedly.

There was something, however, to which the Malines participants did object. Bourne enclosed in his letter an article from the *Tablet* of 2 December 1922 to help Mercier appreciate 'the present position of Anglicanism.' That article outlined Anglican divisions and was critical of Halifax. What Bourne had no reason to anticipate was that Mercier would pass this on to Portal, who took considerable exception. In Portal's (mistaken) opinion, this indicated 'there are rocks ahead on our side as well as yours.' Portal believed the article demonstrated 'very clearly' Bourne's attitude was the same as that of Merry del Val and Gasquet.[49] Such a miscalculation was disastrous. The Malines participants needed all the friends they could find, and Bourne was disposed to be such. Instead, they chose to demonise him, casting him in the role Vaughan had adopted in the 1890s.[50] Yet, as his covering letter made clear, inclusion of the *Tablet* article did not token Bourne's opposition to the Conferences, simply the desire to sound a necessary note of realism.

Bourne continued to exhibit a benevolent attitude to the Conversations, despite unrelenting criticism from the *Tablet* and the English Jesuits. They claimed the Conversations would reduce the number of individual conversions as Anglicans chose to wait for corporate reunion. Portal tried to counter this negative coverage by asking the Dominican Fr McNabb to write on the subject. McNabb, however, was under censure, it being alleged that he accepted the Anglican branch theory of ecclesiology and minimised the differences between Catholics and Anglicans. The Dominican Master-General only consented to the publication of McNabb's article if the Cardinal approved it. Bourne, and Bidwell, read the article and decided against publication. Bourne felt McNabb's comparison of Mercier with Wiseman served 'no useful purpose,' and would actually harm the cause he sought to promote. 'It does not seem right to suggest that Cardinal Wiseman would have regarded the Church as the Mother Church of the Anglican Establishment. In any case the appellation, if closely analysed, is inaccurate. It might, perhaps, have been used vaguely in 1841. In 1924 it is mischievous and misleading.'[51] With so many in England and Rome searching for evidence of heresy, Bourne's conclusion was prudent rather than obstructive.

Bourne did not content himself with being a passive observer of the events at Malines. Mercier's Pastoral to his clergy on the subject was not universally welcomed in England. One allusion was unfortunate. Mercier cast himself as the Good Samaritan tending the injured and needy Anglican invalid. Not surprisingly, there were English Catholics who took Mercier to be alluding to themselves in his reference to the Levite who passed by 'superbly unfeeling.' H. S. Dean wrote to Bourne, in Rome at the time, protesting against the Pastoral, and Mercier's request that the *Universe* and the *Tablet* publish it 'without curtailment.'[52]

The Cardinal ignored Dean's request that 'something be done in Rome' about the Malines Conversations. On the contrary, he sat down to give Oldmeadow very precise—and he knew unwelcome—instructions as to how the Pastoral should be covered in the *Tablet*. 'Give it the most sympathetic and cordial treatment, and quote largely from it. In a sense the most important words are on p. 7 : "it is sufficient for us to know that we proceed with the agreement of the Supreme Authority, blessed and encouraged by It": which reveals the fact, known to me in confidence all along, that the conversations were held with the knowledge, approbation, and encouragement of the Holy See.'[53] Bourne showed himself as 'delighted as he could be' with Mercier's Pastoral, and when the *Osservatore Romano* published it omitting the reference to papal approval, he suspected foul play. He sent immediately to the newspaper's editorial office 'to inform them of his dissatisfaction, his regrets, and to ask for an explanation.'[54] He succeeded in extracting an acknowledgment of their error.

Bourne himself had written a Pastoral Letter on the Malines Conversations before travelling to Rome, to be published in his absence. Again, he tempered sympathy with realism. Catholics, he wrote, 'have noted with thanksgiving to God that on all sides there is a renewed and intensified longing for such union; and a keen realisation that disunion is evidently contrary to the declared will of our Lord and Saviour, and the cause of untold harm to men. At the same time it is clear that on the part of our fellow-countrymen who do not accept the authority of the Holy See, there is almost complete misapprehension of the sole basis of union which is in conformity with the will of Christ—namely, the frank and complete acceptance of divinely revealed truth ... In the first place our attitude is, and must be, one of intense sympathy manifested both in constant and more fervent prayer for the restoration of England to the unity of Christendom ... and in a readiness to explain and elucidate in every way those teachings of the Catholic Church which are still so often misunderstood and misrepresented by our fellow countrymen.'

While the Cardinal had his own doubts as to the methods and outcome of the Conversations, he had to defend himself on two fronts—against ultramontane Catholics who wished to end the talks at all costs, and High Church Anglicans who believed, and often spoke, nothing but the worst of English Catholics. Bourne alluded to this second group in his Pastoral. 'Unfortunately, there are some who, separated from us, are apparently not prepared to give us credit for this sympathetic attitude.' He had in mind comments like those of the *Church Times*: 'the English Roman Catholics, whose position always leads them to make the worst of us and to prevent any *rapprochement* between Romanism and Anglicanism, have again intervened at Rome with a certain amount of success.'[55] In the face of these critics, the Cardinal made a generous offer. 'There is no sacrifice of place or position that we are not prepared to make in order to attain so great an end—how there is no Bishop among us who would not gladly resign his see and retire into complete obscurity if thereby England could be Catholic again.'

He expressed himself satisfied that such talks should occur 'in France, or in Belgium, or here at home, or in any other country.' In his opinion 'such contact, with the help and guidance of the Holy Spirit, must be productive of good, even though no actual result may be immediately attained.' As he was obliged to do, the Cardinal stipulated only that 'such union must be based on absolute truth and sincerity. There can be no question of compromise built up on the acceptance, or rejection, or mere toleration of a certain number of religious opinions. It can only come from the whole-hearted and sincere acceptance of divinely revealed truths.'[56]

'You wished our Conversations ill'

How was it possible within the space of eighteen months for Bourne to move from a pragmatic, but undoubtedly benign, attitude to a spectacular row with Mercier on the subject, in which the Belgian alleged, 'The impression Your Eminence always gave me was that you wished our Conversations ill; that, as you see it, all the efforts of Catholics should be concentrated on individual conversions, and that to such conversions our meetings at Malines are more a hindrance than a help'[57]?

The answer lay partly in sincere misunderstandings. Mercier misinterpreted Bourne's reality checks for an underlying hostility he did not possess. But over an extended period Bourne was also subject to massive provocation from both the supporters and detractors of the Conversations.

The Malines participants were deeply conscious that, in many ways, their Conversations were a replay of the first tentative efforts at reunion of the 1890s. They were also conscious that most of those earlier protagonists were still active. Once more Halifax and Portal were promoting reunion. The sympathetic Gasparri was now Cardinal Secretary of State, but counterbalanced in Rome by the presence of Merry del Val, Prefect of the Holy Office, and Gasquet, confidant to successive Popes. The latter two feared their earlier victory was to be thrown away and the Anglicans admitted to full communion without the resolution of underlying doctrinal differences.

Portal was most sensitive to the political undercurrents. As early as January 1923 he was writing to Halifax, 'The conflict of rival influences will soon begin at Rome.' He identified their most dangerous adversary. 'The day Merry del Val thinks he can put a spoke in the wheel he will not fail to do so, both for the event in itself and for personal motives with regard to the Cardinal.'[58] Merry del Val had always suspected Mercier of Modernist tendencies, and 'found him deplorably ignorant of English affairs.'[59] He had no higher opinion of Gasparri. 'He knows very little of the true history of the "Anglican Church" or of its present situation and to this day nurses extraordinary delusions.'[60]

Merry del Val and Gasquet had a difficulty, however. Pius XI was consistently supportive of the Malines Conversations. As late as October 1925 Gasquet was unable to make any progress. 'I had an audience of the Holy Father. We discussed the question of the Malines Conference but though I spoke very plainly he still approved of the fact that conversations in private could do no harm. I replied that unfortunately they were regarded as semi-official. He did not put any value on the alleged falling-off of conversions.'[61] Merry del Val vented his frustration. 'Everything is being carried on with the utmost secrecy, here at all events, so that it is impossible to find out who are acting, what they are doing or saying; and any attempt to rectify or to counteract the mischief seems to be resented. I need hardly tell you that *nothing*, absolutely *nothing*, has in any way been revealed to the Holy Office.'

To make any headway in Rome, Merry del Val knew that he needed the cooperation of Bourne as the head of the local church potentially most affected by the Conversations. And Merry del Val did not know exactly where Bourne stood on the issue. His own role in blocking Bourne's cherished dreams of diocesan division meant he did not feel able to approach the English Cardinal directly. He told Moyes that he hoped Bourne would 'not hesitate to speak plainly to [the Pope] for his position entitles him to do so. If he only says what of course is true, that anything that can lead Anglicans to the Church or to the conversion of England, must be welcomed by all Catholics, he will be misunderstood as encouraging what is being done.'[62] Merry del Val also used the English Jesuits as intermediaries. The relevant paragraph of his letter to Woodlock was duly copied to Bourne. 'Surely Cardinal Bourne and the English Bishops will take occasion to make a clear statement and sweep away this false doctrine. I fancy Cardinal Gasquet would be ready to do so and he can do so with the assurance that the true doctrine will be upheld here.'[63] The invidious comparison to Gasquet demonstrated Merry del Val's political acumen, but Bourne had always shown himself capable of withstanding unwelcome pressure from Rome.

Bourne was more susceptible to react to indiscretions committed by the Conversations' supporters, indiscretions the critics magnified and manipulated. The English secular Press reported Portal as having said in a speech in Brussels in September 1926 that 'an agreement was in fact reached at Malines on the principles of the Council of Trent,' the only outstanding difference being the Papacy. It was further claimed that Portal had alleged that the French and Belgian Catholics held a more moderate position on papal claims than the intolerant and rigid English Catholics.[64]

The events leading to the change in Bourne's position really began with Halifax's address to the Anglo-Catholic Congress in the Albert Hall on 9 July 1925. Unwisely, Halifax referred to the contents of Mercier's controversial paper at the Fourth Conversation—without revealing his source. Particularly, he maintained that reunion would not mean Anglicans being asked to deny that they were already a valid Church. Among his audience was the Jesuit, Francis Woodlock, who pounced on the opportunity to open a Press campaign. Portal saw the danger immediately and wrote to Halifax, 'I have read his latest in the *Church Times*; it is essential to avoid all controversy with him and especially any comparison between him and Cardinal Mercier; his goal is obviously to get Cardinal Mercier to respond, whereas good politics demand that he remains silent for the present. There is no doubt that Cardinals Merry del Val and Gasquet are behind Fr Woodlock and push him.'[65] It came to pass exactly as Portal had feared.

His concerns over Mercier were well-founded. Mercier and Bourne were, in some respects, similar: both possessed an essential goodness and simplicity, of which others made use—and a considerable temper. Mercier's own friends recognised that his simplicity 'sometimes landed him in difficulties which might have been avoided ... As M. Portal put it, "His greatness was likely to be better recognised in the next world than it is in this."'[66] Two years earlier Portal had counselled, 'The Cardinal must be careful not to furnish our adversaries with any weapons they can make use of.'[67]

On 2 October 1925 Woodlock wrote in the *Tablet*, 'We have a genuine grievance against the policy of insinuation which during the last two and a half years has suggested that English theologians have presented a different theory of infallibility from that held by their Continental—and less ultramontane—brethren ... It is strongly insinuated that [Cardinal

Mercier] and I hold different doctrines as to the necessity of communion with the Pope as a condition of Catholicity. It is chiefly the mystery as to what passes at Malines which causes all the mischief.'[68]

Mercier rose to the bait. (At the suggestion of Mgr Carton de Wiart, the Belgian Diocesan Treasurer of Westminster, Woodlock had written after the Albert Hall meeting inviting the Belgian Cardinal to repudiate Halifax and confirm his own 'tendentious interpretation' of that meeting.) Mercier expressed his anger in a letter to Woodlock. 'An injustice' had been committed against Halifax. Woodlock had 'declared war on the Malines Conversations' on the basis of words 'falsely attributed' to Portal. Mercier took strong exception to the implication that he and the other Catholic participants held a minimalist line on papal primacy and infallibility, and upbraided Woodlock for his failure to support their efforts towards reunion. The matter might have rested there, but Mercier made the mistake of insisting his letter be published in the *Tablet*.[69]

Oldmeadow claimed that he 'unintentionally' precipitated the crisis.[70] There was nothing 'unintentional' about it. The enemies of Malines in Rome, Westminster, the English Press and the Jesuits had all been manoeuvring towards this moment: the opportunity to enmesh Cardinal Bourne in the dispute. Oldmeadow sent Bourne Mercier's demand. He told his proprietor that he had no wish to be unfair to Mercier by allowing him to engage in an unseemly 'newspaper controversy,' no wish to be unfair to Woodlock, given he had refused to print most of his letters. Oldmeadow related to the Cardinal that Woodlock was support by Moyes, Merry del Val, Gasquet and an unnamed 'distinguished theologian' at Bourne's *alma mater*, St Sulpice.[71] The unspoken question was whether the Archbishop of Westminster would rouse himself to rebut Anglican claims that Catholic teaching was different in England to Belgium and France.

Bourne did react—and with considerable violence. To rebuke an English priest publicly in the pages of the *Tablet*, would, he maintained, 'be a grave error of judgement, productive of serious harm to religion.' It would damage Mercier's own reputation and play directly into the hands of those Anglicans who alleged divisions within Catholicism. Bourne gave expression to pent up frustration. Mercier's behaviour had been all wrong from the outset. 'The Archbishop of Canterbury has been given the fullest information of the proceedings at Malines—I have been excluded from all such knowledge and thereby a grave wrong has been done both to me and to the interests of the Catholic Church in England.' Ever ready to take the slight, Bourne complained, 'The Anglicans are treated as friends—we, the Catholics of England, apparently as untrustworthy.' Given the treatment he had received, the Archbishop of Westminster declared himself 'powerless to intervene' 'to correct or control free-lances like Fr Woodlock.' That letter was written in haste and in passion. [72] As we have seen, Bourne had not been left as 'absolutely in the dark' as he alleged. Otherwise, most of what he said was true, but better left unsaid.

The correspondence between the two Cardinals continued for five weeks. Mercier set out to be conciliatory and assured Bourne that his 'name was never mentioned during our meetings without respectful sympathy.' He made, however, one regrettable hostage to fortune. He told Bourne he had kept silent regarding the Conversations 'to avoid passionate disputes in the Press.'[73] The Englishman chose to interpret this in the worst possible sense. 'Information which can be and has been given in all confidence to the Archbishop of Canterbury and other Protestants cannot safely be entrusted to the Archbishop of Westminster ... Does Your Eminence realise the gravity and the insulting character of such a suggestion?'[74]

Mercier too now abandoned all restraint. He did not place the same trust in Bourne as he did in Davidson because 'the Archbishop of Canterbury always encouraged the Malines Conversations ... The impression Your Eminence always gave me was that you wished our Conversations ill; that, as you see it, all the efforts of Catholics should be concentrated on individual conversions, and that to such conversions our meetings at Malines are more a hindrance than a help.'[75]

Mercier was a seriously ill man at the time, but he did Bourne a disservice. He was forgetting the encouragement the Archbishop of Westminster had given the Conversations at the outset. He was forgetting Bourne's efforts to ensure his 1924 Pastoral Letter was accurately reported in Rome and sympathetically covered in London. He was forgetting Bourne's refusal to associate with Merry del Val's intrigues. Bourne was not inconsistent. He was perfectly sincere in wishing the participants well on the one hand, and on the other doubting their chances of success. As the head of the local Catholic Church, Bourne had a duty to refute Anglican misrepresentations in the field of ecclesiology and Church history. The Malines Conversations had begun as private, informal talks on matters of theological difference. Should they develop into substantive negotiations, Mercier had promised to hand over their conduct to the English hierarchy. The Conversations turned to the consideration of practical details at a disconcertingly early stage. Mercier could be interpreted as reneging on that promise. Neither man emerges well from the correspondence.

The timing of the altercation could not have been worse for the cause of reunion. Bourne had an audience with Pius XI the week after Mercier's final letter. He was still livid as he travelled to Rome and prepared notes in advance of the audience. We know what enraged him most: 'setting aside the English Roman Catholic hierarchy.' Had Mercier really considered the reaction of those Bishops whose very existence he had unilaterally condemned? (Halifax alleged that Mgr Battifol had breached their agreed confidentiality and passed information to Bourne that July.[76]) No wonder Bourne was angry. He also believed Malines was undermining the Church's teaching on papal infallibility and Anglican orders.[77] In the matter of diocesan division, Bourne had discovered Rome's predisposition to take the part of the incumbent Bishop against those who seek to disturb him. Now the principle worked to his advantage.

It would be wrong to suggest that Cardinal Bourne's intervention with the Pope ended the Malines Conversations. There were numerous factors which ensured that would have happened in any event: the deaths of Mercier and Portal, internal difficulties within Anglicanism and the realisation by most participants that the talks had reached a natural conclusion for the immediate future. In other respects, however, Bourne's action may have been decisive. It helped tip the balance of power within the Church in favour of Merry del Val, Gasquet and those English Catholics who wanted no repetition of Malines. A markedly different atmosphere now prevailed in Rome.

In his first Encyclical Letter Pius XI had addressed himself warmly to non-Catholics, 'The Vicar of the Divine Shepherd cannot but repeat and make his own the words ... "And they shall hear My voice, and there shall be one fold and one shepherd." May God soon bring it to pass, as We and all of you and the faithful earnestly pray.'[78] A very different tone prevailed in his Encyclical, *Mortalium Animos* of January 1928. 'Although many non-Catholics may be found who preach loudly fraternal communion in Christ Jesus, yet you will find none at all to whom it ever occurs to submit to and obey the Vicar of Jesus Christ either in His capacity as a teacher or as a governor. Meanwhile they affirm they would willingly treat with the Church of Rome, but on equal terms, that is, as equals with an equal ... This being so, it is clear that the Apostolic See cannot on any terms take part in their assemblies, nor is it lawful for Catholics either to support or work for such enterprises ... There is but one way in which the unity of Christians may be fostered, and that is by furthering the return to the one true Church of Christ those who are separated from it.'[79]

With Malines definitively repudiated, Merry del Val was jubilant. 'I thank God for the Encyclical ... It has been anxious work and I hardly hoped to reach the goal amidst the confusion of those who raised the dust, the failure to understand the situation on the part of many and the ignorance of the facts.'[80] So was the *Tablet*. 'At long last, honest High Anglicans know where they are. For seven years, men whose rightful place is in the Desired Haven have been tossing outside the breakwater in the delusion that the harbour-master's rules were about to be changed and that they might birth under some flag other than the white-and-yellow ... Malines was a *cul de sac*.'[81]

Bourne, however, refused to be pigeonholed alongside the triumphalists. His introduction to the CTS edition of the Encyclical was far more nuanced. Yes, he maintained, efforts such as Malines were bound to fail where the definite teaching of the Church is ignored or rejected, where the Catholic and Protestant understanding of 'unity' diverges so radically. But he returned to an earlier, more eirenic stance, upholding the possibility of salvation for all men of goodwill inside or outside the visible unity of the Church. 'All men must surely labour and hope and pray that in God's own time every human creature may be gathered into that Unity which is undoubtedly according to His will. And it is their duty, whether they be already within or still outside that Unity, by brotherly love and mutual helpfulness and the uprightness of their lives, but without compromise of truth, to hasten the coming of that day.'[82]

'His constant prayers for reunion'

For Bourne's biographer, the most interesting period occurs after the Conversations. Other than taking the opportunity to further disparage Halifax, it is comprehensively ignored by Oldmeadow. After his papal audience in December 1925, with Rome now condemning talks such as Malines, Bourne, like Merry del Val, could have boasted of his vindication—or at least have maintained an honourable silence. He did neither. Whatever his other faults, Bourne was not an opportunist.

Almost immediately he began to soften. He was genuinely distressed by Mercier's terminal illness. At least they had the opportunity to make amends. The week before his death Mercier assured him of his pleasure in knowing 'that the long-standing affection which united [them] was unchanged.'[83] Bourne confided in Mother Clare Arthur, '[His] death is a very real loss to me—we had known one another for 42 years.'[84] He wrote to Halifax, consoling him on the loss of their mutual friend. Both attended the State funeral in Belgium.

Was it guilt at Mercier's death, a sense of shame in having allowed himself to be manipulated by others which now drove Bourne to pursue the goal of reunion in an increasingly hostile environment? One should not exaggerate the transformation. It took a similar form as before: sympathetic, but pragmatic. 'We are quite prepared to explain, but, as I have always said, the one thing we may not and cannot do is to explain away what the Catholic Church teaches.'[85] The pragmatism and the determination not to concede on the essentials are not surprising. The frequent offers to resume contact with the Anglicans are. It is almost as if he felt obliged, on his own terms, to assume the mantle of the dead Belgian Cardinal.

The Fifth Conversation, scheduled for January 1926 simply to draw up an account of the preceding four, was postponed due to Mercier's death. Halifax and Van Roey, Mercier's successor, promised to keep Bourne updated and to send him a copy of the report.[86] Suddenly, Bourne seemed to contemplate not a formal winding up of the Conversations, but rather their substantive continuation. Having been approached by Halifax about the possibility of a meeting with English Catholic theologians, FitzAlan assured his fellow peer of the Cardinal's 'willingness to continue the discussions.'[87] FitzAlan met twice with Bourne, whom he found 'very sympathetic to the idea' of such a conference chaired by FitzAlan.[88] Alternatively, if asked to send delegates to Malines, Bourne proposed Bishop Bidwell, Canon Myers, Lord Lovat and Algernon Cecil.[89] Nothing came of the suggestion and Bourne's intention seems primarily didactic, but it demonstrates a striking desire to maintain contact with the Anglicans.

Halifax still doubted Bourne's sincerity. A year later he was claiming 'that Cardinal Bourne and other English Catholics have been making hostile representations to [the Pope] as to what has been done at Malines.' Despite protestations to the contrary from Battifol, for Halifax Bourne's 'real attitude' was displayed 'by his public utterances in England [ie the York controversy].'[90] There was a failure to appreciate that publicly the Cardinal had to defend the truth of the Church's position, but that privately he was willing to enter into constructive dialogue. Bourne outlined his objective in his 1927 Lenten Pastoral: 'The return of our separated brethren to the unity of that one Church.' A few months later he made a pitch to further this at a much higher level.

Sir James Marchant, theological reader for the publishing house Longmans, had come into contact with Bourne in connection with various anthologies he published. Their conversations turned to the subject of reunion. One of his Catholic correspondents felt Marchant had scored a rare success. 'His Eminence will meet you with all kindness. You have conquered a man who is not easily so taken.'[91] Marchant now appointed himself mediator between Westminster and Canterbury with a view to breathing new life into the corpse of reunion.

In November 1927 he wrote enigmatically to Davidson, requesting an interview. 'I have a delicate and important matter to put before your Grace, dealing with a serious misunderstanding in which you have most unwittingly become involved in connection with the Roman Hierarchy and which I feel certain you would like to be informed, and to clear away.'[92] When they met, Marchant told the Archbishop of Canterbury of the Cardinal's 'distress' at the Malines talks being arranged and held 'without any communication with himself as representing the Roman Church in England and under an apparent supposition that he (Cardinal Bourne) would be adverse to any approaches towards mutual explanations between Romans and Anglicans in England. Quite the contrary, I can assure you, is the case. The Cardinal's eyes were filled with tears when he spoke to me of his longing to see more friendly relations established and his constant prayers for reunion.' According to Marchant, the Cardinal had asked him to tell the Archbishop that 'he would be most eager to promote mutual explanation and friendly relationship.'

Davidson remained guarded. He had heard nothing to lead him 'to suppose that Cardinal Bourne desired to depart in any way from the attitude he has taken with regard to Roman Catholicism and Anglicanism. He has throughout maintained that the conversion of individuals and the bringing of them into the fold is the only policy he could further in England, and his addresses and references to Anglicanism have never indicated, so far as I have observed, any desire for corporate conversations or approaches or for ultimate corporate reunion save by absorption.' Marchant said he thought Bourne would be making contact after the Malines Reports were published in January 1928 'about his wish to promote better relations and even to discuss the question of reunion.' Was

Bourne now to assume Mercier's role in promoting unity? Davidson remained unconvinced, committing himself only to say any communication he received from the Cardinal would be given 'the most respectful and cordial consideration.'[93]

This narrowest window of encouragement was sufficient opening for Marchant. One suspects he overplayed significantly his conversation with Davidson. The moment he returned from Lambeth, he was writing to the Cardinal, 'I had a long and intimate talk with the Archbishop of Canterbury ... and I have a report to give to you which I feel you will be much pleased to hear.'[94] This was followed up with a visit to the Cardinal a few days later. Then Marchant proceeded to dangle the bait again in the direction of Lambeth. 'I have a direct message of *importance* to deliver to you personally from Cardinal Bourne. Would you kindly give me an interview at your convenience?'[95] Uncertain whether Marchant was trying to manipulate both parties or was himself party to a wider Roman conspiracy, Davidson determined there were to be no more games. He wrote politely, but firmly, to Bourne saying that if had anything of importance to communicate, then he would like to hear from him directly.[96]

Marchant derived great satisfaction from creating an atmosphere of intrigue, but there was substance to his suggestiveness. Bourne had a proposal to make. 'I should be quite prepared to depute two or three competent persons to enter into discussion with others chosen by Your Grace, to see if in this way explanation of points of difference might lead to closer mutual understanding.' Marchant had implied that Davidson had already mooted the possibility, counselling that such talks be limited to Catholics and Anglicans, rather than including the Nonconformists. (There is nothing in Davidson's correspondence or reaction supporting this suggestion.) Bourne concluded by asking whether they might meet at the Athenaeum 'to discuss matters more fully' after his return from Rome in the New Year.[97]

The two men met at their club in February 1928. They spoke openly about the Malines Conversation, and Bourne's supposed hostility to them, 'a hostility which he entirely repudiates.' The Cardinal repeated his earlier offer. 'He said that he is practically ready to arrange for any talks we like between Anglicans and Roman Catholics in England, although he is not very hopeful that much would eventuate from them.'[98] It is difficult to see what more the Cardinal could have done. But Davidson did not wish to pursue the matter. He 'was not very clear that further conferences would prove of value.'⁹⁹ He had been badly scarred since their last contact. On 15 December the revised Prayer Book, a project in which he had invested much time and energy, had been unexpectedly defeated in the House of Commons due largely to popular fear and dislike of Anglo-Catholicism. The Archbishop had no wish to give his opponents further ammunition by agreeing to consort with Papist theologians. Aged eighty, he decided to throw in the towel and retired later that year.

'A few fireside, informal talks over tea'

Evincing a 'deep spirituality and lofty idealism,'¹⁰⁰ Sir James Marchant was a curious and colourful character. In his work on Malines John Dick erroneously describes him as a Roman Catholic. He belongs rather to the pages of Peter Anson or A. N. Wilson. At various times aligned to the Anglicans, Congregationalists and Presbyterians, he was a religious free spirit. Davidson's successor, Cosmo Lang, had the measure of Marchant: 'He is in many ways an interesting and useful man and has a knack of getting people together on important public matters. But he seems to have an incurable taste for subterranean methods and for keeping himself in the forefront of public attention. He is always speaking to me as if he had the confidence of Cardinal Bourne. But when Cardinal Bourne is asked about him he rather shrugs his shoulders and smiles and implies that Marchant makes more of this friendliness than the facts warrant.'¹⁰¹

Lang was rightly suspicious. Consistency had no part in Marchant's psychological makeup. At one moment he was telling Bourne of his desire to bring Anglicans 'to submission to the Catholic Roman Church.'¹⁰² At another he himself was considering episcopal ministry in the Free Churches. Then he was offering himself for ordained ministry within the Church of England.¹⁰³ When the Anglicans declined such an exotic candidate, Marchant showed no rancour. He simply changed his request to support for his claim for an increased Government pension. There is no indication of malice. He probably deceived himself more than others. In one of his last letters, the Cardinal gently indicated that he understood Marchant. 'I know and appreciate deeply the difficulties of your position and I understand your good faith. At the same time in the eyes of the world at large that position, as you will readily recognise yourself, is anomalous and perplexing. You are on the very threshold and still hesitate to enter ... May God guide you and bring you safely in His own time to the harbour of rest.'¹⁰⁴

But from the summer of 1927 Marchant was encouraging Bourne in the direction he was already thinking: 'to bring together a group of devout, catholic-minded scholars.' Marchant played to his audience. 'It would *not* be a reunion Committee, but its primary object would be as stated above. I have always felt that the *first* thing to do would be to approach Your Eminence and to submit the suggestion for your consideration.'[105] He strengthened his case in the Cardinal's eyes by writing to the Press urging the French and Belgians to refrain from meddling in English ecclesiastical affairs.[106] He also implied more than the circumstances could probably bear, confiding to the Cardinal 'an important Bishop,' 'one of my oldest and most influential friends in the C of E,' had asked him to visit. 'There is more behind the invitation that I can refer to.'[107] If the 'important Bishop,' was Frank Woods of Winchester, whom Marchant saw at other times and who wrote for him, then such a meeting is unlikely to have had great significance for Catholic-Anglican reunion.

Two years later Marchant tried the same approach with Lang as he had with Davidson. The Cardinal, he maintained, was 'really hurt' by suggestions he had discountenanced the Malines Conversations. 'He said, "I am myself the son of a convert and I know what grievous misunderstandings there are on both sides which need clearing away if only that we might dwell together in brotherly accord to differ as we needs must." I know that he would favour conversations here, at home.' Then Marchant advanced his proposal—and his own continuing involvement—having obviously raised the matter in some form with Bourne first. 'Do you think that in quite an informal and friendly way a few Anglicans might meet a few Romans to talk over the position of Rome and to elicit explanations? .... [Marchant discounted the Malines participants.] But men like say Dr Garvie, the Bishop of Oxford—I mention names which occur to one as competent. But I must not presume to suggest names to Your Grace. Cardinal Bourne, I think, had in mind Abbot Butler and his own Bishop colleague. Perhaps three to begin with. I asked him a little time ago whether I should not drop out of the role of being, as it were, a convenient medium for the moment. But he urged me to continue doing what I am trying to do.'[108]

Lang was dismissive, finding Marchant 'very tiresome.' In his view 'no good purpose would be served by any such conversations between Bourne and his friends and Anglicans in this country as Marchant suggests. I find it very difficult to know how far this man is pursuing obscure efforts and intrigues of his own or how far he carries any weight with Cardinal Bourne or other persons.'[109] He wrote to Marchant telling him so. 'I am not prepared to take part in countenancing or having cognizance of conversations of this kind.' He saw no better chance of success than Malines, the papal Encyclical put paid to such discussions and he did not wish to prejudice the impending Lambeth Conference where Christian unity was again on the agenda. But Lang left one loophole. 'If [conversations] can be arranged between representatives of these Churches privately as between Christian men, I have no sort of objection.'[110] It was all Marchant needed.

With the Lambeth Conference over, Marchant returned to Lang, wondering whether he felt able to contact Bourne 'over the matter of friendly conversations on English soil of an informal character.' Or, at the very least, to give such talks his blessing. Marchant had been industriously working away on the other side too, and produced the names of three Catholics: 'devout and learned men—and I may say liberal-minded in the best sense of that word—belonging to the Roman Church [who] would be quite happy to meet in friendly conversations. They are Archbishop Goodier, Dr Abbot Butler and the Right Rev Dr D'Arcy.' They 'would not be in any sense whatever formally appointed or be formal representatives,' but they had the Cardinal's blessing for this work.[111] This represented a great advance by Bourne. These were not pedestrian curial officials such as he had previously suggested, but men of imagination and theological stature. Marchant reassured Lang: 'They are good scholars and certainly represent a different type to those we are accustomed to think of.'[112]

Suffering ill health, Lang delayed replying for four months. He consulted William Temple in York, who advised against treating Bourne as Lang's equivalent. Canterbury ought to be dealing directly with the Vatican—and *Mortalium Animos* precluded this.[113] Lang was not prepared to initiate talks, but he repeated his previous position. 'There is nothing to prevent private informal conversations taking place between members of these Churches and I could have no possible objection to such informal conversations.'[114]

Marchant lost no time. By 14 May 1931 there had already taken place in his private room at the Thackeray Hotel in Great Russell Street (his London residence) 'a few fireside, informal talks over tea, envisaging *the problems.*' According to Marchant, the Cardinal knew and approved of the talks.[115]

The Catholics were led by Alban Goodier, the Jesuit former Archbishop of Bombay and spiritual writer, described by Bourne as 'a true and sincere friend and counsellor in my public work.'[116] The other Catholics were Cuthbert Butler, former Abbot of Downside, a Church historian and writer on mysticism, Fr Bede Jarrett, Provincial of the English Dominicans, and the Oxford Jesuit, Fr Martin D'Arcy. The identity of the non-Catholics is less certain. Marchant refers to a private meeting on reunion addressed by Dr Garvie, Dr Orchard and Dr Scott.[117] The latter was Herbert Scott, an Oxfordshire clergyman and Anglican scholar, who had written on reunion. But the first two were Congregationalist ministers. (William Orchard made free use of Catholic ritual in his Mayfair Chapel and was to convert the following year.) Goodier suggests, however, that all those he was talking to were Anglican clergy and implies the conversations continued up to April 1932.[118]

The Thackeray Hotel talks were 'under the seal of the confessional.' Marchant maintained that no one knew of them save the participants, Cardinal Bourne and Archbishop Lang. That confidence was better kept than at Malines—with the result that it is difficult to uncover what was actually said.

What we do know is that the Anglican participants set out their position. A Memorandum was drafted on 18 June 1931—it is this which is in the Westminster Archives. In a slightly amended form it was given to Cardinal Bourne in October to take to his audience with Pius XI two months later.[119]

That memorandum stated the Anglo-Papalist position within the Church of England. The Anglo-Papalists were a phenomenon largely incapable of comprehension to both Catholics and most of their co-religionists. They were Anglicans who believed there was no doctrinal 'difference between themselves and the Holy Roman Church.' They accepted as infallibly true not only the teaching of the pre-Reformation Church, but also the subsequent Councils and papal pronouncements. They celebrated the Roman liturgy, and to all intents and purposes were indistinguishable from Roman Catholics—save that they were not in communion with Rome. That they regretted, and they viewed unity with Rome as their ultimate objective. They argued that they remained in the Anglican Communion because the Church of England had 'not forfeited her inherent share in the life of the Universal Church,' and was the cultural expression of the Church in England. They believed in the validity of their Anglican orders, and sought corporate reunion between Rome and Canterbury. They maintained that this position was shared by 400 Anglican clergy in England and overseas.

At the request of the Catholic participants, the Memorandum gave terms for union which might be 'finally acceptable to the Anglican church.' Those drafting the document purported to speak for the wider Church of England. Their proposals did not differ significantly from the position reached at Malines: the Archbishop of Canterbury to be created a Patriarch of the Western Church, the Anglicans to have their own canon law and the nomination of Bishops, a vernacular liturgy, the regularisation of orders and the retention of married clergy. Two differences, however, would have appealed to Bourne: the existing Catholic hierarchy would remain, and many of these concessions would only be temporary. The Memorandum argued optimistically that dogmatic union was more easily attainable than commonly thought—because the English were not interested in dogma. It also held out the prospect of major movement, if only Rome adjusted her attitude. 'Many Catholic-minded people in England are being alienated from Rome by the harsh language used of them by some Roman Catholic newspapers and even in some pulpits.'

In many ways this contact was potentially more significant than Malines. Here was a group of Anglican clergy who sought union, rather than mere recognition. It seemed obvious that there should be discussion with them, but, in fact, there had been no official contact between the Anglo-Papalists and the English Catholic hierarchy. There was no Anglo-Papalist present at the Malines Conversations. Yes, of course, they were even less representative of Anglicanism than the Anglo-Catholics, but at least they spoke the same language and professed the same aim as Rome. They held out great hopes. 'It is only necessary for contact to be made, for Rome to make some definite advance, and these inarticulate voices would become a chorus for unity.' It was argued that the English were natural Catholics—opposed to both Communism and extreme nationalism. 'Once corporate union was attained, England would be the greatest defender of the Papacy.'[120]

Marchant offered blandishments to Bourne. 'I am sure that Your Eminence has done a far, far better thing than Cardinal Mercier was misled into attempting.' All that was needed was for the Holy Father, 'under [Bourne's] personal inspiration' to offer a word of encouragement. Marchant allowed his imagination free rein, saying no doubt the Cardinal would receive this group 'in a year or so,' in the process making one or two of them Bishops. 'What a glorious thing it would be if, during your reign as Archbishop of Westminster, such a movement began as should in the long run bring England again to the feet of the Holy Father!'[121]

What happened to these fancies in the cold light of day? Archbishop Goodier was a practical Lancastrian and an English Jesuit defined by opposition to Anglicanism. He displayed little sympathy for the Anglo-Papalists. 'The more I have thought about the outcome of these conversations, the more I am disappointed, not to say annoyed.' He queried whether even these Anglicans were genuine in seeking union, rather than recognition.[122] Ultimately, he was no more yielding than Moyes. He advised the Cardinal against continuing the London talks. 'If they think that we are anxious to receive them on their own terms they must be undeceived, and this seems the only way ... Conversion can only be individual and can never be *en masse* ... Whatever they themselves may claim, the Church to which they pay allegiance is heretical, and that only on that understanding can further conversations be possible. They know they are wrong, but they hope they may be partly right.'[123]

What of Bourne's own position? Tantalisingly, we have little direct evidence. Obviously, he allowed the talks to proceed—with rather more enthusiasm than Lang did for the Anglicans. Most tellingly, Bourne was prepared to present the Anglo-Papalist Memorandum to Pope Pius XI. He would not have done so if he did not approve of the talks or if he did not hope for future progress. Given the definitive papal rejection of all matters ecumenical three years earlier, his action demonstrated integrity and courage. We do not know how Bourne handled this, whether seriously urging the document's merits or whimsically fulfilling a pledge to Marchant. There is, however, a record of Pius XI's reaction. He received the Memorandum 'sympathetically, but did not see what more he could say or do than he had already said and done.'[124] And it seems no more was said and done during the little time Bourne had remaining at Westminster. The Anglo-Papalist clergy wanted 'simply to know that the Holy Father prayed for them and had listened with a Father's heart to their faltering plea.'[125] Their representative expressed himself 'more than satisfied' with the Pope's response.[126]

John Dick's assessment is fundamentally correct.

> After the death of Mercier, and even after *Mortalium Animos*, Bourne remained surprisingly ecumenical. He was clearly misrep-

resented by his biographer and misunderstood by Halifax and Portal, who were somewhat battle-scarred by their experiences with Cardinal Vaughan ... [Bourne] wanted to be open to the Anglicans but found himself bound to defend, sometimes against the Anglicans, important elements of English Roman Catholic history since the sixteenth century. He looked for understanding and yet was often not understood. He was a tragic figure not a hero. Francis Bourne was the restless leader of a restless Church which was slowly edging out of the narrow Ultramontanism it had been confined to by his predecessors at Westminster.[127]

Notes

1. Editorial, *Tablet*, 27 January 1934.
2. Viscount Halifax, *Church Times*, 14 May 1880, cited H. Hemmer, *Fernand Portal (1855–1926): Apostle of Unity* (London: Macmillan & Co Ltd, 1961), p. 14.
3. Halifax to Portal, 11 July 1894, cited Hemmer, *Fernand Portal*, pp. 33–34.
4. Davidson, cited Oldmeadow, *Francis Cardinal Bourne*, ii, p. 361.
5. Portal, *Les Ordinations anglicanes*, 1894, cited Hemmer, *Fernand Portal*, pp. 32–33.
6. Encyclical, Report of Lambeth Conference, 1920, p. 11.
7. Report of the Sub-Committee on Relation to and Reunion with Episcopal Churches, *Report of Lambeth Conference, 1920*, p. 145.
8. *Tablet*, 31 May 1919, p. 675.
9. Moyes, *Tablet*, 15 March 1919, p. 297.
10. Keating, Pastoral, *Tablet*, 15 May 1920, p. 653.
11. Encyclical, *Report of Lambeth Conference, 1920*, p. 12.
12. 'Appeal,' *Report of Lambeth Conference, 1920*, pp. 28–29.
13. Report of the Sub-Committee on Relation to and Reunion with Episcopal Churches, *Report of Lambeth Conference, 1920*, p. 144.
14. FAB, St John's, Islington, 26 September 1920, *Tablet*, 2 October 1920, p. 449.
15. FAB, Homily, Westminster Cathedral, 15 November 1918, *Tablet*, p. 576.
16. Mercier, Memorandum to Benedict XV, December 1920, cited R. Aubert, 'The History of the Malines Conversations,' in *One in Christ*, 1 (1967), pp. 58–59.
17. B. Barlow, OSM, *'A brother knocking at the door': The Malines Conversations, 1921–1925* (Norwich: The Canterbury Press, 1996), p. 48.
18. Mercier to Davidson, 21 May 1921, cited Bell, *Randall Davidson*, pp. 1254–1255.
19. Walker to FAB, 30 October 1920, AAW, Hi. II/184.
20. FAB to Walker, 9 November 1920 (copy); Moyes Memorandum, AAW, Hi. II/184.
21. Walker to FAB, 12 November 1920; FAB to Walker, 15 November 1920 (copy), AAW, Hi. II/184.

22 Mercier, Pastoral, 18 January 1924.
23 Mercier to FAB, 8 November 1925, AAW, Bo. III/124/4/2.
24 Lang to Davidson, 10 October 1921 (copy), LPL, Lang Papers, 59/138–9.
25 Davidson to Mercier, 12 October 1921, cited Bell, *Randall Davidson*, p. 1255.
26 Mercier, Pastoral, 18 January 1924.
27 J. A. Robinson to Mercier, 17 December 1821, MAA, Box 1, No. 12, cited Barlow, '*A brother knocking at the door,*' p.72.
28 Editorial, *Tablet*, 2 December 1922, p. 720.
29 F. Woodlock, SJ, *Times*, 2 January 1923.
30 Walker to Mercier, 13 June 1922, MAA, B1/6, cited Barlow, '*A brother knocking at the door,*' p. 80.
31 Gasparri to Mercier, 25 Nov 22, MAA, B1, cited Barlow, '*A brother knocking at the door,*' p. 88; Mercier to Davidson, 10 January 1923, cited Bell, *Randall Davidson*, p. 1258.
32 Davidson to Mercier, 24 March 1923, cited Bell, *Randall Davidson*, p. 1267.
33 Davidson, Speech to the Upper House of Convocation, 6 February 1924, cited *The Conversations at Malines, 1921–1925* (Oxford: OUP, 1927), p. 54.
34 Mercier, Pastoral, 18 January 1924.
35 Halifax to Portal, 19 August 1925, Portal Papers, Paris, cited Barlow, '*A brother knocking at the door,*' p. 163.
36 Lord Stamfordham to Davidson, 5 June 1925, LPL, Davidson Papers, cited J. Dick, *The Malines Conversations Revisited* (Leuven: Leuven University Press, 1989), p. 144.
37 Lang to Davidson, 10 October 1921 (copy), LPL, Lang Papers, 59/138–9.
38 J. G. Lockhart, *Charles Lindley, Viscount Halifax* (London: Centenary Press, 1936), p. 340.
39 W. Frere to Oldmeadow, 23 February 1935, AAW, Bo. III/124/4/1.
40 Halifax to Portal, 29 November 1921, Portal Papers, Paris, cited Barlow, '*A brother knocking at the door,*' pp. 59–60.
41 Oldmeadow, *Francis Cardinal Bourne*, ii, pp. 363–364.
42 FAB to Mercier, 29 October 1925, AAW, Bo. III, 124/4/1.
43 Mercier to FAB, 7 December 1925, AAW, Bo. III/124/4/2.
44 Bell, Memorandum of interview with Walker, 20 April 1922, LPL, Lang Papers, 59/149–50.
45 FAB to Halifax, 24 September 1922; Halifax to FAB, 27 September 1922, AAW, Bo. I/78.
46 Halifax to Mercier, 1 December 1922, MAA, Malines Conversations 1922, AI 13, cited R. Aubert, 'Cardinal Mercier, Cardinal Bourne and the Malines Conversations' in *One in Christ*, 4, (1968), p. 374n.
47 Mercier to FAB, 30 November 1922, (copy), MAA, Malines Conversations, 1922, B II 1, cited Aubert, 'Cardinal Mercier, Cardinal Bourne and the Malines Conversations,' p. 375.

48 FAB to Mercier, 4 December 1922, MAA, B1, cited Barlow, '*A brother knocking at the door,*' p. 90.
49 Portal to Halifax, 10 January 1923, Halifax Malines Papers, File A4 271, Box 2, cited Barlow, '*A brother knocking at the door,*' p. 129.
50 Beauduin to Halifax, 29 December 1923, cited Barlow, '*A brother knocking at the door,*' pp. 121–122.
51 FAB to McNabb, 18 April 1924, AAW, Bo. V/91b.
52 Dean to FAB, 4 February 1924, AAW, Hi. II/184.
53 FAB to Oldmeadow, 6 February 1924, AAW, Bo. III, 124/4/2.
54 Fr Sordet, CSsR, to Mercier, 7 February 1924, cited Aubert, 'Cardinal Mercier, Cardinal Bourne and the Malines Conversations,' p.377.
55 Cited *Times*, 3 March 1924.
56 FAB Pastoral, 20 January 1924, read on 2 March 1924.
57 Mercier to FAB, 7 December 1925, AAW, Bo. III/124/4/2.
58 Portal to Halifax, 10 January 1923; Portal to Halifax, 16 January 1923, Halifax Malines Papers, File A4 271, Box 2, cited Barlow, '*A brother knocking at the door,*' p. 91.
59 Burton, Diary, 4 May 1926, CDA.
60 Merry del Val to FAB, 7 February 1930, AAW, Bo. III/124/4/2.
61 Gasquet Diary, 24 October 1925, cited Leslie, *Cardinal Gasquet*, p. 255.
62 Merry del Val to Moyes, 14 February 1925, AAW, Moyes/127.
63 Merry del Val to Woodlock, 28 July 1925, copied by Woodlock to FAB, 29 October 1925, AAW, Bo. III/124/4/1.
64 *Tablet*, 3 October 1925, p. 432; Aubert, 'Cardinal Mercier, Cardinal Bourne and the Malines Conversations,' p. 378.
65 Portal to Halifax, 17 July 1925, Halifax Malines Papers, A4 271, Box 7, cited Barlow, '*A brother knocking at the door.*' p. 162.
66 Bell, *Randall Davidson*, p. 1288.
67 Portal to Halifax, 10 January 1923, Halifax Malines Papers, File A4 271, Box 2, cited Barlow, '*A brother knocking at the door,*' p. 91.
68 Woodlock to Editor, *Tablet*, 10 October 1925, p. 485.
69 Mercier to Woodlock, 26 October 1925 (copy), AAW, Bo. III/124/4/1.
70 Oldmeadow, *Francis Cardinal Bourne*, ii, p. 381.
71 Oldmeadow to FAB, 28 October 1925, AAW, Bo. III/124/4/1.
72 FAB to Mercier, 29 October 1925, (copy), AAW, Bo. III/124/4/1.
73 Mercier to FAB, 8 November 1925, AAW, Bo. III/124/4/2.
74 FAB to Mercier, 17 November 1925, AAW, Bo. III/124/4/2.
75 Mercier to FAB, 7 December 1925, AAW, Bo. III/124/4/2.
76 B. Kidd to Davidson, 22 November 1927, LPL, Davidson Papers, 466/304.
77 FAB, *Aide-memoire*, 14 December 1925, AAW, Bo. III, 124/4/1.
78 Pius XI, *Ubi Arcano Dei*, 23 December 1922.

79   Pius XI, *Mortalium Animos*, 6 January 1928.
80   Merry del Val to Woodlock, 24 January 1928, ABSI, BH/6, cited Dick, *The Malines Conversations Revisited*, pp. 180–181.
81   Editorial, *Tablet*, 14 January 1928, p. 38.
82   FAB, Introduction to Pius XI, *Mortalium Annos*, CTS (London, 1928).
83   Canon Dessain, Malines, to FAB, 15 January 1926, AAW, Bo. III/124/4/2.
84   FAB to Arthur, 21 February 1926, BDA.
85   FAB, Catholic Writers' Day, 25 November 1927, *Tablet*, 3 December 1927, p. 727.
86   Halifax to FAB, 31 January 1926; Van Roey to FAB, 29 March 1926, AAW, Bo. III/124/4/2.
87   FitzAlan to FAB, 2 May 1926, AAW, Bo. III/124/4/2.
88   FitzAlan to Halifax, 7 May 1926, BIY, Malines Papers of Lord Halifax, Box 8/9.
89   FAB to FitzAlan, 4 May 1926, AAW, Bo. III/124/4/2.
90   Halifax to Hemmer, 18 September 1927, (draft), LPL, Davidson Papers, 466/251.
91   W. Barry to Marchant, 29 November 1927, OUL, Marchant MS, English Lett. 314/149.
92   Marchant to Davidson, 15 November 1927, LPL, Davidson Papers, 466/293.
93   Davidson, Memorandum of interview with Marchant, 22 November 1927, LPL, Davidson Papers, 466/309.
94   Marchant to FAB, 22 November 1927, quoted in FAB to Davidson, 6 December 1927, LPL, Davidson Papers, 466/329.
95   Marchant to Davidson, 2 December 1927, LPL, Davidson Papers, 466/327.
96   Davidson to FAB, 3 December 1927, (copy), LPL, Davidson Papers, 466/328.
97   FAB to Davidson, 6 December 1927, LPL, Davidson Papers, 466/329.
98   Davidson, Memorandum of interview with FAB, 16 February 1928, LPL, Davidson Papers, 466/381.
99   Bell, *Randall Davidson*, p. 1302.
100 Editorial, *Tablet*, 26 November 1927, p. 689.
101 Lang to Stamfordham, 22 November 1929 (copy), LPL, Lang Papers, 97/212–13.
102 Marchant to FAB, 25 July 1927, AAW, Bo./Marchant.
103 Marchant to Lang, 28 February 1932, LPL, Lang Papers, 112/161.
104 FAB to Marchant, 9 March 1933, OUL, Marchant MS, English Lett. 314/235.
105 Marchant to FAB, 25 July 1927, AAW, Bo./Marchant.
106 Marchant to Editor, *Times*, 3 October 1927.
107 Marchant to FAB, 20 October 1927, Bo./Marchant.
108 Marchant to Lang, 12 November 1929, LPL, Lang Papers, 97/208.
109 Lang to Davidson, 22 November 1929 (copy), LPL, Lang Papers, 97/209.
110 Lang to Marchant, 22 November 1929 (copy), LPL, Lang Papers, 97/210.
111 Marchant to Lang, 29 December 1930, LPL, Lang Papers, 107/18–19.
112 Marchant to Lang, 14 May 31, LPL, Lang Papers, 107/22–24.

[113] Temple to Lang, 6 January 1931, LPL, Lang Papers, 107/20.
[114] Lang to Marchant, 2 May 1931, LPL, Lang Papers, 107/21.
[115] Merchant to Lang, 14 May 1931, LPL, Lang Papers, 107/22–24.
[116] FAB to Lépicier, 17 February 1928, AGOSM, Lépicier Papers.
[117] Marchant to Bell, 21 October 1931, LPL Bell Papers, 212/7.
[118] Goodier to FAB, 19 April 1932, AAW, Bo./Marchant.
[119] Memorandum, 18 June 1931, AAW, Bo. I/107; Marchant to Goodier, 24 October 1931, AAW, Bo. I/107.
[120] Memorandum, 18 June 1931, AAW, Bo. I/107.
[121] Marchant to FAB, 1 July 1931, AAW, Bo. I/107.
[122] Goodier to FAB, 28 October 1931, AAW, Bo. I/108.
[123] Goodier to FAB, 19 April 1932, AAW, Bo./Marchant.
[124] Goodier to FAB, 21 February 1932, AAW, Bo./Marchant.
[125] Marchant to FAB, 28 November 1931, Bo./Marchant.
[126] Goodier to FAB, 21 February 1932, AAW, Bo./Marchant.
[127] Dick, *The Malines Conversations Revisited*, pp.191–192.

Chapter 23

The General Strike

'A sin against the obedience which we owe to God'

The General Strike was the result of a prolonged dispute in an uncompetitive coal mining industry as miners sought improved working conditions while pit owners attempted to reduce pay. When the miners were locked out of their pits on 30 April 1926 and talks with the Government broke down, the General Council of the Trades Union Congress called a General Strike. For nine days between 4 and 13 May large numbers of workers in the rail, transport, construction, printing and utility industries came out on strike in support of the miners, while the Government attempted to replace them with civilian volunteers. It made for a tense time, but scarcely the revolutionary situation some in the Government and Press claimed. The Government reached an agreement with the other unions, leaving the miners to return to work later in the year on such terms and to such jobs as they could salvage.

On the Sunday of the General Strike Cardinal Bourne mounted the pulpit at Westminster Cathedral to preach on the moral principles involved. He reminded Catholics of their duty to pray for 'a just and lasting peace.' But he did not limit himself to platitudes and calls for spiritual assistance. Clearly and concisely, he enunciated his view. 'There is no moral justification for a general strike of this character. It is a direct challenge to a lawfully constituted authority and inflicts, without adequate reason, immense discomfort and injury on millions of our fellow countrymen. It is therefore a sin against the obedience which we owe to God, Who is the source of that authority; and against the charity and brotherly love which are due to our brethren. All are bound to uphold and assist the Government, which is the lawfully constituted authority of the country and represents, therefore, in its own appointed sphere, the authority of God Himself.'[1]

Until the 1920s Cardinal Bourne was generally viewed as socially progressive. That one phrase—the Strike constituted a sin against

God—comprehensively destroyed or, depending upon one's perspective, redeemed his reputation. It caused uproar and resulted in the heaviest postbag on any one issue during his time at Westminster.

The country as a whole, and Catholics in particular, ought to have been less surprised, delighted or outraged by the Cardinal's statement. Bourne enjoyed a constant record of seeking to improve the conditions of the industrial working class, but his pronouncements on the morality of strikes had always been carefully nuanced, and he had consistently rejected anything suggestive of class warfare.

Speaking to Catholic trade unionists, the Cardinal had addressed the issue at the 1912 Catholic Congress in Norwich. Allowing the lawfulness of strikes, he begged strikers to consider first what they were contemplating. But he was equally insistent in his demands on employers. Workers must ask themselves whether the reasons for a strike 'were sufficient to justify them in inflicting upon the whole community perhaps tremendous sufferings and dislocation of society ... The same remarks apply to the owners of capital and employers when they take into their hands the tremendous weapon of a lock-out ... The power of capital and the power of labour carry enormous responsibilities to the State and to God.'[2]

He returned to the subject the following year. The Cardinal again admitted the necessity of strikes and lock-outs 'in extreme cases,' but there was there was one matter he thought could 'hardly ever be justified.' 'The idea of the universal or general strike seems to me contrary to every principle of justice and charity. I know well that these extreme methods, in this and other political controversies, are being justified on the ground that there is now a real war being waged between capital and labour; and that in war all means, however terrible, may be lawfully employed. The argument, to my judgment, is absolutely fallacious. It is not strictly correct to define the industrial conflict as a state of war. At most, the term may be used analogously, and analogies are to be employed warily and with circumspection. And no such lame and halting analogy can justify in God's sight the criminal acts which sabotage and the universal strike most certainly involve.'[3] He repeated his claim in the immediate aftermath of the War. 'The dislocation of industry by reckless strikes or heartless lock-outs is a sin in many cases against the mutual charity and goodwill which men owe to one another.'[4]

The Cardinal's pronouncement in May 1926 was, therefore, scarcely novel. There is no reason to question his sincerity, but there was another matter playing on his mind. It was in his interest to support publicly the 'constitutional' card played by the Baldwin Government. It was Bourne's longstanding objective to achieve the repeal of remaining anti-Catholic legislation. He did not allow the Government's preoccupation with industrial relations to deflect him from writing directly to the Prime Minister requesting his support for the Roman Catholic Relief Bill then before Parliament.[5] Bourne's 'clear and strong pronouncement' on the morality of the General Strike did not go unnoticed. He did not allow it to. The Cardinal sent a copy to Baldwin, who immediately thanked him for his support.[6]

But, if the Cardinal was looking to be rewarded, then the Government were also prepared to make full use of his statement. At a time when controversially the Archbishop of Canterbury was denied coverage on the BBC and in the Government newspaper, *The British Gazette*, Bourne's homily was reported on the BBC the evening it was delivered. The Benedictine, Bede Camm, wrote from Cambridge to tell the Cardinal that the Government had sent 8,000 copies of his homily for distribution there.[7]

Less gracious and welcome than Baldwin's letter was a note the Cardinal received the same day from the *Daily Mail's* proprietor, Lord Northcliffe: 'Your endeavours to support our cause and your support of the Government do not pass unrecorded. You have our blessing on your noble work. The complete subjugation of the workers is now almost accomplished.'[8] Bourne was prepared to use the crisis to advance the cause of Catholic equality; but 'the complete subjugation of the workers' was no part of his agenda.

But that is how it appeared to some. No amount of hostile correspondence would cause the Cardinal to change his mind, but some must have pained him. One Catholic non-striking worker wrote, 'Are you so out of touch with the Catholic population of this country that the appalling result of your declaration is lost in the midst of your desire to toady to the aristocracy of this country? ... I am afraid that you have done irreparable harm to "the Church" among Our Lord's own people—the poor.'[9] An anonymous writer attributed ignoble motives to him. 'You are out looking for converts when more people are leaving it through your attitude. Look after those of the Church and get others after.'[10] Five Catholic Labour MPs, normally deferential to ecclesiastical authority, took exception to the Cardinal's words. 'As members of the working class, we have the right to protect the standard of life of those who labour, and when the mine-owners endeavour to lower the standard of life of the miners, it is our bounden duty to stand by them ... We protest against a high dignitary of Holy Church making a statement which neither the morality nor the theology of our faith justifies.'[11]

But the tenor of the correspondence the Cardinal received was far from uniform. On the whole, the Catholic laity opposed his statement. The episcopate was divided. Keating in Liverpool indicated to Fr McNabb that he would have taken a different line, but felt that it would 'never do' for a Catholic Bishop 'to publicly disown the Cardinal's lead.'[12] Amigo sought to manipulate the situation, writing to a number of Bishops complaining that the Cardinal's statement had created resentment among the poor, who looked to the Church for comfort and support. There was, however, no common mind among the Bishops, and Amigo did not receive the response he anticipated. Bishop Thorman of Hexham & Newcastle 'thought that Bourne's pronouncement "caused no real perturbation;" that the clergy had "heard no question or complaint but rather acknowledge that his Eminence had power aright to speak."'[13] Bishop Henshaw of Salford felt that the trade union movement had been hijacked by political extremists, the General Strike damaged both the country as a whole and the working class in particular and, therefore, it 'was a sin.' On this matter, Bourne was more representative than Amigo.[14]

The Dominican, Fr John-Baptist Reeve, spoke of the CSG's members' 'shock and embarrassment' at the Cardinal's pronouncement, and could only suggest that Bourne 'had been misinformed on a question of fact.'[15] But there is little evidence that his opinion was widely shared by other Catholic priests. The *Leeds Mercury* quoted four local priests who endorsed absolutely every word of the Cardinal's statement.[16] Bede Camm thought it 'magnificent and courageous.' A priest in Liverpool wrote to say 'that your clear and fearless words on the strike have made a great impression here. One of the millers of the north of Liverpool told me that your manifesto absolutely stopped the strike of some 500 men. He also told me that more than one of his Protestant friends have expressed their gratitude to you for the clear lead that you have given to the men.'[17]

Generally non-Catholics were loudest in the Cardinal's praise. The *Times* led the Establishment's chorus of appreciation. In its opinion Bourne had 'illustrated afresh both the discipline of his Church and his own grasp of Christian ethics.'[18] The Tory convert Algernon Cecil claimed that the Cardinal's clear lead 'had given many people quite a new feeling towards Catholicism. They were completely in sympathy with His Eminence, and they made no bones about saying so.'[19] But it was not just the great and the good who were vociferous in their admiration of the Cardinal's stance. An Anglican correspondent of the *Yorkshire Herald* voiced his opinion 'that it is the Church of Rome which has at this time taken the man's part in striking a blow, and a very powerful one too, on the side of the liberty of the individual and against that immoral power which has sought to deprive the individual of that liberty.'[20] A Nonconformist mother who had lost two sons in the First World War thanked the Cardinal for standing up against possible revolution and in favour of the democratic principles for which her sons had given their lives.[21]

Amigo noted that within a matter of days of his controversial homily the Cardinal had begun 'a campaign defending the attitude taken.'[22] More distasteful to Bourne than the honest criticism received was Northcliffe's attempt to enlist him as a supporter of the unacceptable face of capitalism. When the *Tablet* reappeared after the Strike it made no secret of its contempt for the 'cheap journalism' and undignified partisanship of the *British Gazette* run by Northcliffe and Churchill.

The Cardinal spoke on the BBC three days after the end of the Strike in very measured terms. 'Truly God has watched over and guided and blessed the nation and the people in this time of terrific stress ... [We pray] men and women of every rank and order may be so directed by obedience to constituted authority, and by brotherly love, that, all bitterness of recrimination being avoided, they may gradually reach a peaceful and permanent understanding, fair and just to all concerned therein.' He deliberately sought prayers for the miners, praising their 'many brave and unselfish characteristics' and hoping they might 'at last receive a solution of their grievous economic difficulties.'[23] Two years later he personally contributed to relieve distress among the mining community, urging his fellow Catholics to do likewise.[24] But there was no dilution of the original pronouncement. The first post-Strike *Tablet* editorial reiterated Bourne's position. 'On the merits of the coal dispute Catholics are as free as ever to form their opinions; but on the General Strike we have heard the words of our spiritual leader and we know that it is opposed to the teachings of the Catholic Church.'[25]

Was the Cardinal right to have spoken out so strongly? There is no doubting his courage and principle. Although the working class constituted the great majority of his flock, the Cardinal had made it consistently clear that it was no part of his brief to defend them in all their actions. Labour, as well as capital, was capable of damaging the common good and, if this were the case, it was his duty to speak out. Whether Bourne was right to view the General Strike as an organised threat to legitimate authority is, with hindsight, questionable—although the offer of funding from Soviet Russia aroused widespread suspicion.[26] Bourne's stance was honestly shared at the time by a significant portion of national opinion when it was by no means clear that the general dispute would end swiftly and peaceably.

The Methodists acknowledged that the Cardinal could be relied upon for a 'no nonsense' approach. It was this clarity people sought, and Bourne provided, in time of crisis.[27] He restated the matter in the early days of the return of industrial peace. 'In party politics, which divided men into different ranks, the Church did not interfere; but the simple issue recently before them, when constituted authority was opposed, was more far-reaching than a political question, and had to be answered by Christian ethics. It had to be remembered that all properly constituted authority came from God.'[28] Having judged that 'constituted authority' was at threat, Bourne acted conscientiously and courageously.

'The charge of disingenuousness'[29]

The General Strike brought Cardinal Bourne into conflict not only with workers and trades unionists, but also the Church of England. There was much irritation in Anglican quarters that a Roman prelate had been allowed to play the patriotic card to the appreciation of the British Establishment and the detriment of Lambeth Palace. Henson in Durham could be relied upon to express the matter robustly. 'What could be more unfortunate—I might almost say grotesque—than a procedure that made it possible for Cardinal Bourne to become the mouthpiece of public sentiment and civic duty—a role which belongs pre-eminently to the National Church, and therein conspicuously to the Primate.'[30] Sharp practice by the Cardinal was alleged.

During the rail strike of 1919 Christian leaders had united in an appeal to the nation. The Cardinal had joined the Archbishop of Canterbury, the Bishop of London and Free Churchmen in deploring both the strike and a descent into class warfare. An 'appeal to reason and justice' was made for 'really worthy conditions of life for all grades of industrial workers.'³¹ Randall Davidson felt a similar approach was possible in 1926.

Initially, Davidson's position was equivalent to that expressed in the Cardinal's controversial homily. In a Lords speech on the second day of the Strike the Archbishop declared it 'so intolerable that every effort is needed, is justifiably called for and ought to be supported, which the Government may make to bring that condition of things as speedily as possible to an end. The thing does not seem to me really to bear discussion or to admit of argument, so obvious do the facts seem to be.'³² However, just two days later on 7 May a delegation of Anglicans and Nonconformists persuaded Davidson that the matter was indeed open to discussion and argument, and he adopted a more conciliatory tone towards the strikers.

At Lambeth Anglicans and Nonconformists drafted their proposals in a document, *The Crisis: Appeal from the Churches*. 'Representatives of the Christian Churches in England' called for a negotiated settlement based on three conditions to occur 'simultaneously and concurrently': the TUC ending the Strike, the Government's offer of short-term financial assistance to the mining industry and the employers' retracting lower wage scales.³³ They then set out to secure the agreement of the Prime Minister, the Leader of the Opposition and the Cardinal. The Archbishop felt such agreement had been attained and prepared to broadcast the Appeal on the BBC that evening. At the last moment the BBC refused permission to broadcast. Davidson alleged political interference. Although denied by the Director-General of the BBC, the Archbishop's suspicions must have been increased when the BBC relayed the Cardinal's more strident statement on 9 May.

Davidson's *Appeal* was published in the Press on 8 May—to a storm of criticism from those who felt that he had betrayed the Government in its defence of law and order. The First Lord of the Admiralty spoke for his class: 'Our Archbishop has been very foolish in joining the free churches in a very woolly and cowardly declaration about the Strike. Cardinal Bourne has done much better, and declared the General Strike to be a crime against God. I wish our church could be a little more clear in discerning fundamental right from fundamental wrong—and not be always trying to condone the un-Christian behaviour of the mob because they are poor.'³⁴ The Dean of St. Paul's was equally critical. 'The Bishops have come out of it very badly, bleating for a compromise while the nation was fighting for its life. Cardinal Bourne won golden opinions by saying what our Bishops were too cowardly to say: 'This strike is a sin against God.'"³⁵

Davidson was stung by the unfavourable comparison. He turned on two hostile Tory MPs he encountered in Parliament. 'Nall was very angry with me for our message and thought with Major Kindersley, who was with him, that we had done great harm and that the Church would suffer discredit. They were very outspoken, but quite reasonable too. I showed them that they did not really understand what had passed and assured them that I was quite unrepentant about the message, believing it to have done good. They amused me by saying, "What a contrast—your attitude and that of Bourne." I asked, "Are you aware that Bourne wholly approved of all that we said and himself suggested some of the words we inserted?" This staggered them and amazed them. I think they felt a little abashed.'"³⁶

The Archbishop of Canterbury felt obliged to defend himself by revealing *the truth of the matter*. Henson expressed what Davidson merely implied. 'The wily Cardinal was quick to seize the opportunity of presenting himself to the public in the character of the good citizen in vivid contrast with the fumbling and untimely peacemaking of the Primate. If he knew, and had assented to, the Archbishop's proposals, his conduct can hardly be purged from the charge of disingenuousness.'³⁷ Is *the truth of the matter* that, in a moment of national crisis, Cardinal Bourne acted disingenuously and opportunistically simply to gain popularity and political concessions?

Rather it was Davidson who lacked consistency. The tone of the *Appeal* was far removed from his condemnation of the Strike two days earlier. But what actually happened on 7 May that allowed accusations of bad faith to be levelled against Bourne? Approval of the *Appeal* had to be gained very rapidly, in the days before electronic communication, if an agreed statement was to be broadcast to the nation that evening. The Archbishop went to Downing Street, while Baldwin was in Cabinet, attempting to negotiate with him through his secretary.

Meanwhile Davidson sent his chaplain with a copy of the *Appeal* to Bourne. Finding him out, the chaplain left the following note: 'The Archbishop of Canterbury (subject to the consent of the Government) is broadcasting tonight the enclosed statement. His Grace wished that the Cardinal Archbishop should see the statement, in confidence, before it is made ... He does not expect His Eminence will necessarily make any statement on the document. If His Eminence felt disposed, however, to state his approval to the Archbishop of Canterbury, it would be welcomed, as he expects to be asked before broadcasting—in private conversations— with whom it was that he had consulted.'[38]

The Cardinal sent his reply as soon as he returned. Unfortunately, we lack a copy of that response and must rely on what Davidson reported to others. Writing to the Director-General of the BBC the next day, the Archbishop of Canterbury acknowledged at least implicitly that Bourne's role in drafting the *Appeal* was less direct than that of Anglican and Free Church leaders but, nevertheless, 'Cardinal Bourne has expressed his full concurrence in it.'[39] The Archbishop returned to the subject in a memorandum he dictated two weeks later. The Cardinal had 'caused a message to be sent expressing his agreement with the document, but asking (like Ramsay MacDonald) that the withdrawal of the Strike should be the first of the three suggestions.'[40] Davidson is tantalisingly vague. Did Bourne simply ask that the three conditions the *Appeal* laid down for a settlement be listed in a different order? Or, more fundamentally, did Bourne disagree with the conditions being implemented 'simultaneously and concurrently'—in which case he supported the Government's position that the General Strike be called off first?

In fact, the Cardinal's exact intention is of little consequence. The controversy was a manufactured one, reflecting Davidson's discomfiture in the face of Anglican criticism rather than duplicity on Bourne's part. Events of 7 May were fast moving. Davidson obviously felt that he had the Cardinal's support for the *Appeal*—and there is no particular reason to doubt that, at least in general terms, this was the case. Bourne never denied the claim later. However, it is not fair to make a direct comparison between the *Appeal* of 7 May and the homily of 9 May. The former was an appeal for a settlement to the General Strike on the part of several Church leaders, the latter a pronouncement on its morality by one leader in particular. There is no inconsistency between the Cardinal seeking a negotiated settlement to the General Strike and maintaining that the Strike lacked 'moral justification.'

Seven years later the *News Chronicle* reported a sensationalist address, 'Cardinal and Primate: Allegation of a Broken Pact,' delivered in Cambridge by an Anglican cleric. Dr W. W. Longford alleged, 'As a matter of fact, there was a deliberate arrangement between the Primate and the Archbishop of Westminster, which the Archbishop of Westminster broke in order to gain popularity with the nation.' As a matter of fact, Longford had form. The Cardinal had had cause to warn him shortly after the General Strike in connection with libellous articles he had written on the French hierarchy. The Cambridge speech was nothing more than an opportunistic attempt at revenge against an ailing man. There was no substance to Longford's charge, which the *Tablet* could rightly dismiss: no pact with the Archbishop of Canterbury had been broken because no pact existed.[41] One might disagree with Bourne's stance in the General Strike, but he was not guilty of deception.

Notes

1. FAB Homily at High Mass, Westminster Cathedral, 9 May 26, CTS Pamphlet.
2. FAB, Address, National Conference of Catholic Trades Unionists, Norwich, August 1912, cited Oldmeadow, *Francis Cardinal Bourne*, ii, p. 216.
3. FAB, Address on syndicalism, Leicester, 11 February 1913, *Tablet*, 15 February 1913, p. 245.
4. FAB, 'The Duty of Catholics at the Dawn of Peace,' *WCC*, December 1918, p. 224.
5. FAB to Baldwin, 1 May 1926, copy, AAW, Bo. I/108.
6. 10 May 1926, Bo. V/77.
7. B. Camm, OSB, to FAB, 15 May 1926, AAW, Bo. V/77.
8. Lord Northcliffe to FAB, 10 May 1926, Bo. V/77.
9. J. Wall to FAB, 10 May 1926, AAW, Bo. V/77.
10. Anonymous to FAB, u/d, AAW, Bo. V/77.
11. J. Scurr, H. Murnin, J. Tinker, M. Connolly & J. Sullivan to FAB, 10 May 1926, AAW, Bo. V/77.
12. Keating to McNabb, 14 May 1926, LAA, Keating Papers, Series 4 I A/6, cited Aspden, *Fortress Church*, p. 169.
13. Bishop J. Thorman to Amigo, 9 June 1926, SAA, Amigo Papers, Correspondence with Bishops, cited Aspden, *Fortress Church*, p. 172.
14. Bishop T. Henshaw to Amigo, 11 June 26, SAA, Correspondence with Bishops, cited Aspden, *Fortress Church*, p. 172.
15. J.-B. Reeve, OP, *The Christian Democrat*, June 1926, cited Aspden, *Fortress Church*, pp. 168–169.
16. *Leeds Mercury*, 11 May 1926.
17. J. A. Burge, OSB, Liverpool to FAB, 13 May 1926, AAW, Bo. V/77.
18. *Times*, 11 May 1926.
19. A. Cecil at National Catholic Congress, 1926, cited Aspden, *Fortress Church*, p. 173.
20. G. Jalland to Editor, *Yorkshire Herald*, 15 May 1926.

21 Harriet Eller to FAB, 17 May 1926, AAW, Bo. V/77.
22 Amigo to Henshaw, 6 June 1926, cited Clifton, *Amigo*, pp. 110–111.
23 FAB, BBC broadcast, 16 May 1926, *Tablet*, 22 May 1926, p. 665.
24 *Times*, 21 April 1928.
25 Editorial, *Tablet*, 15 May 1926, p. 638.
26 *Tablet*, 22 May 1926, p. 644.
27 *Methodist Recorder*, 27 May 1926.
28 FAB, Our Lady of Victories, Kensington, 24 May 1926, *Tablet*, 29 May 1926, p. 697.
29 Henson, Diary, 14 June 1926, cited Aspden, *Fortress Church*, p. 167.
30 Henson to Davidson, 9 June 1926, cited Bell, *Randall Davidson*, p. 1316.
31 Joint Appeal to the Nation, *Times*, 2 October 1919.
32 Davidson, House of Lords, 5 May 1926, cited Bell, *Randall Davidson*, p. 1306.
33 *The Crisis: Appeal from the Churches*, cited Bell, *Randall Davidson*, p. 1308.
34 W. Bridgeman to his mother, 9 May 1926, Shropshire Archives, Bridgeman Family Records, 4629/1/1926/37.
35 Dean Inge, *Diary of a Dean*, p. 111.
36 Davidson, Memorandum, cited Bell, *Randall Davidson*, pp. 1312–1313.
37 Henson, Diary, 14 June 1926, cited Aspden, *Fortress Church*, pp. 166–167.
38 Rev F. D. V. Narborough to FAB, 7 May 1926 (copy), AAW, Bo. V/77.
39 Davidson to J.C.W. Reith, 8 May 1926, cited Bell, *Randall Davidson*, p. 1309.
40 Davidson, Memorandum, dictated 23 May 1926, LPL, Davidson Papers, 15/85–86.
41 *Tablet*, 2 September 1933, pp. 306–307.

Chapter 24

The Metropolitan of Metroland

'A good organiser'

Every Archbishop of Westminster acquires significant national and international responsibilities. In championing Bourne's candidacy, Bishop Cahill argued that his three predecessors had flourished in this capacity—to the detriment of the ordinary life of the Diocese. The next Archbishop 'should be rather a good organiser than a brilliant public man.'[1] That was Bourne's reputation, and that is what he delivered over three decades. His successor's biographer noted 'the efficient state in which the archdiocese had been bequeathed by Cardinal Bourne … Westminster was a well-ordered diocese.'[2] Another Archbishop of Westminster agreed with this assessment, noting that, 'By far the greater time of his time and energy were devoted to purely diocesan affairs.'[3]

Bourne's method was not to implement new policies, but rather to bring order and efficiency to the existing situation. He had little desire for 'new decrees. I regard with reluctance new legislation unless it be absolutely necessary.'[4]

Immediately the new Archbishop established an atmosphere and a routine conducive to work. Vaughan had envisaged the Westminster Cathedral clergy being part of his household. Bourne found them a distraction. The two establishments, although under the same roof, were physically separated—as they had been at Southwark. The Archbishop's time was too valuable to be squandered by casual visitors. No one was to be granted an interview without a prior appointment—a rule applied even to his own curial officials. Bourne maintained this discipline by limiting keys to Archbishop's House to his two private secretaries.

Save when travel, visitations or Cathedral ceremony imposed their own timetable, Bourne's day was methodical and precise. Rising at 6 am, he said his Mass at 7 am and allowed himself thirty minutes before breakfast to read the *Times*. He opened and sorted his post before seeing his private secretaries at 9.30 for dictation, never delegating responsibility for correspondence. The secretaries were asked to arrange interviews and organise the details of ceremonial and travel. The rest of the morning was spent in seeing appointments. The Diocesan Treasurer, Chancellor, Cathedral Administrator and Editor of the *Tablet* each had their allocated weekly time.

Deemed efficient and hard-working by his contemporaries, Bourne's day appears distinctly leisurely to us. After lunch at 1 pm no further commitments were scheduled until 5 pm. Having recited the breviary, the Cardinal was free to walk and undertake private visits. The Athenaeum and Hooley's presbytery in Clapham Park were favoured afternoon venues before tea at Archbishop's House at 4.30 pm. Visitors were seen again between 5 and 7 pm. Dinner was eaten with his secretaries; non-clerical guests were rare and the simple fare was accompanied normally by nothing more than mineral water. Bourne retired to his room to read for a couple of hours. His lights went out as the clock struck 10 pm.[5]

A reporter from the *Westminster Cathedral Chronicle* allowed access to Archbishop's House in the early years of Bourne's occupancy was surprised by its austerity and practicality. Even in the first decade of the twentieth century the Archbishop's private study was equipped with telephones, typewriters 'and all the paraphernalia of modern life.'[6] The new Archbishop quickly dispensed with the services of the carriage and horses, given by the Duke of Norfolk and the Southwark laity, replacing them in 1907 by a car.[7] Bourne was never slow to adopt modern technology.

The eccentric convert novelist, Mgr Robert Hugh Benson, bequeathed to the Archbishops of Westminster his modest country house at Hare Street in Hertfordshire. With his interest in the occult, the Hare Street interior was very much Benson's own creation. The Cardinal's presence was 'incongruous' in this 'stage *set* for R.H.B.'[8] Nevertheless, this was where Bourne relaxed, enjoying the gardens and surrounding country. The visitors' book attests to the regular presence of various priest friends from his Southwark days.

The charges of autocracy levelled against Bourne in Southwark are not sustained by the evidence. In Westminster too he sought advice. At 11 am every Monday (or Thursday) the Archbishop met with his auxiliary Bishops, Vicar-General, Treasurer, Chancellor and one of the private secretaries. The Archbishop's 'Council' discussed clergy appointments, any proposals for new churches and schools and other diocesan business.[9]

But having consulted, he had no difficulties in taking decisions: 'I am always ... willing to listen to any representations that may be made to me. But, ultimately, it is for me to decide, and then I expect my priests to give me that obedience which is due to me from them; and to carry out their duties in the way that it belongs to me to decide.'[10]

Feeling particularly vulnerable to criticism in the continuing dispute with Southwark, Bourne asked the Jesuit Fr Considine for a meticulously honest assessment of the Archbishop's standing in the eyes of his clergy. Considine obliged. The gains achieved by a more efficient regime were readily acknowledged. However, the Jesuit noted a charge previously levelled in Southwark 'that the older clergy find it difficult to get the ear of the Archbishop, who is therefore thrown more upon the information of younger men ... [The] distribution of work under various departments ... sometimes forces persons, whether lay or clerical, to settle important matters with subordinates upon which they wished contact with the "Chief" himself.'[11]

Appointed young, the Archbishop may not have felt comfortable with more mature counsel. Instead, he surrounded himself with young assistants—but then they grew old together. Bourne's loyalty to his staff during his long tenure at Westminster was legendary. Mgr Carton de Wiart spent more than a quarter of a century at Archbishop's House, mostly as diocesan Treasurer. Arthur Jackman was Principal Private Secretary for a similar length of time, to be succeeded by George Coote, who had been Second Private Secretary since 1912 and remained until Bourne's death in 1935. Canon Lionel Evans accumulated in excess of 25 years in Archbishop's House as Assistant Secretary and then Chancellor. It produced consistency and experience, but did little to encourage new talent and new ideas. Bourne's successor felt change was long overdue. Hinsley dispensed with the services of Coote, 'a good man and devoted' but 'not acceptable to many outside Archbishop's House.' Hinsley quickly formed the opinion that Coote 'and a few others have complete knowledge of everything and nobody else knows what's what.'[12]

'He was a father to me'

Rome took to heart Cahill's criticism of Vaughan's stewardship of Westminster. Bourne was charged by the Holy See 'to build up a body of clergy sufficient for our needs, ordained for and permanently attached to the Diocese.' In 1903 Westminster was ordaining few priests of its own, relying—not always happily—on the religious orders and priests imported from elsewhere. A generation on, the Cardinal could report that this deficiency had been plugged. By 1927 Westminster had 125 students studying for the priesthood.[13] This was much more than the result of a successful recruitment drive; it reflected Bourne's relationship with his clergy.

The Bishop's first duty is as a father to his priests, especially to those in any kind of difficulty. Bourne had provided that paternal affection and assurance to the boys in his charge at West Grinstead and his seminarians at Wonersh. But appointed Bishop of Southwark too young, hyper-sensitivity to criticism resulted in insecurity. Only with the younger priests he himself had formed could he relax sufficiently to offer the stability of a father figure.

Three decades in Westminster gave Bourne a renewed confidence and competence in his dealings with his clergy. As in Southwark, he began with aspirants to the priesthood. His simplicity and conviction inspired those in formation. Speaking at the Jesuit-run pre-seminary college, the Cardinal 'outlined so beautifully the sublimity of the call to the priesthood, and explained what the motive must be inspiring all work in a priest's life—personal love of Our Lord and zeal for souls ... [A priest's vocation story] was one of God's romances.'[14] Bourne knew what he was about when it came to those training for the priesthood. More practically, he made a point of meeting every seminarian at least once a year to ensure he gained 'a personal knowledge of those who were afterwards to become his helpers in the work for souls in the diocese of Westminster.'[15] A desirable and humane practice not as obvious to as many Bishops as one might expect. Canon Reggie Fuller, one of the last priests to be ordained by Bourne, recalled seventy years on, 'he could be the kindest of men; he was a father to me.'[16]

Fuelled by allegations of his antipathy to Irish nationalism, the reputation persisted for decades that Bourne (himself half-Irish) preferred his priests to be English. Irish priests, it was said, would find a warmer reception from the Gibraltarian Amigo. Jackman refuted the claim, 'If he desired a native clergy, was he not justified in doing all he could, as he did, to encourage vocations to, and educate students for, the priesthood in his own land, instead of borrowing from other countries?'[17] Fuller agreed: Bourne was an Englishman who was perfectly happy to accept Irish seminarians—he needed them. Fuller studied with a number of Irish at St Edmund's but most were from families settled in the Diocese. Other Bishops accepted Irish-born and -trained priests because they lacked either local vocations or the funds to put their own candidates through seminary. Bourne was largely free from such constraints. Yet it simply 'would not have crossed Bourne's mind to exclude Irish priests' from Westminster.[18]

Parish visitations formed a major part of the routine, allowing Bourne to gain acquaintance with the priests and people of London, Middlesex, Hertfordshire and (until 1917) Essex. It was a gruelling schedule: three parishes each week, other commitments permitting. Bourne's industry and normality stood him in good stead in the parish setting. 'His visitation addresses were always extraordinarily lucid, courageous, and to the point, and always different, with some new idea. There was never that monotonous repetition that one would think inseparable from such discourses.'[19] Having one's immediate superior present was not a welcome experience for all priests, but in Bourne they found one who 'came in the guise of counsellor, protector and encourager.'[20]

Simply to be known to and noticed by their Archbishop was all most priests asked. Bourne's attention to detail served him well. 'His Eminence's recollection of name and face was remarkable. At some largely-attended gathering, where scores of persons pressed about him to do him homage, he would greet by name some young priest whom he not seen, perhaps, for many months. He remembered who they were, where they were, all about them. It made them feel—what was indeed the fact—that in their persons as well as in their work the Archbishop kept them in mind.'[21]

Bourne shared his priorities with his clergy. Westminster priests could, he felt, apply themselves more to study and to parish administration. More important by far, however, was the spiritual life. As their father in God, he recommended 'a spirit of prayer,' adoration of the Blessed Sacrament and frequent Confession, and deprecated frequent 'allusion to money matters.'[22] Just occasionally the Cardinal spoke more freely of his appreciation and affection for his priests. 'We are a reticent people,' he acknowledged. 'It is not often that we allow to spring to our lips the thoughts which are deepest in our hearts. While I thank you most sincerely for your good wishes, and for your prayers, may I thank you too for giving me this opportunity of revealing for a moment something of the feeling that is ever in my mind and heart towards you, my brethren of the secular and regular clergy.'[23]

Bourne's auxiliary recalled that the Cardinal 'took a great personal interest in his priests and was always glad to see them and ready with sympathy and advice in all their concerns. As he was undemonstrative, this was not always realised; and some were inclined, at times, to keep aloof when they would have been gladly welcomed.'[24] For someone perceived as austere, Bourne was remarkably tolerant and patient in his dealings with his clergy. Jackman remembered, 'He never crushed the bruised reed, and personally I don't remember his suspending any priest ... His strength was in his restraint, and he didn't mind, or rather wouldn't be influenced by, the suggestion that he was weak.'[25]

The Westminster Archives contain ample testimony to his forbearance and concern. In 1911 Mgr Poyer wrote to the Archbishop of his intellectual difficulties, his inability to subscribe to the anti-Modernist oath and his doubt even whether he could remain a Catholic. Bourne dropped everything to reply, regretting his lack of any previous intimation of this personal crisis. 'I know not if I could have helped you, but certainly you would have had my fullest sympathy. And the knowledge of your difficulties would have made clearer to me many things which perplexed me in your attitude. I trust that you will come and see me and speak with all frankness ... I beg Our Lord to guide and comfort you and I will not forget you at the altar.'[26] After his interview, Poyer wrote, 'A thousand thanks for your sweetness and goodness yesterday. I shall never forget it and how I wish I had come to you before!'[27] How different and how appealing Bourne emerges from these private encounters with his priests.

The Cardinal was not afraid to confront the Vatican in defence of his priests. In 1919 the Holy Office censured a book by Dr John Vance, Vice-President of St Edmund's. Cardinal Bisleti at the Congregation for Seminaries demanded his dismissal. In Bourne's opinion, Vance was being punished simply for taking the line of Mercier's Thomistic school. Incensed by the perceived injustice, he successfully sought the Pope's intervention. The Cardinal later claimed he would have otherwise resigned. In a tone characteristic of his dealings with Rome, he thundered, 'Let the Holy Office have the courage and straightforwardness to attack Cardinal Mercier and his teaching openly, or to point out wherein Dr Vance has departed from that teaching. To condemn that teaching indirectly by attacking at the outset of his career a good and very earnest young priest is a proceeding I dare not characterise.'[28]

This concern for his clergy and willingness to do whatever he could on their behalf did not prevent Bourne speaking firmly when the occasion required. One Westminster priest felt the force of his paternal correction: 'You have unfortunately the repute of being very carping and critical, both of your superiors and of your brethren. I have heard this from many sources so that reluctantly I am forced to believe it. I would exhort you to do all in your power to overcome this tendency which undoubtedly gives scandal and must have a very harmful effect on your own spiritual life. Nothing impedes the action of the Holy Spirit so much so much as a critical spirit for it prevents the blessing of God resting upon us and our work, which can be blessed only in proportion to our union with the Will of God in our regard. Criticism is the very opposite of whole-hearted acceptance of the Divine Will and hinders very greatly our own sanctification and the work entrusted to us by Our Divine Master.'[29]

When he succeeded as Archbishop of Westminster in 1935, Hinsley found the position a difficult one to fill. Were it not for his stirring wartime addresses, he is likely to have suffered by comparison to his predecessor. The clergy 'could never feel that he had his pulse on their activities. The long and fatherly reign of Cardinal Bourne had made it difficult for anyone to take his place in their particular sphere.'[30]

'The Lay People's Cardinal'

Anyone who believes the English Church prior to the Second Vatican Council was a priest-ridden institution with a servile laity should spend time in Catholic diocesan archives. It was not only the Duke of Norfolk and the Catholic aristocracy who felt able to treat an Archbishop as their equal. Ordinary men and women when sufficiently aroused had no inhibitions in telling a Prince of the Church exactly what they thought of him.

Bourne was no clericalist. Already in Southwark he had agreed 'to place the financial affairs of the mission in the hands of a representative council, and thus put into practice a principle which had been much discussed in theory. The experiment had, so far, been more than justified.'[31] Arriving in Westminster, the new Archbishop wrote, 'I count much on the support of the laity, for I shall need help of every kind if I am to accomplish anything.'[32]

It was the local government politician, Sir John Gilbert, who gave Bourne the unexpected accolade of 'the Lay People's Cardinal.' He substantiated his claim. Bourne had 'made the Catholic laity realise what they could and should do for the Catholic cause.' Gilbert praised his 'determined efforts ... consistently made throughout the whole of his episcopate to give the laity regular opportunities of coming into contact with him.' In particular, Gilbert appreciated 'the remarkable encouragement which the Cardinal had always given to Catholic organisations mainly composed of laity, and in persuading the Catholic laity to take their share in public life.'[33]

Bourne did not fear lay involvement. He perceived it as neither a threat nor a challenge. Indeed, in many areas he called it into being. 'All over England the clergy are looking to lay help and lay assistance in almost every department of their work. We now have set on foot in various parts of England various associations and federations for uniting Catholics in defence of Catholic interests. Why is it that these associations and federations, although they have made very real progress, do not make the progress that they ought to make? Simply and solely because the educated laymen are not there in sufficient numbers, or, if they exist in sufficient numbers, are not ready to give their cooperation.'[34]

With an expanding Catholic middle class and an increasingly articulate and organised working class, Bourne was the right man at the right time to direct the growth in number and scope of Catholic organisations involved in national life and charitable work. It played to his administrative gifts. 'It was all part of his thoroughness; and with it went an amazing memory for faces and associations. He had the names of secretaries and treasurers at his fingertips, he never confused the persons or their offices, and he found time, moreover, to master the contents of almost any number of reports.'[35] The Cardinal expressed his admiration and gratitude for the Westminster laity 'who were prepared, when their ordinary day's work was over, to give their evenings so generously and so devotedly in defence of Catholic interests.'[36] However generous and devoted, the laity no doubted appreciated his 'horror of long speeches and of meetings overrunning their advertised time.'[37]

From the outset Bourne felt that the Catholic laity would only be truly effective if the energy and skills of Catholic women were fully mobilised. A *Tablet* editorial reflected its proprietor's views: 'We are writing these lines to stir up our Catholic women. Catholic women in Parliament will not only defend the Church, in such matters as education, but they will, in our honest belief, turn out to be the best friends of the people.'[38] The Cardinal believed that the laity in general, and the CWL in particular, had a special role to play in catechesis and reaching out to the lapsed, 'stemming the leakage' in the phraseology of the day.[39]

There was nothing nominal about Bourne's involvement with Catholic organisations. In Westminster, as in Southwark, he surrounded himself with their lay leadership and was instrumental in transforming the CTS annual conference into the National Catholic Congress. Meeting for the first time in Leeds in 1910 it brought together the whole spectrum of organised Catholic activity. Any issue, social, educational, charitable and spiritual, could be debated and systematic action promoted. Catholic organisations, often specialist and regional, were given a national platform. Bourne provided the impetus—not without opposition. The Cardinal's plan to take the National Congresses beyond the industrial heartlands of Catholicism was hotly contested by the Duke of Norfolk. At least Norfolk had the grace to admit his mistake after the success of the 1912 Norwich Congress.[40] Such success was not accidental, but the result of meticulous and coordinated planning. 'At intervals for months beforehand [the Cardinal] was accustomed to call the delegates of the constituent societies to Archbishop's House, to scrutinise the details of organisation, and to follow in all their particulars the various propositions put before it.'[41] Industry and application were rewarded.

Bourne further harnessed the skills of the laity by promoting the Catholic Evidence Guild, presiding over its inaugural meeting in April 1918. Two diocesan priests were assigned to assist in the formation of volunteers but, from the beginning, it was largely a lay initiative under the leadership of the New Zealander, Vernon Redwood. The objective was to present the Catholic Faith coherently to a non-Catholic audience. From its launch the Cardinal appreciated priests were not best fitted for the task. 'The work of exposition and explanation must be done mainly by laymen.'[42] Beneath the crucifix, a public speaker expounded Catholic doctrine at Speakers' Corner in Hyde Park and forty other locations across the Diocese. Within a year 160 laity were being trained for the work. The Catholic Evidence Guild speaker became a familiar character to Londoners.

The Cardinal countered objections directly. Volunteers would be asked 'by what authority do you lay folk stand up on the platform to expound the truths of the Catholic Faith? Who sent you? By whose authority do you speak?' They spoke, the Cardinal asserted, by *his* authority, by authority of the Bishop. And he regularised their status with Rome, conferring on speakers the canonical status of catechist.[43] Even Merry del Val and Gasquet conceded the service performed for the Church in Bourne's encouragement of the Catholic Evidence Guild.[44]

Frank Sheed's involvement with the Catholic Evidence Guild gave him the opportunity to view the Cardinal's *modus operandi* first hand. Provided the layman accepted basic boundaries, he exercised a light touch. 'I had nothing but kindness from him. He gave me two rules, "Don't ask my advice. Just tell me what you're doing. I'll stop you if I think it necessary." He never did. Another time he put it even more concisely: "I never start anything. But I never stop anything" ... We got along splendidly.'[45] The experience of Sheed's wife was similar. 'Quietly, with an occasional pull that reminded us he held the reins, the Cardinal supported us. When we published the first edition of our *Training Outlines* he wrote the introduction—suggesting that priests might find the book useful in preparing their sermons. It is hard today to realise how revolutionary such a remark appeared.'[46]

John Gilbert was the Cardinal's model layman: competent, connected and, above all, 'loyal.'[47] By the standards of his day, Bourne gave Catholic lay leadership considerable latitude. Nevertheless, he indicated from the outset his expectation that this leadership be correctly channelled. In his opinion 'there were a number of questions affecting Catholic interests which could be handled by the laity, if only the laity set about it in the right way ... One thing his Eminence impressed upon laymen in their work for the Church, and that was to organise it in such a way as to be a help, and not a hindrance to the clergy.'[48]

Bourne's most significant clash came not with the rank and file laity but with James Hope, the Duke of Norfolk's nephew. Possibly an ageing Cardinal recalled the Fitzalan Howards' reluctance to accept his leadership in the education crisis a generation earlier. Hope wrote on parish reform in the correspondence pages of the *Tablet*. His stated motive was the relief of 'the clergy from harassing burdens they ought never to bear.'[49] He followed this up with a paper delivered to the Wiseman Society. Hope and a couple of diplomats drafted a memorandum for circulation among eminent laymen.[50] Genuine concerns were aired. Parishes were sometimes subject to unnecessary debt and waste as a result of priests, lacking experience and expertise, supervising financial and property matters. Instances were cited of priests keeping parish assets in their personal accounts which were then successfully claimed by the priest's family after his death. The proffered solution was a committee of enquiry composed of clergy and laity. Hope prejudged the outcome of such an inquiry by anticipating the creation of lay committees in parishes 'to assist the parish priest in matters of finance, building and dealings with non-Catholic official bodies.'[51]

It was not the nature of the proposed reforms which irked the Cardinal as much as the manner in which Hope pursued them. He met Hope and his colleagues in the spring of 1928 and outlined his objections to their proposals. Hope assured the Cardinal that they were acting in 'no hyper-critical or subversive spirit,' and then proceeded, with what could only have appeared as aristocratic hauteur in the Cardinal's eyes, to ignore his objections and press their case in their memorandum bearing the signatures of 87 of the Catholic great and the good.'[52] The Cardinal chose to deal with the perceived impertinence by simply ignoring it.

Two years later Hope resumed his campaign. The Cardinal brought the subject to the Bishops' Low Week meeting. The Bishops conceded the crux of Hope's concern: 'any parish priest is free to form a committee to assist him in the temporal concerns of his parish' with his Bishop's consent, which would not be unreasonably refused.[53] But Hope was not prepared to let matters rest and work for reform at this practical, parochial level. He still wanted his grand inquiry to determine how parishes should be run and developed schemes to this end. This was too much for Bourne. The Bishops had given no such approval for 'a committee of enquiry.' Experience had shown no desire for lay committees. Financial incompetence was not an exclusively clerical preserve. The Cardinal tartly informed Lord Rankeillour (the recently ennobled Hope), 'I have just had a striking example of the inadequacy and futility of lay control which has resulted in my being asked to find several hundreds of pounds to pay debts which ought never to have been incurred.'[54] Hope continued to push his hobby horse with Hinsley, who was more affable—but, ultimately, no more forthcoming. For Bourne, Hope was quite simply the wrong type of layman against whom he had earlier cautioned.

'The extension of God's Kingdom'

Bourne's lifetime witnessed massive population growth in the Greater London area: from 3.1 million in the year of his birth to more than 8 million at the time of his death. In the earlier period much of that growth occurred along the railway lines of South London. In the twentieth century the expansion of the Underground and Metropolitan Lines produced huge increases in the northern and western districts of the capital.

How successful was the Church in meeting the demands this growth entailed in terms of the provision of priests, churches and schools? Trusting in Providence, the Cardinal's aspirations matched the increase in population. Opening a new church in Hatfield in 1930, he made reference to Our Lord's commission of His apostles and to St Augustine's mission to Kent. 'There were many instances where a few Catholics at the setting up of a new church had grown into hundreds. If the Church had men and funds, she would re-establish a church in every town and village.'[55] That was the stated desire: the provision of 'spiritual help in the shape of a church with a resident priest in every new locality where Catholics are likely to reside.'[56] Nor was the Cardinal a mere functionalist, referring to 'a right instinct in the English mind—that it attaches great importance to the externals of worship. The people of this country were not attracted, but were repelled, when they saw our worship taking place in anything like mean surroundings; they liked to see something more worthy of the Majesty of God, and were more likely to be attracted by our churches and go into them if they were stately and dignified buildings.'[57]

How was this to be effected? The Cardinal had little doubt. 'Where the development of the Catholic Church in this country is concerned, you cannot buy too much land, and though I can count many instances where we have bought far too little, I do not know of a single instance where we acquired too much.'[58] When Fr Henry England learnt of the sale of a former Wesleyan Chapel in Pimlico in 1916, Bourne's response was direct and immediate: 'Whatever you do, don't miss it.'[59]

Planning for such expansion was, however, neither systematic nor centralised. It is wrong to expect it to have been. The Catholic Church lacked the resources and the personnel to have developed such a strategy. London's residential development was itself largely piecemeal.

The initiative often came from the locality. In 1913 Catholic families wrote to the Cardinal asking for help in securing a priest and church in Manor Park, where there was now an estimated Catholic population of 1,600.[60] Elsewhere, the Cardinal relied on the local clergy and religious to identify needs and draw these to his attention.[61] Then it was down to the competence and sheer pertinacity of the priest sent to open a new mission. Bourne acknowledged it required 'a man of exceptional organising ability and zeal for work, and with a sufficiency of means to support him through the first years when there was practically no income.'[62] A priest's work was made lighter, however, by the knowledge that he had the Cardinal's 'continued kindness and interest.'[63] More practical assistance came in the form of donations from the Cardinal's private means[64] and his inducement of others to part with their cash to fund new parishes, churches and schools.[65]

As in Southwark, the Cardinal successfully attracted the support of the wealthy, especially converts, enthusing them with his vision for the expansion of Catholic truth. Parishes in Ruislip, Burnt Oak, Welwyn Garden City and elsewhere owed their churches to such benefactors. The Cardinal interested himself in the development of Catholic life in Hertfordshire. He encouraged the Catholic Missionary Society's 'motor chapel' tours of the county to those towns lacking a church, seeing this as a prelude to the placing of 'a permanent priest in the town.'[66] Taking pride in the Church's growth in Hertfordshire, towards the end of his life Bourne noted 'there remained only one or two towns still without facilities for Mass.'[67] He also encouraged the Diocesan Missionaries of Our Lady of Compassion (subsequently the Catholic Missionary Society) in their work in rural Essex.

Canon Fuller recalled the Cardinal's speech at the centenary of Catholic Emancipation, detailing the Church's progress, the number of churches built. 'He gave out all the usual platitudes—he was very good at that.'[68] This he did formally each year in his Trinity Sunday Pastoral Letter, listing the new churches opened and any temporary churches and Mass centres. He pleaded with his people for the resources to fund 'the work of the extension of God's Kingdom by means of new churches and other centres of religious influence.'[69] To this end, he listed annually those places in Westminster most in need of a church. Generally, a church was then erected within the space of a few years.

Diocesan statistics published from 1916 show a healthy increase in the practising Catholic population in Westminster. The annual figure for baptisms, probably depressed by the War, was a little over 5,000 in 1916. By Bourne's final year it had risen to 7,300—even after Brentwood had been split from the Diocese. The annual number of conversions at the end of the War was in the region of 1,500. Peaking at 2,000 in the early 1920s, it then fell back to the earlier level. (Still good in comparison to the figure of 699 a century on.) Most encouraging was the 50% increase in the number of marriages to 3,000 by the mid-1930s (compared to a current figure of just 1,169.)

The Cardinal was not averse to enumerating the visible signs of the expansion of Catholicism in his episcopate. But it went deeper than an obsession with bricks and mortar. 'Statistics,' he said, 'show a remarkable increase in the number of Catholics, and will show more. But mere statistics do not mean much. Along with an increase in numbers there is a steady growth of Catholic influence and the attention given to Catholic opinion.'[70] Those closest to Bourne were given a privileged insight into his true motivation. Lépicier praised his friend's unstinting efforts in the development of the nation's spiritual life, evidenced particularly by his concern for female religious communities. 'He referred to the foundation of twenty-five new Carmels, in which Cardinal Bourne had taken so great a part, as twenty-five defences against the assaults of the Evil One.'[71]

'To retain a place within the national system of education'[72]

In Bourne's early years in Westminster Catholic schools were involved in an epic struggle for their very survival. Simultaneously, and subsequently, the Church had also to meet the educational demands imposed both by a growing population and increased expectations.

Controlling the London County Council from 1904, the Liberals applied financial pressure against denominational education. Reports highlighted deficiencies in the physical plant. Bring your school buildings up to standard, the Church was told, or face closure. The Archbishop appealed, on the basis of information provided by the Committee of the Diocesan Association of Voluntary Schools, for more than £100,000 to ensure compliance in Westminster. Three schools had to be re-built entirely; many others required urgent work.[73] Bourne seldom had problems raising money, associating himself with appeals, applying to those with cash. By 1908 £113,000 had been spent on Catholic elementary schools within Westminster. The religious orders provided almost half of this, the balance coming from parish loans, fundraising and individual donations.[74]

Bourne valued education for its own sake. The young Archbishop noted, 'The need of the school was absolutely urgent, because the future work of the Catholic Church in London would depend upon the education of our children.'[75] But for the vast majority of Catholic children education ceased when they left their elementary school. In 1905 there were 37,561 children in Catholic elementary schools in Westminster, only 3,448 in secondary schools. And the latter were mainly girls (of whom a third were non-Catholic) in convent schools.[76] James Driscoll wrote in 1911, when there were just 11 Catholic secondary schools in the whole country (only one in Middlesex, and none in London) recognised by Board of Education—as opposed to 525 non-Catholic schools: 'If there is one class of Catholics which has suffered in the past as regards educational facilities for their children, it is our middle class, especially our lower-middle class. To the parents of this class, as a rule, we have offered no opportunity for the education of their sons, except the boarding school in the country or the elementary school in the town.'[77] Without such schools, Catholic boys would be lost to non-Catholic schools—and, potentially, to the Faith.

The need had been identified eight years earlier. Reflecting on his own experience, Bourne wrote in his first Westminster Pastoral Letter of 'the urgent necessity of providing a sound teaching in suitable schools for those who require an education beyond that which is to be found in our elementary schools ... the history of middle class day schools for boys is a tale of anxiety, disappointment and failure ... it ought not to be impossible to set on foot, to furnish and staff some three or four first-class day schools for boys, which, for a time at least, would meet the requirements of our Catholic boys in London.' This was not simply left at the level of aspiration. Even before his return from collecting the pallium in Rome, the Archbishop had formed a small committee for the purpose, its members drawn from priests from both sides of the Thames.[78] The following year a 'Secondary Education Council' was established, meeting at Archbishop's House.[79]

An opportunity to begin to remedy the situation arose almost immediately. It was resolved that the memorial to Cardinal Vaughan should take 'the form of a secondary day school in Westminster.' A

Catholic grammar school 'under the shadow of the Cathedral' was envisaged, 'controlled by an effective body of governors, composed chiefly of laymen.'[80] Spiralling costs forced the sale of a site near the Cathedral. A decade passed before the Cardinal Vaughan Memorial School was fully functioning in Kensington.

By the end of his reign, Bourne had his 'three or four' day schools for boys, with new Catholic grammar schools in Finchley and Gunnersbury, but the vision was too limited. He himself acknowledged, 'Many more such secondary schools are needed. In no direction is still further progress more urgent.'[81] With respect to Finchley Catholic Grammar School, the Cardinal recounted how when the local priest 'had gone to him with a scheme he readily agreed to its advisability: he was always glad when priests went to him with new schemes of development.'[82] By the 1930s it was no longer acceptable to sit back and await the proposals of parish priests for the development of secondary education. More concerted action was required from the hierarchy.

Westminster Cathedral: 'a true centre of spiritual life'

For half a century after the restoration of the hierarchy London's principal Catholic church remained Bourne's former cathedral, St George's, Southwark. Various proposals were mooted for a new cathedral north of the Thames, but the metropolitan diocese had to make do with pro-cathedrals in the City and Kensington until Cardinal Vaughan finally commissioned John Bentley to design Westminster Cathedral in its strikingly original 'Christian Byzantine' style. Bentley died in March 1902 and Vaughan in June 1903 when the Cathedral was structurally complete, but the interior little more than a shell. The vast inner gloom of unadorned brickwork caused one Methodist Liberal MP—no friend to the Church—to exclaim 'in derision that the Roman Catholics had set out to build a cathedral and had finished by producing a railway terminus.'[83]

It fell to Bourne to decorate and develop the Cathedral. For more than three decades it was a source of much anxiety for, and criticism of, the Archbishop. Vaughan had been adamant that Bentley's vision was to be implemented in its entirety; but often detailed plans were lacking. There was a constant stream of critical letters in the *Tablet* and secular Press, claiming to know Bentley's intentions and criticising the subsequent decisions of the authorities. A correspondent in the *Observer*, for example, denounced 'the deplorable blunders and errors of taste and judgment in the slowly progressing decoration of the Cathedral.'[84] Architectural purists wanted nothing to jar with Bentley's Byzantine concept. Others clamoured for a more devotional interior better aligned to Gothic sensibilities.

Bourne accepted the responsibility with the utmost gravity. He never doubted that he was planning for the premier church of the British Empire and for generations of Catholics yet to be born. So he took himself off—and sent others—to study the mosaics of Sicily, Ravenna and Venice. Recognising that completion of the decoration might take a century or more, the Cardinal established the Cathedral's own school of mosaic workers. Nothing was done hurriedly. Oldmeadow recalled, 'Cardinal Bourne gave long thought to the Cathedral Sanctuary. When he was worried about the visibility of the choirmaster, perched up on the retro-choir, he caused a model of some proposed screen-work to be erected; and I remember sitting with him for nearly an hour on the organ-bench over the narthex while he pondered and discussed the effect.'[85]

Wherever practical, Bourne gave effect to Vaughan's and Bentley's original intentions. After Bentley's death, John Marshall, his deputy, was allowed to oversee the development of the Cathedral for the next generation. (Continuity was further ensured by then appointing Marshall's deputy, Laurence Shattock, as his successor.) Bourne's relationship with Marshall reflected that with most of his subordinates: strong criticism combined with stubborn loyalty. To his regret, the Cardinal allowed Marshall to persuade him to commission his fellow Nonconformist, Robert Anning Bell, for the Lady Chapel altar piece and the tympanum over the great west door. 'The result was the greatest disappointment I had received in connection with the building of the Cathedral. I came to the conclusion that no non-Catholic could be safely trusted with work of this character.'[86] Eric Gill felt he had been commissioned to carve Stations of the Cross for the Cathedral less on grounds of faith than economy. Bourne and Marshall shared their painful disappointment, querying the practicality of work in 'very low relief' given the lighting conditions in the Cathedral. More colour and conventional figures had been anticipated.[87] Nevertheless, with amendments, Bourne allowed these exceptional and poignant carvings to remain. Gill expressed his gratitude 'that people are now taking a more sympathetic view of the Stations.'[88]

Disappointments did not prevent the Cardinal giving a very spirited defence of Marshall in the face of criticism from the artistic and Catholic establishment. The Catholic antiquarian Everard Green was particularly scathing. 'Can nothing be done to stop the destruction of the interior of the late Mr Bentley's superb Cathedral Church of Westminster? Since his death incompetency seems to have run riot ... That the marble decorations of [the Blessed Sacrament] Chapel and in the Lady Chapel savour of restaurant and music hall design few will care to deny, and one weeps to think of the huge cost and the unscholarly results.'[89] The Cardinal faced similar objections at the Catholic Dining Society meeting he addressed in May 1912. He met specific criticisms with courtesy and common sense. But the underlying disapproval of the *cognoscenti* lay in their disapproval of Marshall. In their view, a mere architect could not be entrusted with the internal decoration of the Cathedral. Marshall's association with Bentley, his ability and his study of Church mosaics counted for nothing. 'The Cardinal has completely failed to grasp what, as it seems to me, *must* be the cardinal principle: that the superintendence of the internal decoration of a building designed for mosaic in the manner in which the Cathedral is designed for mosaic must or should be given to a decorative artist.'[90]

More public criticism came from the convert Edward Hutton in response to Gilbert Pownall's 'pretty pretty' mosaics in the Lady Chapel and the sanctuary arch. Those in the Lady Chapel were judged 'meaningless, weak and incoherent.' Hutton saved his strongest invective for the sanctuary arch, the most extensive area of mosaics completed to date, opining on 'the empty puerility of its design, the weakness and clumsiness of its drawing and, not least, the ugliness and crudity of its colour.' He meant his words to be felt by the highest authority. 'One wonders, indeed, whether those finally responsible for these works have any real knowledge of their undertaking.'[91]

The Cardinal could not allow such criticism in the pages of the national Press to go unanswered, however much he felt it to be simply 'an illogical tirade.' It gave him the opportunity, after thirty years of responsibility, to expound his vision for the Cathedral and explain his methodology. He met the experts head on. 'It must ever be borne in mind that the Cathedral is not a museum of art, but a house of prayer. Primarily we must seek the honour and glory of God in all that is undertaken. Secondly, we must take care that there is nothing which would hinder, and that everything shall assist, the piety of the ordinary faithful Catholic. It had been suggested to Cardinal Vaughan that he should form a committee of leading artists to guide him in the work. He listened to the suggestion, but he never carried it out. The same suggestion was often made to me, but I soon came to see that, were any such committee formed, I should be placed in front of clamant, loud-voiced, contradictory opinions, and have thrust upon me the unenviable task of deciding between them. I saw the only course to pursue was to study the question as closely as I could myself, to see for myself all the great examples of mosaic work that were available to me and to seek individual advice from the best sources at home and abroad.'[92]

The Cardinal tempered fidelity to the architect's intention with his concerns for the primary purpose of a Catholic cathedral and practicality. He accepted, on the whole, that sculpture was not a part of Byzantine ecclesiastical architecture. Therefore, he removed a Gothic statue of Our Lady. But, at the same time, he would not deprive the Catholic faithful of necessary aids to devotion, even where these represented developments from the early Church. So he installed statues of the Sacred Heart and St Peter. The purists maintained that Stations of the Cross had no place in a Byzantine basilica. The Cardinal responded, 'The Cathedral is not a basilica but a parish church, and as such must include the Stations of the Cross.' He was told that, for the aesthetic integrity of the whole, it was essential that the entire Cathedral was paved in marble. The Cardinal suggested his critics take note of the British climate and the difficulty of cleaning marble.[93] More questionable was his decision to remove the great hanging crucifix—as it obscured the central figure of the Christ in Majesty on the sanctuary arch. It was inevitable that such an iconic feature of the Cathedral would later be restored to its original position.

Today's worshipper and visitor must judge for himself the success of Bourne's contribution. We owe him more than we realise. With architectural Modernism no longer unchallenged, some of Bourne's most controversial decisions, such as Pownall's mosaics in the Lady Chapel, are among the Cathedral's best loved features. One project, however, is no longer extant. When the Cathedral was designed, critics hailed it as an extravagant folly: there was no way that it would be filled by practising Catholics. Such a judgment rapidly proved misplaced. By 1904 the Sunday Mass attendance at the Cathedral was in the region of 6,000. The Cardinal sought a yet greater space for national Catholic gatherings. For years after its construction, the land adjacent to the Cathedral was disfigured by thousands of tons of debris from the excavation of the foundations. At the Cardinal's instigation, this was cleared to make way for a vast open air church, with a capacity four or five times that of the Cathedral itself. It was to be 'a centre of the Catholic activities in the metropolis.' This outdoor church was used for the centenary of Catholic Emancipation and on other occasions, but this time it was the Cardinal who had overlooked the constraints of the British climate.[94]

Since Bourne the Archbishops of Westminster have not tended to see the completion of the internal decoration of the Cathedral as a priority, wanting to incur neither the expense nor the controversy. Bourne moved cautiously and exercised commendable restraint, but he never shirked the responsibility. Vast sums were expended because he believed this was important. Up to its opening in 1903 the Cathedral had cost £198,000, including the acquisition of the site and construction. By 1927 almost as much again had been spent on internal decoration, with major projects still being commissioned.[95] Bourne's first biographer rightly regrets there is no monument to his subject in the Cathedral.

The internal decoration of Westminster Cathedral, however, was only a means to an end. Bourne always had that ultimate purpose clearly in mind. 'The Cathedral has become a living reality and a true centre of spiritual life. It is the home of the Sacred Liturgy of the Church, rendered every day with great accuracy and completeness ... At the same time due place is given to the preaching of the Word of God.'[96] The Cathedral had, what the Cardinal described, 'a twofold mission and ministry.' It was to act as a focal point, gathering the Catholics of the country and Empire for great national and international events. 'But the chief mission of the Cathedral, the one which stands paramount and intangible above and beyond all others, is that of its daily service, in which, day by day, month by month, year in and year out, it gives to God in the public prayer of the Church, on behalf of the people, the worship which is His due.'[97] The liturgical life of the Cathedral, and its musical expression, inspiring Catholic and non-Catholic alike, is again reflective of the Cardinal's quiet direction and determination.

Once more Bourne was proceeding along the lines laid down by his predecessor, but it was for him to implement and maintain the liturgical standards of the Cathedral on a daily basis and for the great ceremonies of the Church's year and the nation's life. In this he was well served for three decades by the Cathedral Administrator, Mgr Howlett. Each day a dozen Masses were said, High Mass and the Divine Office were sung and Confessions were heard.

The Archbishop knew the power of good liturgy to draw people to Christ and His Church. Describing the services of Holy Week and Easter, the *Tablet* maintained, they had been celebrated with more 'care and completeness' than at any time in England since the Reformation. 'The large crowds of people that have been devoutly attending them prove that the liturgical functions of the Church have a wonderful power of attracting people to the House of God and of making them realise the meaning of the great drama of the Passion and Resurrection.'[98] Bourne allowed the liturgy to point to the continuity between the Church over which he presided and the pre-Reformation English Church. His own enthronement and the rite for the induction of Cathedral canons were modelled on medieval English precedents.

Today Westminster Cathedral is synonymous with the world's finest Church music. Once more, Bourne needs to be more widely credited for this legacy. The Cathedral was opened as the struggle as to the nature of Church music was reaching its climax. The standard line was: 'If you have Mozart and fiddles you'll fill the Church; if you have Palestrina and plainchant you'll empty it.'[99] Vaughan rejected the popular wisdom by opting for Gregorian chant and Counter-Reformation polyphony, especially English composers such as Byrd, Tallis and Tye. He intended it to be sung by Benedictine monks, but his attempts to found a monastic community to serve the Cathedral came to naught. He settled for the next best thing. Richard Terry was the lay director of music at Downside, a convert and former choral scholar at King's, Cambridge.[100] It was an inspired choice.

When Pope Pius X issued his *Motu Proprio* requiring the Church to give primacy to chant and simple polyphony, Terry was able to state 'there was found nothing to alter in the music of the Cathedral.' He added that the new Archbishop continued to uphold both the letter and the spirit of the papal document.[101] Bourne forbade an orchestral Mass setting at his first St Patrick's Day Mass at Soho Square, but his musical views allowed of some flexibility. Some argued the Cathedral gave greater priority to polyphony than Rome envisaged. Nor was modern or non-Catholic music off limits, if deemed appropriate. The Cardinal admired César Franck, while the Cathedral also sang the music of Holst, Wood, Howells and Vaughan Williams.[102]

At a papal audience in 1903, Bourne elicited Pius X's approval for the Cathedral's use of the plainchant of Solesmes. 'Speaking of sacred music generally [the Pope] told the Archbishop that he earnestly desired that music of the very highest class should be sedulously cultivated in Westminster Cathedral.'[103] Within a very short space of time Terry ensured that the Cathedral Choir was recognised as one of the finest in Europe. Its influence in terms of technique and repertoire was extended as a result of the Eucharistic Congress, and recordings were made as early as 1910.[104]

The sound Terry achieved was the result of two developments previously unknown in English Catholic cathedrals: the use of 15 paid, professional male voices and the establishment of a choir school, 24 boys singing in the Cathedral in return for receiving an education.[105] Musical excellence came at considerable expense. By 1905 the Cathedral Choir cost £2,000 p.a. Vaughan's endowment met only half of this. But Bourne consistently rejected advice to scale back the Cathedral's music. He was told to limit music to Sundays and feast days, to dispense with the male voices altogether, to rely on priests and boys chanting in a side chapel. Financial constraints eventually forced a reduction in the number of male voices, but otherwise the tradition and full range of sung services were maintained. And this despite difficulties Terry himself presented. In 1911 Bourne had to insist that he cut back his outside commitments, attend rehearsals in person and pursue proper procedures in dismissing choristers. When Terry resigned in 1924, the Cardinal was able to replace him with two priests who had trained under him and who maintained the Choir's outstanding reputation.[106]

Vaughan's and Terry's role in the Cathedral's musical tradition are well documented. It was left to Terry's successor to acknowledge the vital part played by Bourne.

> One name will stand out when the complete history of Catholic music is written—the name of Francis Cardinal Bourne ... Without him no progress would have been made. Cardinal Vaughan founded the choir; Cardinal Bourne saved it from destruction. In 1904–05 a heavy debt had accumulated and the financial position was serious. Voices were not wanting to counsel economy and to plead for the abolition of the choir as constituted.

It was pointed out that the boys, with the priests, could render the required music. Plainsong would suffice. Terry's ideal was in gravest danger. The Cardinal, in face of all difficulties, took the large-hearted decision. The ideal must be upheld; the choir must be saved at all costs.[107]

'Our venerable College of St Edmund'

As a youth, Francis Bourne had more personal experience of various seminaries and religious houses than perhaps any other priest of his age. He felt passionately about the formation of priests and came to prominence as the co-founder of a seminary. Predictably, on arriving in Westminster he identified seminary education as his priority. 'Almost all the questions which demand our special care at the present moment ... are connected with education. We begin with the most important—that, indeed, which is the foundation of all our other work—the training in knowledge and virtue of those who aspire to the Ecclesiastical State.' Referring to the lack of a home-grown clergy, he indicated his intention to provide future priestly formation 'within the Diocese itself.' This would necessarily involve his old *alma mater*, 'our venerable College of St Edmund.'[108] Bourne's views on seminaries both inspired his supporters and perturbed his opponents when his name was mentioned as Vaughan's successor.

Gasquet expressed the views of many in the English Church when he wrote that Bourne's 'notion of education is far too *foreign* to please most people.'[109] It was feared that Bourne would supplant the leisurely and gentlemanly 'Douai tradition' with a more rigorous Tridentine version of seminary formation—as Manning had attempted at Hammersmith. Then there was the issue of the Central Seminary at Oscott founded just six years earlier. Given his vigorous defence of individual diocesan seminaries, what would be the new Archbishop's stance towards this centralised venture? The Church did not have to wait long for an answer.

'The Central Seminary is doomed'[110]

Writing just 15 years after Bourne's death, the Church historian, Fr Philip Hughes, painted a rosy picture of the Central Seminary and gave a correspondingly negative assessment of the new Archbishop's actions. 'The Central Seminary was very speedily a remarkable success, and it gave every promise of becoming the long desiderated, national centre of

Catholic thought. But Vaughan's reign was short. Within six years of the new Oscott venture he was dead; and when, in his place, the founder of the Southwark diocesan seminary was named archbishop, the older policy was restored and the Central Seminary, deprived of its main support, ceased to be: after forty years one can safely say a major tragedy.'[111] Unsurprisingly, the Bishop of Birmingham took a similar view at the time. He saw the Central Seminary as Vaughan's 'greatest work,' after that of the foreign missions, a real advance in education which Bourne was intent on wrecking.[112]

The facts do not support such a simplistic analysis. Oscott's future, as the national home seminary (excepting Ushaw and Wonersh), was already unravelling prior to Bourne's appointment to Westminster. Vaughan had agreed to transfer his philosophy and theology students to Oscott on the understanding that Birmingham sent its own junior seminarians to study the humanities at St Edmund's. Birmingham failed to honour this agreement, sending no seminarians to Ware after 1900.[113] Not only was St Edmund's deprived of the fee income, but it resulted in a massive imbalance of lay boys (more than 100) over those destined for the Church (just 26).

Matters came to a head just after Vaughan's death. In July 1903 Bernard Ward, the College President, voiced to Mgr Fenton, the diocesan administrator, his alarm that the ecclesiastical status of St Edmund's was being jeopardised by the lack of seminarians—a concern Vaughan had considered unimportant. Added to this were financial problems caused by Westminster's investment in Oscott, with no compensating contribution from external seminarians at Ware. The number of clerical and lay students combined was too few to make the College financially feasible. Although only temporarily responsible for the Diocese, Fenton acted immediately. He informed Oscott that Westminster would be sending no further philosophy students there. Westminster seminarians would remain at St Edmund's until the new Archbishop determined the future diocesan policy.[114]

Everyone knew Bourne's preference for independent diocesan seminaries. But he was compelled by circumstances to act more urgently than he might have wished. Ward confirms that the new Archbishop 'had practically no alternative but to re-establish a School of Divinity here, to say the least, at a much earlier date than would have otherwise have been the case.'[115]

From the outset, Bourne gave clear indications of his intentions. His first Mass as Archbishop in Westminster was offered at St Edmund's. He assured those present that 'the College must always be in his thoughts as being the very centre of all his work, since, without an efficient and holy clergy, nothing could be done ... Thus he begged them all, superiors as well as students, to believe that all his action with regard to the College would ever be in the interest of religion and in love for the College itself.'[116] He made the same point to his Vicar-General: 'The interests of the College are very dear to me, and they will be safe in my hands.'[117]

But first he consulted others. On his arrival in Westminster, the new Archbishop questioned Bernard Ward. Prudently, Ward restricted himself to information derived from his experience of eleven years as President, rather than proffering his own solutions.[118] Bourne suffered no uncertainty as to the course of action to be taken. 'The indications of Providence were so clear that I could have no doubt as to the will of God in this matter.'[119] So on 18 December 1903 he summoned the Cathedral Chapter to ask if they agreed with him that St Edmund's should be maintained as an ecclesiastical college and, if so, that the formation of Westminster seminarians should be concentrated there. The Archbishop assured the Canons that he was 'prepared to consider most carefully' any better suggestion they might have. But he guided their ruminations by disclosing that the Pope himself expected him 'to found a *real Seminary in the Diocese of Westminster.*' The Chapter unanimously agreed with their Archbishop.[120] To be fair, however, this was only the logical conclusion to the step taken by Fenton earlier in the year.

The Archbishop justified his reversal of the policies of his immediate two predecessors. He referred to 'the experiment' of the preceding 35 years, maintaining that he was merely restoring continuity with the earlier practice of training Westminster's priests at St Edmund's. He was not saying that Vaughan would have taken the same decision had he lived, but faced with 'the grave contingencies' then existing, Vaughan too would have been obliged to reconsider the whole question of the Central Seminary.[121]

Few in Westminster needed convincing of the change in policy. Convincing the Oscott authorities was another matter. While Westminster was only one of the dioceses supporting the Central Seminary, everyone was conscious that its commitment was crucial. The Central Seminary raised the stakes after Fenton's initial decision by stating that any seminarian who had not studied philosophy at Oscott was barred from studying theology there.[122] The Archbishop tried to soften the blow by giving Mgr Parkinson, Oscott's Rector, advance notice of his decision, explaining his rationale and requesting that existing Westminster seminarians be allowed to complete their theology there.[123]

In the days before an individual Bishop's independence was constrained by episcopal conferences, no one seriously questioned Bourne's right to take this decision. Although others might regret it, the dispute arose less from the principle than over the money. Bishop Ilsley held that the funds invested in Oscott should remain with Birmingham to meet the ongoing costs of the Central Seminary. But once Westminster announced the withdrawal of its seminarians, other Bishops looked longingly at their £2,000 endowments. Northampton and Portsmouth felt their commitment to the Central Seminary was 'a very dear commodity' they could not afford.[124]

The battle lines were drawn. Ilsley wrote to Rome in defence of Oscott and encouraged other Bishops to do likewise.[125] Hedley supported the Central Seminary, but most Bishops agreed with Riddell: 'Archbishop Bourne is right in restoring Old Hall as the Westminster seminary: for years I have held that it was a mistake for Cardinal Manning to transfer his students to Hammersmith and another mistake for Cardinal Vaughan not to take them back to Old Hall when he sold Hammersmith. Archbishop Bourne is repairing these two mistakes and I could not oppose him.' Most Bishops preferred independent diocesan seminaries, rejecting the claim that the paucity of Catholics made this impractical in England. Riddell specifically cited the example of Wonersh.[126] For Cahill financial matters were most pressing. Small dioceses were getting a raw deal. Sending few seminarians to Oscott themselves, they felt their capital investment was subsidising richer dioceses.[127]

Bourne played to the concerns of his brother Bishops. He assured them St Edmund's would be open to any seminarians they wished to send, 'but I have no intention of creating a central Seminary there under joint control, and am indeed very strongly opposed to any such idea. You are perfectly right to retain your complete freedom of choice.'[128] The Archbishop was on firm ground defending his concept of seminary formation in Rome. Ward, who was with him, wrote back admiringly of his approach.[129] Once Ilsley had raised the matter in Rome, Bourne felt able to press his case for a ruling that any Bishop was free to withdraw his seminarians *and* his capital investment from Oscott, coordinating similar requests from the Bishops whom he knew to be sympathetic.[130]

At the meeting of Bishops constituting the Oscott Board summoned by the Archbishop on 4 May 1905, Cahill proposed the dissolution of the Central Seminary and the return of capital to the respective dioceses. Birmingham and Newport & Menevia supported the retention of Oscott, but were outvoted by Westminster, Northampton, Clifton and Portsmouth.[131] Requiring Rome's approval, the matter dragged on for a further four years, but Bourne prevailed. 'One hears in Rome that there are cardinals in Propaganda who think that in matters of ecclesiastical administration the Archbishop of Westminster knows best.'[132]

The Central Seminary was dead. Bourne had a fully-constituted major Seminary in Westminster much more rapidly than he had dared hope. Was he right to push for such a change? Was it not a retrograde step, depriving young priests of the advantages of pooled resources and learning? There were those who argued this. Smaller dioceses could hardly hope to make such provision independently. But the founding of Wonersh and the restoration of St Edmund's, along with other English seminaries at home and overseas, offered Bishops considerable choice in the formation they wished their students to receive. Then Bourne was not the Bishop of a smaller diocese. Of course, he sought efficient and effective ecclesiastical education. But his method of achieving this was not national or regional collaboration, but rather expanding 'considerably' the number of students to justify independent seminaries.[133] In both Southwark and Westminster he successfully accomplished this.

It depends on one's expectations of a Seminary. Bourne's position was consistent. While never denying the need for further education for the few, a seminary was not a Catholic university, but the provider of spiritual formation for future parochial clergy united heart and mind with their Bishop. It is difficult to dispute that. But Bourne's role in the demise of the Central Seminary meant Amigo found a ready ally in the person of Ilsley in the subsequent battles between Westminster and Southwark.

'Separated to some extent'[134]

While the restoration of the Seminary at St Edmund's was welcomed in Westminster, there was much uncertainty as to the form it would take. The President, Bernard Ward, embodied old ways. He wrote of St Edmund's, 'The system of discipline in force is substantially the same as that of the English College at Douai. It is held to be of the greatest importance to train boys gradually by allowing them a reasonable amount of liberty, increasing as they grow older, to habits of self-command and true manliness, based on solid Christian principles.'[135] That sounded like the manifesto of any Victorian public school. Canon Fuller, a seminarian at St Edmund's in Bourne's time, recalled that the Cardinal 'was devoted to the Sulpician Fathers.' The Sulpician system aimed at turning out good priests; 'the Douai tradition' sought something much broader.[136] On ecclesiastical education Bourne had a clear vision and determination. Contemporaries naturally speculated as to whether he 'would at once proceed to remodel St Edmund's College on the lines of St John's Seminary.'[137]

The new Archbishop provided grounds for such suspicion. One of his first acts was to send Bernard Ward to St Sulpice to see how things were done there. Ward found his hosts 'very congenial,' but learned little from them. His English character was immune to French spirituality. He attended 'a most go-ahead lecture,' but his correspondence home dwelt on food, the weather and Test match scores.[138] Bourne persevered. Two months later he sent Edwin Burton and Edward Myers. They were a little more thorough, engaging in long conversations with the Sulpicians 'on the method of training students and forming the priestly character.' However, when asked to adopt change, Burton resorted to a familiar device of the English Catholic Church: change was unnecessary because the desired policy was already being pursued—in a manner appropriate to the English character. Burton assured his Archbishop 'that the spirit of St Sulpice in its essentials of learning and holiness seems so akin to the spirit of our own St Edmund's that we may enter on the work as a thing not new to us.' Politely, he was stating that St Edmund's would continue as it always had.

An example. Burton and Myers were unable to avoid noticing the Sulpician emphasis on 'the familial intercourse between priests and students.' Burton maintained that there would be no difficulty in securing this at St Edmund's 'as it already exists.' [139] Eighteen years later this was still not the case. Bourne had to labour the point to Myers, by then President of St Edmund's: 'Many of our students are from comparatively humble homes and the presence of a priest having his meals with them and CONVERSING WITH THEM is an instinctive good training in good manners and a means of keeping conversation at a useful and instructive level ... I am always afraid of ecclesiastical students coming to regard the priests in charge of them primarily as schoolmasters who are only concerned with teaching them, and not about the rest of their life and training.'[140] Vance, the Vice-President, resented the fact that the clergy were expected to live with the seminarians and share their food.[141] Bourne failed to inculcate this basic Sulpician practice into seminary life.

Why was this the case? Firstly, he was unable to devote the time and detailed attention to St Edmund's which he had lavished upon Wonersh. As Archbishop of Westminster, he was simply too preoccupied. Almost immediately, the education crisis and the fight for the survival of the Catholic schools were unleashed upon the English Church. But Bourne was generally determined and industrious when he thought an important principle at stake. There was another consideration at play here. Canon Fuller identified it decades later: uncharacteristically, Bourne hesitated, torn between two traditions.[142]

Wonersh was a new foundation. As Bourne's views of seminary formation coincided with his Bishop's, he was given a largely free hand to introduce 'foreign' practices. By contrast, at Ware he encountered an established institution with a history stretching back over three centuries. The Archbishop disputed the assumption that he was hostile to its customs. 'Many thought that I would gradually banish the lay-students from St Edmund's. Such a thought never entered my mind. I went there as a lay student in 1875 and it was there that my own vocation to the priesthood took definite shape.'[143] He denied that he was an iconoclast. 'It has always been my principle that every institution should develop on the lines of its own traditions; and ... St Edmund's College has very special, very precious and in some ways a unique tradition.' Bourne valued a school run by diocesan priests, not leaving education as a preserve of the religious orders. He even acknowledged, from his own experience, certain benefits accruing from a 'mixed' education, which might provide 'the basis of solid and lasting sympathy and friendship between clergy and laity.'[144]

And yet ... Bourne could not ignore the Church's teaching since Trent that this was not the way things were to be done. Those destined for the priesthood were to receive a formation apart. A view he supported, and had implemented in Southwark. For almost twenty years, the Archbishop sought to reconcile two apparently irreconcilable traditions. Vance gave a cynical account of how a solution was arrived at, thinking his Archbishop well-intentioned, but self-deluded. As interpreted by Vance, Bourne convinced himself that Our Lady personally resolved the problem during a pilgrimage to Lourdes. It was an example, he maintained, of the Archbishop's 'Inner Light' syndrome, 'one of the worst of the soul's afflictions and disasters.'[145]

In fact, the resolution of the issue was both more prosaic and more spiritually authentic. The Cardinal recounts how this unfolded gradually in the years 1917–1920 as the result of prolonged prayer and reflection. By 1919 St Edmund's was in crisis. The older buildings were falling apart, there was a deficit of £15,000 on the current account and the number of lay boys far exceeded the seminarians. Action was unavoidable, a solution towards which he had been moving 'for a long time.'[146] The Cardinal consulted widely—the authorities at St Edmund's, the diocesan curia and Catholic laymen with sons in education. And, yes, he sought Our Lady's guidance during his pilgrimage to Lourdes in November 1919, asking her, that if his scheme met with divine approval, to give him the means to carry it out. Within a month of returning to England, the Cardinal was informed that he had been named the residuary legatee of a Mrs Fitzgerald, providing him with over £50,000. Vance was sceptical about trusting to divine providence; the Cardinal was not.[147]

With this windfall and other legacies and donations, the reorganisation of St Edmund's began. A house system was introduced with two objectives. The first made perfect sense, retaining the lay boys at St Edmund's while providing an appropriate formation for seminarians. So the College was divided into three parts: St Hugh's Preparatory School; Allen Hall, the Senior Seminary with its own chapel and refectory; the School, itself now divided into three houses, named after Vicars Apostolic. Challoner and Talbot Houses were for lay boys. Douglass House was essentially the Junior Seminary, for boys considering the possibility of priesthood. While joining the lay boys for study and sport, Douglass House attended Mass with the Allen Hall seminarians and received spiritual formation appropriate for their age.

If the Cardinal had left matters there, his scheme would have been readily understood and may well have suceeded. The problem was he cherished another ambition. He sought to transform St Edmund's into a Catholic Winchester or Eton as they had existed prior to the Reformation and felt the house system would ensure this.[148] The convert Ronald Knox thus found himself a schoolmaster at St Edmund's to add lustre to the

Cardinal's project. Catholic parents did not take to the idea. For once, Vance's analysis was more accurate than his superior's. He admitted snobbery and the ability of the established Catholic public schools to offer discounted fees played their part. Nevertheless, the suggestion that St Edmund's might become a major public school was fundamentally flawed. Firstly, the College as a whole was run by its President. No School could flourish without its own Headmaster. More importantly, St Edmund's was 'a Seminary, and that ends it. So again putting boys in cassocks is all wrong from this point of view. So is Douglass House. The modern parent wants the school to be a school; and nothing else ... It is always the same story: the laity do not want their boys to be educated with or like Church boys ... You will never get lay boys to come in satisfactory numbers, nor of the *quality* you want, to any place where there are Church boys who are differentiated and made a kind of *petit seminaire*.'[149]

Vance's advice to the Cardinal was not appreciated. He was dismissed as Vice-President in 1926. But the idea of St Edmund's being a major public school with lay and clerical elements had to be abandoned.

'The use of arms'

Cardinal Bourne had no qualms about schoolboys engaging in army exercises. In an article written before the First World War, 'he advocated general military training for all in the schools, so as to have the nation always prepared for war.' Ward, as College President, was firmly opposed to seminarians having any such role and blocked the introduction of a Cadet Corps at St Edmund's. The Cardinal had to content himself with praising such drill as was permitted and encouraging 'the further idea of general training in the use of arms which he, for one, believed to be the only true guarantee for the peace and safety of the country.' But within a week of Ward's resignation in 1916 the formation of a uniformed Corps was announced.[150] Bourne derived great satisfaction from inspecting them on St Edmund's Day that year. 'I saw the troop on my arrival and expressed my appreciation of all that they had accomplished during a short space of time. I feel that they are performing all that I had hoped of them. Because I feel that the work of the College cannot be regarded as complete without a Cadet Corps.'[151]

Ward may no longer have been President of St Edmund's, but, as a Bishop since 1917 and with seminarians at the College, he was not without influence. He expressed his deep unease at seminarians participating in any form of military service and only stayed his hand so as not to cause difficulty at a time of national crisis.¹⁵² But a month after the Armistice he gave the College notice that all Brentwood students should be withdrawn from the Cadet Corps. In Bourne's absence in the Mediterranean, Myers acceded to Ward's request.¹⁵³

The ensuing altercation reflects well on neither the Cardinal nor the Bishop. Had Ward left matters there, it is possible that Bourne would have respected his right to act as he chose in relation to his own seminarians. But the Bishop of Brentwood immediately raised the stakes on receiving the answer he sought from St Edmund's. He decided that his students, although exempted themselves, were endangered by their very presence at the College 'surrounded by other church students undergoing that training, with consequent danger of militarist influence.' The former President gave notice that his seminarians were to be withdrawn from St Edmund's entirely.¹⁵⁴ Furthermore, Ward involved Cardinal Bisleti at the Congregation of Seminaries.¹⁵⁵

Back from his travels in the Near East and the Balkans, Bourne regarded this as extreme provocation and rescinded any further exemption from the Corps.¹⁵⁶ He fired off a furious letter to Bisleti, claiming, somewhat disingenuously, that he had no knowledge of the nature of Ward's objections and that Ward was acting under the influence of his Irish Vicar-General,¹⁵⁷ a man 'of somewhat violent temper.' The Cardinal was also less than forthright in maintaining that the Corps' activity constituted 'simply gymnastic and physical exercises.' Rather more to the point, Bourne stated any school with social aspirations was expected to have a Cadet Corps. 'Public opinion attaches great importance to them and parents insist on them for their children.'¹⁵⁸

Bisleti was better informed, and was not about to overturn the prohibition on clerics carrying arms to appease English middle class parents. He wrote on 1 September 1919 reminding Bourne a Cadet Corps was forbidden in a seminary.¹⁵⁹ Ushaw, which received the same decree, immediately dissolved their Corps and cancelled an order for army rifles.¹⁶⁰ Bourne, by contrast, over reacted. At most he ought to have made use of the house system he was about to introduce and distinguished lay boys and junior seminarians. Instead, he sent another intemperate letter to the Vatican, asking Archbishop Cerretti to intervene directly with the Pope regarding Bisleti's 'absolutely deplorable' decree. Implausibly, he argued that the events at St Edmund's would damage Catholic interests at the Versailles Peace Conference. In reality, he feared more that the 'parents of better families' would not send their children to a school which lacked its own Cadet Corps; patriotic opinion demanded it.[161]

His 'terrible letter' did Bourne no good at all. It played into the hands of Gasquet, Merry del Val and Hinsley, who were able to present him in the worst possible light. The whole Vatican 'from the Pope downwards' was 'indignant' with him.[162] The Cardinal delayed promulgating the decree at St Edmund's for several months so that the staff there 'professed to disbelieve in its existence,' but Bisleti happily obliged in distributing copies to Bourne's suffragans and eventually he had to comply.[163] The chastening experience was apparent over a decade later when the question of a Cadet Corps arose at the new Catholic grammar school in Gunnersbury. The Cardinal lamely informed the headmaster, 'We are all of the opinion that it would be unwise in present circumstances to start a Cadet Corps. The Scout organisation is at the present day in every way more useful.'[164] Not Bourne at his best.

'His concentration on St Edmund's'

Over three decades Bourne poured resources into St Edmund's. With the restoration of the Seminary, he commissioned the architect of Wonersh, Frederick Walters, to design accommodation and facilities for the influx of the new men. Work on the 'Divines' Wing,' later known as Allen Hall, comprising fifty rooms for the seminarians, began in spring 1904. Structurally, it was largely complete by that September. Together with a new Shrine Chapel of St Edmund, Allen Hall was formally opened in May 1905. A less persistent man might have abandoned his plans when the new building went up in flames within a decade. Bourne patiently set out about rebuilding, only on a grander scale.

The Fitzgerald bequest gave the Cardinal free rein to implement his proposed improvements to the College. To facilitate the new house system, new classrooms were erected, old buildings re-roofed and redecorated as St Edmund's underwent 'a peaceful siege at the hands of an army of workmen.'[165] The Cardinal himself regarded the Galilee Chapel, an extension to the College Chapel, as the most important of all his works, serving both as a memorial to the War dead and acting as 'a parish church' for the lay boys at the School.[166] But it did not finish with the development of the early 1920s. Right to the end the Cardinal was continuing to lavish money on St Edmund's. A new wing to Allen Hall was initiated in 1930 to accommodate the growing number of seminarians. The Golden Jubilee gift of £1,800 from his clergy was spent improving the College Chapel sanctuary.

This largesse did not meet with universal approval. Fifteen years after the Cardinal's death, Fr Gordon Wheeler criticised 'his concentration on St Edmund's to the detriment of provision for primary education in the new suburbs.'[167] It was an objection Bourne had anticipated, pointing out that, although he spent well over £100,000 on St Edmund's, little or none of this had come from general diocesan resources; at no time had he ever made an appeal to fund these improvements. The initial cost of building Allen Hall had been met, appropriately enough, from the sale proceeds of St Thomas's Seminary, Hammersmith. Then the Cardinal was remarkably successful at attracting both priestly vocations and the donations and bequests required to pay for their formation.[168]

Whether or not one approves of his priorities, Cardinal Bourne undoubtedly constitutes one of the major benefactors of Allen Hall. With his decision to restore the Seminary to Westminster, he is also one of the most decisive influences on its history. It is unjust that he remains virtually unknown to the Seminary community today.

Notes

1. Cahill to Gotti, u/d, SCPF, 102/1904, f. 289, rr. 54–55.
2. Hagerty, *Cardinal Hinsley*, p. 209.
3. J. C. Heenan, *Cardinal Hinsley* (London: Burns Oates & Washbourne Ltd, 1944), p. 76.
4. FAB, Allocution at the Westminster Diocesan Synod, 6 October 1925.
5. Canon G. Coote to Hinsley, 18 May 1935, AAW, Bo. IV/5/2; Jackman, 'Francis Cardinal Bourne,' *Dublin Review*, April 1935, pp. 177–195; FAB, St Bede's, Clapham Park, 16 May 1932, *Tablet*, 21 May 1932, p. 672; S. Seuffert, 'Francis Cardinal Bourne,' Fr Claude Williamson (ed.), *Great Catholics*, Catholic Book Club (London, 1939), p. 487.
6. D. Hamilton, 'A Visit to Archbishop's House,' *WCC*, January 1910, p. 12.
7. Jackman, 'Francis Cardinal Bourne,' *Dublin Review*, April 1935.
8. Caraman, *C. C. Martindale*, p. 125.
9. Coote to Hinsley, 18 May 1935, AAW, Bo. IV/5/2.
10. FAB to Fr A. Purdie, 4 April 1930, draft, AAW, Bo. I/98/16.
11. Considine to FAB, 8 June 1911, AAW, Bo. III/124/5.
12. Hinsley to Fr V. Elwes, 5 & 21 May, 20 June 1935, AAW, Hi/Misc., cited Hagerty, *Cardinal Hinsley*, p. 211.
13. FAB, Advent Pastoral 1927.

14 FAB, Address, Campion House, Osterley, 23 June 1921, *Tablet*, 2 July 1921, p. 15.
15 *Rogito* enclosed in FAB's tomb, cited *WCC*, February 35, p. 3.
16 Fuller, Interview, 7 November 2001.
17 Jackman, *Irish Catholic*, 13 June 1940.
18 Fuller, Interview, 7 November 2001.
19 Jackman, 'Francis Cardinal Bourne,' *Dublin Review*, April 1935, pp. 177–195.
20 Canon Ring, Jubilee Presentation, 26 April 1922, *Tablet*, 29 April 1922, p. 546.
21 Elliot Anstruther, 'Francis Cardinal Bourne,' *Dublin Review*, April 1935, p. 191.
22 FAB, Allocution, Westminster Synod, 23 October 1906; FAB, Allocution, Westminster Synod, 6 October 1925.
23 FAB, Reply to the chapter and clergy on Silver Jubilee of Episcopacy, *WCC*, July 1921, pp. 127–128.
24 Butt, cited Oldmeadow, *Francis Cardinal Bourne*, ii, p. 346.
25 Jackman, 'Reminiscences of Cardinal Bourne,' *Wonersh Magazine*, May 1936, p. 109.
26 FAB to Mgr Poyer, 16 May 1911, AAW, Bo. III/47/11.
27 Poyer to FAB, 18 May 1911, AAW, Bo. III/47/12.
28 FAB to Cerretti, 14 September 1919 (copy), AAW, Bo. III/124/6; FAB to Lépicier, 30 December 1928, AAW, Bo. I/112.
29 FAB to Fr J. Reany, 25 October 1929, copy, AAW, Bo. I/98/17.
30 Wheeler, 'The Archdiocese of Westminster,' Beck (ed.), *The English Catholics 1850–1950*, p. 182.
31 Fr Cooney, Clergy Dinner, St. Thomas', Wandsworth, *Tablet*, 22 February 1902, p. 314.
32 FAB to Ward, 1903, cited Ward, *Insurrection versus Resurrection*, p. 150.
33 Gilbert, Jubilee Presentation, 26 April 1922, *Tablet*, 29 April 1922, p. 546.
34 FAB, Radcliffe College, 30 July 1913, *Tablet*, 9 August 1913, p. 217.
35 Anstruther, *Tablet*, 5 January 1935, p. 8.
36 FAB to WCF, 22 May 1917, *Tablet*, 26 May 1917, p. 661.
37 Fletcher, *O, Call Back Yesterday*, p. 113.
38 Editorial, *Tablet*, 9 June 1923, p. 756.
39 FAB to CWL, 26 November 1922, *Tablet*, 9 December 1922, p. 786; FAB, CWL AGM, 29 January 1923, *Tablet*, 3 February 1923, p. 165.
40 Norfolk, Norwich, 5 August 1912, *Tablet*, 10 August 1912, p. 229.
41 Anstruther, *Tablet*, 5 January 1935, p. 8.
42 FAB, Preface to CEG Handbook, cited *Tablet*, 2 November 1918, p. 500.
43 FAB, CEG AGM, 21 October 1921, *WCC*, November 1921, p. 208.
44 Sheed, *The Church and I*, p. 45; Gasquet, 'The Catholic Evidence Guild,' *WCC*, December 1919, p. 224.
45 Sheed, *The Church and I*, p. 83.
46 Ward, *Unfinished Business*, p. 91.

47 FAB, University of London Catholic Society, 10 February 1930, *Tablet*, 15 February 1930, p. 215.
48 FAB to WCF, 22 May 1917, *Tablet*, 26 May 1917, p. 661.
49 J. Hope to Editor, *Tablet*, 13 November 1926, p. 660.
50 Hope to FitzAlan, 21 March 1928, AAW, Hi. II/163.
51 Memorandum, AAW, Hi. II/163.
52 Hope and H. Norman to FAB, 20 December 1928, AAW, Hi. II/163.
53 FAB to Hope, 15 April 1931 (copy), AAW, Hi. II/163.
54 FAB to Rankeillour, 3 July 1934 (copy), AAW, Hi. II/163.
55 FAB, Homily, Hatfield, 12 February 1930, *Tablet*, 22 February 1930, p. 237.
56 FAB, Trinity Sunday Pastoral 1912.
57 FAB, Ponders End, 25 September 1921, *Tablet*, 1 October 1921, p. 441.
58 FAB, St Mary's Twickenham, 23 June 1927, *Tablet*, 2 July 1927, p. 15.
59 Fr H. England, 'The Pimlico Mission,' *WCC*, December 1936, p. 227.
60 *Tablet*, 26 July 1913, p. 138.
61 FAB, Blessed Sacrament Church, Copenhagen Street, *Tablet*, 6 November 1915, p. 596.
62 FAB, Royston, 25 June 1921, *Tablet*, 2 July 1921, p. 24.
63 Fr Barton Brown to FAB, 17 June 1916, AAW, Bo. I/92.
64 FAB to Barton Brown, 16 June 1919, AAW, Bo. I/92.
65 FAB, St Michael's, Ashford, 13 November 1927, *Tablet*, 19 November 1927, p. 676.
66 FAB, Royston, 25 June 1921, *Tablet*, 2 July 1921, p. 24.
67 FAB, Abbots Langley, 11 October 1931, *Tablet*, 17 October 1931, p. 504.
68 Fuller, Interview, 7 November 2001.
69 FAB, Trinity Sunday Pastoral, 1927.
70 FAB, Salesian College, Battersea, 18 December 1924, *Tablet*, 3 January 1925, p. 28.
71 Lépicier, Paris, 18 May 1929, *Tablet*, 25 May 1929, p. 722.
72 *Tablet*, 8 September 1923, p. 306.
73 *Tablet*, 29 June 1907, p. 1029.
74 *Tablet*, 23 May 1908, p. 805.
75 FAB, Meeting, 7 June 1904, *Tablet*, 11 June 1904, p. 942.
76 *Tablet*, 16 September 1905, pp. 474–476.
77 J. Driscoll, 'Our Secondary Schools,' *Tablet*, 1 April 1911, p. 486.
78 FAB, Pastoral Letter, 29 December 1903.
79 *Tablet*, 11 June 1904, p. 924.
80 *Tablet*, 11 June 1904, pp. 922, 925.
81 FAB, 'The Church's Opportunity,' *Clergy Review*, February 1931, p. 122.
82 FAB, Finchley, 27 June 1931, *Tablet*, 4 July 1931, p. 20.
83 Oldmeadow, 'Westminster Cathedral and What the Cardinal Archbishop has done for It,' *WCC*, May 1922, p. 84.

84 P. G. Konody, *Observer*, 3 October 1915.
85 Oldmeadow, *Francis Cardinal Bourne*, ii, p. 337n.
86 FAB, Christmas Message, *WCC*, January 1934, p. 3.
87 J. Marshall to E. Gill, 18 September 1914 (copy), AAW, Bo. V/49c.
88 Gill to Jackman, 4 September 1917, AAW, Bo. V/49c.
89 E. Green, FSA, to Editor, *Tablet*, 30 April 1910, p. 696.
90 G. Siordet to W. Ward, 3 June 1912, SAUL, Ward Family Papers, ms 38347/VII/271/2.
91 E. Hutton to Editor, *Daily Telegraph*, 7 December 1933.
92 FAB, Christmas Message, *WCC*, January 1934, p. 2.
93 Siordet to Ward, 3 June 1912, SAUL, Ward Family Papers, ms 38347/VII/271/2.
94 Oldmeadow, *Francis Cardinal Bourne*, ii, pp. 298-299; *Tablet*, 8 March 1919, p. 288.
95 *WCC*, December 1927, p. 236.
96 FAB, Pastoral, 8 January 1905, *Tablet*, 7 January 1905, p. 28.
97 FAB, 29 June 1920, 25th anniversary of laying of foundation stone, *Tablet*, 3 July 1920, pp. 29-30.
98 *Tablet*, 29 April 1905, p. 662.
99 R. R. Terry, 'The Cathedral and its Music: II,' *WCC*, 1907, p. 22
100 P. Doyle, *Westminster Cathedral 1895-1995* (London: Geoffrey Chapman, 1995), p. 53.
101 Terry, 'The Cathedral and its Music: I,' *WCC*, February 1907, p. 25.
102 Oldmeadow, *Francis Cardinal Bourne*, ii, p. 338; Doyle, *Westminster Cathedral 1895-1995*, pp. 60-62.
103 FAB, Audience, 6 November 1903, *Tablet*, 14 November 1903, p. 773.
104 *WCC*, September 1909, p. 228; January 1910, p. 5.
105 Terry, 'The Cathedral and its Music: II,' p. 25.
106 Doyle, *Westminster Cathedral 1895-1995*, pp. 55-59.
107 Fr L. Long, 'A Song School Jubilee,' *Tablet*, 2 October 1926, p. 431.
108 FAB, Pastoral Letter, 29 December 1903.
109 FAG to Fleming, 2 June 1903, cited Leslie, *Cardinal Gasquet*, p. 80.
110 Ilsley to Riddell, 5 March 1904, NorDA, FIV.10.
111 Fr P. Hughes, 'The Coming Century,' Beck (ed.), *The English Catholics 1850-1950*, p. 36.
112 Ilsley to Riddell, 1 March 1904, NorDA, FIV.10.
113 Ward to Fenton, u/d (autumn 1903), copy, AAW, SEC XIV/17/86.
114 Ward to FAB, 5 October 1903, AAW, SEC XIV/17/85; Fenton to Mgr H. Parkinson, 10 July 1903 (copy), BAA, OCA/CS6, Rector's Report to the Bishops.
115 Ward to Fenton, u/d (autumn 1903), copy, AAW, SEC XIV/17/86.
116 FAB, Homily, St Edmund's, 4 October 1903, *Tablet*, 10 October 1903, p. 595.
117 FAB to Fenton, 25 October 1903, AAW, SEC XIV/17/87.

[118] Ward to FAB, 5 October 1903, AAW, SEC XIV/17/85; Ward to Fenton, u/d (autumn 1903), copy, AAW, SEC XIV/17/86.
[119] FAB, Speech to St Edmund's Academia, 22 September 1904, cited Oldmeadow, *Francis Cardinal Bourne*, i, p. 247.
[120] Provost Johnson to Chapter, 16 December 1903, AAW, Bo. I/116; Chapter Resolution, 18 December 1903, AAW, Bo. I/116.
[121] FAB, Speech at St Edmund's, 24 May 1905, cited Oldmeadow, *Francis Cardinal Bourne*, i, p. 247.
[122] Meeting, Oscott, 13 October 1903, BAA, OCA/CS/C3, Board of Bishops' Minute Book, pp. 44–45.
[123] FAB to Parkinson, 25 December 1903, AAW, Bo 4/2/3–1(copy); FAB to Parkinson, 4 January 1904, BAA/PC.
[124] Riddell to Cahill, 5 January 1904, NorDA, Riddell, FIV.10; Cahill to Riddell, 6 January 1904, NorDA, FIV.10.
[125] Ilsley to Riddell, 1 March 1904, NorDA, FIV.10.
[126] Riddell to Ilsley (copy), 4 March 1904, NorDA, FIV.10.
[127] Cahill to Burton, 27 March 1905, CDA, Burton Papers, Correspondence 1902–05.
[128] FAB to Burton, 19 January 1905, CDA, Burton Papers, Correspondence 1902–05.
[129] Ward to Burton, Rome, 8 May 1904, AAW, Ward Papers, SEC XVA/26.
[130] FAB to Burton, 17 January 1905, CDA, Burton Papers, Correspondence 1902–05.
[131] Meeting, Archbishop's House, 4 May 1905, BAA, OCA/CS/C3, Board of Bishops' Minute Book, p. 48.
[132] Mgr Prior, Rector of Beda, to Ilsley, 1906, cited M. Williams, *Oscott College in the Twentieth Century* (Leominster: Gracewing, 2001), p. 13.
[133] FAB Pastoral, *Tablet*, 16 July 1904, p. 112.
[134] FAB, *Ecclesiastical Training*, p. 1.
[135] Ward, 'St Edmund's College,' *WCC*, May 1909, pp. 133.
[136] Fuller, Interview, 7 November 2001.
[137] FAB, 'Reorganisation of St Edmund's College,' *WCC*, May 1923.
[138] Ward to Burton, 24 January 1904, AAW, SEC XIV/15A/9; Ward to Burton, 26 January 1904, AAW, SEC XIV/15A/10.
[139] Burton to FAB, 28 March 1904, AAW, Bo. I/116.
[140] FAB to Myers, 30 November 1922 (copy), AAW, Bo. I/108.
[141] Canon J. Vance, 'Notes on St Edmund's College,' January 1960, AAW, Bo. I/110.
[142] Fuller, interview, 7 November 2001.
[143] FAB notebook, 5 April 1920, cited Oldmeadow, *Francis Cardinal Bourne*, ii, p. 169.
[144] FAB, 'Reorganisation of St Edmund's College,' *WCC*, May 1923.
[145] Vance, 'Notes on St Edmund's College,' January 1960, AAW, Bo. I/110.
[146] FAB, 'Reorganisation of St Edmund's College,' *WCC*, May 1923.
[147] FAB notebook, 5 April 1920, cited Oldmeadow, *Francis Cardinal Bourne*, ii, pp. 169–170.

148 FAB, 'Reorganisation of St Edmund's College,' *WCC*, May 1923.
149 Vance to FAB, 1 March 1926, AAW, Bo. I/108.
150 Ward to Hinsley, 28 April 1919 (copy), BDA, K2/d; FAB, Speech Day, St Edmund's, 1 July 1913, *Tablet*, 5 July 1913, p. 18.
151 FAB, St Edmund's, 16 November 1916, *Tablet*, 25 November 1916, pp. 709–710.
152 Ward to Burton, 29 Dec 1917, AAW, SEC XIV/15B/97.
153 Ward to Myers, 31 December 1918, copy, AAW, Bo. I/116; Myers to Ward, 15 January 1919, copy, AAW, Bo. I/116.
154 Ward to Myers, 17 January 1919, AAW, Bo. I/116.
155 For the precise sequence of events see Fr S. Foster, 'Prelates at War: Cardinal Bourne, Bishop Ward and the St Edmund's College Cadet Corps Dispute,' in *Recusant History* 30, 2 (2010), pp. 343–376.
156 Fr T. E. Flynn, Prefect of Studies, to Ward, 25 April 1919 (copy), AAW, Bo. III/124/6.
157 Mgr William O'Grady, ironically chosen by Ward on Bourne's advice to smooth Ward's relations with the Irish clergy in Brentwood.
158 FAB to Bisleti, 29 April 1919, AAW, Bo. III/124/6.
159 Decree, Congregation for Seminaries to English Archbishops, 6 August 1919 (copy), BDA, K2/d; Bisletti to FAB, 1 September 1919, AAW, Bo. III/124/6.
160 Whiteside to FAB, 6 October 1919, AAW, Bo. III/124/6.
161 FAB to Cerretti, 14 September 1919 (copy), AAW, Bo. III/124/6.
162 Hinsley to Ward, 26 October 1919, BDA, K2/d.
163 Ward to Gasquet, 31 December 1919, DAA, Gasquet, 889.
164 FAB to Fr J. Warren, 3 May 1932 (copy), AAW, Hi. II/108.
165 *Tablet*, 1 January 1921, p. 9.
166 *Tablet*, 26 November 1921, p. 700.
167 Wheeler, 'The Archdiocese of Westminster,' Beck (ed.), *The English Catholics 1850–1950*, p. 174.
168 FAB, St Edmund's, 16 November 1930, *Tablet*, 22 November 1930, p. 687.

Chapter 25

Noctem Quietam et Finem Perfectum

'I have not been very well of late'[1]

Given his industrious reputation, Bourne's correspondence, reads at times surprisingly like that of a semi-invalid. He was constantly seeking medical advice; 'thorough examinations' by the doctor were a regular occurrence.

Yet these were not the life-threatening conditions of his childhood. The Cardinal's voice, never strong, was a perennial cause for concern. The strain of public speaking told upon him. Overtaxing his vocal chords, he withdrew from engagements, seeking cures in the South of France and Switzerland.[2] 'Severe attacks of influenza' also necessitated lengthy periods of convalescence overseas.[3] Often the diagnosis was simply exhaustion. The prescription was invariably the same: 'complete rest and change.'[4] The complaint preceded the increased workload of Westminster. As Bishop of Southwark, Bourne found himself suffering from fatigue and awarded himself 'some weeks resting in Italy.'[5] His contemporaries could be less than sympathetic. During one lengthy absence from the Diocese, Bidwell shared with Merry del Val his opinion that there was not 'much the matter with the Cardinal.'[6]

The Fitzalan Howards concluded at an early stage that Bourne's afflictions were largely psychosomatic. In 1904 Talbot told his brother of the Archbishop's plans for recuperation in Perthshire, noting there was 'nothing wrong but general depression of the nervous system.'[7] Confirmation of this analysis was provided by Bourne's 1917 denouement with the hierarchy over diocesan division which led to a complete collapse of health and three months at Hare Street away from official business. The Cardinal was not slow in sharing with his episcopal brethren his diagnosis of his condition. 'I need not disguise the fact that Low Week was an intensely painful experience to me, and had much to do with my recent illness.'[8] The Bishops were basically decent men and, whatever their disagreements, the fact there was no recurrence of that 'painful experience' over the next two decades can be explained, not just by an underdeveloped sense of collegiality and the realisation he was not to be changed, but also by genuine concern for Bourne's wellbeing. The Cardinal himself felt this to be the case. 'My brethren realising, I imagine, the real cause of my breakdown in health have since then been much more considerate.'[9]

Whether or not psychosomatic, the effects of the 1917 conflict were apparent to all. One layman commented, 'I think he is in very poor health. I saw him yesterday but not to speak to; he looks an old man and his hair is quite white.'[10] And the Cardinal was still in his mid-fifties. Overwork brought on another 'severe attack of illness' early in 1920 resulting in two months of 'rest in a suitable climate'[11] Amigo dared to dream, sharing with Gasquet his aspiration, 'You might still change places.'[12] While Bourne himself hoped to 'regain full health,' he contemplated the alternative with equanimity. 'I shall go home, in a chronic increasing condition of ill-health, gradually limiting my activities, necessitating precautions, and leading slowly or rapidly to the end.'[13] Such musings were unduly pessimistic. Medical attention and two months in the Mediterranean wrought their cure. By the end of April the Cardinal was able to confide, 'I [am] ... restored to my usual good if not extremely robust health.'[14]

'Sorrow and grave anxiety'[15]

Given his earlier health, the Cardinal was remarkably fit as the 1920s gave way to the 1930s. Another thorough medical examination in 1928 revealed, 'I am sound in every part, and that for one of my age I have a first-class life.'[16] His schedule for the summer and autumn of 1932 was as full as it had been a generation earlier. In June he opened a further extension at St Edmund's to accommodate the growing number of seminarians; a new lecture hall was added in November. August saw him acting as Papal Legate at the consecration of Buckfast Abbey. He was preaching at Cambridge and Edinburgh. At one point he was opening new buildings for Catholic schools on a daily basis. Presiding at the opening of new offices for the CWL in October provided a moment of particular pleasure. Then there were episcopal consecrations and priestly ordinations, the normal round of meetings and dinners for Catholic institutions, in addition to the everyday routine of diocesan administration. A cold prevented the Cardinal presiding at a meeting of the Catholic Prisoners' Aid Society with the Jesuits at Farm Street on 24 November

Noctem Quietam et Finem Perfectum

1932, but he left London that evening on the boat train for his *ad limina* visit to Rome.[17] The probability was that he would remain at the helm in Westminster for another decade.

No one was prepared, therefore, for the stream of telegrams from Rome just days later. Arriving at his preferred residence in the Eternal City, the Redemptorist house in the Via Merulana, the Cardinal's 'slight cold' had deteriorated significantly on the journey. He was admitted immediately to the Calvary Hospital of the Little Company of Mary ('the Blue Nuns') suffering from bronchial cold and gastric flu. By 1 December his condition had taken a turn for the worse 'such as to occasion the utmost anxiety. The state of his heart shows increasing weakening.'[18]

Something else unexpected occurred: a huge outpouring of sympathy for the Cardinal. Constitutionally incapable of appealing for affection in health, it came unsought in illness. The hospital where he was being nursed saw a constant flow of visitors: cardinals, bishops, members of the Roman aristocracy and the English community in Rome. Pius XI sent his blessing; George V conveyed sympathy and best wishes.[19] Across his Diocese and England prayers were offered and the Blessed Sacrament exposed for his recovery. Every night the BBC announced the latest bulletin on the Cardinal's health. Even those elements of the secular Press not normally sympathetic to the Catholic Church expressed their solicitude and concern.[20] Anticipating his loss, there was a general acknowledgement that over three decades he had led his co-religionists to a position of prominence and respectability in English society.

By the end of the first week of December a corner had been turned. Although still weak, the Cardinal's temperature and pulse had returned to normal. He was able to celebrate Midnight Mass and attend an audience with the Pope. But, still an invalid, he sailed with his Private Secretary on a liner out of Naples on 28 December. Arriving in Tilbury a week later, Bourne returned immediately to Archbishop's House for two weeks. Avoiding public duties, he still attempted the routine governance of the Diocese. However, it was not to be business as normal, but two long years of gradual decline—interspersed with moments of improved health and activity.

'Not completely cured'[21]

As Hitler became German Chancellor at the end of January 1933, the Cardinal was convalescing at a convent on the Isle of Wight. He did not allow himself long enough. By early February he was back in London transacting business and paying numerous visits. The result while staying with the Blue Sisters at St Leonard's-on-Sea on St Patrick's Day was 'a sudden onset of pulmonary oedema, which threatened to become grave in the extreme.'[22] The threat was taken sufficiently seriously that the Cardinal was anointed by his auxiliary, Butt. There was an improvement, but this time Bourne had to consent to a more prolonged period of rest.[23]

Not until June was the *Cathedral Chronicle* able to publish again a full schedule of public appearances for the Cardinal. Pre-eminent among them was a trip to Liverpool as Papal Legate to lay the foundation stone of the proposed vast new Lutyens Cathedral of Christ the King. But six hours before his departure the Cardinal suffered a further serious relapse; the Cardinal Archbishop of Armagh stood in for him at Liverpool. In reporting Bourne's incapacity, the *Tablet* implicitly condemned Archbishop Downey's project. It was just as well, the journal opined, that Bourne had not collapsed at the ceremony lest the baser type of non-Catholic interpreted this 'as heaven's rebuke of a pretentious scheme hatched by the Archbishop of Liverpool in a mood of unspiritual megalomania.' Even although the Cardinal recovered, the incident led to an acceptance that his future public appearances would be limited.[24]

In September 1933 he made his final overseas trip—to Paris for the fiftieth anniversary reunion of his St Sulpice classmates. The following month he made his first public speech in almost a year. It was too much. A chill contracted at the end of November led to confinement to his bed. Although partially recovered by mid-December, public participation in the Christmas liturgies was out of the question.[25] His Private Secretary described his condition at the end of 1933. 'His Eminence has not been able to write a single letter this Christmas ... There has been no progress these last weeks. He sadly developed bad insomnia ... Hence he is very often exhausted.'[26]

But God was good. He permitted a final few months of health for the celebration of three events close to the Cardinal's heart. In April he presided at a rally to mark John Bosco's canonisation and visited the Salesians in Battersea whose house he had helped found so many years before. 11 June 1934 was the Cardinal's Golden Jubilee of priesthood. Despite Canon St John's death that month, the Cardinal was able to attend the various celebrations of the occasion. Bishops, priests, religious and the laity thronged Westminster Cathedral for a Solemn Mass of

Noctem Quietam et Finem Perfectum

Thanksgiving. Thousands spontaneously knelt before Archbishop's House to receive his blessing from the balcony, and then treated him to hearty and prolonged cheering. The affection and respect evinced during his illness in Rome were renewed by the Catholic faithful.[27] One suspects, however, that he was most touched by the Pope's tribute. 'Among your many and varied activities on behalf of souls, there is one which merits special praise; We refer to the zeal and energy with which you have ever promoted the sound education of the young, and particularly of those destined for the priesthood. It must indeed be a great consolation to you to reflect that you have devoted nearly the whole of your life to this work of education.'[28] In confirmation of the accolade, the Cardinal travelled to St Edmund's the following day to conclude his anniversary celebrations at the School and Seminary.

Under Henry VIII England's great shrine to Our Lady at Walsingham suffered the same fate as every other religious house in the country. But by 1896, the Slipper Chapel—the final stage on the pilgrim route—was back in Catholic hands. Disputes between the benefactress, the Benedictines and the Diocese delayed matters, but in August 1934 the first national Catholic pilgrimage in four hundred years visited Walsingham. How appropriate that it was led by Cardinal Bourne, who had done so much to emphasize continuity with the pre-Reformation Church. A day pilgrimage to rural Norfolk was a major ordeal in the 1930s, but the weakened Cardinal persevered in leading more than 10,000 pilgrims first to Mass in Norwich, and then on to Benediction by the Slipper Chapel itself. The consequences were all the Cardinal could have prayed for. The event caught the national imagination—even beyond Catholic circles. The *Times* wrote approvingly, 'Such ground cannot but be holy; and it is good to think that the holiness of the holy land of Walsingham is once more recognised and honoured.'[29] It was to be the Cardinal's final significant public function.

Go forth, faithful Christian

Although Cardinal Bourne continued to receive occasional visitors and conduct a limited amount of business, the priests and people of Westminster knew that all was not well when Bishop Butt informed them there would be no Advent Pastoral Letter that year. One of the nursing sisters supplied the details. 'My news isn't good, His Eminence is really very ill. I told you some time ago that the kidneys were not acting properly and now [he] has extensive dropsy! Legs very swollen. Dr Parkinson came a week ago and found him much worse than he expected, in fact he said it was only a question of weeks than of months. His Eminence has been told and though it was a shock at first, he is now quite happy and resigned.'[30] The Private Secretary confirmed this. 'The medical facts are gloomy; the double dose of last resort treatment has little response: that is the black medical side. Yet we—I—see him daily in his best moments, chatting and reasonably bright, almost expecting him to say: "We'll go down to the Cathedral and see the latest mosaic work." All the time I know he is physically unable to walk there and back.'[31]

By 30 December the bulletins from Archbishop's House were preparing the Catholic faithful for the inevitable. Bishop Butt had already performed his final duty for his longstanding friend in reading to him the Profession of Faith for his assent. As the old year slipped away, the Cardinal's words became fewer and fainter. Towards the evening of 31 December, Mgr Coote read the 'Jesus Psalter' to the Cardinal, who could only reply, 'Tired ... Comforting.'[32] As the nurse left the room for a short while in the first half hour of 1935 Cardinal Bourne slipped quietly and peacefully into eternity.

'An unending stream of silent mourners'[33]

In the official biography, Oldmeadow writes disapprovingly of the funeral rites accorded to his late employer which he thought 'less impressive' than those of Cardinal Vaughan 32 years earlier. Oldmeadow regretted the fact that the lying-in state took place, not in the Cathedral, but in the adjoining Hall.[34] But surely Bourne would have approved the arrangement: designed to ensure that the liturgical life of the Cathedral, which he had done so much to establish, should not be disturbed. More important than the venue was the fact, recorded by both the Catholic and secular Press, that over two days thousand upon thousand took the opportunity to pray and pay their final respects as they passed the coffin in silent procession.

On the morning of Friday, 4 January 1935 thousands of ordinary men and women waited in the cold for the Cathedral doors to open 2 ½ hours before the funeral. The Solemn Requiem Mass for Cardinal Bourne was sung by Archbishop Mostyn of Cardiff in the presence of the Cardinal Archbishops of Paris and Gniezno and the arrayed ranks of archbishops, bishops, abbots and priests. Twenty countries sent representatives.

Noctem Quietam et Finem Perfectum

Oldmeadow and the *Tablet* noted one significant absence. With the exception of the Lords of the Admiralty, there was no one to represent the British Crown or Government. Why the insulting omission, Oldmeadow queried, given Queen Victoria had sent a wreath for Cardinal Manning forty years earlier?[35] We know now the decision not to send a royal representative was taken on the advice of the Archbishop of Canterbury, from whom Buckingham Palace sought guidance.[36] Ironically, one of Bourne's last comments had been to praise Archbishop Lang's homily at the marriage of the Duke and Duchess of Kent.[37]

The Requiem over, a cortege of thirty cars, accompanied by Cardinal Hlond drove slowly through the London streets into the Hertfordshire countryside. Groups of mourners gathered at the roadside to watch its passing. Cardinal Bourne was being brought to rest at the seminary he loved and restored at St Edmund's, Ware. There his body was buried before the altar of the Galilee Chapel which was his gift to the College.

But the story does not end quite there. Westminster tradition has it that one of the priest secretaries was heard running down the corridors of Archbishop's House in the early hours of New Year's Day 1935 calling for a doctor. Given the Cardinal had already been certified dead, it was thought that the man was touched by grief. But, no; he had just discovered the Cardinal's written request: that his heart be removed and placed in the chapel at Wonersh. Bourne was not a man to forget his first love. And there his heart remains to this day, beside the altar of his patron, St Francis de Sales. In death, as in life, Francis Bourne was shared by two Seminaries, two Dioceses.

Notes

1. FAB to Lépicier, 27 February 1920, AGOSM, Lépicier Papers.
2. *Tablet*, 28 August 1909, p. 346; Oldmeadow, *Francis Cardinal Bourne*, ii, p. 92.
3. *WCC*, January 1910, p. 3; Oldmeadow, *Francis Cardinal Bourne*, ii, p. 94.
4. Talbot to Norfolk, ACA, 3 April 1904.
5. FAB to Ledochowski, 14 August 1901, SCPF, 102/1901, f. 211, r. 468.
6. Merry del Val to Broadhead, 5 April 1920, UCA, Broadhead Papers, OS/J/54.
7. Talbot to Norfolk, ACA, 3 April 1904.
8. FAB to Keating, 7 July 1917, NorDA, FV.1.
9. FAB to Lépicier, 2 October 1918, AGOSM, Lépicier Papers.
10. Robertson to Glancey, 9 September 1917, BAA, E261.

11. Copy of medical certificate dated 18 February 1920 enclosed under FAB to Amigo, 23 February 1920, SAA, Bourne Papers, Letters to Amigo.
12. Amigo to Gasquet, 25 February 1920, DAA, Gasquet, 917A.
13. FAB notebook, 22 March 1920, cited Oldmeadow, *Francis Cardinal Bourne*, ii, p. 168.
14. FAB notebook, Fiesole, 30 April 1920, cited Oldmeadow, *Francis Cardinal Bourne*, ii, p. 171.
15. *Tablet*, 3 December 1932, p. 732.
16. FAB to Arthur, 22 March 1928, BDA.
17. *Tablet*, 26 November 1932, p. 707.
18. *Tablet*, 3 December 1932, p. 732.
19. Rome correspondent, *Tablet*, 10 December 1932, p. 789.
20. *Tablet*, 10 December 1932, pp. 773, 779.
21. *Rogito* enclosed in FAB's tomb, cited *WCC*, February 1935, p. 6.
22. *Tablet*, 25 March 1933, p. 376.
23. *Rogito* enclosed in FAB's tomb, cited *WCC*, February 1935, p. 6.
24. Editorial, *Tablet*, 10 June 1933, p. 717.
25. *Tablet*, 16 December 1933, p. 807.
26. Coote to Arthur, 31 December 1933, BDA.
27. *WCC*, July 34, p. 137; *Tablet*, 16 June 1934, p. 752.
28. Pius XI to FAB, 8 June 1934.
29. *Times*, 18 August 1934, cited *WCC*, September 1934, p. 173.
30. Sr Winifred to Arthur, 15 November 1934, BDA.
31. Coote to Arthur, 15 November 1934, BDA.
32. Oldmeadow, *Francis Cardinal Bourne*, ii, p. 340.
33. *Times*, 3 January 1935.
34. Oldmeadow, *Francis Cardinal Bourne*, ii, pp. 340–341.
35. *Ibid.*, ii, p. 341; *Tablet*, 12 January 1935, p. 36.
36. Lang to Sir Clive Wigram, George V's Private Secretary, 19 January 1934, cited Moloney, *Westminster, Whitehall and the Vatican*, p. 83.
37. FitzAlan, BBC Tribute broadcast, 4 January 1935.

Chapter 26

'From first to last a man of God'[1]

'Little indeed on which to form any idea of the man'[2]

Ernest Oldmeadow contested furiously the reviews of his biography.[3] The most crushing came from one who had known the Cardinal better than any other, Arthur Jackman, intimately acquainted with Bourne for over forty years, his secretary for a generation. Conceding the magnitude of the task undertaken, Jackman made the telling point that the biographer had no personal knowledge of his subject in his early years—and had failed to make use of those who did. It was not that Oldmeadow sought to disguise the Cardinal's shortcomings. He readily acknowledged that Bourne was not 'a considerable scholar, an orator, a man of letters ... his was not a brilliant intellect.'[4] But Oldmeadow's approach was simply to marshal the facts, interpreted by his own adversarial approach, from the dry and functional correspondence held by the Westminster Archives.

The result was a dull and depressing tome virtually unread today. Jackman wrote with regret, 'People who were familiar with the Cardinal for many years will look almost in vain for any trace of the forthright, candid, simple and kindly man they knew, pitied and loved so well. The soul is wanting.'[5] Those familiar with the Cardinal chose not to write an alternative biography. So he became 'a neglected and much maligned figure.'[6] Yet it is possible to piece together from contemporary fragments a more balanced and accurate assessment of Francis, Cardinal Bourne.

'A great English Cardinal'[7]

In January 1935 the national Press obituaries were not uncritical, but they were fair and overwhelmingly appreciative of Bourne's qualities, his leadership of the Catholic Church and his place in public life. Individuals too delivered a similar verdict. As Minister for Education, H. A. L. Fisher had enjoyed close contact with the Cardinal. A non-Catholic, he wrote to FitzAlan after Bourne's death to say, 'How much I came to respect and admire Cardinal Bourne ... I always felt his integrity, strength and intelligent appreciation of views other than his own and of the difficulties with which we were confronted. His death is a great loss to the country.'[8] This was not simply a natural desire to avoid speaking ill of the dead. It reflected the tenor of assessments composed at other significant moments in Bourne's life.

It was felt that he had been tested by fire in his early days in Westminster, and proven his worth. A French cleric summarised Bourne's achievement in the Education Crisis. 'Less wisely counselled, English Catholics might have emerged with diminished strength, compromised by opposition to the Liberal party, practically bound to the Conservatives, and, without having its powerful social position, condemned to share the fate of the Established Church. Instead of that, they emerged freer than ever, and delivered from any appearance of solidarity with the Conservative party.'[9] The *Times* concurred. The survival of the Catholic schools in the State sector given the forces ranged against them ranked 'in the category of political miracles; but it may not have been brought to a triumph without the calmness and tact of the Archbishop.'[10]

There was similar praise for Bourne's handling of the confrontation with the Liberal Government during the 1908 Eucharistic Congress. The Bishop of Northampton spoke for the hierarchy in lauding Bourne's achievement. 'We have proved by experience the soundness of his judgement, the calmness of his temper, his courage at a crisis, and his tenacity of purpose. In him we have come to recognise a leader who can lead, a leader whom we can follow with confidence and enthusiasm.'[11] Again, a view widely shared by non-Catholics that, by virtue of 'his tact and reasonableness,' it was Bourne who had won the 'moral victory.' The Cardinal's role in the Irish Troubles and the General Strike was more contentious, but also recognised as further evidence of his courage and principle. Bourne's sympathy for 'the humbler classes' was demonstrated by his refusal to bow to the demands of 'the stiffer Tories among his flock' and condemn the nascent Labour Party.[12] Never afraid to venture into the arena of public affairs when the good of the Church demanded it, Bourne 'was no politician.' People do not look their priests for expediency, intrigue or posturing. The Cardinal stood for something 'far more important and that was what God wanted of him then and there ... [His] first duty was to be what God wanted him to be, and to do what God wanted him to do.'[13]

'From first to last a man of God'

All his obituaries spoke of the Cardinal's patriotism. Again, it was a Frenchman who had noted this during the First World War, writing, 'The problem today is to widen for Catholicism in England a way of approach which is largely and honourably assured for it. But in [the English] ... Catholicism has still to be implanted as a factor of the national life and to make the national services of Catholicism clear to English public opinion. And it is just this task which, if we are not mistaken, Cardinal Bourne has undertaken, and in which he has already largely succeeded.'[14]

Ignoring his Irish mother, the national Press pronounced Bourne the quintessential Englishman. They claimed to find in his character all that was typical of the race and which made for their greatness. The Cardinal was, they maintained, understated and efficient, practical and dependable. 'To do his duty quietly and steadily, without fuss or sentimentality, was his consistent ambition.' 'His patience and perseverance enabled him to succeed where a more superficially brilliant man would probably have failed.'[15] The English were having held up to themselves all those self-deprecating qualities they imagined made for their imperial destiny—and they approved. Foreign Office dispatches caught the same tone. The British Legation in Rome wrote to Whitehall, 'It would have been easy to find an archbishop with greater intellectual attainments or of superior social status ... , but it probably would not have been possible to find anyone so discreet, so reliable and so essentially English, alike in his modesty, his pertinacity and his shrewdness.'[16]

At his Silver Jubilee of episcopacy, the *Daily Telegraph* judged, 'Never has the Roman Catholic Church, during the last 300 years, been in a stronger position in this country than it is today, and never has it made more rapid strides, in the course of any period of eighteen years, than it has made in the eighteen years which have passed since Cardinal Bourne came to Westminster.' To a significant extent, it was a personal achievement. Fourteen years later, the *Times* stated, 'The death of Cardinal Bourne ... is a grave loss, not only to his own communion, by whom he will be deeply mourned, but also to the nation at large.' Most pleasing to the Cardinal would have been the newspaper's assertion that non-Catholic Englishmen looked to him as 'a statesmanlike champion of religious education, but also a courageous opponent of all those modern movements and influences which are calculated, openly or subtly, to sap the foundations of family life and indeed the whole structure of the community.'[17]

Contemporaries observed the similarities between Cardinal and King, whose reign Bourne's tenure at Westminster broadly spanned. George V and Bourne 'were both heroes of the middle classes. They were aloof, unimaginative, yet clear sighted and strong of will ... They were both respected and in the twilight of their years mellowed so that they grew in stature.'[18] In an age of rapid domestic change and conflict and dictatorship overseas, the stability provided by their common sense, moderation and sheer commitment to duty should never be under-estimated. God dealt generously with the English in leadership of Church and State in the early twentieth century.

'A great churchman'

Writing for the *Westminster Cathedral Chronicle*, Archbishop Downey of Liverpool made an unexpected comparison. In his opinion, Bourne 'undoubtedly takes rank as a great churchman, more akin in spirit to Cardinal Manning than to any other of his predecessors in the See of Westminster. For the second and fourth archbishop had much in common: the same essential sanity of outlook, the same prudence in action, the same sureness of touch, the same natural reserve, the same warm-heartedness under a grave exterior, the same compassion for the multitude. Both alike won the profound respect and admiration of their non-Catholic fellow-countrymen.'[19] Remembering Manning's position in the English Establishment and his popularity with the working classes, Downey's judgment may be queried. More obvious was Goodier's comparison to another English cardinal. 'Like Newman, though he steeled himself more than Newman to conceal it, he was intensely sensitive ... Wounds of more than forty years ago would open and bleed from time to time.'[20]

Bourne was especially sensitive to perceived slights from the Vatican and from his brother Bishops—partly the consequence of insecurity. His appointments to Southwark and Westminster came at too young an age. His Private Secretary noted: Bourne's 'great fault' as Bishop of Southwark 'was his youth, and naturally enough the elder men felt it.'[21] Nor was he at ease in his dealings with the Roman Curia. What others called charm and compromise, Bourne condemned as superfluity or insincerity. As a result, despite his frequent travels, he lacked the influence which the Cardinal Archbishop of the British Empire's principal city might have exercised in the universal Church. Even his much publicised visit to the Near East after the First World War was of little enduring significance.

Conflict within the hierarchy caused Bourne much pain and thwarted some of his most cherished plans. He was unfortunate in counting two consummate intriguers, Amigo and Gasquet, among his opponents. But Bourne must bear his share of the responsibility. In an ecclesiastical context Gasquet's warning was reasonable: 'You are regarded as too determined to have everything your own way and to consider everyone against you personally, who does not agree with your way of thinking.'[22] One could disagree with him and still be committed to the advancement of the Catholic faith in England, but Bourne did not see it that way. If charm and collaboration had formed part of the Cardinal's repertoire, how much more he might have achieved. Instead, his unhelpful comment to an auxiliary was: 'Hardly ever have I planned a useful bit of work without the Devil putting it into the head of some good man to spoil it.'[23] Bourne did not manage fraternal conflict well, but it is telling that there was no other member of the hierarchy with the stature to unify and pacify.

Episcopal animosity might excite historians trawling through diocesan archives, but it was hidden from ordinary Catholics of the time. Bourne's lack of pretence and finesse struck a chord with the average worshipper in the pew. His evident sincerity allowed an auxiliary to recall, 'In his public utterances in the pulpit and elsewhere, he was extraordinarily convincing.'[24]

Even by contemporary standards, the objectives Bourne set himself on arrival in Westminster were extremely focused on the internal life of the Church. He enumerated these: 'the proper organisation of the Cathedral, Archbishop's House, Clergy House, and Curia; the reconstruction of St Edmund's College with philosophical and theological studies: the Cathedral Choir School: the foundation of a secondary day-school.'[25] Some would criticise this approach as narrow and parochial, but Bourne was wise. He knew his limitations. If he could help form a good and holy priesthood, his priests in turn would spread the blessings of sound teaching and pastoral care among their people.

His concentration on the training and life of his priests was deliberate—and fruitful—as demonstrated by the increase in priestly vocations over which he presided in both Southwark and Westminster. The formation of the young drew out Bourne's higher qualities as Jackman recollected: 'His was a magnetic personality, and in those days his high ideals of what a priest, and even a church student, should be, while they aroused much criticism, fired the enthusiasm of the young levites entrusted to his care ... He was more a father than a president of the college; revered, respected, and feared—yes, but only as a loving parent; for he always mixed with us, and save for breakfast, all his meals were in our dining room. To be in his group at recreation was much sought after. This alone has struck me as sufficient evidence of the real filial affection that existed.'[26] Many priests, especially of an older generation, never succeeded in penetrating Bourne's reserve. But plenty did. To those experiencing moral or doctrinal difficulties he could provide a vital lifeline.

'The Cardinal is a sphinx'[27]

A puzzle to many of his contemporaries, what kind of a man was Bourne? He was not easily known. Frank Sheed recollected a meeting when a layman had the audacity to speak of Bourne in his presence 'as "our much loved Cardinal, may I dare call him our Francis?" The Cardinal never looked more glacial.'[28] Lord FitzAlan conceded, 'To understand the Cardinal, one had to be on intimate terms with him. He had a reserve which sometimes gave an impression almost of coldness, but to an individual in a time of trial or sorrow he would unbend with an overwhelming rush of sympathy.'[29] Archbishop Goodier's experience was similar. 'By nature the Cardinal was among the shyest of men, so shy that he would remain almost hidden in his shell; still, as is the case with most shy men, once the shell was broken he revealed himself with all the simplicity, the spontaneity, of any innocent child ... he would reveal himself as one who was true from beginning to end.'[30]

While he consorted with many in the course of his duty, the Cardinal had few, if any, close friends. He was unfailingly loyal to his acquaintance and subordinates, but he unwound to very few. Those who received his confidence were women in positions of authority. It is easy to see him seeking the affection and assurance withheld by a stern mother. One was Mother Clare Arthur, foundress of the Ursuline sisters in Brentwood. The other to whom Bourne revealed himself unreservedly was also a female religious superior, Mother Janet Stuart. To her he poured out his heart on his mother's death in 1900. 'She felt the nature of my sorrow, and the special loneliness in which I stood owing ... and with extraordinary tact she sought to make those first days of loss less terrible to bear ... During my stay, in a wonderful way she made it easy for me to speak to her.' He turned to her again when the burden of Westminster fell on his shoulders. Even after her move to Belgium in 1911, her letters continued to offer him 'every service of guidance, encouragement, and help that was in her power to do.'[31] Goodier, however, described the Cardinal's relations with Mother Stuart not in terms of friendship and affection, but rather 'respect' and 'veneration.'[32]

His tendency to reserve was partly innate, partly cultivated. For half his life, Bourne had no close family members. No one was more conscious of the need to protect priestly confidences, no one more sensitive to misinterpretation. Bourne alluded to this at the consecration of a brother Bishop. 'A Bishop is frequently misunderstood. He has constantly to take action based on knowledge of which he is absolutely sure but which in charity and as a duty of conscience he can communicate to no living soul. With such knowledge he has to act; and unless he has the confidence of his people he will certainly be misunderstood and will have to leave the clearing of the misunderstanding first to God and then to the confidence of his friends.'[33] And the Cardinal was not in the habit of confiding to friends. He followed his own advice: 'Do not burden others with your sorrow. If it is a matter which your superiors can remedy, your way is clear; if not, keep it locked up in your heart until you kneel before the Tabernacle, and then pour forth the heavy secret to Him who alone can fully understand your sorrow and renew your courage.'[34] Bourne harboured an inveterate mistrust of the loquacious. 'We may take it for granted,' he maintained, 'that many a high intent has been hindered because there has been too much talking.'[35]

It was not that he lacked humanity. Even Oldmeadow refers to Bourne's notebooks. These, 'though expressed with the utmost delicacy, make it plain that, after renouncing the world, he had to fight the flesh and the devil like any other young man.' Jackman refers to another struggle. 'There was no mistaking the fact that he had Irish blood, of which one symptom was a mixture of mildness and a quick temper, notwithstanding that, after the example of his great patron, St Francis de Sales, the latter was extraordinarily well under control and made him very holy.'[36]

There were those who admired the Cardinal for his firmness and conviction. But Goodier admitted 'at times he was over-strong, over-determined.'[37] Others were less charitable. One Bishop wrote: 'I know he is difficult to move. I know he is instinctively against things which are not his own "conceits" … he is apt to be touchy and to look on any initiative except his own as the work of an enemy bent on discrediting him.'³⁸ Vance offered his analysis: 'When Cardinal Bourne conceived an idea and held it firmly, nothing could rid him of it and nobody could reason him out of it ... He was a man of considerable holiness but was afflicted by the "Inner Light" and by an obstinacy of judgment which was unusually developed.'³⁹ This was certainly evident in the manner in which the Cardinal expressed himself. His divinely-inspired insights might have been alarming had the other Bishops not grown familiar with his ways and learnt to ignore or parry them accordingly.

That the Cardinal took difficult decisions to prayer, especially to his daily Mass, and there found guidance ought to have been unremarkable. But with Bourne it was so to a very marked degree. 'Such implicit trust in the guidance of Providence, such decision, with human reasons coming only in the second place, was a feature of the Cardinal's mentality which struck one as peculiarly his own.'⁴⁰ This could cause him to reject the legitimate views of others. Yet it is difficult to think of a case where this adversely affected the interests of the Church—save, if one accepted its merits, his own scheme for diocesan division. Another contemporary shared Vance's view—without the hyperbole. 'Around him [the Cardinal] gathered a few devoted friends, but not advisers. He sought information before he made a decision, he gathered his facts, analysed them, and then decided on his course of action. "When we know the facts we will decide," he said on more than one occasion.'⁴¹ But this was how Bishops were expected to behave. A lack of collegiality might have produced certain failings, but there was no retreat behind institutional bureaucracy. Bourne was prepared to lead and, on balance, did so wisely and well.

Glimpses of Bourne's essential kindness have been seen. He was always willing to be inconvenienced for a priest in crisis, to defend a victim of injustice. As Cardinal Archbishop of Westminster, he never forgot his more humble origins in Clapham. Forty years later he was paying a small allowance to an old family servant, arranging for her care by Ursuline sisters.⁴² Many charities and good causes received personal donations from the Cardinal over the years.

Those who knew him best make reference to the Cardinal's 'simplicity.' Within the constraints of his office, many attested to his modesty of lifestyle. But it was more than a lack of extravagance. A successor in Westminster knew him as 'a man of great personal simplicity without a trace of conceit or self-indulgence.'⁴³ It is a different picture than that painted by Amigo and Gasquet. But one senses that Jackman understood the Cardinal better. 'He was often deceived by insincere people, because he was in some respects as simple as a child, and he could get quite angry if one suggested wrong motives. Tiresome people often got their way more easily than the more yielding. His judgment of character was sometimes warped, or, rather, influenced too favourably if he liked the person in question.'[44] It was as if he had failed to develop those defence mechanisms which come to most with age. Goodier spoke of his 'intense personal affection. He found a child's delight in a childlike proof of love; he loved many far more than they ever knew, he was hurt when those he loved failed him.'[45] There was a lack of psychological and emotional sophistication that is surprising for a Cardinal Archbishop. But then it was not to the sophisticated that Our Lord promised to the kingdom of God.

'The freedom of the soul'

Those who knew him remarked how the Cardinal's apparent and profound spirituality brought warmth to an otherwise reserved personality. *Intellectually*, he reminded his priests, they were all aware that the efficacy of their priesthood depended upon 'close and intimate union with Our Lord' attained through prayer and dependence upon and submission to the Holy Spirit. But how difficult to attain in practice.[46] Jackman relates how the Cardinal's determination was brought to bear upon his spiritual life and made to serve his personal sanctification.[47] There was order and method to the interior life based upon his daily Mass, the breviary, meditation and frequent Confession.

Bourne acknowledged two pre-eminent companions, both French, in his own spiritual life. He discovered St Francis de Sales at a young age and remained faithful. The saint's fundamental humanity and moderation were an enduring influence. 'I am glad that you get on well with St Francis of Sales,' he wrote to a female religious. 'He will guide you very quietly but very far.'[48] His other choice of spiritual guide is revealing: neither a great martyr for the faith nor an illustrious prelate, but a humble French girl who died in obscurity during his own lifetime. Bourne's admiration for the Carmelite, St Thérèse of Lisieux, as God's gift to the modern Church, was unbounded. He spoke of her life as marking 'an epoch in the spiritual life of the world.' Bourne was implacably imposed to Jansenism and the spiritual damage it caused the young by etching upon their minds 'the terrible judgments and punishments of Almighty God.'

In Thérèse he discovered an ally for promoting a more authentic spirituality: 'the ideal of the loving Father Who would be obeyed through love.' He recognised that her Little Way—'to make *little* sacrifices, to do *little* things, for the love of God'—would instinctively and automatically appeal to the practical English.[49] He never ceased to extol her as a spiritual guide, not least to the many Carmels he opened and promoted.

Thérèse meant much to the Cardinal. He wrote to Mother Clare Arthur, 'I have studied her life very closely, and it is quite extraordinary in its wonderful simplicity.'[50] What particularly appealed was the example of spiritual liberty. Von Hügel recalled the Cardinal saying that 'the Little Flower' had taught him 'how little human direction certain souls need—God is their Director.'[51] The tremendous energy and confidence of the Victorians brought great gains for English Christianity, but sometimes at the risk of an insistence on obedience and control in what should have remained most intimate and free, the relationship of the individual soul to its Creator. It is to Bourne's great credit that he always insisted on this liberty. He realised that love could never be forced; the attempt to do so could be highly destructive.

He traced this principle in the prefaces he was asked to write for numerous spiritual works. There he criticised the restrictive practices which had kept many souls 'too far from the Master's feet by over-systematic tracing of the avenues of approach.'[52] He expressed frustration, even anger, at unnecessary and petty control, which had produced only 'constraint, much suffering, sterile uniformity, ultimate impotence, final decay. And individual existences, with their special gifts and powers, have been sacrificed all the time.'[53]

The Cardinal praised Blessed Columba Marmion for offering a better path. 'Many are held back by the want of simplicity, the discouraging complexity and the exaggerated refinement and multiplication of detail, which have lessened the value of so many modern spiritual books. The main object of striving has been obscured by too great insistence on the methods of attaining, and the freedom of the soul under the guidance of the Holy Ghost has been impaired. Abbot Marmion carries us back again to a wider and more wholesome tradition.'[54] Rules and regulations must always remain but means, Bourne insisted, 'and never usurp the one essential end, the union of the individual soul with God.'[55]

Bourne never compromised on the essential, but then displayed surprising flexibility as to how this might be achieved in his own life and by others. He himself insisted on at least half an hour's daily meditation, but personally found this easier later in the day when other distractions were less pressing. He suggested, for those who found it helpful, a similar adjustment to his own priests, 'putting vocal prayer in the morning, and leaving mental prayer, preferably before the Blessed Sacrament, to the late afternoon or evening hours.'[56] Goodier commented, 'Prayer was to him a very simple thing, a realisation rather than a form, a life rather than an act, a being with God rather than a speaking to Him.'[57]

Difficulties and opposition were to be taken to prayer. The Cardinal spoke from experience when he wrote to Mother Arthur, 'These great crises in life, so painful when they first manifest themselves, are full of His grace if we know how to discern and use it—and bring us very rapidly more closely to Him.'[58] It is in the spiritual life, the essence of the priesthood, that Bourne finally emerges unequivocally as a warm and attractive character, allowing his life to be informed in every respect by what he believed. FitzAlan spoke the truth when in his tribute he referred to the 'communion with his God' which was 'the chief feature' of Bourne's life.[59]

Ne cede malis

Was Francis Bourne a truly great Archbishop of Westminster? In terms of personal accomplishments, possibly not. He was, however, entirely appropriate. In many ways he was the first genuinely modern holder of the office, able to move his Church forward confidently into the twentieth century.

As Jackman noted, the Cardinal possessed moral courage, a perennial quality required of a Bishop. This was exercised at the individual level. 'Once he was convinced someone was in the wrong, he fearlessly informed the erring one in interview or letter, and did not seem to care what *he* lost in consequence.'[60] That same moral courage was exercised at the national level, and was appreciated beyond the Catholic Church. The *Times* commented, 'His pastorals and his greater speeches ... were the outcome of conscientious thinking and they always embodied definite principles.'[61]

Cardinal Bourne never failed in the Bishop's duty to act as a sentinel and a prophetic voice to his age. With clarity and perseverance, he defined and defended the most important issues for English Christianity for coming generations: the divinity of Christ and orthodox moral teaching, especially with regard to marriage and the family. This he summarised in the 1929 centennial celebrations of Emancipation: 'This, then, as it appears to me, is the special mission of the Catholic Church in this country in the second century of our recovered freedom which is opening out before us, namely to strengthen and uphold that Christianity which is based upon and rooted in belief in the Divinity of Jesus Christ Our Lord, and to maintain the tradition of the Christian moral life ... [Catholics] have it in their power to render to this England, which we all love so dearly, a service of the extent of which no one can today forecast and the value of which God alone can tell.'[62]

It was his self-possessed strength in pursuit of this mission which led Archbishop Downey to praise him: 'He was, indeed, the just and determined man whom nothing could shake from his settled purpose. His episcopal motto is a true index to his character: *ne cede malis*, "yield not to the powers of evil." And the Virgilian line continues, *sed contra audentior ito*, "but meet them with still greater firmness."'[63]

Notes

1. Goodier, 'Cardinal Bourne,' *The Month* (1935), p. 111.
2. Jackman, *Irish Catholic*, u/d cutting.
3. Oldmeadow to Editor, *Catholic Herald*, 7 June 1940.
4. Oldmeadow, *Francis Cardinal Bourne*, i, pp. xi-xii.
5. Jackman to Editor of *Catholic Herald*, 31 May 1940.
6. Aspden, *Fortress Church*, p. 12.
7. Editorial, *Times*, 2 January 1935.
8. Fisher to FitzAlan, 1935, cited, Oldmeadow, *Francis Cardinal Bourne*, ii, p. 145.
9. Vanneufville, *Le Correspondant*, December 1917, cited *Tablet*, 26 January 1918, p. 126.
10. *Times*, 1 January 1935.
11. Keating, Annual Catholic Reunion, Birmingham, 24 January 1909, *Tablet*, 30 January 1909, p. 179.
12. *Times*, 1 January 1935.
13. Goodier, 'Cardinal Bourne,' *The Month* (1935), p. 111.
14. Vanneufville, *Le Correspondant*, December 1917, cited *Tablet*, 26 January 1918, p. 125.
15. *Times*, 1 January 1935; Editorial, *Times*, 2 January 1935.
16. H. Montgomery to A. Eden, Annual Report 1935, 9 January 1936, cited Hachey (ed.), *Anglo-Vatican Relations, 1914–1939*, p. 295.
17. *Times*, 1 January 1935; Editorial, *Times*, 2 January 1935.

18 Seuffert, 'Francis Cardinal Bourne,' p. 481.
19 Archbishop Downey, 'Francis Cardinal Bourne,' *WCC*, April 1935, p. 50.
20 Goodier, 'Cardinal Bourne,' *The Month* (1935), p. 114.
21 Jackman, 'An Appreciation,' *Catholic Times*, 4 January 1935, p. 2.
22 Gasquet to FAB, u/d draft, Summer/early autumn 1917?, DAA, Gasquet, 917A.
23 Cited Oldmeadow, *Francis Cardinal Bourne*, i, p. 236.
24 Butt, cited Oldmeadow, *Francis Cardinal Bourne*, ii, p. 346.
25 FAB notebook, 22 March 1920, cited Oldmeadow, *Francis Cardinal Bourne*, ii, p. 168.
26 Jackman, 'An Appreciation,' *Catholic Times*, 4 January 1935, p. 2.
27 Fr Basil Maturin to J. Ward, 1 July 1913, copy, SAUL, Ward Family Papers, ms 38347/VII/199/2/9.
28 Sheed, *The Church and I*, p. 171.
29 Fitzalan, BBC Tribute broadcast, 4 January 1935.
30 Goodier, 'Cardinal Bourne,' *The Month* (1935), p. 110.
31 FAB memorandum, 13 August 1915, cited Jackman, 'Reminiscences of Cardinal Bourne,' *Wonersh Magazine*, May 1935, pp. 24–25.
32 Goodier, 'Cardinal Bourne,' *The Month* (1935), p. 109.
33 FAB speech, 25 February 1908, cited Oldmeadow, *Francis Cardinal Bourne*, i, p. 271.
34 FAB homily, English College, Lisbon, 6 October 1922, *Tablet*, 21 October 1922, p. 532.
35 FAB speech, Ushaw centenary, 28 July 1908, *Tablet*, 1 August 1908, p. 180.
36 Jackman, *Irish Catholic*, 13 June 1940.
37 Goodier, 'Cardinal Bourne,' *The Month* (1935), p. 111.
38 Dunn to Whiteside, 25 March 1920 (copy), NotDA, G.04.01, cited Aspden, *Fortress Church*, p. 119.
39 Vance, 'Notes on St Edmund's College,' January 1960, AAW, I/110.
40 Goodier, 'Cardinal Bourne,' *The Month*, (1935), p. 112.
41 Seuffert, *'Francis Cardinal Bourne,'* p. 483.
42 FAB to Arthur, 1 January 1906 (copy), BDA.
43 Heenan, *Cardinal Hinsley*, p. 21.
44 Jackman, 'Francis Cardinal Bourne,' *The Dublin Review*, April 1935.
45 Goodier, 'Cardinal Bourne,' *The Month* (1935), p. 114.
46 FAB, *Allocution at the Diocesan Synod*, 6 October 1925, p. 3.
47 Jackman, 'Reminiscences of Cardinal Bourne,' *Wonersh Magazine*, November 1935, p. 85.
48 FAB to Arthur, 7 November 1896 (copy).
49 FAB, Kensington Carmel, 16 October 1923, *Tablet*, 20 October 1923, p. 494.
50 FAB to Arthur, 26 October 1923 (copy), BDA.
51 de la Bedoyère, *The Life of Baron von Hügel*, p. 350.

52 FAB, 'Preface,' C. S. Durrant, *A Link between Flemish Mystics and English Martyrs* (London: Burns Oates & Washbourne Ltd, 1925), p. vi.
53 FAB, 'Introduction,' M. Monahan, *Life and Letters of Janet Erskine Stuart* (London: Longmans, 1922), p. vii.
54 FAB, 'Preface,' Abbot C. Marmion, *Christ the Life of the Soul* (London: Sands & Co, 1925), p. 11.
55 FAB, 'Introduction,' Monahan, *Life and Letters of Janet Erskine Stuart*, p. viii.
56 FAB, Allocution at the Diocesan Synod, 6 October 1925, p. 6.
57 Goodier, 'Cardinal Bourne,' *The Month* (1935), p. 112.
58 FAB to Arthur, 13 April 1927, BDA (copy).
59 Fitzalan, Tribute, 4 January 1935.
60 Jackman, 'Francis Cardinal Bourne,' *Dublin Review*, April 1935.
61 *Times*, 1 January 1935.
62 FAB, 'Education and Morality,' National Catholic Congress, Royal Albert Hall, 13 September 1929, cited FAB, *Congress Addresses*, pp. 200–201.
63 Downey, 'Francis Cardinal Bourne,' *WCC*, April 1935, p. 49.

Sources and Bibliography

Primary Sources

Archives of the Archbishop of Westminster
Bourne Papers
Hinsley Papers
Moyes Papers
Roman Letters
St Edmund's College Archives
Acta of the Bishops' Conference of England and Wales
Westminster Diocesan Almanac and Directory

Arundel Castle Archives
15th Duke of Norfolk Papers
Viscount FitzAlan, Family Correspondence

Birmingham Archdiocesan Archives
Central Seminary Papers
Ilsley Papers
Parkinson Correspondence

Bodleian Library, Oxford
Asquith Papers
Fisher Diary
Marchant Papers

Brentwood Diocesan Archives
Doubleday Papers
Mother Clare Arthur Papers
Ward Papers

Clifton Diocesan Archives
Burton Papers

Downside Abbey Archives
Gasquet Papers

House of Lords Records Office
Lloyd George Papers

Lambeth Palace Library
Bishop Bell Papers
Archbishop Davidson Papers
Archbishop Lang Papers

National Archives
Home Office Papers
Foreign Office Papers
War Office Papers

National Library of Ireland
John Redmond Papers

Northampton Diocesan Archives
Keating Papers
Riddell Papers

Nottingham Diocesan Archives
Brindle Papers
Dunn Papers

Portsmouth Diocesan Archives
Cahill Papers

Sources and Bibliography

Rome, Sacred Congregation for the Propagation of the Faith

St Andrew's University Library
Ley papers
Von Hügel Papers
Ward Family Papers

St John's Seminary, Wonersh, Archives

Servite General Archives, Rome
Archivio Generale (Storico)—Lépicier Papers

Sheffield University Library
Hewins Manuscripts

Southwark Archdiocesan Archives
Amigo Papers
Bourne Papers
Chaplains' Papers
Chapter Records

Ushaw College Archives
Bourne Family Papers
Broadhead Papers

Magazines, Newspapers and Periodicals
Catholic Herald
Catholic Times
Clergy Review
Daily Telegraph
The Dublin Review
Evening Standard

The Month
The Ransomer
Salesian Bulletin
The Shield
South London Press
The Tablet
The Times
Truth
The Universe
Ushaw Magazine
The Venerabile
Westminster Cathedral Chronicle
The Wonersh Magazine

Primary Printed Sources

Catholic Directory of England and Wales

Oxford Dictionary of National Biography

F. A., Cardinal Bourne, *Ecclesiastical Training* (London: Burns Oates & Washbourne Ltd, 1926)

F. A., Cardinal Bourne, 'The Catholic Apostolic Roman Church', in J. Marchant (ed.), *The Reunion of Christendom: A Survey of the Present Position* (London: Cassell & Co, 1929)

F. A., Cardinal Bourne, *Congress Addresses* (London: Burns, Oates & Washbourne Ltd, 1929)

F. A., Cardinal Bourne, *Occasional Sermons* (London: Sheed & Ward, 1930)

R. J. Dingle, *Cardinal Bourne at Westminster* (London: Burns, Oates & Washbourne Ltd, 1934)

W. Meynell (ed.), *A Record of the Sayings and Doings of Francis, Fourth Archbishop of Westminster* (London: Burns & Oates, 1911)

A British Cardinal's Visit to the Western Front (London: 1918)

The Story of the Congress (London: Burns & Oates, 1908)

Report of Lambeth Conference, 1920 (London: SPCK, 1920)

Sources and Bibliography

Report of the Nineteenth Eucharistic Congress (London: Sands & Co, 1909)

The Conversations at Malines 1921–1925 (Oxford: OUP, 1927)

Secondary Printed Sources

Books

P. Ackroyd, *London: The Biography* (London: Chatto & Windus, 2000)

L. Andrews, *The Education Act 1918* (London: Routledge & Kegan Paul, 1976)

K. Aspden, *Fortress Church: The English Roman Catholic Bishops and Politics 1903–63* (Leominster: Gracewing, 2002)

A. Auffray, SDB, *Saint Don Bosco* (Macclesfield: St. Dominic Savio House, 1964)

B. Barlow, 'A Brother Knocking at the Door': *The Malines Conversations 1921–1925* (Norwich: Canterbury Press, 1996)

J. Barr, *A Line in the Sand: Britain, France and the Struggle that Shaped the Middle East* (London: Simon & Schuster, 2011)

G. Beck (ed.), *The English Catholics 1850–1950* (London: Burns & Oates, 1950)

G. K. A. Bell, *Randall Davidson*, 3rd ed. (London: OUP, 1952)

B. Bogan, *The Great Link: A History of St George's Cathedral*, 2nd ed. (London: Burns & Oates, 1958)

D. G. Boyce, *Englishmen and Irish Troubles: British Public Opinion and the Making of Irish Policy 1918–1922* (London: Jonathan Cape, 1972)

M. J. Broadley, *Louis Charles Casartelli: A Bishop in Peace and War* (Manchester: Koinonia Press, 2006)

W. Brown, *Through Windows of Memory* (London: Sands & Co Ltd, 1946)

P. Caraman, SJ, *C. C. Martindale: A Biography* (London: Longmans, 1967)

G. Clegg, *Clapham Past* (London: Historical Publications Ltd, 1998)

M. Clifton & D. Goddard, *The Shrine of Our Lady of Consolation & St Francis West Grinstead: A Short History*

M. Clifton, *Amigo: Friend of the Poor* (Leominster: Fowler Wright Books Ltd, 1987)

M. Clifton, *A History of the Archdiocese of Southwark* (London: The Saint Austin Press, 2000)

M. Cruickshank, *Church and State in English Education* (London: Macmillan, 1964)

M. de la Bedoyère, *The Life of Baron von Hügel* (London: J. M. Dent & Sons Ltd, 1951)

J. A. Dick, *The Malines Conversations Revisited* (Leuven: Leuven University Press, 1989)

P. Doyle, *Westminster Cathedral 1895–1995* (London: Geoffrey Chapman, 1995)

S. Finnegan, *In Hope of Harvest: The Story of St John's Seminary* (Wonersh: The Wonersh Press, 2011)

M. Fletcher, *O, Call Back Yesterday* (Ware: The Old Hall Press, 2000)

S. Foster, *A History of the Diocese of Brentwood, 1917–1992* (Brentwood: Diocese of Brentwood, 1994)

P. Galloway, *A Passionate Humility: Frederick Oakeley and the Oxford Movement* (Leominster: Gracewing, 1999)

W. T. Gribbin, *St Edmund's College Bicentenary Book, 1793–1993* (Old Hall Green, 1993)

J. Hagerty, *Cardinal Hinsley* (Oxford: Family Publications, 2008)

A. Hastings (ed.), *Bishops and Writers: Aspects of the Evolution of Modern English Catholicism* (Wheathampstead: Anthony Clarke, 1977)

A. Hastings, *A History of English Christianity 1920–1990* (London: SCM Press, 1991)

S. Hastings, *Evelyn Waugh: A Biography* (London: Sinclair-Stevenson, 1994)

J. C., Cardinal Heenan, *Cardinal Hinsley* (London: Burns Oates & Washbourne Ltd, 1944)

J. C., Cardinal Heenan, *Not the Whole Truth* (London: Hodder & Stoughton, 1972)

H. Hemmer, *Fernand Portal (1855–1926): Apostle of Unity* (London: Macmillan, 1961)

J. B. Hogan, *Clerical Studies* (Boston: Marlier, Callnan & Co, 1898)

T. Hooley, *A Seminary in the Making* (London: Longmans, Green and Co Ltd, 1927)

R. Jenkins, *Asquith* (London: Collins, 1964)

T. Johnstone & J. Hagerty, *The Cross on the Sword: Catholic Chaplains in the Forces* (London: Geoffrey Chapman, 1996)

R. Jonas, *France and the Cult of the Sacred Heart* (Berkeley: University of California Press, 2000)

Sources and Bibliography

S. Leslie, *The Passing Chapter* (London: Cassells, 1934)

S. Leslie, *Cardinal Gasquet: A Memoir* (London: Burns Oates, 1953)

D. Miller, *Church, State & Nation in Ireland, 1898–1921* (Pittsburgh: University of Pittsburgh Press, 1973)

M. McInally, *Edward Ilsley: Archbishop of Birmingham* (London: Burns & Oates, 2002)

T. Moloney, *Westminster, Whitehall and the Vatican* (London: Burns & Oates, 1985)

M. Monahan, *Life and Letters of Janet Erskine Stuart* (London: Longmans, Green and Co, 1922)

J. Murphy, *Church, State and Schools in Britain, 1800–1970* (London: Routledge and Kegan Paul, 1971)

E. Oldmeadow, *Francis Cardinal Bourne*, 2 vols. (London: Burns Oates & Washbourne Ltd, 1940 & 1944)

R. O'Neil, MHM, *Cardinal Herbert Vaughan* (Tunbridge Wells: Burns & Oates, 1995)

J. Pollard, *The Unknown Pope: Benedict XV (1914–1922) and the Pursuit of Peace* (London: Geoffrey Chapman, 1999)

A. Randall, *A Vatican Assignment* (London: William Heinemann Ltd, 1956)

B. Reardon, *Roman Catholic Modernism* (London: A. & C. Black, 1970)

P. Rogers, *Westminster Cathedral: From Darkness to Light* (London: Burns & Oates, 2003)

H. Rope, *Benedict XV* (London: The Catholic Book Club, 1940)

G. Stebbing, CSSR, *History of St. Mary's, Clapham* (London: Sands & Co., 1935)

F. Valentine, OP, *Father Vincent McNabb* (London: Burns & Oates, 1955)

A. Vidler, *A Variety of Catholic Modernists* (Cambridge: CUP, 1970)

M. Ward, *Insurrection versus Resurrection* (London: Sheed & Ward, 1937)

M. Ward, *Unfinished Business* (London: Sheed & Ward, 1964)

R. Watt, *Robert Hugh Benson: Captain in God's Army* (London: Burns & Oates, 1918)

E. Waugh, *The Life of Ronald Knox* (London: Chapman & Hall, 1959)

M. Williams, *Oscott College in the Twentieth Century* (Leominster: Gracewing, 2001)

P. Williamson, *Stanley Baldwin* (Cambridge: CUP, 1999)

K. Wykeham-George, OP, & G. Mathew, OP, *Bede Jarrett* (London: Blackfriars Publications, 1952)

M. Yelton, *Anglican Papalism 1900–1960: An Illustrated History* (Norwich: Canterbury Press, 2008)

Articles

K. Aspden, 'The English Roman Catholic Bishops and the Social Order, 1918–1926' in *Recusant History*, 25, 4 (2001), pp. 543–64

R. Aubert, 'The History of the Malines Conversations,' in *One in Christ*, 1 (1967), pp. 56–66

R. Aubert, 'Cardinal Mercier, Cardinal Bourne and the Malines Conversations,' *One in Christ*, 4 (1968), pp. 372–379

A. Bellenger, OSB, 'Cardinal Gasquet (1846–1929): an English Roman,' in *Recusant History*, 24,4 (1999), pp. 552–560

J. Cashman, 'The 1906 Education Bill: Catholic Peers and Irish Nationalists,' in *Recusant History*, 18,4 (1987), pp. 422–439

J. Davies, 'Catholic Representatives in Parliament: The North West of England, 1918–1945,' in *Recusant History*, 26,2 (2002), pp. 359–383

J. Davies, '"War is a Scourge": The First Year of the Great War 1914–1915: Catholics and Pastoral Guidance' in *Recusant History*, 30,3 (2011), pp. 485–500

P. Doyle, 'Charles Plater and the Origins of the Catholic Social Guild,' in *Recusant History*, 21,3 (1993), pp. 401–417

P. Doyle, '"To Whom Should We Turn?": Aspects of the Relationship between the English and Welsh Hierarchy and Rome, 1880s–1920s,' in *Recusant History*, 29,4 (2009), pp. 523–539

J. M. Fewster, 'The Royal Declaration against Transubstantiation and the Struggle against Religious Discrimination in the Early Twentieth Century,' in *Recusant History*, 30,4 (2011), pp. 555–572

S. Foster, 'A Bishop for Essex: Bernard Ward and the Diocese of Brentwood,' in *Recusant History*, 21,4 (1993), pp. 556–571

S. Foster, 'Bernard Ward: Edmundian and Historian,' in S. Gilley (ed.), *Victorian Churches and Churchmen* (Woodbridge: Catholic Record Society, 2005), pp. 163–182

Sources and Bibliography

S. Foster, 'Prelates at War: Cardinal Bourne, Bishop Ward and the St Edmund's College Cadet Corps Dispute' in *Recusant History*, 30,2 (2010), pp. 343–376

T. Horwood, 'Public Opinion and the 1908 Eucharistic Congress,' in *Recusant History*, 25,1 (2000), pp. 120–131

N. Lash, 'Modernism, aggiornamento and the night battle,' in A. Hastings (ed.), *Bishops and Writers* (Wheathampstead: Anthony Clarke, 1977), pp. 51–79

G. I. T. Machin, 'The Liberal Government and the Eucharistic Procession of 1908,' in Journal of *Ecclesiastical History*, 34 (1983), pp. 559–583

V. A. McClelland, 'Bourne, Norfolk and the Irish Parliamentarians: Roman Catholics and the Education Bill of 1906,' in *Recusant History*, 23,2 (1996), pp. 228–256

V. A. McClelland, 'St Edmund's College, Ware and St Edmund's College, Cambridge: Historical Connections and Early Tribulations,' in *Recusant History*, 23,4 (1997), pp. 470–482

P. Scotti, OSB, 'Wilfrid Ward and The Dublin Review,' in *Downside Review* (July 1999), pp. 191–216

S. Seuffert, 'Francis Cardinal Bourne,' in C. Williamson (ed.), *Great Catholics* (London: Catholic Book Club, 1939), pp. 481–490

M. Snape, 'British Catholicism and the British Army in the First World War,' in *Recusant History*, 26,2 (2002), pp. 314–358

Y. Taouk, 'The Guild of the Pope's Peace: A British Peace Movement in the First World War,' in *Recusant History*, 29,2 (2008), pp. 252–271

M. J. Weaver, 'George Tyrrell and the Joint Pastoral Letter,' in *Downside Review*, 99 (January 1981), pp. 18–39

Index

Members of the Church are indexed under the latest title used in the text.

Admiralty 332, 336, 338, 573
Amigo, Bishop Peter 88, 128, 366, 374, 375, 382, 433–434, 460–461, 518, 519, 530, 568, 582
   cardinalate, accused of blocking FAB's 240, 241, 242
   diocesan division 283, 284–293, 296–308
   FAB, criticism of 182, 363, 419
   FAB, collaboration with and affection for 88, 89, 91, 120, 251–252, 257, 275–276
   FAB, dispute with 251–276, 313, 553, 579
   hierarchy, relations with 180, 314, 315, 317
   Ireland 396, 399, 400, 401, 404, 407, 408, 411
   military chaplains/bishop 334, 336, 338, 339, 340
   Modernism 212, 213, 219, 229, 239
   Rome, appeal to 266–267, 269, 270–272
   Southwark, appointment as Bishop of 117, 119–120, 121, 122, 123, 251
   Southwark, Vicar–General of 96, 118, 120
   transfer, proposed from Southwark 268, 270–271, 283, 285, 286, 288, 289, 296, 310
   World War I 326, 342, 345
Anglicans 364, 405, 418, 444, 457, 469, 470, 471, 472, 479–484, 486, 496, 505–508
   Anglo–Papalists 507–508, 509
   competition with 198, 296, 308, 310, 313
   cooperation with 442–443, 450–451, 455–456, 475, 476, 520
   denominational schools 134–135, 138, 142, 143, 157, 164, 169, 170, 171, 172, 179, 181
   General Strike 520, 521–523
   military chaplains 334, 335, 340
Anning Bell, Robert 543
Anti-Catholic legislation 200, 203, 420, 426, 428–429
   Roman Catholic Relief Act 1926 429–430, 517
   Royal Declaration 426–428
anti-Catholicism 99n., 198, 290, 332
anti-Semitism 367–368, 375
Antrobus, Fr Frederick 81
Apostolicae Curae (1896) 480
Appeal to All Christian People (1920) 481, 482–483, 484
Arabs 368–369, 370
Arthur, Mother Clare 84, 98, 501, 580, 584, 585
Asquith, Herbert 303, 331, 333, 427–428
   education 169–170, 171
   Eucharistic Congress 200, 201–203, 204, 205, 206, 208
Assumption, Warwick Street 6
Athenaeum 475, 503, 528

Baden-Powell, Sir Robert 463
Bagshawe, Archbishop Edward 223–224
Baldwin, Stanley 429, 430, 517, 522
Balfour, Arthur 136, 153, 157, 345, 363, 367, 369, 380
Banfi, Fr Serafino 83
Barrett, Fr George 65, 83
Barton Brown, Mgr Henry 473

Batiffol, Mgr Pierre 486, 499, 501
Battersea 58, 570
BBC 517, 519, 521, 523, 569
Beauduin, Dom Lambert, OSB 488
Belgium 13, 14, 16, 25, 27, 46–47, 325, 326, 328, 344, 346, 348, 359
Bell, Rev George 486, 490
Belloc, Hilaire 141, 146–147
Benedict XV, Pope 175, 176, 233, 312, 316, 343, 481
   diocesan division 284, 289–290, 296, 297, 298, 299, 302, 303, 304, 305, 306, 307, 308, 363, 367, 380, 407
   military chaplains/bishop 337, 338
   Peace Note (1917) 346–349
   World War I 343, 344, 345–349
Benson, Fr Robert Hugh 291, 318, 473, 528
Bentinck, Lord Henry 402
Bentley, John 40, 542, 543, 544
Bergh, Abbot Thomas, OSB 213, 220, 269, 273, 453–454
Bidwell, Bishop Manuel 179, 182, 183, 224, 342, 454, 492, 501, 567
   Amigo–FAB dispute 268, 271, 272
   London, unification as one Diocese 283, 284, 285
   military chaplains/bishop 331, 332, 334, 336, 339, 340
Billot, Louis, Cardinal, SJ 366
Birrell, Augustine 141, 143, 144, 145, 150, 151, 152, 154, 155, 156, 157, 170
birth control 456–460, 476
Bishop, William 124–125, 256, 257
Bisleti, Gaetano, Cardinal 377, 532, 558, 559
Blackheath 52, 53, 54, 58, 64
Blackfriars, Oxford 189
Blundell, Francis 183, 429
Booth, General William 443, 475
Boris II, King of Bulgaria 362, 367
Bourne, Agnes 13, 28

Bourne, Charles 2, 13, 28
Bourne, Edward 2, 3, 4, 6, 13, 29, 39, 40, 52
Bourne, Ellen (née Byrne) 5–6, 7, 13, 22, 23, 24, 25–26, 28, 29, 30, 31, 36, 43, 45, 52, 57, 97, 387, 580
Bourne, Francis, Cardinal
   Amigo, dispute with 251–276
   anti-Catholic legislation 420, 427–430, 517
   anti-Semitism 367–368, 370, 375
   assessment of 575–578, 585–586
   birth control 456–460, 476
   Canada 360–361
   Cardinal, creation as 207, 239–248, 380
   Catholic Party, opposition to 420–421, 424–425
   Catholic Women's League 326, 366–367, 460, 461–463, 535, 568
   character 26, 52, 122, 129, 240, 246–247, 272, 325, 387, 577, 578, 579, 580–583, 585, 586
   childhood 11–18
   clergy, relations with 230–231, 530–533, 539
   Coadjutor Bishop 82–83, 84
   continuity with medieval Church, emphasizes 115–116, 205, 312–313, 418, 470–471, 547, 556, 571
   converts 472, 473–475, 498, 502
   COPEC 450–456, 476
   curate 52–64
   death 572
   dictators 373–376
   diocesan divisions, proposals for 271, 281, 282–311
   doctrine 441, 442, 470, 472, 585, 586
   education, commitment to 116, 133, 134, 135, 147, 171, 187, 188, 541, 571
   Education Crisis, leadership during 136–172, 281, 576
   educational reform, subsequent proposals 173–187

Index

Eucharistic Congress (London 1908) 198–208, 244, 281, 427, 576
evangelisation 117, 291–292, 295, 310–311, 472, 538
financial misconduct, allegations of 124–129, 256, 269
formation of clergy 42, 65–67, 69–71, 75, 77, 87–88, 530, 549, 553, 554–556, 579–580
funeral and burial 572–573
further studies 46–47
General Strike 429, 450, 515–516, 517–524, 576
health 13, 21, 26, 29, 31, 39, 41, 42, 47, 51, 73, 173, 176, 180, 308, 315, 454, 567–570, 571–572
hierarchy, relations with 122–123, 128, 145, 161, 175–176, 281, 300, 301–302, 303, 304, 307, 308, 311, 312, 313–315, 316–318, 381, 397, 405, 408, 567–568, 578, 579
Holy See's unofficial representative in London 343–344, 381–382
international affairs 357–359, 362
Ireland 6, 387–412, 530–531, 576
Labour Party 430–436, 576
laity, relations with 449, 533–537
League of Nations 371–373, 376, 475
Malines Conversations 479, 488–501, 502, 503, 505
military/naval chaplains/bishop 91, 92, 93–95, 108, 110, 329, 331–334, 336–340
Modernism 128, 211–233, 239–240, 241, 242
morality 441, 456, 476, 585, 586
Near Eastern & Balkan tour 362–367, 578
non–Catholics, relations with 470–471, 472, 475–476
Pastoral Letters 116, 147–148, 229, 326, 328–329, 363, 373, 405, 407, 411, 442, 445, 493, 502, 539, 541, 571, 585
patriotism 325, 326, 329, 365, 373, 388, 417, 418, 577
politics 418–422, 576

Primate of England & Wales, proposed 312–313
religious life 39, 56–58
reunion 481–482, 483, 484, 493–494, 500, 501–503, 505–506, 508–510
Roman Curia, dealings with 87, 122, 127, 175–176, 243, 272, 293, 296–297, 300, 307, 311, 338, 367, 376–378, 400, 532–533, 558–559, 578
Rome, FAB's visits to 76, 84, 95, 96, 97, 110, 115, 120, 122, 164, 180, 247, 254, 267, 270, 291, 293, 296, 297, 298, 337, 342, 357, 362, 407, 492–493, 499, 548, 552, 569
routine 527–529
schooldays 21–32, 35–36
seminarian 36–46
Seminary Rector 64–78, 83
social teaching 431, 435, 444–449, 516
Southwark, Bishop of 83–98, 118–119
Southwark, alleged subsequent interference in 117–118, 119, 121, 255, 259, 263, 267, 273, 274–275
spirituality 38, 52–53, 582, 583–585
St Edmund's College 31–32, 35, 36, 37, 38, 549, 550–560, 573, 579
Temperance 116, 442–444, 475
vocation 35–36, 529–530, 579
Westminster, appointment as Archbishop 103, 107–113, 115
Westminster, as diocesan Bishop 527–536, 538–542
Westminster Cathedral 542–549
Westminster Catholic Federation 146, 327, 422–425, 460
World War I 177, 295, 303, 325–351, 375, 444, 445
Zionism 368–371
Bourne, Harry 7–8, 13, 17, 21, 22, 23, 24–25, 26, 27, 28–29
Bourne, Henry (grandfather) 1, 2, 3, 4–5
Bourne, Henry (father) 2, 3, 4, 5, 6, 7, 13, 14, 15, 16, 17, 18, 21, 22–24, 25, 26, 387

Bourne, Sarah (née Hodson) 1, 2, 4, 13, 29, 52
Brade, Sir Reginald 342
Braye, Lord 428
Brentwood (Essex), Diocese of 284, 296, 297, 298, 300, 302, 308, 309, 311
Brighton (Sussex), proposed Diocese of 264, 268, 271, 286, 287, 288, 291, 296, 297
Brindle, Bishop Robert 104, 158
Brodrick, St John 95
Brotherton, Fr Albert 73
Brown, Bishop William 205, 337, 405
    education 145, 150, 151, 154–155, 156, 160, 170, 179–180
    Amigo–FAB dispute 258, 259, 262, 265, 268, 269, 270, 272, 273, 285–286
Buckfast Abbey 568
Burns, Fr Cecil 230, 231
Burns, Thomas 424–425, 432, 433, 434
Burnt Oak 539
Burton, Fr Edwin 252, 255, 554
Burton, Bishop George Ambrose 143, 159, 161, 205, 316
Butler, Abbot Cuthbert 505, 506, 507
Butt, Bishop John 56–57, 58, 59, 60, 81, 82, 84, 85, 86, 87, 258, 273, 421
    criticism of 72, 81
    founds Seminary 63–64, 67, 68, 74, 75, 76, 77
    illness and death 81, 82, 83
Butt, Bishop Joseph 99n., 212, 570, 571, 572
    cardinalate, FAB's 240, 241, 242
    Rector of St John's Seminary 83, 212, 213, 253–254
Byrne, John 5
Byrne, Mary 5–6, 13, 14, 23, 25, 26, 29, 31, 43, 45, 52, 97

Byrne, Matilda 5

Cahill, Bishop John 92, 93, 124, 125, 128, 147, 207, 244, 317–318, 529, 552, 553
    cardinalate, defends FAB's cause 240, 241, 242
    Westminster, promotes FAB's candidacy for 107–108, 109, 110, 527
Camberwell 27, 29, 37, 39, 51, 52, 53, 54
Cambridge
    Diocese, proposed of 291, 298, 300, 305, 310
    University 189
Camm, Fr Bede, OSB 240, 241, 517, 518
Campbell–Bannerman, Sir Henry 139, 141–142, 152, 155, 166, 169
Canada 360–361
Cardinal Vaughan Memorial School 541–542
Carey, Fr Thomas 392–394
Carmelites 540
Carton de Wiart, Mgr Maurice 497, 529
Cary–Elwes, Bishop Dudley Charles 310
Casartelli, Bishop Louis 47, 317, 328, 330, 347, 359, 396, 404, 422, 424, 425
    diocesan division 299, 300, 301, 306
    education 147, 158, 169, 175, 176, 177
    Labour Party 430, 432, 433
Casement, Sir Roger 392–394
Catholic Action 425
Catholic Church in England & Wales
    converts 335, 472–475
    expansion 12, 311, 538, 577
    Provinces, new 246, 264, 268, 269, 290, 292, 293, 310, 311–312
    Primate of, proposed 312–313

Index

Catholic Council for International Relations 357–358, 375
Catholic Education Council 138, 145, 151, 154, 158, 159, 160, 180
Catholic Evidence Guild 535–536
Catholic Land Movement 449
Catholic Missionary Society 539
Catholic Party, proposals for 420–421, 424–425
Catholic Prisoners' Aid Society 325, 568
Catholic Social Guild 432–433, 444–447, 449, 451, 452, 453, 455, 460, 518
Catholic Trades Unionists 432, 434, 516
Catholic Truth Society 447, 458, 535
Catholic Union 396, 397, 404, 425–426, 432, 433, 446, 458
Catholic Women's League 326–327, 366–367, 460, 461–463, 535, 568
Cecil, Algernon 501, 518–519
Cecil, Lord Robert 143, 345, 372
Central Seminary 74, 75, 107, 240, 549–553
Cerretti, Archbishop Bonavenrura 290, 558
Charity Commissioners 126, 127, 128, 156, 257, 261
Churchill, Winston 169, 199, 206, 332, 519
Clapham 7, 12–13, 14–15, 18n., 25, 51, 582
Clifford, Dr John 137, 141, 143, 144, 172, 475
Clune, Archbishop Patrick 409
Coats, Stuart 433
Coffin, Bishop Robert 7, 8, 14, 15, 21, 51, 52, 58, 60n.
Communism 310, 375, 508
Conan Doyle, Arthur 359

Concistorial Congregation 271–272, 284, 290, 297, 298, 299, 300, 312, 338, 339
   FAB's membership of 298, 300, 318
Congo 359, 392
Connelly, Canon 67, 68, 92
conscription 341–342
Conservative Party 418–419, 420
   denominational education 136, 137, 138, 139, 150, 153, 162, 181, 185, 576
Considine, Fr Daniel, SJ 212, 232, 529
converts 472, 473–475, 492, 495, 502, 509, 540
Coote, Mgr Charles 115, 119
Coote, Mgr George 529, 572
COPEC 451–456, 476
Cotter, Bishop William 267, 301, 317, 399, 400, 476
Crewe, Earl of 201
Croke Robinson, Mgr Walter 224
Crookall, Provost 41
Curzon, Lord 397
Czechoslovakia 462

Dalston 26, 27
Danell, Bishop James 39, 41, 42, 51, 59, 63
D'Arcy, Fr Martin, SJ 506, 507
Davidson, Archbishop Randall 372, 400, 405, 442, 443, 456, 469–470, 475
   education 144, 153, 170, 171, 173, 179
   General Strike 517, 520, 521, 522–524
   Malines Conversations 483, 484–485, 486, 487, 488, 490, 491, 498, 503
   reunion 502, 503–504
Davies, Thomas 180–181
Dawes Trust 86, 88, 124–125, 129, 257, 259–260, 261, 266, 269
Dawson, Lord 457

De Lai, Gaetano, Cardinal 267, 268, 269, 270, 271, 283, 284, 286, 287, 288, 292, 296, 297, 298, 299, 300, 302, 307, 309, 338, 340, 401
Dean, H. S. 492
Denis, Mgr Jean-Marie 59, 60
Derby, Earl of 341
de Salis, Count 343, 345
Dessoulavy, Fr Charles 212, 213
de Verteuil, Alexander 27
D'Houet, Mother Mary Madeleine, FCJ 5
dictators 373–376
Dillon, John 146, 152, 155, 156, 160, 162, 395
diocesan division 270, 271, 274, 281–311
  background 281–283, 305, 307
  Low Week meeting, 1917 291, 299, 300, 301, 303–308, 339, 567
  Oscott meeting, 15 March 1917 301, 304, 305, 307, 314
disarmament 375–376
divorce 456, 460, 475, 476
Dodsworth, Rev 4
Dominicans 39, 60, 189
Doreau, Dom 63
Doubleday, Bishop Arthur 254, 255, 274, 285
Downey, Archbishop Richard 183, 570, 578, 586
Downside, Abbey 106, 107, 108
Driberg, Tom 473
Driscoll, Canon James 541
Drummond, Sir Eric 372
Dubois, Louis-Ernest, Cardinal 366, 384n.
Duchemin, Mgr Charles 291, 310, 320n.
Duchesne, Fr Louis 214, 232
Dublin 5, 388, 391
Dublin Review 222, 223, 224, 225, 232

Dundalk 27
Dunn, Bishop Thomas 177, 297, 299, 300, 301, 302, 305, 309, 316, 339, 397, 399, 405, 406, 452, 475

Ebbsfleet 84
education—see also universities and Westminster, Archdiocese of, schools
  Church's commitment to Catholic schools 133–134, 135, 144
  Hadow Report 181, 186
  secondary schools 165–166, 177, 181, 186–187
  teacher training colleges 166
  voucher system, proposal 185–186
Education Act 1902 108, 116, 136–137, 138, 139, 146, 172
Education Bill 1906 127, 142–163
Education Bill (Special Religious Instruction) Bill 1907 163–165
Education Bill (No. 1) 1908 167–169
Education Bill (No. 2) 1908 170–171
Education Bill 1917 173–177
Education Act 1918 177–179
Education Bill 1921 180–181
Education Bill 1929 182
Education Bill 1930 182–183
Education Bill 1931 184–185
Education Regulations 1907 regarding secondary schools 165–166, 177, 187
Education Regulations 1907 regarding teacher training 166
Edward VII 198, 201, 206, 243, 376, 417, 427, 428
Egypt 1, 3, 4, 23–24, 362, 365, 366
Ellis, Frances 98
English College, Douai 21, 30, 42, 275, 549, 554
English College, Rome 41–42, 247, 378–379
England, Fr Henry 538

Eppstein, John 358
Escarguel, Edward 65
Eucharistic Congress (Metz, 1907) 198
Eucharistic Congress (London, 1908) 197–208, 244, 427, 548
Eucharistic Congress (Montreal, 1910) 360–361
Eucharistic Congress (Dublin, 1932) 410
Evans, Canon Lionel 529

Fascism 373, 374
Fenton, Bishop Patrick 115, 119, 121–122, 123, 550, 551
Ferdinand, King of Rumania 363
Finchley Catholic Grammar School 542
Fisher, Herbert 173–174, 175, 176, 177, 178, 179, 180, 575–576
FitzAlan, Viscount (Lord Edmund Talbot) 418, 429, 430, 501, 567, 580, 585
   Education Crisis 156, 161, 162
   Ireland 381, 409, 410
   as political intermediary 95, 175, 178, 184, 331, 369, 380, 382, 428
Fitzgerald bequest 556, 559
Fleming, Fr David 77, 120, 121, 243, 246, 376–377
Fletcher, Margaret 461, 462, 466n.
Fooks, Edward 86, 259, 260
Ford, Fr Thomas 52, 54
France 38, 77, 84, 325, 329, 358, 364, 366, 369, 376
Frere, Dr Walter 485, 489
Füchter, Fr Albert 73
Fuller, Canon Reggie 275, 378, 530–531, 539, 554, 555

Gardner, Lucy 451
Garvie, Dr Alfred 505, 507
Gasparri, Pietro, Cardinal 337, 348, 365, 380, 407, 486, 490, 494, 495
Gasquet, Aidan, Cardinal, OSB 77, 121, 128, 175, 231, 232, 239, 246, 274, 309, 400, 407, 433, 536, 549, 568, 582
   diocesan division 283, 297, 298, 299, 301, 302, 304, 305, 306, 311
   FAB, opposition to 106–107, 120–121, 128–129, 299, 338, 339, 559, 579
   Malines Conversations 491, 494, 495, 496, 497, 499
   military chaplains/bishop 334, 337, 338, 339, 340
   Modernism 216, 229
   Westminster, candidate for 104, 106–107, 108, 109, 111, 112, 113, 339
   World War I 343, 344, 345, 347
General Strike 429, 450, 476, 515–524
George V 363, 409, 417, 428, 488, 569, 578
Gibbons, James, Cardinal 199, 380
Gilbert, Sir John 122, 130–131n., 149, 165, 168, 179, 198, 262, 265, 449, 534, 536
Gill, Eric 543
Giustini, Filippo, Cardinal 366, 383n.
Gladstone, Herbert 201, 202, 206
Glancey, Canon Michael 270
Goodier, Archbishop Alban, SJ 310, 318, 506, 507, 509, 578, 580, 581, 582, 585
Gore, Bishop Charles 486
Gotti, Antonio, Cardinal 105, 109, 111, 118–119, 122, 126, 128, 164, 212
Grant, Bishop Thomas 14, 92, 282
Green, Everard 544
Greenhithe 15–17, 21, 23, 24, 25
Guild of the Pope's Peace 349
Gunnersbury Catholic Grammar School 542, 559

605

Haig, General Douglas 177, 330
Halifax, Charles, 2nd Viscount 479–480, 484–485, 486, 488, 489, 490–491, 494, 496, 497, 499, 500, 501, 510
Hare Street House 308, 389, 528, 567
Harnack, Adolf 215
Hatfield 473, 538
Healy, Tim 142, 144
Henderson, Arthur 381
Hedley, Archbishop Cuthbert, OSB 224, 231, 269, 281, 296, 312, 313, 327, 552
    Westminster, candidate for 104, 105–106, 109, 112
Hemmer, Fr Hippolyte 486
Hemptine, Abbot Hildebrand, OSB 107
Henfield 65, 73
Henry, Sir Edward 201
Henshaw, Bishop Thomas 517
Henson, Bishop Hensley 469, 471, 485, 520, 522
Herbert, Dennis 429
Hereford, proposed Diocese of 298
Heron's Ghyll 52
Hertfordshire 30, 284, 539
Hewins, William 401, 445
hierarchy
    cooperation with non–Catholics 451, 452, 455, 475
    Labour Party 430, 432–433, 434
    Low Week meetings—see also diocesan divisions 164, 315, 317, 408, 430, 537
    Rome, relations with 300, 301, 303, 304, 306, 307, 315, 316, 381
    Standing Committee, proposed 315–316
Hinsley, Arthur, Cardinal 285, 311, 316, 372, 529, 533, 537, 559
Hitler, Adolf 374, 375, 569

Hlond, August, Cardinal 572, 573
Hoare, Sir Samuel 365
Hogan, Fr John Baptist 43, 44–45, 212, 214, 217, 223
Holderstock, Fr 4
Holy See
    British diplomatic representation at 343–344, 381
    representation in London 343, 381–382
Hooley, Fr Thomas 253, 254, 265, 528
Hope, James—see Rankeillour, Lord
Hopper, Fr 273
House of Lords
    education 143, 153–154, 155, 157, 158, 162, 172, 184, 185
Howard, Edward, Cardinal 38
Howard, Sir Henry 343
Howlett, Mgr Martin 547
Hutton, Edward 544

Ilsley, Archbishop Edward 180, 288, 309
    Amigo–FAB dispute 268, 269, 313
    Central Seminary 75, 550, 552, 553
    diocesan division 287, 296, 299, 301, 303, 306
Inge, Dean William 448, 521–522
IRA 397, 400, 401, 402, 403
Ireland
    British reprisals 397, 402, 403, 405, 408
    conscription 395
    Easter Rising 391–392
    Home Rule 387, 389–391, 394, 397
    military/naval chaplains/bishop 329, 331, 332, 333–334, 337, 338, 339
    Troubles 397–409
Irish hierarchy 398, 404, 405, 407, 408
    conscription 396
    military chaplains 334, 337, 338, 339, 431
Irish Parliamentary Party 332, 345, 388, 394, 397, 450

Index

denominational education 139, 140–141, 145, 146, 148–149, 151, 152, 155, 156, 157, 158, 159–160, 161, 163, 169, 172, 388–389
Isle of Wight 29, 569
Islington 2, 6–7
Italy 325, 330, 344–345, 348, 366, 369, 379, 380

Jackman, Canon Arthur 70, 284, 289, 312, 401, 402, 403, 411, 529, 530, 532, 575, 579, 581, 582, 583, 585
Jarrett, Fr Bede, OP 291, 310, 318, 486, 507
Jarrow Hunger March 450
Jerusalem 325, 362, 364, 365, 368
Johnson, Mgr 118
Johnson, Fr Vernon 474–475
Johnson, Bishop William 115
Joynson Hicks, Sir William 429

Kean, Bishop Godric 366
Keating, Archbishop Frederick 313, 314, 347, 366, 404, 433, 448, 452, 454, 481, 518, 576
   Amigo–FAB dispute 269, 270, 273
   diocesan division 287, 291, 292–293, 298, 299, 300, 303, 305, 306, 307–308, 310
Keating, Joseph, SJ 371
Keatinge, Bishop William 334, 335, 340
Keatinge, Canon 119
Keily, Bishop John 303, 305, 308
Kensit, John 200
Kent (Rochester), proposed Diocese of 297–298, 300, 305
Kent, Fr Frederick 73
Keogh, Fr 41
Kerr, Lord Walter 404
Kidd, Dr Beresford 486
King, Thomas 122, 262, 269
Kitchener, Herbert, Lord 331

Knox, Fr Ronald 474, 556

Labouchere, Henry 123
Labour Party 140, 183, 184, 430–436, 450, 453
Lacordaire, Fr Jean–Baptiste–Henri, OP, 39
Laing, Rev Robert 29
Lambeth Conference (1920) 456, 481, 482, 483, 484, 485
Lambeth Conference (1930) 458, 506
Lamentabili (1907) 211, 226
Lancaster, Diocese of 310, 311
Lang, Archbishop Cosmo 471, 481, 488, 504, 505–506, 507, 509, 573
Lansbury, George 450
Lansdowne, Marquess of 154, 162
Larkin, Rev Denis Larkin 73
Lateran Treaty (1929) 380–381
League of Nations 369, 371–373, 376, 475
Le Grave, Fr 31, 37
Leo XIII, Pope 76, 82, 84, 109, 445, 446, 480, 489
Leonard, Bishop John 93–94
Lépicier, Alexis, Cardinal 279n., 377, 401, 540
   Amigo–FAB dispute, attempt to negotiate 268, 271, 272, 285
   diocesan division 283, 284, 289, 295, 296, 308, 309
Lex Orandi (1903) 218–219
Liberal Catholicism—see also Modernism
   Joint Pastoral Letter 226
Liberal Party 418, 430
   denominational education 134, 137–138, 139, 140, 141, 146, 147–148, 149, 150, 153, 165, 169, 203, 419–420, 540, 576
Lincoln, proposed Diocese of 296, 297, 298, 300, 305, 309
Liverpool Cathedral 570

Little Company of Mary 569, 570
Lloyd George, David 369, 370, 381, 419, 431
   education 139, 151, 173, 178
   Ireland 394, 395, 397, 398, 404, 408, 409, 410
   World War I 303, 327, 342
Logue, Michael, Cardinal 408
   military chaplains 333–334, 337, 339
Loisy, Fr Alfred 213, 214, 215–216, 217, 218, 219, 220, 221, 227, 232
London
   expansion 11, 12, 14, 283, 538
   unification, proposed as one Diocese 264, 265, 271, 282–290, 293, 401
   University 188, 449
London County Council 13, 138, 169, 285, 289, 450, 540
London Oratory 51, 474
Long, Walter 395–396
Longford, Dr W. W. 523–524
Louvain, Catholic University 46, 47
Lovat, Lord 501

MacDermot, Mary 5
MacDonald, Ramsay 434, 523
MacSwiney, Terence 399–400, 411
MacVeagh, Jeremiah 406, 407
Malines Conversations 476, 479, 482–483, 484–501, 502, 503, 505, 508
Malta 248
Marlborough, Charles, 9th Duke of 472
Marmion, Bl Columba 584
Manning, Henry, Cardinal 7, 30, 31, 38, 40, 73, 74, 90, 106, 109, 135, 231, 239, 282–283, 406, 419, 442, 549, 552, 573, 578
Mannix, Archbishop Daniel 399, 400, 411
Manor Park 539
Mara, William 423, 437n.

Marchant, Sir James 502, 503, 504–506, 507, 508, 509
The Margaret Chapel 3
Marshall, John 543, 544
Martindale, Fr Cyril, SJ 357, 358
McBride, Professor 457
McIlroy, Professor 458
McIntyre, Archbishop John 300, 453, 455
McKenna, Reginald 163, 164, 165, 166, 167, 168
McNabb, Vincent, OP 204, 444, 486, 492
Mercier, Desiré, Cardinal 47, 199, 224, 242, 404, 471, 500–501, 503, 532
   Malines Conversations 482, 483, 484–488, 489, 490, 491, 492, 493, 494, 495, 496–497, 498, 499, 508
Merry del Val, Rafael, Cardinal 106, 121, 127, 128, 129, 207, 239, 243, 246, 312, 313, 338, 339, 368, 377, 391, 407, 446, 448, 473, 480, 536, 559
   Amigo–FAB dispute 258, 265, 267, 269, 271, 272
   cardinalate, rumours blocking FAB's 240, 241, 242–243
   diocesan division 287, 288, 291, 292, 293, 294, 299, 302, 305, 306, 307
   Malines Conversations 491, 494, 495, 496, 497, 498, 499, 500
   Modernism 105, 211, 212, 213, 216, 218, 219, 220, 221, 222, 226, 228, 229, 242, 495
   Westminster, candidate for 104–105, 110, 111
Mignot, Archbishop Eudoxee-Irénée 214–215, 216, 244
military bishop 95, 336–341
military chaplains 92
   Boer War 92–94
   FAB's 1903 reforms 91, 93, 94, 95, 108, 110–111

Index

World War I 329, 331–340, 342
Mivart, St George 230
Modernism 111, 211–233, 455
Monthly Register 232
Mooney, Leo 430
Moore, Provost 118, 119
Moran, Patrick, Cardinal 112, 113
Morant, Robert 150
Morgan, Fr Emmanuel 93
Mortalium Animos (1928) 499–500, 506
Mortlake 55, 56, 57, 58, 64
Mostyn, Archbishop Francis 183, 572
Moyes, Canon James 434, 481, 483, 495, 497
Murnane, Canon Edward 125
Mussolini, Benito 373, 374
Myers, Canon Edward 501, 554, 558

National Catholic Congresses 207, 535
    Leeds (1910) 428, 535
    Newcastle (1911) 379
    Norwich (1912) 361, 516, 535
    Cardiff (1913) 293, 294, 297, 307, 325
    Liverpool (1920) 460
    London (1929) 459
The Nation's Crisis (1918) 445–447
naval chaplains 331, 332, 340, 363
Nazism 371, 372, 374–375
Newman, John Henry, Cardinal 3, 4, 7, 216–217, 222, 223, 224, 578
Nonconformists 116–117, 179, 181, 453, 469, 470
    denominational schools, opposition to 134, 136, 137, 141, 142, 143, 157, 163, 167, 171–172, 183
Norfolk, Henry, 15th Duke of 82, 87, 120, 188, 199, 216, 222, 224, 271, 272, 312, 343, 349, 359, 390, 423, 426, 475, 528, 535
    Commission on Southwark finances 257, 258, 261, 262, 266, 267
    diocesan division 286, 288
    Education Crisis, role in 138, 139, 140, 145, 149, 150, 154, 158–163, 170
    Westminster, appointment of Archbishop 103, 105–106, 110
Northcliffe, Lord 517, 519

Oakley, Canon Frederick 3–4, 6
O'Dwyer, Bishop Edward 157, 224–225
O'Grady, Mgr William 558, 565n.
O'Halloran, Canon Michael 120, 121
O'Hara, Leo SJ 454, 455
Oldmeadow, Ernest 112–113, 117, 123, 159, 471, 473–474
    biography 12–13, 575
    Malines Conversations 488, 489–490, 491, 492, 497, 500
Orchard, Dr William 507
Orthodox Church 344, 362, 363, 364, 365, 482, 485
Oscott—see Central Seminary
Ostend, 27
Our Lady Help of Christians, Blackheath 52, 53–54
Our Lady of Consolation, West Grinstead 58–59
Our Lady of Victories, Kensington High Street 41
Oxford
    proposed Diocese of 310
    University 189, 472

Pacelli, Mgr Eugenio 337, 381
pacifism 327, 349–350
Palestine 364, 366, 368–371, 373, 417
Pan–Christian Conference, Geneva 481, 482
Paris 27, 29, 30, 38, 42–43, 46, 127, 156, 570
Parkinson, Mgr Henry 444, 552
Parkminster 63, 64
Pascendi (1907) 211, 212, 213, 219, 221, 224, 226–227, 228

Patmore, Henry 27
Patterson, Mgr James 31, 36, 37
Percy, Lord Eustace 181, 182, 186, 419, 435
Petre, Maud 219, 220
Petworth 86, 108, 125, 126, 258
Pimlico 538
Pius X, Pope 109, 115, 123, 128, 199, 207, 211, 219, 226, 228, 232, 240, 243, 244, 246, 248, 271, 283, 295, 310, 313, 342, 368, 376–377, 473, 547, 548
Pius XI, Pope 290, 425, 435, 486, 490, 491, 495, 499, 507, 509, 569
Plater, Fr Charles, SJ 329, 398, 401, 445, 451, 452
Plumstead 85–86
Poland 325, 346, 362, 376
Ponsonby, Lord 184
Pooley, Joshua 65
Portal, Fr Fernand 479, 480, 482, 484, 485, 488, 489, 491, 492, 494–495, 496, 497, 499, 510
Portsmouth, Diocese of 63, 86, 126
Portugal 198, 359, 417
Pownall, Gilbert 544, 545
Poyer, Mgr 230–231, 532
Preston, proposed Diocese of 298
Prior, Dr John 81
prisoners of war 327, 346
Propaganda Fide 105, 109, 110, 112, 120, 122, 123, 126, 127, 552
Protestant Alliance 200

Quadragesimo Anno (1931) 435

Rampolla, Mariano, Cardinal 224, 343
Randall, Sir Alec 381
Rankeillour, Lord 536–537
Rawlinson, Fr Stephen, OSB 95, 336
Redmond, John 388–389, 394, 422, 427, 428
Education Crisis 140–141, 144, 145, 146, 148, 150, 151, 152, 154, 155, 156, 157, 158, 159, 160, 161, 162, 163, 166, 172, 185, 389
World War I 332, 391
Redwood, Vernon 535
Reed Lewis, William 123–124, 126, 127, 128–129
Reeve, Fr John–Baptist, OP 518
reunion 479–483, 484, 485, 486, 487–488, 489, 490, 492, 493–494, 496, 497, 500, 501–503, 505–506, 507–508
Richard, Francois, Cardinal 45, 84, 216
Riddell, Bishop Arthur 107, 552
Ripon, Marquess of
  Education Crisis 146, 150, 151, 152, 156
  Eucharistic Congress 202, 206
Robertson, Charles 319n., 472, 473
Robinson, Dr Armitage 485
Roehampton 55, 97, 218
Romaine, William 86
Roman Question 379–381
Rooney, Canon James 151, 152
Ruislip 539
Runciman, Walter 169, 170, 171, 197
Russell, Charles 168, 423, 424
Russia 344, 367–368, 372, 375, 475, 520
Ryan, Fr Edward 93, 94

Salesians 46, 56, 57–58, 66, 70, 570
Salford Catholic Federation 176, 422, 424, 430, 432, 433
Salisbury, Marquess of 427
Samuel, Sir Herbert 369
Santa Sophia, Istanbul 344, 362, 364, 365
Scannell, Canon 119
Schobel, Fr Victor 74, 75
schools—see education and Westminster, Archdiocese of

Index

Scott, Dr Herbert 507
Scouts 463, 559
Scurr, John 183, 184
Seaford 69
self–determination 368, 373–374
Shattock, Laurence 543
Sheed, Frank 536, 580
Sheerness 54
Sheil, Fr Denis 240, 241
Sinn Féin 389, 392, 394, 396, 397, 399, 402, 405, 407
Si qua est (1911) 269, 287, 290, 293, 294, 296, 307, 310, 312, 313, 314
social teaching of the Church 430–450
Socialism 425, 430, 431–432, 433, 434, 435
Society of Secular Priests 88, 89–91
South Tyrol 373
Southwark, Chapter of canons 37, 39, 41, 86, 87, 96, 110, 286
   Amigo's appointment to Southwark 120, 121, 123
   FAB's appointment to Southwark 81, 83–84
   FAB's appointment to Westminster 118, 119, 252
   FAB's creation as Cardinal, reaction to 264, 265, 266, 273, 283
Southwark, Diocese of 36, 54
   Bishop's House 83, 85, 97
   expansion 85, 98
   financial situation 84–87, 98, 124–126, 257–258, 266, 268–269, 271, 287–288, 297
   seminary for 63
Southwark Rescue Society 85, 86, 98, 261, 262, 263
St Aloysius's, Somers Town 4
St Augustine's, Walworth 91, 98
St Bede's, Clapham Park 91, 98, 265, 528
St Charles's House, Begbroke Place 472, 473
St Edmund's College, Ware 21, 30–31, 40, 74, 88, 115, 256, 275, 377, 531, 568, 571, 573
   Cadets Corps 557–559
   development and expansion 559–560
   FAB's schooldays 30, 31–32, 35
   FAB as a seminarian 36, 37, 38, 39, 260
   reorganisation of 553–557
   restoration of Seminary 549, 550–553, 579
   staff 230, 554–555, 556–557
St Edmund's House, Cambridge 188
St Francis de Sales 38, 46, 89, 573, 581, 583
St George's Cathedral, Southwark 82–83, 84, 85, 91, 97, 273, 274, 282, 286, 400, 542
St James's, Spanish Place 31, 198, 417
St John, Canon Edward 65, 68, 85, 86, 87, 96, 98, 99n., 115, 120, 121, 122, 123, 125, 257, 258, 260, 266, 270, 285, 570
   Amigo–FAB dispute, as a cause of 258, 260–264, 267, 268, 273
St John Berchman's School 91
St John Bosco 46, 56, 57, 58, 66, 570
St John the Evangelist, Duncan Terrace 6
St John's Seminary 110, 573
   buildings 68, 76–77
   foundation 64
   expansion 75–76
   FAB's later dealings with 118, 252–253, 254–255, 256, 274
   Henfield, early days at 65–67, 73
   Modernism, accusations of 212–214, 239, 240, 255, 268
   spiritual formation 66, 71
   staff 69, 73, 76, 83, 253
   studies 65, 68–69, 76
   Wonersh, move to 67–68
St Leonard's-on-Sea 570

St Mary's, Clapham 7, 12, 14, 15, 51–52, 64, 91, 248
St Mary Magdalen's, Mortlake 55, 56
St Nicholas's Home, Highgate 460
St Sulpice Seminary, Paris 42–46, 66, 73, 214, 554, 570
St Thérèse of Lisieux 474, 583–584
St Thomas's Seminary, Hammersmith 40–42, 74, 549, 552, 560
Stanbrook 88
Stanfield, Fr Francis 36
Stopes, Marie 456, 457, 458, 460
Storrs, General Sir Ronald 364, 369
Streeter, Ada 453
Stuart, Mother Janet 97, 247, 248, 256, 273, 580–581
Sulpicians 42, 43–44, 64, 70, 88, 91, 554, 555
Surmont, Canon Edmund 40–41
Sutherland, Halliday 458
Sykes, Sir Mark 178, 397

Tablet 221, 231, 239, 306, 374, 380, 491–492, 497, 528
Talbot, Lord Edmund—see FitzAlan, Viscount
Taranto 362
Taunton, Fr Ethelred 104, 108, 124, 126, 127, 128, 129, 242
Temperance 116, 442–444, 475
Temple, Archbishop William 451, 452, 485, 506
Terry, Richard 547, 548, 549
Thackeray Hotel talks 506, 507
Thorman, Bishop Joseph 518
Todd, Canon William 53
Tonks, Joseph 73
Troubridge, Admiral 363
Truth 123, 124, 125–126, 256, 257, 259
Tunbridge Wells 51
Turin 38, 46, 57, 58

Treaty of Rome (1915) 344–345
Trevelyan, Sir Charles 182, 183
Tynan, Canon 157
Tyrrell, Fr George, SJ 212, 213, 214, 215, 218–220, 224, 227, 231, 232, 242
unemployment 449–450
universities
    Catholic contribution to academic life 188–189
    Catholic university/faculty 188, 189
    further studies for priests 75, 188, 472
Urquhart, Francis 453
Ushaw 21, 22, 24, 26, 28, 29, 35, 47, 82, 105, 558

Vance, Canon John 377, 532–533, 555, 556, 557, 582
Vannutelli, Vincent, Cardinal 199, 200, 388
Van Roey, Jozef–Ernest, Cardinal 485, 501
Vatican—see Holy See
Vaughan, Herbert, Cardinal 76–77, 81, 82, 83, 84, 86, 88, 89, 103–104, 106, 108, 109, 116, 135, 136, 225, 230, 231, 419, 480, 527, 529
    seminary formation, policy on 73–74, 75, 549–550, 551, 552
    Westminster Cathedral 542, 543, 545, 547, 548
Verdier, Jean, Cardinal 572
Versailles Peace Conference 351, 368, 380, 559
Victoria, Queen 417, 573
von Hügel, Baron Friedrich 107, 115, 232, 584
    Modernism 214, 215, 216, 218, 220–222, 225, 239

Wales, new Province of 296, 297, 311
Walker, Leslie, SJ 452–453, 454, 455, 483, 484, 486, 490

Walsingham 571
Walters, Frederick 68, 559
War Office 92, 93, 94, 95, 331, 332, 333, 334, 335, 336–337, 338, 340, 342
Ward, Bishop Bernard 177, 232, 307–308
   Bishop of Brentwood 298, 300, 302, 309
   Cadet Corps dispute 557–558
   President of St Edmund's College 550, 551, 552, 553–554, 557
Ward, Josephine 233, 490
Ward, Maisie 45, 218, 221, 225, 226, 227, 536
Ward, Wilfrid 207, 232, 475–476
   Modernism 213, 220, 221, 222–225, 226, 233, 239, 242
Ward, William George 3, 4
Warwick, Fr James 120
Waugh, Evelyn 473–474
Weathers, Bishop William 38, 40, 41
Weekly Register 231
Weld–Blundell, Fr Odo, OSB 332
Welwyn Garden City 539
Wenham, Canon John 55–56
West Grinstead 59–60, 64, 65, 73, 90
Westminster, Archdiocese of 36, 74
   administration 109, 527, 528–529, 531, 579
   Archbishop, appointment of 103, 104
   Archbishop's House 199, 527, 569, 572, 573, 579
   clergy, FAB's relations with 530–533, 539
   expansion 539–540
   military chaplains 95, 331, 333, 334
   relations with other Dioceses 299, 311–314
   schools 116, 540–542, 560
   vocations, FAB's promotion of 529–530, 549, 553, 560
Westminster Cathedral 281, 289, 327, 391, 403–404, 515, 579
   building and decoration 115, 125, 198, 542–546, 572
   liturgy 115–116, 199, 205, 206, 248, 546–547, 570, 572
   music 547–549, 579
Westminster Catholic Federation 146, 327, 422–425, 445, 447, 460
Westminster, Chapter of canons 104, 107, 110, 115, 551
Whelahan, Fr Thomas 85–86
Whiteside, Archbishop Thomas 82, 174, 176, 180, 246, 305, 309, 310, 311, 398, 475
   Amigo–FAB dispute 268, 269
   diocesan division 287, 300, 306, 307
Wilkinson, Fr Francis 24
Williams, Archbishop Thomas 425, 460
Wilson, President Woodrow 347, 380
Wingate, Sir Reginald 366
Wiseman, Nicholas, Cardinal 222, 224, 248, 282, 492
women's suffrage 460
Wonersh—see St John's Seminary
Woodchester 39
Woodlock, Fr Francis, SJ 485, 495, 496–497, 498
Woods, Bishop Frank 505
World Missionary Conference, Edinburgh (1910) 480
World War I 295, 315, 325–351, 375, 442, 444, 445, 480, 482

York Controversy 471, 501
Yugoslavia 363, 367

Zionism 368–371

www.ingramcontent.com/pod-product-compliance
Lightning Source LLC
Chambersburg PA
CBHW071429300426
44114CB00013B/1359